THE ORIENTAL INSTITUTE OF THE UNIVERSITY OF CHICAGO

ASSYRIOLOGICAL STUDIES · NO. 20

SUMEROLOGICAL STUDIES
IN HONOR OF
THORKILD JACOBSEN

ON HIS
SEVENTIETH BIRTHDAY
June 7, 1974

THE ORIENTAL INSTITUTE OF THE UNIVERSITY OF CHICAGO

ASSYRIOLOGICAL STUDIES · NO. 20

THE UNIVERSITY OF CHICAGO PRESS · CHICAGO AND LONDON

International Standard Book Number: 0–226–62282–7
Library of Congress Catalog Card Number: 75–42584

THE UNIVERSITY OF CHICAGO PRESS, CHICAGO 60637
THE UNIVERSITY OF CHICAGO PRESS, LTD., LONDON

EDITOR'S FOREWORD

Planning a *Festschrift* to honor Professor Jacobsen was joyful, if formidable. The breadth and depth of his contribution to our understanding of Mesopotamian civilization left one unable easily to conceive of a truly fitting tribute; no random collection of articles seemed quite adequate.

Instead, we set out to solicit specific articles covering the field of Sumerology that would include a critical description of the course taken by scholarly research up to the present, an analysis of the approaches that have been used in the research, and a prospectus on the techniques and problems that should prove fruitful to future investigation.

The volume was limited to the study of Sumerian civilization even though Sumerology constitutes only one of the fields to which Professor Jacobsen has made a fundamental contribution, for it was hoped that an opportunity would be provided to the Sumerologist—all too often reluctant to venture into the synthesis of his studies—to approach from a broader perspective. It was also hoped that the volume would serve as a bench mark, and, at the very least, Sumerology would honor itself by being associated with Professor Jacobsen.

Sumerian studies were divided into the sub-fields of history, geography, art, archeology, economy and social structure, law, language, lexicography and the lexical tradition, schools, religion, and literature; articles were pledged to cover these areas, each to be accompanied by a selective bibliography. The titles of the essays and the manner of presentation and approach were left to the respective authors. Unfortunately, articles on history, art and archeology, and religion failed to join their fellows in the volume, and the bibliography on Sumerian writing and grammar was supplied by the editor.

Professors T. Abusch, J. A. Brinkman, W. W. Hallo, B. A. Levine, and W. L. Moran were kind enough to lend their names, advice and help toward the completion and publication of the volume.

STEPHEN J. LIEBERMAN

June 7, 1974

NOTE: For typographic simplicity we have represented ħ by h and g̃, ŋ by ḡ.

TABLE OF CONTENTS

PAGE

ABBREVIATIONS ix

THORKILD JACOBSEN: PHILOLOGIST, ARCHEOLOGIST, HISTORIAN. *Samuel Noah Kramer* 1

GEOGRAPHIE. *Hans J. Nissen* 9

SUMERIAN ADMINISTRATIVE DOCUMENTS: AN ESSAY. *Tom B. Jones* . . 41

ZUM SUMERISCHEN EID. *Dietz Otto Edzard* 63

ANCIENT WRITING AND ANCIENT WRITTEN LANGUAGE: PITFALLS AND PECULIARITIES IN THE STUDY OF SUMERIAN. *I. M. Diakonoff* . . 99

LEXICOGRAPHY. *M. Civil* 123

THE OLD BABYLONIAN EDUBA. *Å. Sjöberg* 159

TOWARD A HISTORY OF SUMERIAN LITERATURE. *William W. Hallo* . 181

FORMALE GESICHTSPUNKTE IN DER SUMERISCHEN LITERATUR. *Claus Wilcke* 205

LIST OF ABBREVIATIONS

A   lexical series á A = *nâqu.*
AASF   Suomalaisen Tiedeakatemia. Annales Academiae scientiarum
             Fennicae. Helsinki, 1909———.
AB   Assyriologische Bibliothek. Leipzig, 1881–1927.
ABAW   Akademie der Wissenschaften, Munich. Philos.-hist. Kl.
             Abhandlungen. Munich, 1835———.
AfO   Archiv für Orientforschung. Berlin, etc., 1926———.
AHw   W. von Soden. Akkadisches Handwörterbuch. Wiesbaden,
             1965———.
AJA   American Journal of Archaeology. Baltimore, etc., 1888———.
ANET   J. B. Pritchard, ed. Ancient Near Eastern Texts Relating to
             the Old Testament. Princeton, 2d ed., 1955; 3d ed., 1969.
             Supplementary Texts and Pictures, ed. by J. B. Pritchard.
             Princeton, 1969.
AnOr   Analecta Orientalia. Rome, 1931———.
Antagal   lexical series a n - t a - ǧ á l = *šaqû.*
AOAT   Alter Orient und Altes Testament. Neukirchen-Vluyn, 1969———.
AOS   American Oriental Series. New Haven, 1924———.
ArOr   Archiv Orientální. Prague, 1929———.
AS   Chicago. University. Oriental Institute. Assyriological Studies.
             Chicago, 1931———.
ASKT   P. Haupt. Akkadische und sumerische Keilschrifttexte.
             Leipzig, 1881–82.
ATU   A. Falkenstein. Archaische Texte aus Uruk. Berlin and
             Leipzig, 1936.
BA   Beiträge zur Assyriologie. Leipzig, 1890–1927.
Bab   Babyloniaca; Études de philologie assyro-babylonienne.
             Paris, 1907–37.
BASOR   American Schools of Oriental Research. Bulletin. South
             Hadley, Mass., etc., 1919———.
BE   Pennsylvania. University. Babylonian Expedition. The Baby-
             lonian Expedition of the University of Pennsylvania.
             Series A: Cuneiform Texts. Philadelphia, 1893–1914.
BIN   Babylonian Inscriptions in the Collection of James B. Nies,
             Yale University. New Haven, 1917———.

BiOr	Bibliotheca Orientalis. Leiden, 1944——.
BL	S. Langdon. Babylonian Liturgies. Paris, 1913.
BWL	W. G. Lambert. Babylonian Wisdom Literature. Oxford, 1960.
C	consonant.
CAD	Chicago. University. Oriental Institute. The Assyrian Diction-ary. Ed. by I. J. Gelb, *et al.* Chicago and Glückstadt, 1956——.
CBS	tablets in the collections of the University Museum of the University of Pennsylvania, Philadelphia.
CRRA	Compte rendu de la Rencontre assyriologique internationale.
	II. Compte rendu de la seconde Rencontre assyriolo-gique internationale. Paris, 1951.
	III. Compte rendu de la troisième Rencontre assyrio-logique internationale. Leiden, 1954.
	VII. P. Garelli, ed. Gilgameš et sa legende. Paris, 1960.
	XVII. Actes de la XVIIᵉ Rencontre assyriologique inter-nationale. Han-sur-Heure, 1970.
	XVIII. Gesellschaftsklassen im Alten Zweistromland und in den angrenzenden Gebieten. XVIII. Rencontre assyriologique internationale. *ABAW* NF Heft 75. Munich, 1972.
	XIX. P. Garelli, ed. Le palais et la royauté. Paris, 1974.
CT	British Museum. Cuneiform Texts from Babylonian Tablets in the British Museum. London, 1896——.
Erimhuš	lexical series e r i m - ḫ u š = *anantu.*
Fara III	A. Deimel. Die Inschriften von Fara III: Wirtschaftstexte aus Fara. Wissenschaftliche Veröffentlichung der Deut-schen Orient-Gesellschaft, Vol. 43. Leipzig, 1923.
GSG	A. Poebel. Grundzüge der sumerischen Grammatik. Rostock, 1923.
Gudea Cyl.	*TCL* VIII.
Gudea Statues	E. de Sarzec. Découvertes en Chaldée. Paris, 1884–1912.
HAV	Hilprecht Anniversary Volume: Studies in Assyriology and Archaeology. Leipzig, 1909.
Hh	See Uh.
HKL	R. Borger. Handbuch der Keilschriftliteratur. Berlin, 1967——.
HLC	Haverford College. Library. Haverford Library Collection of Cuneiform Tablets or Documents from the Temple Archives of Telloh. Ed. by G. A. Barton. Philadelphia and London, 1905–14.
HS	tablets in the Hilprecht-Sammlung, University of Jena.
HSAO	Heidelberger Studien zum alten Orient. Ed. by D. O. Edzard. Wiesbaden, 1967.
HSM	tablets in the Harvard Semitic Museum, Cambridge, Mass.

HSS	Harvard Semitic Series. Cambridge, Mass., 1912——.
HUCA	Hebrew Union College, Cincinnati. Annual. 1914——.
IJAL	International Journal of American Linguistics. New York, etc., 1917——.
ISET	M. Çığ and H. Kızılyay. Sumer Edebî Tablet ve Parçalari I. Ankara, 1969.
ITT	Istanbul. Arkeoloji müzeleri. Inventaire des tablettes de Tello. Paris, 1910–21.
JAOS	American Oriental Society. Journal. New Haven, 1849——.
JCS	Journal of Cuneiform Studies. New Haven, 1947——.
JEOL	Vooraziatisch-Egyptisch Genootschap "Ex Oriente Lux," Leyden. Jaarbericht. Leiden, 1933——.
JNES	Journal of Near Eastern Studies. Chicago, 1942——.
KAR	E. Ebeling. Keilschrifttexte aus Assur religiösen Inhalts I–II. Wissenschaftliche Veröffentlichungen der Deutschen Orient-Gesellschaft, Vols. 28 and 34. Leipzig, 1915–19 and 1920–23.
KBo	Keilschrifttexte aus Boghazköi. Wissenschaftliche Veröffent-lichungen der Deutschen Orient-Gesellschaft, Vols. 30, 36, 68–70, 72, 73, 77–80. Leipzig, 1916——.
L	tablets in the Lagash collection of the Museum of the Ancient Orient in Istanbul.
LSS	Leipziger semitistische Studien. Leipzig, 1903——.
MAD	Chicago. University. Oriental Institute. Materials for the Assyrian Dictionary. Chicago, 1952——.
MAH	tablets in the collection of the Musée d'Art et d'Histoire, Geneva.
MBI	G. A. Barton. Miscellaneous Babylonian Inscriptions. New Haven, 1918.
MDOG	Deutsche Orient-Gesellschaft, Berlin. Mitteilungen. 1899——.
MDP	France. Mission archéologique en Iran. Mémoires de la Délégation en Perse. Paris, 1900——.
MIO	Berlin. Akademie der Wissenschaften. Mitteilungen der Instituts für Orientforschung. Berlin, 1953——.
MNS	Å. Sjöberg. Der Mondgott Nanna-Suen in der sumerischen Überlieferung I. Stockholm, 1960.
MSL	B. Landsberger, ed. Materialien zum sumerischen Lexikon. Rome, 1937——.
MVAG	Berlin. Vorderasiatisch-Ägyptische Gesellschaft. Mitteilungen. Berlin, Leipzig, 1896——.
N	tablets in the collections of the University Museum of the University of Pennsylvania, Philadelphia.
NB	Neo-Babylonian.
NBC	tablets in the Babylonian Collection of Yale University Library, New Haven.

NFT	G. Cros. Nouvelles fouilles de Tello. Paris, 1910.
NG	A. Falkenstein. Die neusumerischen Gerichtsurkunden. Munich, 1956–57.
Ni.	tablets in the Nippur collection of the Museum of the Ancient Orient, Istanbul.
Nikolski	M. V. Nikolski. Dokumenty Chozjajstvennoj otčetnosti drevnejšej ěpochi Chaldei iz sobranija N. P. Lichačeva. St. Petersburg and Moscow, 1908–15.
NRVN	M. Çığ and H. Kızılyay. Neusumerische Rechts- und Verwaltungsurkunden aus Nippur I. Ankara, 1965.
NT	field numbers of tablets excavated at Nippur (preceded by the number of the season).
O	tablets in the Musées royaux d'art et d'histoire, Brussels.
OB	Old Babylonian.
OBTR	R. J. Lau. Old Babylonian Temple Records. New York, 1906.
OECT	Oxford Editions of Cuneiform Inscriptions [Texts]. London, etc., 1923——.
OIP	Chicago. University. Oriental Institute. Oriental Institute Publications. Chicago, 1924——.
OLZ	Orientalistische Literaturzeitung. Berlin, etc., 1898——.
Or	Orientalia. Rome, 1920–30; new series, 1932——.
OrS	Orientalia Suecana. Uppsala, 1952——.
PAPS	American Philosophical Society. Proceedings. Philadelphia, 1840——.
PBS	Pennsylvania. University. University Museum. Babylonian Section. Publications. Philadelphia, 1911——.
PRAK	H. de Genouillac. Fouilles françaises d'el-ʾAkhymer. Premières recherches archéologiques à Kich I–II. Paris, 1924–25.
R	H. C. Rawlinson. The Cuneiform Inscriptions of Western Asia I–V. London, 1861–1909. Preceded by volume number.
RA	Revue d'Assyriologie et d'archéologie orientale. Paris, 1884——.
REC	F. Thureau-Dangin. Recherches sur l'origine de l'écriture cuneiform. Paris, 1898–99.
RIAA	Brussels. Musées royaux d'art et d'histoire. Recueil des inscriptions de l'Asie antérieure des Musées royaux du cinquantenaire à Bruxelles. Ed. by L. Speleers. Brussels, 1925.
RLA	Reallexikon der Assyriologie. Berlin, etc., 1932——.
RSO	Rivista degli studi orientali. Rome, 1907——.
RTC	F. Thureau-Dangin. Recueil de tablettes chaldéenes. Paris, 1903.
SAHG	A. Falkenstein and W. von Soden. Sumerische und akkadische Hymnen und Gebete. Zurich and Stuttgart, 1953.
SBH	G. A. Reisner. Sumerisch-babylonische Hymnen nach Thontafeln griechischer Zeit. Berlin, 1896.

SEM	E. Chiera. Cuneiform Series III: Sumerian Epics and Myths. *OIP* XV. Chicago, 1934.
SGL	A. Falkenstein and J. J. A. van Dijk. Sumerische Götterlieder I–II. Heidelberg, 1959–60.
SKIZ	W. H. P. Römer. Sumerische "Königshymnen" der Isin-Zeit. Leiden, 1965.
SKly	J. Krecher. Sumerische Kultlyrik. Wiesbaden, 1966.
ŠL	A. Deimel. Šumerisches Lexikon. Rome, 1930–50.
SLTNi	S. N. Kramer. Sumerian Literary Texts from Nippur in the Museum of the Ancient Orient at Istanbul. Annual of the American Schools of Oriental Research XXIII. New Haven, 1944.
SP	E. I. Gordon. Sumerian Proverbs. Philadelphia, 1959. Other proverb collections in *JAOS*, Vol. 77 (1957) p. 67, *JCS* XII (1958) 1, 43, and *BiOr* XVII (1960) 122.
SR	D. O. Edzard. Sumerische Rechtsurkunden des III. Jahrtausends aus der Zeit vor der III. Dynastie von Ur. Munich, 1968.
SRT	E. Chiera. Sumerian Religious Texts. Upland, Pa., 1924.
SSA	J. J. A. van Dijk. La sagesse suméro-accadienne. Leiden, 1953.
StOr	Suomen itämainen seura, Helsinki. Studia Orientalia. Helsinki, 1925——.
StP	Studia Pohl. Rome, 1967——.
StP M	Studia Pohl. Series Major. Rome, 1969——.
StSem	Studi Semitici. Rome, 1958——.
STVC	E. Chiera. Cuneiform Series IV: Sumerian Texts of Varied Contents. *OIP* XVI. Chicago, 1934.
SZ RomAbt	Zeitschrift der Savigny-Stiftung für Rechtsgeschichte. Romanistische Abteilung. Weimar, 1880——.
TAD	Türk Arkeoloji Dergisi. Istanbul, Ankara, 1933——.
TCL	Paris. Musée national du Louvre. Textes cunéiformes. Paris, 1910——.
TCS	Texts from Cuneiform Sources. Locust Valley, 1966——.
TIM	Texts in the Iraq Museum. Baghdad and Wiesbaden, 1964——.
TIOT	T. Jacobsen. Toward the Image of Tammuz and Other Essays on Mesopotamian History and Culture. Ed. by W. L. Moran. *HSS* XXI. Cambridge, Mass., 1970.
TLB	Nederlandsch Archaeologisch-Philologisch Institut voor het nabije oosten, Leyden. Tabulae Cuneiformae a F. M. Th. de Liagre Böhl Collectae. Leiden, 1954——.
TMH	Jena. Universität. Texte und Materialien der Frau Professor Hilprecht Collection of Babylonian Antiquities im Eigentum der Universität Jena. Leipzig, 1932——.
TUU	H. Sauren. Topographie der Provinz Umma, nach den Urkunden der Zeit III. Dynastie von Ur I: Kanäle und Bewässerungsanlagen. Heidelberg, 1966.

UCS	R. M. Adams and H. J. Nissen. The Uruk Countryside. Chicago, 1972.
UDT	J. B. Nies. Ur Dynasty Tablets. *AB* XXV. Leipzig, 1920.
UET	Joint Expedition of the British Museum and of the Museum of the University of Pennsylvania. Ur Excavations, Texts. London, 1928———.
UF	Ugarit-Forschungen. Neukirchen-Vluyn, 1969———.
Uh	lexical series ur$_5$-ra = *ḫubullu*. Published in *MSL* V–XII.
UM	tablets in the collections of the University Museum of the University of Pennsylvania, Philadelphia.
UNL	G. Pettinato. Untersuchungen zur neusumerischen Landwirtschaft I–II. Istituto Orientale di Napoli. Ricerche II–III. Napoli, 1967.
UVB	Notgemeinschaft der Deutschen Wissenschaft. Vorläufige Bericht über die von der Deutschen Forschungsgemeinschaft in Uruk-Warka unternommenen Ausgrabungen I–XI. Abhandlungen der Preussischen Akademie der Wissenschaften. Phil.-hist. Kl. Berlin, 1930–41.
	Deutsche Warka Expedition. Vorläufige Bericht über die vom Deutschen Archäologischen Institut und der Deutschen Orient-Gesellschaft aus Mitteln der Deutschen Forschungsgemeinschaft unternommenen Ausgrabungen in Uruk-Warka XII–XXII. Abhandlungen der Deutschen Orient-Gesellschaft. Berlin, 1956———.
V	vowel.
VAB	Vorderasiatische Bibliothek. Leipzig, 1907———.
VAT	tablets in the collections of the Staatliche Museen, Berlin.
VDI	Vestnik Drevneĭ Istorii. Moscow, 1937———.
VS	Berlin. Staatliche Museen. Vorderasiatische Schriftdenkmaler der Königliche Museen. Leipzig, etc., 1907———.
WO	Welt des Orients. Göttingen, 1947———.
WZJ	Jena. Universität. Wissenschaftliche Zeitschrift der Friedrich-Schiller-Universität Jena, gesellschafts- und sprachwissenschaftliche Reihe. Jena. 1951———.
YBC	tablets in the Babylonian Collection, Yale University Library, New Haven.
YNER	Yale Near Eastern Researches. New Haven, 1967———.
YOS	Yale Oriental Series. Babylonian Texts. New Haven, 1915———.
ZA	Zeitschrift für Assyriologie und verwandte Gebiete. Leipzig, etc., 1881———.
ZDMG	Deutsche Morgenländische Gesellschaft. Zeitschrift. Leipzig, 1847———.
ZZB	D. O. Edzard. Die "Zweite Zwischenzeit" Babyloniens. Wiesbaden, 1957.

THORKILD JACOBSEN: PHILOLOGIST, ARCHEOLOGIST, HISTORIAN

Samuel Noah Kramer

Philadelphia

As I have had occasion to write some years ago,[1] it takes all kinds of scholars to make up the world of learning and to add, be it ever so much or ever so little, to human knowledge. There is the narrow specialist, who concentrates all his life's work on a limited, restricted area of investigation, and his direct opposite, who spreads his talents far and wide over varied and diversified fields of inquiry. There is the researcher obsessed with details and minutiae, the eternal "card-collector," incapable of fusing them into a coherent synthesis, or refusing to do so on principle, and there is his polar antithesis, who, unworried by the sparse, limited data at his disposal, does not hesitate to construct elaborate theories and generalizations. But rare indeed is the scholar who possesses these varied talents and virtues in the proper productive proportion, whose learning is deep and whose interests are broad, who assembles with patience and discrimination the multiform relevant concrete details, penetrates their contents, and comes up with a cogent synthesis that is stimulating and challenging. Thorkild Jacobsen, whose contributions and publications I have followed closely and profitably for more than four decades, is a prime example of this exceptional, blessed, scholarly species. As even a cursory survey of his numerous published works reveals, he has contributed significantly and seminally to a broad spectrum of Mesopotamian studies, to philology and archeology, culture and history, religion and mythology, government, administration, and law. His generalizations and syntheses, original and perceptive, are nearly always firmly grounded on concrete, detailed, discriminately selected and judiciously marshalled data, both philological and archeological.

Nor is it only as scholar and researcher that Professor Jacobsen has advanced significantly the state of Mesopotamian studies. During a crucial period in the history of the Oriental Institute of the University of Chicago, he was its director and chief administrator and, as such, was largely responsible for bringing to its faculty during the late forties several eminent cuneiformists, all refugees, who vitalized and enriched American cuneiform scholarship as a whole. It was during those years, too, that he conceived, originated, and organized the Nippur

1. See my review of A. Leo Oppenheim's *Ancient Mesopotamia* in *Archaeology*, Vol. 19 (1966) p. 138.

1

Expedition, which started as a joint enterprise of the Oriental Institute and the University Museum[2] and not only made many new inscriptional and archeological discoveries but also helped to clarify to some extent the rather perplexing excavations of the University of Pennsylvania's Peters-Hilprecht expedition of 1889–98. Add to this his role in the preparation and publication of the *Assyrian Dictionary* both as editor and contributor,[3] and it is not too much to say that Mesopotamian studies, both American and worldwide, would never have reached their present stage of progress but for the vision and inspiration, the dedication and devotion of Thorkild Jacobsen.

Let us now take a closer look at some of Jacobsen's more impressive scholarly contributions over the decades. As early as 1934, while still epigrapher of the Oriental Institute Iraq Expedition under the direction of Henri Frankfort, he published the monograph *Philological Notes on Eshnunna and Its Inscriptions* (*AS*, No. 6), consisting of three essays: "The Name of Eshnunna," "The E-sikil Inscription of Shulgi," and "A Letter from Eshnunna and an Assyrian Law." In this monograph, written some four decades ago, the scholarly competence and approach that became the "trademark" of Jacobsen's contributions were already in evidence: the knowledge and utilization of Akkadian as well as Sumerian, close attention to both philological and archeological detail, the shaping of generalizations and syntheses significant for the culture and history of Mesopotamia as a whole. As epigrapher, "and not only as epigrapher,"[4] of the Iraq Expedition, he continued to contribute to its publications in one form and another for years after its excavations had ceased and thus added immensely to their scientific value.[5]

For Jacobsen, 1939 was a banner year in terms of publications. In that year appeared three outstanding contributions to cuneiform research: the epoch-making *The Sumerian King List* (*AS*, No. 11), the long-delayed *Cuneiform Texts in the National Museum, Copenhagen* (Leiden), and the challenging "The Assumed Conflict between the Sumerians and Semites in Early Mesopotamia" (*JAOS*, Vol. 59). This last was intended as something of a "shocker," since it attempted to demolish the generally current view that the history of war-torn Mesopotamia was essentially a deadly struggle between two racial groups, the Sumerians and the Semites. By and large the arguments put forward are reasonably cogent,[6] although there is one document the article makes much of, only

2. See T. Jacobsen and J. A. Wilson, "The Oriental Institute: Thirty Years and the Present," *JNES* VIII (1949) 243.

3. See Introduction to Volume A, Part 1, of the *CAD*, pp. xiv–xxiii, and *JNES* VIII 243–44.

4. So Henri Frankfort in his Foreword to this monograph.

5. See *TIOT*, "Bibliography," pp. 471 ff., item Nos. 5, 6, 11, 13, 14, 15, 16.

6. Among these arguments are (1) the fact that a statue of Lugalzaggesi, who was presumably a true-blue Sumerian, has engraved on it an inscription in Akkadian; (2) the fact that Sargon the Great, a model Semite, was nevertheless chosen by Ur-Zababa, a presumably Sumerian ruler of Kish, as his vizier; and (3) the assertions in Sargon's inscriptions that it was primarily the Sumerian gods, and especially Enlil himself, who granted him victory over the Sumerian Lugalzaggesi.

the initial section of which was known in 1939,[7] that is hardly helpful for its thesis.[8] Nevertheless, there are some indications that there was considerable friction between Sumerian and Semite, and that there was at least a rudimentary consciousness of their racial and linguistic differences.[9]

Though published in 1939, *Cuneiform Texts in the National Museum, Copenhagen* actually went to press six years earlier, but for reasons beyond the author's control, its printing "dragged out" until 1939. Its eighty texts, both Sumerian and Akkadian, are almost all economic, administrative, and legal in character and range in date from Urukagina to Cyrus. Jacobsen's copies, transliterations, synopses, and especially the vocabulary to the texts from the period of the Third Dynasty of Ur foreshadow the scholarly qualities that are the hallmark of his later contributions.

But it is the third of his 1939 publications, *The Sumerian King List*, a monograph that has become a Sumerological classic and an indispensable tool for all students of Mesopotamian history, that came as a kind of breath-taking revelation to the world of cuneiform scholarship. The central core of the book is "A Critical Edition of the Text, with Translation and Notes," that presents the contents of the King List according to all available documents together with accompanying notes that make up the larger part of each page and are brimful of highly detailed, informative, stimulating, and challenging comment on the text, the variants, and the lacunae, as well as on the names of the rulers: their reading, meaning, and the relevant references in cuneiform literature. Preceding this focal textual presentation is a chapter on textual problems that includes an analysis of the "individual manuscripts" demonstrating their derivation from a single original, as well as a minutely detailed study of the multitudinous variants,

7. For bibliographical details, see *ANET* (3d ed.) pp. 646–47.

8. Take, for example, the assertion in the article that "there can be no doubt that he [the author of the composition] is in full sympathy with Agade, with the riches which came to it, with its wise, joyous, militant inhabitants, and with the peace and security which then reigned. He is certainly not describing the rise and downfall of a hereditary, hated, racial enemy" (*TIOT*, p. 191). As is now evident from the composition as a whole, its author was a dire enemy of Agade, full of bitterness and rage, because of the ravaging and pillaging of Enlil's Ekur in Nippur by Naram-Sin, whose Semitic origin may have been in the poet's mind.

9. Thus, Sargon, in his efforts to keep his rebellious Sumerian subjects under control, found it advisable to place garrisons made up of Akkadians in the Sumerian cities (see *TIOT*, p. 155 and n. 103), thereby indicating that he could not trust the loyalty of garrisons made up of Sumerians, who may have felt themselves different from the Akkadians either racially or linguistically, or both. Similarly, the fact that, during the Agade dynasty, Semitic Akkadian came to be used evermore even in Sumerian cities suggests a certain rivalry between Sumerian and Semite; *a priori* it is difficult to suppose that Sumerian men of letters were not disturbed by this development and "took it lying down," as it were. Finally, to take an example from later days, the fact that Ibbi-Sin, whose name, to be sure, is Semitic, designates the treacherous Išbi-Erra, who is about to usurp his throne, as one "who is not of Sumerian seed" (see A. Falkenstein, "Ibbīsîn—Išbiᵓerra," *ZA*, Vol. 49 [1949] p. 61, line 18) points to a certain patriotic pride in being Sumerian (see also *The Sumerians* [Chicago, 1963] pp. 287–88).

to determine their genealogy. Following the "central textual core" is a chapter devoted to the composition of the document, including a persuasive but not very convincing attempt to arrive at the date of the "first edition" by means of "internal evidence," as well as a brilliant, closely reasoned analysis of the nature of the source material available to the author, and his methodology in integrating them into a coherent whole. Next comes a concluding chapter on the historical value of the King List followed by a tabular arrangement of the chronology of the Mesopotamian rulers down to the First Dynasty of Babylon with accompanying absolute dates that are now sadly "out of date." So, too, are quite a good many other parts of the book. After all, it was a pioneering monograph written more than thirty years ago, and since then new evidence has become available that invalidates many of the inferences, emendations, and restorations that pervade the book. Nevertheless, it still stands as an all-important, fundamental contribution, basic for the chronological framework of Mesopotamian history, and virtually all scholars would be most grateful to its author for a revised version of this invaluable monograph.[10]

In 1943 appeared another of Jacobsen's outstanding, provocative publications, this time concerned with the nature and history of the Mesopotamian political structure. The article, "Primitive Democracy in Ancient Mesopotamia" (*JNES* II), sets out to demonstrate that "prehistoric Mesopotamia was organized politically along democratic lines, not as was historic Mesopotamia, along autocratic." In its quest for supporting evidence, the article helps to illuminate the relatively democratic character of the judicial branches of the governments of Assyria and Babylonia, as well as the impressive political role of the people's assembly in the early days of Sumerian history. To be sure, as is carefully pointed out in the paper, there are but few traces of this very ancient assembly in the texts, but its existence and prominence can be inferred from what is known about the assembly of the gods, since, according to the author "in the domain of the gods we have a reflection of older forms, of the terrestrial Mesopotamian state as it was in prehistoric times."[11]

10. The most penetrating and valuable critique of the book is that of F. R. Kraus, "Zur Liste der älteren Könige von Babylonien," *ZA*, Vol. 50 (1952) pp. 29–60; most of its objections and strictures, especially those in regard to the date of the original composition of the King List and the "genealogy" of its various versions, are, in my opinion, well taken. But Kraus's most important contribution was the transliteration of several fragments in the Istanbul Museum of the Ancient Orient that he recognized as belonging to the very same King List piece in the University Museum in Philadelphia that was published by Leon Legrain in *PBS* XIII (1922) as No. 1. Kraus's masterful reconstruction of the text of these fragments and the detailed commentary that follows modify and rectify a number of Jacobsen's readings, restorations, and emendations, especially those concerned with the rulers of the Second Dynasty of Uruk (see now the copies of the three fragments in "A 'Fulbright' in Turkey," *University Museum Bulletin*, Vol. 17, No. 2 [1952] pp. 3–56).

11. See also "Early Political Development in Mesopotamia," *TIOT*, pp. 370–74, nn. 10–20 for additional argumentation concerning the idea of primitive democracy and the role of the assembly in early Mesopotamia.

In 1946, another productive publication year, there appeared the "popular" *The Intellectual Adventure of Ancient Man* (Chicago), with Jacobsen as one of its main contributors, a detailed scholarly review of my *Sumerian Literary Texts from Nippur in the Museum of the Ancient Orient in Istanbul* (in *BASOR*, No. 102), and a superb, comprehensive critique of my *Sumerian Mythology* (in *JNES* V). The latter had appeared two years earlier, in 1944, after a decade of intense, concentrated study of some of the unpublished Sumerian literary tablets and fragments in Istanbul and Philadelphia and in a sense broke new ground in Sumerological research, for until then Sumerian mythology was virtually *terra incognita*, or so I thought. But Jacobsen for one, it seems, had been devoting much of his time and energy to all the available Sumerian literary documents, and especially the large important group that had been published between the years 1930 and 1944. And so when *Sumerian Mythology*, a book that was preliminary and introductory in character, made its appearance, he was well prepared to study, analyze, and dissect its contents with a penetrating eye, a discerning mind, and a not unwilling heart, and his review-article is chock-full of constructive corrections, revisions, and suggestions that shed considerable new light on the myths of Sumer.[12]

12. For an evaluation of some of Jacobsen's contributions to Sumerian mythology, see my review of the *Intellectual Adventure of Ancient Man* in *JCS* II (1948) 39–70 (also the new, enlarged introductory Preface to the revised *Sumerian Mythology* [Philadelphia, 1972]). On this occasion it may be useful to examine the very interesting suggestion in Jacobsen's review-article that there was a Sumerian version of the creation of man according to which it was the earth that produced man in primeval days, that the first man grew up from the earth like plants, and that it was Enlil who broke through the crust of the earth with his newly created pickaxe so that the first man developed below could "sprout forth" (see *TIOT*, pp. 111–14, and now G. Pettinato, *Das Altorientalische Menschenbild* [Heidelberg, 1971] pp. 29–33 and 82–85). His evidence derives primarily from the initial 24 lines of the ^{giš}al composition that he analyzes with his customary penetration and erudition. Nevertheless, there is some reason to remain skeptical and unconvinced. The passage concerned is full of difficulties and obscurities both in reading (there are quite a number of tantalizing variants) and in translation (single words, full lines and even groups of lines). Thus, to take but one example, the statement "it [the uzu-mú-a that is assumed to stand for ki-uzu-mú-a] is a *frequently* mentioned sacred spot in Nippur, and our text [the ^{giš}al document] shows with *all desirable clarity* the reason for its sacred character" (italics mine) is, to say the least, a bit of an exaggeration. Or take the statement immediately following: "for the first men grew up from the earth like plants according to a tradition vouched for also in the introductory lines of the myth of Enki and E-engurra: a-ri-a nam-ba-tar-ra-ba / mu hé-gál ana[sic] ù-tu-da / ukù-e ú-šim-ge$_{18}$ ki in-dar-a-ba, "When destinies had been determined for (all) engendered things, / When in the year (known as) 'Abundance, born in heaven, . . .' / The people had broken through the ground like grass (lit.: plants and herbs)." (This composition was edited in 1969 by A. A. al-Fouadi in his dissertation for the Department of Oriental Studies of the University of Pennsylvania, under the title "Enki's Journey to Nippur.") I would suggest a different reading and rendering of these lines, thus: u$_4$-ri-a nam ba-tar-ra-ba / mu hé-gál an ù-tu-da / kalam-e ú-šim-gim ki in-dar-a-ba, "In a distant day, when fates had been decreed / In a year when hegal, heaven-born, / Had covered the land like plants and herbs." In support of this reading and rendering, note the following: (1) the reading u$_4$-ri-a, as Al-Fouadi notes in his list of

In the years following 1946, Jacobsen has continued to publish stimulating, illuminating articles concerned with Mesopotamian myth and religion[13] as well as Mesopotamian political history,[14] and such miscellaneous studies as those concerned with the administration of the textile industry,[15] aspects of law and legal practices,[16] Sumerian proverbs,[17] and the Sumerian verb.[18] Finally, beginning in 1954, there has appeared a whole series of publications dealing with archeological investigations undertaken in various regions of Sumer and distinguished by an innovative, imaginative methodology first conceived by Jacobsen as early as 1937 that utilizes a ceramic surface survey in conjunction with relevant inscriptional material.[19] The results of these investigations have

---

variants, is found in six manuscripts as opposed to only one for a-ri-a; (2) the mu of the second line, it is not unreasonable to assume, parallels the u₄ of the preceding line; (3) the verb ki—dar, which originally meant "to break through the ground," developed a second-ary meaning "to cover," in the sense of "to occupy the surface of," just as, for example, the verb ki—ág, which originally meant "to measure the ground," developed a secondary meaning "to love"; (4) the rendering I suggest is much more appropriate as an introduction to a composition that glorifies Enki's building of his engur-temple and his journey by boat to Nippur, in which mankind plays no role whatever.

13. See *TIOT*, pp. 1–15, 16–38, 39–47, 52–72, 73–103.

14. *Ibid.*, pp. 132–56 and 173–86. The former, "Early Political Development in Meso-potamia," a comprehensive survey of the development of Mesopotamian political forms from "primitive democracy" to "primitive monarchy," is a ground-breaking contribution to Sumerological research; its 115 notes are brimful of translations that are invaluable for the cuneiformist, even if he should disagree with some of the arguments and conclusions. The latter, "The Reign of Ibbī-Suen," concerns primarily the catastrophic events that marked the end of the Third Dynasty of Ur. But because of the insufficient source material available at the time the article was written, it suffers from a serious misapprehension of the Ibbi-Sin—Išbi-Erra correspondence as sketched in *TIOT*, pp. 175–77. This is not the place, however, to go into details. Suffice to say that *OECT* V, a volume in preparation by Gurney and Kramer, will present textual evidence for quite a different profile of the corres-pondence, one that is particularly revealing for the bitter-sweet relationship between Ibbi-Sin and the treacherous, Machiavellian Išbi-Erra.

15. See *TIOT*, pp. 216–29.

16. A comparison of the *TIOT* translation of that text (2 NT 54) with that in my *History Begins at Sumer* (New York, 1959) pp. 51–55 will show that the two renderings agree in most essentials, except for the concluding lines: according to the former, the wife who knew about the murder of her husband but remained silent is adjudged guilty of murder, whereas according to the latter she is declared not guilty. These diametrically opposed renderings, however, are not capricious; as *TIOT*, p. 201, n. 44, indicates, two of the three available duplicates omit the crucial line that includes the wife among the guilty, but one, 3 NT 273, a text not available to me at the time the book was written, adds it. Now methodologically speaking, I believe that Jacobsen is quite justified in preferring the fuller version as the authentic text, and it is the *TIOT* interpretation of the verdict that should be taken as correct. Nevertheless, it is very strange that a line so crucial to the meaning of the verdict should be omitted in two of the three extant versions, and this, together with the fact that the real meaning of several other lines in the document is by no means assured, should be borne in mind by the interested scholar.

17. See *TIOT*, "Bibliography," p. 472, No. 20.

18. See *ibid.*, "Bibliography," pp. 471 ff., No. 18 and pp. 245–70.

19. See *ibid.*, "Bibliography," pp. 471 ff., Nos. 44, 52, 53, 54 and pp. 231–44.

only partially been published to date, but it is already apparent that they have opened up new untapped sources for the study of Mesopotamian history and culture.[20]

So much for this brief, all too inadequate overview of Jacobsen's more important contributions to Mesopotamian studies. In conclusion, it may not be out of place to close this "Introduction" with some relevant comment on the nature and substance of the scholarly cooperation and collaboration between Jacobsen and myself over the years. While we had met from time to time in the Oriental Institute in the 1930's and the early 1940's, it was not until the end of the Second World War that our mutual interest in the recovery and restoration of the Sumerian literary documents brought us closer together. For it was then that Jacobsen conceived the project of excavating at Nippur, a site which in addition to its other archeological inducements and attractions, held out the promise of yielding a substantial number of Sumerian literary tablets and fragments. Since Nippur had been excavated by the University of Pennsylvania toward the end of the last century, he naturally turned to me, then Curator of the Tablet Collection of the University Museum, to help him persuade its Director, Froelich Rainey, to make it a joint Oriental Institute–University Museum enterprise, a task that I undertook and fulfilled with no little relish and joy. In its first three seasons, the expedition excavated many hundreds of Sumerian literary pieces, most of them small fragments, and casts of all except the very small ones were brought to the Oriental Institute. Consequently, I had the not unpleasant duty of travelling from time to time to Chicago to try, together with Jacobsen, to identify and classify their contents. It was during the years 1947–55, therefore, that our collaboration, always casual and informal, was at its closest, as is evident from several of Jacobsen's publications.[21] As for my scholarly debt to him, it has been noted, at least to some extent, throughout my publications. But such public acknowledgments only evidence the more obvious, ostensible share of the indebtedness. Thorkild Jacobsen, to repeat a phrase I had occasion to use in my review of *Toward the Image of Tammuz*,[22] is a "heroic" figure in cuneiform research, and the seminal, inspiring thrust of his original, imaginative, challenging contributions is deep and subtle, and not readily put in words, nor easily itemized.

BIBLIOGRAPHY

Jacobsen, Thorkild. *Toward the Image of Tammuz and Other Essays in Mesopotamian History and Culture.* Ed. by William L. Moran. *HSS* XXI. Cambridge, Mass., 1970.

20. For details and bibliographical references, see *ibid.*, pp. 427–28, n. 1.
21. See for example *ibid.*, pp. 471 ff., Nos. 7, 32, 37, 80, and pp. 157–72, 104–31.
22. *The Catholic Biblical Quarterly*, Vol. 33 (1971) pp. 266–68.

GEOGRAPHIE

Hans J. Nissen

Berlin

EINLEITUNG

Zum gegenwärtigen Zeitpunkt eine Zusammenfassung unserer Kenntnisse der Sumerischen Geographie schreiben zu wollen ist ein sehr schwieriges Unternehmen, da wir uns wissenschaftsgeschichtlich in einer Phase befinden, in der gerade auf dem angesprochenen Gebiet neue theoretische Ansätze sich in den Vordergrund schieben, ohne dass das Grundmaterial schon in genügender Weise zur Verfügung stehen würde. Dennoch mag es gerade vor der Formulierung neuer Konzepte nützlich sein, eine Bestandsaufnahme zu machen, um so deutlicher auf die Lücken aufmerksam machen zu können.

Diese Neubestimmung wird nötig und ermöglicht durch die in anderen Bereichen akzeptierte Erkenntnis, dass die geographischen Verhältnisse einen wesentlichen Einfluss auf die Ausbildung von lokalen Kulturgruppen haben und vor allem auch auf die Frage, wo konkret sich solche Entwicklungen vollziehen.[1] Die in der Geschichtswissenschaft und somit auch in der Archäologie vermehrt hervortretenden Bestrebungen, Phänomene nicht nur zu konstatieren sondern auch systematisch zu erklären, muss sich also in besonderem Masse auf eine genaue Kenntnis der äusseren Lebensumstände stützen, da oft nur auf diese Weise Erklärungsmöglichkeiten angeboten werden können.

In den letzten Jahren sind Techniken, die die Bereitstellung vieler Einzelbeobachtungen ermöglichen, entwickelt worden, vor allem als Ergebnis der technologischen Entwicklung[2] im Rahmen der archäologischen Feldforschung, die somit in die Lage versetzt wurde, tatsächliche Überreste der alten Umwelt wieder zu gewinnen.[3] Schwieriger ist die Lage bei der Auswertung der Texte, also der

---

1. K. Butzer, *Environment and Archaeology* (2. Aufl.; Chicago, 1972) Kap. 32 und 34.

2. In steigendem Masse stellen die Naturwissenschaften Techniken zur Wiedergewinnung der Umweltsbedingungen im Altertum zur Verfügung. Eine Übersicht bietet: D. Brothwell und E. Higgs, Hrsg., *Science in Archaeology* (2. Aufl.; London, 1965). Die Anwendung einiger dieser Techniken zur Rekonstruktion eines Teils der alten Umwelt bieten die verschiedenen Beiträge in P. J. Ucko und G. W. Dimbleby, Hrsg., *The Domestication and Exploitation of Plants and Animals* (London, 1969).

3. Für einen Versuch, die auf diese Weise gewonnenen Erkenntnisse mit bereits bekannten Tatsachen in ein Gesamtbild einzubringen, vgl. K. V. Flannery, "The Ecology of Early Food Production in Mesopotamia," *Science*, Bd. 147 (1965) S. 1247–56.

anderen Richtung, aus der wir wesentliche Informationen über die alte Umwelt erfahren könnten. Hier ist das Problem noch nie als Ganzes angegangen worden, wenn auch eine Reihe von Untersuchungen von Teilproblemen bereitsteht. Wie jedoch noch weiter unten auszuführen sein wird, betreffen diese nur Teilaspekte, vor allem im Bereich der Identifizierung und der Lokalisierung von Orten und Wasserläufen, und auch dies oft nur auf kleinere geographische Räume beschränkt.[4] Kaum einmal jedoch ist der Versuch gemacht worden, die in den verschiedenen Textgruppen vorhandenen Bemerkungen über die Landschaft zu sammeln und daraus zusammen mit den vorhandenen Informationen über die Fluss- und Siedlungssysteme eine vollständiges Bild der geographischen Verhältnisse zu zeichnen.[5] Diese Grundvoraussetzungen zu erarbeiten ginge allerdings weit über den Rahmen dieses kurzen Abrisses hinaus, der die Aufgabe hat, einen Überblick über das Problem und einen Ausblick zu geben.

GANG DER FORSCHUNG

Ausgehend von der Interessenlage der frühen Reisenden und dann auch der frühen Ausgräber war die Identifizierung von Ruinen mit aus der Bibel oder anderen alten Quellen bekannten Orten eines der wichtigsten Anliegen. Die Sitte, Ziegel ihrer Bauwerke mit Inschriften zu versehen, aus denen oft Art und vor allem Standort des betreffenden Gebäudes hervorgehen, machte die Aufgabe der Identifizierung anhand von Oberflächenfunden auf Ruinen relativ einfach— nach der Entzifferung der Schrift—so dass bis in die Jahre vor dem zweiten Weltkrieg der äussere Rahmen der Besiedlung des babylonischen Raumes mehr oder minder festlag.[6] Seither ist nur wenig dazugekommen, doch sei hier vor allem auf die Lösung des komplizierten Problems der Namen der Hauptorte des Gebietes von Lagaš angeführt, die über die reine Identifikation hinaus wichtige Informationen für einen Teil der Geschichte der Frühdynastischen Zeit (FD) bis zur Ur-III Zeit geliefert hat.[7] Die letzten "klassischen" Identifizierungen—Fund eines Ziegels mit Ortsnamen auf einer bisher nicht benannten Ruine—gelangen mit der Identifizierung des modernen Madain mit dem alten

---

4. Vgl. dazu Th. Jacobsen, "The Waters of Ur," *Iraq* XXII (1960) 174–85 (*TIOT*, S. 231–43); A. Falkenstein, *Die Inschriften Gudeas von Lagaš* I (*AnOr*, Bd. 30 [Rom, 1966]); *TUU; UCS*, S. 41–54; J. Renger, "Zur Lokalisierung von Karkar," *AfO* XXIII (1971) 73–78; C. Wilcke, "Der aktuelle Bezug der Sammlung der sumerischen Tempelhymnen und ein Fragment eines Klageliedes," *ZA*, Bd. 62 (1972) S. 35–61.

5. Einen Überblick für einen begrenzten geographischen Bereich gibt *TUU*, S. 86–89.

6. Zu einer Geschichte der frühen Reisenden vgl. A. Parrot, *Archéologie mésopotamienne* I, *Les Étappes* (Paris, 1946); S. A. Pallis, *The Antiquity of Iraq* (Copenhagen, 1956) Kap. II.

7. A. Goetze, in *Sumer* XI (1955) 127–28; Th. Jacobsen, "Early Political Development in Mesopotamia," *ZA*, Bd. 52 (1957) S. 96–99 (*TIOT*, S. 134–47); ders. "La Géographie et les voies de communication du pays de Sumer," *RA* LII (1958) 127–29; ders., in *Iraq* XXII 177; ders. "A Survey of the Girsu Region," *Sumer* XXV (1969) 105; Falkenstein, *AnOr*, Bd. 30, S. 17–21.

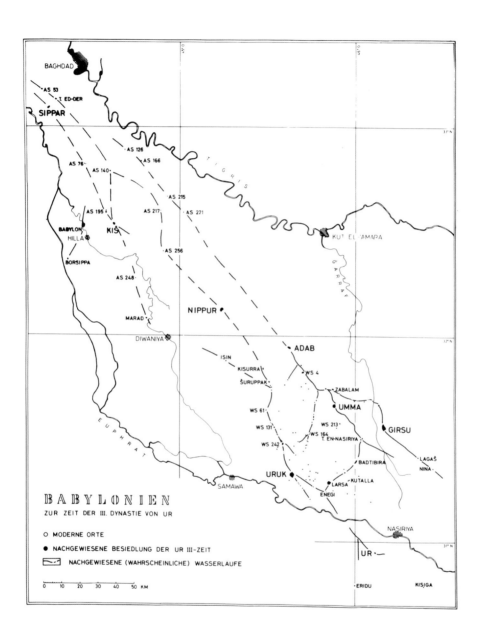

BAGHDAD

AS 53
T. ED-DER
SIPPAR

AS 126
AS 166
AS 76
AS 140
AS 215
AS 195
AS 217
AS 221
BABYLON
HILLA
KIŠ
BORSIPPA
AS 256
AS 248
MARAD
NIPPUR
DIWANIYA
T I G R I S
KUT EL AMARA
G A R R A F

ADAB
ISIN
WS 4
KISURRA
ŠURUPPAK
ZABALAM
UMMA
WS 61
WS 131
WS 213
GIRSU
WS 164
T. EN-NASIRIYA
WS 242
LAGAŠ
NINA
BADTIBIRA
E U P H R A T
URUK
KUTALLA
SAMAWA
LARSA
ENEGI

BABYLONIEN
ZUR ZEIT DER III. DYNASTIE VON UR

O MODERNE ORTE
● NACHGEWIESENE BESIEDLUNG DER UR III-ZEIT
NACHGEWIESENE (WAHRSCHEINLICHE) WASSERLAUFE

0   10   20   30   40   50 KM

NASIRIYA

UR

ERIDU   KISIGA

Bad-Tibira[8] und des modernen Ibzeikh mit dem alten Zabalam.[9] Dass noch
viel zu tun ist, zeigt die Tatsache, dass nicht einmal die Lage so bedeutender alter
Städte wie Akkad,[10] Akšak, Larak oder Keši[11] bekannt ist, geschweige denn die
Lage von kleineren aus der Literatur wohlbekannten Orten wie Guʾabba,[12]
Urusagrig,[13] Enegi, Karkar, Apisala, KI.AN[14] oder kleineren Dörfern im Ein-
zugsgebiet grösserer Städte.[15]

Die in den dreissiger Jahren unseres Jahrhunderts einsetzenden Bemühungen,
die grossen Städte Babyloniens in ihrer Umgebung erfassen zu wollen,[16]
führten allerdings zu genaueren Untersuchungen der Oberfläche grösserer Teile
Süd-Mesopotamiens mit dem Ziel der genauen kartographischen Aufnahme
aller Spuren menschlicher Einwirkung auf die Landschaft, primär aller Ruinen
alter Siedlungen.[17] Die auf diese Weise gewonnenen Informationen über Einzel-

8. V. Crawford, "The Location of Bad-Tibira," *Iraq* XXII (1960) 197–99.

9. Goetze, in *Sumer* XI 127–28; Jacobsen, in *Iraq* XXII 177; *UCS*, S. 217.

10. Zum Problem der Lokalisierung von Akkad, vgl. Gibson, *The City and Area of Kish*
(Coconut Grove, Miami, 1972) S. 6–7.

11. Zur wahrscheinlichen Identifizierung von Keši als dem heiligen Bezirk von Urusagrig
vgl. Wilcke, in *ZA*, Bd. 62, S. 55.

12. Zur Gleichsetzung von é-ᵈnin-mar-ki mit Guʾabba s. Wilcke, in *ZA*, Bd. 62, S. 47
(bereitsvermutet von Falkenstein, *AnOr*, Bd. 30, S. 27–28).

13. S. Anm. 11.

14. S. dazu die Versuche *UCS*, S. 50–53.

15. S. die Aufstellung der Orte im Bereich von Lagaš in Falkenstein, *AnOr*, Bd. 30, S.
22–39.

16. Die frühesten waren die durch R. Koldewey angeregten Untersuchungen der Umgebung von Fara durch W. Andrae, "Die Umgebung von Fara und Abu Ḥaṭab," *MDOG*,
Nr. 16 (1903) S. 24 ff.; es folgten die Untersuchungen der Umgebung von Uruk (E. Heinrich
und A. Falkenstein, "Forschungen in der Umgebung von Warka," *UVB*, Bd. 9 [1938]
S. 31–38 und Taf. 18), von Tello (A. Parrot, *Tello: Vingt Campagnes de Fouilles* [Paris,
1948] S. 9–13 und Fig. 2) und des Diyala Gebietes (Forschungen von Th. Jacobsen in den
Jahren 1936–37, deren Ergebnisse von R. McC. Adams in *Land behind Baghdad* [Chicago,
1965], mit verwertet sind; cf. dort S. 119).

17. Eine Zusammenfassung der Surveys und ihrer Publikationen bis 1958 findet sich in
Jacobsen, in *Iraq* XXII 174–75 mit Anm. 1. Seitdem sind zu nennen:
1966: Umgebung von Ur und Eridu durch H. T. Wright. Im ganzen noch unveröffentlicht;
Teile verwendet in Wright, *Rural Production* (Ann Arbor, 1969) S. 25–32.
1966/67: Umgebung von Kish durch McGuire Gibson. Publiziert zusammen mit einer
ausführlicheren Darstellung des Survey of Central Akkad (1956/57) in: Gibson, *Kish*.
1967: Umgebung von Uruk durch R. McC. Adams und H. J. Nissen. Veröffentlicht als
UCS.
1968/69: Umgebung von Nippur durch R. McC. Adams. Unveröffentlicht.
1969: Umgebung von Tello durch Th. Jacobsen. Vorbericht erschienen in *Sumer* XXV 103–9.
Es fehlen vor allem noch Untersuchungen der Gebiete westlich des heutigen Euphrats, um
Isin, um Adab und des Gebietes zwischen dem Ur/Eridu und dem Uruk Survey. Systema-
tischer Erforschung bedürfen ferner die Gebiete entlang des Tigris südlich von Jarjaraya,
ebenso der gesamte Bereich östlich des Šaṭṭ el-Ġarrāf, in dem bis jetzt nur die grösseren
Ruinen aufgenommen wurden. Freilich dürfte ein Survey mit dem Ziel der Aufnahme
kleinerer Siedlungen und Wasserläufe auf erhebliche Schwierigkeiten stossen, da intensive
Bewässerung bzw. Dauersümpfe kaum Überreste an der Oberfläche erkennen lassen.

siedlungen und Siedlungssysteme werden uns sicher bei den genannten Problemen der Identifizierung weiterhelfen.

Die Tatsache, dass die meisten der alten Ruinen nicht an den modernen Flussläufen liegen, führte schon früh zu Überlegungen, dass die Flüsse in alter Zeit einen anderen Verlauf hatten als heute.[18] Gleiches sagten die Texte aus, wenn sie Fara, Larsa, Uruk und Ur am Euphrat liegen lassen, obwohl alle diese Ruinen heutzutage oft recht weit vom Euphrat entfernt liegen. Eine genauere Überprüfung aber war natürlich kaum möglich, da alte Kanäle oder sogar Flüsse nicht so klar erkennbare Reste auf der Oberfläche hinterlassen wie alte Städte, und so ist uns die eindeutige Identifizierung mit alten Kanalnamen in keinem einzigen Fall möglich. Hilfe bieten uns hier allerdings die Texte, die uns bisweilen berichten, dass der Ort *x* am Kanal *y* lag und uns so den Kanal lokalisieren lassen, wenn wir die Lage des Ortes *x* kennen.[19] Leider sind die Schreiber der alten Wirtschaftstexte keine Freunde von redundanter Ausdrucksweise gewesen. Da die Leser derartiger Tafeln selbstverständlich wussten, welche Orte mit welchem Kanal zusammengehörten, war eine bestimmte Stelle, die in einem Text angegeben werden sollte, durch den Ortsnamen *oder* den Kanalnamen eindeutig bestimmt, so dass die Nennung von Ortsnamen *und* Kanalnamen eine Redundanz dargestellt hätte. Es kommt dazu, dass die Bewohner einer Ortschaft von dem vorbeifliessenden Wasserlauf wahrscheinlich nur als von "dem Fluss" oder "dem Kanal" sprachen, eine Übung, der sich die Texte aus der betreffenden Stadt anschlossen.[20]

In vielen Fällen unüberwindliche Schwierigkeiten bewirkt auch der Brauch, Teilabschnitte der Hauptwasserläufe gesondert zu benennen oder alten Kanälen nach einer Reinigung oder Vergrösserung neue Namen zu geben.[21] Detailliertere Untersuchungen der Bildung von Kanalnamen könnten uns hier weiterhelfen.

Im Verlaufe der genannten Surveys wurden nun vereinzelt noch auf der Oberfläche sichtbare Spuren früherer Wasserläufe und Kanäle registriert, vor allem führten jedoch die seit den fünfziger Jahren vorliegenden Luftaufnahmen zur Aufdeckung zusammenhängender Kanalnetze.

Eine Möglichkeit zur weiteren Verfeinerung brachten die Erfolge in der Aufstellung einer recht kleinteiligen Keramikabfolge für das alte Südmesopotamien, die die alten Siedlungsreste oft sehr genau durch die Oberflächenfunde

---

18. S. C. S. Fisher, *Excavations at Nippur* (Philadelphia, 1905) S. 28; L. W. King, *A History of Sumer and Akkad* (London, 1923) S. 7 ff. und die Karte am Ende des Buches. J. Jordan, *Uruk-Warka* ("Wissenschaftliche Veröffentlichungen der Deutschen Orient-Gesellschaft," Bd. 51 [Leipzig, 1928]) S. 3–4 sieht im Lauf des Šaṭṭ el-Kar den alten Euphratlauf, im direkt nach Uruk führenden Šaṭṭ en-Nil einen Seitenkanal. Cf. dazu W. K. Loftus, *Travels and Researches in Chaldaea and Susiana* (London, 1857) Plan nach S. 160 und S. 161 ff.

19. *TUU*, S. 32.

20. *Ibid.*, S. 128; *UCS*, S. 42*b*.

21. *TUU*, S. 128 mit Anm. 70; *UCS*, S. 44*a* und *b*.

datieren liessen.[22] Da angenommen werden kann, dass Siedlung und dabeiliegender Wasserlauf gleichzeitig existierten, konnten so auch die an sich nicht datierbaren Kanäle zum Teil bestimmten Perioden zugewiesen werden. Leider war es bis jetzt nur in wenigen Fällen möglich—vor allem bei den Hauptkanälen—solche im Gelände fixierten Wasserläufe mit Hilfe der schriftlichen Nachrichten zu identifizieren, doch könnten hier mit Erfolg detailliertere Surveys, vor allem der Gebiete um Umma, Lagaš und Ur, für die wir viele Kanalnamen kennen, eingesetzt werden.

Bedauerlicherweise ist die oben genannte Möglichkeit der Identifizierung alter Wasserläufe auf wenige Fälle beschränkt, und somit stellt ein Verfahren, das von den mageren Informationen der Texte ausgehend wenigstens die ungefähre Lage, die Strömungsrichtung und Grösse festzulegen sucht, immer noch die einzige Möglichkeit dar, ein etwas detaillierteres Bild zu zeigen.[23]

Sind wir so im Bereich der Siedlungen und Wasserläufe auch noch etwas davon entfernt, ein zusammenhängendes detailliertes Bild zeichnen zu können, so ist dort die Situation doch unvergleichlich viel besser als im Bereich der Wiedergewinnung der alten Landschaft, die ja schliesslich den weitgehend bestimmenden Hintergrund für die Entwicklung der Siedlungs- und Wassersysteme abgegeben hat.

In der Periode der frühen Entdeckungen wurden genaue Überlegungen über die die grösseren Orte umgebende Landschaft kaum angestellt, wie ja auch dieser Aspekt bei den im letzten Viertel des vorigen Jahrhunderts einsetzenden grösseren Grabungen völlig vernachlässigt wurde.

Einzelheiten wurden in älterer Zeit zur Frage der antiken Landschaft von der Philologie beigesteuert, ausser der Identifikation von Tier- und Pflanzennamen[24] bisweilen auch Namen von Siedlungs- und Landschaftsformen.[25] Erst in neuerer Zeit aber richtete sich die Aufmerksamkeit auf die Landschaft als Ganzes, auf Beziehung und Verteilung der einzelnen Landschaftsformen.[26]

---

22. Unsere Kenntnis der Keramikabfolge wurde vor allem durch die Untersuchungen in Nippur erweitert (zusammengefasst von D. P. Hansen, "The Relative Chronology of Mesopotamia, Part II," R. W. Ehrich, Hrsg., *Chronologies in Old World Archaeology* (Chicago, 1965) S. 201–13. S. auch D. E. McCown, R. C. Haines, und D. P. Hansen, *Nippur* I (*OIP* LXXVIII [Chicago, 1967]), weiterhin durch die verschiedenen Grabungen in Uruk (H. J. Lenzen, "Die Keramik," *UVB* XXI [1965] 36–42; H. J. Nissen, "Grabung in den Quadraten K/L XII in Uruk-Warka," *Baghdader Mitteilungen*, Bd. 5 [1970] S. 101–91), Ur (Wright, *Rural Production*, S. 61–74) und durch die während des Uruk-Surveys gefundene Keramik (*UCS*, S. 97–104).

23. Cf. die auf diese Weise zusammengestellten Skizzen *TUU*, S. 212 oder Wilcke, in *ZA*, Bd. 62, S. 57.

24. B. Landsberger, *Die Fauna des Alten Mesopotamien* (Leipzig, 1934); R. C. Thompson, *A Dictionary of Assyrian Botany* (London, 1949).

25. Die Diskussion der verschiedenen Termini und ihre gegenseitige Abgrenzung ist nie als Ganzes angegangen worden. Zu Einzeldiskussionen, vgl. *SGL* I 41–42 (u r u – á - d a m – maš-gána, "Stadt—Dorf—Zeltlager"); Falkenstein, *AnOr*, Bd. 30, S. 39–41: é-duru₅– uru-sag—maš-ga-na-sag. Cf. auch infra die Diskussion zu e d e n, a m b a r.

26. *TUU*, S. 86–89; *UCS*, S. 1–8 und passim.

Schon früh waren zum allgemein akzeptierten Bestandteil jeglicher kultur-
geschichtlicher Betrachtung Mesopotamiens Aussagen geworden, die auf zwei
Grundbeobachtungen zurückgehen: einmal, dass Südbabylonien ein Flussdel-
tagebiet ist, das wie alle auf diese Weise entstandenen Gebiete allmählich sich
aus einem Sumpfgebiet in festes Land verwandelt, dabei aber immer die Neigung
zur Sumpfbildung behält.[27] Die zweite Beobachtung war, dass in Babylonien
nicht genügend Regen fällt, um einen Regenfeldbau zu ermöglichen, dass also
jeglicher Anbau nur auf künstlicher Bewässerung beruhen konnte.[28] Beides sah
man in Texten historischer Zeit bestätigt und fühlte sich berechtigt, beide
Annahmen in Untersuchungen über die frühe Entwicklung der Kultur in
Babylonien einsetzen zu können.[29]

Aus der Tatsache, dass im Norden Mesopotamiens prähistorische Schichten
gefunden wurden, die sich lückenlos bis ins Neolithikum zurückverfolgen liessen,
dass ähnliche Bemühungen für Babylonien aber zu der Einsicht führten, dass
der gesamte babylonische Raum vor der sog. ʿUbaid Zeit nicht oder nur ganz
spärlich besiedelt gewesen war, zog man den Schluss, dass zu der Zeit, als in den
angrenzenden Gebieten sich bereits spätneolithische Kulturen ausgebildet
hatten, der Süden Mesopotamiens noch völlig versumpft und somit für jegliche
Besiedlung ungeeignet war.[30]

Überlegungen über den Ursprung der sog. Hochkulturen in Babylonien
bezogen meist die zweite Beobachtung, die der Notwendigkeit künstlicher
Bewässerung, in der Weise ein, dass die zur Unterhaltung eines Kanalnetzes,
das man als Voraussetzung für die Durchführung künstlicher Bewässerung
ansah, notwendige Organisation und Verwaltung den Anstoss gegeben habe,
auch in anderen Bereichen des Zusammenlebens vergleichbare Organisations-
prinzipien zu befolgen, was zur Bildung von Städten und schliesslich von Staaten
führte.[31]

Dabei wurde wenig Wert auf eine Verbindung dieser beiden Aussagen gelegt,
die in einer Erklärung der Verhältnisse während des Überganges von Sumpf-
landschaft zu einer Landschaft, die nur durch Kanäle Wasser zugeleitet be-
kommt, hätte bestehen müssen.

27. Bereits J. de Morgan, *Recherches archéologiques* (*MDP* I [1900]) 4–32; vgl. auch
A. Moortgat, *Die Entstehung der sumerischen Hochkultur* ("Der alte Orient," Bd. 43
[Leipzig, 1945]) S. 10, 16; A. L. Perkins, *The Comparative Archeology of Early Mesopotamia*
("Studies in Ancient Oriental Civilization," No. 25 [Chicago, 1949]) S. 73.

28. S. die Diskussion und Tabellen bei E. Wirth, *Agrargeographie des Iraq* (Hamburg,
1962) S. 13 ff. Bereits ausgesprochen von Herodot: Buch I Kap. 193.

29. So z.B. A. Falkenstein, "Die Ur- und Frühgeschichte des Alten Vorderasien," E.
Cassin, J. Bottéro, und J. Vercoutter, Hrsg., *Fischer Weltgeschichte*, Bd. 2 (Frankfurt, 1965)
S. 28–29.

30. Cf. Anm. 27.

31. S. R. J. Braidwood, *The Near East and the Foundations for Civilization* ("Condon
Lectures" [Eugene, Ore., 1952]) S. 39–40; K. A. Wittfogel, *Oriental Despotism* (New Haven,
1957); R. Coulborn, *The Origin of Civilized Societies* (Princeton, 1959). Eine erste Entgegnung
erfuhr diese Idee durch R. McC. Adams in C. H. Kraeling und R. McC. Adams, Hrsg., *City
Invincible* (Chicago, 1960) S. 27 und Diskussion, S. 34 ff.

Die Folge war, dass man sich berechtigt sah, auch für die Frühzeit diejenigen landschaftlichen Verhältnisse anzunehmen, die man aus den Texten späterer Jahrhunderte erschliessen konnte: weite von Getreide bestandene Flächen soweit die Bewässerungssysteme reichen, jenseits davon Weideland, sowie intensiv bewässerte Palmen- und Gemüsegärten in der Nähe der Siedlungen.

Erst die von den Untersuchungen im Diyala Gebiet initiierten Studien über die Rolle der Bodenzusammensetzung für die Landwirtschaft und, damit zusammenhängend, über Vorkommen und Ausbreitung von Bodenversalzung im Altertum störten dieses Bild einer im ganzen stabilen Umwelt.[32] Durch den Nachweis der Ausbreitung der Versalzung des Bodens zu bestimmten Zeiten konnten erstmals plausibel Erklärungen für die Veränderung von Siedlungssystemen in diesen Zeiten gegeben werden, und es wurde somit nicht nur deutlich, dass die Umwelt und mithin auch das Landschaftsbild im Altertum und seither sich verändert hatte, sondern dass diese Veränderungen ganz konkrete Folgerungen für das Leben im babylonischen Raum hatten.[33]

Verschiedene Untersuchungen an schriftlich überliefertem Material erweiterten in der Folgezeit unseren Horizont—so mehrten sich die Zeugnisse für einen Wald- und Sumpfgürtel entlang eines Teils des östlichen Euphratarms[34]—doch der Natur der Texte entsprechend handelte es sich meist um Momentaufnahmen, noch dazu für Zeiten, die in der Gesamtentwicklung der Kultur in Babylonien recht spät liegen, so dass sie wenig geeignet waren, die herrschende Meinung zu ändern. Versuche, durch Pollenanalysen das Vegetationsbild zu den verschiedenen Zeiten und damit das jeweilige Landschaftsbild zu rekonstruieren, scheiterten daran, dass sich im extrem trockenen Boden Babyloniens kaum Pollen erhalten haben.[35] Untersuchungen über das Klima stecken ebenfalls noch ganz in den

32. Th. Jacobsen und R. McC. Adams, "Salt and Silt in Ancient Mesopotamian Agriculture," *Science*, Bd. 138 (1958) S. 1251–58; Th. Jacobsen, "Salinity and Irrigation Agriculture in Antiquity" (Diyala Basin Project, "Report on Essential Results" [mimeograph., 1958]).

33. Jacobsen und Adams, in *Science*, Bd. 138, S. 1251–52; R. McC. Adams, "The Study of Ancient Mesopotamian Settlement Patterns and the Problem of Urban Origins," *Sumer* XXV (1969) 111–24.

34. Zu Waldvorkommen s. infra den Abschnitt "Wald." Die Existenz von Sumpfgebieten kann man aus den reichen Rohrerträgen einzelner "Felder" erschliessen. Siehe dazu unten. Die modernen dichten Dünengürtel im Bereich Adab, Tell Jidr, Zabalam und Umma gehen sicher darauf zurück, dass dieses Gebiet als ehemaliges Überschwemmungsland eine spärliche Vegetation zuliess, an der sich die Flugsande anlagern konnten. Cf. dazu Heinrich und Falkenstein, in *UVB*, Bd. 9, S. 32.

35. Während der Grabung 1967 wurden in Uruk vier Proben für Pollenuntersuchungen aus Späturuk Schichten der Grabung in K/L XII gesammelt und Herrn Dr. G. Lang von den Landessammlungen für Naturkunde in Karlsruhe zur Untersuchung übergeben. In zwei Proben fand sich nichts, in den beiden anderen "einige Cyperaceen, eine Chenopodiacee und ein Quercus-ähnlicher Typ." Die Befürchtung, dass die Pollenkörner der extremen Trockenheit nicht standgehalten haben, hat sich so leider bestätigt. Die Untersuchungen wurden wegen der mageren Ergebnisse nicht fortgesetzt.

Inzwischen sind im amerikanischen Südwesten, wo die klimatischen Bedingungen denen des Iraq entsprechen, Techniken entwickelt worden, die durch Anreicherungsverfahren

Anfängen,[36] und so sind es wiederum die archäologischen Oberflächenuntersuchungen, die den Anstoss dazu gaben, die Entwicklung der Landschaftsformen in einem anderen Rahmen zu sehen als dies bisher geschehen war.[37]

DER HEUTIGE STAND DER KENNTNISSE DER GEOGRAPHISCHEN VERHÄLTNISSE

Diese Untersuchungen ermöglichen uns, folgendes Bild in groben Linien zu zeichnen:

Nur wenig wissen wir über die sog. ᶜUbaid Zeit, die früheste aus der wir Reste menschlichen Lebens in Babylonien haben. Siedlungen aus dieser Zeit sind zu wenig zahlreich und liegen so verstreut, dass man weder über die Beziehungen der Siedlungen untereinander noch über die Situation der Wasserläufe etwas aussagen kann.[38] Das Argument, dass Siedlungen dieser und vorausgehender Perioden nur nicht gefunden seien, weil sie von späteren Schwemmanlagerungen überdeckt seien,[39] hat nicht ganz an Kraft verloren, muss jedoch wesentlich modifiziert werden, nachdem wenig nördlich von Uruk die Reste einer früh (vor?) ᶜUbaid-zeitlichen Siedlung auf der heutigen Oberfläche gefunden wurden.[40] Das Überlagerungsargument dürfte daher im wesentlichen nur auf den Bereich des heutigen Euphratlaufes (Eridu, Qalᶜa des Ḫaǧǧi Mohammed, Ras el ᶜAmiye)[41]

---

dennoch gute Ergebnisse erzielen. Vgl. dazu J. Schoenwetter, "The Pollen Analysis of Eighteen Archaeological Sites in Arizona and New Mexico," P. S. Martin *et al.*, *Chapters in the Prehistory of Eastern Arizona* I ("Fieldiana: Anthropology," Bd. 53 [Chicago, 1962]) 168–209; ders., "Pollen Survey of the Chuska Valley," A. H. Harris *et al.*, *An Archaeological Survey of the Chuska Valley and the Chaco Plateau, New Mexico* I, *Natural Science Studies* (Museum of New Mexico "Research Records," Nr. 4 [Santa Fe, 1967]) 72–103.

Reichere Untersuchungen, die jedoch nur sehr allgemein für unser Gebiet herangezogen werden dürfen, liegen vor für den Westiran. Zusammenfassung und Literatur bei W. van Zeist, "Reflections on Prehistoric Environments in the Near East," Ucko und Dimbleby, *The Domestication and Exploitation of Plants and Animals*, S. 35–46.

36. Zusätzlich zu W. van Zeists Artikel, zitiert in Anm. 35, vgl. auch Flannery, in *Science*, Bd. 147, S. 1247–56.

37. Vor allem *UCS*, Kap. 2 und 3.

38. R. M. Adams, "Survey of Ancient Water Courses and Settlements in Central Iraq," *Sumer* XIV (1958) 102 und Fig. 2; ders., *Land behind Baghdad*, S. 34–35 und Fig. 2. Allerdings müssen die entsprechenden Karten für die ᶜUbaid-Perioden beträchtlich geändert werden, da viele der dort eingetragenen Orte lediglich nach dem Vorkommen von Tonsicheln datiert wurden, die als "index fossil" für die ᶜUbaid Zeit aufgefasst wurde. Durch neuere Untersuchungen (*UCS*, S. 208–9) hat sich jedoch eine längere Verbreitungsdauer der Tonsicheln herausgestellt, so dass die betreffenden Orte neu datiert werden müssen (Adams bei Gibson, *Kish*, S. 184). Die Karten Gibson, *Kish*, Fig. 6 und *UCS*, Fig. 2 berücksichtigen diese Veränderung.

39. D. Stronach, "Ras al ᶜAmiya," *Iraq* XXIII (1961) 124; Falkenstein, in Cassin, Bottéro, und Vercoutter, *Fischer Weltgeschichte*, Bd. 2 (1965) S. 29.

40. *UCS*, S. 9 zu WS 298, S. 98, 174–77.

41. *Ibid.*, S. 6–8, 9.

zutreffen, ebenso mit einiger Sicherheit auf das Gebiet des heutigen Sumpfgebietes im Süden des Landes.[42] Das eben Gesagte trifft auch für die folgenden
Jahrhunderte der sog. Früh-Uruk Zeit zu, für die zwar etwas mehr Siedlungen
vorhanden sind, deren Zahl aber bei weitem nicht ausreicht, um ein besseres
Bild zu liefern.[43]

Erst mit der Spät-Uruk Zeit betreten wir historische Räume, für die so reich-
haltige Informationen vorliegen, dass wir über die blosse Feststellung der Existenz von Siedlungen hinauskommen. Genauere Zahlen liegen immerhin für
einen recht grossen Teil des babylonischen Raumes vor, so dass mit einiger
Berechtigung allgemeine Aussagen gemacht werden können.[44] Das Auffallendste
ist die Vermehrung der Siedlungen, die nun so dicht beieinander liegen, dass mit
Methoden der Siedlungsforschung bestimmte Aussagen über die Beziehungen
der Siedlungen untereinander gemacht werden können.[45] Obwohl selbstverständlich zu vermuten ist, dass es mehrere Modelle des gegenseitigen Verhält-
nisses gab—die wir im einzelnen noch nicht immer voneinander trennen,
geschweige denn jeweils benennen können—ist doch vor allem eines klar:
nämlich dass es bereits in dieser Zeit ausgeprägte Hierarchien von Siedlungen
gibt, d.h. also feste Abhängigkeitsverhältnisse. Wegen der grossen Zahl von
Siedlungen ist es nun auch zum ersten Mal möglich, das gleichzeitige System der
Wasserläufe mit einiger Genauigkeit wiederzugewinnen. Es ergibt sich, dass das
vorherrschende Element zu dieser Zeit nicht grosse Flüsse, geschweige denn
Kanäle waren, sondern eine Vielzahl kleiner, sich durch das flache Land
windender Wasserläufe, die sich verzweigen, sich wieder treffen und derart
netzförmig das Land überziehen, dass man den Eindruck eines Gebietes bekom-
mt, das über keinen Wassermangel verfügt, ja möglicherweise sogar die Situation
der Wasserrinnen in einem sumpfigen Gebiet wiedergibt.

Die Gesamtsituation ändert sich in der folgenden Ǧemdet Nasr Zeit: zwar
behält das Wassersystem denselben Charakter,[46] doch bahnt sich eine Entwicklung an, die in der folgenden Frühdynastischen Zeit deutlicher wird: die Ausbildung geraderer Wasserläufe. Sichtbarer sind die Veränderungen bei den
Siedlungen: die Zahl nimmt ab, dafür steigt die Durchschnittsgrösse, und zwar
zeigt sich, dass diejenigen Siedlungen bestehen bleiben und sich vergrössern, die

42. Eine Zusammenfassung der Diskussion um den Verlauf der Küstenlinie des Persischen
Golfes im Altertum findet sich bei Gibson, *Kish*, S. 16–17.

43. Als gesonderte Keramikgruppe zur Datierung von Siedlungen während eines Surveys
nur verwandt im Uruk Survey (*UCS*, S. 9–10 und Fig. 2) und im Nippur-Survey (unpubli-
ziert).

44. Für das Uruk-Gebiet: *UCS*, S. 11–12 und Fig. 3; für Zentral-Akkad mit Kish:
Gibson, *Kish*, S. 48, 184–85, Fig. 6 und map 2. S. auch Adams, in *Sumer* XXV 114–16.

45. Dies gilt vor allem für den Süden des Landes (*UCS*, S. 17–23 und Fig. 3) während die
Veränderungen in Nordbabylonien anders verlaufen (Adams bei Gibson, *Kish*, S. 184–85).

46. *UCS*, Fig. 4. Der Siedlungsplan *UCS*, Fig. 12 stellt wegen seiner modernen Parallelen
mit Sicherheit den Grundriss einer Sumpfsiedlung dar und beweist damit die Existenz
ausgedehnter Sumpfgebiete nördlich von Uruk noch während der Ǧemdet Nasr Zeit
(*UCS*, S. 25).

unter den Siedlungen der früheren Zeit nach den Regeln der Siedlungsgeographie als die jeweiligen Zentren bezeichnet werden mussten.[47] Dieser Trend zur Konzentration hat wahrscheinlich verschiedene Gründe, politische und wirtschaftliche,[48] aber wahrscheinlich auch solche, die uns in diesem Zusammenhang weiter interessieren müssen.

Diese Gründe werden in den Veränderungen sichtbar, die in der folgenden FD-I Zeit zu fassen sind. Der Trend zur Konzentration bei den Siedlungen hält an, und gleichzeitig wird nun auch eine Parallelerscheinung bei den Wasserläufen sichtbar: der netzartige Charakter weicht zugunsten einiger weniger grösserer Wasserläufe, die nun grosse Teile des Landes, die vorher von kleinen Wasserläufen durchflossen worden waren, ohne direkte Wasserversorgung lassen.[49] Die Siedlungen, die sich in diesen jetzt unversorgten Gebieten befanden, verschwinden, und dafür werden die Siedlungen an den nun Vorrang gewinnenden Wasserläufen grösser. Auch diese Entwicklung ist auf politische und wirtschaftliche Gründe u.a. zurückzuführen,[50] doch wird hier eine andere Entwicklung unübersehbar: ein generelles Zurückgehen des Wassers, das, von dieser neuen Situation aus gesehen, von der Spät-Uruk Zeit ab kontinuierlich eine Grundlage für alle weiteren Entwicklungen abgab. Worauf dieser Rückgang zurückzuführen ist, ist unklar, doch spielten Trockenlegung von sumpfigen Gebieten[51] und erhöhte Verdunstung durch Vergrösserung der Anbauflächen[52] sicher eine grosse Rolle.

Der Trend zur Konzentration bei den Siedlungen ist somit wahrscheinlich auch als Antwort auf die sich verschlechternden Wasserverhältnisse anzusehen, denn an dieser Stelle in der Gesamtentwicklung treten völlig neue Notwendigkeiten und Probleme auf, die nur mit neuen Mitteln zu lösen sind. War in den vorhergehenden Zeiten immer genug Wasser vorhanden, in so vielen Wasserläufen oder Wasserflächen, dass man das Wasser jeweils nur durch kleine Stichgräben auf das danebenliegende Land bringen musste,[53] tritt nun zum ersten Mal

47. *Ibid.*, S. 18–23, 27–28.

48. Zusätzlich zu *UCS*, Kap. 2; vgl. H. J. Nissen, "The City Wall of Uruk," in P. J. Ucko, R. Tringham und G. W. Dimbleby, Hrsg., *Man, Settlement and Urbanism* (London, 1972) S. 796.

49. *UCS*, S. 18–21, Fig. 8.

50. Vgl. Anm. 48.

51. Für einen literarischen Beleg dafür, dass die Umgebung von Uruk noch nach der Gründung der Stadt versumpft war und erst trocken gelegt werden musste s. C. Wilcke, *Das Lugalbandaepos* (Wiesbaden, 1969) S. 119 zu den Zeilen 294–301.

52. Dies kann erschlossen werden aus der ständig anwachsenden Gesamtbesiedlungsfläche (= Addition der Flächen aller während einer Periode besiedelten Orte) im Gebiet des Uruk-Survey:

Spät-Uruk Zeit	*ca.*	440 ha
Ǧemdet Nasr Zeit	*ca.*	500 ha
Frühdynastisch I	*ca.*	950 ha
Frühdynastisch II–III	*ca.*	1050 ha
Ur-III Zeit	*ca.*	1350 ha

53. P. Buringh, "Living Conditions in the Lower Mesopotamian Plain in Ancient Times," *Sumer* XIII (1957) 38–41; Wright, *Rural Production*, S. 19–20; *UCS*, S. 12.

die Situation ein, dass das Land entlang der wenigen Wasserläufe nicht mehr ausreicht, um die Versorgung sicherzustellen. Man ist daher gezwungen, Wasser mit Hilfe von Kanälen in diejenigen Gebiete zu bringen, die früher von kleineren Wasserläufen durchzogen waren, die aber nun ausgetrocknet waren. So scheint dies der Zeitpunkt zu sein, wo zum ersten Mal grosse Gemeinschaftsaufgaben im Bereich der Wasserversorgung nötig wurden, und der Zug zur Konzentration dürfte auch unter diesem Gesichtspunkt zu sehen sein.

Wenn in der eben behandelten FD-I Zeit sich auch zum ersten Mal so etwas wie ein relativ stabiles System von wenigen grossen Wasserläufen auszubilden scheint, so wird doch durch die sichtbaren Veränderungen zur nächsten Zeit hin auch hier eine Differenzierung möglich.[54] Die schon erwähnte Tendenz der Siedlungen, sich an die verbleibenden Wasserläufe zu verlagern, scheint sich viel stärker als Bewegung nach Osten als nach Westen auszuwirken, also an den östlichen Euphratarm mehr als an den westlichen. Der Grund dürfte darin zu sehen sein, dass aus irgendwelchen Gründen der östliche Euphratarm der bedeutendere, weil mehr Wasser führende, wurde.[55] Die Auswirkungen sind enorm: Erhalt der Substanz oder sogar Verringerung der Grösse bei den Siedlungen am westlichen Euphratarm, Vermehrung und Vergrösserung der Siedlungen am östlichen Euphratarm, eine Entwicklung von der vor allem Umma profitiert, das nun am Ende von FD-I erst die Grösse einer Uruk vergleichbaren Stadt annahm.[56]

Leider sind wir nur ungenügend über die Situation im Bereich des Staates von Lagaš unterrichtet, insbesondere über die Frage, woher das Hauptbewässerungswasser für dieses Gebiet kam.[57] Die vielen Belege für Kanäle, die vom östlichen Euphratarm nach Südosten in das Gebiet von Lagaš abzweigen,[58] die Ergebnisse des Uruk-Surveys und des Surveys der Girsu-Region für dieses Gebiet[59] sowie der lange Streit zwischen Umma und Lagaš um Wasser und Grenzgebiete[60] zeigen alle, dass normalerweise der Euphrat der Hauptwasserlieferant war. Das Wasser des Tigris wurde nur selten herangezogen, wohl mit dem Ziel,

54. *UCS*, S. 18–19 und Fig. 6.

55. Dieser östliche Arm des Euphrat ist in der neueren Literatur meist als Iturungal angesprochen worden, doch wird diese Auffassung nicht von den Texten getragen. Dazu und zum allgemeinen Problem vgl. *UCS*, S. 42–46.

56. *Ibid.*, S. 18; Nissen, in Ucko, Tringham, und Dimbleby, *Man, Settlement and Urbanism*, S. 796.

57. Die Diskussion ist in letzter Zeit wieder etwas aufgelebt durch die Beiträge von E. de Vaumas, "L'écoulement des eaux en Mésopotamie et la provenance des eaux de Tello," *Iraq* XXVII (1965) 81–99; *TUU*, S. 119–25; Jacobsen, in *Sumer* XXV 105–6 (letzterer mit einem plausibeln Vorschlag für die Lokalisierung des alten Tigrislaufes).

58. *TUU*, S. 12–13 und passim zu den Kanälen Gibil, Kunagara und Magurra, sowie die Skizze auf S. 212. Vgl. dazu die Bemerkungen *UCS*, S. 52 mit Anm. 70.

59. *UCS*, Fig. 17; Jacobsen, in *Sumer* XXV 103–8.

60. Für eine Zusammenfassung und Erklärung dieses Streites vgl. Jacobsen, in *Sumer* XXV 104; für einen zusätzlichen Erklärungsversuch vgl. Nissen, in Ucko, Tringham, und Dimbleby, *Man, Settlement and Urbanism*, S. 796.

der Kontrolle durch Umma zu entgehen.[61] Das so entstandene plötzliche
Überangebot von Wasser mag eine der gefährlichsten Entwicklungen für
bewässertes Land unterstützt haben: die Versalzung, die im Gebiet von Lagaš
zur Frühdynastischen Zeit erstmals nachzuweisen ist, und dort die Verlagerung
des politischen Schwerpunktes im Gebiet von Lagaš nach Norden zur Folge
gehabt hat.[62]

Doch wenn auch mit der Ausbildung der Flussysteme, der Einführung
der Grosskanäle, dem Auf- und Ausbau der Systeme der zentralen Orte am
Anfang von FD-II die meisten der Einzelheiten vorhanden sind, die in den
folgenden geschichtlichen Perioden den Hintergrund abgaben, vor dem sich
alles abspielt, so ist mit dieser Situation doch keineswegs ein stabiler Zustand
erreicht. Freilich wissen wir trotz der nun einsetzenden grossen Zahl von Texten
relativ wenig über die folgenden Zeiten von FD-III und Akkad, doch können
wir aus einigen Anhaltspunkten schliessen, dass besonders einer der Trends, die
wir für die frühere Zeit vermutet hatten, auch weiter anhält: der Rückgang des
Wassers.

Die Tatsache, dass zwar Uruk eine bedeutende Stadt bleibt und in den politischen Auseinandersetzungen eine führende Rolle einnimmt, kann nicht darüber
hinwegsehen lassen, dass nach Aussage der Erforschung der Ruine die Grösse
der Besiedlungsfläche innerhalb der Stadtmauer rapide abgenommen hat:
weite Flächen sind während der Ğemdet Nasr und vor allem der FD-I Zeit zum
letzten Mal besiedelt, ganz zu schweigen von den weiten Besiedlungsflächen
ausserhalb der Stadtmauer aus der FD-I Zeit,[63] die alle nie wieder besiedelt
wurden. Besiedlungsschichten der FD-III Zeit finden sich vor allem im engeren
Bereich um das Hauptheiligtum Eanna, während von der Besiedlung in der
Akkadischen Zeit noch weniger bekannt ist.[64] Diese Entwicklung ist wohl
kaum zu trennen von den Anhaltspunkten für die Ur-III und die folgende Zeit,
dass der an Uruk vorbeifliessende Euphratarm so gut wie kein Wasser mehr
führte.[65] Dies dürfte im grösseren Zusammenhang mit dem Rückgang des
Wassers zu sehen sein, wobei der westliche Arm mehr betroffen wurde als der
östliche. Dieser neuerlichen Verknappung des Wassers konnte nun nicht mehr

61. Jacobsen, in *Sumer* XXV 104–5; bereits Jacobsen und Adams, in *Science*, Bd. 138,
S. 1252.

62. Jacobsen und Adams, in *Science*, Bd. 138, S. 1252. Die Versalzung ist aber keineswegs
auf das Gebiet von Lagaš in der FD-III Zeit beschränkt, wie aus der Vielzahl der Felder von
Lagaš, Umma und Ur aus der Ur III Zeit hervorgeht, die als "am Brackwasser gelegen
(a-uri)" oder "versalzen (ki-mun, ki-mun-gál, du₆-mun)" bezeichnet werden:
Lagaš   *UNL* I, FN 84, 272, 329, 366a, 586, 724.
Umma *UNL* I, FN 8, 18, 216, 275, 366b, 399, 450b, 473, 482, 518, 585, 680, 746, 768, 815.
Ur   *UNL* I, FN 244, 346, 551.

63. Nissen, in Ucko, Tringham, und Dimbleby, *Man, Settlement and Urbanism*, S. 794
mit Anm. 16 und 17.

64. Reste der akkadischen Zeit wurden in Uruk innerhalb der Stadtmauer nur auf den
ganz im Norden liegenden Hügeln gefunden (Eigene Beobachtungen an Lesefunden).

65. *UCS*, S. 46–47.

dadurch begegnet werden, dass man entweder mit dem Wasser seine Siedlung
verlagerte, oder dass man durch Intensivierung der Heranleitung oder Nutzung
des Wassers die Effektivität verbesserte, sondern sie führte sehr wahrscheinlich
zu echten Engpässen, wovon in erster Linie diejenigen betroffen waren, die am
unteren Teil eines Flusses oder Kanals sassen. Die dauernden politischen und
kriegerischen Auseinandersetzungen zwischen den Städten während der FD-III
Zeit dürften nicht zuletzt darauf zurückgehen, dass die auf diese Weise Be-
nachteiligten versuchten, sich auf anderem als friedlichem Wege das zum
Überleben nötige Wasser zu sichern.

Ein interessantes Detail soll hier aufgegriffen werden, weil es zeigt, wie sehr
sich grundlegende Änderungen noch in historischer Zeit vollzogen haben.
Vergleicht man die Karten für das Uruk-Survey–Gebiet für die FD-I Zeit und
die Ur-III Zeit im Hinblick auf Lage und Wasserversorgung von Bad-Tibira[66]
miteinander, so fällt auf, dass in der FD-I Zeit der als alt bekannte Ort Bad-
Tibira[67] an einem der kleineren von NW nach SO verlaufenden Wasserläufe
liegt; keine Spur von der in späterer Zeit wichtigen Querverbindung Bad-
Tibira—Larsa. In der Ur-III Zeit dagegen (und wahrscheinlich schon etwas
älter) nimmt der Ort eine derartige Form an, dass zwingend geschlossen werden
muss, dass er nun an einem NO-SW verlaufenden Kanal lag, der bei Tell en-
Nasiriya von einem Hauptausläufer des östlichen Euphratarmes abgezweigt
worden war. Dies unterstreicht nicht nur einmal mehr die Annahme, dass die
entscheidende Verlagerung des östlichen Euphratarms an die uns aus der Ur-III
Zeit geläufige Stelle in oder nach die FD-I Zeit[68] gesetzt werden muss, und
berichtet uns nicht nur von der Fertigkeit der damaligen Wasserbauer, die Fluss-
ableitungen durchzuführen verstanden, sondern ist ein weiteres Anzeichen für
die Wasserknappheit im westlichen Euphratarm, da durch diese neue Verbindung die Wasserversorgung von Uruk und Ur[69] sichergestellt wurde.

Wegen der besonderen Bedeutung, die die Natur der Bewässerungssysteme
für jegliche kulturhistorische Diskussion hat, soll hier noch einmal auf die Frage
des frühesten Auftretens grosser Kanalsysteme eingegangen werden. Oben
wurde schon bemerkt, dass Kanäle im eigentlichen Sinn erst in oder nach FD-I
zum ersten Mal auftauchen. Die nächste Frage wäre nun, ob die Vielzahl von
Einrichtungen in Verbindung mit Kanälen, die uns aus der Ur-III Zeit bekannt
sind,[70] schon zugleich mit den Kanälen eingeführt wurden.

---

66. *UCS*, Fig. 5 und 6.

67. In der "sumerischen Königsliste" ist Bad-Tibira als zweite Stadt in der Reihe der
vorsintflutlichen Herrschaftszentren angegeben: Th. Jacobsen, *The Sumerian King List*
(*AS*, Nr. 11 [1939]) S. 70–73.

68. Wahrscheinlich am Beginn von FD-II, da Umma, das an diesem neuen Wasserlauf
liegt, kaum Reste aus der FD-I Zeit aufwies (siehe dazu aber die einschränkenden Bemerkungen *UCS*, S. 227 zu WS 197).

69. Für eine entsprechende Information aus einer späteren Zeit cf. den Nur-Adad Text:
J. van Dijk, "Une insurrection générale au pays de Larša avant l'avènement de Nūradad,"
JCS XIX (1965) 1–25; behandelt *UCS*, S. 49.

70. S. die Zusammenstellung *TUU*, S. 47–65.

Es braucht nicht betont zu werden, dass wir keinerlei direkte Nachrichten für diese Frage haben. Anhaltspunkte können aber aus den Funktionen dieser Einrichtungen gewonnen werden, die nämlich zum grössten Teil bestimmt zu sein scheinen, Wasser so lange wie möglich zur Bewässerung verfügbar zu halten, wozu besonders die vielerlei Arten von Becken zu zählen sind, die an verschiedenen Stellen aus den Kanälen Wasser abzweigen, um es bei Niedrigwasser wieder in den Kanal abgeben zu können.[71] Im Sinne der obigen Annahme einer Verschlechterung der Wassersituation ist zu vermuten, dass diese Zusatzeinrichtungen erst nach und nach geschaffen wurden, um der Verringerung des Wassers zu begegnen. Dazu passt, dass von den ganzen Termini für derartige Einrichtungen kein einziger in eindeutiger Verwendung als Ausdruck für eine Bewässerungseinrichtung vor der FD-III Zeit belegt ist, und es fällt ferner auf, dass alle Termini Ausdrücke der normalen Sprache sind, wie Mund, Becken, Torhaus, Verschluss,[72] die nur durch Zusätze oder ihre Verbindung mit Kanalnamen als Termini des Bewässerungswesens erkenntlich sind. Wären Kanäle und ihre Zusatzeinrichtungen schon mit der Frühzeit des Ackerbaus in Babylonien verknüpft, sollte man spezielle termini technici erwarten. Zugleich fällt auf, dass der einzige Beruf, der speziell mit Kanälen zu tun hat, der gú-gal (auch kù-gal) "Kanalinspektor o.ä.,"[73] der später so etwas wie eine Wassersteuer (gugallûtu)[74] einzutreiben hatte, in der akkadischen Zeit zum ersten Mal auftaucht. Bezeichnenderweise finden wir ihn weder in den Wirtschaftstexten der FD-III Zeit noch in den sonst sehr ausführlichen Berufsnamenlisten der Fara-Zeit,[75] geschweige denn in den älteren Textgruppen.[76] Statt spezieller Berufe wurden für die Arbeiten an den Kanälen und den einzelnen Teilen der Bewässerungs-systeme guruš und geme, "Arbeiter" und "Arbeiterinnen," eingesetzt, wohl unter einem ugula, "Aufseher."[77]

Es wird also deutlich, dass zumindest von der ausgehenden frühgeschichtlichen Zeit an *eine* Entwicklung sich kontinuierlich vollzogen hat: der Rückgang des nach Südbabylonien gelangenden Euphratwassers, der eine entscheidende Gefährdung der Existenz bedeutete. Auf die dauernde Verschlechterung

71. Kun-zi-da, nag-ku₅, bar-lá, behandelt in *TUU*, S. 50–51, 54–56, 61–62.

72. Ka, "Mund" > "Zusammenfluss oder Abzweig von Wasserläufen"; kun, "Becken"; dub-lá, "Torbau"; kéš-du, "schliessen" > "Wehr." Siehe die Einzeldiskussionen weiter unter.

73. A. Salonen, *Agricultura Mesopotamica* (Helsinki, 1968) S. 339; die von Jacobsen, in *ZA*, Bd. 52, S. 123, Anm. 71 vertretene Etymologie von ensí, "city-ruler," als en-si-ak, "manager of the arable land," in Kraeling und Adams, *City Invincible*, S. 38, herangezogen, um zu zeigen, dass es bereits in der Frühzeit einen staatlichen Verwalter des bebauten Landes und damit der Bewässerungsanlagen gab, erfährt einen entscheidenden Widerspruch durch die These, dass ensí dem vorsumerischen Sprachgut angehöre (*CAD*, Bd. I/J, S. 266).

74. *CAD*, s.v. *gugallu* und *gugallûtu*.

75. S. die frühdynastischen Lú-Listen in *MSL* XII.

76. Ur (*UET* II), Ğemdet Nasr (*OECT* VII), Uruk (*ATU*; "Remarks on the Uruk IVa and III Forerunners" of the ED Lú A-List, *MSL* XII 4–8 und Pl. I).

77. *TUU*, S. 66–83 und passim; selten auch guruš-šà-sahara (*TUU*, S. 73 mit Anm. 219).

wurden im Laufe der Zeit immer neue Antworten gefunden, die freilich nie eine endgültige Lösung darstellen konnten. Auf diese dauernde Veränderung soll hier noch einmal hingewiesen werden, da hieraus folgt, dass die Verhältnisse zu einer Zeit keinesfalls auf die einer anderen Zeit übertragen werden können.

DIE GEOGRAPHISCHEN VERHÄLTNISSE ZUR ZEIT DER 3. DYNASTIE VON UR

Im folgenden soll versucht werden durch Klärung und gegenseitige Abgrenzung der zur dieser Zeit gebräuchlichen Termini für geographische Einzelheiten, sowie durch Herbeiziehung der uns von den archäologischen Untersuchungen bekannten Informationen ein Bild von den geographischen Verhältnissen der Ur-III Zeit zu zeichnen. Dabei ist leider die Einschränkung zu betonen, dass so gut wie nichts über Nordbabylonien ausgesagt werden kann aus Mangel an schriftlicher Überlieferung.[78] Dies ist besonders schmerzlich, da wir aus der Entwicklung während der älteren und der jüngeren[79] Perioden wissen, dass die Verhältnisse vom Süden nicht in den Norden übertragen werden dürfen.

Auf eine weitere Einschränkung ist bereits hingewiesen worden: die Aufzeichnungen beschränken sich auf diejenigen Informationen, die festzuhalten für den geregelten Ablauf der wirtschaftlichen Vorgänge absolut notwendig waren. Alles allgemein Bekannte wird weggelassen mit der Folge, dass vieles gerade für uns Interessante verschwiegen wird. Dazu gehört, dass der zu einer Siedlung gehörige Wasserlauf einfach "der Kanal" genannt wird, und dass die Lage eines Feldes zur Siedlung nur selten angegeben wird.[80] Trotz dieser Einschränkungen sollen in den folgenden Abschnitten die Wasserversorgung, die Siedlungsformen und die Landschaftsformen behandelt werden, wobei jeweils am Anfang die zum Themenkreis gehörigen sumerischen Termini genannt und behandelt werden, gefolgt von einer allgemeinen Beschreibung der Systeme und der Gesamtsituation.

78. Cf. die Zusammenstellung der Quellen der Ur III Zeit in *UNL* I, Teil 1, 4–5.

79. Durch die Gründung neuer Städte und Kanäle unter den Vorgängern Hammurapi's von Babylon (Sumula'el, *ZZB*, S. 124; Apilsîn, *ZZB*, S. 152; Sînmuballiṭ, *ZZB*, S. 152–53) wurde der Umfang der landwirtschaftlich genutzten Fläche in Nordbabylonien erheblich ausgedehnt. Der dadurch erhöhte Wasserverbrauch war sicher ein wesentlicher Grund für die Wasserverknappung im Süden, vor allem im Larsa Rimsîn's (dazu Renger, in *AfO* XXIII 77–78). Zur Kolonisierung des nordbabylonischen Raumes vergleiche die Ergebnisse des Survey of Central Akkad: Adams, in *Sumer* XIV 102–3 und ders., Gibson, *Kish* S. 186. Wann diese Bemühungen eingesetzt haben, muss aus Mangel an Informationen im Dunkeln bleiben.

80. S. oben Anm. 20.

Die Wasserversorgung

Für Wasserläufe sind drei Ausdrücke bekannt:

i_7: scheint ziemlich unterschiedslos für Flüsse und grössere Kanäle gebraucht worden zu sein.[81] Ein Kriterium scheint zu sein, dass ein i_7 mit Booten befahren werden kann.[82]

e: offenbar kleiner als i_7, da nie Schiffstransporte belegt sind. Bisweilen kann e den Kanal in einem frühen Stadium vor Füllung mit Wasser bezeichnen.[83]

pa_5 bzw. pa_4-a-da-ga: die kleinsten Bewässerungsgräben.[84]

Da e wahrscheinlich eine Spezialbezeichnung darstellt handelt es sich im wesentlichen um einen Gegensatz i_7:pa_5. Nach modernen Beispielen[85] dürfte es sich um den Gegensatz handeln zwischen den Wasserläufen, die das Wasser bis dicht an die Verbrauchsstelle, d. h. die zu bewässernden Felder bringt, und den Gräben, die dann das Wasser aus diesen Kanälen auf die Felder bringen und die Verteilung auf den Feldern übernehmen.

Wenige der in den Texten bezeugten Zusatzeinrichtungen an den Kanälen[86] lassen sich eindeutig bestimmen. Zu den interessanteren zählen die verschiedenen Einrichtungen zur Absperrung oder Abdämmung, die in einem Land und einer Situation, in der jegliches Wasser mit Hilfe langer Kanäle an das zu bewässernde Land gebracht werden muss, in dem also nie genug Wasser vorhanden ist, um alle Felder gleichzeitig zu bewässern, unbedingt notwendig für das Funktionieren eines Bewässerungssystems sind.

Nach modernen Beispielen zu schliessen hat man vor allem mit zwei Arten von Absperrvorrichtungen zu rechnen: (a) die grösser bemessenen, die das Wasser in den grösseren Kanälen und (b) die kleineren, die das Wasser in den auf die Felder führenden Gräben regulieren. Beide sind am Beginn der jeweiligen Kanäle zu erwarten, bzw. auch zusätzlich im Verlaufe solcher Kanäle, die sich in mehrere gleichwertige Kanäle aufspalten. Während es sich bei (a) um grössere gemauerte und mit Toren versehene Anlagen handelt, sind die unter (b) genannten Anlagen wohl lediglich Erdwälle, die bei Bedarf schnell errichtet oder entfernt werden.[87]

Bei Durchsicht der in der Ur-III Zeit gebrauchten termini fällt auf, dass es nur Bezeichnungen für einigermassen aufwendige Sperrvorrichtungen gibt, was die Annahme rechtfertigt, dass auch in alter Zeit die kleinen Bewässerungsgräben durch Erdwälle verschlossen und durch ihre Wegnahme wieder geöffnet werden

---

81. *TUU*, S. 35.

82. *Ibid.*, S. 36.

83. *ZZB*, S. 112, Anm. 567; Jacobsen, "Salinity and Irrigation Agriculture," S. 6: "pa_5 often run along the top of artificial dykes (e) to preserve desirable elevation"; *TUU*, S. 40: "Bewässerungsgraben, Kanaldamm."

84. *TUU*, S. 42 und vorhergehende Anm.

85. Wirth, *Agrargeographie*, S. 95–96, Abb. 25; Adams, *Land behind Baghdad*, S. 19.

86. S. die Bezeichnungen bei *TUU*, S. 47–65.

87. S. Anm. 85.

konnten. In den Texten tauchen in diesen Fällen lediglich die Ausdrücke für öffnen und schliessen auf, keine Bezeichnung für den Wall selbst.[88]

Als Bezeichnung für das Wehr selbst kennen wir ^{giš}kéš-du = akk. *erretu ša nâri*, doch taucht sie selten auf,[89] vor allem kaum in Wirtschaftsurkunden der Ur III Zeit.[90] Nicht direkt bekannt sind die Absperrvorrichtungen in Verbindung mit anderen Einrichtungen an Kanälen, dem kun-zi-da,[91] nag-ku₅,[92] zwei Arten von Becken, die geöffnet und geschlossen werden konnten. Sie konnten aus Holz sein, werden also sicher auch feste Einrichtungen gewesen sein.[93]

Am interessantesten scheint die grosse komplexe Anlage des dub-lá ^{d}utu zu sein, die in Texten aus Umma wiederholt auftaucht. Ihre Lage wird als östlich unweit von Umma bestimmt.[94] Die Anlage bestand aus mehreren Teilen, die auch sonst alleine als Bewässerungseinrichtungen bekannt sind, wie Wehre, mehrere Arten von Becken, während das Kernstück offenbar eine dub-lá genannte Einrichtung war. Dub-lá ist eigentlich ein Torbau,[95] am besten bekannt vom dub-lá-mah in Ur, wo es sich nach den archäologischen Resten um ein Bauwerk handelt das mit zwei hintereinanderliegenden Räumen genau dem Typ des Mehrkammertores entspricht.[96] Ein solches Bauwerk entspricht dem, was man von einer Schleuse erwarten sollte, und so sollte einen nicht wundern, dass eine offenbar sehr aufwendige Bewässerungseinrichtung so benannt wird. Selbstverständlich ist uns die genaue Lage unbekannt, doch soll hier eine Hypothese über Ort und Funktion aufgestellt werden.

In der Nähe von Umma gibt es eine Stelle, an der die Existenz eines Wehrs mit Schleuse gefordert werden muss und schwierige Strömungsverhältnisse

---

88. *TUU*, S. 71–72.

89. Die klarsten Belege sind Eannatum Galet A vii 8–13 und Entemena Brique A iii 10 ff. (E. Sollberger und J.-R. Kupper, *Inscriptions royales sumériennes et akkadiennes* [Paris, 1971] S. 59, 68), woraus hervorgeht, dass die Wehre aus gebrannten Ziegeln errichtet waren.

90. *TUU*, S. 51–52. Der einzige einigermassen sichere Beleg ist a-šà kéš-du, *UNL* I, FN 181 (ohne ^{giš}!), und wahrscheinlich kéš-du nag-su^{ki}, *TUU*, S. 52, Anm. 121; *NG* I 31, Anm. 3.

91. Schwierig zu beantworten ist die Frage, wo sich das kunzida eines Kanals befunden hat. Diejenigen, die in kun = akk. *zibbatu*, "Schwanz," im Gegensatz zu ka, "Abzweigstelle," sehen (Literatur, *TUU*, S. 49), setzen auch das kunzida an die Mündung, d.h. das Ende eines Kanals. Ausdrücke wie: kun-zi-da ka i₇-i-si-in^{ki}, "das kunzida am ka des Isin-Kanals" (Jahresdatum Sumuᵓel 14) ergeben dann aber keinen Sinn. Mit F. R. Kraus, "Provinzen des neusumerischen Reiches von Ur," *ZA*, Bd. 51 (1955) S. 53 ist dagegen kun wohl auch in Verbindung mit Kanälen als "Becken" zu übersetzen, kunzida als eine besondere Art von Becken. Bei diesem Vorgehen löst sich auch die Merkwürdigkeit auf, dass in einigen Fällen ka, "Abzweigstelle," und kun, "Mündung," an derselben Stelle gelegen haben müssten (*TUU*, S. 50).

92. *TUU*, S. 54–56; Salonen, *Agricultura*, S. 223–28.

93. *TUU*, S. 56 mit Anm. 134.

94. *Ibid.*, S. 59–61, 189–90.

95. W. Heimpel, *Tierbilder in der sumerischen Literatur* (StP, Bd. 2 [1968]) S. 323–26.

96. C. L. Woolley, *Ur Excavations* V (Oxford, 1939) 28, VIII (London, 1965) 9–16 mit Taf. 48–51.

zudem das Vorhandensein einer recht komplizierten Anlage wahrscheinlich machen: die Stelle wenig westlich von Zabalam und nordöstlich von Umma, an der der von Adab kommende östliche Euphratarm sich in den über Zabalam nach Apisala und in den nach Umma—Bad-Tibira fliessenden Arm trennt. Dabei ist zu vermuten, dass der in gerader Richtung nach Zabalam weiterfliessende Wasserlauf dem Beharrungsvermögen von Strömungen eher entgegenkommt als der fast im rechten Winkel abzweigende Arm; dass also ohne Gegenmassnahmen der Zabalam-Arm an Bedeutung gewinnt auf Kosten des nach Süden abgehenden Armes.

Von der Bedeutung der Wasserverbindung Adab–Umma–Bad-Tibira–Larsa–Ur als Haupthandelsstrasse der Zeit der 3. Dynastie von Ur aus gesehen ist es daher äusserst wichtig, an diesen gefährdeten Stellen Massnahmen zu ergreifen, die dafür sorgen, dass in dem für die Wirtschaft wichtigeren Wasserlauf genügend Wasser bleibt. Dies ist nur so zu erreichen, dass man an dieser Abzweigstelle im nach Osten führenden Arm, der aber ebenfalls eine Bedeutung als Handelsstrasse hatte, eine grosse Anlage errichtete, die einmal in der Lage war, die Hauptströmung umzuleiten, das Wasser zugleich etwas anzustauen, so dass es leicht in die gewünschte Richtung abzuleiten war, und eine Vorrichtung einzubauen, die dieses Bauwerk nicht als allzu grosses Hindernis für die Schifffahrt erscheinen liess.[97]

Mit den genannten Spezial- und Zusatzeinrichtungen befand sich offenbar das Bewässerungssystem der Ur-III Zeit auf einer hohen Stufe der Organisation, die es den Bewohnern gestattete, den grösstmöglichen Nutzen aus dem Wasser in den vorhandenen Kanälen zu ziehen. Neben den mit dem Ausbau des bestehenden Systems einhergehenden Arbeiten an den Kanälen und ihren Anlagen[98] zeigen jedoch zwei Dinge, dass man durch Anlage bzw. Neubelebung grösserer Kanäle sich bemühte, das System insgesamt zu vergrössern. Hier ist einmal die Neuanlage eines grösseren, auch von Schiffen befahrenen Kanals zu nennen, der durch seinen Namen "Amar-Su'ena Kanal" das Alter seiner Entstehung zu erkennen gibt.[99] Leider sind die Belege zu wenig zahlreich, um eine Lokalisierung durchführen zu können, doch muss er im Umkreis von Umma gelegen haben,[100]

97. Hier soll auf Tell Khaita = WS 170 (*UCS*, S. 226) hingewiesen werden, das an einer Stelle liegt, an der so etwas wie das dubla-ᵈutu zu erwarten wäre. Der Tell scheint eine künstliche Aufschüttung oder eine grosse Ziegelsetzung zu bergen, keinen Siedlungshügel. Er ist deshalb auch nicht durch Oberflächenfunde zu datieren.

98. *TUU*, S. 66–69.

99. Durch veschiedene Texte sind wir über die Neuanlage (Vergrösserung) dieses Kanals unterrichtet, *TUU*, S. 66, 97–104.

100. *Ibid*., S. 97; *UCS*, S. 47. Die dort vorgeschlagene Lokalisierung wird von Wilcke, in *ZA*, Bd. 62, S. 56–59 mit guten Gründen bestritten. Bei der hier zugrunde gelegten Deutung von kunzida als eine Art von Becken (vgl. Anm. 91) ist das Diagramm bei Wilcke allerdings zu ändern, da Šešdua dann nicht den Endpunkt des Amar-Su'ena-Kanals markieren muss. Es entfällt ferner die Annahme, dass der Kanal zwei Tagereisen lang gewesen sei, und somit das Hauptargument für die in *UCS*, S. 47, Anm. 40 ausgesprochene Ablehnung der Identifizierung des A.-Kanals mit dem Wasserlauf, der nordwestlich von Umma den östlichen Euphrat erlässt und dann über Tell Jīd in Richtung Uruk fliesst. Bei Annahme

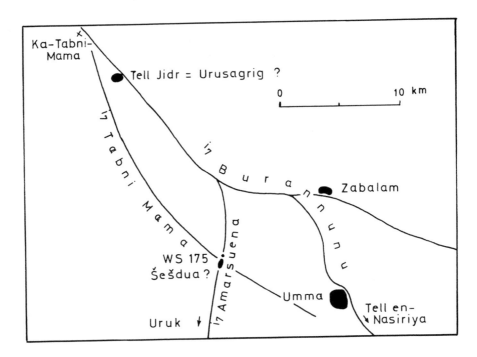

wie die obige Karte zeigt. Der andere Punkt betrifft die lediglich vom Survey zu
erschliessenden Bemühungen desselben Herrschers Amar-Su᾿ena, den westlichen Arm des Euphrats von Fara nach Uruk neu zu beleben.[101]

Im ganzen dürfen jedoch diese und andere Massnahmen nicht so sehr unter
der Überschrift Expansion der landwirtschaftlichen Nutzfläche gesehen werden,
sondern eher als Versuche, der Wasserverknappung Herr zu werden.

DIE SIEDLUNGSSYSTEME

Leider müssen auch hier Einschränkungen vorangestellt werden. Denn obwohl
wir für die Ur-III Zeit weitaus am meisten Informationen sowohl durch Texte
als auch durch die Surveys besitzen, ist es doch nur in sehr wenigen Fällen
möglich, diese beiden Quellen gemeinsam für die Rekonstruktion einzusetzen.
Dies liegt vor allem daran, dass die Gebiete, für die wir über die besten inschrift-

---

dieser Möglichkeit und der wieder wahrscheinlicher werdenden Identifizierung von Keši/
Urusagrig mit Tell Jidr (s. Anm. 11) ergäbe sich aus den Angaben für den A.-Kanal und
den Ergebnissen des Surveys (*UCS*, Fig. 17) die Situation auf der beigefügten Karte; so
würde verständlich, dass der Amar-Su᾿ena-Kanal später die umstrittene Grenzlinie zwischen
Isin und Larsa sein konnte (Wilcke, in *ZA*, Bd. 62, S. 58).
101. *UCS*, S. 47.

lichen Zeugnisse verfügen, die Gebiete um Lagaš und Umma,[102] noch zu wenig archäologisch untersucht sind; die archäologisch gut erforschten Gebiete um Uruk und Nippur dagegen werden kaum durch inschriftliche Quellen beleuchtet. Dennoch ist vielleicht eine allgemeine Linie in einem generellen Ansteigen der Zahl der Siedlungen von der frühdynastischen zur Ur-III Zeit hin zu bemerken. Dies ist vor allem im Gebiet des Uruk-Surveys zu beobachten,[103] weniger im Gebiet des Kiš-Surveys.[104]

Bei diesem Trend scheint bedeutsam, dass vor allem die Zahlen bei den kleinen und mittleren Ortsgrössen ansteigen, während sich im Bereich von Siedlungen um 100 ha und darüber kaum Verschiebungen ergeben. Diese Beobachtung wird sehr schön durch eine Untersuchung der Texte aus Tello/ Lagaš bestätigt, wo gegenüber 22 Siedlungen für die FD-III und 34 für die akk. Zeit, 94 Siedlungen für die Ur-III Zeit bezeugt sind, und die Verschiebung offensichtlich hauptsächlich auf das Konto der kleinen Siedlungen geht,[105] während die bedeutenden Orte bereits aus älterer Zeit bekannt sind.

Es tritt somit eine Siedlungsform wieder stärker auf, das vermutlich nur von einer Familie oder Familiengemeinschaft bewohnte Gehöft bzw. Dorf, die in den davorliegenden Zeiten sehr zurückgegangen war,[106] äusserlich wohl gut zu erklären durch die unruhigen Verhältnisse zur späteren FD Zeit und der Akkad Zeit, durch die wohl kleine unbefestigte Siedlungen am ehesten in Mitleidenschaft gezogen worden waren. Die wohl etwas ruhigeren Zeiten unter der 3. Dynastie von Ur dagegen erlaubten wieder Siedlungen ausserhalb der befestigten Städte.

Doch ist hier ein spezieller Punkt von Interesse: da die Effektivität der Landwirtschaft sinkt, je weiter die Felder von der Siedlung entfernt sind, gibt es eine unsichtbare Grenze um jede Siedlung, ausserhalb derer Land von Bauern dieser Siedlung nicht bestellt werden kann. Dabei ist der Radius bei grossen Siedlungen genauso gross wie bei kleinen, da er von der menschlichen Laufgeschwindigkeit abhängt. Das auf diese Weise um eine städtische Siedlung sich gruppierende Land genügte offenbar während der späten Frühdynastischen Zeit, um die

102. In beiden Bereichen wären intensive Geländeuntersuchungen sehr wünschenswert, doch sähen sich solche Unternehmungen vor grosse Probleme gestellt, da das Gebiet im östlichen Halbkreis um Umma zum grossen Teil von Dünen bedeckt ist oder sich im Bewässerungsgebiet des Šaṭṭ el-Ġarrāf befindet. Letzteres trifft auch für den grössten Teil des Gebietes von Lagaš zu, während andere Teile im Dauersumpfgebiet liegen.

103. Bei der Gegenüberstellung von 44 Siedlungen der FD-III Zeit (*UCS*, S. 21) und 89 der Ur-III Zeit (*UCS*, S. 37) ist allerdings zu berücksichtigen, dass bei der Datierung der Orte mit Hilfe der Keramik zwischen den Perioden von Ur III und Isin/Larsa nicht unterschieden werden konnte. Es ist daher möglich, dass einige der der Ur-III Zeit zugeschriebenen Orte—vor allem die nicht an den grossen Kanälen gelegenen Orte nordöstlich und östlich von Uruk—erst aus der Isin/Larsa Zeit stammen.

104. Gibson, *Kish*, Table 3, S. 49.

105. Vgl. hierzu die vielen mit é-d u r u₅, "Dorf," und é, "Gehöft," zusammengesetzten Ortsnamen, Falkenstein, *AnOr*, Bd. 30, S. 25–27, 39–41.

106. *UCS*, Fig. 7, S. 17.

Nahrungsversorgung der Bevölkerung der Stadt sicherzustellen. Und das, obwohl wir wissen, dass es zumindest am Ende der Frühdynastischen Zeit Sitte war, Felder (oder nur Teile davon?) brach liegen zu lassen.[107]

Es war jedoch auch schon davon gesprochen worden, dass gerade während dieser Zeit die zunehmende Versalzung des Bodens Teile des südlichen Bereiches von Lagaš und von Ur das Land unbestellbar machte, und so grosse Siedlungen in ihrer Ausdehnung sehr schrumpften oder ganz aufgegeben werden mussten.[108] Könnte man nicht annehmen, dass für die so in die bestehenden Siedlungen flutenden Menschen das städtische Umland nicht mehr genügte, so dass die landwirtschaftliche Nutzfläche vergrössert werden musste? Da im Bereich der bestehenden Siedlungen alles verfügbare Land bereits bebaut war, ergab sich notwendigerweise der Zwang, neue Siedlungen zu gründen.

Denkbar ist allerdings auch, dass der Bereich Uruk–Umma–Lagaš die Getreideproduktion erhöhen musste, um andere Teile des Gesamtbereiches mit zu versorgen,[109] z.B. Ur, das möglicherweise ebenfalls hart von der Versalzung getroffen war,[110] aber wegen der Bedeutung als Hafenstadt nicht wie das Lagaš-Gebiet mit der Verlagerung von Siedlungen antworten konnte.

DIE LANDSCHAFTSFORMEN

Wie bereits bemerkt, ist über diesen Bereich bis jetzt am wenigsten gearbeitet worden, auch sind direkte Landschaftsbeschreibungen nicht aus der Literatur zu gewinnen. Indirekt tragen zu unserem Themenkreis die Erwähnungen bestimmter Formen in den Wirtschaftstexten bei, sei es, dass die Lage eines bestimmten Feldes durch seine Nähe zu einem "Wald" (= tir) präzisiert wird, oder dass daraus, dass von einem Feld sehr oft Rohrlieferungen gemeldet werden, geschlossen werden kann, dass es an sumpfiges Gebiet grenzte oder versumpfte Gebiete einschloss. Es liegen somit genügend Informationen vor, die es erlauben, das Vorhandensein bestimmter Landschaftsformen zu konstatieren.

So gut wie keine Nachrichten besitzen wir dagegen über die genaue Lokalisation bestimmter Landschaftsformen und, damit zusammenhängend, über Beziehungen von Einzelformen untereinander oder zu den Siedlungen oder gar

107. Jacobsen, "Salinity and Irrigation Agriculture," S. 65–66.

108. Dazu passt, dass nach Ausweis der Oberflächenfunde auf el-Hiba und Surġul diese Orte bis auf kleine Bereiche (heilige Bezirke?) während der FD-III Zeit aufgegeben wurden (Jacobsen, in *RA* LII 128 und eigene Beobachtungen). Dies wird durch die neuen Untersuchungen in el-Hiba bestätigt; s. D. P. Hansen, "Al-Hiba, 1968–1969, A Preliminary Report," *Artibus Asiae* XXXII (1970) 243–50, bes. 244.

109. Cf. dazu, dass in den wenigen Texten, die von Gerste oder Mehltransporten handeln, Umma, Kamari oder Apisala als Lieferanten auftauchen und Ur und Nippur als Zielorte (*TUU*, S. 131, 133, Anm. 80, 135, 139, 165). Zur Annahme, dass Ur möglicherweise auf Importe angewiesen war, s. *UNL* I, Teil 1, 11–12.

110. Vgl. dazu die Felder von Ur, die am Brackwasser lagen (*UNL* I, FN 244 und 551) sowie ein Feld, dessen Bodenqualität mit du₆-mun, "Salzhügel," angegeben wird (*UNL* I, FN 346).

über die flächenmässige Verteilung der einzelnen Landschaftsformen. Gemäss den heutigen Verhältnissen haben wir an Landschaftsformen—ausserhalb der Siedlungen—folgendes zu erwarten: intensiv kultiviertes Land, Ackerland, Weideland, Sumpfgebiete, "Wald," Steppe und Wüste.

Intensiv kultiviertes Land.—Angesprochen sind hier Gärten, in denen Dinge angebaut werden, die intensiver Pflege und intensiver Bewässerung bedürfen. Zu nennen sind vor allem die kiri$_6$, "Gärten," die zunächst als Baumgärten aufzufassen sind, meist wohl Palmgärten, aber auch mit anderen Obstbäumen bestanden.[111] Unter den Bäumen wurde wohl Gemüse ange-pflanzt.[112] Es ist zu vermuten, dass diese Gärten immer direkt an einem Haupt-kanal—der also immer Wasser führte—lagen[113] und in der Nähe der jeweiligen Siedlungen, obwohl die Belege sehr spärlich sind. Nicht recht in unser Bild passt, dass einmal 600 Bund Rohr als aus einem Garten stammend bezeichnet werden.[114]

Ackerland.—Wir sind über Felder weitaus besser unterrichtet, da die Art der Feldbestellung, Zahl der Arbeiter und ihre Entlohnung sowie Nutzungsabgaben die Grösse der Felder weit über die Buchführung eines Gartens hinausging und so diese Einzelheiten viel eher in schriftlicher Form niedergelegt wurden. Eingehende Vorarbeiten erleichtern zudem eine Zusammenfassung.[115]

Die Zahl der Texte und Einzelinformationen—insgesamt sind uns einstweilen 881 Felder mit Namen bekannt—darf allerdings nicht darüber hinwegtäuschen, dass diese Texte nur einen Bruchteil der damaligen landwirtschaftlichen Nutz-fläche erfassen. Gegenüber einer vermuteten landwirtschaftlichen Nutzfläche von 3000–5000 km² für Lagaš[116] ist durch Texte insgesamt nur eine Fläche von 705 km² belegt, die sich rapide verringert, wenn man methodisch einwand-freier vorgeht und nur Angaben aus Texten zusammenzählt, die aus demselben Jahr stammen.[117]

111. Z. B. wurde ein Teil des Gibil-Feldes in der Gemarkung Apisala als Palmgarten mit 405 Stämmen verpachtet (*UNL* I, FN 366). Zu anderen Früchten vgl. H. Sauren, *Wirtschaftsurkunden aus der Zeit der III. Dynastie von Ur im Besitz des Musée d'Art et d'Histoire in Genf* (Naples, 1969) No. 279 ii 1′–4′ und passim, wo von einem Garten mit Dattelpalmen und Granatapfelsträuchern die Rede ist.

112. *TUU*, S. 86; für moderne Beispiele vgl. E. Wirth, *Agrargeographie*, S. 52–53.

113. *TUU*, S. 130; *BIN* V, Nr. 255 Rs. 18: kiri$_6$ da-i$_7$-da, "Garten in der Nähe des Kanals" (wohl der Hauptkanal gemeint). *TUU*, S. 122, *ITT* III, Nr. 6447: kiri$_6$ ^{giš}gišimmar gú i$_7$-idigna-ka, "Palmgarten am Ufer des Tigris-Kanals."

114. *TUU*, S. 117.

115. *UNL*; Salonen, *Agricultura*.

116. *UNL* I, Teil 1, 11.

117. Die Fläche von 705 km² ergibt sich aus einer Addition aller jemals aus Tello belegten Felderangaben ohne Rücksicht darauf, ob und wie sie datiert sind. Für einzelne Jahre getrennt errechnen sich:

Šulgi 46	53,9 km²
Amar-Su'ena 1	192,3 km²
Amar-Su'ena 7	60,6 km²
Šū-Su'en 1	45,1 km²
Ibbi-Su'en 3	19,5 km²

Dass selbst eine Fläche von 705 km² unrealistisch ist, geht auch aus der Überlegung hervor, dass unter der Voraussetzung, dass der Ertrag eines i k u Land (= 3600 qm) durchschnittlich 300 s i l à Gerste (1 s i l à = 0,82 liter) beträgt,[118] und dass 2 s i l à die normale tägliche Getreideration eines Arbeiters beträgt,[119] der Gesamtertrag aus 705 km² nur reichen würde, um 76.500 Menschen[120] ein Jahr lang zu versorgen, bzw. 21.200 Menschen, wenn man die Gesamtfläche von 192,3 km² für das Jahr Amar-Su'ena 1 zugrunde legt.[121] Dabei ist zu beachten, dass, eine nicht unbeträchtliche Menge von Getreide an Tiere verfüttert wurde.[122] Ein Ansatz von 3000 km² landwirtschaftlicher Nutzfläche für Lagaš erscheint von daher durchaus realistisch.[123]

Ähnliche Überlegungen für andere Städte anzustellen verbietet sich durch die bei weitem geringere Menge an Informationen. So beträgt die 705 km² für Lagaš entsprechende Zahl nur 279 km² für das Gebiet Umma,[124] dem eine Schätzung von etwa 1000 km² gegenübersteht.[125]

Von den Informationen her ist also keine Auskunft über die Grösse der landwirtschaftlichen Nutzfläche einer Stadt im Verhältnis zu ihrer Grösse zu erhalten.

Weideland.—Wir betreten hier wieder einen recht ungesicherten Bereich, da es einmal an einer grösseren Untersuchung über die Viehwirtschaft der Ur-III Zeit fehlt, zum anderen kein Terminus für Weide oder Weideland im Sumerischen existiert. So sind wir darauf angewiesen, ein lückenhaftes Bild aus den wenigen Nachrichten zu erschliessen.

118. Eine Zusammenstellung der in *UNL* bei den einzelnen Feldern gebuchten Ernteerträge ergibt, dass der Ertrag von 1 i k u zwischen 0,9 und 2,7 g u r Gerste schwanken kann. Als sicherer Durchschnittswert wird hier ein Ertrag von 1 g u r Gerste (= 300 s i l à) pro 1 i k u Land angenommen.

119. I. J. Gelb, "The Ancient Mesopotamian Ration System," *JNES* XXIV (1965) 232–33.

120. Die gesamte landwirtschaftliche Nutzfläche beträgt 190.270 i k u mit einem angenommenen Gesamtertrag von *ca.* 56 Millionen s i l à Gerste.

121. Landwirtschaftliche Nutzfläche: 51.925 i k u mit einem angenommenen Gesamtertrag von 15,5 Millionen s i l à Gerste.

122. Vgl. den im folgenden erwähnten Text: N. Schneider, "Der Viehbestand des é - g a l in Lagaš," *AfO* IV (1927) 206–8 und die allgemeinen Bemerkungen von A. Salonen, *Agricultura*, S. 392: Pflugrinder erhalten normalerweise 3 g u r Gerste für das Pflügen von 1 b u r Feld.

123. Dabei würde sich der angenommene Gesamtertrag immerhin auf 231 Millionen s i l à Gerste belaufen.

124. Vgl. Anm. 117. Für einzelne Jahre getrennt ergeben sich folgende Zahlen:

Šulgi 46	30,3 km² (178,7 km²)
Amar-Su'ena 1	39,4 km² (187,8 km²)
Amar-Su'ena 7	72,6 km² (220,9 km²)
Šū-Su'en 1	61,5 km² (209,8 km²)
Ibbi-Su'en 3	42,7 km² (191,0 km²)

Die Zahlen in Klammern ergeben sich durch die Addition des Feldes *UNL* I, FN 794, das zwar für die betreffenden Jahre belegt ist, nicht aber ausdrücklich als jeweils ganz bebaut.

125. *UNL* I, Teil 1, 11.

Man wird davon ausgehen können, dass es zwei Arten von Viehhaltung gab:
die eine nahe bei oder in der Siedlung, die andere in Herdenform, wobei vermutlich verschiedene ökologische Räume genutzt wurden.

Dass alle Arten von Vieh bei Siedlungen gehalten wurden, ist uns aus Texten
bekannt, wobei aber vermutlich nur die Fälle aufgezeichnet wurden, wo es sich
um abgabenpflichtige Viehhaltung handelte. Die grossen Haushalte unterhielten
riesige Vieh"ställe," wie z.B. ein Palast in Girsu über Futtergerste für eine grosse
Anzahl von Schafen, Kühen und Ochsen abrechnet.[126] Diese sind in 5 Herden
unter je einem Oberhirten eingeteilt. Drei Monate lang werden eine wechselnde
Anzahl von Tieren mit Gerste gefüttert; allerdings sind die monatlichen Rationen
pro Schaf (2/3–2 s i l à) so gering, dass entweder daran zu denken ist, dass jedes
Tier nur einmal im Monat auf diese Weise gefüttert wurde, oder die angegebene
Zahl von Tieren durch die Zahl der Monatstage zu dividieren ist, bevor man die
Anzahl der den ganzen Monat im Stall befindlichen Tiere erhält.

Ich möchte an die erste Möglichkeit denken, d.h. dass sich die Tiere jeweils
nur einen oder wenige Tage zwischen zwei Austrieben im Pferch aufhielten[127]
und während dieser Zeit gefüttert werden mussten. Die Weide ist also auch für
diese Tiere als das Normale anzusehen. Wo wurde geweidet? Aus vielen Texten
wissen wir, dass Felder oder Teile von Feldern zu Weidezwecken benutzt wurden,[128] wobei zu vermuten ist, dass Teile (vielleicht der während eines Jahres
brachliegende Teil) das ganze Jahr als Weide benutzt wurden, während nach
der Ernte das ganze Feld zur Beweidung freigegeben wurde.[129] Für diese Annahme spricht, dass bei einigen Feldern Vieh als zum Feld gehörig aufgeführt ist,[130]
wie auch aus den sehr viel häufigeren Fällen hervorgeht, wo Tiere unter den
Opfergaben oder sonstigen Abgaben eines Feldes auftauchen.[131]

Neben diesen Herden, die bisweilen eine ansehnliche Grösse erreichen konnten,[132] müssen aber Herden der oben angeführten Art stehen, die nicht an Felder,
also an feste Standorte, gebunden waren, sondern das nicht ständig kultivierbare und das nicht kultivierbare Land nutzten. Dazu werden einmal Gebiete
gehören, die für eine Bewässerung zu hoch liegen, dann aber auch die Flächen,
die am Ende von Kanalsystemen liegen und somit nur in Jahren grösseren
Wasseranfalls bewässert werden können.

Zu diesen Gebieten dürfte vor allem der e d e n genannte Bereich gehört haben.
E d e n wird normalerweise mit Ebene, Steppe, Wüste übersetzt[133] und bezeichnet

---

126. Schneider, in *AfO* IV 206–8.

127. Zur Schur? Die Gerstezuteilungen des Textes fanden in den ersten drei Monaten
des babylonischen Jahres statt, die Schafschur "meist am Ende des Jahres" (F. R. Kraus,
Staatliche Viehhaltung in altbabylonischen Lande Larsa [Amsterdam, 1966] S. 46–50).

128. In *UNL* I bei vielen Feldern notiert: FN 9, 40, etc.

129. *Ibid.*, FN 67 C.

130. *Ibid.*, FN 217, 407, 459, 526, 586.

131. *Ibid.*, FN 29, 40, 57, 59, 74, 81, 122, 356, 373, 427, 469, 473, 481b, 514, 518, 626, 859.

132. *Ibid.*, FN 217: 1654 + x Schafe, 535 + x Zicklein.

133. *CAD*, *AHw*, s.v. *edinnu*.

in literarischen Texten vorzugsweise das nicht kultivierbare Land,[134] in dem wilde Tiere leben.[135] Aus der engen Verbindung von dem Hirten Dumuzi mit dem eden zog man ferner den Schluss, dass das eden wohl vornehmlich als Weidegrund genutzt worden sei.[136] Verbindungen von Ortsnamen und eden wurden als die Steppe des oder bei dem betreffenden Ort,[137] übersetzt und die stehenden Verbindungen an-eden und gú-eden als Hohe Steppe[138] bzw. Rand der Steppe.[139]

Erst in Verbindung mit dem Survey of Ancient Watercourses, bei dem man zwischen den beiden Haupteuphratarmen in Südbabylonien eine weitgehend fundleere Fläche gefunden hatte, machte Jacobsen den Vorschlag, das eden etwa mit dem modernen Begriff der Ǧezire gleichzusetzen. Er fand seine Ansicht dadurch bestätigt, dass rund um dieses fundleere Gebiet sich die Städte Zabalam, Umma, Bad-Tibira, und Uruk finden, die alle Kultorte des Hirten Dumuzi sind. An-eden und gú-eden fasst er als spezielle Teile des eden auf: eden wäre also die Bezeichnung für einen geographisch fest umrissenen Bereich gewesen.[140] Gegen diese Annahme spricht jedoch, dass bisweilen eden im Zusammenhang mit Orten gebraucht ist, die mit Sicherheit nicht direkt mit dem Gebiet zwischen den beiden Euphratarmen in Verbindung stehen. Zu nennen ist hier vor allem das gú-edena, das nach allem, was wir wissen, durch den östlichen Euphratarm und den damit verbundenen Anbaugürtel von der "Ǧezire" getrennt ist.[141] Einen weiteren Hinweis auf die Existenz eines eden in der Nähe von Lagaš gibt der Name eines Feldes im Bereich dieser Provinz,

---

134. Besonders gut illustriert durch *VS* II, Nr. 25 viii 8–10 (*SKly*, S. 74 und Kommentar, S. 206–7), wo unter mehreren Massnahmen Enlils, die gegen das Wohl des Landes und der Menschen gerichtet sind, gesagt wird: "die Menschen hat er wie Samen in der Steppe ausgestreut," d.h. unfruchtbar gemacht. Samen in der Steppe ausstreuen ist ebenso gegen eine funktionierende Landwirtschaft gerichtet—weil kein Ertrag zu erwarten ist—wie das vorher genannte "den Fluss verderbliches Wasser führen lassen."

135. Z.B. Gudea Zyl. B. XII 7–11. Cf. auch Heimpel, *StP*, Bd. 2, S. 76 zu alim-edena. Er sieht im Element -eden nach Tiernamen einen Hinweis darauf, dass das Tier wild ist, wie anše-eden-na = akk. *sirrimum*, "Wildesel" (Uh XI 46). Dazu noch gù-eden-na = akk. *arnabu*, "Hase" (Uh XIV 155), ᵈnin-kilim-eden-na = akk. *ajaṣu*, "Wiesel" (Uh XIV 204).

136. Jacobsen, in *RA* LII 129.

137. Jacobsen, in *Iraq* XXII 181.

138. "High eden," Jacobsen, in *RA* LII 129; "hochliegender, nicht unter Kultur stehender Teil der Steppe," Falkenstein, *NG* II 301 zu 2; "Hohe Steppe," Wilcke, in *ZA*, Bd. 62, S. 55.

139. "Edge of the desert," Th. Jacobsen, "The Reign of Ibbī-Suen," *JCS* VII (1953) 40, Anm. 47 (*TIOT*, S. 413); "bord du desert," Sollberger und Kupper, *Inscriptions royales* S. 305.

140. Th. Jacobsen, in *Archaeology*, Bd. 7 (1954) S. 53–54; ders., in *RA* LII 129.

141. *TUU*, S. 13. Nach den Informationen *UNL* I, FN 399 war das gú-edena eine Gemarkung im Bereich von Umma, die mit 1045 ha eine beträchtliche Grösse besass. Es war gut bewässertes Land, zum Teil wohl sogar versumpft (cf. dazu Gudea Zyl. B XII 1), da reiche Rohrlieferungen von dort gemeldet werden.

a-šà si-gar-eden-na, "Feld (namens) Riegel der Steppe."[142] Ein weiteres
Beispiel ist der eden-eriduga^{ki} genannte Kanal bei Eridu.[143] Somit wird
eden ganz allgemein das nicht bewässerbare Land bezeichnen, gleich in welcher
Gegend, während geographisch bestimmte eden-Bereiche durch eden mit
Zusatz bezeichnet wurden.

In der Tat gibt es Anzeichen dafür, dass der ganze von Jacobsen für eden
in Anspruch genommene Bereich an-eden genannt wurde.[144] Gú-eden a wäre
dann nicht als "der an das eden angrenzende Bereich" zu übersetzen, sondern
mit einem leicht verschobenen Bedeutungsansatz von gú als "das kultivierte
eden."[145]

Zwar wird an der Annahme festzuhalten sein, dass das eden, wenn überhaupt
dann als Weidegebiet genutzt wurde, doch ist aus den Belegen weder die Art
noch die Intensität dieser Nutzung zu erschliessen, und vor allem darf man nicht
den umgekehrten Schluss ziehen, dass der ganze Bereich des eden diesem Zweck
diente, da nicht auszuschliessen ist, dass einzelne Teile mehr wüstenartigen als
steppenartigen Charakter hatten.

Sumpfgebiete.—Die Existenz von Sumpfgebieten in Südbabylonien im Altertum ist nie umstritten gewesen. Auch dass dies nicht nur in der Frühzeit der
Fall war, sondern auch für spätere, historische Zeit zutraf, geht eindeutig aus
den Texten hervor. Schwierig wird es allerdings, wenn wir den Umfang und die
geographische Lage der Sumpfgebiete zu einer Zeit erschliessen wollen. Obwohl

142. Sauren, *Genf*, No. 90:18.

143. Jacobsen, in *Iraq* XXII 181.

144. Vgl. Anm. 11. Da Urusagrig = *Āl-Šarrākē* einige Male in Wirtschaftstexten
auftaucht und so seine Lage in der Nähe von Adab bestimmt werden kann, ist somit auch
Keši festgelegt. Aus Wilckes Argumentation ergibt sich aber nicht zwingend eine Lage
nördlich von Adab, und so möchte ich gegen meine Einwände *UCS*, S. 50–52 s.v. Dabrum
und Keši doch wieder eine Identifizierung von Keši/Urusagrig mit Tell Jidr in Erwägung
ziehen. Aus der Gleichung Keši = Teil von Urusagrig geht nur hervor, dass der Ort an
einem Fluss lag, und so dürfte die Lesung von 2. Urklage Zeile 146 (*PBS* X/2, Nr. 4 Rs. 3)
keši^{ki} an-eden-(/dè)-na-aš dù-a, "zum Hoch-Eden hin gebaut" (*ZZB*, Anm. 242;
zuletzt G. Gragg, *The Keš Temple Hymn* [*TCS* III (1969)] S. 162*b*) der Lesung von Wilcke,
in *ZA*, Bd. 62, S. 55, keši^{ki} an-eden-na dili dù-a, "Keši, das einsam in der 'hohen
Steppe' steht," vorzuziehen sein. Der von Wilcke gezogene Schluss, dass der heilige Bezirk
von Urusagrig ausserhalb der Stadt in der hohen Steppe gelegen habe, ist eine unseren
sonstigen Kenntnissen entgegengesetzte und durch die Texte nicht gestützte Annahme. Bei
dem zur Stützung herangezogenen keši^{ki} uru_x(= EN), "hochgelegenes Keši," ist nicht
berücksichtigt, dass die Belege für uru_x(= EN) bei Å. Sjöberg und E. Bergmann, *The
Collection of the Sumerian Temple Hymns* (*TCS* III) S. 62–64 eher eine Bedeutung "herrlich,
gewaltig" als "hoch" nahe legen. Das an-eden ist somit belegt für die Nähe von Keši/
Urusagrig = Tell Jidr(?), Zabalam (Jacobsen, in *RA* LII 129) und Larsa (van Dijk, in *JCS*
XIX 6, Z. 79).

145. Das Bedeutungsfeld von gú, "Rand," umfasst nicht nur den Rand als Trennungs-
linie bzw. das Ufer eines Kanals oder die Meeresküste, sondern spricht auch die Randzone
eines Wasserlaufes an, als besonders fruchtbar, da gut zu bewässern. Vgl. dazu *SKIZ*, S.
257 zu 46 ff. Gú-eden a wäre somit "die (bewässerte bzw. unter Kultivation genommene)
Randzone der Steppe."

es spezielle Ausdrücke für Sumpfgebiete und Röhricht gibt, sind wir doch auf die recht wenigen Fälle angewiesen, in denen Namen von Orten oder Feldern nach einem in der Nähe befindlichen Sumpfgebiet benannt sind oder diese geographische Nähe in anderer Weise beschrieben wird.

Hier ist vor allem ein Ort ambar[ki] im Bereich von Lagaš zu erwähnen, der von der FD-III Zeit bis in die Ur-III Zeit belegt ist, wobei oft der "Wald" von Ambar (tir-ambar[ki]) erwähnt ist.[146] Ambar ist verhältnismässig oft als Bestandteil von Feldernamen belegt, entweder mit Zusatz eines Ortsnamens, der uns das Feld aus dem Namen lokalisieren lässt,[147] oder auf Tafeln einer bestimmten Herkunft, die uns das Feld in einen bestimmten Bereich verweisen lassen.[148] Dabei ist auffällig, dass neben der unerwarteten Bezeugung eines Sumpfgebietes bei Šuruppak in erwarteter Weise solche Gebiete bei Lagaš und Ur belegt sind. Man vermisst Umma, das nach Aussage anderer Texte über recht ausgedehnte Sumpfgebiete verfügt haben muss. Hier ist vor allem an die vielen Beispiele zu denken, in denen Rohr als Erzeugnis eines Feldes genannt wird.[149] Es erscheint allerdings fraglich, ob dies uneingeschränkt das Vorhandensein von Sumpfgebieten signalisiert; denn bei Durchsicht der entsprechenden Felder zeigt sich, dass mit einer Ausnahme eines Feldes in der Gemarkung Apisala[150] alle anderen Fälle von Tafeln aus Umma bekannt sind. Sind diese Gegensätze aufzulösen, indem man sich auf die relativ geringe Informationsmenge beruft, oder muss man entgegen der herkömmlichen Meinung einen Unterschied zwischen ambar und einem Gebiet, auf dem Rohr wächst, machen? Auf letzteres deutet vor allem Gudea Zyl. B XII 1–2 (s. auch XIV 28) hin, wo ambar mit Fischen als Ertrag und giš gi mit Rohrertrag angesprochen ist. Doch fällt es schwer, diese Unterscheidung nachzuvollziehen, da ein Röhricht ohne Fische kaum vorstellbar ist. Dass ambar möglicherweise nicht Sumpfgebiet bedeutet,[151] könnte auch die Tatsache zeigen, dass nicht ein einziges der ambar im Namen enthaltenden Felder Rohr als

146. *UNL* I, FN 5: a-šà a-ambar[ki], "Feld am Wasser von Ambar" (Tello Text); *UNL* I, FN 129: a-šà a-zé igi-ambar[ki]-ta, "F. des Aze vor Ambar" (Tello Text); vgl. auch Falkenstein, *AnOr*, Bd. 30, S. 22.

147. A-šà ambar lagaša[ki] (*UNL* I, FN 84, 529), a-šà ambar èš šà nina[ki] (*UNL* I, FN 81).

148. Šuruppak: *UNL* I, FN 77; Lagaš: *UNL* I, FN 76, 78, 79, 80, 82, 86, 87; Ur: *UNL* I, FN 83, 85, 148.

149. Als alleiniges Erzeugnis gebucht: *UNL* I, FN 338, 394, 480. Zusammen mit Gerste: *UNL* I, FN 8, 10, 40, 69, 74, 101, 230, 275, 281, 303, 399, 405, 447, 460, 463, 746. Interessant erscheint der Wechsel von sig[7], "schneiden," und zé, "ausreissen," in Verbindung mit Rohr, denn das erste scheint auf eine Art Ernte hinzudeuten, während "ausreissen" mehr auf die Vorbereitung zur Anlage eines Feldes(?) gehen könnte.

150. *UNL* I, FN 658. Vgl. ferner Salonen, *Agricultura*, S. 279: 3600 sa gi gu-kilib-ba 15-ta gá-nun en-gaba-gina-ta é-te-na-šè, "3600 Bündel Rohr in Packen zu 15 Stück von der Tenne von E. nach Etena," wobei Etena am Tigriskanal nördlich von Apisala anzusetzen ist (*TUU*, S. 121).

151. Cf. A. Falkenstein, "Die Ibbīsîn-Klage," *WO* I (1947–52) 378, 380, Z. 47, "Teich"; desgleichen *SAHG*, S. 175.

Ertrag ausweist.[152] Dass nach Ausweis unserer recht zahlreichen Texte, die
eine Art auf bestimmte Gebiete beschränkt sein soll, die andere auf ein von der
ersten Art ausgelassenes Gebiet, ist kaum anzunehmen, und so zeigt dieses
Beispiel, wie wenig wir selbst in Fällen, in denen wir über statistisch ausreichendes
Material zu verfügen glauben, uns auf die Textinformationen verlassen können.

Wald.—Die Übersetzung "Wald" für t i r[153] ist beibehalten worden, obwohl
sie das Bedeutungsfeld von t i r wahrscheinlich nicht trifft. Zwar wird von
Holzlieferungen aus t i r genannten Gebieten für Stauwehranlagen berichtet,[154]
doch darf man sich darunter keine Wälder in unserem Sinne vorstellen. Von ihrer
Lage im engsten (Überschwemmungs-) Bereich des östlichen Euphratarmes und
im Gebiet von Lagaš und der dadurch nahe gelegten räumlichen Nähe zu Sumpfgebieten ist eher zu schliessen, dass es sich um Uferwald oder Uferdickicht
handelt. Dazu würde auch passen, dass š e g₉ und š e g₉ - b a r, "Wildschweine," die
Tiere der t i r sind.[155]

Steppe, Wüste.—Unser Material lässt nicht erkennen, ob im Sumerischen
ein Unterschied zwischen diesen beiden Landschaftsformen gemacht wurde.
Dies wird von daher verständlich, dass eigentlich kaum eine Situation vorstellbar
ist, in der Texte über das vollständig unbewohnbare und nicht nutzbare Gebiet
hätten berichten sollen. Selbst literarische Texte, die einen Gegensatz bewohnt
—unbewohnt, zivilisiert—unzivilisiert ansprechen, können mit dem Ausdruck
für Steppe auskommen. Für den Sesshaften ist das ausserhalb der eigenen
Sphäre liegende Land alles gleich unbewohnbar.

Hauptbezeichnung ist das bereits behandelte e d e n.[156] Daneben taucht nur
vereinzelt ein anderer Begriff auf, der aber nicht weiter zu bestimmen ist:
k i - ú š = akk. *baliltu/balītu*, "Steppe," das bisweilen als Qualitätsbezeichnung
des Bodens eines Feldes auftaucht.[157] S ù (g) = akk. *hurbu*, "leer, wüst," ebenfalls als Qualitätsbezeichnung für Felder gebraucht,[158] stellt dagegen wahrscheinlich nur eine Bezeichnung für vorübergehend unbebautes Gelände dar,

---

152. Soweit für die in Anm. 147 und 148 genannten Felder eine Nutzung angegeben ist,
ist entweder Gersteanbau genannt oder eine Nutzung als Weideland.

153. *TUU*, S. 56 mit Anm. 134, S. 61 mit Anm. 157, S. 89 mit Anm. 279.

154. T i r ist belegt für folgende zu lokalisierenden Orte: t i r - k i s u r a – a d a b^{ki}, t i r -
z a b a l a m^{ki}, sowie für folgende Orte, die ungefähr lokalisiert werden können: flussaufwärts
von Umma: bei Elugala; flussabwärts: bei Kamari, Makurra, Nagsu, Ukunuti, AN.ZA.GÀR
(am Girsu Kanal). Ferner bei TU.RU.DU, Garšana, BALA.TI.IM.KU.KU, Igala, Paʾenku,
Šunamugi (Belege in *TUU*, S. 11, 24, 88). Im Lagaš-Gebiet sind belegt t i r - a m b a r^{ki} und
t i r - b a - b i l₄ - l a, Falkenstein, *AnOr*, Bd. 30, S. 22, 37.

155. B. Landsberger, "Tin and Lead: The Adventures of Two Vocables," *JNES* XXIV
(1965) 296, Anm. 40.

156. Vgl. supra unter "Weideland."

157. *CAD* s.v. *balītu*. *UNL* I, FN 7, Anm. 6: "Teil eines Feldes, der unbebaut war und
deshalb gut als Viehweide geeignet."

158. *UNL* I, Teil 2, 243.

wie die Gesetzesbestimmung zeigt: n u - u n - u r u$_x$ (= APIN) šà-sù-ga ì-gar,
"(if) he did not plow (the land) and caused it to become arid."[159]

ZUSAMMENFASSUNG UND AUSBLICK

Trotz der Fülle des Materials ist so auch für die Ur-III Zeit kein zusammenhängendes Bild zu zeichnen. Dies ist deswegen bedauerlich, weil einerseits die
alleinige Konstatierung der Existenz bestimmter Landschaftsformen und anderer
geographischer Einzelheiten nicht befriedigt, andererseits in einer überwiegend
agrarisch ausgerichteten Kultur eine genaue Kenntnis der geographischen
Verhältnisse uns instand setzen könnte, Wesentliches über Möglichkeiten und
Ausrichtung des Wirtschaftssystems auszusagen.

Aufgrund der Zufallsauswahl und der speziellen Zielsetzung der meisten
Texte, die weite Bereiche völlig auslassen, ist allerdings auch nicht zu erwarten,
dass wir jemals Informationen über alle Einzelheiten, und vor allem über das
flächenmässige Verhältnis der einzelnen Landschaftsformen, bekommen könnten.

An dieser Stelle tritt die archäologische Feldforschung ins Blickfeld; denn sie
wäre in der Lage, einige der Fragen zu beantworten. Dazu wären vor allem zwei
Dinge nötig: Fortführung, Nachlese und Ausbau der Surveys des Landes und
die Vermessung von zwei bis drei west-östlichen Transversalen durch Babylonien. Durch systematische Untersuchungen der Überreste der alten Flora
durch Pollenanalyse und Flotation ergänzt, wäre dann die Basis gegeben, eine
historische Geographie auf weniger heuristischer Grundlage aufbauen zu
können.

BIBLIOGRAPHIE

Adams, R. McC. "Settlements in Ancient Akkad." *Archaeology*, Bd. 10, Nr.
4 (1957) S. 270–73.
———. "Survey of Ancient Water Courses and Settlements in Central Iraq."
Sumer XIV (1958) 101–3.
———. *Land behind Baghdad*. Chicago, 1965.
———. *The Evolution of Urban Societies*. Chicago, 1965.
———. "The Study of Ancient Mesopotamian Settlement Patterns and the
Problem of Urban Origins." *Sumer* XXV (1969) 111–24.
Adams, R. McC., und H. J. Nissen. *The Uruk Countryside*. Chicago, 1972.
Andrae, W. "Die Umgebung von Fara und Abu Hatab." *MDOG*, Nr. 16 (1903)
S. 24–30.
Braidwood, R. J. *The Near East and the Foundations for Civilization*. "Condon
Lectures." Eugene, Ore., 1952.

159. O. R. Gurney und S. N. Kramer, "Two Fragments of Sumerian Laws," *Studies in
Honor of Benno Landsberger* (*AS*, Nr. 16 [1965]) S. 19.

Buringh, P. "Living Conditions in the Lower Mesopotamian Plain in Ancient Times." *Sumer* XIII (1957) 30–46.

Butzer, K. *Environment and. Archaeology.* 2. Aufl. Chicago, 1972.

Crawford, V. "The Location of Bad-Tibira." *Iraq* XXII (1960) 197–99.

Edzard, D. O. *Die "zweite Zwischenzeit" Babyloniens.* Wiesbaden, 1957.

Edzard, D. O., und G. Farber-Flügge. *Die Orts- und Gewässernamen der Zeit der 3. Dynastie von Ur.* "Tübinger Atlas des Vorderen Orients," Beihefte, Reihe B, 7. Wiesbaden, 1974 (konnte nicht mehr benutzt werden).

Falkenstein, A. *Die Inschriften Gudeas von Lagaš* I. AnOr, Bd. 30. Rom, 1966.

Flannery, K. V. "The Ecology of Early Food Production in Mesopotamia." *Science,* Bd. 147 (1965) S. 1247–56.

Gibson, McGuire. *The City and Area of Kish.* Coconut Grove, Miami, 1972.

Goetze, A. "Archaeological Survey of Ancient Canals." *Sumer* XI (1955) 127–28.

Great Britain, Naval Intelligence Division. *Iraq and the Persian Gulf.* "Geographical Handbook Series" B.R. 524. Oxford, 1944.

Heinrich, E., und A. Falkenstein. "Forschungen in der Umgebung von Warka." *UVB* IX (1938) 31–38.

Hommel, F. "Ethnologie und Geographie des Alten Orients." *Handbuch der Altertumswissenschaft* III, 1.1 München, 1926.

Jacobsen, Th. "Mesopotamian Mound Survey." *Archaeology,* Bd. 7 (1954) S. 53–54.

———. "Early Political Development in Mesopotamia." *ZA,* Bd. 52 (1957) S. 91–140.

———. "La Géographie et les voies de communication du pays de Sumer." *RA* LII (1958) 127–29.

———. "Salinity and Irrigation Agriculture in Antiquity." Diyala Basin Project, "Report on Essential Results June 1 '57–June 1 '58." Mimeograph. 1958.

———. "The Waters of Ur." *Iraq* XXII (1960) 174–85.

———. "A Survey of the Girsu (Telloh) Region." *Sumer* XXV (1969) 103–9.

Jacobsen, Th., und R. McC. Adams, "Salt and Silt in Ancient Mesopotamian Agriculture." *Science,* Bd. 138 (1958) S. 1251–58.

Lees, G. M., und N. L. Falcon. "The Geographical History of the Mesopotamian Plains." *Geographical Journal,* Bd. 118 (1952) S. 24–39.

Pettinato, G. *Untersuchungen zur neusumerischen Landwirtschaft* I und II. Istituto Orientale di Napoli, "Ricerche" II und III. Napoli, 1967.

Renger, J. "Zur Lokalisierung von Karkar." *AfO* XXIII (1971) 73–78.

Salonen, A. *Agricultura Mesopotamica.* AASF Ser. B, Tom 149. Helsinki, 1968.

Sauren, H. *Topographie der Provinz Umma, nach den Urkunden der Zeit III. Dynastie von Ur* I: *Kanäle und Bewässerungsanlagen.* Heidelberg, 1966.

Schilstra, J. "Irrigation as a Soil and Relief-forming Factor in the Lower Mesopotamian Plain." *Netherlands Journal of Agricultural Science* X (1962) 179–93.

Ucko, P. J., und G. W. Dimbleby, Hrsg. *The Domestication and Exploitation of Plants and Animals.* London, 1969.

Ucko, P. J., R. Tringham und G. W. Dimbleby, Hrsg. *Man, Settlement and Urbanism.* London, 1972.

Vaumas, É. de. "Études irakiennes, Première Serie." *Bulletin de la Société de Géographie d'Égypte* XXVIII (1955) 125–92.

――――. "Études irakiennes, Deuxième Serie; le controle et l'utilisation des eaux du Tigre et de l'Euphrate." *Révue de Géographie alpine* XLVI (1958) 307.

――――. "L'Écoulement des eaux en Mésopotamie et la provenance des eaux de Tello." *Iraq* XXVII (1965) 81–99.

Wilcke, C. "Der aktuelle Bezug der Sammlung der sumerischen Tempelhymnen und ein Fragment eines Klageliedes." *ZA*, Bd. 62 (1972) S. 35–61.

Wirth, E. *Agrargeographie des Iraks.* "Hamburger Geographische Studien," Heft 13. Hamburg, 1962.

Wright, H. T. *The Administration of Rural Production in an Early Mesopotamian Town.* Museum of Anthropology, University of Michigan "Anthropological Papers," Nr. 38. Ann Arbor, 1969.

SUMERIAN ADMINISTRATIVE DOCUMENTS: AN ESSAY

Tom B. Jones

Minneapolis

It was in Paris, October 12, 1894, at the weekly *séance* of the Académie des Inscriptions et Belles-Lettres that Léon Heuzey made the first public announcement of a novel and very important discovery.[1] Consul Ernest de Sarzec in his eighth season of excavation at Telloh had found "un gisement de tablettes d'argile couvertes d'inscriptions cunéiformes," some 30,000 documents comprising the archives of ancient "Lagash" for a period beginning with pre-Sargonic times and ending with the fall of the Ur III dynasty. Discovered in the interior of a small mound, the tablets were all carefully filed on five or six layers or shelves in two distinct but adjacent galleries of brick construction. At least 5000 tablets were said to be in perfect condition, and an equal number were only slightly damaged; for the rest, there was hope that the fragments of many could be identified and reassembled. Paleographic comparison with the inscriptions of the rulers of Lagash, texts found in earlier campaigns, permitted the assignment of the tablets to specific periods, and the new documents, from a cursory examination, appeared to be accounts, lists of offerings, and inventories along with contracts in the form of case tablets bearing the seals of witnesses or scribes.

Unfortunately, de Sarzec was not able to take possession of the whole archive since it was plundered by natives who sold thousands of the tablets to dealers in Baghdad. It is usually said that the clandestine digging took place after de Sarzec's departure in 1894,[2] but a rather confused account of the proceedings by E. A. W. Budge[3] suggests that the natives, urged on by the dealers in Baghdad, had already discovered the mound and removed some of its contents before de Sarzec was allowed to "find" it. We shall return to this point, but for the moment it can be noted that more than 3000 of the tablets excavated by de Sarzec in 1894 reached Istanbul in sufficiently good condition to merit later publication.[4] The clandestine finds of natives, without doubt considerably less

---

1. *Compte Rendu de l'Académie des inscriptions et belles-lettres* XXII (1894) 344–45, 359–62.

2. A. Parrot, *Tello* (Paris, 1948) p. 20; *idem*, *Archéologie mésopotamienne* I (Paris, 1946) 133; C. H. W. Johns, *Cuneiform Inscriptions . . . in the Library of J. Pierpont Morgan* (New York, 1908) p. 16.

3. E. A. W. Budge, *Rise and Progress of Assyriology* (London, 1925) pp. 199–202.

4. *Inventaire des tablettes de Tello* II (Paris, 1910) 1–3.

than the estimated 35,000 tablets, were soon dumped on the market and dispersed to the winds after "an archaeologist at that time resident in Baghdad" told
the dealers that "the inscriptions on them were not historical, but were chiefly
accounts....."[5] This identification of the nature of the tablets, while perfectly
correct, was not made without intended malice, for the "archaeologist" was
Henri Pognon, the lifelong enemy of Léon Heuzey.[6]

The scorn of Pognon for the "laundry lists" of Telloh was anything but novel
then, and it continued to be the characteristic stance of Assyriologists for
decades to come. In 1904 Hilprecht, with his customary and universal disdain,
criticized de Sarzec for carelessness in not providing guards at Telloh, and at the
same time he minimized the importance of the archive de Sarzec had found. "A
large number of the stolen tablets," said Hilprecht, "are still in the hands of the
antiquity dealers. At first sought by the latter in the sure expectation of an
extraordinary gain, this archaeological contraband began recently to disappoint
them, the comparatively uninteresting and monotonous contents of the average
clay tablet from Tellô offering too little attraction to most of the Assyriological
students."[7]

Although the possibilities for historical research presented by the archives
of Telloh and the similar deposits soon to be discovered at Drehem and Jokha
were dimly and imperfectly recognized by a few scholars, conditions were
unfavorable for any protracted and systematic study of these new materials. It
was not just that too little was known about the Sumerian language itself, for an
even greater obstacle to progress was the rapid and uncontrollable dispersal
of the clandestine finds. Truly definitive research on archives of such magnitude
must wait until they could in large part be reassembled. A few hundred tablets
here or a few thousand there would not suffice, but when the holdings of the
major collectors had been published, they could be combined, and the real
work could begin. It is only recently that the volume of published texts has
reached a level at which profitable exploitation is feasible; and, as a result,
important studies have already made their appearance. Ultimately, the des-
pised "laundry lists" will provide not only the details of Sumerian social,
economic, and administrative organization, but also they may reveal something
new and unsuspected about the larger aspects of life in Mesopotamia in the third
millennium B.C.

Eight decades have passed since de Sarzec found the archives at Telloh, and
if we follow step by step the developments from that time to the present in this
small area of Sumerology we shall find the materials for an interesting and
instructive chapter in the history of scholarship. The story can best be told with
special reference to the most numerous class of documents, those of Ur III.[8]

5. Budge, *Rise and Progress*, p. 201.
6. Parrot, *Archéologie mésopotamienne* I 369.
7. H. V. Hilprecht, *Excavations in Assyria and Babylonia* (Philadelphia, 1904) p. 248.
8. This is not to suggest that research on Sargonic and Proto-Imperial texts has been
unimportant or lacking in value, but the Ur III records serve the present purpose more
directly and economically.

For the most part precisely dated and thus amenable to chronological arrangement, the Ur III records are concerned with a great variety of subjects. Consequently, they have attracted more attention than earlier Sumerian documents of a similar kind which are more limited in number and scope.

Officially, it all began with Heuzey's announcement of de Sarzec's finds of 1894, echoed by Ward's remarks to the American Oriental Society in New Haven in the following year,[9] but it seems likely that de Sarzec had been anticipated by his own diggers since Scheil reported having seen tablets from Telloh on the upper Tigris in May, 1894.[10] Moreover, there are other facts that may bear on this question:

Large numbers of the tablets acquired by dealers in Baghdad were sold to the British Museum, the Berlin Museum, the Louvre, and other major institutions, while smaller lots were purchased by libraries and museums elsewhere, and by private persons. D. Z. Noorian, who had served as interpreter for the American excavators at Nippur, sold 400–500 tablets (including more than 250 Ur III texts) to a buyer who in turn presented them to Columbia University. Some of these tablets were published by W. R. Arnold[11] as early as 1896, and the rest were exploited in detail by R. J. Lau[12] ten years later. The E. A. Hoffman collection at the General Theological Seminary, published by H. Radau[13] in 1900, had been purchased in 1896 from Noorian in New York, where the Haverford tablets, too, were bought from Gullabi Gulbenkian in 1901.[14] Presumably, the Telloh texts published by the British Museum from 1896 to 1900 and Reisner's Berlin collection also came from the clandestine finds of 1894.[15]

If, then, we tabulate by years the numbers of tablets contained in the publications of these collections and compare them by means of a graph with a similar tabulation of the texts found by de Sarzec and conveyed to Istanbul,[16] it becomes immediately apparent that a gaping hole was made in the Telloh archives by the clandestine diggers, who seem to have concentrated on the area in which the tablets dated from Shulgi 44 to Amar-Sin 5 were collected. The fact that de Sarzec and his successors at Telloh did not find many tablets dating from this period strongly suggests that the archive had been plundered before de Sarzec's arrival in 1894.

At first and up to about 1910–12 work on the Telloh material went as well as could be expected. An essential preliminary was the publication of as many of

9. W. H. Ward, in *JAOS* XVI (1895) p. ccv.

10. Parrot, *Tello*, p. 21.

11. *Ancient Babylonian Temple Records* (New York, 1896).

12. *Old Babylonian Temple Records* (New York, 1906).

13. *Early Babylonian History* (New York, 1900).

14. G. A. Barton, *Haverford Library Collection of Cuneiform Tablets* I (Philadelphia, 1905) 5, and Barton's paper summarized in *AJA* VI (1902) 36–37.

15. *Cuneiform Texts from Babylonian Tablets in the British Museum* (London); *Tempelurkunden aus Telloh* (Berlin, 1901).

16. Texts contained in *ITT* II–III as well as *ITT* IV; F. Thureau-Dangin, *Recueil de tablettes chaldéennes* (Paris, 1903); C. Virolleaud, *Comptabilité chaldéenne* (Poitiers, 1903).

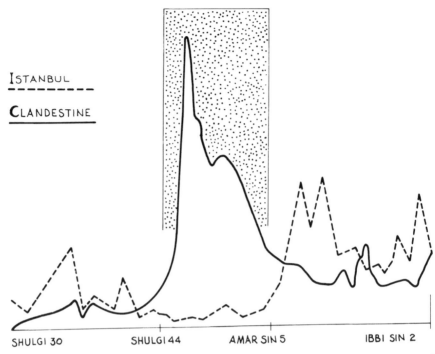

ISTANBUL

CLANDESTINE

SHULGI 30   SHULGI 44   AMAR SIN 5   IBBI SIN 2

Fig. 1.—Relative numbers of dated tablets found by French excavators and secured by clandestine diggers

the tablets as possible, particularly from the larger collections. The British Museum led the way with the publication of *Cuneiform Texts from Babylonian Tablets in the British Museum*, Part I (1896), followed by Parts III and V (1898), VII (1899), and IX and X (1900). Radau and Reisner were not far behind (1900, 1901); the first volume of the Haverford collection appeared in 1905,[17] Lau's Columbia texts in 1906, and the smaller group of Amherst tablets in 1908.[18] Because of their location at Istanbul, de Sarzec's tablets were delayed somewhat in publication. Virolleaud and Thureau-Dangin were able to make a few of the Ur III texts available by 1903,[19] but large numbers of the Istanbul tablets were not accessible to scholars until the appearance of *Inventaire des tablettes de Telloh*, Vol. II in 1910 and Vols. III and IV in 1912.

By 1910 more than 2500 Ur III texts from Telloh had been published, and there had been some attempts at evaluation and interpretation of the material. Progress had been made in establishing the sequence of the year formulas, the order of the Lagash months was known, and there had been discussions of certain categories of texts.[20] There had not been time, however, for a consolida-

17. The remaining two volumes of *HLC* were completed by 1915.
18. T. G. Pinches, *The Amherst Tablets*, Part I (London, 1908).
19. See n. 16, above.
20. Radau, *Early Babylonian History*, pp. 238 ff., 287 ff., 319 ff.

tion of the published texts, which in turn might lead to an overall survey of the significance of this material for historical reconstruction. A fairly typical discussion is that of C. H. W. Johns in his introduction to the calendar of the J. Pierpont Morgan collection published in 1908:

"De Sarzec, at the close of his campaign of 1894, laid bare a collection of some thirty thousand tablets.... Had it been possible to keep them together, as they dated from every year, almost every day, of a very long period, and concerned the most minute affairs of the temple officials and many of the principal inhabitants of the city, it might have been possible to reconstruct the municipal annals of Telloh for the third millennium B.C. with a completeness far greater than that of a European city in the Middle Ages. It was too late in the year to remove such an immense accumulation, and before De Sarzec could resume operations the natives had carried off the bulk of the tablets. The archives were thus scattered, and almost every museum in Europe and America possesses Telloh tablets of this collection. From their numbers, and divorced as they were from their true connection, seemingly dry and uninteresting, they became a drug in the market, and not readily finding buyers, quantities have been destroyed....

"A very large number of all the collections of tablets from Telloh come from temple archives. The purpose of these tablets was to record some payment or donation made from the temple stores or received from worshippers, tenants, etc., as offerings, rents or dues. There was a large number of people who regularly received certain allowances in food, drink, or other goods. By what title they received such things we are rarely, if ever, told. It is certain, however, that particular families, descended from the original group who formed the first settlers of the city, or deriving from them by conquest, purchase or adoption, had the right to so many days at a particular altar, temple gate or other site about the place.... A temple was in many respects like a medieval monastery. It had lands and endowments. Possibly all the land of the city had once belonged to the god.... Private property in land had, however, already arrived. The temple received much revenue from its lands and tenants of houses, buildings, or other property. It also lent out from its enormous stores of goods paid in kind, crops, herds, flocks, etc. Especially frequent are advances of corn, oil, wine, wool, even silver. Such loans usually name a fixed period for repayment. ... It is probable that the borrowers, if not all citizens, had a customary right to borrow of the temple in time of need. It was a form of collective charity.... The steward of the temple had, of course, to account for all that he allowed out...."[21]

Unhappily, two events put an end to what had seemed a promising development in the study of the Telloh archive. The first of these was the discovery of the huge archives of Drehem and Jokha, which immediately engaged the attention of scholars who might otherwise have worked on the Telloh material;

---

21. Johns, *Cuneiform Inscriptions*, pp. 16–20.

instead, their efforts were concentrated on collecting and publishing the new Drehem and Jokha texts. The second event was the onset of the First World War, which slowed scholarly activity and disrupted international communication among scholars. A bit more of the Telloh archive was to be published during the war years by Hussey, Barton, and Nies,[22] but even the publication of the Drehem and Jokha tablets fell off as the war went on; also among the casualties were the Ur III texts from Nippur, which had begun to be published by D. W. Myhrman in 1910.[23]

Unlike Telloh, Drehem and Jokha were not the object of formal archeological excavation. Rather, the mounds were opened by natives who sold the tablets to dealers in Baghdad. Once more the market was inundated by "laundry lists," and the dealers were in despair as the oversupply drove prices down.[24] The new tablets were more widely dispersed than those from Telloh, and, even worse, many found their way into numerous small private collections ranging in size anywhere from one to a dozen tablets.[25] Because of a lack of proper cleaning and baking, many tablets were soon in such bad condition that they disintegrated and so were lost to scholarship.

The Drehem find was the first of the two to be made, presumably in 1909, but possibly as early as 1908. The discovery was publicly announced in 1910 by F. Thureau-Dangin, who published thirteen of the new texts.[26] In the following year the same scholar identified the Drehem months and established their order.[27] Then, large collections began to be published: Genouillac, *Tablettes de Dréhem*; Langdon, *Tablets from the Archives of Drehem*; and Genouillac, *La trouvaille de Dréhem*, all at Paris in 1911; and in 1912 came *CT* XXXII and Legrain, *Les temps des rois d'Ur* (Paris). Smaller collections were also published between 1911 and 1915.[28]

Before we treat the Drehem discovery in detail, however, that of Jokha must be discussed. This find, too, was announced by Thureau-Dangin, who in 1911 commenced his article on the names of the months at Umma (Jokha) with the exclamation: "After Drehem, Jokha!"[29] Actually, the site of Jokha had been known for twenty years. It had been visited by both Scheil and Peters in the last

22. M. I. Hussey, *Sumerian Tablets in the Harvard Semitic Museum*, Part II (*HSS* IV [Cambridge, Mass., 1915]); *HLC* III (1915); and J. B. Nies, *Ur Dynasty Tablets from Telloh and Drehem* (*AB* XXV [1919]).

23. *Sumerian Administrative Documents* (*BE* III [Philadelphia, 1910]).

24. A Baghdad dealer once described the situation to me with the utmost animation and even pathos—20 years after the event.

25. In the United States, for example, the tablets marketed by E. J. Banks (1925–35) are ubiquitous.

26. "La trouvaille de Dréhem," *RA* VII (1910) 186–91.

27. "Notes assyriologiques," *RA* VIII (1911) 84–88.

28. L. Delaporte, "Tablettes de Dréhem," *RA* VIII (1911) 183–98; E. Dhorme, "Tablettes de Dréhem à Jerusalem," *RA* IX (1912) 39–56; E. Margolis, *Sumerian Temple Documents* (New York, 1915); W. M. Nesbit, *Sumerian Records from Drehem* (New York, 1914).

29. "Notes assyriologiques," *RA* VIII (1911) 152.

decade of the nineteenth century,[30] and tablets from the mound were already in circulation before 1911: in the J. Pierpont Morgan collection, for example, there were two that had been bought from Scheil, and others were included in Myhrman's publication of the Nippur texts.[31] Moreover, Scheil himself in 1911 identified Jokha as the site of ancient Umma.[32]

Publication of the Umma texts followed hard on the heels of the new find: Bedale, *Sumerian Tablets from Umma in the John Rylands Library* (Manchester, 1915), and Contenau, *Contributions à l'histoire économique d'Umma* (Paris, 1915) and *Umma sous la dynastie d'Ur* (Paris, 1916).

Nevertheless, complications developed. There were, on the one hand, large collections that contained tablets from both Drehem and Jokha, and it was not always possible to distinguish one variety from another when the tablets lacked month dates, and so a certain amount of confusion was introduced. Drehem and Jokha texts, to cite only two examples, were mixed together in C. E. Keiser's *Cuneiform Bullae of the Third Millennium* (New Haven, 1914) and in his *Selected Temple Documents of the Ur Dynasty* (New Haven, 1919). Although the two categories were clearly separated by Nikolsky,[33] and the Telloh and Drehem material was also divided by Nies,[34] the fact that the Ur III administrative texts were being published by *collection* rather than by *archive* was bound to have an unfavorable psychological effect: it suggested that the archives had a uniformity of content and could be treated as a whole rather than separately.

On the other hand, there were, if only briefly, certain encouraging signs that research on the administrative documents was entering upon a new and more mature phase. Groups of texts relating to specific subjects were attracting attention. The juridical texts and those dealing with date culture, metals, and the textile industry were analyzed in brief articles.[35] Contenau, a leader in this development, divided his publications of the Umma collections by subject categories of texts. Even more ambitious was Keiser's monograph *Patesis of the Ur Dynasty* (New Haven, 1919). Far and away the most successful effort was that of Legrain in his introduction to *Les temps des rois d'Ur* as he put together in 47 pages all that he and others had learned about the Drehem archive.

The year 1919 marked the end of a phase in the study of the Ur III texts. We shall consider subsequent developments presently, but it is worth noting here that by 1919 perhaps as many as 5000 texts had been published. Of these, more than 3200 were from Telloh, and Drehem and Umma accounted for more than

---

30. G. Contenau, *Contributions à l'histoire économique d'Umma* (Paris, 1915) p. vii.

31. Johns, *Cuneiform Inscriptions*, p. ix; *BE* III 1.

32. "Une nouvelle dynastie Suméro-accadienne," *Compte Rendu de l'Académie des inscriptions et belles lettres* (1911) 318–27.

33. *Documents de comptabilité administrative* II (Moscow, 1915).

34. *UDT*.

35. Scheil, "L'exploitation des dattiers," *RA* X (1913) 1–9; Contenau, "Tablettes de comptabilité relatives à l'industrie du cuivre à Umma," *RA* XII (1915) 15–25; *idem*, "Tablettes de comptabilité relatives à l'industrie du vêtement à Umma," *RA* XII (1915) 146–57; and several others.

1000 and 600, respectively. After 1919 the publication of Telloh texts was minimal, a fact that tended to discourage further research, but the Drehem and Jokha materials continued to be made available in large volume. Strangely enough, this fact did not greatly stimulate further researches of the sort that had characterized the period 1911–19, and we shall next describe and analyze this phenomenon.

Between 1920 and the beginning of the Second World War many large collections of Ur III texts were published—usually in autograph copy with indexes of names (personal, divine, place, etc.) and Sumerian terms.[36] With few exceptions, little or no commentary was provided. The main efforts of the editors seemed to be aimed at making the texts available; the responsibility for their interpretation was left to others—if such there were! In this manner, more than 5000 texts were published. For the most part the collections were the usual mixture of Drehem and Umma material.[37] The impact of the Ur III texts from Ur (*UET* III), which added a new archive to the list, was not apparent until after 1947, when the indexes were finally published. Moreover, the Nippur archive remained dormant after Myhrman's publication of 171 texts in 1910, and the texts from Adab excavated by Banks before the First World War have never been published.[38]

In all fairness, it should be emphasized that research on the Ur III documents or any such large body of texts must necessarily pass through several stages: one, the publication of scattered collections; two, the amalgamation of this material into a single corpus; and three, interpretation. While the publication of a large collection is anything but the work of a moment, the labor involved in stage two is immense. It comprehends, among other things, the making of endless lists in order to provide an apparatus with which to begin the process of interpretation. The archive must be reconstructed chronologically; a prosopography has to be compiled; indexes of technical and administrative terms are necessary; and so on. Few people had, or have, the stomach for it! Moreover, in the period now under consideration there was other, and to most, more interesting work to be done on the literary texts, on Sumerian grammar, on the Proto-Imperial texts, and the like. Another limiting factor was that there were few Sumerologists—specialists who worked only in Sumerian; most were Assyriologists concerned with the full range of Mesopotamian cuneiform materials who found little time to nibble at Sumerian.

36. E. Chiera, *Selected Temple Accounts from Telloh, Yokha, and Drehem* (Princeton, 1922); C. F. Jean, *Šumer et Akkad* (Paris, 1923); Y. Nakahara, *The Sumerian Tablets in the Imperial Library of Kyoto* (Tokyo, 1928); H. F. Lutz, *Sumerian Temple Records of the Late Ur-Dynasty* (Berkeley, 1928); G. Boson, *Tavolette cuneiformi sumere degli archivi di Drehem e di Djoha della ultima dinastia di Ur* (Milan, 1936); G. G. Hackman, *Temple Documents of the Third Dynasty of Ur from Umma* (*BIN* V [New Haven, 1937]); A. Pohl, *Rechts- und Verwaltungsurkunden der III. Dynastie von Ur* (Leipzig, 1937); and others to be mentioned below.

37. There were a few exceptions: *ITT* V contained only Telloh materials, *TCL* V only Umma, and *UET* III only Ur III.

38. Except for those published by S. Langdon, "Ten Tablets from the Archives of Adab," *RA* XIX (1922) 187–94.

As a consequence, most of the collecting and organizing of the Ur III documents in the period 1920–39—and even later—was done by two persons: Nikolaus Schneider, whose published works spanned the years 1925–50, and the Rev. T. Fish, who began to publish in 1924 and continued to 1958. Schneider was the editor of four major collections totalling nearly 1200 Drehem and Umma texts,[39] but in addition his elaborate indexes and his lists of deities, officials, personal names, cult and administrative terms, and Sumerian names for animals, plants, and the like, were extremely comprehensive and included citations from virtually every Drehem and Umma collection published up to the time each list was compiled.[40] Subsequently, based on the apparatus he had assembled, Schneider produced a score of valuable articles and monographs.[41]

Fish was to edit two major collections[42] and to publish various tablets from others. Unlike Schneider, he began by writing short articles on various subjects suggested by individual tablets or groups of tablets and only later began to accumulate and publish lists and indexes, especially in his own vehicle, *Manchester Cuneiform Studies* (1951–58). Useful, though not entirely accurate, were his chronological lists of tablets from Lagash, Drehem, and Umma.[43] In his wide-ranging articles Fish touched upon subjects, mainly economic, that required larger treatment and did receive it ultimately from later scholars.[44] It also seems fair to say that of the two, Fish was more historically minded than Schneider and saw more clearly the possibilities of the Ur III documents for historical reconstruction. His article on the Sumerian city of Nippur demonstrated this even though the volume of material available to him was inadequate for his purpose.[45]

Another and very important phase of Neo-Sumerian studies began in 1939 with Thorkild Jacobsen's publication of the Copenhagen documents.[46] At home in Sumerian in a way not evident among his predecessors who had dealt with the Ur III texts, Jacobsen's philological commentary had a genuine, comforting

39. "Keilschrifturkunden aus Drehem und Djoḫa," *Or*, No. 18 (1925) pp. I–XVII, "Die Geschäftsurkunden aus Drehem und Djoka in den Staatlichen Museen (VAT) zu Berlin," *Or*, Nos. 47–49 (1930), *Die Drehem- und Djoḫa-Urkunden der Strassburger Universitäts- und Landesbibliothek* (*AnOr*, Vol. 1 [1931]), and *Die Drehem- und Djoḫatexte im Kloster Montserrat* (*AnOr*, Vol. 7 [1932]).

40. In almost every issue of *Orientalia* between 1925 and 1930.

41. For a partial listing, see T. B. Jones and J. W. Snyder, *Sumerian Economic Texts from the Third Ur Dynasty* (Minneapolis, 1961) pp. 350–51, and A. Leo Oppenheim, *Catalogue of the Cuneiform Tablets of the Wilberforce Eames Babylonian Collection* (*AOS* XXXII [New Haven, 1948]) p. 223.

42. *The "Behrens" Collection of Sumerian Tablets in the Manchester Museum* (Manchester, 1926) and *Catalogue of Sumerian Tablets in the John Rylands Library* (Manchester, 1932).

43. *Manchester Cuneiform Studies* V (1955) 33–35, 61–91, 92–114.

44. For a partial listing, see Jones and Snyder, *Sumerian Economic Texts from the Third Ur Dynasty*, pp. 348–39, and Oppenheim, *Eames*, pp. 217–18.

45. "The Sumerian City of Nippur in the Period of the Third Dynasty of Ur," *Iraq* V (1938) 157 ff.

46. *Cuneiform Texts in the National Museum, Copenhagen* (Leiden, 1939).

ring and a thoroughness that set a standard for the future. His intuitive genius for things Sumerian, which was to be demonstrated over and over in the years to come, was already apparent in this early publication.

The intervening war years were even more disruptive of publication and scholarly intercourse than those of World War I, but when something like normalcy returned, it was significant that the first major publication of Ur III texts was produced in 1948 by A. Leo Oppenheim, one of the most brilliant and versatile Assyriologists of the twentieth century.[47] As in Jacobsen's catalog, so also in Oppenheim's, the philological commentary was rich and thorough and would provide scholars and students alike with an indispensable aid to further research.

The work of Jacobsen and Oppenheim, combined with the publication of Legrain's indexes and calendar for the *UET* III texts (1947), established a firm foundation on which a new edifice of scholarship could be built, and this structure was buttressed shortly thereafter by Adam Falkenstein's three-volume *Die neusumerischen Gerichtsurkunden* (Munich, 1956–57). Falkenstein's elucidation of the juridical documents contributed to the understanding of closely related Ur III administrative texts. In addition, this great scholar appears to have recognized the possibilities of the administrative texts and to have called them to the attention of his students with conspicuous results. Interest and activity in research on the Ur III materials was further stimulated by the publication of new texts, perhaps as many as 5000 by 1972.[48] Thus, the essential conditions for promoting a new and more mature phase of study had been met: a large body of text material was available; the integration of the text collections was well begun; and greater familiarity with the Sumerian language had been achieved.

Yet, when all these things had been done, when such preliminary work was well along if not completed, it was not entirely clear what the next step should

47. Oppenheim, *Eames*.

48. C. Gordon, *Smith College Tablets* ("Smith College Studies in History" XXXVIII [Northampton, 1952]); M. Çığ, H. Kızılyay, and A. Salonen, *Die Puzriš-Dagan-Texte der Istanbuler Archäologischen Museen*, Part I (*AASF*, Series B, Vol. 92 [Helsinki, 1954]); K. Oberhuber, *Sumerische und akkadische Keilschriftdenkmäler der Archäologischen Museums zu Florenz* (2 vols.; Innsbruck, 1958–60); E. Szchlechter, *Tablettes juridiques et administratives de la IIIe Dynastie d'Ur et de la Ire Dynastie Babylonienne* (2 vols.; Paris, 1963); W. W. Hallo, *Sumerian Archival Texts* (*TLB* III [Leiden, 1963]); N. Forde, *Nebraska Cuneiform Texts of the Sumerian Ur III Dynasty* (Lawrence, Kan., 1967); M. Lambert, *Tablettes économiques de Lagash* (Paris, 1968); H. Sauren, *Wirtschafturkunden aus der Zeit der III. Dynastie von Ur im Besitz des Musée d'Art et d'Histoire in Genf* (Naples, 1969); J. P. Grégoire, *Archives administratives sumériennes* (Paris, 1970); C. E. Keiser, *Neo-Sumerian Account Texts from Drehem* (*BIN* III [New Haven, 1971]); D. I. Owen and G. D. Young, "Cuneiform Texts in the Museum of Fine Arts, Boston," *JCS* XXIII (1970) 68–75; Owen and Young, "Ur III Texts in the Zion Research Library, Boston," *JCS* XXIII (1970) 95–115; S. Levi and P. Artzi, "Sumerian and Akkadian Documents from Public and Private Collections in Israel," *ᶜAtiqot* IV (1971); D. I. Owen, "Neo-Sumerian Texts from American Collections, I," *JCS* XXIV (1972) 137–73. And others to be mentioned below.

be. On the analogy of research on Akkadian documents, a number of possibilities suggested themselves. One might study a single class of Babylonian or Assyrian texts: a type of contract, the form of legal decisions or diplomatic agreements, and so on. The Old Assyrian (Cappadocian) documents had been arranged according to class by Julius Lewy. Without denying the utility of this approach, it was admittedly one of expediency, since the early collections of the Old Assyrian texts were derived from clandestine sources with the result that their archival unity had been disrupted and could not easily be restored. More recently, when new tablets have been recovered by archeological excavation, the integrity of the individual archives has been preserved, thus allowing a different sort of treatment more conducive to historical research. An alternative approach was the study of an activity: Mesopotamian agriculture, metal-working, textile manufacture, and the like. Experience has shown this to be a viable method of study providing the volume of texts is adequate and the study is made in sufficient depth, but in such case it is most profitable to limit the chronological period under consideration or to divide the discussion by chronological periods; often a good monograph has been marred by the tacit assumption that there was little change in an activity over a period of two thousand years. Again, one might choose to deal with various aspects of a single large archive: what has been done and what has been projected in the case of Mari texts provides a good example of this approach.

If now we survey the progress of research on the Ur III documents in this third quarter of our century, we shall see that scholars have approached the material in various ways. The matter is interesting, and it can also be instructive, since future workers in the area may profit by observing both the successes and the mistakes of their predecessors.

The advantage and convenience of working with the texts of a single archive already collected in a single volume and provided with comprehensive indexes did not escape the alert Jacobsen, who in 1953 published his fascinating paper on the textile industry at Ur.[49] This study was drawn from published texts, most of which date from the reign of Ibbi-Sin.[50] In consequence, it could not be nor was it intended to be comprehensive or final, but it called attention to an important subject and demonstrated once again the extraordinary acumen of Jacobsen himself. Although not concerned with the same period, Oppenheim's paper on the seagoing merchants of Ur also showed the possibilities of research in the Ur archives.[51]

A different tack was taken by W. W. Hallo and J. B. Curtis in their article on merchants' balanced accounts.[52] In this instance a single group of texts, num-

---

49. T. Jacobsen, "On the Textile Industry at Ur under Ibbi-Sîn," *Studia Orientalia Ioanni Pedersen Dedicata* (Hauniae, 1953) pp. 172–87 (*TIOT*, pp. 216–29).

50. *UET* III.

51. A. Leo Oppenheim, "The Seafaring Merchants of Ur," *JAOS*, Vol. 74 (1954) pp. 6–17.

52. "Money and Merchants in Ur III," *HUCA* XXX (1959) 103–39.

bering only 16 at the time, was studied. The results were useful, but the article necessarily left unresolved questions that could be answered only by research on all varieties of texts in which the "merchants" appeared. A definitive monograph on this subject is soon to be published by N. W. Førde.

The study of an activity, metal-working in Ur III, was published by Limet in 1960.[53] By limiting his subject chronologically to a single period and by employing all the evidence (published and unpublished texts and the lexicographical material), Limet achieved a thorough and basic monograph that all but exhausted the subject and possessed two other distinct advantages: it could be combined with similar treatments of metal-working devoted to other periods of Mesopotamian history in order to make a historical survey of the topic covering all of pre-classical antiquity, or it could provide material for a chapter in a comprehensive study of economics and governmental organization under the Third Dynasty of Ur.

In 1966 Sollberger published his work on the Ur III "letter orders."[54] This was an example of a different approach, that of assembling all the documents of a certain class. Undeniable as the utility and scholarly excellence of this study are, it is not above criticism on other grounds because the texts were arranged alphabetically by the names of the addressees without regard to their archive of origin and without any attempt to distinguish from one another orders addressed to different persons who possessed identical names.[55] Falkenstein's earlier treatment of a class of documents, the *Gerichtsurkunden*, did not have to take such problems into account because almost all the documents came from the Telloh archive. Somewhat earlier, Nikolaus Schneider, in his paper on archive labels, had lumped them all together without regard to archive, but, although he does not seem to have realized it, his method of arranging the subgroups by key phrases more or less automatically separated the labels by archive and thus averted what might have been a minor disaster.[56]

In contrast to this rather undiscriminating way of treating the documents, it should be mentioned that Limet in addition to surveying the Ur III metalworking industry as a whole very wisely chose to discuss separately the evidence for Ur, Drehem, Umma, and Telloh. The same procedure has been followed in the admirable monograph of Waetzold on the Ur III textile industry.[57] On the whole, it may be said that this approach of studying an activity in the framework of a limited chronological period is one of the most successful and open-ended thus far attempted and deserves to be encouraged.

---

53. *Le travail du métal au pays de Sumer au temps de la IIIe Dynastie d'Ur* (Paris, 1960). One should not neglect to add his immensely useful *L'anthroponymie sumérienne* (Paris, 1968).

54. *Business and Administrative Correspondence under the Kings of Ur* (*TCS* I [1966]).

55. See Jones, in *JAOS*, Vol. 89 (1969) pp. 162–65 for a criticism of this.

56. N. Schneider, "Die Urkundenbehälter von Ur III und ihre archivalische Systematik," *Or*, n.s., Vol. 9 (1940) pp. 1–16.

57. *Untersuchungen zur neusumerischen Textilindustrie* (Rome, 1972).

This is not to say, however, that the study of an activity is the only approach possible or preferable under present conditions. On the contrary, the decade 1960–70 saw the publication of a number of very ambitious and useful undertakings concerned with a variety of topics: Amorites in Ur III,[58] topography of Umma,[59] fields and field names,[60] aspects of the bureaucracy at Telloh.[61] Nor should one neglect to mention Gelb's masterly article on the ration system, in which he achieved the results of a monograph in hardly more than a dozen pages![62]

The contributions to Neo-Sumerian mentioned above deal either with some general phase of Ur III or with the sites of Jokha and Telloh, but it remains to speak of Drehem and several matters related to it.

A volume of previously unpublished Ur III economic texts with an accompanying commentary that appeared in 1961 was the work of two historians by no means expert in Sumerology,[63] and an estimate of its value (or lack of it) can best be obtained from the reviews by Goetze, Lambert, and Sollberger.[64] The first was kind enough to say that it employed a "patiently developed and executed new approach to these seemingly boresome and barren tablets." The "method" consisted of the simple expedient of setting in their chronological order the published administrative texts relating to a particular subject and by this means reconstructing the ledgers of selected Sumerian bureaucrats. Then, by an analysis of the data assembled in this way, an attempt was made to comprehend the organization of an office or a bureau and the operation of its machinery. One of the concrete results of such an approach was the demonstration that officials at Drehem, for example, did move from lesser to more important posts. From this one might infer the existence of a bureaucratic organization far more sophisticated than had hitherto been suspected.

Inspired (or, more properly, goaded) by this publication, Goetze wrote his impressive article on the šakkanakku officials of Ur III,[65] a major contribution to the subject of Sumerian political organization. This was by no means the only Neo-Sumerian topic that this great scholar illuminated with the light of his prodigious learning. One has only to glance at the *Journal of Cuneiform Studies* to see that the field ranked high among his many interests.[66]

58. G. Buccellati, *The Amorites of the Ur III Period* (Naples, 1966).

59. H. Sauren, *Topographie des Provinz Umma nach den Urkunden der Zeit der III Dynastie von Ur* (Bamberg, 1966).

60. G. Pettinato, *Untersuchungen zur neusumerischen Landwirtschaft* I (Naples, 1967), and *Die runden Tafeln* (*AnOr*, Vol. 45 [1969]).

61. M. Lambert, "Les archives de Urabba fils de Bazig," *RA* LIV (1960) 114–30, and "La vie économique d'un quartier de Lagash," *RA* LV (1961) 77–146.

62. "The Ancient Mesopotamian Ration System," *JNES* XXIV (1965) 230–43.

63. Jones and Snyder, *Sumerian Economic Texts from the Third Ur Dynasty.*

64. Goetze, in *JCS* XVII (1963) 33–37; Lambert, in *RA* LVI (1962) 217–19; Sollberger, in *AfO* XXI (1966) 89–92.

65. A. Goetze, "Šakkanakkus of the Ur III Empire," *JCS* XVII (1963) 1–31.

66. See, e.g., "Umma Texts Concerning Reed Mats," *JCS* II (1948) 165–202, and many other articles including a number in the series "Texts and Fragments."

Also on the subject of Sumerian political organization, W. W. Hallo's dissertation on the ensis of Ur III carried forward the work begun by Keiser.[67] In 1960 he followed this with an important article on the bala and more recently has published other useful papers.[68] Moreover, S. T. Kang, a student of Hallo's, has written on Drehem texts dealing with women and the meaning of maškim and gìr.[69]

Looking back on the accomplishments of three-quarters of a century and particularly at the progress of the last decade, it is clear that much has been done, but it is also evident that what we have seen is only a beginning. Many subjects remain to be investigated and ultimately combined in a grand synthesis which will give a full picture of Mesopotamia in the Ur III period. Moreover, while many texts have now been published, thousands more lie neglected in collections great and small, and it should be emphasized that the publication of this material is much to be desired for several reasons. Not only will it fill out and buttress our present knowledge, but it will also open the doors to new topics for study. Given the large base of the already published texts, the addition of even a few hundred more increases geometrically the possibilities for exploitation. The consequences of the availability of new texts can be illustrated by a single example:

In 1961 H. H. Figulla produced a catalogue or calendar of 3000 tablets (almost all unpublished) in the British Museum.[70] About two-thirds of them were Ur III texts from Telloh. Even though the catalogue merely summarized the contents of each tablet in the briefest possible manner, the information provided was sufficient in many instances for certain kinds of investigation. In particular, we may consider the interesting case of the tablets from the forty-seventh year of Shulgi and the activities of an official named Bazi.[71]

Before the appearance of Figulla's catalogue only about 70 Telloh tablets from Shulgi 47 had been published. These were to be found mostly in publications of Barton, Nies, and Reisner; the excavators of Telloh had published only 7 because this part of the archive had already been plundered. Figulla's catalogue added about 200 new Shulgi 47 texts, nearly three times the number previously available. Of this lot about 85 came from the accounts of Bazi, whereas only 20 of his tablets had been known before, most of these published by Nies. What was even more interesting was that nearly 70 of the 85 new tablets of Bazi had come to the British Museum in a single shipment of 735 assorted tablets on March 28, 1896. In addition to those of Bazi there were about 50

67. "The Ensi's of the Ur III Dynasty," (Ph.D. diss.; Chicago, 1953).

68. "A Sumerian Amphictyony," *JCS* XIV (1960) 88–114; "The House of Ur-Meme," *JNES*, Vol. 31 (1972) pp. 87–95; "Contributions to Neo-Sumerian," *HUCA* XXIX (1958) 69–128; and others.

69. *Sumerian Economic Texts from the Drehem Archive* (Urbana, 1972). See now also K. Maekawa, "Agricultural Production in Ancient Sumer," *Zinbun*, Vol. 13 (1974) pp. 1–60.

70. *Catalogue of the Babylonian Tablets in the British Museum* I (London, 1961).

71. Bazi was the principal of the Urabba studied by Lambert. See n. 61 above.

other texts from Shulgi 47 in the shipment. Of this total of 120 texts a large number of those dated by month came from months VIII–X and had to do with the disbursement of barley. It was thus apparent that this portion of the archive was reasonably intact, allowing for broken or damaged tablets not offered for sale, although a small part had gone to the collection published by Nies.

It is not clear from the records of Shulgi 47 whether Bazi had all the responsibilities attested for him in later years when he was directly concerned with fields and with metals and other commodities. Rather, his accounts for Shulgi 47 tell us only about his operations in connection with barley, but this by itself is important. We can follow Bazi through the year as he engages in activities typical of a number of similar functionaries at Telloh yet more fully illustrated in his case because of the number of texts. We see him dispatching large quantities of grain to Nippur; still more grain was sent by boat to local granaries and milling establishments; throughout the year quantities of barley were transferred to other officials; seed grain was paid out; wages and rations of grain were distributed to workers. By combining the other texts of Shulgi 47 with those of Bazi we can round out the picture and show graphically the relative numbers of payments and disbursements as well as the time of year when such operations occurred. Seed grain, for example, was provided for the farmers in months V–X: feed for animals was necessary at the end of summer when all forage had run out. The movement of grain by boat to Nippur and the local storehouses and processing establishments took place during the harvest season in months XI–XII and immediately afterwards in the early months of the new year. Bazi's own shipments to Nippur were heaviest in month IV. The largest transfers of grain to other officials occurred in months IV and X when in the former case stores were being accumulated for the oncoming season of ploughing and planting and in the latter when huge quantities were necessary to pay the harvest hands.

The accompanying figures (Figs. 2–4) show the numbers of surviving (published) texts for each month of Shulgi 47, the month by month distribution of texts relating to specific activities, and Bazi's own expenditures for the year. Of the 8000 kur of the known disbursements by Bazi for this year, 4000 were sent to Nippur, 1200 were transferred to officials, and smaller amounts were expended for seed, rations and wages, milling, and offerings.

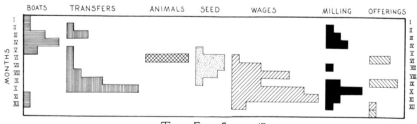

Texts From Shulgi 47

Fig. 2.—Relative numbers of texts relating to each activity month by month

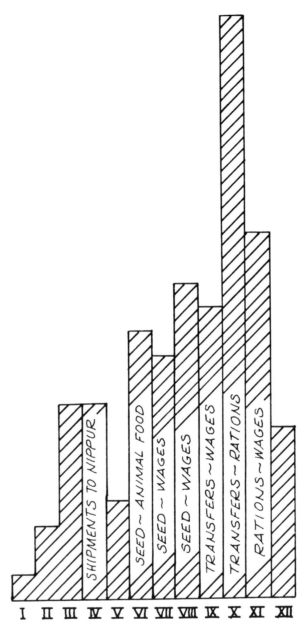

Fig. 3.—Main expenditures by month

Bazi was only one of a number of officials responsible for the disbursement of grain, but from the information provided by his records we are encouraged to look further into the matter in our attempt to discover something more about

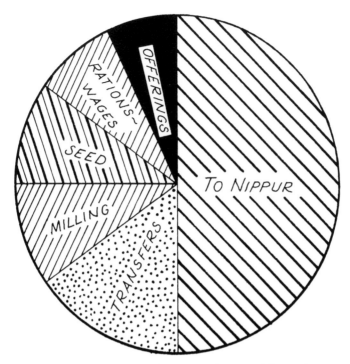

Fig. 4.—Relative amounts (in k u r) expended by Bazi for various purposes

the processes of disbursement and distribution. Although Figulla's catalogue does not help us with this, an archive of considerable proportions survives from Shulgi 41. Some of these texts were carried off by the clandestine diggers, but most were excavated by de Sarzec in 1898 and 1900.[72] From the data provided by this archive it is possible to construct a "flow chart" illustrating the ways in which grain of each year's harvest was moved from local storehouses to larger granaries and milling establishments, and also shipped off to Nippur and Ur.

As a preface to this discussion, it should be stated that in the territory of Lagash a dozen or more temple establishments were responsible for cultivating most of the arable land (see the discussion of Amar-Sin 2 below). The main crop was barley, and in any given year the yield averaged better than two million bushels. About half of this amount was consumed by the cost of production (wages for workers, feed for the draft animals, and the like), and a quarter went to the king as royal tax. The remaining 25 per cent accrued to the priests. From this they fed themselves, paid out seed grain, sent large quantities to Nippur, provided the grain for milling, and so on.

The surviving texts from the archive of Shulgi 41, which we are about to discuss, do not involve all the temple establishments, but the activities disclosed

72. *ITT* IV.

may be considered typical of the organization as a whole. It is also worth noting that of the approximately 60 published texts of Shulgi 41, at least 45 belonged to the archive in question or to related accounts, and of this total of 60 more than 50 were found by de Sarzec.

We may begin with *OBTR*, No. 252, dated in the fourth month, the account tablet of Ur-dingirra, sanga of the divine Shulgi. With a "capital" of more than 3700 kur of barley, he dispatched 1400 kur by boat to unspecified destinations (revealed by other texts as we shall presently see); nearly 1400 went to Ur-dam, agent of Ur-Nanše, for storage and ultimate distribution in the same manner as illustrated by the accounts of Bazi; most of the remainder was stored by Ur-dingirra in local barns.

Among the persons to whom Ur-dingirra dispensed barley to be transported by boat was Abbamu, the ship captain, who received 196 kur. From Abbamu's own records (*CT* VII, Pl. 33a) we learn that in addition to this amount of 196 kur from Ur-dingirra he received grain from the priests of Igalim and Ningishzida and from another official probably connected with the temple of Ningirsu. This grain was then taken by Abbamu to Urgishgigir, the granary superintendent. One hundred and seventy-three kur, turned over by Ur-dingirra to Ludimma, another boatman, was then transferred by the latter (*ITT* IV, No. 7497) to Ur-ᵈNIM.MARᵏⁱ (*ITT* IV, No. 7151) and others for shipment to Ur and Nippur. Amu, still another boatman, performed a similar function,[73] while Lu-ᵈNinmug (*CT* VII, Pl. 21b) received grain from the establishments of Nindara, Dumuzi, and Ningirsu, some of which he passed on to Ludugga for shipments to Nippur as well as for making payments to Ludimma and others. In still another set of transactions, Namhani (*RTC*, No. 423) paid grain to the establishment of URU × KARᵏⁱ, which was then transferred to Nabasha and to Urgishgigir, the granary superintendent (*CT* VII, Pl. 31b). The data from the texts just cited together with other documents from the archive[74] can be assembled from the "flow chart" shown in Figure 5.

A much smaller group of tablets dated in the second year of Amar-Sin provides important information far out of proportion to the number of texts involved. One tablet (*CT* X, Pls. 18–19) records the share of the barley crop that accrued to each of about a dozen priestly establishments of the city-state of Lagash: the grand total was 84,666 kur (col. v, ll. 19–21). A companion tablet (*CT* VII, Pl. 8) sets forth in detail how the priests expended this income. The 84,666 kur (col. 1, ll. 1–3) heads the list of items making up the "capital," but the yield of Amar-Sin 2 was below average so that in order to meet expenses the priests had to dip into stores of old grain (ll. 5–7) and even add "new" grain

73. Amu appears in *OBTR*, No. 252, *CT* IX, Pl. 41, *ITT* IV, Nos. 7073, 7088, 7177, 7500, 7503.

74. The pertinent texts are *CT* VII, Pls. 21b, 31a, 33a; *CT* IX, Pls. 38, 41; *UDT*, No. 64; *RTC*, No. 423; *OBTR*, Nos. 242, 252; *ITT* IV, Nos. 7039, 7073, 7088, 7151, 7177, 7182, 7194, 7215, 7226, 7261, 7500, 7503, 7510, 7652, 7678, 7715, 7728, 7749, 7773, 7799, 7858, 7882, 8028, 8122.

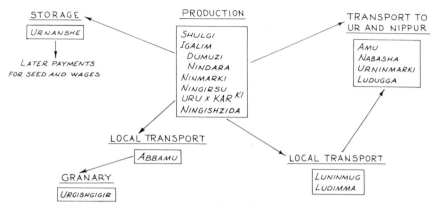

Fig. 5.—Flow chart

(ll. 8–9) that would have been counted as revenue for the following year. The expenditures for Amar-Sin 2 included 49,790 kur as royal tax, allotments to various priestly corporations in the territory of Lagash, and amounts set aside for seed and other expenses incidental to the annual planting. At the end of the list was an item of 14,400 kur sent to Nippur.

Now, while these records are themselves extremely useful and interesting, when combined with other data they lead to conclusions that are indeed startling. Briefly stated, certain bits of evidence have always suggested that there was a high degree of organization and planning in the Ur III period. The *runden Tafeln*, for example, those field surveys that assign cultivators to definite plots and specify the crops and amount of seed to be sown, are mostly dated in the first month of the year, right after the harvest, and several months in advance of the fall sowing and planting. This more than implies the most careful and systematic planning. Again, one may point to the "tables of organization" for the temple establishments, annual compilations that are dated not later than the fourth month and specify the numbers of officials and workers assigned to each corporation for that specific year.[75] It does not seem to be a matter of general knowledge that *HSS* IV, No. 4 is a combined table of organization and budget for the temple establishments of Girsu in the year Amar-Sin 2 that sets the numbers of officials and workers for each corporation and the amount of barley assigned to each: the grand total is 12,768 kur. It is fascinating to discover that a basic number or proportion was given to each establishment. The base for Ningirsu was 20: 200 kur was allotted for šabra officials, 100 for the archivists, and there were to be 20 overseers of oxen, and so forth; NIN.MAR^{ki} had a base of 19 with 190 for the šabra officials, 95 for archivists, and there were to be 19 overseers of oxen; similar figures for Nindara (base 7) were 70, 35, and 7; and so on. The date of this budget was the first month of the year, and like most budgets it was more of a hope than a reality: in the final accounting (*CT* VII,

75. For examples, see *ITT* II, Nos. 865, 907, 3536, and 4192.

Pl. 8 col. 2, ll. 2–4) the priests got only 12,270 kur, 500 less than projected. Man proposes, God disposes!

HSS IV, No. 4 seems to have been only one part of the grand budget for the city-state of Lagash, for one can see the outlines of the general principles on which Ur III budgets were based. This may be explained as follows:

Barley was seeded at an average rate of 460–70 silà per bur, as an examination of the "round tablets" and similar texts will show. In text No. 5 (G. Reisner, *Tempelurkunden aus Telloh* [Berlin, 1901]), for example, which is dated in Shulgi 47, the priests used 5678 kur to plant 3667 bur in barley. In Amar-Sin 2 5190 kur was employed for seed grain (*CT* VII, pl. 8). Thus, the amount of land under cultivation by the priests in that year was about 3312 bur.[76]

There are numerous indications that in budgeting in this period a yield of 60 kur per bur was assumed. Half of this, as we have said, was expected to defray the cost of production, and the remainder was divided equally between the king and the priests. If, for example, we divide the amount of the royal tax, 49,790 kur (*CT* VII, Pl. 8) by 15, we get a figure of 3319 bur for the land under cultivation in Amar-Sin 2. This compares favorably with the area of 3312 given above. Doubling the royal tax, incidentally, gives 99,580 kur, only 15 less than the 99,595 stated as the "capital" of the priests in the same document; this was the revenue projected by the priests though in fact the yield fell nearly 15,000 kur short (84,666) of their estimate.[77]

Even more clearly demonstrating the budgeting practice is *RTC*, No. 407, in which for Shulgi 28(?), 30, and 32 we are given the figures for (*a*) the area under cultivation, (*b*) the projected yield calculated at the priestly share of 30 kur per bur, and (*c*) the actual yield accruing to the priests along with the surplus or the deficit for each year. In the first year an area of $4134\frac{1}{2}$ bur was cultivated; this would be 248,070 kur at 60 kur per bur. The priests expected 124,035 according to *RTC*, No. 407 and actually had a surplus of about 5000 kur. In the second year, however, with 4190 bur they expected 125,700 but fell short by about 7500 kur. In the third year they planted 4261 bur with a projection of 127,830 and missed their goal by a horrendous 49,406! Something must have gone very wrong.

Parenthetically, from data of this sort it is possible to estimate the normal yield per unit of seed. We have only to divide the yield by the amount of seed grain (60 kur by 460–70 sila) to see that the average is a yield between 38- and

76. $\dfrac{5190}{1.567}$ (5190 bur at 470 silà per bur).

77. The land cultivated by the priests increased in area in the middle years of Shulgi and then dropped rather sharply:

Shulgi	28	4134 bur	(*RTC*, No. 407)
	30	4190	(*RTC*, No. 407)
	32	4261	(*RTC*, No. 407)
	47	3667	(*TUT*, No. 5)
Amar-Sin	2	3312	(*CT* VII, Pl. 8)
Shu-Sin	7	3102	(*ITT* II, No. 629)

39-fold. This falls nicely between the estimate of 36-fold for the Neo-Babylonian period and 41 for the age of Urukagina.[78]

Enough has been said, one hopes, to demonstrate the possibilities of the Ur III documents. Many types of the operations they record have still to be investigated, and there are also thorny problems long recognized but still unsolved, among them two that are particularly irritating:

The first has to do with archive labels, the tags attached to the baskets in which tablets were filed according to subject and date. In those instances in which we possess a great many tablets of the same year dealing with the same type of transaction conducted by a single official—the receipts and expenditures of Abbashagga at Drehem in Amar-Sin 5, for example—one would expect to find an appropriate label. Instead, the labels we have do not seem to be associated with any large category of existing texts.

The second problem involves the "letter orders." In no case do we have a tablet confirming compliance with a specific order: we cannot match an order with a tablet recording the precise receipt or expenditure required by the order itself.[79]

To sum up, there has indeed been progress in four-score years with marked acceleration during the past two decades, and there is every reason to think that the pace will quicken.

SELECTED BIBLIOGRAPHY

Goetze, Albrecht. "Šakkanakkus of the Ur III Empire." *JCS* XVII (1963) 1–31.

Jones, Tom B., and John W. Snyder. *Sumerian Economic Texts from the Third Ur Dynasty*. Minneapolis, 1961.

Legrain, Léon. *Les temps des rois d'Ur*. Paris, 1912.

Limet, Henri. *Le travail du métal au pays de Sumer au temps de la III⁰ dynastie d'Ur*. Paris, 1960.

Oppenheim, A. Leo. *Catalogue of the Cuneiform Tablets of the Wilberforce Eames Babylonian Collection in the New York Public Library*. *AOS* XXXII New Haven, 1948.

Sollberger, Edmund. *Business and Administrative Correspondence under the Kings of Ur*. *TCS* I. Locust Valley, N.Y., 1966.

Waetzoldt, Hartmut. *Untersuchungen zur neusumerischen Textilindustrie*. Rome, 1972.

---

78. See *RLA* I 16–20 (*Ackerbau*); H. Prinz, "Babyloniens Landwirtschaft einst und jetzt," *Weltwirtschaftliches Archiv* VIII (1916) 1–28; and T. Jones, "Ancient Mesopotamian Agriculture," *Agricultural History* XXVI (1952) 449.

79. For the complications of this, see my review of Sollberger, *TCS* I, in *JAOS*, Vol. 89, pp. 162–65.

ZUM SUMERISCHEN EID

Dietz Otto Edzard

München

Die ehrenvolle Aufgabe, Thorkild Jacobsen einen Aufsatz zu widmen, der den Forschungsstand auf dem Gebiet des "Sumerian Law" zusammenfassen und fördern sollte, war dem Autor eine Last wie jedem, der weiss, dass der Jubilar die Aufgabe besser hätte lösen können. Es schien angesichts der umfangreichen und vielfältigen Materie ratsam, sich auf einen Sektor zu beschränken, der dennoch wichtig genug ist, das System zu erhellen. Das ist der Eid bei den Sumerern. Ein bindender Ausspruch, der mit mancherlei Riten und Gesten verbunden sein kann, spielt in allen Rechtssystemen eine zentrale Rolle. Der Sprechende verpflichtet sich zu einer künftigen Handlung oder Unterlassung (promissorischer Eid), oder er beteuert, dass er etwas (nicht) getan habe, dass etwas (nicht) geschehen sei (assertorischer Eid). 1914 trat Johannes Pedersen mit seinem bis heute nicht überholten Buch *Der Eid bei den Semiten* hervor.[1] Dieses Buch behandelt weit mehr als nur den vor Gericht und im Zusammenhang mit Rechtsfällen geleisteten Eid. Die Übergänge sind fliessend vom Eid zum Fluch und Bann oder vom Eid zum Gelübde. All dies auf den Spuren Pedersens auch hier einzubeziehen, erwies sich bald als unmöglich.[2] Der Hauptgrund dafür war, wie bisher immer wieder in der Sumerologie, der unumgängliche Zwang, vom Versuch der grosszügigen Überschau ins philologische Detail hinabzusteigen.

Mit dem sumerischen Eid ist gemeint der in sumerischen Texten sumerisch formulierte Eid.[3] Er wird hier nicht zum ersten Mal behandelt. A. Falkenstein hat ihn im Zusammenhang mit den Gerichtsurkunden der III. Dynastie von Ur

---

1. Die vorangegangene dänische Ausgabe trug den Titel *Den semitiske Ed* (Kopenhagen, 1914). Vgl. aus neuerer Zeit E. Gräf, *Das Rechtswesen der heutigen Beduinen* (o. J. [1955–57]) bes. S. 56 ff.

2. Folgende Themen verdienen weitere und ausführlichere Behandlung: Eid und Gelübde in der schönen Literatur; Eid und Beschwörung; der Eid in der Umgangssprache (Eid und verbaler Modus); die sprachliche Form des Eides in der sumerisch-akkadischen Symbiose.

3. Das will sagen, dass wir in erster Linie Eide in einer Sprache, nicht bei einem Volke, meinen; aber auf der anderen Seite bestreiten wir nicht, dass die Semantik der Eidesformeln in der Sprache X Rückschlüsse auf Anschauungen primär der Sprecher dieser Sprache erlauben.

dargestellt.[4] Aber es fehlte noch eine Zusammenfassung, die auch andere Perioden und andere Textgattungen berücksichtigt. Die Terminologie bot noch viele Probleme. Es stellte sich heraus, dass in der Fachliteratur noch keine klare und einheitliche Meinung über die Verteilung der Verben TAR = tar und TAR = ku₅(-d/r) sowie ihrer Zusammensetzungen herrscht. Das machte einen leidig langen Exkurs notwendig.

All dies sind Gründe, die den Verfasser dazu bewogen haben, den ursprünglich vorgesehenen Titel "Der sumerische Eid" kleinlaut in "Zum sumerischen Eid" abzuändern.

Dieser Aufsatz hat folgende Gliederung:

   I. Die Eide in der "Geierstele" des Eanatum von Lagaš
      A. Exkurs: nam-tar, nam-ku₅ und Verwandtes
      B. Nam-ku₅ in der "Geierstele"
      C. Mu-pà in der "Geierstele"
      D. Zi-GN in der "Geierstele"

  II. Der promissorische Eid
      A. Sargonische Beispiele
      B. Neusumerische Beispiele
      C. Altbabylonische Zeit
      D. Mu-lugal
      E. Zi-lugal

 III. Der assertorische Eid
      A. Sargonische Beispiele
      B. Neusumerische Beispiele
      C. Geltung des Eides
      D. Assertorischer Eid und Ordal

  IV. Zusammenfassung

I. DIE EIDE IN DER "GEIERSTELE" DES EANATUM VON LAGAŠ

Die ältesten bisher überlieferten Belege für sumerische Eide stammen aus dem Text der "Geierstele" (*ca.* 2470 v. Chr.).[5] Der Text von Kol. xvi, Z. 12 bis Rs. v 41 ist in sechs Abschnitte aufgegliedert, die—bis auf den sechsten—weitgehend gleich lauten und daher, obwohl zu einem beträchtlichen Teil zerstört,

---

4. *NG* I 63–72.
5. Literatur bis 1964 bei M. Falkner und E. Sollberger, "Geierstele," *RLA* III 94–95. Neue Übersetzung von E. Sollberger in J.-R. Kupper und E. Sollberger, *Inscriptions royales sumériennes et akkadiennes* (Paris, 1971) S. 50–54. Die von M.-Th. Barrelet, "Peut-on remettre en question la 'Restitution matérielle de la Stèle des Vautours'?" *JNES*, Bd. 29 (1970) S. 233–58, in Frage gestellte Rekonstruktion der "G." kann wenigstens vom Text her nicht erschüttert werden; s. E. Sollberger, zitiert in *JNES*, Bd. 29, S. 256.

wechselseitig ergänzt werden können. In der Deutung besteht bisher kein Konsens. Selbst eine so wichtige Frage wie die Verteilung von Verbalformen der 1. und 3. Person, d.h. von direkter Rede und Bericht, wird von den Autoren verschieden beantwortet. Anerkannt ist, dass Eanatum seinen Gegner, den Herrscher von Umma, verpflichtet, eine ihm zudiktierte Grenze einzuhalten. Der "Mann von Umma" schwört nacheinander bei Enlil von Nippur, Ninhursanga von Keši, Enki von Eridu, Suʾen von Ur, Utu von Larsa und bei Ninki. Kol. xvi, Z. 12–Kol. xvii, Z. 20 (1. Abschnitt, ergänzt nach den Parallelen) lauten:

xvi 12 lú-umm[a^k]$^!$-ra	Eanatum gab
é-an-na-túm-m e	dem Mann von Umma
sa-šuš-gal-	das grosse Fangnetz
15 ^{d}en-líl-lá	des Enlil
e-na-sum	(und)
nam e-na-ta-ku$_5$	schwor ihm dabei.[6]
18 lú-umma^{ki}-ke$_4$	Dabei schwor auch
é-an-na-túm-ra	der Mann von Umma
nam mu-na-ku$_5$-de$_6$	dem Eanatum:[7]
21 zi-^{d}en-líl	"Beim Leben Enlils,
lugal-an-ki-ka	des Königs von Himmel und Erde![8]
a-šà-^{d}nin-gír-su-ka	Ich werde das Feld des Ningirsu

6. Sollberger (*Inscriptions royales*, S. 50–53): "Moi, E-ana-tuma, sur l'homme d'Umma j'ai lancé… et (par ce filet) je lui ai prêté serment," d.h. in der I. Person.

Die Lesung der Königsnamens ist umstritten: E a n a t u m oder E a n a t u m a ? Sollberger analysiert -tuma(DU)-me mit -me als Kopula -me(n), "ich bin"; ich möchte -túm-me vorziehen mit Ergativpostposition -e. Entscheidend ist die Schreibung des Dativs é-an-na-DU-ra in Kol. xvi, Z. 19, wenn wir die altsumerische Schreibregel gelten lassen, wonach die konsonantisch anlautende Dativpostposition -ra, -r nur nach Konsonantenauslaut geschrieben wurde: ^{d}en-líl-ra, ^{d}en-ki(-k)-ra, aber ^{d}nanna(-r). Vgl. *GSG* § 356, wo aber die lautliche Interpretation in eine rein orthographische umzumünzen ist. Diesem Befund liegt Silbenzählung zugrunde und die Tatsache, dass man eine Silbe der Struktur KVK entweder durch KVK-Zeichen oder nur durch KV-Zeichen ausdrückte, aber noch nicht durch Kombination von KV + VK. Auf den Namen é-an-na-DU angewandt, bedeutet das, dass wir den Dativ é-an-na-DU-ra silbenmässig in e/a/na/tum/ra zerlegen können, aber nicht in *e/a/na/tu/ma(r).

Der Vollname des Königs (vgl. Sollberger, *Inscriptions royales*, S. 57, Anm. 1) é-an-na-^{d}inanna-ib-gal-ka-ka-a-DU (Kol. v, Z. 26–28) hilft bei der Analyse vorerst nicht weiter; er ist m.E. nicht sicher erklärt. Th. Jacobsen ("Early Political Development in Mesopotamia," *ZA*, Bd. 52 [1957] S. 131 [*TIOT*, S. 391–92] Anm. 90,6), Sollberger und andere folgen A. Poebel ("Zur Geierstele," *OLZ*, Bd. 14 [1911] S. 198–200), der DU = túm(a) = *wasmum*, "würdig (für)" deutete. Dabei bleibt aber das plene-a (-ka-a-DU) unberücksichtigt, das durchaus ein Verbalpräfix sein könnte, so dass wir eine finite Verbalform vor uns hätten.

7. Für das Syntagma (Folge Präteritum-Präsens) s. unten Anm. 69.

8. Z. 21–39 fasse ich als den in direkter Rede gesprochenen Eid des "Mannes von Umma" auf; s. schon A. Falkenstein, "Zur Grammatik der altsumerischen Sprache," *AfO* XVIII (1957) 92, Anm. 15.

24 ur₅ ì-kú	(nur) gegen Zins(?) essen.⁹
ꜣeꜣ BAD-šè na-e	Den Graben will ich nicht . . . .¹⁰
d[a-rí-da-gal-la-šè]	[. . . . .]¹¹
27 [ki-sur-ra-]	[werde ich die Grenze]
[ᵈnin-gír-su-ka-ke₄]	[des Ningirsu bestimmt]
[ba-ra-mu-bal-e]	[nicht überschreiten.]
30 [e pa₄-bi]	[Deich und Graben werde ich]
[šu-bal ba-ra-ak-ke₄]	[bestimmt nicht ändern.]
[na-rú-a-bi]	[Die Stelen dort werde ich]
33 [ba-ra-kur₆-re₆]	[bestimmt nicht ausreissen.]
[u₄-da mu-bal-e]	[Wenn ich (dennoch) überschreite,]
[sa-šuš-gal-]	[dann soll das grosse Fangnetz]
36 [ᵈen-líl-lá]	[des Enlil, vermittels dessen]
[nam e-ta-ku₅-rá]	[ich geschworen habe,]
[ummaᵏⁱ-a]	[über Umma]
39 [an-ta hé-šuš]	[herabfallen."]
[é-an-na-túm-me]	[Eanatum weiss fürwahr]
[gal na-ga-mu-zu]	[mehr als andere.]¹²
42 [tuᵐᵘšᵉⁿ-min-nam]	[Zwei Tauben legte er]
[igi-ba šimₓ(= REC 391)	[Antimonschminke auf die Augen,]
ba-ni-g̃ar]	[steckte ihnen]
[eren sag̃-ba ì-mi-du₈]	[Zedern(blätter)¹³ an den Kopf]
45 [ᵈen-líl-ra]	[(und) liess sie zu Enlil]
xvii [nibruᵏⁱ-šè]	[nach Nippur]
[šu e-ma-ni-ba]	[losfliegen:]
3 [tuᵐᵘšᵉⁿ nibruᵏⁱ-šè	["Tauben, auf nach Nippur!"]
DU.DU-ba(?)]¹⁴	
[é-an-na-túm-me]	[Eanatum]
[KA a-ku₅-de₆]	[. . . . t]:¹⁵

9. Sehr unsicher; man würde *ur₅-ra oder *ur₅-šè erwarten. Sollberger (*Inscriptions royales*, S. 50–54): "Un déluge a devoré le champ de Ningirsu."

10. Mir unklar. Sollberger (*Inscriptions royales*): "J'ai décrété un talus de barrage." Na-e wäre aber die im präsentischen Konjugationsmuster gebrauchte *marû*-Form.

11. Wohl mit Sollberger (*Inscriptions royales*): "au grand jamais" oder eine ähnliche Zeitbestimmung.

12. Versuch, in der Übersetzung der Präfixhäufung na-+-(i)nga- gerecht zu werden.

13. Sollberger (*Inscriptions royales*, S. 51–53): "de la résine de cèdre"; C. Wilcke (*Lugalbandaepos*, [Wiesbaden, 1969] S. 153–54): "Weisszedern(zweige)."

14. Ergänzung eines Imperativs (nach Kol. xix, Z. 17) unsicher.

15. Sollberger (*Inscriptions royales*, S. 52) nimmt diese beiden Zeilen nur in Kol. xix, Z. 18–19 an, wo tatsächlich erhalten. Er übersetzt dort (zusammen mit Z. 17): "Les carpes qui sont au service de l'Apsu, moi, E-ana-tuma, je leur rendis hommage." Fasst man dort Z. 17 hingegen als Imperativ auf (suhurᵏᵘ⁶ abzu-šè DU.DU-ba, "Karpfen, auf zum Abzu!"), so stehen Z. 18–19 für sich. Die Verbalform KA a-ku₅-de₆ ist mir unklar; besteht (so Sollberger) ein Zusammenhang mit KA-tar, das—idiomatisch—mit *dalīla dalālu*, "huldigen, preisen," übersetzt wird? Einer Lesung tar würde die Orthographie TAR.DU widersprechen (s. unten I A 7).

6 [lugal-mu]   ["Wenn gegen meinen Herrn]
  [^{d}en-líl-ra]   [Enlil]
  [a-ba du$_{11}$-ga]-nà   auf [irgend jemandes Geheiss]
9 [a-ba šár-ra-na   oder sonstige weitere Rede
  lú umma^{ki}-a^{16} jemand, der in Umma
  inim-da gur-ra-da-am$_6$ rückfällig wird—
12 u$_4$ an-dù   . . . .
  inim an-ǧál   . . . .—
  u$_4$-da inim-ba   gegen diese Abmachung
15 šu ì-bal-e   verstösst,
  sa-šuš-gal-   so soll das grosse Fangnetz
  ^{d}en-líl-lá   des Enlil, vermittels dessen
18 nam e-ta-ku$_5$-rá   er geschworen hat,
  umma^{ki} über Umma
  an-ta hé-šuš^{17} herabfallen!"

Von dieser fünfmal wiederholten Form weicht die Fassung des Eides bei Ninki ab. Rs. iii 2 bis v 41 lauten:

iii [é-an-na-túm-me(?)]   [Eanatum(?)]
  3 [. . . . . . .]   [. . . . .]
    [lú(?)]-um[ma^{ki} (x)]   lässt [den Mann von(?)] Um[ma],
    lu[gal . . .-ra(?)]   Kö[nig. . .],
  6 mu-^{d}nin-ki-ka   den Namen der Ninki
    mu-ni-pà-dè   anrufen.^{18}
    lú-umma^{ki}-ke$_4$ Es schwört
  9 é-an-na-túm-ra   der Mann von Umma
    nam mu-na-ku$_5$-de$_6$ dem Eanatum:
    zi-^{d}n[in]-ki-[ka]   "Beim Leben der Ninki!
  12 [a-šà-^{d}nin-gír-su-ka [Ich werde das Feld des Ningirsu,
    (etc.)]   etc.]"
 v ^{d}nin-ki   "Ninki, bei der ich ihn

---

16. Lú umma^{ki}-a ist nicht = lú-umma^{ki}-ke$_4$, also keine Genitivverbindung; daher "jemand in Umma."

17. Sollberger (*Inscriptions royales*) sieht keinen syntaktischen Zusammenhang von Kol. xvii, Z. 6 bis Z. 20. Er fasst Kol. xvii, Z. 6–11 als Fragesatz auf und schliesst Z. 12–13 an: "Tant que le jour se fera, (cette) parole sera."
Ich möchte so analysieren: lugalmu . . .-ra . . . lu Umma'a inimda gurada'am (= gur-ad-a-am) . . . uda inimba šu ibale . . . , "jemand, der in Umma gegen meinen Herrn . . . rückfällig wird, . . . wenn er gegen diese Abmachung verstösst. . . ." Z. 8–9 sind ein adverbialer Zusatz. Zu Z. 12–13, m.E. eine Parenthese, vgl. *SR*, S. 90, Nr. 43 v 7–vi 1; ich halte aber die damalige Deutung nicht mehr für sicher und wage zur Zeit keine Übersetzung.

18. Wohl nicht "er lässt ihn 'Name der Ninki' ausrufen," da in Z. 11 zi- und nicht mu-^{d}nin-ki-ka folgt.

33 nam-ni ma-ni-ku₅-rá	für mich habe schwören lassen,[19]
umma^ki	möge veranlassen,
muš ki-ta g̀iri-ba	dass eine Schlange aus dem
36 su₁₁ hé-mi-dù-dù-e	Boden Umma in den Fuss beisst.
umma^ki	Wenn Umma
e-bi bal-e-da-bi	diesen Kanal hier überschreitet,
39 g̀iri-bi	möge Ninki
^dnin-ki-ke₄	(Ummas) Fuss
ki hé-da-kar-ré	vom Erdboden hinwegraffen!"

In dem Teil der "Geierstele," der mit Eiden zu tun hat (*ca.* 40% vom Gesamttext), kommen folgende Wendungen vor, die für die Eidesleistung relevant sind:

nam e-na-ta-ku₅ (Kol. xvi, Z. 17)	"er schwor ihm dabei / vermittels dessen"
nam mu-na-ku₅-de₆ (Kol. xvi, Z. 20)	"er schwört ihm"
nam e-ta-ku₅-rá (Kol. xvi Z. 37, Kol. xvii, Z. 18)	"bei dem / vermittels dessen er / ich "geschworen hat / habe"
zi-GN (Kol. xvi, Z. 21)	"(beim) Leben der Gottheit NN"
mu-GN mu-ni-pà-dè (Rs. iii 6–7)	"er veranlasst ihn, den Namen der Gottheit NN anzurufen"
nam-ni ma-ni-ku₅-rá (Rs. v 33)	"bei der ich ihn für mich habe schwören lassen"

Wir geben mu-pà, "den Namen rufen" wörtlich wieder, was auch sinnvoll ist.[20] Dagegen übersetzen wir nam-ku₅ nur aus dem Kontext heraus mit "schwören," ohne die Einzelglieder dieses zusammengesetzten Verbums zu berücksichtigen; allerdings auch ohne zu wissen, ob eine analytische Übersetzung noch angebracht ist. Wenn wir nämlich nam e-na-ta-ku₅ formal durch "er schnitt ihm damit NAM" wiedergeben, ist nichts gewonnen; wir können uns darunter nichts vorstellen (s. unten I A 3). Wenn nun ferner unter den Sumerologen noch grösste Unsicherheit betr. Verteilung der beiden Verben nam-tar und nam-ku₅ herrscht, so scheint ein Exkurs über TAR und seine Zusammensetzungen unumgänglich. Der hier folgende Versuch ist freilich in keiner Weise erschöpfend gedacht.

A. EXKURS: nam-tar, nam-ku₅ UND VERWANDTES

1. Èn-tar

èn-tar, "fragen, sich kümmern um"; konstruiert mit dem Dativ Sing. und dem Lokativ-Terminativ Plural der Person, dem (Lokativ-) Terminativ der

---

19. Ich halte mich eng an Sollberger (*Inscriptions royales*): "par qui il m'a prêté serment," möchte den Satz aber kausativisch übersetzen; vgl. unten Anm. 37.

20. *Watûm*, "finden," als Entsprechung zu pà(-d) ist gewiss eine aus "rufen, hervorrufen" weiterentwickelte Bedeutung.

Sache, oft aber auch absolut, d.h. ohne dimensionales Objekt; *hamṭu* und *marû* lauten tar.[21]

Nichtfinit *hamṭu*: ᵈnanše nu-mu-un-su-a saĝ-èn-tar-ra-ni, "Nanše ist es, die sich in erster Linie um die Witwe kümmert," Nanše-Hymne, Z. 22.[22]

èn-tar hat hier die Funktion von dub-sar, d.h. eines von der *hamṭu*-Basis aus gebildeten Verbalnomens.[23]

Nichtfinit *marû*: èn tar-re-da-ni, "wie er fragt," Schooldays, Z. 34.

èn tar-re-dam, "ist nachzuprüfen," in Ur III-Wirtschaftstexten häufiger Vermerk; s. M. Yoshikawa, in *Or*, NS, Bd. 37 (1968) S. 408.

Finit *hamṭu* im Präteritum: PN-ra èn ù-na-tar, "nachdem du NN gefragt hast," *TCS* I, Nr. 306:3–4.

èn ba-na-tarᵃʳ, "(G.) wurde verhört," *NG*, Nr. 138:11.

èn [b]a(!)-ne-tar-ra, "als man sie (eos) verhörte," *NG*, Nr. 89:11; vgl. 101:12.

Finit *hamṭu* in freier Reduplikation: níg-libir-ra-bi èn hé-bí-tar-tar, "um das Alte kümmere ich mich immer wieder," Šulgi B 275; vgl. Schreiber und missratener Sohn, Z. 50.

Finit *marû* im Präsens: u₄-da èn-mu mu-ra-tar-re, "wenn er dich nach mir fragt," Enlil und Ninlil I, Z. 69 ‖ [96] ‖ 122.

ama-me èn [li]-bí-in-tar-re-dè-en, "wir können uns [nicht] um unsere Mutter kümmern," F. Ali, "Letter Collection B" 13:6.[24]

é-ir₁₁-da-na-ka in-bi hé-tar-e, "er möge sich um das Haus seines Sklaven kümmern," *RTC*, Nr. 84 Rs. 9 (s. 5); vor Ur III.

Sowohl für das nominale wie für das verbale Glied liegt die Lesung fest: Wechsel in/èn in Ur III;[25] Komplementierung von TAR durch ar, d.h. tarᵃʳ.

21. Im Folgenden wird versucht, bei Belegen möglichst weitgehend nach der *hamṭu*- und *marû*-Basis zu scheiden. Für die nicht-finiten Verbalformen vgl. Verf., "Ḥamṭu, marû und freie Reduplikation beim sumerischen Verbum," *ZA*, Bd. 62 (1972) S. 1–34 (2. Teil und Fortsetzung von *ZA*, Bd. 61 [1971] S. 208–32). Da die dritte Folge des Aufsatzes noch aussteht, sei hier ein Teil der vorläufigen Ergebnisse kurz mitgeteilt (dieses Resümee schliesst selbstverständlich die Arbeiten und Ergebnisse anderer, bes. von M. Yoshikawa, aber auch die Auseinandersetzung mit ihnen, dankbar ein): Die *hamṭu*-Basis ist gewöhnlich mit dem Konjugationsmuster des Präteritums verbunden, die *marû*-Basis mit dem des Präsens-Futur; das Morphem /ED/ ist mit der *hamṭu*-Basis inkompatibel. Beim "intransitiv-passiven" Verbum, das nur ein Konjugationsmuster kennt (die "Normalform"), können trotzdem durch die Verwendung verschiedener *hamṭu*- und *marû*-Basen zwei Stufen (Tempus, Aspekt?) unterschieden werden. Hier ist wieder /ED/ nur mit *marû* vereinbar. Umgekehrt ist eine "intransitiv-passive" Verbalform mit /ED/ in ihrer Funktion zwangsläufig "Präsens-Futur." Bei bestimmten Verben greift die *marû*-Basis auch auf den Plural des Präteritums (belegt nur in der 3. Person Plural) über, so bei dug₄/e, wo Sing. bí-in-dug₄, Plural bí-in-eš (= bi-in-dug, bi-n-e-(e)š).

22. Für nähere Aufschlüsselung literarischer Belege s. den Anhang S. 94–95.

23. Vgl. Verf., *ZA*, Bd. 62, S. 5–6.

24. Auffällig die abweichende Rektion. "Sumerian Letters" (Ph.D. diss., University of Pennsylvania, 1964).

25. S. auch für šA-tar (= èn-tar) E. Sollberger, *Business and Administrative Correspondence under the Kings of Ur* (*TCS* I [1966]) S. 115, Nr. 194.

TAR+e wird altbab. gewöhnlich tar-re geschrieben (älter selten tar-e, *RTC*, Nr. 84 Rs. 9), altsum. und sargonisch vermutlich tar-ré;[26] tar+a wird tar-ra geschrieben, offenbar nicht *tar-rá.[27]

Etymologie: vorausgesetzt, èn sei dasselbe Wort wie èn = *mati*, "wann?" wäre zu erwägen "jemandem (den Ausruf) 'wann' abschneiden" im Sinne von "auf seinen Ruf eingehen, sich um ihn kümmern." Dann wäre allerdings "fragen" eine sekundäre Wortbedeutung.

2. Nam-tar

nam-tar, (bisher konventionell) "das Schicksal entscheiden"; Rektion: Lokativ-Terminativ der Person und Sache in der Präfixkette; Dativ der Person, Lokativ der Sache beim nominalen Satzteil; *hamṭu* und *marû* tar; zu unterscheiden von nam-šè tar.[28]

Nichtfinit *hamṭu*: sipa-zi ᵈutu-ù nam-tar-ra-ra, "dem rechten Hirten, dem Utu das Schicksal entschieden hat," *SRT*, Nr. 15:47′ (Šulgi Q).

Nichtfinit *marû*: gi-dur kuru₅-dè nam tar-re-dè, "die Nabelschnur durchzutrennen, das Schicksal zu entscheiden," *SRT*, Nr. 6 iii 2 (Nr. 7:13).[29]

Nichtfinit *hamṭu* in freier Reduplikation: nin . . . nam-tar-tar-re, "Herrin, . . . , die alles Schicksal entscheidet," Gudea Zyl. A iv 9.

Finit *hamṭu* im Kohortativ: lugal nam gi₄-rí-ib-tarᵃʳ nam-du₁₀ gú-mu-rí-ib-tarᵃʳ, "König, das Schicksal will ich dir entscheiden, gutes Schicksal will ich dir entscheiden," *TCL* XV, Nr. 13:47 (Šulgi D 264).

Finit *marû*: an-da bára-gal-la dúr mu-da-an-ğar, ᵈen-líl-da kalam-ma-na nam mu-un-di-ni-ib-tar-re, "Zusammen mit An hat sie auf dem grossen Postament Platz genommen, (woraufhin) sie zusammen mit Enlil ihrem Lande das Schicksal entscheidet," Inanna/Iddin-Dagān (Isin 6*), Z. 25–26 (*SKIZ*, S. 129).

Selten ist abweichende Rektion oder absolute Verwendung des Verbums, d.h. ohne Objekt.

Dativ in der Präfixkette: u₄ ᵈnin-gír-su-ke₄ gír-nun-ta sᵃˡ-du₁₁-ga-ni ba-pà-da-a é-ninnu-[t]a [na]m-n[i] mu-na-[ta]r-ra-[a], "als

---

26. Sargonisch belegt bei nam-tar: PN nam-tar-ré-dè = Namtared+ Ergativ postposition, *PBS* IX, Nr. 5 ii 3.

27. Einmal altbab. belegt bei dem parallel zu beurteilenden nam-tar: [lugal-me-èn] sipa nam-tar-rá-ni-e [z]i ğá-ğá-ğá in-ga-me-na-ta, "da ich, der König, auch der Hirte bin, dessen Schicksalsentscheidung Leben schafft," Šulgi C 74 (Lesung und Übersetzung abweichend von G. Castellino, *Two Šulgi Hymns (BC)* (StSem, Nr. 42 [1972]) S. 252–53.

28. Nam-šè tar (im Folgenden nicht weiter behandelt) steht, wenn der Inhalt der Handlung von nam-tar im selben Satz beschrieben ist, z.B. mu-hé-ğál-la nam-šè tar-ra-àm, "dem ein Jahr des Überflusses als Sch. e. worden ist," Šulgi Q (*SRT*, Nr. 15) Z. 46′.

29. W. Römer, "Einige Beobachtungen zur Göttin Nini(n)sina auf Grund von Quellen der Ur III-Zeit und der altbabylonischen Periode," *Lišān mithurti* (*AOAT* I [1969]) S. 295, Z. 75; geklärt durch Th. Jacobsen, "Notes on Nintur," *Or*, NS, Bd. 42 (1973) S. 291 mit Anm. 65.

Ningirsu vom 'Hohen Wege' aus seine Opferzuweisung gefordert und ihm (Entemena) vom Eninnu aus das Schicksal entschieden hatte," Sollberger, *Corpus des inscriptions* "*royales*" *présargoniques de Lagaš* (Genève, 1956), Entemena 35 iii 1–6.

ubur-kù-mu-a nam ma-ra-ni-tar, "an meinen reinen Brüsten habe ich (Ninsuna) dir (Šulgi) das Schicksal entschieden," *SLTNi*, Nr. 80:25 (Šulgi P 25).

Lokativ in der Präfixkette: ^{d}a-nun-na-[ke$_4$-n]e túg-ga-ni ba-an-dab$_5$-bé-eš, x im-ma-an-AG-eš, nam im-[ma]-TAR-eš, šu-x im-[m]a-an-búr-ru-uš, "die Anuna-Götter packten sie (Ninhursanga) an ihrem Gewand, machten . . ., . . .ten, . . . ten," Enki und Ninhursanga, Z. 246–49. Hier ist Klärung durch Duplikate erwünscht; liegt überhaupt nam-tar vor?[30]

Absolut: arhuš ma-ra-an-tuk-àm na-ám-zu in-tar-ra-àm, "er hat Mitleid zu dir gefasst, hat dein Schicksal entschieden," Nippur-Klage, Z. 155 (*PBS* X/4, Nr. 1 iv 19).

Wie bei èn-tar ist auch bei nam-tar die Lesung über alle Zweifel erhaben. Nicht nur wird TAR gelegentlich durch ar verdeutlicht (tar^{ar}); das akkadische Lehnwort, der Dämonenname *namtaru*, beseitigt alle Unsicherheit. Ebenfalls wie bei èn-tar wird tar + e gewöhnlich dargestellt durch tar-re, sargonisch tar-ré (s. Anm. 26), und tar + a durch tar-ra (für eine Ausnahme s. Anm. 27).

Was aber bedeutet nam-tar? Unsere Übersetzungen "Schicksal entscheiden," "decree the fate," "décréer le destin," etc., beruhen allesamt auf der akkadischen Phrase *šīmtam šâmum*, "die Bestimmung bestimmen," die sich schon durch ihre Paronomasie als genuin akkadisch und somit als sinngemässe, nicht aber wörtliche Übersetzung entpuppt.[31]

Nam ist umstritten. Die Gleichung = *šīmtu*, "Bestimmung, Geschick, Schicksal," hilft uns nicht weiter, da sie aus nam-tar isoliert und der akkadischen Wendung verpflichtet ist. Nach A. Falkenstein[32] wäre nam erstarrte Kurzform von *ana'am (ana-àm), "was ist es?" dabei bezog F. sich vor allem auf die nam-Komposita vom Typ nam-lugal, die er als *"was-ist-es: König" = "das was (den) König (ausmacht)" = "Königtum" erklärte. F. konnte bei dieser Herleitung begründen, weshalb nam-Komposita keine Genitivverbindungen sind. Doch wurde diese These angefochten.[33]

30. Immerhin ist nam-ku$_5$ unwahrscheinlich, da die Form sonst -ku$_5$-ru-uš lauten sollte; s. allerdings für Ausnahmen Anm. 50.

31. Zum sog. "tautologischen Infinitiv" und verwandten Erscheinungen vgl. G. Goldenberg, in *Israel Oriental Studies* I (1971) 36–85, wo viele Beispiele aus semitischen und nichtsemitischen Sprachen.

Von der gängigen Übersetzung "Schicksal entscheiden" hat sich Th. Jacobsen distanziert: "'to command with absolute authority and effectivity' . . . used of the sentence imposed by a judge" (*ZA*, Bd. 52, S. 101–2, Anm. 13), ohne aber auf die Rektionsverhältnisse einzugehen.

32. *Das Sumerische* (Leiden, 1959) S. 35, § 15,2.

33. Vgl. Sollberger, *TCS* I 155, Nr. 507; implicite G. Steiner, "Die Bezeichnungen von 'Gruppen' und 'Klassen' durch Abstrakta in Sprachen des Alten Orients," *CRRA* XVIII 193–94.

Wir wissen jetzt, dass neusum. und altbab. n a m in "Fara" n á m (*ATU*, Nr. 502, ähnlich wie TÚG) entsprechen kann und umgekehrt.[34] Die frühdynastischen Vorläufer der lexikalischen Listen mit Menschenklassen (Lú, *MSL* XII 3–21) enthalten mehrere Einträge mit NÁM, was die Autoren n á m lesen. Sind es mit Präfix n á m - (jüngeres n a m -) gebildete Abstrakta? Wenn das zutrifft, ist die Verwendung des Zeichens NAM = s í m, s í n auch als n a m womöglich sekundär. Es ist ferner denkbar, dass n á m ursprünglich etwas Gewandartiges war und dass daher die Ähnlichkeit des Zeichens mit dem für "Stoff, Gewand" (TÚG = t ú g) rührt.

Das ist alles spekulativ. Doch erschweren derlei Überlegungen ein Festhalten an Falkensteins Etymologie. Wenn wir tatsächlich n á m > n a m als etwas von Hause aus Konkretes auffassen dürfen, wird die Verbindung mit einem Verbum des Schneidens wie t a r und auch k u₅ (s. I A 5) verständlich. Andererseits ist eine grammatische Schwierigkeit zuzugeben: n a m -Komposita sind, wie oben gesagt, keine Genitivverbindungen. Freilich ist die sumerische Nominalkomposition noch nicht genügend untersucht, und gerade archaische Bildungen geben noch Fragen auf.

Wir arbeiten im Folgenden mit der Hypothese, dass n a m - t a r zwar akkadisch eine Entsprechung "Schicksal bestimmen" oder ähnlich hat, im Sumerischen aber zunächst "NAM schneiden" bedeutete, wobei nicht bekannt ist, welche speziellere Art des Schneidens, Trennens t a r meinte. Zwecks weiterer Klärung wenden wir uns der Rektion des Verbums zu.

Wenn eine Handlung zu jemandes Gunsten durchgeführt wird, so pflegt die begünstigte Person im Dativ zu stehen: s u m, "geben" (mu-na-sum), b a, "zuteilen" (ì-na-ba), a-r u, "weihen" (a mu-na-ru), d í m, "machen," und d ù, "bauen" (mu-na-dím, -dù) usw. Anders n a m - t a r. Hier enthält zwar die begünstigte Person die Dativpostposition -r a; aber in der Infixkette stellt das rückbezügliche Morphem einen Lokativ-Terminativ dar[35] (E n l i l e Š u l g i r a n a m mu-ni-in-tar). Nam-tar teilt diese Rektion mit s a g - e - e š r i g₇, "schenken." G. Gragg nimmt in seiner jüngsten Studie *Sumerian Dimensional Infixes* in Anlehnung an A. Poebel und A. Falkenstein "erstarrten Gebrauch des Infixes" an, "where the infix seems to have no connection either with the goal of the action, or with the place where it takes place."[36]

Diese Erklärung befriedigt nicht, da nicht gesagt wird, von welcher ursprünglichen Funktion her die Form "erstarrt" ist. Eine andere Lösung liegt näher. Wir gehen von der sumerischen Kausativkonstruktion aus. Ein akkadischer Satz vom Typ *šarrum šakkanakkam ālam ušēpiš*, "der König hat den General eine Stadt bauen lassen," kann bekanntlich nicht mit doppeltem Akkusativ ins

---

34. R. D. Biggs, "The Abū Ṣalābīkh Tablets," *JCS* XX (1966) 81, Anm. 57 und 59: ŠA-n á m = altbab. na-nam; "An Archaic Sumerian Version of the Kesh Temple Hymn," *ZA*, Bd. 61 (1971) S. 204: nam-nun = altbab. nám-nun.

35. Analog auch die Rektion erweiterter Wendungen wie nam-tar-ra-šà-ge-guru₇-a-zu ǧá-e ga-mu-ri-ib-tar, "eine Schicksalsentscheidung nach deinen Wünschen will ich dir zukommen lassen," Lugalbanda und Enmerkar A, Z. 166 (Übers. C. Wilcke).

36. *AOAT* Sonderreihe 5 (1973) S. 80.

Sumerische übersetzt werden. In diesem Satz würde das veranlasste Subjekt, d.h. der erste der beiden Akkusative, durch einen Dativ dargestellt werden: *lugal-e šagin-ra . . . ; doch wird šagin-ra beileibe nicht durch ein Dativinfix beim Verbum aufgenommen. Denn ein Satz *lugal-e šagin-ra uru mu-na-an-dù würde ja bedeuten "der König hat dem General eine Stadt gebaut"! Der Satz lautete vielmehr *lugal-e šagin-ra uru mu-ni-in-dù.[37] Das ist nun eben die Konstruktion, die wir als die bei nam-tar normale kennen gelernt haben. Wir dürfen daraufhin einen Satz ᵈen-líl-le šul-gi-ra nam mu-ni-in-tar nicht mehr übersetzen *"Enlil hat dem Šulgi das Schicksal entschieden" und auch nicht wörtlich *"Enlil hat dem Šulgi NAM geschnitten," sondern nur wörtlich "Enlil hat Šulgi veranlasst, NAM zu schneiden" im Sinne von "Enlil hat Šulgi gestattet, an dem, was NAM ist, teilzuhaben."

Das hätte, wenn es richtig gedacht ist und wir es strikt befolgen, grosse Konsequenzen für unsere Vorstellung vom Verhältnis Gott: Mensch in der sumerischen Religion. Nicht die Gottheit "entscheidet dem Menschen das Schicksal," sondern sie lässt zu, dass er sich einen gebührenden Anteil nimmt. Zugleich aber sehen wir, wie all unser Bemühen um Einsicht in Erscheinungen der altorientalischen Kultur zuallererst ein rein philologisches ist.

3. Di-ku₅(-d/r)

di-ku₅(-d/r), "eine Rechtssache entscheiden"; für die mögliche Verteilung von *hamṭu* und *marû* s. unten I A 7; dub-sar-Typus di-ku₅, "Richter," mit Vokalauslaut.

Nichtfinites *hamṭu*: di-TAR-a-ĝá šu-ni íb-bal-e-a, "(und) wer sich über das von mir entschiedene Recht hinwegsetzt," Gudea Statue B viii 17–18.

Hier liegt "Hiatus"-Schreibung vor; nach Analogie anderer Verbindungen mit ku₅(-d/r) (s. I A 4–6) dürfen wir aber di-kur₅-a einsetzen.[38]

Nichtfinites *marû*: du₆-ur-saĝ-e-ne di ku₅-ru-dè hé-du₇, "der 'Heldenhügel' ist wahrlich geeignet für das Rechtsprechen," *VS* X, Nr. 197 iii 20; hiernach TAR-dè = kuru₅-dè[39] in di-kalam-ma kuru₅-dè GA. RAŠ[40]-kalam-ma bar-re-dè, "das Recht des Landes zu sprechen, die

---

37. Vgl. für Kausativbildungen Th. Jacobsen, *MSL* IV 28*–30*; "About the Sumerian Verb," *Studies in Honor of Benno Landsberger* (*AS*, No. 16 [1965]) pp. 93–94 mit Anm. 16 [*TIOT*, S. 264 und 456–57]); s. auch G. Flügge, *Der Mythos "Inanna und Enki" unter besonderer Berücksichtigung der Liste der me* (*StP*, Bd. 10 [1973]) S. 66–69.

38. Vgl. u.a. noch ki-di-dab₅-ba ù nam-erím-kur₅-a-ba, "am Orte des Rechtsspruch-Erteilens und des Eidleistens," *NG*, Nr. 126:16–17 für Schreibung TAR-a im Falle eines anderen zusammengesetzten Verbums (s. I A 6).

39. Wir könnten auch kur₅-(u)dè transliterieren. Vgl. M. Civil, "The Sumerian Writing System: Some Problems," *Or*, NS, Bd. 42 (1973) S. 33–34, der im Falle lugal-ni statt lugala-ni vielmehr lugal-ani empfiehlt. Solange unser Umschriftsystem aber nicht radikal reformiert ist (und bedarf es dessen?), sollte man der traditionellen Methode den Vorzug geben, "überhängende" Vokale, wenn überhaupt, zusammen mit der vorangehenden Silbe auszudrücken.

40. Gemeint ga-eš₈, Variante zu gewöhnlichem ka-aš; s. dazu J. Klein, "Sum. ga-raš = Akk. *purussû*," *JCS* XXIII (1971) 118 mit S. N. Kramer, in *BiOr* VII (1950) 77, Anm. 6.

Entscheidung für das Land zu fällen," Šulgi F (*TMH* NF IV, Nr. 11:26).

ki-di-ku₅-ru-bi-šè (1 Var. -kuru₅-), "zu dem Orte, der Recht entscheidet," Nungal-Hymne, Z. 35 (*AfO* XXIV [1973] 30).[41]

Präsens: [e]n-kur-ra di-gal mu-ku₅-de₆(DU)-en ka-aš-mah mu-bar-re-en, "Herr des Berglandes, grosse Rechtssprüche verkündest du, die grössten Entscheidungen triffst du," *ISET* I 96, Ni. 2781 Vs. 20.

e-ne di-kur-ra ì-ku₅-dè, "er (Ur-Nammu) spricht Recht über das Bergland," Ur-Nammus Tod, Z. 144.

di mu-un-da-ku₅-ru-ne (Var. mu-na-kuru₅-ne), "(die Anuna-Götter) sprechen Recht mit Bezug auf sie (Inanna)," Inannas Gang zur Unterwelt, Z. 163.

Freie Reduplikation: di-si-sa-am-gu-ku = *di-si-sá-ku₅-ku₅, "immer/überall gerades Recht sprechend," *Sumer* XIII (1957) 83, Z. 2.

Der dub-sar-Typus (s. Anm. 23) di-ku₅, "Richter," endet vokalisch, enthält also eine defektive Form der Basis. Der Plural lautet di-ku₅-ne (*NG*, Nr. 1:5); im Genitiv steht [in]im-di-ku₅, "Wort des Richters" (*NG*, Nr. 113:41); bei Antritt der Kopula haben wir di-ku₅-àm (Šulgi A 84 [Var. M]). J. Krecher hat als Alternative zu di-ku₅ di-kuru₅ erwogen.[42] Mit einer solchen Form würde sich aber die neben di-ku₅-ne bezeugte Pluralform di-ku₅-e-ne (*NG*, Nr. 202:8; Codex Lipit-Eštar, Z. 30) nicht vereinbaren lassen; denn *di-kuru₅-ene ist kaum möglich; man würde *di-kuru₅-ne oder aber *di-ku₅-ru-ne erwarten.

ku₅(-d/r) folgt bei Antritt von -e komplizierteren Regeln als tar; s. die Zusammenstellung in I A 7; dort auch zur Frage des Konsonantenauslauts.

Als Grundbedeutung von di-ku₅(-d/r) ist wohl anzusetzen "eine Rechtsangelegenheit abschneiden" im Sinne von "die R. durch Entscheidung beenden"; ein Verbum des "Schneidens, Trennens" für "entscheiden" ist vielen Sprachen einschliesslich des Deutschen gemein. Die Übersetzung von di beruht dagegen nur auf unserer Interpretation von akkadisch *dīnum*. Wir wissen nicht, ob diese Entsprechung ursprünglich ist. Sollte di gleicher Herkunft sein wie die nichtfinite *marû*-Basis di zu dug₄/e, "sprechen"?[43] Oder wäre di ein sehr altes akkadisches Lehnwort?

---

41. A. Falkenstein, *NG* III 98, nahm auch ein Partizip di-ku₅-ra, "Recht sprechend" an; doch steht -ra an der zitierten Stelle (*STVC*, Nr. 133 ii 3′) vor einer Lücke, so dass gar nicht sicher ist, ob es zu di-ku₅ gehört.

42. "Verschlusslaute und Betonung im Sumerischen," *Lišān mitḫurti* (*AOAT* I [1969]) S. 171, Anm. 19.

43. Unsere Umschrift di ist nur approximativ. Di kommt altsum. nicht als freier Silbenwert vor und ist auch dem altakk. Syllabar noch so gut wie unbekannt. I. J. Gelb nennt in *Old Akkadian Writing and Grammar* (*MAD*, Nr. 2 [2. Aufl., 1961]) S. 105, Nr. 266 nur das Sumerogramm TU.DI.DA = *dudittum* (Herkunft des Wortes unbekannt). Die von ihm weiter zitierten Ausnahmen sind die PN "A-ba-(ᵈ)Da-di" und "DINGIR-Da-di" (ebd. Nachtrag S. 212); dies sind in Wirklichkeit sumerische Namen: a-ba-(an)-da-sá, "wer kann mit ihm/ihr wetteifern?" bzw. der daraus verkürzte Name an-da-sá.

4. Nam-ku₅(-d/r)

nam-ku₅(-d/r), "verfluchen";[44] für die mögliche Verteilung von *ḫamṭu* und *marû* s. unten I A 7; Person oder Sache, die der Fluch trifft, stehen überwiegend im Komitativ.[45]

Nichtfinit *ḫamṭu*: im ᵈen-ki-ke₄ nam-ku₅-rá (Var. W, AA) / nam-ku₅-da (Var. A, D) hé-a, "es sei ein Lehm(platz), den Enki verflucht hat," Fluch über Akkade, Z. 335; s. 237, 239.

Präteritum: ki-bal-da nam im-ma-da-an-ku₅, "sie verfluchte das aufsässige Land," *SRT*, Nr. 6 iii 34 (Nr. 7:45).

uru an-né nam ba-ku₅-da-a-gim (Var. D) / ba-TAR-gim (Var. J) / ... -rá-a-gim (Var. "O"), "wie eine Stadt, die An verflucht hat," Inanna und Ebiḫ, Z. 48.

Präsens: nam ḫa-ba-an-da-ku₅-ru-ne, "sie mögen ihn verfluchen," *UET* I, Nr. 100:31 (Šū-ilišu); vgl. *AfO* XIX (1959–60) 8, Kol. iv', Z. 12 (Šū-Su'en); hiernach auch TAR.NE = kuru₅-dè in nam ḫa-ba-an-da-kuru₅-ne, *UET* I, Nr. 57:14 (Šulgi).

Zu den Schreibregeln für ku₅(-d/r)+Vokal sowie für den Konsonanten im Auslaut s. die Zusammenstellung in I A 7.

Etymologie: Wir übersetzen "verfluchen" wegen der Gleichung mit akk. *arārum*. Das kann aber nicht die Grundbedeutung sein. Nam x-da ku₅ heisst wörtlich "mit/bei jemanden/einer Sache NAM abschneiden." Es ist möglich, aber kaum noch zu beweisen, dass hier ein uralter Analogiezauber zugrunde liegt, bei dem der Verfluchende einen Streifen von Gewand des mit Fluch zu Belegenden an sich brachte. Dies freilich unter der Voraussetzung, dass unser Versuch einer Herleitung von nam aus nám nicht völlig irrig ist (s. I A 2). Vgl. noch Anm. 57.

Nam-tar und nam-ku₅(-d/r) sind im Kontext kaum zu verwechseln. Wenn auf TAR noch eine Silbe folgt, werden verschiedene orthographische Regeln befolgt. Auch ist die Präfixkette verschieden konstruiert.

Gerade die Rektion warnt aber auch davor, dass wir unser nam-ku₅(-d/r), "verfluchen," mit dem nam-ku₅ der "Geierstele" verbinden. Dort steht die betroffene Person im Dativ; nam-ku₅ hat dort dieselbe Rektion wie das sogleich zu behandelnde nam-erím-ku₅ (I A 5).

5. Nam-erím-ku₅(-d/r)

nam-erím-ku₅(-d/r), "einen assertorischen Eid leisten";[46] für die mögliche Verteilung von *ḫamṭu* und *marû* s. unten I A 7; die Person, der man schwört, steht im Dativ.[47]

Nichtfinites *marû*: nam-erím ku₅-ru-dè ba-an-sum-mu-uš, "sie

---

44. Konventionelle Übersetzung; s. unten die Diskussion.

45. Im Folgenden nur wenige Belege; weiteres Material bei W. Römer, *SKIZ*, S. 101–2 mit S. 125–26, Anm. 13, 14.

46. Interpretierende Übersetzung; s. unten die Diskussion zur Etymologie.

47. S. auch noch ausführlicher Abschnitt III.

(gaben ihn zum . . . =) veranlassten ihn, den assertorischen Eid zu schwören,"
HSM 1384:22 (Enlil-bāni);[48] vgl. *STVC*, Nr. 86 ii 3–6.[49]

nam-erím-bi ku$_5$-ru-dè nu-un-še-e, "den assertorischen Eid wollte er
nicht leisten," *NG*, Nr. 209:8–10.

Präteritum: nam-erím-bi nu-un-ku$_5$, mu nam-erím-bi nu-un-
[k]u$_5$-da, "er leistete den assertorischen Eid nicht; weil er den assertorischen
Eid nicht leistete," HSM 1384:24–25.

[n]am-erím-bi in-kur$_5$-eš(!), "sie haben den assertorischen Eid geleistet," *NG*, Nr. 78:15'.[50]

Präsens: na-ám-erim ma-ku$_5$-dè-en, "du wirst mir schwören," *SRT*, Nr.
31:13–16; s. 25.[51]

nam-erím-bi i-ku$_5$-de$_6$, "er wird den assertorischen Eid leisten," *NG*,
Nr. 215:15.

nam-erím-bi i-kuru$_5$-ne, "sie werden den assertorischen Eid leisten,"
NG, Nr. 127:19.

U. ù dam-ni nam-erím ha-ma-ku$_5$-re bí-in-du$_{11}$, nam-erím-bi
ba-ku$_5$-da,[52] "'U. und seine Frau sollen mir (jeder)[53] den assertorischen Eid
leisten' erklärte er; wenn darüber der assertorischer Eid geleistet wird, (. . .),"
NG, Nr. 195:27'–29'.

Ausserhalb der Sphäre unserer Gerichtsurkunden steht der literarische Beleg:
^{d}nin-hur-saĝ-ĝá-ke$_4$ mu(-)^{d}en-ki nam-erím ba-an-ku$_5$, "Ninhursanga . . .," Enki und Ninmah, Z. 218. Diese Zeile ist mir unklar; vielleicht
führen Duplikate weiter.[54]

Zu den Schreibregeln für ku$_5$(-d/r)+Vokal sowie für den Konsonanten im
Auslaut s. die Zusammenstellung in I A 7.

Die Lesung NE.RU = erím liegt fest einerseits durch den Lokativ nam-
NE.RU-ma in *NG*, Nr. 30:9, andererseits durch verschiedene unorthographische
Schreibungen.[55]

48. Gerichtsurkunde im Harvard Semitic Museum, die ich mit freundlicher Erlaubnis des
verewigten G. Ernest Wright, zitiere.

49. Das weitere dort leider schlecht erhalten: túg(-)nam-erím-[ma(?)], [x (x)]
ga(?) KA $^⌈$x$^⌉$ [x (x)] (abgebrochen).

50. Auffälligerweise nicht -ku$_5$-ru-uš; eš steht sehr eng am Rand; wollte der Schreiber
abkürzen? S. aber auch *ZA*, Bd. 53 (1959) S. 70, Nr. 11:5.

51. Mir von C. Wilcke nachgewiesen (s.a. unten I B). Inanna verlangt von Dumuzi die
Bestätigung, dass er früher keine Liebesaffären gehabt habe.

52. Das -da in ba-ku$_5$-da ist unklar; nach A. Falkensteins Kommentar ist es in TAR
hineingeschrieben.

53. Obwohl logisch ein pluralisches Subjekt vorliegt, ist die Verbalform Singular.
Individualisierung der Einzelglieder des Pluralsubjekts erklärt vielleicht auch die Verwendung
von Sing. in-pà in altbab. Urkunden bei mehreren Schwörenden (Hinweis von H. Petschow;
vgl. M. San Nicolò, *Die Schlussklauseln der altbabylonischen Kauf- und Tauschverträge*
[2. Aufl., München, 1974] S. 62 f.).

54. S. N. Kramer hat in *Enki and Ninhursag: A Sumerian "Paradise" Myth* (*BASOR*
"Supplementary Studies," Nr. 1 [New Haven, 1945]) S. 10 übersetzt: "(Thereupon) Ninhursag cursed Enki's name"; so auch *ANET* (2. Aufl.) S. 40. Man würde *mu-^{d}en-ki-ga-
ka erwarten.

55. Vgl. unten Anm. 94.

Etymologie: nam-erím-ku₅ ist eine Erweiterung von nam-ku₅; allerdings ist die Verschiedenheit der Rektion zu beachten. Wörtlich übersetzen wir "jemandem ein böses NAM / etwas Böses abschneiden." Vielleicht sollte eine solche Wendung ursprünglich ausdrücken, dass sich der Schwörende bei seiner Aussage von Bösem, Falschem, Widrigem distanzierte. Dies würde besonders einleuchten, wenn die Formel zunächst auf eine negative, Böses abstreitende Eidesaussage beschränkt gewesen wäre. Leider wissen wir aber nichts über das Alter der Formel, für die uns die ältesten Belege aus der altakk. Zeit vorliegen.[56] A. Falkensteins Deutung "den Bann 'schneiden'" geht bereits von einem nam-erím aus, dessen Übersetzung akk. *māmītu* verpflichtet ist.

6. Ku₅(-d/r) ohne festes Objekt

ku₅(-d/r) ohne festes Objekt "abschneiden"; das Verbum regiert den Akkusativ; für mögliche Verteilung von *ḫamṭu* und *marû* s. unten I A 7.

Nichtfinit *ḫamṭu*: áb amar-bi ku₅-da-gim, "wie eine Kuh, deren Kalb man (von ihr) getrennt hat," Nippur-Klage, Z. 67.

Nichtfinit *marû*: umbin-ku₅-ru, "Coiffeur," Proverb Collection 3.124 (s. *SP* 2.113); vgl. dazu in freier Reduplikation umbin-ku₅-ku₅, Inannas Gang zur Unterwelt, Z. 320.

Präteritum: níg-du₁₀ bí-ib-ku₅-ru-uš-àm, "sie haben das Gute abgeschnitten," Nippur-Klage, Z. 63.

Präsens: mu-na-ku₅-dè ba-kú, "(Isimud) schneidet ihm (Enki) (die Pflanze) ab, und (Enki) beisst hinein," Enki und Ninhursaga, Z. 202, 204, 206. Dass wir hier nicht etwa *mu-na-kuru₅-dè zu lesen haben, zeigt Z. 208 mu-na-bu-re, "er reisst ihm (die Pflanze) aus," d.h. eine Form eindeutig ohne /ED/.

túg-3-tab-ba lú nu-ku₅-de (Var. -da), "ein dreifältiges Tuch kann niemand abschneiden," Gilgamesch und Huwawa, Z. 107.

pa-bi ì-ku₅-ru-ne, "sie schneiden die Äste davon ab," Gilgamesch und Huwawa, Z. 140.

nam-tar-ra-ni hé-da₅-kuru₅-ne, "(An, Enlil, etc.) mögen ihm sein NAMTARA wegschneiden," Gudea Statue B ix 5.[57]

Während ich unschwer Beispiele für ku₅(-d/r) mit freiem Objekt finde, ist mir das bei tar nicht möglich. Unklar der folgende Beleg:

an-ga-àm éš-gim ì-TAR-re-en, "auch . . .st du wie ein Seil," Dialog 2, Z. 70.

Angesichts von túg . . . ku₅ (oben Gilgamesch und Huwawa, Z. 107) könnte man für ku₅ plädieren; doch spricht -re eher für tar.[58]

---

56. S. unten Abschnitt III.

57. Gemeint wohl "das was er durch Gewährung von nam-tar erlangt hat." Die Rektion (Komitativinfix) ist dieselbe wie bei nam-ku₅(-d/r) (oben I A 5), und der Kontext, eine Fluchformel, stimmt ebenfalls mit dem bei nam-ku₅(-d/r) geläufigen überein. Es erhebt sich daher die Frage, ob nam-ku₅(-d/r) etwa eine aus nam-tar-ra ku(-d/r) verkürzte Wendung ist.

58. Für eine Ausnahme s. aber I A 5 (*NG*, Nr. 195:27').

7. Resümee zum morphologischen Befund

Es gibt bisher keinen Anhaltspunkt dafür, dass das Verbum tar verschiedene Basen für *hamṭu* und *marû* hatte. Es verhielt sich offenbar wie s a r, "schreiben," oder k a r, "wegnehmen." Tar + Morphem /a/ wird so gut wie ausschliesslich tar-ra geschrieben; der m.W. älteste Beleg ist nam-tar-ra in Sollberger, *Corpus*, Ukg. 4–5 vii 20; eine Ausnahme tar-rá s. in Anm. 27. Tar + Morphem /e/ bzw. + e-haltiges Morphem wird altsum. tar-ré, neusum. und jünger tar-re geschrieben, niemals aber *tar-re₆(DU).[59]

Viel verzwickter sind die Verhältnisse bei k u₅(-d/r). Anhand der Belege aus I A 3–6 können wir als Arbeitshypothese das folgende "Paradigma" aufstellen, das sich—wohlgemerkt—ganz mechanisch an unserer Umschriftweise orientiert:

Präteritum	Präsens
*iku(d/r)	ikuden
*iku(d/r)	ikuden[60]
inku(d/r)[61]	ikude,[62] ikure[63]
. . . . .	*ikurunden
. . . . .	*ikurunzen
inkuruš[64]	ikurune[65]

Wir erkennen eine für Präteritum und Präsens Plural gültige Basis k u₅-r, die ein antretendes [e] zu [u] assimiliert. Die Singularbasis des Präteritums lautet k u₅-d/r, die des Präsens k u₅-d mit möglicher Ausnahme k u₅-r, so dass vielleicht auch hier k u₅-d/r anzusetzen ist. Anders als beim Plural unterbleibt im Singular die Assimilation eines antretenden [e].

Mit der Pluralbasis k u₅-r stimmt die Basis des nichtfiniten *marû* überein; wir kennen folgende Formen: k u r u, k u r u d e, k u r u d a m.[66]

Dagegen können wir die nichtfinite *hamṭu*-Basis übereinstimmend mit der Basis Präteritum Singular wieder als k u₅-d/r definieren: k u d/r a.[67]

Schliesslich ist für d i - k u₅(-d/r) ein "d u b - s a r - T y p u s" zu nennen, wo die Basis in einer weiteren Spielform, nämlich defektiv als k u erscheint (s. oben I A 2).

Wir fassen den Befund zusammen: Rein mechanisch stellen wir vier Formen fest: (1) k u mit Vokalauslaut, (2) k u(d/r), das ein folgendes [e] nicht assimiliert, (3) k u(d) mit seltener Variante k u(r), ebenfalls ohne Einwirkung auf folgendes [e], und (4) k u(r), das ein folgendes [e] zu [u] assimiliert. Kategorie

---

59. Die bei E. Sollberger, *Le Système verbal dans les inscriptions "royales" présargoniques de Lagaš* (Genève, 1952) S. 243, s.v. n a m - t a r zitierten Beispiele gehören zu n a m - k u₅.

60. Ma-ku₅-dè-en, I A 5; mu-ku₅-de₆-en, I A 3.

61. Nu-un-ku₅-da, I A 5; ba-ku₅-da, I A 4; . . .-rá, I A 4.

62. Mu-na-ku₅-dè, I A 6; ì-ku₅-de₆, I A 5.

63. Ì-ku₅-re, I A 6.

64. Bí-ib-ku₅-ru-uš-àm, I A 6; aber auch in-kur₅-eš, I A 5.

65. Ì-ku₅-ru-ne, I A 6; ha-ba-an-da-ku₅-ru-ne, I A 4; mu-un-da-ku₅-ru-ne, I A 3.

66. Ku₅-ru, I A 6; ku₅-ru-dè, ku₅-ru-dam, I A 5.

67. Ku₅-da, ku₅-rá, I A 4; ku₅-da, I A 6.

(4) gehört zum nichtfiniten *marû* sowie zum Präsens und Präteritum Plural; (2) entfällt auf nichtfinites *hamṭu* sowie auf Präteritum Singular. Soweit könnten wir (2) k u (d / r) als die *hamṭu*-, (4) k u (r) als die *marû*-Basis definieren. Eindringen von *marû* auch in den Plural des Präteritums könnte als eine Parallele zu d u g₄ /e angesehen werden (vgl. oben Anm. 21).

Aber unsere Rechnung geht nicht so glatt auf. Widersprüchlich verhält sich (3), d.h. die für Singular Präsens festgestellte Form. Selbst wenn wir bei ihr den Auslautkonsonanten (d / r) nicht mit dem der Basis Präsens Plural (r) konfrontieren, bleibt doch die verschiedene Reaktion von angehängtem [e] in Singular (i k u d e) und Plural (i k u r u -). Wir müssen also ausser einer möglichen Verteilung von *hamṭu*- und *marû*-Formen auch noch mit verschiedenen Singular- und Pluralbasen rechnen.

Mehrfach wurde betont, dass wir bei dieser Erörterung mechanisch von unserer Umschrift ausgehen. Uns ist klar, dass diese Umschrift den Konsonantenauslaut nur unvollkommen darstellt. Es handelt sich um eine phonetische (wir können noch nicht ohne Weiteres sagen: phonologische) Grösse, für deren Wiedergabe man zunächst das—leider schon mit "Werten" überlastete— Zeichen DU verwendete. Ausser k u₅ (-d / r) haben noch andere Verben sowie (nach J. Bauer) Substantive diesen Auslaut.[68]

Unser vorläufiges Ergebnis haben wir oben in der Transliteration von "Geierstele," Kol. xvi, Z. 12–Kol. xvii, Z. 20 vorweggenommen und das dortige n a m . . .-TAR.DU teils mit - k u₅ - d e₆, teils mit - k u₅ - r á umschrieben, je nachdem, ob wir mit einer Präsens- oder einer nominalisierten Präteritalform rechnen.

Nach diesem überlangen Exkurs wenden wir uns der Bedeutung von n a m - k u₅ in der "Geierstele" zu.

B. N a m - k u₅ IN DER "GEIERSTELE"

n a m - k u₅ (-d / r) mit Dativrektion ist in der "Geierstele" reziprok gebraucht. Eanatum gab dem Manne von Umma das Fangnetz Enlils, und n a m e - n a - t a - k u₅, "er schnitt ihm vermittels (dieses Netzes) NAM ab" (Präteritum), woraufhin oder wobei nun der Mann von Umma seinerseits dem Eanatum n a m m u - n a - k u₅ - d e₆, "NAM abschneidet" (Präsens).[69] Wie spielte sich die Handlung ab?

68. Als ich diesen Aufsatz schon abgeschlossen hatte, machte mir J. Bauer freundlicherweise ein Ms. zugänglich, das auf einen Vortrag beim XXIX. Internationalen Orientalistenkongress (Paris, 1973) zurückgeht: "Zum /dr/-Phonem des Sumerischen." Bauer behandelt ausser Verben wie k u₅, s ù u.a. auch Nomina wie g u₄, e n k u ₓ(= ZAG.HA) u.a. vorwiegend auf Grund altsum. Texte. Er rekonstruiert einen vokalisch mehrwertigen Lautwert DU = d r a, d r e, für den er als Parallele im graphischen System GÁ = ĝá, ĝeₓ heranzieht. Bei t a r und k u₅ kommt Bauer, was die "Verlängerung" um -a oder -e betrifft, zu den gleichen Ergebnissen wie wir oben: altsum. t a r + a = tar-ra, + e = t a r - r é, k u₅ (-d/r) + a = k u₅-rá, + e = k u₅-DU. Auf das Gesamtparadigma von k u₅ (-d/r) geht Bauer entsprechend dem in andere Richtung gehenden Zweck seines Aufsatzes nicht ein. (S. jetzt *WO* VIII/1 [1975] 1–9.)

69. Zu beachten die Folge Präteritum-Präsens, die—zumindest im altbab. Sumerisch nachweisbar—ausdrücken kann, dass die Handlung B (Präsens) mit der von A (Präteritum) gleichzeitig verläuft. Vgl. Verf., *ZA*, Bd. 61, S. 230, Anm. 78.

War es eine zweiseitige Abmachung, bei der auch Eanatum eine Verpflichtung einging, deren Wortlaut nur nicht verewigt wurde? Dergleichen liesse sich zumindest grammatisch begründen. Oder war es ein einseitiger Akt, wie es zumindest nach dem Bildinhalt der Stele ganz den Anschein hat? Wir können diese Frage letztlich nicht entscheiden, da wir nicht dabei gewesen sind! Sollte die Handlung einseitig gewesen sein, müssten wir als Bedeutung für nam-ku$_5$ zweierlei annehmen: (1) "den Eid leisten, die Verpflichtung (bei einem Göttersymbol) eingehen" und (2) "jemanden zur Leistung eines Eides, zum Eingehen einer Verpflichtung veranlassen."

Zu beachten ist aber, dass die Form nam e-na-ta-ku$_5$ nicht ohne Weiteres kausativ *"er liess ihn dabei schwören" übersetzt werden darf (vgl. Anm. 37). Hingegen enthält der sechste Eidesabschnitt, der bei Ninki geschworene, Formen, die wir glaubten, kausativ auffassen zu dürfen: mu-...mu-ni-pà-dè (s. I C) und nam-ni ma-ni-ku$_5$-rá, "bei der ich ihn für mich habe schwören lassen." War etwa nach der monotonen Wiederholung in den Eidesabschnitten 1–5 im sechsten eine Steigerung beabsichtigt, durch die auch sinnmässig der letztliche Triumph des Eanatum zum Ausdruck kam?

Eine sichere Entscheidung ist kaum möglich. Unser Urteil wäre leichter, wenn die Zahl altsumerischer Belege für die Eidesleistung grösser wäre. Schwierig ist auch, dass die bei Eanatum gebrauchte Formel nam-ku$_5$ mit Dativ nicht unmittelbar mit einer jüngeren verbunden werden kann. Nam-ku$_5$, "verfluchen" (I A 4), weicht in der Rektion ab, was Konsequenzen für die Bedeutung hat. Nam-erím-ku$_5$ (I A 5) hat zwar ebenfalls Dativrektion, bezieht sich aber anders als das nam-ku$_5$ der "Geierstele" nicht auf etwas Zukünftiges. D.h. wenn wir die Eide der "Geierstele" nach den Kategorien "promissorisch" oder "assertorisch" klassifizieren, so trifft die erste Kategorie zu. Nam-erím-ku$_5$ ist aber spätestens seit der neusumerischen Zeit Ausdrucksmittel schlechthin für die zweite Eideskategorie, die assertorische. Falls wir dennoch eine Beziehung herstellen wollen, müssen wir mit einer Entwicklung im Rechtsformular rechnen, die von einer freien Verwendungsmöglichkeit von nam-ku$_5$ zur ausschliesslichen Verwendung von nam-erím-ku$_5$ im assertorischen Eide führte.

Dass eine strenge Scheidung noch nicht bestand, lehrt immerhin der sechste Eidesabschnitt. Eanatum lässt seinen Rivalen "den Namen der Ninki anrufen"; er veranlasst ihn zu einem Ausspruch, der in der jüngeren Sprache regelmässig den promissorischen Eid begleitet; die Reaktion darauf ist aber trotzdem wie in den vorigen fünf Abschnitten: nam mu-na-ku$_5$-de$_6$.

Es kann sein, dass die formularmässige Trennung nach promissorischem und assertorischem Eid eine Errungenschaft der Akkade-Zeit war.

C. Mu-pà(-d) IN DER "GEIERSTELE"

Die Wendung nam e-na-ta-ku$_5$ der Eidesabschnitte 1–5 ist im sechsten Abschnitt ersetzt durch mu-GN(-ak) mu-ni-pà-dè. Wir übersetzen "er lässt ihn den Namen der Ninki anrufen," d.h. als Kausativ; denn "er hat . . .

angerufen" müsste ja heissen mu- . . . mu-(n)-pà oder e-(n)-pà.[70] Was ist
der Grund für die abweichende Phraseologie? Wir sähen vielleicht klarer, wenn
der Anfang des sechsten Abschnitts voll erhalten wäre.[71]

In Abschnitt 6 ist die Gottheit unmittelbar der Garant des Eides; es fehlt das
vorher jedesmal erwähnte Fangnetz der Gottheit. Entsprechend lesen wir in
Rs. v 22–23 denn auch nicht *x (Gegenstand) nam e-ta-ku_5-rá, ". . . bei
dem er geschworen hat," sondern GN nam-ni ma-ni-ku_5-rá, "Ninki, bei
der ich ihn für mich habe schwören lassen."

Der sechste Abschnitt bietet noch mehr Besonderheiten. Die Verbalform
mu- . . . mu-ni-pà-dè ist Präsens ebenso wie das folgende nam mu-na-ku_5-
de_6. Die Folge der "Tempora" ist also anders als in den Abschnitten 1–5,
wo wir die Folge Präteritum-Präsens so zu interpretieren versucht haben, dass
die Handlung B mit der Handlung A gleichzeitig ist (s. Anm. 69). Das könnte
für die Gesamtdeutung von Gewicht sein. Im Gegensatz zur—möglicherweise—
reziproken Eidesleistung in Abschnitt 1–5 ergreift in Abschnitt 6 Eanatum
allein die Initiative und zwingt den Gegner zum Schwur.

Wir haben in der "Geierstele" den bisher wohl ältesten Beleg für mu-pà(-d),
"Namen anrufen," von einem Menschen gesagt, der sich an einen Gott wendet.
Umgekehrt kann auch die Gottheit den Menschen rufen: Hier ist das seit
Eanatum immer wiederkehrende Herrscherepithet mu-pà-da-GN, "den Gott
NN bei Namen gerufen hat" zu nennen. Der Ausdruck war zwischen Mensch
und Gott reziprok verwendbar, aber in einer jeweils ganz verschiedenen Bedeu-
tung.

D. Zi-GN IN DER "GEIERSTELE"

Der Anruf zi-^{d}en-líl (Kol. xv, Z. 21–22), [zi-^{d}nin-hur-saĝ-ka] (Kol.
xvii, Z. 30), [zi-^{d}en-ki . . .-ka] (Kol. xviii, Z. 33–34), [zi-^{d}su$^{\circ}$en-. . .-ka]
(Kol. xx, Z. 10–12), zi-^{d}utu-[. . .-ka] (Rs. i 11–12), zi-^{d}n[in]-ki-[ka]
(Rs. iii 11), "beim Leben des Enlil!" etc. leitet in der direkten Rede den promissorischen Eid ein. Die Formel zi-GN ist uns in jüngeren Rechtsurkunden nur
noch verhältnismässig selten erhalten. Ein Grund dafür ist vielleicht, dass uns
promissorische Eide überwiegend in indirekter Rede überliefert sind. Ein
zweiter, dass für gewöhnlich der König angerufen wird und dass hier die
Wendung mu-lugal, "Name des Königs," entweder seit eh und je üblich war
oder aber älteres zi-lugal, "Leben des Königs," verdrängt hat.[72]

Wir kennen die Formel ausserhalb der Gerichtssphäre in Erzählungen; hier
steht sie am Anfang eines Gelübdes, das der Held der Erzählung ablegt.[73] Aber

70. Vgl. oben I A 2 mit Anm. 37.
71. Vgl. oben I.
72. Vgl. *NG* I 63, Anm. 6, und III 142, s.v. mu-lugal.
73. Vgl. Gilgamesch und Huwawa, Z. 92–94: zi ama-mu ^{d}nin-sún-ka a-a-mu kù
^{d}lugal-bàn-da, en-na lú-bi lú-u$_x$(= ULÙ) hé-a dingir hé-a
im-ma-ab-za-àm, gìri kur-šè gub-ba-mu uru-šè ba-ra-gub-bé, "Beim Leben
meiner Mutter Ninsuna, beim Leben meines Vaters, des hellen Lugalbanda, bis jener Mann
dort, sei er ein Mensch, sei er ein Gott, es nicht erfahren hat, werde ich meinen zum Bergland
gerichteten (Fuss =) Weg gewisslich nicht (zurück) zur Stadt richten!"

auch die bekannte Beschwörungsformel zi-an-na hé-pà zi-ki-a hé-pà,
"das Leben des Himmels sei angerufen, das Leben der Erde sei angerufen!"
gehört hierher;[74] denn sie bezweckte, etwas Bevorstehendes nach dem Willen
des Beschwörers zu garantieren, sei es positiv, sei es negativ, und insofern
besteht Verwandtschaft zum promissorischen Eid.

Die Formeln "Leben der Gottheit!" und "das Leben der Gottheit anrufen"
erinnern schliesslich an das akk. *nīš* (aAK *na'āš*) *ilim tamûm* (*wamā'um*), "beim
Leben des Gottes schwören." Dort ist zwar zi = *nīšum/na'āšum*, "Leben";
aber die Grundbedeutung von *wamā'um* (und dem davon abgeleiteten *tamā'um*)
kennen wir noch nicht.

II. DER PROMISSORISCHE EID

Wenn sich eine Vertragspartei verpflichtet, künftighin etwas zu tun oder zu
unterlassen, so bekundet sie das unter Anrufung einer Gottheit oder des Königs
oder auch beider. Die grundlegende Formel ist mu-GN/lugal[75] . . . -pà,
". . . . hat den Namen von Gott NN/des Königs angerufen." Dafür kann in der
Akkade-Zeit auch kürzer nur mu-GN/KN stehen. Viel seltener ist zi-lugal
(. . .-pà) "das Leben des Königs (anrufen)"; s. dazu unten II E. Der Inhalt des
Eides wird überwiegend in der direkten Rede wiedergegeben. Die syntaktische
Konstruktion, d.h. die Art der Verknüpfung von Eidesinhalt und Formel, ist
zunächst uneinheitlich. In der Ur III-Zeit verfestigt sie sich: Die Formel folgt
auf einen nominalisierten Satz (Eidesinhalt), der einen vorangesetzten Genitiv
darstellt, seltener auf . . . LAL-ede, LAL-eda oder LAL-edam; schliesslich kann
sie auch asyndetisch an einen nichtnominalisierten Satz angeschlossen sein.

A. Sargonische Beispiele

mu-lugal-šè, imim-bi al-til$_x$(= KUL), "Beim Namen des Königs!
Die Angelegenheit ist beendet," *PBS* IX, Nr. 5 ii 13–14 (Ende) (*SR*, Nr. 65).

---

74. A. Falkenstein leitete zi-lugal unmittelbar von zi-GN in der Beschwörung ab.

75. Mu-lugal wird zu Recht als Genitivverbindung aufgefasst. Sie ist exakt nachweisbar
in mu-lugal-ka-ni, "seinen Namen des Königs," besser "sein 'beim Namen des Königs!'"
(*NG*, Nr. 205:62; s. I 64 mit Anm. 1). Neusumerisch werden auch sonstige Verbindungen
mit lugal als Rektum einer Genitivverbindung stets ohne -la geschrieben; "mu-lugal-la"
in *NG*, Nr. 122:8 ist ein Versehen. Als "erstarrte" Schreibung wurde mu-lugal in der
altbab. Zeit weiter gebraucht; doch gibt es Ausnahmen: mu-lugal-la, *Texts in the Iraq
Museum* IV, Nr. 8:27, 16:26; mu-lugal-la-bi, *TIM* IV, Nr. 26:14. Merkwürdig ist
LUGAL.AL in *NRVN* I, Nr. 202 Rs. 2, 238:5, beide Mal in der Formel mu-LUGAL.AL-bi
in-pà. Hier liegt wohl kaum mit H. Sauren, "Untersuchungen zur Schrift- und Lautlehre
der neusumerischen Urkunden aus Nippur," *ZA*, Bd. 59 (1969) S. 48 und 50, "eine bewusst
unvollständige Wiedergabe des Sprachbildes," vor. *NRVN* I, Nr. 193:13 mu-LUGAL.AL-bi
al-pà gibt vielleicht die Lösung: Hier Dittographie von AL, in Nr. 202 und 238 Kontamina-
tion zwischen mu-lugal-bi in-pà und al-pà.

mu-ᵈnin-IN-na-šè, ᴵN. dumu-A., ᴵL. dumu-S., lú lú nu-ba-gi₄-gi₄, inim-bi al-til, "Beim Namen der Nin²insina(?)!⁷⁶ Nesag, der Sohn des Amar-abzu, und Lu-dingira, der Sohn des S., werden deswegen keine Ansprüche mehr gegeneinander stellen.⁷⁷ Die Angelegenheit ist beendet," *BIN* VIII, Nr. 158:34–40 (Ende) (*SR*, Nr. 20).

mu-KN-šè, lú lú nu-ba-gi₄-gi₄-da, "Beim Namen des Narām-Su²en dafür, dass sie deswegen keine Ansprüche gegeneinander mehr stellen werden," *BIN* VIII, Nr. 162:5–6 (*SR*, Nr. 71). Ähnlich mu-lugal, lú lú nu-ba-gi₄-gi₄-da-a, inim-bi al-tilₓ(= KUL), *PBS* IX, Nr. 4 i 12–ii 2 (*SR*, Nr. 56); s. Kol. ii, Z. 10–12; s. a. I. J. Gelb, *Sargonic Texts in the Louvre Museum* (*MAD*, Nr. 4 [1970]) Nr. 170:1–6 (*SR*, Nr. 85a).

U.-ke₄, mu-KN..., in-pa, N.-ra, kúr la-ba-gi₄-gi₄-da-šè, "Ur-lugala hat den Namen des Narām-Su²en ..., angerufen dafür, dass er deswegen künftig gegen die Ningula keine Ansprüche mehr stellen werde," *BIN* VIII, Nr. 164:1–6 (*SR*, Nr. 85); vgl. Nr. 167:13–16 (*SR*, Nr. 84).

lú-ki-inim-ma-bi-me, lú lú la-ba-gi₄-gi₄-da, mu-lugal ba-pà, "... waren die Zeugen dabei. Dafür dass keiner gegen den anderen mehr Ansprüche stellen wird, wurde der Name des Königs angerufen," *JCS* XX 126–27, Z. 16–19 (Ende) (*SR*, Nr. 78a).

Selten findet sich mu-...pà mit Komitativ.⁷⁸ Die betreffenden Texte sind leider lückenhaft, so dass unsere Deutung nur vorläufig sein kann.

MAD, Nr. 4, Nr. 14: Sammelurkunde über zwei Eidesfälle (1. Grundstück; 2. Ninra [Sklavin?])⁷⁹

1 (iku) gána [...]	1 Iku Feld [...]
uš-[da-d]a ([...])⁸⁰	[m]it Uš[da] ([...])
3 [.....]	[.....................]
kúr [...]	künftig [...],
inim-ma	hat Inima zusammen mit ihm
6 mᶠuˈ-nᶠaˈ-rᶠaˈ-ᶠaˈm-ᵈsu²en	den Namen des Narām-Su²en

76. Der Versuch, die Stadt ᴵN(ᵏⁱ) mit Insin/Issin zu identifizieren, mag kühn wirken. Er bedarf sicheren Beweises. Es fällt immerhin auf, dass der Name der Stadt Issin (konventionell Isin) im Laufe der Geschichte immer wieder anders geschrieben wurde: in-sín(NAM) in dumu-ᵈnin-in-sín-ka-ke₄, "Sohn der Nin²insina," *CT* XXXVI, Pl. 3, No. 109930:5 (Lu-Utu, Ensi von Umma), von Å. Sjöberg, "Die göttliche Abstammung der sumerisch-babylonischen Herrscher," *OrS* XXI (1972) 93, zitiert, aber anders gelesen; neusum. in-siᵏⁱ, in-si-inᵏⁱ, i-si-inᵏⁱ, in-si-naᵏⁱ (Genitiv); altbab. i-si-inᵏⁱ; mittelbab. PA.ŠEᵏⁱ (volksetymologische Schreibung nach *išinnu*, "Halm"), EZEN (= *isinnu*, "Fest") in ᵈnin-EZEN-na = Nin²issina (Adad-apla-iddina II., unpubl. Isin 1973). (Zum selben Ergebnis gelangte J. N. Postgate, *Sumer* XXX [1974] 207–9.)

77. Konstruiert im Singular; wörtlich: "N...., L...., einer wird gegen den anderen deswegen nicht zurückkehren."

78. Vgl. *NG*, Nr. 104:7 in nichtrekonstruierbarem Kontext.

79. S. a. J. Krecher, "Neue sumerische Rechtsurkunden des 3. Jahrtausends," *ZA*, Bd. 63 (1974) S. 258–61.

80. Nach dem Photo hat Z. 2 vielleicht noch eine eingerückte Zeile.

in-da-[p]a   angerufen.
sá-lim-mu dumu-é-mah-   Salimmu, der Sohn des Emahda,
   da-ke$_4$
9 bar-nin-ra-ka   hat wegen der Ninra
uš-[da]-da   zusammen mit Ušda
mu-na-r[a-a]m-^{d}su^{ɔ}en   den Namen des Narām-Su^{ɔ}en
12 in-da-pa kúr inim nin-ra   angerufen dafür, dass er künftig betr.
                                  Ninra

inim-ma nu-g̃á-g̃á-šè   gegen Inima nicht klagen werde.
(eine Zeile frei)
(4 Zeugen)   . . . .
lú-ki-inim-ma-bi-me   waren die Zeugen dabei.
(eine Zeile frei)
21 ur-kal-ga   Urkalga,
lú-erén KU.KU-IN^{ki} Soldat, wohnhaft in Issin(?)
mu gi$_4$ NE PA $^{\ulcorner}$x$^{\urcorner}$ . . . .

MAD, Nr. 4, Nr. 15[81]

10 su$_{11}$-lum gur kù-ta   10 Kor Datteln statt Silber,
u$_4$ su$_{11}$-lum 1 kù gín-a   als 3 Scheffel 2 Seah Datteln
3 3 (n.) 2 (b.) al-ág̃-g̃á   für 1 Sekel Silber abgewogen wurden,
uš dumu-sag̃-du$_5$-ke$_4$ hat uš, der Sohn des Katasterleiters,
uš dumu-sagi$_x$(= SILÀ.ŠU.   dem uš, dem Sohn des obersten
   DU$_8$)-mah-ra   Mundschenken,
6 kù 10 kù gín-šè   für 10 Sekel Silber
ì-na-sum   gegeben.
kù-gána-ka še gána-bi   . . . .
9 30 še gur kù-ta gú ba-g̃ar   wurden 30 Kor Gerste anstelle
                                  des Silbers angelastet.
mu-šar-kà-lí-šarri^{ri} Den Namen des Šar-kali-šarrī,
lugal-a-kà-dè^{ki}-ka   Königs von Akkade,
12 uš dumu-sagi$_x$(=   haben uš, der Sohn des obersten
   SILÀ.ŠU.DU$_8$)-mah   Mundschenken,
me-ɔan-né   und Meɔane,
dumu-lugal-kal-zi-bì   der Sohn des Lugal-kalzi,
15 uš dumu-sag̃-du$_5$-ka-šè   hinsichtlich des uš, des Sohnes des
                                  Katasterleiters,
in-da-[p]a   gemeinsam angerufen.[82]
u$_4$ gána-ka še-zu 1 kù   "Wenn auf dem Felde deine Gerste,
   gín   1 Sekel,
18 30 še gur-t$^{\ulcorner}$a$^{\urcorner}$ 30 še-bi gur   je 30 Kor Gerste...
g[a-r]a-[...]   wollen [wir] dir [...]"
in-na-$^{\ulcorner}$e$^{\urcorner}$-[éš][83]   haben [sie] zu ihm gesagt.

81. S. a. Krecher, in *ZA*, Bd. 63, S. 247–50.
82. Das Subjekt U. M.-bi ist im Sumerischen als Singular konstruiert.
83. Nach dem Photo eher so statt mit I. J. Gelb in-na-$^{\ulcorner}$ag$^{\urcorner}$.

21 inim-bi a[l-til]   Die Angelegenheit [ist beendet].
   (3 Zeugen)   . . . .
   me-šeš-šeš dub-sar-bì   Mešeššeš war der Schreiber.

Nr. 14 ist inhaltlich unklar, da am Anfang zu schlecht erhalten. Die Urkunde zerfällt in zwei Teile: Z. 1–7 und Z. 8–13. Da in beiden die Personen Ušda und Inima vorkommen, gehören sie gewiss zusammen. Dagegen ist Salimmu zuvor nicht genannt. Er leistet den promissorischen Eid, und zwar zusammen mit Ušda, so dass sich die Verwendung des Komitativinfixes erklärt. Welche Funktion Salimmu hatte, wissen wir nicht.

Nr. 15 behandelt in Z. 1–7 die Übergabe (Verkauf?) von Datteln. Die Kursangabe in Z. 2–3 ist zu vergleichen mit *BIN* VIII, Nr. 179:1–2 (*SR*, Nr. 18):15 Kor Datteln = 30 Sekel Silber. Es folgt eine mir unklare Klausel (Z. 8–9). Im folgenden Eid ist eine vorher nicht genannte Person Meʾane hinzugezogen, die gemeinsam mit dem Empfänger (Käufer?) schwört. In Z. 17–19 folgt der Eid im Wortlaut, leider an entscheidender Stelle zerstört.

B. Neusumerische Beispiele

In der neusumerischen Zeit überwiegt die Folge nominalisierter Satz+mu-lugal-bi...-pà.

nu-ù-gi$_4$-gi$_4$-da U. mu-lugal-bi in-pà, "dafür, dass er keine weiteren Ansprüche mehr stellen werde, hat Utu-baʾe den Namen des Königs angerufen," *NG*, Nr. 9:3′–5′.

Wie das plene -ù (= *i) zeigt, ist die Verbalform finit, d.h. *nu-i-gigi-(e)d-a(-ak). Vgl. im Plural:

ir$_{11}$-da la-ba-gi$_4$-gi$_4$-dè-ša-a [m]u-l[uga]l-[b]i ì-p[à-dè-eš], "dafür, dass sie auf den Sklaven keine Ansprüche mehr stellen werden, haben (die Söhne des U.) etc.," *NG*, Nr. 64:17′–18′. Die Verbalform lautet *la-ba-gigi-(e)d-eš-a(-ak).

inim-ama-ne-ne nu-ù-ub-kúr-ne-a mu-lugal-bi in-pà-dè-eš, "dafür, dass sie das Wort ihrer Mutter nicht ändern werden, haben etc." *NG*, Nr. 99:44–46. Analyse: *nu-i-b-kur-ene-a(-ak).

Bei jedem nominalisierten Satz, der ja selbst wieder ein Nomen darstellt, ist nach dem Kasus zu fragen. In dem uns vorliegenden Syntagma ist es ein Genitiv. Das geht besonders deutlich aus der Schreibung mit plene -a in *NG*, Nr. 64 hervor. Die Konstruktion lautet demnach: . . . V (= finites Verbum)+/a/ (Nominalisator)+/a(k)/ (Genitivpostposition) mu-lugal-bi . . .-pà; -bi dient zur Wiederaufnahme des Genitivs, und das ganze Syntagma lässt sich zurückführen auf die Formel X-ak Y-bi...-pà.

Seltener ist die Wiedergabe des Verbums im Satz, der die eidliche Aussage zusammenfasst, durch LAL-ede:[84]

---

84. Für LAL-eda, LAL-edam s. Verf., "Das sumerische Verbalmorphem /ed/ in den alt und neusumerischen Texten," *HSAO*, S. 47–48.

42 še gur áĝ-e-dè mu-lugal-bi in-pà-dè-eš, "42 Kor Gerste abzu-
messen, (dafür) haben sie den Namen des Königs angerufen," *NRVN* I, Nr.
56:10–12; vgl. Nr. 55:6–7, 68:3–7.

Wenn trotz fehlendem Genitiv mu-lugal-bi gesagt wird, werden wir wohl
Anwendung einer schon erstarrten Formel annehmen dürfen.

Sehr selten ist die Form LAL-ede hinter mu- . . . . . .-pà nachgestellt, so
nu-gi₄-gi₄-dè in *NRVN* I, Nr. 8 Rs. 1'–2'.

mu-lugal(-bi) . . .-pà steht hinter nicht-nominalisiertem Satz:

in-na-a[b-s]u-su mu-lugal-bi in-pà, ". . . wird er ihm erstatten.
Dafür hat er den Namen des Königs angerufen," *NRVN* I, Nr. 54:4–5; vgl.
Nr. 53:5–8.

Die nicht-nominalisierte eidliche Aussage kann auch in der 1. Person wiedergegeben sein; es folgt in dem Fall noch ein verbum dicendi: bí-duₗₗ, "hat er
erklärt," *NRVN* I, Nr. 49:13; in-na-duₗₗ, "hat er zu ihm gesagt," *NRVN* I,
Nr. 227:7'.

Die Formel mu-lugal . . .-pà kommt gelegentlich in Urkunden auch vor,
ohne dass der Inhalt des Eides aufgeführt wird:

K . . .-ke₄ B . . .-ka nam-dam-šè mu-lugal-ka-ni in-pà, "Kamu
hat der Baba-izu mit Bezug auf die Ehe sein 'beim Namen des Königs!' aus-
gerufen," *NG*, Nr. 205:60–62.

In *NG*, Nr. 1 wird nach der Feststellung, dass Ur-Nanše und Ša-šunigin
heiraten, nur gesagt, dass sie igi-di-ku₅-ne-šè mu-lugal-bi in-pàd-eš,
"vor den Richtern dafür den Namen des Königs angerufen haben" (Z. 5–6).

Eine—beabsichtigte?—Formularabweichung weist *NRVN* I, Nr. 3:7–9 auf:

inim-ba lú nu-ᵣuᵀb(?)-gi₄-gi₄-da mu-lugal ì-ĝál, "dafür, dass niemand auf die Angelegenheit zurückkommen wird, ist der Name des Königs
vorhanden."

Möglicherweise wird hier garantiert unter Hinweis auf einen bereits geleisteten Eid.

C. ALTBABYLONISCHE ZEIT

In der altbabylonischen Zeit überwiegt Konstruktion mit LAL-ede; vgl.
z.B.:

u₄-kúr-šè lú lú-ra nu-gi₄-gi₄-dè mu-lugal teš-bi in-pà-dè-eš,
"künftighin keine weiteren Ansprüche gegeneinander zu stellen, dafür haben
sie gemeinsam den Namen des Königs angerufen," *BE* VI/2, Nr. 23:24 (*VAB*
V, Nr. 190), Samsuᵓiluna 11.

Aber auch die finite Konstruktion kommt weiter vor:

u₄-kúr-šè lú lú-ù-ra inim nu-ĝá-ĝá-ne-a [m]u-lugal-bi in-pà-
dè-eš, "dafür, dass sie gegeneinander nicht klagen werden, haben sie etc.,"
BE VI/2, Nr. 22:22–24 (*VAB* V, Nr. 191), Samsuᵓiluna 13.

D. Mu-lugal

Wenn der promissorische Eid in direkter Rede zitiert wird, so finden wir ihn mit mu-lugal, "Name des Königs!" eingeleitet, was wir idiomatisch gewiss mit "beim König!" übersetzen dürfen; vgl.:

mu-lugal, U.-ra, lú ba-ra-ba-dù, túg ba-ùr, "Beim König! Den Ur-Lumma soll niemand behindern. Er hat verzichtet," *ITT* IV, Nr. 7001:3–6 (sargonisch).

[m]u-lugal, ba-ra-ab-gi$_4$-gi$_4$-dè, "(dass) 'Beim König! Ich werde darauf gewiss nicht zurückkommen' (Ur-Baba zu Ur-Lumma gesagt hat)," *NG*, Nr. 164 i 2′–3′.[85]

Mit einem durch mu-lugal eingeleiteten promissorischen Eid gleichwertig ist die folgende Aussage:

G., ir$_{11}$-U.-ka, ba-an-da-zah, mu-dab$_5$, igi-ni in-ĝar, mu-lugal u$_4$ a-rá-2(!)-ka, ì-zah-dè-na, ga-hul bí-in-du$_{11}$ (Liste von drei Richtern; Datum), "Gūgu, der Sklave des Ur-Nungala, war diesem entlaufen. Man griff ihn auf. Er trat (vor Gericht) auf und sagte: 'Beim König! Wenn ich ein zweites Mal entlaufe, will ich zugrundegehen,'" *NRVN* I, Nr. 1:1–8.

Hier ruft der "Täter" Verderben auf sich herab für den Fall, dass er sein Delikt wiederholen sollte—nicht anders, als es unter Eanatum der "Mann von Umma" tat.

E. Zi-lugal

Viel seltener als mu-lugal ist uns zi-lugal, "Leben des Königs," als Einleitung einer Aussage überliefert; dass solche Aussagen promissorische Eide seien, lässt sich zunächst wegen der Parallele mu-lugal annehmen. Zu zi-GN vgl. oben I D. Die hier folgenden Beispiele wurden schon von A. L. Oppenheim[86] und A. Falkenstein[87] zitiert. In keinem der Fälle können wir die Person des zugehörigen Verbums eindeutig festlegen.

ITT II, Nr. 2730, und III, Nr. 4847, sind mit zi-lugal eingeleitete Zusicherungen seitens des Ur-Baba, des Tempelverwalters (sanga) der Ninsuna, bzw. des Ursaga, des Tempelverwalters vom Bagara(d), Bewässerung betreffend (1. oder 3. Person).

Eine durch zi-lugal eingeführte negative Aussage in *ITT* V, Nr. 6866 Rs. 7–10 ist leider nicht mehr verwertbar;[88] unvollständig auch *ITT* II, Nr. 3512 Rs. 1′–5′.[89]

Einen sicheren Beleg für zi-lugal-bi pà, das gewiss der Formel mu-lugal-bi pà nachgebildet ist, haben wir in *YOS* IV, Nr. 19:

iti-ezen-mah-ta, lú-kisal(?)(-)mu-x, u$_4$-10 za-la-a, 15 u$_8$ 15 zeh$_x$(= SAL.ÁŠ.GÀR), zi-lugal-bi ì-pà, 1 udu íb-su-su (3 Zeugen),

---

85. Anders als A. Falkenstein möchte ich direkte Rede annehmen.

86. *Catalogue of the Cuneiform Tablets of the Wilberforce Eames Babylonian Collection* (*AOS* XXXII [1948]) S. 140 zu TT 1.

87. *NG* I 63, Anm. 6.

88. Zi-lugal ⌜x⌝ [. . .], ba-ra-⌜x⌝-[. . .], bí-[(in-)du$_{11}$], é-ᵈ[. . .].

89. L[ú-ki-inim-ma-bi-me], mu-[. . .], um-ma(-)[. . .], íb-[. . .], zi-lugal ì-⌜x⌝ [. . .]; ⌜x⌝ in der Kopie nicht Anfang von PÀD.

"Als vom Monat IX. (Puzriš-Dagān) der 10. Tag vergangen war,[90] hat L. (betreffend) 15 Mutterschafe und 15 Ziegen das Leben des Königs angerufen: Ich werde/er wird[91] 1 Stück Kleinvieh ersetzen."

Die Frage, ob mu-lugal oder zi-lugal primär sei, ob beide miteinander konkurrierten, bis sich mu-lugal als alleinige Formel durchsetzte, oder ob die beiden Formeln in ihrer rechtlichen Implikation voneinander abwichen, können wir nicht sicher beantworten. Der zeitliche Abstand zwischen Eanatum (*ca.* 2470) mit Belegen für zi-GN (aber nicht zi-KN oder zi-lugal) und Narām-Suʾen von Akkade (*ca.* 2270) mit Belegen für mu-KN (pà)— jeweils als Einleitung promissorischer Eide—beträgt volle zwei Jahrhunderte oder mehr. Die Belegstatistik von der altakk. bis zur altbab. Zeit lässt allerdings vermuten, dass—zumindest beim Eide, der sich auf den König berief—mu-lugal die Regel war. Zi-lugal war dann entweder eine seltene Analogieform; es war entlehnt aus der Beschwörung (vgl. Anm. 74); oder aber es war in seiner rechtlichen Funktion etwas von mu-lugal überhaupt Unterschiedenes.

III. DER ASSERTORISCHE EID

Der Eid, mit dem jemand etwas schon Geschehenes oder etwas Gegenwärtiges als wahr hinstellt oder abstreitet, wurde im Sumerischen, wie längst erkannt, ganz anders formuliert als der promissorische Eid. Verwendet wurde als Nomen nam-erím mit dem Verbum ku₅(-d/r) (vgl. schon oben I A 5) oder aber nam-erím mit der Kopula -àm. Seltener ist nam-erím in Verbindung mit anderen Verben (gur, sum; s. unten). Wenn der assertorische Eid zitiert wird, dann genau wie der promissorische für gewöhnlich indirekt und nicht in direkter Rede.

A. SARGONISCHE BEISPIELE

Unsere ältesten Belege stammen aus der Akkade-Zeit:
(Ur-sisi hat bei U. ein Guthaben) ba-da-gur, nam-erím-e, šu-a ba-ğál, "(U.) hat es Ur-sisi gegenüber bestritten. (Da wurde U.) zum Schwören des assertorischen Eides (veranlasst). Es war (wie sich herausstellte) vorhanden," *BIN* VIII, Nr. 169: 7–8 (*SR*, Nr. 81 mit Kommentar).

ù nam-erím, nu-ga-ma-ku₅, di-bi di hé-bé, "auch hat er mir den assertorischen Eid nicht geleistet; in dieser Rechtssache mögest du den Prozess führen," *ITT* II, Nr. 2758 Rs. 2′–5′ (*SR*, Nr. 96).

---

90. Ist der Text in Ordnung? Die Übersetzung nimmt stillschweigend an, dass Z. 2 und 3 vertauscht sind. Zeichen x am Ende von Z. 2 wie "2/3." Statt u₄-10 za-la-a vielleicht u₄-14 ⟨zal⟩-la-a.

91. Wir kennen den näheren Sachverhalt nicht. Entweder wörtliche Versicherung in 1. oder in 3. Person konstatierte Verpflichtung.

B. Neusumerische Beispiele

Überaus reichlich ist das Material in den neusumerischen Gerichtsurkunden. Wir unterscheiden die folgenden hauptsächlichen Fälle:

1. Nominalisierter Satz (im Lokativ)+PN_1 (PN_2 etc.) nam-erím-àm; PN steht dabei nicht im Ergativ, und nam-erím-àm steht auch bei pluralischem Subjekt. Das vorangehende Satzgefüge kann ungeheuer kompliziert und verschachtelt sein wie z.B. in *NG*, Nr. 75:2–21:

> $U._1$ ir_{11}-$U._2$ ì-me-àm, $L._1$ ù $L._2$ dumu-$U._2$-ke_4-ne
> igi-bi ib-^{gá}ĝar^{ar}
> mu-lugal $U._1$ ir_{11}-ra ama-gi_4^{ki}-ni hé-^{gá}ĝar^{ar}
> dumu-lú-dili-gin_7-na-àm hé-dím
> bí-in-du_{11}-ga
> ù
> ir_{11}-da ama-gi_4^{ki}-ni ba-^{gá}ĝar^{ar}-kam
> PN_1 (bis) PN_7 $U._1$-ke_4 in-pà-da
> PN_8 PN_9 PN_{10} nam-erím-àm

> "Dass betr. $U._1$, der ein Sklave des $U._2$ gewesen war,
> $L._1$ und $L._2$, die Söhne des $U._2$, aufgetreten sind (und):
> 'Beim Namen des Königs! Des Sklaven $U._1$ Freilassung
> möge verfügt werden, und er möge werden wie der Sohn
> eines Individuums'
> erklärt haben
> und dass (ferner) dafür,
> dass des Sklaven Freilassung bewirkt wurde,
> $U._1$ den PN_1, PN_2 etc. (als Zeugen) gerufen hat—
> das haben PN_8, PN_9 und PN_{10} beeidigt."

Hier wird assertorisch beschworen, dass früher ein promissorischer Eid (eingeleitet durch mu-lugal) geleistet worden ist; vgl. ähnlich *NG*, Nr. 14:2–9.

Nam-erím-àm kann auch gesagt werden, ohne dass der Eidesinhalt wiedergegeben wird:

[U. m]a[r-d]ú nam-erím-àm, "[Ur-Šulgira, der Amur]ru, leistete den assertorischen Eid," *NG*, Nr. 52:23'.

2. Dem nominalisierten Satz (im Lokativ) folgt nam-erím(-bi) ì-/in-ku_5, bei pluralischem Subjekt íb-ku_5 (z.B. *NG*, Nr. 67:11):

D., U.-na-an-na, ⌜ú⌝ nu-ù-da-nú-a, nam-erím in-ku_5, "Damkala hat beeidigt, dass ausser Ur-balangkuga niemand bei ihr geschlafen habe," *NG*, Nr. 24:9'–12'.

Nominalisierung + Kasus (Lokativ) werden gewöhnlich nur durch Silbenzeichen (Konsonant+)a dargestellt; nur noch selten finden wir die altsum. Orthographie -(K)a-a, z.B.:

nu-ù-na-an-sum-ma-a (. . . nam-erím-bi in-ku_5), "dass er es ihr nicht gegeben hat (etc.)," *NG*, Nr. 126:9–11.

Hier ist der Kasus durch eigenes Silbenzeichen dargestellt. Wir vermuten einen Lokativ;[92] wörtlich würde es heissen: "Daran, dass . . . , hat er das Böse abgeschnitten."

3. Wenn der assertorische Eid noch bevorsteht, heisst es nam-erím-bi ku$_5$-ru/kuru$_5$-dam (NG, Nr. 62:12–13 und oft). Hier ist, wie NG, Nr. 210 iv 9–10 u.ö. zeigen, der Ergativ erforderlich. Kurudam steht jedoch auch bei pluralischem Subjekt (vgl. III B 1):[93] "PN$_1$ (und PN$_2$ etc.) soll(en) den assertorischen Eid leisten."

4. Wird der Eid durch einen Dritten veranlasst, so steht nam-erím-bi ba-sum, "er wurde zum assertorischer Eid gegeben," NG, Nr. 69:7 oder nam-erím ku$_5$-ru-dè ba-sum, "er wurde hingegeben, den assertorischen Eid zu leisten," NG, Nr. 110:10–11.

U.-ke$_4$, L.-ra, di ì-da-an-du$_{11}$, U. nam-bi-ri(!)(HU)-ì[94] ba-sum, nam-bi-ri(!)-e un-ku$_5$ (. . . bí-du$_{11}$), "Ur-Nuska hat gegen Lu-Su'en prozessiert. Ur-Nuska wurde zum assertorischer Eid gegeben, und nachdem er den assertorischen Eid geleistet hatte, (hat er '. . .' erklärt)," NRVN I, Nr. 2:1–5.[95]

Hierher gehört auch nam-erím-ma ba-ni-dab$_5$, "er wurde zum assertorischer Eid gezwungen," wörtlich "er wurde veranlasst, an das nam-erím zu greifen," NG, Nr. 30:8–9.

C. Geltung des Eides

A. Falkenstein hat darauf hingewiesen, dass der assertorische Eid im Tempel geleistet wurde.[96] Auf die Weise erhöhte sich zweifellos noch die Wirksamkeit des Eides. In solchen Fällen wurden Götterembleme zur Hilfe genommen, was aber in der neusumerischen Zeit nur ausnahmsweise vermerkt wird:[97]

U.-e šà-bi-ta nu-ù-ma-ra-è-a, U. gíri-AN.NA-k[a] nam-erím-àm, "dass er, Urmes, daraus nichts entnommen hat, hat Urmes beim eisernen Dolch beschworen," NG, Nr. 205:53–54.[98]

Der vor der Aussage zu leistende assertorische Eid galt offenbar als untrügliches Beweismittel. Er überwog die Zeugenablehnung seitens einer Partei. Er

92. Formal, d.h. vom orthographischen Befund her, ist auch ein Genitiv möglich. Ein Lokativ ist aber als Parallele zur Dativrektion bei Personen das Wahrscheinlichere.

93. Vgl. Verf., HSAO, S. 39 mit Erklärungsversuch.

94. Zur behelfsmässigen Darstellung von gesprochenem *nambri(m) vgl. Verf., BiOr XXV (1968) 354–55; H. Sauren, in ZA, Bd. 59, S. 23; J. Krecher, in AOAT I 193 mit Anm. 59a. Bei Sauren und Krecher sind noch weitere unorthographische Schreibungen notiert.

95. Aus diesem Text geht deutlich hervor, dass die Eidesleistung vor der Aussage stattfand.

96. NG I 65. Dass dies ausschliesslich der Fall war, lässt sich allerdings nicht beweisen.

97. Für die altbab. Zeit s. nach wie vor A. Walther, Das altbabylonische Gerichtswesen (LSS VI/4–6 [1917]) S. 192, 196–208; J. Renger, "Götternamen in der altbabylonischen Zeit," HSAO, 138–71.

98. Vgl. NG I 65 mit Anm, 5.

wurde der Sicherheit halber auch dann verlangt, wenn der Sachverhalt bereits geklärt zu sein schien wie in *NG*, Nr. 62:12–13. Andererseits notiert *NG*, Nr. 99:30–31 den Verzicht auf einen assertorischen Eid, weil übereinstimmende Aussagen vorlagen. In *NG*, Nr. 212:11–14 gilt der assertorische Eid, nachdem die Zeugen verstorben sind, als genügendes Beweismittel: mu-bi-šè L.-e nam-erím-bi un-ku₅ ir₁₁ ba-an-túm-mu, "deshalb darf Lugal-Emahe, nachdem er den assertorischen Eid geleistet hat, den Sklaven mitnehmen."

Die Möglichkeit des Meineides wurde offensichtlich nicht in Betracht gezogen —oder als das geringere Übel angesehen. Die Furcht vor göttlicher Strafe[99] spiegelt sich wider in den nicht seltenen Fällen, wo eine Partei den assertorischen Eid verweigert: nam-erím-bi-ta im-ma-ra-gur-ra, "weil er vor einem assertorischen Eid darüber zauderte," *NG*, Nr. 205:23; vgl. Nr. 113:53, und s. Band III, S. 118. Ähnlich *NG*, Nr. 209:8–10: nam-erím ku₅-ru-dè nu-un-še-e, "den assertorischen Eid zu leisten, weigerte er sich";[100] s. noch oben I A 5 zu HSM 1384:24–25.

D. Assertorischer Eid und Ordal

Wenn der assertorische Eid ein so entscheidendes Gewicht hatte, müssen wir fragen, wann und weshalb man anstelle der Eidesleistung das Flussordal als Beweismittel vorzog oder sogar anzuwenden gezwungen war; d.h. wann die Beweislast der Partei abgenommen und die Entscheidung der Gottheit anvertraut wurde. Leider ist unser Quellenmaterial auf diesem Sektor noch sehr dürftig und überdies nicht eindeutig.[101] Wir fassen uns hier zum Thema kurz; eine ausführlichere Darstellung der Materie ist zu erwarten.[102]

Im sargonischen Ordalprotokoll *TMH* V, Nr. 159 (*SR*, Nr. 99; vgl. Nr. 98) sind vorwiegend Realien Gegenstand und, wenn wir die äusserst knappen Sätze richtig verstehen, Anlass für Ordale: Feld, Sklave, Silber, Kleinvieh, Korn. Wir wissen aber nicht, ob das Ordal jedesmal auch vollzogen wurde. Möglich ist (vgl. *SR*, S. 159), dass oft bereits die Androhung des Ordals Schuld und Unschuld zu klären vermochte, d.h. dass ein Zurückschrecken vor dem Ordal in der gleichen Weise als Eingeständnis der Partei gewertet wurde wie die Ablehnung des assertorischen Eides.

La Trouvaille de Dréhem (Paris, 1911) Nr. 85 (Ur III) gibt als Anlass für die Stiftung von zwei Silberringen (je 10 Sekel Gewicht) durch zwei Frauen (eine

---

99. B. Meissner lässt in seinen "Neuarabischen Geschichten aus dem Iraq" (*BA* V) erzählen, wie peinliche Folgen ein falscher Eid hatte, den eine des Diebstahls verdächtigte Frau beim ᶜAmrān ibn ᶜAbi schwor: ḫallafōha tzarrib ğīr, "kaum hatte man sie schwören lassen, da begann sie, Pech zu kacken" (S. 100).

100. Die Verteilung der Basen še und še(-g) beim Verbum "genehm sein; gern haben, wollen" muss noch untersucht werden.

101. A. Falkenstein, "Eine gesiegelte Tontafel der altsumerischen Zeit," *AfO* XIV (1941–44) 333–36 (s. jetzt auch *SR*, Nr. 98); J. Klíma, "L'Ordalie par le Fleuve en Elam," *RA* LXVI (1972) 41, Anm. 1 mit einer (überwiegend aufs Akkadische bezogenen) Bibliographie.

102. Freundliche Mitteilung von Dr. Tikvah Frymer, Detroit.

Musikantin und die Amme einer Prinzessin) an: u$_4$ ^{d}i$_7$-lú-ru-gú-ta, ì-im-
e-re-éš-ša-a, "als sie vom (göttlichen) Fluss gekommen waren" (Z. 5–6).[103]
Offenbar handelt es sich um eine Dankesgabe nach günstigem Ausgang. Leider
kennen wir nicht den Grund für das Ordal.

NG, Nr. 24:9'–12' (s. oben III B 2) bietet uns den Fall einer Frau,[104] die ihre—
doch wohl angezweifelte—eheliche Treue durch das Ablegen eines assertorischen
Eides bekundete, falls der weitgehend zerstörte Test nicht etwa anders zu
ergänzen ist. Zum Eid bei Vorwurf des Ehebruchs vgl. sonst KH §§ 131, 132.
Vielleicht war hier aber das Ordal eher üblich. Codex Ur-Nammu § 11 sieht
jedenfalls für die des Ehebruchs bezichtigte Ehefrau das Flussordal vor.[105]

Codex Ur-Nammu § 10 handelt ebenfalls von Bezichtigung und daraufhin
vorzunehmendem Ordal. Inhalt der Bezichtigung ist wohl—trotz der von J. J.
Finkelstein geäusserten Zweifel—Zauberei.[106] Es wäre begreiflich, wenn das
Ordal bei Verdacht des Ehebruchs oder der Zauberei ausschliesslich oder doch
mit Vorliebe als Beweismittel gedient hätte. Im ersten Fall könnte die Frau nach
Ansicht des Gerichtes Gefühle entwickelt haben, die sie instandsetzten, die beim
Göttereid gegebenen psychologischen Hemmnisse zu überwinden. Im Falle
der Zauberei mochte das Gericht der Meinung sein, dass der oder die Beschul-
digte in den Besitz magischer Kräfte gelangt war, die den Göttereid neutralisier-
ten. All dies war bei Streitfällen aus Rechtsgeschäften sowie bei Sach- und
Körperdelikten nicht gegeben.

IV. ZUSAMMENFASSUNG

Wir haben versucht, den Eid in sumerischen Verträgen und Gerichtsurkunden
von Eanatums "Geierstele" bis zum Ende der neusumerischen Zeit, d.h.
während eines halben Jahrtausends, zu verfolgen. Eine solche Untersuchung
wird dadurch sehr erschwert, dass die Belege verschieden dicht gestreut sind.
Die von A. Falkenstein vorgenommene grundsätzliche Trennung von promissorischem und assertorischem Eid bewährt sich auch für die Ur III vorangehenden Jahrhunderte. Doch scheint es, dass die Ur III geläufige scharfe terminolo-
gische Trennung zwischen beiden Eidesarten das Ergebnis einer längeren
Entwicklung und vielleicht letztlich eine Errungenschaft der Akkade-Zeit
gewesen ist.

Unter Eanatum wird der promissorische Eid in der direkten Rede mit zi-GN,

103. S. a. schon A. Falkenstein, NG I 62, Anm. 6.

104. Unglücklicherweise ist der Anfang des Textes zerstört; wir haben also nicht die letzte
Sicherheit darüber, dass die den Eid leistende Damkala Ehefrau des Ur-balangkuga war,
mit dem allein sie laut Eid geschlafen haben will.

105. Letzte Edition des Codex Ur-Nammu von J. J. Finkelstein, "The Laws of Ur-
Nammu," JCS XXII (1968) 66–82.

106. Ebd., S. 74 zu Z. 271. Lies dort aber wohl am ehesten nam-KA×LI-zu = nam-
uš$_7$-zu.

"Leben der Gottheit NN," eingeleitet (s. I D). Einmal, im sechsten Eidesabschnitt der Stele, bezeichnet Eanatum das Veranlassen eines solchen Eides durch das Verbum mu-GN pà, "den Namen der Gottheit NN anrufen" (s. I C). Dagegen heisst es mit Bezug auf den "Mann von Umma," der den Eid leistet, stets—auch im sechsten Abschnitt—nam-ku₅, und dieses Verbum wird in den Abschnitten 1–5 auch auf Eanatum bezogen. Nam-ku₅ hat in jeder Richtung: Eanatum → Gegner und Gegner → Eanatum Dativrektion (s. I B). In jüngerer Zeit kennen wir nam-ku₅ mit dieser Rektion nicht mehr, wohl aber ein nam-ku₅ mit Komitativ und in der—zumindest akkadisch so entsprechenden—Bedeutung "verfluchen" (s. I A 4).

In der sargonischen Zeit haben wir das auch für Ur III typische Bild. Der promissorische Eid ist terminologisch fest verbunden mit der Wendung mu-... (pà), wobei auf mu das Wort lugal, "König," oder Königsname folgt (s. II A). Die syntaktische Verbindung zwischen mu-... pà und dem Eidesinhalt ist verschieden: Asyndese mit Eidesinhalt in direkter Rede; Syndese mit Eidesinhalt in direkter Rede nominalisiert, wobei das neu entstandene "Nomen" im Genitiv steht (s. II B); Syndese mit indirekter Rede und der Verbalform als LAL-ede, LAL-eda oder LAL-edam konstruiert (s. II B.). Belege für zi-lugal (pà), "das Leben des Königs (anrufen)," sind bisher so selten, dass wir nicht sicher sagen können, ob es ein Synonym zu mu-... pà war oder etwas funktionell Verschiedenes (s. II E). Der assertorische Eid ist terminologisch verbunden mit der Wendung nam-erím ku₅ oder nam-erím-àm (s. III).

Sowohl die Wendung nam-erím ku₅ als auch das nam-ku₅ der "Geierstele" waren Anlass zu einem langen Exkurs über nam-tar, nam-ku₅ und Verwandtes (s. I A). Der Versuch, diese Wendungen etymologisch zu klären, kann in keiner Weise als schon gelungen bezeichnet werden. Doch war der Versuch unerlässlich. Denn wenn wir—ein zentrales Anliegen auch der Keilschriftrechte—die Rechtsterminologie und das Rechtsverständnis eines Volkes in seiner historischen Entwicklung verstehen wollen, dann ist eine genaue Kenntnis dessen, was die Wörter wirklich bedeutet haben, allererste Voraussetzung. Im Gegensatz zu mu-... pà werden für nam(-erím) ku₅ bisher aber nur Scheinübersetzungen verwendet, und zwar Übersetzungen auf Grund der akkadischen Entsprechungen.

Es erwies sich in diesem Zusammenhang als nötig, auch die Frage nach der Bedeutung des nominalen Elementes nam neu zu stellen. A. Falkensteins Etymologie nam < *anaʾam (a-na-àm) ist fraglich. Es scheint so, als sei nam in "Fara" mit nám (Zeichen ähnlich wie TÚG) vertauschbar gewesen. Das öffnet Spekulationen den Weg, ohne aber zu einem sicheren Ergebnis zu führen (vgl. I A 2). Bei einer genauen Analyse der Rektionen von nam-tar und nam-ku₅ fiel auf, dass unsere für nam-tar gängige Übersetzung "jemandem das Schicksal entscheiden" nicht zutreffen kann; sie ist einzig und allein akkadischem šīmtam šâmum verpflichtet. Die normale Rektion von nam-tar (Lokativ-Terminativ in der Infixkette, Dativ der betroffenen Person) legt eine kausative Wendung nahe: *"jemanden veranlassen, NAM zu schneiden" (I A 2).

Nur mit grösster Zurückhaltung haben wir für nam-ku₅ vorgeschlagen "(jemandem) NAM abschneiden" und dabei NAM auf etwas Konkretes (Gewandartiges?) zurückgeführt (s. I A 5).[107]

Unser Tasten, Raten und letztliches Unvermögen, wirklich sichere Erkenntnisse über den sumerischen Eid zu gewinnen, geht darauf zurück, dass wir ein sumerisches Gerichtsverfahren mit seinen Eiden oder einen Vertrag nur in Andeutungen und Ausschnitten kennen—und auch das nur in Fällen, die schriftlich fixiert wurden. Die Texte geben nur einen schwachen Abglanz der Wirklichkeit wieder, und es ist unmöglich, alle begleitenden Umstände zu rekonstruieren. Daher auch unsere Schwierigkeit, eine strenge Grenze zwischen assertorischem Eid und Ordal zu ziehen (s. III D). So erschöpfende Berichte, wie wir sie etwa über Rechtsfälle der arabischen Beduinen haben,[108] wird uns keine Tontafel jemals schenken. Das ist ärgerlich; aber es gibt der produktiven Phantasie reichlich Nahrung. Phantasie und Intuition, verbunden mit intimer Text- und Sachkenntnis und unerbittlicher grammatischer Genauigkeit, Stärken Thorkild Jacobsens, können in Zukunft wohl auch das Recht und Rechtsleben der Sumerer weiter aufzuhellen helfen.

Zitatenschlüssel für literarische Texte (soweit kein eindeutiger Hinweis auf Originalpublikationen gegeben).

Dialog 2 (Enkita und Enki-hegal) Z. 70: *ISET* I 123, Ni. 9497 ii 14; *ISET* I 148, Ni. 4384 i 5; *Or*, NS, Bd. 22 (1953) Taf. XXXVI, Ni. 4114+4139 Vs. 3′; *UET* VI, Nr. 152 i 20 (Ms. C. Wilcke).

Enki und Ninhursanga, nach S. N. Kramer, *BASOR* "Supplementary Studies," Nr. 1 (New Haven, 1945) S. 10 ff.

Enlil und Ninlil, Kol. i, Z. 69: *MBI*, Nr. 4 ii 24′; Z. 122: *MBI*, Nr. 4 iv 3 und *SEM*, Nr. 77 iii 11′.

Fluch über Akkade, nach A. Falkenstein, in *ZA*, Bd. 57 (1965) S. 50–64 und eigener Textzusammenstellung.

Gilgamesch und Huwawa, nach S. N. Kramer, *JCS* I (1947) 8–23 und eigener Textzusammenstellung.

Inanna und Ebih, Z. 48: *PBS* X/4, Nr. 9 Rs. 22 (D); *UET* VI, Nr. 13:15 (J); N 1117 ("O") nach eigener Textzusammenstellung und MSS B. Eichler und Å. Sjöberg.

Inannas Gang zur Unterwelt, nach S. N. Kramer, *JCS* V (1951) 1–14 und eigener Textzusammenstellung.

Nippur-Klage, Z. 63: *PBS* X/4, Nr. 1 ii 4′ und *SLTNi*, Nr. 101 Vs. 10; Z. 67: *PBS* X/4, Nr. 1 ii 12′ und *SLTNi*, Nr. 101 Vs. 14.

---

107. Da die Grundbedeutung von ku₅(-d/r), "abschneiden," ist, dürfen wir nam-ku₅ nicht etwa mit dem arabischen "Eide des Trennens" (scil. zwischen Lüge und Wahrheit) in Verbindung bringen; vgl. dazu E. Gräf, *Das Rechtswesen der heutigen Beduinen*, S. 62.

108. Vgl. E. Gräf, *Das Rechtswesen*.

Schooldays, nach S. N. Kramer, *JAOS*, Bd. 69 (1949) S. 201–4 (Museum Monograph [Philadelphia]) und eigener Textzusammenstellung.

Schreiber und missratener Sohn, Z. 50: *TCL* XVI, Nr. 45:4; *TMH* NF III, Nr. 40+41+*TMH* NF IV, Nr. 39 i 28′ (join C. Wilcke). S. jetzt Å. Sjöberg, in *JCS* XXV (1973) 105–69.

Ur-Nammus Tod, Z. 144: S. N. Kramer, *JCS* XXI (1967) 115, Z. 143.

BIBLIOGRAPHIE IN AUSWAHL

Im Folgenden keine Textpublikationen und -bearbeitungen, soweit diese nicht unter speziell juristischen Gesichtspunkten erfolgt sind.

Es werden nur Arbeiten aufgeführt, die sich ganz oder überwiegend auf sumerische Texte beziehen. Die Frage, ob von "sumerischem Recht" gesprochen werden darf, die der Herausgeber und der Verfasser bejahen, ist kontrovers. Vgl. Literatur bei D. O. Edzard, *Sumerisches Rechtsurkunden*, S. 10 mit Anm. 1, die dezidierte Stellungnahme von F. R. Kraus, in *Genava*, NS, VIII 295, sowie dessen Arbeit *Sumerer und Akkader: Ein Problem der altmesopotamischen Geschichte* (Amsterdam, 1970).

Allgemeines

Cardascia, G., und J. Klíma. *Droits cunéiformes*. A/2. Introduction bibliographique à l'histoire du droit et à l'ethnologie juridique. Herausgegeben von J. Gilissen. Bruxelles, 1966.

Haase, R. *Einführung in das Studium keilschriftlicher Rechtsquellen*. Wiesbaden, 1965.

Klíma, J. "Gesetze." *RLA* III (1966) 246–51.

Korošec, V. "Keilschriftrecht." In *Orientalisches Recht. Handbuch der Orientalistik*. Herausgegeben von B. Spuler. 1 Abt., Ergänzungsband III, S. 49–219. Leiden, 1964.

Kraus, F. R. "Ein zentrales Problem des altmesopotamischen Rechtes: Was ist der Codex Hammu-rabi?" *Genava*, NS, VIII (1958) 283–96.

Speiser, E. A. "Cuneiform Law and the History of Civilisation." *PAPS*, Bd. 107 (1963) S. 536–641.

"Reformen" des Uru-KA-gina

Diakonoff, I. M. "Some Remarks on the 'Reforms' of Urukagina." *RA* LII (1958) 1–15.

Hruška, B. "Die innere Struktur der Reformtexte Urukaginas von Lagaš." *ArOr*, Bd. 41 (1973) S. 4–13, 104–32.

Lambert, M. "Les réformes d'Urukagina." *RA* L (1956) 169–84.

Thureau-Dangin, F. "Urukagina." In *Die sumerischen und akkadischen Königsinschriften*. *VAB* I 42–57. Leipzig, 1907.

"*Codices*"

CODEX UR-NAMMU

Finkelstein, J. J. "The Laws of Ur-Nammu." *JCS* XXII (1969) 66–82. Schliesst Gurney-Kramer ein.

Gurney, O. R., und S. N. Kramer. "Two Fragments of Sumerian Law." In *Studies in Honor of Benno Landsberger. AS*, Nr. 16, S. 13–19. Chicago, 1965.

Kramer, S. N. "Ur-Nammu Law Code." *Or*, NS, Bd. 23 (1954) S. 40–48. Mit "Appendix: Notes by A. Falkenstein," S. 48–51.

Anschliessende Studien

Finkelstein, J. J. "Sex Offenses in Sumerian Law." *JAOS*, Bd. 86 (1966) S. 355–72.

Klíma, J. "La patria potestas dans les nouveaux fragments législatifs sumériens." In *Symbolae Iuridicae et Historicae Martino David Dedicatae* II. Herausgegeben von J. A. Ankum, R. Feenstra und W. F. Leemans. Leiden, 1968. Korrekturen dazu von D. O. Edzard, in *BiOr* XXX (1973) 194–96.

Lambert, M. "Le code d'Ur-Nammu." *RA* XLIX (1955) 169–77.

Petschow, H. "Neufunde zu keilschriftlichen Rechtssammlungen." *SZ Rom. Abt.* LXXXV (1968) 2–12.

CODEX LIPIT-IŠTAR

Civil, M. "New Sumerian Law Fragments." In *Studies in Honor of Benno Landsberger. AS*, Nr. 16, S. 1–4. Chicago, 1965.

Nougayrol, J. "Un fragment oublié du code (en) sumérien." *RA* XLVI (1952) 53–55.

Steele, F. R. "The Code of Lipit-Ishtar." *AJA* LII (1948) 425–50. (Nachdruck als "Museum Monograph." Philadelphia, o.J.).

―――. "An Additional Fragment of the Lipit-Ishtar Code Tablet from Nippur." *ArOr* XVIII/1–2 (1950) 489–93.

Anschliessende Studien

Kramer, S. N. (Übersetzung). *ANET*, S. 159–61. 2. Aufl. Princeton, 1955.

Lettinga, J. "Het sumerische wetboek van Lipitistar, koning van Isin." *JEOL*, Bd. 12 (1951–52) S. 249–63.

Szlechter, E. "Le code de Lipit-Ištar." *RA* LI (1957) 57–82 und 177–96, *RA* LII (1958) 74–90.

Selms, A. van. "The Best Man and Bride—From Sumer to St. John." *JNES* IX (1950) 65–75.

Wilcke, C. "Einige Erwägungen zum § 29 des Codex Lipitestar." *WO* IV (1966) 153–62.

FRAGMENTE VON "CODICES"

Civil, M. "New Sumerian Law Fragments." In *Studies in Honor of Benno Landsberger. AS*, Nr. 16, S. 4–8. Chicago, 1965.

Clay, A. T. "No. 28. Sumerian Prototype of the Ḥammurabi Code." *Miscellaneous Inscriptions in the Yale Babylonian Collection. YOS* I 18–27. New Haven, 1915.

Anschliessende Studien

Klíma, J. "Au sujet de nouveaux textes législatifs de la Babylonie ancienne." *ArOr*, Bd. 35 (1967) S. 121–27.

Petschow, H. "Zu § 3 des Fragments der Rechtssammlung YBT I 28." *ZA*, Bd. 58 (1967) S. 1–4. Dort Anm. 1 weitere Bibliographie.

———. "Neufunde zu keilschriftlichen Rechtssammlungen." *SZ Rom. Abt.* LXXXV (1968) 17–21.

Edikte

Kraus, F. R. *Ein Edikt des Königs Ammi-ṣaduqa von Babylon.* "Studia et Documenta ad Iura Orientis Antiqui Pertinentia" V. Leiden, 1958. Dort S. 194–209 zu (sumerischen) Erlässen der Könige von Isin und Larsa.

Ur_5-ra = *ḫubullu; ana ittišu*

Landsberger, B. *Die Serie ana ittišu. MSL* I. Rom, 1937.

———. *The Series* ḪAR-ra = *ḫubullu*: *Tablets I–IV. MSL* V. Rom, 1957. Dort S. 1–81 Tafel I und II mit Termini und Phrasen aus dem Rechtsleben. Nachträge in *MSL* IX 157–58. Rom, 1967.

Textbearbeitungen, systematisch

Bauer, J. (Rezension zu Edzard). *ZA*, Bd. 61 (1972) S. 316–25.

Çığ, M., H. Kızılyay, und A. Falkenstein. "Neue Rechts- und Gerichtsurkunden der Ur III-Zeit aus Lagaš aus den Sammlungen der Istanbuler Archäologischen Museen." *ZA*, Bd. 53 (1959) S. 51–92.

Dijk, J. van. "Neusumerische Gerichtsurkunden in Bagdad." *ZA*, Bd. 55 (1963) S. 70–90.

Edzard, D. O. *Sumerische Rechtsurkunden des III. Jahrtausends aus der Zeit vor der III. Dynastie von Ur. ABAW* NF Bd. 67. München, 1968.

Falkenstein, A. *Die neusumerischen Gerichtsurkunden.* I: *Einleitung und systematische Darstellung;* II: *Umschrift, Übersetzung und Kommentar;* III: *Nachträge, Berichtigungen, Indizes und Kopien. ABAW* NF Bd. 39, 40, 44. München, 1956–57.

Kraus, F. R. "Di-til.la. Sumerische Prozessprotokolle und Verwandtes aus der Zeit der III. Dynastie von Ur." *BiOr* XV (1958) 70–84. Rezension zu Falkenstein.

Krecher, J. "Neue sumerische Rechtsurkunden des 3. Jahrtausends." *ZA*, Bd. 63 (1974) S. 145–271.

Matouš, L. "Einige Bermerkungen zu altsumerischen Rechtsurkunden." *ArOr*, Bd. 39 (1971) S. 1–15. Rezension zu Edzard.

Petschow, H. (Rezension zu Edzard). *SZ Rom. Abt.* LXXV (1958) 381–88.

Einzelstudien

Diakonoff, I. M. "Sale of Land in Pre-Sargonic Sumer." In *Papers Presented by the Soviet Delegation to the XXIIId International Congress of Orientalists*, Heft 4, S. 5–32. Moscow, 1954.

———. "Kupl'a-prodaža zemli v drevnejšem Šumere i vopros o šumerskoj obščine." *VDI*, Bd. 54 (1955) S. 10–40. Ausführlichere russische Fassung des Vorigen.

Edzard, D. O. "Die *bukānum*-Formel der altbabylonischen Kaufverträge und ihre sumerische Entsprechung." *ZA*, Bd. 60 (1970) S. 8–53. S. besonders S. 9–13.

Eilers, W. *Gesellschaftsformen im altbabylonischen Recht.* "Leipziger rechtswissenschaftliche Studien" LXV. Leipzig, 1931. Nachdruck, 1970.

Jacobsen, Th. "An Ancient Mesopotamian Trial for Homicide." *Analecta Biblica*, Bd. 12 (1959) S. 130–50. Nachdruck, *TIOT*, S. 193–214 und 421–22.

Kraus, F. R. "Nippur und Isin nach altbabylonischen Rechtsurkunden." *JCS* III (1951) 1–228. S. 89–117 betr. das sumerische Vertragsformular in Urkunden aus Isin.

Kraus, F. R. "Neue Rechtsurkunden der altbabylonischen Zeit." *WO* II/2 (1955) 120–36. Rezension von *UET* V; behandelt besonders das sumerische Formular der Rechtsurkunden aus Ur.

Matouš, L. "Les contrats de partage de Larsa provenant des archives d'Iddin-Amurrum." *ArOr* XVII/2 (1949) 142–73.

———. "Les contrats de vente d'immeuble provenant de Larsa." *ArOr* XVIII/4 (1950) 11–67.

Owen, D. I. "A Unique Letter-Order in the University of North Carolina." *JCS* XXIV (1972) 133–34. Wichtig für das Verständnis des Zusammenhangs zwischen šu-ba-n-ti-Urkunde und brieflicher Anweisung.

Petschow, H. "Zu den Stilformen antiker Gesetze und Rechtssammlungen." *SZ Rom. Abt.* LXXXII (1965) 24–38. S. besonders S. 25–27.

Pritsch, E. "Zur juristischen Bedeutung der šu-ba-n-ti-Formel." *Bonner Biblische Beiträge*, Bd. 1 (1950) S. 172–87.

Sauren, H. "Zum Bürgschaftsrecht in neusumerischer Zeit." *ZA*, Bd. 60 (1970) S. 70–87.

Szlechter, E. "Six contrats d'adoption d'Ur." *Mélanges H. Lévy-Bruhl*, S. 287–96. Paris, 1959.

Wilcke, C. "Ku-li." *ZA*, Bd. 54 (1969) S. 65–99.

ANCIENT WRITING AND ANCIENT WRITTEN LANGUAGE: PITFALLS AND PECULIARITIES IN THE STUDY OF SUMERIAN

I. M. DIAKONOFF

Leningrad

ek yngwaR Þorkildi runoR worahto

One of our leading Sumerologists told me a few years ago, "The longer I work on Sumerian grammar, the less I understand it"—an admission with which many a Sumerologist would agree! It is a joke well known among Assyriologists that there are as many Sumerian languages as there are Sumerologists. It is true that we are in possession of a number of profound studies of that elusive language, one of the most prominent being the study of the Sumerian verb by Thorkild Jacobsen in *Studies in Honor of Benno Landsberger*; however, we are still very far from anything like a community of opinion on the main grammatical issues needed for further common progress, as one can see in the diverging approaches to the Sumerian verb in the works of R. Jestin, E. Sollberger, I. T. Kaneva, M. Yoshikawa, and D. O. Edzard, to name only the authors of papers specifically devoted to the verb.[1]

I do not and cannot pretend to suggest a general solution, or to give a passkey to all the secret chambers of Sumerian; however, I will try to attract notice to at least some important points to which sufficient attention, to my mind, has not been paid and which may to a certain extent throw some new light on the ground where we stand at present in regard to Sumerian language.[2]

1. R. Jestin, *Le verbe sumérien*, Vols. I–III (Paris, 1943–54); E. Sollberger, *Le système verbal dans les inscriptions "royales" présargoniques de Lagaš* (Geneva, 1952); I. T. Kaneva, "Glagoly dviženija [Verbs of Motion]," *Assiriologija i egiptologija* (Leningrad, 1965); *idem*, "Sprjaženie šumerskogo glagola [Conjugation of the Sumerian Verb]" (with English summary), *Peredneaziatskij sbornik* II (Moscow, 1966); *idem*, "Participles in Sumerian," *MIO* XVI (1970) 541–65; M. Yoshikawa, "On the Grammatical Function of -e- of the Sumerian Verbal Suffix -e-dè/-e-da(m)," *JNES*, Vol. 27 (1968) pp. 251–61; *idem*, "The *Marû* and *Ḫamṭu* Aspects in the Sumerian Verbal System," *Or*, n.s., Vol. 37 (1968) pp. 401–16 (M. Yoshikawa's Japanese monograph on the Sumerian verb has not been accessible to me); D. O. Edzard, "*Ḫamṭu, marû* und freie Reduplikation beim sumerischen Verbum" I, *ZA*, Vol. 61 (1971) pp. 208–32, and II, *ZA*, Vol. 62 (1972) pp. 1–34.

2. This paper was written before the important articles by M. Civil and G. Gragg published in *Or*, n.s., Vol. 42 (1973) fasc. 1–2 (*Festschrift* for I. J. Gelb) became accessible to me. Civil ("The Sumerian Writing System: Some Problems," pp. 21–34) and Gragg ("Linguistics, Method, and Extinct Languages: The Case of Sumerian," pp. 78–96) cover, to a great

A language as an object of linguistic study is usually either a spoken language written down in a phonetic or phonological transcription, or a language which has come down to us in writing designed to render more or less adequately all the units of speech, such as phonemes, morphemes, and lexemes. But, are the linguistic techniques created for the study of languages in this sense fully applicable to Sumerian (or to other *ancient* written languages)? The answer is no. Before the Greeks in the West and the Indians in the East each invented a system of writing consisting of symbols which were conceived as referents of all the phonemes (or groups of phonemes) existing in the language, writing was not designed for rendering spoken language as such; its function was mainly mnemonic. This can be shown even in the case of the so-called phonetic writing systems, that is, the alphabetic and the syllabic ones. I. J. Gelb has already pointed out that, for example, the Phoenician "alphabet" was actually not an alphabet at all,[3] because its symbols were polyphonic, 𐤀 standing for ʾa, ʾu, ʾi, and ʾ∅, and (later) also for ā and the like, 𐤁 for ba, bu, bi, b∅, and, we may add, also for bā, bū, bī, bba, bbu, bbi, and the like. This, however, is not all. It has long been suspected that there were more consonantal phonemes in Canaanite and Phoenician than there were "letters," because of the Greek transcriptions Τύρος and Σιδών, Ἀραβία and Γόμορρα, where Greek τ and σ, zero and γ stand for two Phoenician written symbols only, namely, ṣ and ʿ (but correspond to *four* Proto-Semitic phonemes, *ṭ, and *ṣ, *ʿ, and *ġ, respectively). The Greek transcriptions of Semitic are perhaps not always consistent, and opinions on this point have differed. Let us, therefore, take another case. Everybody seems to agree that at least Ugaritic retained all or most of the Proto-Semitic consonantal phonemes. There is only some difference of opinion on the reason for the inconsistency in the rendering of the Proto-Semitic consonants /*ġ/ = ġ, ʿ, /*ḏ/ = ḏ, z̄₁, /*ṣ̌/ = š, ṭ in Ugaritic. But then, how are we to explain the existence of a shorter variant of the Ugaritic "alphabet," with only 22 consonantal symbols, instead of the 30 (or 31?) of the main variant? This can only mean that the speakers of Ugaritic, *after* having invented a writing system rendering (more or less exactly) *all* the consonantal phonemes of their language, decided to drop a number of the already invented symbols and to express, in several

---

extent, the same ground, and their results (especially Civil's) are a great advance in Sumerian philology and, moreover, in the study of extinct languages generally. After reading Civil's and Gragg's contributions, however, I have decided to publish my own paper without change, for the following reasons: I am not convinced that Sumerian writing can be treated simply as a code of the Sumerian spoken language, even if we introduce the concept of encoding at Civil's P2—P3—P4 levels (phonological) or at the M2—M3—M4 levels (morpholexical), without one-to-one correspondences between phonemes and graphemes, although this is indubitably a useful way of describing the discrepancy between language and writing; however, one does not here take sufficiently into account the mnemonic principle of early writing; moreover, I am convinced that, language being a process, a historical approach to it is and always will be needed, and a transformational, i.e., logical, approach, useful as it may be in many respects, is no adequate substitute for the historical approach.

3. I. J. Gelb, *A Study of Writing* (rev. ed.; Chicago, 1963) pp. 147–53; *idem*, "New Evidence in Favor of the Syllabic Character of West Semitic Writing," *BiOr* XV (1958) 1–7.

cases, two or more phonemes by one symbol.[4] And that is, no doubt, what happened with Phoenician writing, as well. Neither is this process (rather strange as it looks from our modern point of view) at all unique in the history of writing. Exactly the same thing happened with the Germanic runes, for a system of 24 symbols, roughly corresponding to the number of the then existing phonemes, was ousted by another system using only 16 non-univocal symbols! Obviously, the writing in question was not at all meant to be as true a rendering of the spoken language as possible.[5] Moreover, everyone who has read Phoenician or Ugaritic, on the one hand, and Akkadian, on the other, knows that although it is much easier to *learn* the Phoenician or Ugaritic writing system, it is much more difficult to *read* and *understand* Phoenician and Ugaritic than Akkadian, and that not only because we know the Akkadian vocabulary better. Reading Ugaritic is a process of solving riddles (much more so than reading Akkadian, although there, too, an element of decipherment is always present). Of course, it is a process of solving riddles only if you do not know what the text is about. If it is a list of expenditures and recipients—especially if you know the gentlemen in question personally—nothing is easier than reading an Ugaritic text. The same is true if it is a religious text continuously in use in temple service, and the reader is the person performing the service, but not otherwise. Precisely this shows that the function of writing was, initially, mnemonic.

4. This was only a continuation of a process that had been going on for a long time. The Proto-Byblian writing system, which has about a hundred signs, includes practically all signs used as letters of the Phoenician, South Arabian, and Asianic alphabets. One hundred signs are exactly as many as needed if it were used for a Semitic language with a Proto-Semitic consonantal system, and if it applied separate symbols for -Ca-, -Ci-, and -Cu- sequences, one of them being used also for -C∅-, as in Mycenaean and in "Hittite Hieroglyphic"—and in the case of the ʾāläph, also in Ugaritic. A comparison by A. M. Kondratov of the frequencies of Proto-Byblian signs in the various positions with the frequencies of the syllables in a number of ancient Semitic texts which were re-written by me in accordance with a reconstructed Proto-Semitic vocalic and consonantal system (the sequence -C∅- being equated with -Ca-) revealed the coincidence of frequencies between Proto-Byblian ⟨, ⊓, ⊓, ∘, ⅂ and Semitic *ma* (*na*), *ba, ta* (*ti*), ʿ*a,* ʾ*a,* respectively (variants refer to the basic dialect selected). Also ✕ is probably *t* + a vowel. This possibly shows that Phoenician and related alphabets may have been nothing else but the Proto-Byblian writing system condensed by the use of only one sign for all vocalic combinations with one and the same consonant. The throwing together of acoustically similar consonants in Phoenician (and Ugaritic) would then be just another step toward making the writing system easier to learn (and more difficult for strangers to decipher). Note that the short *e* and *a* were still omitted in many Carian and other Asianic inscriptions; see I. M. D'jakonov, "Karijskij alfavit . . . ," *VDI* 1967, No. 100, pp. 240 ff.; V. V. Ševoroškin, *Issledovanija po dešifrovke karijskikh nadpisej* (Moscow, 1965) pp. 309 ff. (the forms in question are underlined).

5. This is probably also the reason why the Ugaritic scribes could use either *d* or $\bar{z}_1$ for /d/, and either *ṣ* or *ṭ* for /ṣ́/, etc., just as the Akkadian scribe could use either TUN or DU for /ṭu/, etc. There is no absolute necessity to connect this phenomenon with phonetics or phonemics—both of them discoveries of a later age. Note that if the use of Hebrew ʿ and *ṣ* for two phonemes each is still a matter of doubt, it is at least certain that Hebrew *š* was used for two distinct phonemes (the graphemic distinction between /ś/ and /š/ being first introduced by the Masoretes in the early Middle Ages).

The same can be said of the early "syllabic" systems (the term is, of course, wrong, because each sign does not necessarily represent a complete syllable as a unit of speech—still less a morpheme, as has been recently suggested—but only a certain sequence of consonants and vowels). It is well known that Mycenaean A and B, Cypriote, "Hittite (or Luwian) Hieroglyphic" and the "Old Persian"[6] operate with symbols representing each a consonant + a vowel (or zero). It has been suggested that in the case of at least the first three systems (since they undoubtedly are genetically connected) this can be explained by the derivation of the scripts in question from one that had been invented for a language characterized phonetically by the exclusive predominance of -CV- sequences. But surely the inventors of the later branches of this hypothetical script (if it has ever existed), that is, of such branches as the Archaic Greek or Luwian and similar writing systems, could just as well invent signs needed for the -VC- sequences, since they introduced a number of changes into the original system anyway. The users of "Hittite Hieroglyphic" knew Hittite Cuneiform, too, but this did not induce them to change their system of writing for one more "readable" from our point of view, that is, more adequately reproducing the phonetic (or phonemic) aspect of their speech. Moreover, all the aforementioned "syllabic" systems with the exception of the "Old Persian" fail to distinguish between the voiced, the voiceless, and the aspirated stops, although the difference between them could not but be felt quite clearly by the inventors of the scripts in question: we cannot accept the notion that *all* the languages concerned were similar to the German *sächselnd* dialects. An analogy is again furnished by the Germanic runes: the later Scandinavian futhorc did not distinguish between voiced and voiceless consonants after the ninth century A.D., although no corresponding phonetic process is known to have occurred in the Scandinavian dialects.

Another typical characteristic of nearly all quasi-"phonetic" writing systems (and of systems with quasi-"phonetic" elements used alongside logographic or ideographic ones) is that they fail to express $-n\#$ and often also $-s\#$ (sometimes also other sounds) in *In-* and *Auslaut*. This is true of Old Sumerian (-me instead of -me-eš: probably a point in favor of E. Sollberger's suggestion that we should read /s/ for š!),[7] of "Hittite Hieroglyphic," Mycenaean, Cypriote, Old Persian, later Runic (as distinct from the earlier Runic derived from the phonetic Italic scripts) and probably of other writing systems of the ancient type, as well.

6. I. M. Diakonoff, "The Origin of the 'Old Persian' Writing System and the Ancient Oriental Epigraphic and Annalistic Tradition," *W. B. Henning Memorial Volume* (London, 1970) pp. 106 ff.

7. Also $-m\#$ ($-b\#$ allophonic?) and perhaps other consonants were omitted in *In-* and *Auslaut*. Cf. M. Civil and R. D. Biggs, "Notes sur des textes sumériens archaïques," *RA* LX (1966) 10, comment on l. 4', and 14. The authors of this paper arrive independently at results which approach my own very closely. The main ideas about the character of Sumerian writing as stated here have, in their essence, been published by me as early as 1940 (*Trudy Otdela Vostoka Gosudarstvennogo Ermitaža* III [Leningrad, 1940] 27–48).

The result is that, for example, in Mycenaean B a word such as *e-ke* may have several hundreds of possible readings! This did not trouble the ancient scribes in the least, however, because they always knew what the general contents of their texts were, and thus their choice was limited to one or, at most, two or three possibilities.

It is important to note that the choice of the sign values was made easier by the use of determinative symbols (incorrectly called "ideograms" by the Mycenologists).

Thus, none of these ancient writing systems was designed to render utterances of speech directly as expressed in the language; they were only systems of aid to memory, used mainly for administrative purposes (and later, to a certain degree, in the cult).

If this is true of the more ancient "alphabetic" and "syllabic" writing systems, then it is still more true of the very first writing systems ever invented by man, and specifically of Sumerian writing. From the time of F. Thureau-Dangin, A. Poebel, and A. Falkenstein, the Sumerian language has been studied mainly at its "classical" stage, that is, from Early Dynastic III to Ur III–Larsam. A. Deimel, it is true, tried his hand at the archaic texts even in his manual of Sumerian, but his linguistic approach was not very rigorous, and "Deimel's Sumerian" has by now been universally abandoned. But also E. Sollberger, attacking Old Sumerian with the most modern linguistic methods of twenty years ago, met with considerable difficulties.[8]

The common mistake seems to be that Sumerian is treated simply as a language, just as if it were a vernacular of some Central African tribe written down in a phonetic transcription. A written language, however—any written language—cannot be investigated by linguistic means and methods alone, if only because an orthography always retains relics not of one but of scores of "synchronic levels" of the language and is strongly influenced by a number of extralinguistic phenomena. Thus, the fashionable methods of descriptive linguistics, as, for example, studying the "levels" of the language each by itself, disregarding all information, however important, if it comes from a level other than the one under consideration (in spite of the inability to explain a number of phenomena from inside that unique level), or looking for "minimal pairs," will here prove futile. In fact, no other "synchronic level" has any reality in linguistics but the one we encounter as the now spoken language (and even then only if we disregard the constant, uninterrupted change of the language which in itself is not a thing but a process, and if we abstract our attention from the multitude of individual peculiarities which constitute a spoken language). A spoken language at one synchronic level cannot simply be compared with the same spoken language at another level:[9] we can only compare a spoken language

8. See note 1.

9. Neither can the still more modern methods of generative linguistics replace a historical approach to the development of languages now dead and reached only through the means of inadequate writing systems.

with a written language, or two stages of a written language between themselves, but a written language does not, as a rule, represent any one particular linguistic synchronic level. Nor do "minimal pairs" exist in a writing system which does not usually register phonemes as such.

Thus, in order to reach a dead language we must get at it through a certain writing system. The first thing to do, therefore, is to study the writing system before we decide on questions of the language structure. I do not think that very much more can be done at present to further the study of the Sumerian language unless we get a better understanding of the workings of the Sumerian writing system. Thorkild Jacobsen's study of the Sumerian verb is and will remain a *tour de force*, and it is difficult to hope we can get much further by purely linguistic methods[10]

In my undergraduate days one of my professors told me that no progress in a field of scholarship is achieved until a pupil has been able to correct his master. But we are still behind our masters in Sumerian in most respects; I am not aware, for instance, that any of the intricate results of Thorkild Jacobsen's study of the Sumerian verb can at present be rigorously and convincingly disproved or improved, even if certain Sumerologists may, rather intuitively, hesitate to accept some of them. From this it follows that the progress in Sumerian linguistics has not lately been so great as we could wish. This is why I suggest we give more attention to the study of the Sumerian writing system, as an aid to the study of the language hidden behind it.

From this point of view it is probably wrong to begin the study of Sumerian with the Neo-Sumerian period, when the original features of the Sumerian writing system had already faded, though its principles certainly continued to be at work. No less wrong, from this point of view, is the now usual system of transcription of Sumerian, which, instead of faithfully transliterating what stands in the text, tries—to my mind, rather unsuccessfully—to create a quasi-phonetic transcription.

What really happened with written Sumerian can be shown most clearly by comparing texts dating from different periods.[11] In what follows we will keep mainly to typologically similar texts, especially to economic temple records, that is, precisely the type of document for which the writing itself was created:

A. Uruk IV

    ATU, No. 297:

obv. 1	7 (gur še)	BA
2	1 (gur še)	GI
right edge	x x x[12]	
rev. 1	6 (gur še BA)	

10. If not directly formulated in the same way, this or a very similar point of view seems to have been reached also by some of the younger Sumerologists, notably M. Civil, R. D. Biggs, and G. Gragg. At least, it seems possible to infer as much from their published work.

11. For similar examples see M. Civil and R. D. Biggs, in *RA* LX 12–13. In some respects their examples, extracted mainly from literary texts, are still more striking.

12. Three(?) unidentified signs, one of them possibly AN; a name or a title?

"7 (gur of barley given as) ration, 1 (gur of barley) returned(?); (responsible for the operation, or recipient) Mr. x x x; (in all) 6 (gur of barley spent in rations)."

Note that many other variants may be plausibly suggested for the text reconstructed here in parentheses.

B. Jemdet Nasr

   ATU, No. 626

rev. i	1	BA 44 ŠE
	2	151 GI
ii	1	BA GI ŠE 195
		(Some signs, probably representing a place name, follow.)

"44 (gur of) barley (given as) ration, 151 (gur of barley) returned(?); barley (given as) ration (and) returned(?); (in all) 195 (gur). Place name(?)."

Note the incomplete rendering of the linguistic contents of the text and the fortuitous sign order, probably unrelated to the syntax of the spoken language.

C. Archaic Ur

   UET II, No. 6

i	1	10 (gur) ŠE
	2	GAL+LÚ+UR
ii	1	4 (gur!)
	2	x-ma-x[13]
	3	x[14]

"10 (gur of) barley (to *or* from) Ur-lugal, 4 (gur of barley to *or* from) Mr. x, [returned?]."

The case relations are not registered!

D. Fara

   Fara III, No. 98

vii	1	AN ŠÈ GÚ
	2	82 GURUŠ
	3	2 (bán) ZÍD TI | ŠU-BA

"In total, 82 men received 2 bán (of) flour."

Note the still free sign order: AN ŠÈ GÚ for gú-an-šè, TI | ŠU-BA[15] probably for

---

13. Certainly a personal name.
14. Probably G[I].
15. Note that one, probably complex, affix, namely -ba-, is here registered in writing.

/šubantieš/ or /šubabtieš/. More morphemes are registered in the less stereo-typed sale texts:

Fara III, No. 38

i 1   ... 11 KUG GÍN SÁM AŠAG$_x$(= GÁNA)

  2   6 AŠAG$_x$(= GÁNA) -bé

ii 1   NAM-MAH

  2   DUMU ^{d}SU+KUR+RU-da-zi

  3   an-na-sím

  4   LÚ-na-nam

iii 1   ŠES

  2   NAM-MAH

  3   LÚ-KI-INIM

  4   GAM-GAM

  5   LÚ SÁM AK

"(So and so much foodstuffs and) 11 shekels of silver (is the) price (of the) field. Its area (is) 6 (iku). (By) Nammah(ane?), son of Suddazi, given to him (should have been /anabsim/?). Lunanam, brother of Nammah(ane?), (was) witness. Gamgam(?) (is) the give(r) (of the) price."

Note the "phonetic" (rebus-type) inclusions -bé, -da-, an-na-sím, -na-nam. But SÁM probably stands for *ní(g)-sá(m) or *ni(g)-sám-(m)a, NAM-MAH for /Nammahane/, LÚ-KI-INIM for *lú-ki-inim-(m)a, AK for *ak-(k)a (punctive, not cursive!). Much of what must have existed in the spoken language is not registered in writing.

E. Early Dynastic III

As is well known, it was about the time of Eanatum of Lagaš that the new system of registering most, though still not all, morphemes in writing was adopted. In the inscriptions of Eanatum's grandfather Ur-Nanše (or Ur-Nazi) E. Sollberger[16] notes seven verbal forms of the type mu + root and only one of the type mu-na-a- + root. This, on the basis of what we know about early Sumerian writing, cannot be taken as meaning that dimensional prefixes were very seldom used in the verb in Ur-Nanše's time, but simply that the scribe thought it sufficient to mark a verbal form as finite by registering a prefix mu- or e- and leaving out all the rest. A more exact picture of the spoken language is given by the texts of the time of Uruinimgena; the question, however, is how exact is it?

Nikolski, Vol. I, No. 6

  rev. (summing up columns)

i 1   gú-an-šè 192 lú še-ba tur-mah-ba

  2   še-bé 24 (gur) 2 (ul) la(l) 1 (bán) gur-SAĞ+GÁL

  3   [š]e-ba tur-mah-ba [lú]-ú-rum

16. *Le système verbal*, p. 123.

4   ᵈBa-Ú
5   Ša(g)₅-ša(g)₅
6   dam Uru-inim-ge-na
7   lugal
8   Lagaš-ka
9   iti(d) ezen DIM₄-kú
ii 1   ᵈNanše(?)-ka
2   En-ik-gal
3   nu-bànda
4   GÁ × NUN ᵈBa-Ú-ta
5   e-ne-ba "4"

"All in all, (for) 192 people, barley ration of their small and big (i.e., everyone); its barley (being) 24 (gur) 2 (ul) minus 1 (bán) (by the) gur-SAG + GÁL(-measure); (it is the) ration of the barley of their small and big, the people (who are) property (of the) goddess Ba-Ú. Ša(g)ša(g), the wife of Uruinimgena, king of Lagaš. Month (called) 'Feast of Gruel(?)-Eating of the Goddess Nanše.' Enikgal, the overseer, portioned (it) out to them from the storehouse of the goddess Ba-Ú. (Year) 4."

Note that even now not all the morphemes are put down in writing: missing are the dative(?) of lú in col. i, 1. 1 and the copula in 1. 2; a genitive marker is missing in /Lagašaka/ (col. i, 1. 8) and possibly one after ᵈBa-Ú in col. i, 1. 4; and the marker of the subject is absent in the final verb. Are we quite sure nothing else has been left out?

F. Ur III

Here we will take a text somewhat different in content from those cited above, although there would not have been any difficulty in finding one that was quite similar.

ITT III, No. 6021

obv. 1   4 ŠE GUR
2   ní(g)-ba LUGAL
3   LÚ-TÚG-me
4   KIŠIB SUKKAL-MAH
rev. 1   iti(d) ezen An-(n)a
2   mu ᵈI-bí-
3   ᵈEN + ZU LUGAL

"4 gur of barley, present (of the) king; (the recipients) are tailors. Seal (of the) sukkal-mah, month 'Feast of An,' year 'Ibbī-Suʾen (became) king.'"

Note the "aid-to-the-memory" way of spelling: ŠE GUR in a syntactical order probably reverse of the one used in spoken language; no marker of the genitive in 11. 2 and 4 (LUGAL, SUKKAL-MAH); -me probably for *-me-eš (hardly LÚ.TÚG.ME as one ideogram?); no copula in rev. 3; of course the archaic reverse order of the signs in ᵈEN + ZU and no reduplication in the Akkadian word *ibbī* are usual features of the "classical" Sumerian spelling.

Compare the text on the seal impressed on the same tablet:

i 1   ᵈI-bí-ᵈEN + ZU
    2   lugal KAL.GA
    3   lugal ŠES.UNU^{ki}-(m)a
    4   lugal an-ub-da-tabtab-(b)a
ii 1   Ìr(ad)-[ᵈNanna(r)]
    2   sukkal-mah
    3   ìr(ad)-da-ni-ir
    4   in-na-ba

"Ibbī-Su°en, the mighty king, the king of Ur, the king of all the four regions of the sky, Ir(ad)-Nanna(r), the sukkal-mah; to his servant (he) to him presented (it)."

Here, too, some morphophonemic elements are lacking, but not more than usual in the normalized "correct" orthography of the epoch; KAL.GA for /kalaga/; in-na-ba for (presumably) /inamba/.

G. Larsam Period

YOS VIII, No. 15: 2–6: ìr(ad) ... šu-ni-a šu-ba-an-ti, "The slave ... from his hand he received."

Note the hypercorrect spelling šu-ni-a (presumably) for /šuna/. But the -n- and -m- in *Inlaut* remain optional also now: nu-mu-gi₄-gi₄-dè (‖ nu-mu-un-gi₄-gi₄-dè) in-ši-sám (‖ in-ši-in-sám) . . . kubabbar sám-til-(1)a-ni-šè in-na-la(1) (‖ in-na-an-la(1)), etc.[17]

Thus, in the beginning, only the stem of the word was written down; later, using the rebus-type procedure, the scribes would add some indications of the morphemes accompanying the stem—just enough to identify the word as, for example, a finite or non-finite verb, or perhaps as a verb in a form pointing to an indirect object not otherwise marked in writing. Even entire words of lesser importance for reproducing the contents of the document might be dropped. It was not until the scribes' mother language was no longer spoken Sumerian that a maximum of morphemes was being regularly registered in writing.

But was it really *necessary* for the scribes to express *all* the morphemes in writing at any period? At least -n and -m in *In-* and *Auslaut* are very often missing even in late Sumerian—probably not because the scribe did not know his Sumerian (a scribe who could write and read, for example, "En-Merkar and the ēn of Aratta," would probably know Sumerian a great deal better than an average modern Sumerologist) but because *he had no need to be reminded* each time of the fact that there was an -n in the *Auslaut*. A scribe who was sure he

17. Examples taken from L. Matouš, "Les contrats de vente d'immeubles provenant de Larsa," *ArOr* XVIII (1950) 11–67.

would not be misunderstood could allow himself to leave out an ending here and an ending there, even as late as Ur III and probably later. Thus, when we use statistics in order to find out whether this or that grammatical element did or did not exist at a certain period in the history of the Sumerian language, it is useful to keep in mind that the "syllabic" signs in Sumerian writing were meant to be only aids to the memory and no more. The better trained the scribe and the more routine the text, the less need there was to express in writing everything that existed in the language; see the Ur III text above (*ITT* III, No. 6021), which omits much more than would be usual in a literary text or a royal inscription of the same epoch.

We said just now that at the beginning of writing only the stem of the word was written down; but is even that correct? I am afraid that the famous passages from A. Falkenstein's *Archaische Texte aus Uruk* (Berlin, 1936) stating that Sumerian writing was a *Wortschrift* and not an *Ideenschrift* has to some degree misled many Sumerologists. Here are the passages in question:

"Der Terminus 'Wortzeichen' ersetzt im folgenden durchweg die übliche Bezeichnung 'Ideogram', die für das sumerische Schriftsystem keine Geltung hat—ebensowenig wie für die akkadische und die weiteren abgeleiteten Schriftarten—, falls man darunter ein der 'Ideen-' oder 'Bilderschrift' zugeordnetes Element versteht . . ." (p. 29, n. 3). This statement is no doubt correct, if we take for granted what Falkenstein writes later:

"Die Frage, ob die ältesten Belege der Schrift Babyloniens noch Reste einer von der Theorie der Schriftentwicklung mehrfach angenommenen Vorstufe der Wortschrift, der 'Ideenschrift', erkennen lassen, ist ziemlich sicher mit nein zu beantworten. Unter Ideenschrift versteht man eine Schriftart, bei der es sich nicht um die Fixierung eines gegliederten sprachlichen Ausdrucks handelt, sondern um *die Darstellung eines ganzen Gedankenkomplexes, der bei der Umsetzung in die Sprache ganz verschiedene Ausdrucksformen annehmen könnte*" (p. 31; italics mine). We need not, however, take this for granted, because Falkenstein's negative attitude to the hypothesis of the existence in Mesopotamia of ideographic writing as defined above is based on an *argumentum ex silentio*. But even if in this case Falkenstein is right, he seems still to be wrong, when he adds: "Der Ausdruck 'Wortzeichen' kann ruhig auch dann gebraucht werden, wenn in Wirklichkeit eine Zeichengruppe zur Darstellung eines Wortes dient" (p. 29, n. 3). Falkenstein fails to notice that not only may several signs stand for one word, but that in hundreds of cases the value of a sign can be chosen from a number of words; indeed, the number of words for which a sign can be used is limited only by the circle of visual or acoustic associations which the picture sign in question calls forth.[18] And can one actually say that the sign BA standing for /ní(g)-ba/, or for /ba-a/, or for /ba-àm/, or for /še-ba/, or for

---

18. The only limitation occurs when an object, although associatively connected with the one depicted by the ideographic sign in question, has already a sign of its own. Thus, the sign FOOT (DU) is used for "stand," "go," "bring," but not for "foot," "sole" which has its own sign (SUHUS).

/munanenba/—we never know exactly what is meant in the archaic texts—bei der Umsetzung in die Sprache keine verschiedene Ausdrucksform annehmen kann?

Of course, by the Early Dynastic III period most of the morphemes were being expressed in writing, and by the Ur III period, virtually all; there was, however, nothing that could prevent a scribe from omitting a sign which he thought superfluous. As for the "stem signs," they still remained ideograms, not logograms; thus, instead of transcribing mu-na-ni-du$_{11}$ or mu-na-ni-dug$_4$, we ought actually to write mu-na-ni-MOUTH; and, of course, DU-DU-ma-ab may mean gen-gen-ma-ab as "free reduplication," or du-du-ma-ab, or túm-túm-(m)a-ab; what really stands in the text is FOOT-FOOT-ma-ab. One may *call* it a logogram, or *Wortzeichen*, if one wishes, and this will be partly correct, because beginning with the ED III period each stem sign in each written context stands for the stem of one particular word; but the sign MOUTH or FOOT does not of itself correspond to any one particular word, and in *this* sense it is *not* a logogram. Nor does it, as we have seen, express the whole word, except in the archaic texts, and there it may stand as a key word to a whole expression which is not written down; see our texts *ATU*, Nos. 297 and 626, above. Besides, a "stem sign" in the archaic texts could express any given form of any word among a number of associatively connected words. Thus, a sign of the archaic Sumerian writing system is not a logogram because it can express less than a whole word and more than a whole word, and because it can express different (even if logically connected) words. By the same reasons it is not a "stem sign," as we provisionally called it above; "ideogram" seems to me, after all, to be the best term, although, of course, not in the sense of an element of a complex pictorial communication which is independent of language, but in the sense of a mnemonic device which by association of ideas could be connected with a number of words existing as elements of the language. With time, in order to convey the necessary information more precisely, more and more units of the spoken language came to be reflected by signs of writing through using various rebus devices, but the whole system was never meant to express all the phonetic or even the morphophonemic elements of the language.

Our next query is closely connected with the concept of Sumerian writing as defined above. Is it necessary always to use in transcription the phonetically shortest form of the possible reading of a sign, for example, ša$_4$ for šag, du$_{11}$ for dug$_4$, pà for pàd, and so forth? To my mind, this method of transcription (1) unnecessarily imitates a phonetic transcription, when actually we have to do with a written language whose writing system was not designed, or in any case not primarily designed, for rendering phonetics and never did render phonetics with any degree of precision; and (2) forces upon the student readings which are not always certain;[19] and (3) doubles the already tremendous efforts neces-

19. Compare the forms of the verb corresponding to Akkadian *nadānu:* Is sì the *marû*-form or a variant reading (such as sum) of sím? And is sig$_{10}$ Emeku or Emesal? Another good example is quoted by Civil and Biggs, in *RA* LX 16 from Ea III 102: e KA = *qabû*, which means that in some cases the sign KA may stand for the *marû*-form e instead of the *hamṭu*-form dug$_4$.

sary for memorizing the Sumerian sign values and vocables (thus, the student must always keep in mind that the participle -a of du_{11} is du_{11}-ga but the participle -a of pà is for some mysterious reason pà-da). It seems much easier to remember that practically all voiced stops and some other consonants are (as in French) mute in *In-* and *Auslaut*.[20] The only difficulty is presented by the shortened reduplicated forms in the *marû*-aspect, as na_8-na_8, *marû* of nag, "to drink," zi-zi, *marû* of zig_x, "to rise," and so forth; see also šu-ba-àm, "let me go free," imperative of šu-bar, ku_4-um-ma-ni, imperative of kur_x, "to enter," and so forth. Here, too, however, we might write -nag-nag (the more so since the *hamṭu*-form in Neo-Sumerian, when not followed by a vocalic suffix, was probably read /na/ and not /nag/!), $-zig_x$-zig_x, and so forth; even in the case of ku_4-um-ma-ni[21] there is no guarantee that the form was not to

20. Since Jestin's discovery of the sound /ǧ/ in Sumerian we are aware of the fact that Old Babylonian and later Sumero-Akkadian syllabaries do not render all the Sumerian phonemes. Here are some other facts, partly noted previously by other scholars, partly new:

1. There were two *l*-sounds in Sumerian; cf. ^{d}En-líl-lá for /enlil-a(k)/ but ^{d}En-líl-la for /*enlil-ra/ and rib ‖ líb. One of the *l*-sounds is dropped in *Auslaut*, as lá for lal#, ǧá ‖ mà for ǧar# (in reduplication) and mal#, bí for bil#, ti for til#; the other is retained, as in bal (which perhaps is only a shortened form of bala ?), gal, dal, hal (but kal<kala(g)), làl, sal (but zal < zala(g)).
2. There were two *r*-sounds in Sumerian, one of them dropped in *Auslaut*, as -r(a) of the dative postposition, ku_4 for kur_x, "to enter," possibly also in bar and ǧar but not in most other cases.
3. There were two *h*-sounds in Sumerian, with the same distinction (ra for rah_x#, du_8 for duh# but retained in mah, etc.). In Emesal h is partly retained, partly > d- (</*g'-/—?).
4. On the evidence of Emesal there were at least two *g*-sounds not counting /ǧ/: dùg (du_{10})~/zeb/, a-gàr~/adar/ (but dugud~/zebed/).
5. There may have been more sibilants than we are aware of. See the evidence of Emesal: sipa(d)~/suba/, sig_4~/šeb/, sím ‖ sum~/zem/ or /zeǧ/, zi(d)~/ zi/, zi ~/ši/.
6. There seems to have been generally some difference between consonants dropped in the *Auslaut* and those retained. Thus, *b* is almost invariably retained (at least there are no indications to the contrary in writing); however, pab> pa_4. Nevertheless, -d# is almost invariably lost (gad and had, "stick," are probably borrowings and may have been read /gat/ and /hat/). Most of the roots in -g# lose this consonant in *Auslaut*, and those which apparently do not (ag, lag, ig, zig [but not zig_x = zi], dug [but not dùg = du_{10} and dug_4 = du_{11}], gug(?), mug, túg [but not tug which is = tuku], ug, and some others) may, at least in some cases, have been pronounced with /k/, e.g., the spellings ag-ga and ak-ka, etc. We may remember that all variants of cuneiform failed to distinguish between voiced, voiceless, and emphatic sounds in signs of the VC type. It is not, however, simply a case of the voiced stops being dropped and voiceless retained, because the voiceless stop in the genitive postposition -ak is dropped. If we are to seek the solution of these phenomena along phonetic lines, one might suppose that the difference was between glottalized and non-glottalized, or between palatalized and non-palatalized, or something of this kind. The genitive postposition might have suffered an irregular development because of its unusually high frequency. Or the difference may have lain in the character of the phonemic tone in the stem. But how are we to know that all or some of these irregularities are not due to the inadequacy of the writing system?

21. S. N. Kramer, "'Inanna's Descent' Continued and Revised," *JCS* V (1961) 6, 1. 125; cf. Edzard, in *ZA*, Vol. 61, p. 225, from which this and some other examples are borrowed.

be read kur$_x$-um-ma-ni simply because of the labial vowel in the stem. In those cases when the Sumerians themselves omitted the final consonant by using an entirely different sign (as in -ǵá-ǵá from ǵar, or šu-ba-àm from šu-bar) we should of course transliterate the forms as they stand in the text; for propaedeutical purposes such forms might be classed with the suppletive *marû*-forms (as e for *hamṭu* dug$_4$, or du for *hamṭu* gen, and so on). If desired, the spelling -na(g)-na(g) may be used. That ǵar-ra is to be read /ǵara/ and not /*ǵarra/ is sufficiently well known, and no special notation is needed in the transliteration of such forms; however, a transliteration of the type ǵar-(r)a is also possible and sometimes desirable. But to be quite precise, we ought to transliterate it as BOWL^{ra} (or else BARLEYCAKE^{ra}), that is, with a "phonetic" complement indicating the reading /ǵara/ instead of /ǵar/, or /munanenǵar/, or /ninda/, or whatever it may be. By the same reasoning TI-ŠU-BA in our Fara text (*Fara* III, No. 98), is in reality TI+ŠU^{ba} (or something like ARROW+HAND^{ba}), that is, an ideogram with a "phonetic" complement pointing to some reading such as /šubantieš/.

The fact that writings of the ǵar-ra (or NINDA^{ra}) type were not abandoned even at the latest stage of Sumerian writing is a proof that this writing system, even when using a maximum of phonetic values created for its signs according to the rebus principle, still remained in its essence a mnemonic system in which an exact rendering of the pronunciation was not aimed at. Thus, when we try to find out the morphophonological structure of the Sumerian language, we must constantly bear in mind that we are not dealing with a language directly but are reconstructing it from a very imperfect mnemonic writing system which had not been basically aimed at the rendering of morphophonemics. Of course, the temptation to explain and to systematize our own arbitrary reconstructions may sometimes prove to be overwhelming.

The next query: If we decide that Sumerian writing was mainly mnemonic and that the morphophonological phenomena were but imperfectly and sometimes carelessly reflected in it, what are we to do with the "unorthographical" spellings and especially with Emesal?[22]

The "unorthographical" spellings may actually be experiments in the creation and use of phonetic instead of mnemonic writing. But since no new signs or methods of expressing sounds in writing were invented, these experiments were bound to fail, because the corpus of Sumerian signs was extremely ill adapted for rendering phonetic distinctions. The tremendous number of homonyms suggests that there must have existed in Sumerian phonemic tones (possibly there was sentence stress but only tone accents in individual words). Yet, except for the crude method of drawing another picture for a homonymous word stem, Sumerian writing had apparently absolutely no means of distinguishing tonally different phonemes.

22. J. Krecher, "Die sumerischen Texte in 'syllabischer' Orthographie," *ZA*, Vol. 58 (1967) pp. 16–65.

The necessity of using some sort of phonetic writing was especially urgent, however, in the case of Emesal texts. So long as the temple service was based on ritual and mythological texts memorized by illiterate officials of the temple,[23] the problem did not arise; but the more the knowledge of Sumerian became the monopoly of highly trained scribes, and the more the temple officials had to resort to the reading of written texts for the correct rendering of the ritual, the more important it became to distinguish Emesal from the "main Sumerian dialect" in writing.

What is Emesal? The original notion that it was a "women's language" has been nearly universally abandoned ever since it appeared that the reading of this term was precisely eme-sal and not, say *eme-mí or *eme-munus or something of the kind and, consequently, that it does not mean "women's language" in word-for-word translation. The deciding vote against the old notion was cast by Thorkild Jacobsen in his notes to E. I. Gordon's *Sumerian Proverbs*.[24] The Akkadian *ummisallu* is, of course, nothing but the transcription of the word, and the precise meaning of another Akkadian name for the Emesal dialect, *lišān ṣilītim*, is not quite clear. It certainly does not mean "elegant language" as once thought; more probably it means "twisted," "slanted sideways" in the sense of "quaint" or "corrupted language," though that meaning does not explain its function at all. There are certainly no indications that it is a territorial or a tribal dialect, although elements of such dialects may be present in Emesal.

Having in so many cases had the privilege of agreeing with Thorkild Jacobsen on so many important questions of Sumerian history and philology (for example, on primitive democracy in Sumer, on the absence of national and racial consciousness or of conflicts based on national and racial rivalry, and the like), I may, perhaps, be allowed this once the privilege of disagreeing. Both internal evidence and anthropological analogies seem to suggest that Emesal, whatever the exact meaning of the term might be, was actually a women's language. Tabooing of the use of "men's" words and "men's" pronunciation is known the world over, more especially among peoples speaking structurally archaic, "ergative" languages. What is more, the difference between a "women's language" and a "main dialect" is very commonly of the same type as the difference between Emesal and the "main Sumerian dialect": this difference is mainly phonetic, with more archaic forms in the "women's dialect," which also

23. See B. Landsberger, in *City Invincible*, ed. by C. H. Kraeling and R. M. Adams (Chicago, 1960) p. 98. It seems to me preferable to avoid the general term "priest" or the like, since no such term existed in Sumerian, and a sanĝa or an ēn, as compared with a šu-i, a gala or a rá-gab, were but more highly placed temple officials. It was precisely because no divine grace was needed for the officials performing the rites in temple that their offices could be bought and sold in small parts after the Ur III period.

24. See the discussion of the problem by F. Thureau-Dangin, "Le rituel du kalû," *RA* XVII (1920) 53, Allotte de la Fuÿe, "Les uš.ku dans les textes archaïques de Lagaš," *RA* XVIII (1921) 101 ff., A. L. Oppenheim, "Mesopotamian Mythology," *Or*, n.s., Vol. 19 (1950) pp. 129–58, E. I. Gordon, *SP*, p. 13, A. Falkenstein, *Das Sumerische* in *Handbuch der Orientalistik* II (Leiden, 1959) 18, *et al.*

differs from the main language in using a limited number of words quite different from those used for the same objects in the language of men;[25] but there are scarcely any grammatical differences. In some languages (for example, in Laki, the native language of my friend and Assyriological colleague, Muhammad Dandamayev) only certain words used by men are taboo for women. But a more typical case is that of Chukchee, in which the "women's language" strongly resembles the Sumerian Emesal. Characterizing the Chukchee language, the well-known anthropologist and linguist V. G. Bogoras writes,[26]

> An interesting feature of Chukchee is the existence of a special women's pronunciation. In contrast to men, the women pronounce only c instead of the men's č and r, especially after palatalized vowels, and likewise cc instead of rk and čg. [Compare in Emesal: š-, -m-, z-, d-, -b, instead of n-, -g̃-, d-, g-, -g.] The r- and č- phonemes are very frequent in the language, so that the speech of the women with their constant c's sounds very different from the speech of the men, and is more difficult to understand. When reproducing the speech of a man, women may pronounce č and r correctly, but in general the use of men's pronunciation is accounted indecent for women.[27] . . . In the dialect of the "Reindeer Chukchees," especially among their western group, there is a tendency to elide -t-, -n- and sometimes -r- in intervocal position, with assimilation of the vowels. In women's pronunciation, however, the original non-contracted forms are always retained. . . . It seems that the contracted forms of the men's pronunciation in the dialect of the "Reindeer Chukchees" is a later development. Cf. men's pronunciation: nĭtvāqāāt, "they live," gãjmītlããt, "they took," qāāt, "reindeer," pl., with women's pronunciation: nĭtvāqēnāt, gãjmītlinãt, qōrāt.[28] [Compare Emesal /umun/, /Amanki/ for Emeku /ēn/ < /ewen/, /Ēnki/ < /Ewenki/.]

Mutatis mutandis, this could be a description of the Sumerian Emesal dialect. Note that Chukchee is also typologically (though not genetically or phonetically) very similar to Sumerian, especially in the verb, since it is also an "ergative" language.

It appears from the existing studies of the problem that Emesal was used (1) for the speech of women and goddesses in epics, proverbs,[29] and similar texts,

25. Cf. gašan for nin, "lady," ta for a-na, "what," in Emesal.

26. *Jazyki i pis'mennost' narodov severa*, ed. J. P. Al'kor, Vol. III, *Jazyki i pis'mennost' paleoaziatskikh narodov*, ed. J. A. Krejnovič (Moscow and Leningrad, 1934) ch. 1.

27. I have been told that when schools with Chukchee as the language of teaching were first opened, little girls blushed and refused to read words containing an r-sound. In the Amerindian Yana language the custom required that men speak to women in the "women's language," and that the "men's language" be used only in conversation between men. Note that an elided r is pronounced /r/ by women!

28. Note that an elided r is pronounced /r/ by women!

29. On the use of Emesal in proverbs see Gordon, *SP*, p. 13. Note that some of these proverbs become meaningless in Akkadian translation because the translation does not indicate that the text is supposed to be spoken by a woman; e.g. *BWL*, proverb 8 (K4327 + 4605 + 4749) iii 3–4, 5–6. Cf. I. M. D'jakonov, in *VDI* 1966, No. 1, p. 15.

(2) for the speech of the messengers and servants of the goddesses, (3) for the speech of incantation singers (gala) in proverbs, and (4) in some hymns and prayers.

Now, we must keep in mind that the messengers and servants of female persons would normally be eunuchs; not being regarded as men, they would probably be expected to use the women's pronunciation. The gala's were regarded as lowly persons,[30] and probably they were typically eunuchs, too.[31] So it seems to be a rather safe guess that the Emesal texts record the speeches, songs and hymns uttered and sung by women and eunuchs. Accordingly, a number of names of household objects and of persons connected with the household have been borrowed into Akkadian from Emesal.[32]

30. See the numerous proverbs obviously making fun of the gala, especially Gordon's proverb (*SP*) 2.98, which is probably to be translated: "The gala is the bottom of the boat."

31. A gala need not *necessarily* have been a eunuch, no more than all singers in an eighteenth- or nineteenth-century choir at the Vatican were castrati; indeed, J. Renger, "Untersuchungen zum Priestertum der altbabylonischen Zeit," *ZA*, Vol. 59 (1969) pp. 192–93, has shown that some gala's had families and that their sons inherited their profession; however, this would probably depend on the cult in which the gala in question acted. The gala's mentioned in Gordon's proverbs 2.100, 101 were, in any case, those employed in the cult of Inana, and it is only the gala's who served goddesses that need concern us in connection with the problem of the Emesal language. The key text is Gordon's proverb 2.99: gala-e dumu-ni a-ha-ba-an-da-ra-ra (var. a-a ba-da-zé-èḡ) uru^{ki} mà-a-gim hé-dù kalam mà-e-gim hé-en-ti. The correct translation was given by T. Jacobsen (Gordon, *SP*, p. 482), but he missed the ironical implication. A parallel proverb exists in Akkadian, only there the gala is replaced by a mule (*BWL*, p. 218, rev. iv 15–18): *sīsû tebû ina muhhi a-ta-ni pa-re-e* (a she-mule, not a jenny-ass, as W. G. Lambert translates!) *ki-i e-lu-ú ki-i šá ra-ak-bu-ú-ma ina uz-ni-šá ú-làh-ha-áš u[m-ma m]u-ú-ru ša tu-ul-li-di ki ia-ti lu la-si-im a-n[a i-me-r]u za-bíl tup-šik-ki la tu-maš-šá-li*, "A lusty stallion, when he mated a she-mule, when he had mounted (her), was whispering into her ear: "Let the foal that you bear be a swift runner like me, do not make it like an [ass] which has to fulfill forced labour." Of course, a she-mule cannot have progeny, and no more could the gala, although the prefix -nda possibly shows that he was not alone in his efforts. The fun of the Sumerian proverb lies partly in the perverse use of the men's and women's dialect: (dumu) a-a zé-èḡ is Emesal, and (dumu) a-ra-ra is also the correct Emesal form for (dumu) a-re-re (or -ri-ri, as it is usually read), but the truly royal speech of the gala is in "men's" Sumerian! The form a-ha-ba-an-da-ra-ra is *marû*, i.e., precative, probably with a conditional shade of meaning, while hé-dù and hé-en-ti are both *hamṭu* and thus affirmative; they need not, however, be in the past tense; the fact that the imperfective aspect is not a present-future, and the perfective not a past tense, can be clearly seen by the study of the verbal forms, e.g., in the "Reform" texts of Uruinimgena. The curious use of the aspects may, in our case, however, also be due to a translation from Akkadian with the help of some late manual which itself contained mistakes as to the classification of *hamṭu*- and *marû*-forms; cf. Edzard, in *ZA*, Vol. 61, p. 212, with a reference to T. Jacobsen, *MSL* IV 36*. The meaning of the proverb is surely: "Should a gala be 'begetting' his son, (he would say): 'He will surely build cities, like me, he will surely make the land live, like me!'" Also, the other proverbs about the gala and his slave and their boasting should be taken in an ironical sense, but space does not allow me to discuss them here.

32. A typical example is Akkadian *šamallû*, "pedlar" (original meaning, "carrier of pack sacks," as one may infer from the picture signs for šaḡan (Emesal šaman) and for the word la(l), "to carry," "to hang up").

Note that no Emesal text is ever written entirely in a "pure" Emesal, that is, completely phonetically. Often ideograms are used without marking that their pronunciation should differ from that in the "main dialect," and sometimes the Emeᴋᴜ forms occur alongside Emesal forms (e.g., hé- instead of dè-). In general, the use in a text of a number of Emesal forms seems to have been a sufficient signal for the reader to use the women's pronunciation, without the scribe's bothering to transcribe every word phonetically as pronounced in Emesal: another feature of mnemonic techniques used in Sumerian writing.

We have in the first part of this paper touched upon some extralinguistic factors hampering the linguistic analysis of Sumerian. In the following we would like to mention some of the pitfalls connected with the commonly recognized facts of Sumerian grammar.

Sumerian is a typical "ergative" language. The definition of the "ergative construction" as applicable to ancient oriental and a number of other languages (North Caucasian, Paleo-Asiatic, Tibetan, and others—but *not* Kartvelian, nor Neo-Iranian and Neo-Indian) has been given in detail by the present author in a number of studies[33] and need not be repeated here in full. An "ergative" language is one which is characterized by contrasting, not passive with active voice, subject with object, and nominative with accusative, but action with state, and ergative with absolute case (usually = zero case), the first expressing the subject of an action, the second the subject of a state—also of a state resulting from an action; such subject of a resulting state corresponds to (but is not identical with) a direct object in languages with a "nominative construction" of the sentence.

Thus, terms such as "transitive" and "intransitive," "active" and "passive," "nominative" and "accusative" refer actually not to the Sumerian grammatical category in question but only to the grammatical category which is generally used in the corresponding cases in the language of the translation; they are, I believe, out of place in the study of Sumerian itself and tend only to obscure the grammatical issues under consideration. For instance, there can be no special "nominative" or "accusative" marker in the prefixes[34] of the Sumerian verb.

---

33. See, e.g., *Hurrisch und Urartäisch* (Munich, 1971) pp. 1–4. For a detailed exposition of the problem, also especially in relation to Sumerian, see I. M. D'jakonov, "Ergativnaja konstrukcija i subjektno-objektnye otnošenija," *Ergativnaja konstrukcija predloženija v jazykakh različnykh tipov* (Leningrad, 1967) pp. 95–115; *idem, Jazyki drevnej Perednej Azii* (Moscow, 1967) pp. 29–33.

34. Instead of the complex terminology involving "preformatives," "profixes," "prefixes," "infixes," and the like, I have suggested using the terms "prefixes of positions 1–6" and "suffixes of positions 1–3" (not subdividing the prefix of each position into its etymological elements terminologically, which obviates the necessity of adhering to or rejecting any particular theory in regard to the origin of the dimensional prefixes; in this way I had hoped to create a terminology which would be acceptable to all Sumerologists). See D'jakonov, *Jazyki...*, p. 66. In fact, all affixes in Sumerian are either prefixes or suffixes, for there exists no infixation in the stem.

There may be expected to exist an ergative marker and an absolute case marker, the latter probably being identical for the subject both of an independent state and of a state resulting from an action. Hence, the suffix -en with a verb of action will mean "me," but with a stative verb it will mean "I." The use of the ergative prefix immediately before the stem will turn the sense of the verbal form from a stative one to one of action (i.e., causative).[35]

A regularly developed "ergative construction" is, for a reason which has not yet been satisfactorily explained, usually connected with a binary system of aspects (punctive and cursive, or perfective and imperfective) in the verb of action;[36] the verb of state dispenses with aspects. Tenses are usually absent or develop in the language at a late stage. Although D. O. Edzard's study of the *hamṭu*- and *marû*-forms has not yet been published in full, it seems clear, both from his and already from M. Yoshikawa's work, that the *hamṭu*-stem is the stem of the punctive (or perfective) aspect of the verb of action, as well as of the aspect-neutral form of the verb of state, and the *marû*-stem is the stem of the cursive (or imperfective) aspect of the verb of action.[37] That some of the *marû*-stems are suppletive in relation to the respective *hamṭu*-stem is nothing out of the ordinary (see Russian *ittí : khodít'*, like the English *go : went*); more curious is the fact that there are not one but two different morphological ways to express the non-suppletive *marû*-stem, namely, "stem + -e" and "stem in (an often incomplete) reduplication." My teacher A. P. Riftin once suggested that the -e suffix of the imperfective aspect might have been a demonstrative pronoun "it" replacing the reduplication of the stem ("stem + it" for "stem + stem").[38] This explanation looks rather attractive but can hardly be proved, unless close analogies to this supposed phenomenon are found elsewhere. At the same time the reduplicated *marû* stem may stand in some kind of genetic connection with what D. O. Edzard calls "freie Reduplikation," or what in Semitic is usually called "stem modification," a phenomenon for which I have suggested the revival of the medieval Latin term "stirps" (Arab. ﺟِﺬ). The history of Afrasian (Hamito-Semitic) languages shows a number of instances of the reduplicated stirps (Hebrew *pi^{cc}ēl*) turning into a durative or habitative aspect of the

35. It seems, however, that the subject of action being expressed in the *marû*-aspect by suffixes, the subject of the resulting state may in this aspect, contrary to the general rule obtaining in "ergative" languages, be expressed by prefixes, viz., by the same prefixes which in the unmarked or *hamṭu*-aspect are used for expression of the subject of action, i.e., there may be a reversal of the markers for the subject of action and subject of state: *hamṭu*: prefix—suffix, *marû*: suffix—prefix. This phenomenon, however, seems not to have occurred completely consistently and is probably of late origin.

36. Note that verbs of motion, inchoative verbs, and a number of other "intransitive" verbs are in many "ergative" languages construed as verbs of action; see Kaneva, in *Assiriologija i egiptologija* (for Sumerian); D'jakonov, *Jazyki. . .* , p. 101 (for Elamite).

37. See n. 1.

38. Originally I thought that reduplicated stems were used for the imperfective aspect only with verbs ending in a vowel, to compensate for the assimilation of the -e suffix by the vowel of the stem (*Jazyki . . .* , p. 77). According to Yoshikawa and Edzard, however, the *marû*-reduplication is not limited to such cases.

main verbal stirps (Hebrew *qāl*), as in Egyptian, in Berber, and elsewhere.

There is more than one pitfall awaiting the linguist who would try to classify all the known stems of Sumerian into *hamṭu, marû,* and reduplicated stirps ("freie Reduplikation"). For one thing, even the linguists of the é-dub-(b)a were not always sure of their ground in their own classification of the stems;[39] there is another important difficulty: as a speaker of a language using aspects, I can attest that all classifications of the meanings of aspect forms have only the value of statistical probabilities. Let us take, for example, the verb cited above, *ittí* : *khodít*: *ja idú* means "I am now going (toward a certain goal)"; *ja khožú* means "I am walking" or "I usually go"; *ja skhožú* means "I shall go." Then, *ja idú v magazín* means "I am going to the shop"; *ja khožú v magazín* means "it is my habit to go to the shop," and *ja skhožú v magazín* means "I shall go to the shop." So far so good. But *ja šol*[40] means "I was going," *ja khodíl* means, in principle, "I went (several times)," "I walked (without a goal)," or "I was walking"; *ja skhodíl* means "I went (only once and then came back)." But *ja šol v magazín* means "I was going to the shop," *ja khodíl v magazín* means "I have (already) been at the shop (probably only once, but at an unspecified time)," and *ja skhodíl v magazín* means "I have been to the shop (and back, at a specified moment)." The Sumerian aspect system may present a picture as complicated.

And the last pitfall is the one from which we started at the very beginning: Sumerian writing being, in its essence, nothing but a system of aids to the memory, a scribe or even a scribal school need not have always bothered to distinguish between the different aspect-stems for our benefit.

The same difficulties beset the linguist working on the "dimensional" prefixes of the verb; the situation here is still more complicated, since this is a category peculiar to Sumerian and to very few languages besides, so that we cannot resort to the help of analogies.

All scholars who have had the audacity, following Thorkild Jacobsen and the other master Sumerologists, to venture into the dangerous field of Sumerian linguistics, know from the start that their life is not going to be all roses and sunshine. I am afraid that I might have made some of the young Sumerologists still more pessimistic. But, nevertheless, I hope that trying to show there are, in this difficult field of scholarship, certain additional difficulties to which sufficient attention is not always given, I have in a way helped to circumvent the pitfalls I have myself pointed out.

BIBLIOGRAPHY

Writing System

Civil, M. "The Sumerian Writing System: Some Problems." *Or*, n.s., Vol. 42 (1973) pp. 21–34.

39. See n. 31.
40. Same stem as *khodít*', but past tense of *ittí*, not *khodít*'!

Civil, M., and R. D. Biggs. "Notes sur des textes sumériens archaïques." *RA* LX (1966) 1–16.

D'jakonov, I. M. *Trudy Otdela Vostoka Gosudarstvennogo Ermitaža* III 27–48. Leningrad, 1940.

Falkenstein, A. *Archaische Texte aus Uruk*. Leipzig, 1936.

Jacobsen, T. "The Inscriptions." In P. Delougaz and S. Lloyd, *Pre-Sargonid Temples in the Diyala Region*, pp. 289–98. *OIP* LVIII. Chicago, 1942.

Lieberman, S. J. *The Sumerian Loanwords in Old-Babylonian Akkadian* I. *HSS*. In press.

Poebel, A. *Die sumerischen Personennamen zur Zeit der Dynastie von Larsam und der ersten Dynastie von Babylon*. Breslau, 1910.

Sollberger, E. "Le syllabaire présargonique de Lagaš." ZA, Vol. 54 (1961) pp. 1–50.

Vaiman, A. A. "K rasšifrovke protošumerskoj pis'mennosti (predvaritel'noje soobščenije)" [On the Decipherment of Proto-Sumerian Script. Preliminary Report]. *Peredneaziatskij sbornik* I (1966) 3–15 [with extensive English summary].

———. "Oboznačenije rabov i rabyn' v protošumerskoj pis'mennosti" [Signs for Slaves and Slave-women in Proto-Sumerian script]. *VDI*, 1974, No. 2, pp. 138–48 [with English summary].

GRAMMARS

D'jakonov, I. M. *Jazyki drevnej Perednej Azii*, pp. 29–33. Moscow, 1967.

Falkenstein, A. *Grammatik der Sprache Gudeas von Lagaš*. *AnOr*, Vols. 28, 29. Rome, 1949–50.

———. *Das Sumerische*. In *Handbuch der Orientalistik*. Ed. by B. Spuler. Vol. 1. Pts. 1 and 2. Leiden, 1959.

Kärki, I. *Die Sprache der sumerischen Königsinschriften der frühaltbabylonischen Zeit*. *StOr* XXXV. Helsinki, 1967.

Poebel, A. *Grundzüge der sumerischen Grammatik*. Rostock, 1923.

STUDIES OF THE VERB

Edzard, D. O. "Ḫamṭu, marû und freie Reduplikation beim sumerischen Verbum." ZA, Vol. 61 (1971) pp. 208–32 and Vol. 62 (1972) pp. 1–34.

Falkenstein, A. "Zum sumerischen Tempussystem." *OLZ* XXIV (1931) 791–94.

Gragg, G. B. *Sumerian Dimensional Infixes*. *AOAT* Sonderreihe 5. Neukirchen-Vluyn, 1973.

Jacobsen, T. "Introduction to the Chicago Grammatical Texts." In *MSL* IV 1*–50*. Rome, 1956.

———. "About the Sumerian Verb." In *Studies in Honor of Benno Landsberger*. *AS*, No. 16, pp. 71–102. Chicago, 1965. Reprinted in *TIOT*, pp. 245–70, 430–66.

Jestin, R. *Le verbe súmerien*. Paris, 1943–45.

Kaneva, I. T. "Glagoly dviženija" [Verbs of Motion]. *Assiriologija i egiptologija.* Leningrad, 1965.

———. "Sprjaženie šumerskogo glagola" [Conjugation of the Sumerian Verb, with English summary]. *Peredneaziatskij sbornik* II (1966) 16–96.

———. "Participles in Sumerian." *MIO* XVI (1970) 541–65.

Kramer, S. N. *The Sumerian Prefix Forms* be- *and* bi- *in the Time of the Earlier Princes of Lagaš. AS,* No. 8. Chicago, 1936.

Krecher, J. "Die pluralischen Verba für 'gehen' und 'stehen' im Sumerischen." *WO* IV (1967–68) 1–11.

Poebel, A. "Die Negation li im Sumerischen." *OLZ* XVII (1914) 158–60.

———. "Die Präfixverbindung eri- in der Inschrift der Geierstele." *ZA,* Vol. 36 (1925) pp. 5–7.

———. "Zur Reihenfolge vor Subjekts- und Kausativelement im aktiven Präteritum und in der u-Form der Sumerischen." *ZA,* Vol. 36 (1925) pp. 9–10.

———. *The Sumerian Prefix Forms* e- *and* i- *in the Time of the Earlier Princes of Lagaš. AS,* No. 2. Chicago, 1931.

———. "The Tenses of the Intransitive Verb in Sumerian." *American Journal of Semitic Languages and Literatures* L (1934) 143–70.

———. "The Root Forms sì(m) and su_{11}(m), 'To Give,' in Sumerian." *JAOS,* Vol. 57 (1937) pp. 35–72.

Scholtz, R. *Die Struktur der sumerischen engeren Verbalpräfixe. MVAG,* Vol. 39/2. Leipzig, 1934.

Sollberger, E. *Le système verbal dans les inscriptions "royales" présargoniques de Lagaš.* Geneva, 1952. Reprinted Wiesbaden, 1971.

Yoshikawa, M. "The *Marû* and *Ḫamṭu* Aspects in the Sumerian Verbal System." *Or,* n.s., Vol. 37 (1968) pp. 401–16.

———. "On the Grammatical Function of -e- of the Sumerian Verbal Suffix -e-dè/-e-da(m)." *JNES,* Vol. 27 (1968) pp. 251–61.

———. "The *Marû*-Conjugation in the Sumerian Verbal System." *Or,* n.s., Vol. 43 (1974) pp. 17–39.

MISCELLANEOUS STUDIES

Civil, M. "From Enki's Headaches to Phonology." *JNES,* Vol. 32 (1973) pp. 57–61.

D'jakonov, I. M. "Ergativnaja konstrukcija i subjektno-objektnye otnošenija." In *Ergativnaja konstrukcija predložonija v jazykakh različnykh tipov.* Leningrad, 1967.

Edzard, D. O. "Sumerische Komposita mit dem 'Nominalpräfix' nu-." *ZA,* Vol. 55 (1963) pp. 91–112.

Falkenstein, A. "Das Potentialis- und Irrealissuffix -e-še des Sumerischen." *Indogermanische Forschungen* LX (1952) 113–30.

———. "Zur Grammatik der altsumerischen Sprache." *AfO* XVIII (1957–58) 89–96.

————. "Untersuchungen zur sumerischen Grammatik." *ZA*, Vol. 45 (1939) pp. 169–94, Vol. 47 (1942) pp. 181–223, Vol. 48 (1944) pp. 69–118, Vol. 53 (1959) pp. 98–105.

Jacobsen, T. "Notes on the Sumerian Genitive." *JNES*, Vol. 32 (1973) pp. 161–66.

————. "Very Ancient Linguistics: Babylonian Grammatical Texts." In D. Hymes, ed., *Studies in the History of Linguistics: Traditions and Paradigms*, pp. 41–62. Bloomington, Ind., 1974.

Kramer, S. N. "Studies in Sumerian Phonetics." *ArOr* VIII (1936) 18–33.

Krecher, J. "Zur sumerischen Grammatik." *ZA*, Vol. 57 (1965) pp. 12–30.

————. "Zum Emesal-Dialekt des Sumerischen." In *HSAO*, pp. 87–110. Wiesbaden, 1967.

————. "Verschlusslaute und Betonung im Sumerischen." In *Lišān miṯḫurti*. *AOAT*, Vol. 1, pp. 157–97. Neukirchen-Vluyn, 1969.

Poebel, A. "Die Genetivkonstruktion im Sumerischen." *Bab* IV (1911) 193–215.

————. *Grammatical Texts. PBS* VI/1. Philadelphia, 1914.

————. *Sumerische Studien. MVAG*, Vol. 26/1. Leipzig, 1921.

————. "Die doppelte Genetivkonstruktion im Sumerischen." *Journal of the Society for Oriental Research* IX (1925) 1–7.

————. "Zu n im Hauptdialekt = š im Emesal." *ZA*, Vol. 38 (1927) pp. 84–87.

————. "The Sumerian Genitive Element." *American Journal of Semitic Languages and Literatures* LI (1935) 145–76.

————. "Another Case of the Predicative Use of the Genitive in Sumerian." *JAOS*, Vol. 58 (1938) pp. 148–50.

Postgate, J. N. "Two Points of Grammar in Gudea." *JCS* XXVI (1974) 16–54.

Salonen, A., and P. Siro. *Studien zur neusumerischen Syntax. AASF*, Vol. 112/2. Helsinki, 1958.

Shaffer, A. "*TA ša kīma A ītenerrubu*: A Study in Native Babylonian Philology." *Or*, n.s., Vol. 38 (1969) pp. 433–46.

Sollberger, E. "Études de linguistique sumérienne." *Cahiers Ferdinand de Saussure*, Vol. 9 (1950) pp. 51–88.

————. "Genre et nombre en sumérien." *Cahiers Ferdinand de Saussure*, Vol. 26 (1969) pp. 151–60.

Thureau-Dangin, F. "Le génitif en sumérien." *RA* VIII (1911) 88–92.

————. "Le génitif en sumérien." *RA* XXXII (1935) 56.

————. "Le suffixe du relatif et le suffixe du génitif en sumérien." *RA* XXXII (1935) 191–98.

LEXICOGRAPHY

M. CIVIL

Chicago

Rather than write an introduction to Sumerian lexicography exclusively for the specialist, I have attempted to make the following pages accessible to interested readers in neighboring fields, following Thorkild Jacobsen's view that Sumerian culture is the "first humanistic culture" and as such must be placed in the wider frame of man's intellectual history. Since so much remains to be done in Sumerian lexicography, however, I could not help expressing my personal views on how the tasks ahead could be carried out, in pages that I am afraid take sometimes a somewhat unpleasant prescriptive tone, for which I apologize to my colleagues.*

1. NATIVE LEXICAL SOURCES

Burdened with all the problems that the paleolinguistic nature of his work entails,[1] the Sumerologist may fail to realize how lucky he is to have at his disposal an enormous wealth of ancient lexical material without which his under-

* In addition to their normal function, [ ] are used on occasion to indicate graphemic transliterations; / / indicate approximate phonemic transcription.

1. The term paleolinguistics has been used occasionally in the somewhat ethnocentric sense of "earlier (i.e., pre-nineteenth-century) stages of the linguistic sciences" (see, e.g., L. Romeo and G. E. Tiberio, "Historiography of Linguistics and Rome's Scholarship," *Language Sciences*, No. 17 [1971] p. 25), but here I apply the term, by analogy with other paleosciences, to the study of languages inaccessible to direct observation. In paleontology, only the anatomy is recoverable and not always whole; the missing anatomical parts and the physiology have to be reconstructed by analogical reasoning and comparative techniques. He who studies a language accessible only through texts has at his disposal only an imperfect and incomplete representation of the utterances of the language, and, because of the lack of informants, the functional, creative process involved in generating these utterances is not recoverable. In particular, if he can assume that the sentences in his corpus are grammatical, he has no means of testing the grammaticality of related sentences not present in the corpus, and, without this test, the study of the generation of sentences is seriously impaired. He has to rely on the relatively poorly known universals of language: the (inductive) structural or distributional universals of the type proposed by Greenberg, and the universal semantic and syntactic claims of the generative grammarians. A formal study of the limitations and methods of paleolinguistics would be most welcome.

standing of the Sumerian language and texts would be very meager indeed. In this section I present a very sketchy outline of some matters well known to the Sumerologist in the perhaps naive hope that outsiders may also be interested in the world's oldest body of lexical works.

1.1. Typology

The Mesopotamian lexicographical legacy is not only imposing in its bulk—the series HAR-ra alone has close to 10,000 entries—but also offers a great diversity of types of compilations.[2] The lexical lists may be unilingual or bilingual, totally or in part. Although the physical arrangement of the languages in the bilingual lists is always the same on the tablets (Sumerian in the left subcolumn, Akkadian in the right),[3] there are reasons to classify them as Sumero-Akkadian or Akkado-Sumerian, depending on which of the two languages provides the criterion for the ordering of the entries (1.2 (g) and (h)). A few examples of polyglot lists are known, mostly Sumerian, Akkadian, and Hittite, with rare examples of Sumerian, Akkadian, and Hurrian, and even Sumerian, Akkadian, Hurrian, and Ugaritic.[4] An isolated type lists the dialectal Emesal spellings alongside the main dialect forms and their Akkadian translations.[5] Although only translations and not definitions of words are given, there are some conventions by which homonyms can be distinguished. The lexical entries may be ordered according to the graphic or phonological shape (sign lists, syllabaries), or according to subjects (thematic lists); explanatory and etymological commentaries are late and relatively rare.

For practical purposes, such as the description of individual manuscripts, it has been found convenient to symbolize the parts of an entry by a numerical code[6] representing the subcolumns in their usual order, from left to right:

0—A vertical wedge preceding the entry in certain types of lists;

1—Sumerian pronunciation of logograms, formulated with the help of a small set of basic syllabograms;[7]

2—Logograms; in late lists it may not always be a faithful imitation of its Old Babylonian shape (the inscribed signs [$sign_1 \times sign_2$] are often written $sign_1 \times sign_2.sign_2$);

3—Sign name; a post-Old-Babylonian innovation, although some sign names can also be found in Old Babylonian non-lexical texts;

2. For some of the lexical lists, see the still useful study of H. S. Schuster, "Die nach Zeichen geordneten sumerisch-akkadischen Vokabulare," *ZA*, Vol. 44 (1938) pp. 217–70. The series published in *MSL*, after Volume XI, are provided with a brief introduction.

3. An exception is the use of Akkadian glosses in unilingual lists, where the gloss may precede the Sumerian entry.

4. For the trilingual lists from Boghazköy, see E. Laroche, *Catalogue des textes hittites* (Paris, 1971) pp. 47–54; for Ugarit, see J. Nougayrol *et al.*, *Ugaritica* V (Paris, 1968) 230–51.

5. Published in *MSL* IV 3–44.

6. Based on the one proposed by Landsberger, *MSL* IX 125.

7. For the concept of basic syllabogram, see, provisionally, Civil, "The Sumerian Writing System: Some Problems," *Or*, n.s., Vol. 42 (1973) p. 29.

4—Akkadian translation;

5', 5", etc.—Translations in other languages.

A code number in parentheses indicates that the item is optional; a code number written as an exponent indicates that the item occurs as a gloss.

1.2. MAIN LEXICAL SERIES

The most important compilations are first described in their final (canonical) form; see 1.3 for their older stages.

(a) Ea group. The purpose of the lists of this family is to give the simple signs of the cuneiform writing system with their pronunciation and Akkadian meanings. The lists are type 0–1–2–(3)–4. They include the main series á : A = *nâqu*, with forty-two tablets and some 14,000 entries, and a shorter recension ea : A = *nâqu*, with eight tablets and 2,400 entries, 70 per cent of which are preserved.[8] Syllabaries A and B, published in *MSL* III, can be considered more or less as direct derivations from intermediate stages of Ea (see introduction to *MSL* XIV).

(b) Diri : SI.A = *atru*. Diri has a purpose similar to that of Ea, but it is limited to compound logograms whose reading cannot be inferred from their individual components; it also includes marginal cases such as reduplications, presence or absence of determinatives, and the like. There are seven tablets of type 1–2–(3)–4, with about 2,100 entries, almost completely preserved except for the last two tablets, which are in fragmentary condition.[9]

(c) HAR-ra = *hubullu*. A thematic collection of twenty-four tablets, HAR-ra = *hubullu* includes legal and administrative terminology (tablets 1 and 2), trees and wooden artifacts (3–7), reeds and reed artifacts (8 and 9), pottery (10), hides and copper (11), other metals (12), domestic (13) and wild (14) animals, parts of the body (15), stones (16), plants (17), birds and fish (18), textiles (19), geographic terms (20–22), food and drinks (23 and 24). It is type 2$^{(1)}$–4. This inventory of material culture had more than 9,700 entries and has been almost entirely reconstructed and published in *MSL* V–XI.

(d) Lú = *ša*. A continuation of the preceding list, Lú = *ša* is a thematic list of professions, kinship terms, and various human activities. It, too, is type 2$^{(1)}$–4. At least four tablets, with 1,300 entries, or about 60 per cent of the whole, are preserved and published in *MSL* XII.

(e) Izi = *išātu*. A collection of compound words (as opposed to the compound logograms of Diri) or simple words, Izi is arranged according to the initial sign by means of the so-called acrographic principle. Thirty or more tablets have been very imperfectly reconstructed, of the type 2$^{(1)}$–4, and published in *MSL* XIII. A large number of the entries that have not been recovered are probably to be found in *Nabnitu*, Erimhuš, and Antagal.

---

8. For a few more details, see Landsberger, "The Third Tablet of the Series Ea A *Nâqu*," *JAOS*, Vol. 88 (1968) p. 133.

9. To be published in *MSL* XV.

(f) Ká-gal = *abullu*. Kagal, which is similar to Izi, has few sections preserved. Its extent and size are not known. It has been published in *MSL* XIII.

(g) SIG₇.ALAN = *nabnītu*. An Akkado-Sumerian vocabulary, *Nabnitu* is grouped by the Sumerian equivalents of Akkadian roots, which in turn are ordered according to the parts of the human body and the activities they perform. It is type 2⁽¹⁾-4. Of thirty-two tablets,[10] only twenty-two are preserved wholly or in part, but originally it must have had approximately 10,500 entries.

(h) Erim-huš = *anantu* and An-ta-gál = *šaqû*. Erimhuš has seven tablets with about 2,000 entries in all; six of them are reasonably well preserved. Antagal has more than ten tablets very poorly preserved. Both are Akkado-Sumerian thematic collections of triplets (occasionally larger sets) of synonyms, or two synonyms and one antonym, or the like. These two collections and *Nabnitu* must be considered as Akkado-Sumerian indexes to the lists Ea, Diri, Izi, Kagal, and the like. The more "logical" and accessible arrangement of items in the former may have been a factor in the restricted diffusion and neglect of the latter.

There are still other secondary lists which are excerpts or local recensions of the ones mentioned above, occasional collections of lexical items for practical purposes, and so on. Typologically, they all can be considered as derived from those already discussed.

(i) Commentaries. Oriented mostly toward the explanation of Akkadian words, this late genre[11] can be of direct interest to the Sumerologist when the text to which the commentary belongs is a lexical one, as in the HAR-gud commentary to (c) or the commentaries to á : A = *nâqu*. Commentaries to Akkadian works, such as omina or medical texts, are of indirect interest because they contain a fair amount of explanation based on entries from the main lists.[12] There are two types of commentaries: the older ones consist of two subcolumns with the word at right explaining the word at left; the late Neo-Babylonian commentaries offer a continuous text with the items separated by the cuneiform equivalent of our colon, indulge freely in etymologies, and frequently use quotations from classical works (Enuma eliš, Gilgameš, Ludlul, omina, etc.) as examples.

---

10. An NB catalogue of this series from Sippar, recently discovered by E. Leichty, shows that the number of tablets was probably much higher.

11. See the somewhat outdated remarks of R. Labat, *Les commentaires assyro-babyloniens sur les présages* (Paris, 1933) pp. 9–23; cf. also G. Meier, "Kommentare aus dem Archiv der Tempelschule in Assur," *AfO* XII (1937–39) 237–46. H. Hunger is preparing for publication a large number of commentaries from Warka. For some considerations about the commentaries from the lexicographer's point of view, see M. Civil, "Medical Commentaries from Nippur," *JNES*, Vol. 33 (1974) pp. 329–38.

12. E. Leichty's statement in "Two Late Commentaries," *AfO* XXIV (1973) 78 that commentaries "quote from lexical texts, but always from the late series like Antagal and Erimḫuš and not from the core lexical works like Ḫḫ or A" may be true for the commentaries he is discussing but does not apply to all commentaries. See my article cited in the preceding note.

1.3. HISTORY

Lexical lists have been found among the oldest tablets discovered at Mesopotamian sites (Uruk IV*a* and III).[13] Among the ones being prepared for publication by H. Nissen there are not only the list of professions (see *MSL* XII 4–24) but also lists of fish, trees, vessels, and artifacts. For the latter half of the Early Dynastic period, lexical lists are extremely abundant from Fara and Abū Ṣalābīkh, but, curiously enough, are almost unknown from Tello. Toward the end of the history of cuneiform writing, lexical tablets were still being copied assiduously in Persian and Seleucid times. Although wooden tablets (waxboards) are attested from the end of the third millennium at least, there seems to be no evidence for copies of lexical lists written on this material.[14] If waxboards were used, however, and are now lost, this could account for some gaps in the textual transmission of lexical texts during the late Old Babylonian and Middle Babylonian periods.

Period I: from the beginning of the cuneiform script until the end of Ur III. The lists are always unilingual; the examples of syllabaries are ambiguous. The lexical tradition shows great uniformity at all sites. As examples, one may quote the list of fish (see M. Civil, "The Home of the Fish," *Iraq* XXIII [1961] 170, n. 9) and birds (M. Civil and R. D. Biggs, "Notes sur des textes sumériens archaïques," *RA* LX [1966] 8, n. 1), whose survival until Ur III times is now confirmed by new fragments from Nippur. The scarcity of lexical texts during the Ur III empire is surprising. Could it be due to the strength of the oral tradition? (see 1.6).

Period II: Isin, Larsa, and Early Old Babylonian. There is a clear break with the textual tradition of the preceding period, and two main innovations: syllabaries, which become extremely common, and the addition of Akkadian translations. The canonical series (1.2 (a) to (f)) are based on originals of this period (proto-series or forerunners).[15] A few important lexical lists, however, such as Ugu-mu (*MSL* IX 49–73), lú-azlag$_2$ = *ašlāku* (*MSL* XII 151–219), and níg-ga = *makkūru* (*MSL* XIII 91–124), did not survive into the canonical period. Most of the tablets preserved, perhaps all (see 1.6), are school exercises. The interesting problems of the textual relationship between the forerunners and the canonical series cannot be discussed here in detail. Among the points worth mentioning: the series HAR-ra started originally with the tree list (Tablet III of the canonical recension). The late Tablets I and II derive from a list of legal terms, phrases from the old collection of "model contracts," and excerpts from Proto-Izi, but were first compiled in Old Babylonian times. The oldest dated

---

13. See *ATU*, pp. 44–47.

14. Of all occurrences of *lēᵓu* as the model for a tablet in H. Hunger, *Babylonische und assyrische Kolophone* (*AOAT*, Vol. 2 [1968]) p. 166, not one is a lexical tablet. (A recently discovered [fall, 1974] tablet of A V/3 is copied from a GIŠ.DA, according to its colophon.)

15. There no longer seems to be any reason to distinguish between proto-series ("Ur Serie") and forerunner ("Vorläufer"); cf. *MSL* II 2. The format of the unilingual series is 2 or 2$^{(4)}$, rarely 2$^{(1)}$.

forerunner to HAR-ra I–II is from the fifteenth year of Samsuiluna. The fore-runner to Tablet XV lists cuts of meat, not parts of the human body (which are to be found in Ugu-mu), and that explains the surprising absence of important parts of the human body in the canonical Tablet XV. The principles of organiza-tion of the lexical entries in Proto-Izi and Proto-Kagal, a combination of mnemotechnical economy and associative digressions, would make a fascinating study.

Period III: Late Old and Middle Babylonian. By a process that can also be detected in the transmission of such literary texts as balag and ér-šèm-ma, there is in late Old Babylonian a branching-off and a certain deterioration of the textual tradition. The main centers (Nippur, Babylon) must have preserved more effectively the tradition of period II, since the canonical recensions are based on copies from these places and are of a better quality than the recensions that are at the source of exportations to peripheral regions (Assur, Boghazköy, Ugarit, Nuzi). Few lexical tablets from period III have been recovered in the south. Erimhuš (above (h)) must date from this period since it is attested in Boghazköy, and SIG₇.ALAN is mentioned in the Kassite text CBS 10938 rev. 14 (*BE* XVII, No. 73*a*). The period ends with the textual stabilization of the lists.

Period IV: Canonical recensions. The origin of the canonical forms of the lists is not clear because of the scarcity of sources during period III. The only thing that can be said is that they must be the product of Babylonian schools before the twelfth century B.C., since the recensions from the time of Tiglath-Pileser I (1115–1077 B.C.) already differ minimally from the ones in the Assur-banipal library and are practically identical with late NB copies coming from Babylon, Sippar, Borsippa, Uruk, and so on. Lists of any consequence do not seem to have been produced during the period, except perhaps for "practical vocabularies" and the very secondary syllabary Á = *idu*. Most, if not all, of the commentaries date from this period.[16]

1.4. GEOGRAPHICAL DIFFUSION

Wherever tablets are found in substantial numbers, lexical texts appear. Mari, which so far has not produced any lexical texts, is an exceptional case. During period II, we have texts from Elam and Cappadocia (unpublished).[17] In period

16. Some OB texts classified as "grammatical" (e.g., Old Babylonian Grammatical Texts XVII [*MSL* IV 47–128, V 196) could very well be bilingual commentaries.

17. V. Scheil, "Vocabulaire pratique," *RA* XVIII (1921) 49 ff. (post Ur III!), and "Quel-ques particularités du sumérien en Elam," *RA* XXII (1925) 45–53. Dossin, *Autres textes sumériens et accadiens* (*MDP* XVIII [1927]), and van der Meer, *Textes scolaires de Suse* (*MDP* XXVII [1935]), include a large number of school exercises of a lexical nature.

M. J. Mellink, "Archeology in Asia Minor," *AJA* LXXIII (1969) 206, *AJA* LXXIV (1970) 160, *AJA* LXXV (1971) 164. Note that if "non-commercial tablets in three columns" refers to subcolumns, it can hardly be HAR-ra, which is 2⁽¹⁾-4, but perhaps it is a Sᵃ vocabulary, unless of course it is a so far unattested format of HAR-ra: 1-2-4, which is after all a con-ceivable format for a peripheral region (compare for instance the Kagal Boghazköy version in *MSL* XIII 149–53). The fact that the tablets have "a distinctive script and vocabulary" could point to an import.

III lists are found in Nuzi, Boghazköy, Alalakh, Ugarit, Palestine, and Tell el-Amarna.[18] All texts can be traced ultimately to the main series described above (1.2). Textual variations are either orthographic, due to local scribal habits, and mostly affect the rendering of the stops, or they are misunderstandings caused by a lack of familiarity with the languages: an Ugarit scribe will write, for example, eme-da-dagal-la for emeda-ga-lá, or will copy materials which were exotic in a town on the Syrian coast, such as fish names and toponyms of Southern Mesopotamia. For scribal misinterpretations in Boghazköy, see the remarks of Güterbock in *MSL* XIII 132–43.

1.5. INTERPRETATION

Taken at their face value, some entries in the native lexical lists appear to be incorrect. There is, to be sure, a fair amount of plain scribal error and misunderstanding, but most of the inaccuracies are to be ascribed to the missing oral component of the lexical tradition on the one hand, and to scribal conventions and abbreviations on the other. Disregard for these factors, especially when the lists are used through modern logogram compilations such as *ŠL* where the entries are listed mechanically with no critical comments, may lead to serious mistakes. Needless to say, the modern compiler has often compounded the problems by his own misreadings and misunderstandings. The case for the inadequacy of *ŠL* and similar collections was convincingly argued by S. N. Kramer many years ago (*Enki and Ninhursag* [*BASOR* "Supplementary Studies," No. 1 (New Haven, 1945)] pp. 31–34). One cannot, however, follow him when he overreacts to the lexical texts described by him as "a huge and more or less amorphous mass" of lists of "all classes and descriptions." Not only is it uncritical to lump together for instance Ea and Á = *idu*, but Kramer, forgetting that without lexical lists he would be unable not only to translate approximately the literary texts, but even to read them, is in fact biting the hand that feeds him. His apparent assumption that a lexical text ought to be derived from bilingual literary texts in order to be reliable is unwarranted and conflicts with what is

18. E.-R. Lacheman, "Nuziana I: Tablettes scolaires," *RA* XXXVI (1939) 81 ff. The Middle Assyrian (MA) lexical tablets, despite their many peculiarities, I consider as part of the main, not peripheral, tradition. Cf. E. Weidner, "Die Bibliothek Tiglatpilesers I.,"*AfO* XVI (1952–53) 197–215. Catalogue of lexical texts from Boghazköy by H. G. Güterbock, apud E. Laroche, *Catalogue*, pp. 47–53. H. Otten and W. von Soden, *Das akkadische-hethitische Vokabular KBo I 44 + KBo XIII 1* ("Studien zu den Boğazköy-Texten" Nr. 7 [Wiesbaden, 1968]). E. von Weiher, "Ein Vokabularfragment aus Boğazköy (*KBo* XVI 87)," *ZA*, Vol. 62 (1972) pp. 109–14 (should have been included in *MSL* XIII, Izi, Boghazköy A and Kagal). D. J. Wiseman, *The Alalakh Tablets* (London, 1953), Nos. 445–47. F. Thureau-Dangin, "Vocabulaires de Ras-Shamra," *Syria* XII (1931) 225 ff., "Nouveaux fragments de vocabulaires de Ras-Shamra," *Syria* XIII (1932) 233 ff.; J. Nougayrol *et al.*, *Ugaritica* V (Paris, 1968) 199–251. Cf. J. Krecher, "Schreiberschulung in Ugarit: die Tradition von Listen und sumerischen Texten," *UF*, Vol. 1 (1969) pp, 131–58. A very large number of texts are being prepared for publication by J. Nougayrol and D. Kennedy. Knudtzon, *Die El-Amarna Tafeln* (*VAB* II [1915]) Nos. 348–54; hand copies in F. Petrie, *Tell el-Amarna* (London, 1894); C. H. Gordon, "The New Amarna Tablets," *Or*, n.s., Vol. 16 (1947) pp. 11–20.

known about the lexical and literary traditions. Nevertheless, Kramer deserves the credit for having clearly established the need for a correct interpretation of the native sources, and for pointing out the dangers involved in swallowing whole what Deimel says. The mistakes of the modern compiler are usually quite easy to detect. Nowadays, only a beginner will be baffled by such oddities as IN.GAM.ZA for in-nu-ha (ŠL 148:50), or will take MUD.HU.ME (ŠL 81:32) for a Sumerian word. The inaccuracies, real or apparent, of the ancient scribe are another matter. A critical appraisal needs first a discussion of the native lexical tradition.

1.6. Oral Tradition

To understand and interpret properly the lexical tradition, one has first to realize the central role that oral instruction necessarily had to play in the training of the scribes, at least in the better known conditions of Nippur.[19] In later times and in other places the situation may have been somewhat different: a scribe from Boghazköy or from Assurbanipal's library may have learned his Sumerian from tablets. The OB Nippur scribe, however, learned to associate sounds and meanings with the signs he was being trained to write from the teacher's oral instruction, and certainly not from consulting a tablet. Otherwise, several facts would remain unexplained: the lack of a pronunciation column in so many tablets, how information which is not included in the most complete copies of Proto-Ea found its way into Ea, the omission of absolutely essential morphophonemic rules, and so on. The lexical lists are only a skeleton, the flesh of the oral teaching is gone forever. Scribal practices, alternative spellings, context analysis, and the like allow us to reconstruct some of the interpretive rules, but the recovery will always be partial. It is difficult to say when this oral tradition was lost. The latest tablets, with their emphasis on the quality of the original, the place where it was obtained, and the collation of the copied text, certainly give the impression of "library" copies that were intended to be read. It seems unlikely that the late NB commentaries, with their accent on etymology, could represent the original form of the oral instruction. The information necessary to interpret the lists is just not found in them. A corollary of the OB Nippur situation is that it is quite likely that we may not have a single "library" or "teacher's" copy among the preserved tablets of that period. The expert scribe was the one who knew the traditional craft by heart; as the trainee was approaching the master's stage, lexical tablets became less and less necessary to him. That may be one of the reasons why so few tablets with the final sections of the lists

---

19. For the transmission of texts in societies with a highly restricted degree of literacy, see J. Goody, ed., *Literacy in Traditional Societies* (Cambridge, 1968), in which suggestive parallels are offered; see also J. Vansina, *Oral Tradition* (Chicago, 1965), historically oriented. Although it has not been so far formally discussed, the concept of an oral tradition accompanying the lexical lists seems to be gaining acceptance; see, e.g., Krecher, in *UF*, Vol. 1, p. 133; M. Civil, "Notes on Sumerian Lexicography, I," *JCS* XX (1966) 120, n. 8.

have been recovered, in contrast to the innumerable tablets with opening sections that have been recovered (see *MSL* XIII 91).

1.7. SCRIBAL CONVENTIONS AND INTERPRETATION PROBLEMS

Leaving aside for the moment elementary scribal errors, it is not always feasible to distinguish between the abbreviating convention and the misinterpretation of the text on the part of the ancient copyist. The examples, which illustrate some of the most frequent scribal conventions, have been chosen in such a way that they will also show how the lexical tradition becomes progressively more explicit (and occasionally deteriorates).[20]

1.7.1. WRITING SYSTEM. (a) "If one of the signs which is part of a Diri compound can have a pronunciation that agrees with some segment of the phonological shape of the compound, assign to the rest a value which will allow the compound to be read as if it were syllabically written." The entry la-a : KAL in Proto-Ea, l. 339 is given in Ea IV 306 as la-a : KAL = *šá* A.KAL^{il-lu} *ni-ʾ-lu šá* A.ME; that is, A.KAL is reinterpreted as e$_4$-la$_6$. Similarly, nu-ú : KU = *re-e-i-a-ú-*[*um*] in Vocab. Proto-Ea, 22:1,[21] is later explained as nu-ú : KU = *šá* ÁB.KU *ú-tul-lu* in Ea I 157; that is, ÁB.KU = unu$_3$. Note that Proto-Ea apparently neglects this crucial information. The ancient scribes rarely made excessive use of this rule which still looks attractive to some modern Sumerologists who like to transliterate PA.TE.SI as en$_5$-si (why not ensi$_2$^{si}?).

(b) "Homophonous signs can share their meanings," for example, tu-ur : TU = *šerru*, and its usual synonyms (A VII/4 66–67) from TUR; še-e : TIR = *nâhu*, *pašāhu* (A VII/4 78–79) and še-e : LUL = *kuṣṣu* (A VII/4 129), the correct logogram in both cases being MÙŠ × A.DI and its variants. This rule goes against the principles of logographic writing, and so it is not surprising to find that it is not applied in genuine Sumerian texts, where such sign confusions appear only as rare textual mistakes.

(c) A number of artificial signs in Ea are never found in actual text occurrences: for instance, urbi(n)gu, written $\frac{LÚ}{LÚ}$ ×, or $\frac{UR}{UR}$ ×, replacing ur-bi—gu$_7$, "to have a fight," in the literary texts; there are many other examples of this, such as the large number of instances of LAGAB with inscribed signs in Ea I 48–131. This is a revival of an old tendency to invent inscribed signs, as shown by the large number of compounds in the Early Dynastic sign lists.

1.7.2. PHONOLOGY. (a) Emesal forms are listed in OB vocabularies with no hint as to their dialectal nature, for example, ta = *minû* (*MSL* II 145, l. 28), although Emesal forms are more or less regularly labeled as such in later lists. (b) Basic syllabograms can have undifferentiated values: [MU] = /mu/ and /g̃u/ in Proto-Ea. Ea resolves the ambiguity at the price of creating a new one:

---

20. See Landsberger, *MSL* IX 143–44 for some of these conventions.
21. Vocab. Proto-Ea is quoted according to *MSL* XIV.

old [MU] = /g̃u/ is replaced by [GU] which now = /g̃u/ and /gu/. The diachronic graphic correspondences solve the problem. (c) Some pronunciations are restricted to some lexical items: gu-u: KU = šá KU.LI *ibru* (Ea I 135),[22] that is, "KU is pronounced /gu/ in the word gu$_5$-li, 'friend.'" The statement is ambiguous, for it can mean "only in" or "as for instance in" (gi-in: KUR = šá ZA.KUR *uqnû* [Ea II 189] applies also to še-gìn for še-gín, "glue," in the Ur III texts). The net result is that one is left in doubt about the pronunciation of *all* instances of KU as a syllabogram! A pronunciation may be restricted without any indication of the fact in the lexical sources: NI can be read líd (Ea II 11) only in líd-ga, an old loanword from Semitic *litku*, obsolete since Sargonic times and as such unfamiliar to the scribes who compiled Ea;[23] the meaning they give (*litiktu*) is approximately correct, but the value is incomplete. Note that in this case the commentary to A II/1 has been preserved, and it too ignores the correct explanation. (d) The example of líd-ga illustrates the occasional survival of obsolete spellings, as in the case of the value zàr of SUM (Ea IV 126), obsolete since Ur III, when it was used in zàr-tab-ba, "pile of sheaves," written zar-tab-ba in Old Babylonian times. (e) Some alternations in spelling, such as s∼š in /sig/∼/šig/ = *šaqummatu* (cf. *MSL* XII 73 ad 846) are perhaps to be explained as the unsystematic updating of original sources from different time periods.

1.7.3. MORPHOLOGY. (a) Verbal root alternations of the type singular/plural, or *hamṭu/marû*, are often, though not always, indicated in later sources, but they appear as simple synonyms in OB lists: [su/tu-uš]: KU and [du-ru]: KU = *wašābum* (Vocab. Proto-Ea, 12:1, 21:2); for the second entry Ea I 144 adds *ša maʾdūti*. In fact, these alternations have often been discovered by context analysis and not in lexical sources, for example, ù-tu (*marû*)/tu-ud (*hamṭu*) (*SP*, p. 125). (b) Unexpected translations such as bu-ú: BU = *ina, ana, -ma* (A VI/1 187–88, 191) must come from a "syllabic" analysis of forms such as á-gùb-bu (< á-gùb-a), "on the left side."

1.7.4. SYNTAX AND SEMANTICS. (a) Some verbal roots have certain meanings only in construction with specific nouns and noun phrases (not only in the so-called compound verbs, but in other syntactic frames as well), but the lexical lists give the restricted meaning without indicating the distributional constraint. Such entries are very common in late vocabularies, but they are attested as early as Old Babylonian. The only indication so far in the lexical lists that zi—gi$_4$ means "to calm down," "to pacify" is gi$_4$ = *nuhhu* (*MSL* II 143, l. 12).[24]

---

22. The gu-u : KU of Ea probably corresponds to one of the two /ku/ values of KU in Proto-Ea, ll. 10–11.

23. On líd-ga see I. J. Gelb, "The Philadelphia Onion Archive," *Studies in Honor of Benno Landsberger* (*AS*, No. 16 [1965]) p. 58 (the correct reading is not among the possibilities listed there). Diri III 28, 32, give the word (with other logograms) as lidda; perhaps an assimilation or a confusion with the measure name ninda$_2$(?).

24. Cf., however, zi-gi-ba-an (Erimhuš IV 151) and zi-in-[gi$_{(4)}$] (*Nabnitu* X 221) both = *šuharruru*.

Selectional restrictions had to be inferred from literary contexts. Although the existence of these semantic restrictions is a very well known fact, and was one of the main arguments in Kramer's criticism of the lexical lists, one can occasionally find in the contemporary literature commentaries such as "in the expression geštu₂-ri, ri = *hasāsu*" (Å. Sjöberg and E. Bergmann, *The Collection of the Sumerian Temple Hymns* [*TCS* III (1969)] p. 54), or "sag-kešda = *it'udu*" (W. W. Hallo and J. van Dijk, *The Exaltation of Inanna* [*YNER*, Vol. 3 (1968)] p. 88).[25] (b) Cases of homonymy are solved in late, though not in older, lists when the specification *ša Y* is added to the Akkadian translation *X*; if *X* is a verb, *Y* can be the subject, the object, and the like. (c) What were the rules for the addition of t-forms or D-forms after the simple verb or, in general, of derivations from a root in the Akkadian column of á : A = *nâqu*? The same question may be asked about the mechanical accumulation of Akkadian synonyms.

1.7.5. ETYMOLOGY. In addition to the omission of part of a compound just mentioned, which can reach extremes such as lá = *erēšu* (from apin-lá), and, still worse, assign a meaning to a phonetic complement as in lá = *ṣehru* (presumably from di₄-di₄-lá), some Akkadian translations are the product of rather involved processes of etymology or word associations. An Old Babylonian Proto-A text gives níg = *jâšim*, which can only be explained as "possession = (what belongs) to me"; it is like translating Latin *mihi* as "property" because of constructions like *mihi est*.

1.7.6. STYLISTICS. (a) Only actual occurrences in context will show that bara₂ = *ašābu* (A I/2 358) is based on a mistranslation of an idiom. Sum. bara₂ can mean "throne (personified)," or "person of royal lineage"; in this meaning the correct Akkadian translation is *āšib parakki*, "the one who sits (or may sit) on a throne." (b) Opposite meanings may be given to the same word, for example, [sa-a]: SIG₇ = *banû* and *la banû* (A V/3 234–35); one of the meanings presumably applies only to ironical discourse. This stylistic device was rightly compared by Landsberger (*MSL* IX 144) with the word pairs called *aḍdad* in Arabic rhetoric: *ʿaǧuzun* can mean both "young girl" and "old woman."[26]

1.7.7. VARIA. As already pointed out by Poebel (*ZA*, Vol. 37 [1927] pp. 252–54), there are some "editorial" conventions in the lexical lists whereby instead of:

$$\text{value}_1 : \text{SIGN}_1 = \text{meaning}_1$$
$$\text{meaning}_2$$
$$\text{value}_2 : \text{SIGN}_1 = \text{meaning}_1$$
$$\text{meaning}_2$$

25. Instead of sag-kešda—ak; the previous remarks of Falkenstein quoted there are more nuanced and avoid the trap.

26. K. Hale has described a curious linguistic tradition among the Walbiri (Central Australia) which makes systematic use of antonymy. For instance, to say "I am sitting on the ground," the men, after the first initiation rites, will say "someone else is standing on the sky" (D. S. Steinberg and L. A. Jakobovits, eds., *Semantics: An Interdisciplinary Reader* [Cambridge, 1971] pp. 472 ff.)

the scribe telescopes the entry and writes:

$$\text{value}_1 : \text{SIGN}_1 = \text{meaning}_1$$
$$\text{value}_2 : \text{SIGN}_1 = \text{meaning}_2$$

with the result that what may be a simple morphophonemic alternation has the appearance of a phonemic contrast. The scribes themselves seem to have forgotten this convention on occasion and created semantic overdifferentiations: $^{du-u}$UL = *nakāpu ša alpi*, $^{ru-u}$UL = *nakāpu ša urīṣi* (*Nabnitu* I 88–89). Ea IV 151–52 gives now: du-u:UL = *nakāpu, asāmu*; ru-u:UL = *kaṣāru*, and so on.[27] It is hardly likely that zugud and zubud are two different words, despite their different translations *patarru* and *zubuttu*, respectively, in Ea IV 115–16 (cf. Civil, in *JNES*, Vol. 32 [1973] p. 60). For other "editorial" conventions, see the introduction to *MSL* XIV. There are many other points to be kept in mind when using the lexical lists, such as incorrect glosses frequent in the late lists (e.g., $^{ku-uš}$Ú = *patānu* in Erimhuš II 296, as well as the more serious u-ra-aš:IB = *nēbettu* in A I/8 39), but the preceding paragraphs give a fair sampling of the most important ones.

1.7.8. SCRIBAL ERRORS. Since most, if not all, of the Old Babylonian lexical lists from Nippur are school exercises, it is not surprising to find in them elementary mistakes, which appear also to a lesser degree in texts of all periods and places. In addition to erroneous substitutions of signs, omissions, and repetitions, there are also cases which show that the scribe simply did not properly understand the entries. The Akkadian equivalents of ú-gu—dé in the lexical lists are *abātu*, "to run away," *āṣû*, "one who goes away," *halāqu*, "to disappear," *lābû*, "howling," "bleating," and *šasû*, "to cry out"; *napardû* in Izi E 315 is possibly a mistake for *naparkû*, "to leave work." All of these meanings belong to the same semantic sphere, except *lābû* and *šasû* (or *šāsû*). One can try to save the reputation of the ancient scribes and assume that the last two forms refer to vocal manifestations of a lost person or animal (see *CAD*, s.v. *lābû*). In all likelihood, however, the scribe simply mixed up ú-gu—dé with gù—dé.

1.7.9. A SAMPLE CASE. In order to understand what kinds of problems the lexicographer is up against when unusual signs, poorly understood Akkadian translations, and scribal errors conspire to confuse the data, let us consider the case of U.PIRIG and its compounds.[28]

The sign U.PIRIG is clearly attested from OB to the Sᵇ syllabary, but it is, nevertheless, an infrequent one. Its reading is fairly well assured: ku-šu (Proto-Ea, l. 577; Sᵇ I 210, with variants ku-uš and ku-šu-um) and glosses

27. Quoted according to *MSL* XIV; the restorations in R. T. Hallock, *The Chicago Syllabary and the Louvre Syllabary* (*AS*, No. 7 [1940]) p. 20, ll. 144 f. have to be corrected.

28. See Å. Sjöberg, "Beiträge zum sumerischen Wörterbuch," *Or*, n.s., Vol. 39 (1970) p. 87, No. 13, for a partial and inconclusive discussion. I will not discuss here the precise meaning of Akk. *pašālu*; it would seem that the traditional "kriechen" (*AHw*, p. 841*b*) could be improved upon.

ku-uš (Erimhuš II 9) and ku-šum (*Nabnitu* B 146); Recip. Ea A iii 12 gives a slightly divergent form, ki-ši. See also below the passage from Antagal III.

The sign appears in the following constructions: (a) kušu alone, (b) kušu—tag, and (c) kušu—ki—tag.

The sign alone (a) is only lexical; if it does appear in context, it has not yet been recognized.

The form kušu—tag (b) is attested (outside of lexical lists) in: anše-edin-na bar-rim$_4$-ma kaš$_4$-di-gin$_x$(= GIM) kušu(!) (collated) ì-tag-tag-ge, "(the messenger)...s like an onager running on dry land" (Enmerkar and the Lord of Aratta, l. 415; S. N. Kramer [Philadelphia, 1952]). The sentence is one of many in this composition that describe traveling messengers. It is attested further in dùr^{ùr} en-gal-gin$_x$(= GIM) kušu ì-tag-tag-ge (Lugalbanda and Hurrum, l. 273, Enmerkar and Enmuškešdanna, l. 46), in úr nitadam$_x$(= SAL.UŠ.DAM)-zu ^{d}dumu-zi-da-ka kušu tag-tag-ga-me-en (for the reference and variants, see Å. Sjöberg, in *Or*, n.s., Vol. 39 [1970] p. 87), in [...] ⌜x⌝ mu-ni-kéš kušu mu-tag-tag-ge, [...máš-a]nše ⟨níg⟩-úr-4-e edin ní-ba lu-a (Enlil and Ninlil II 98–99), and in ⌜x-x⌝-gin$_x$(= GIM) kušu ì-tag-tag-ge (Bird-Fish, l. 147).

The form kušu—ki—tag (c) is found in: inim mah-a-ni-šè ^{d}a-nun-na-ke$_4$-ne kušu ki(!) mu-un-tag-ge-ne (for references, see Sjöberg, in *Or*, n.s., Vol. 39, p. 87).

The history and meaning of the last form is fairly straightforward; the Old Babylonian reference above is translated by *ip-ta-na-ši-lu*. In post-Old-Babylonian times kušu is replaced by kùš, presumably by a scribe who knew the pronunciation but was uncertain about the correct shape of the logogram; he decided to replace it by a homophone. Lexically, we have kùš-ki-tag-ga = *pašālu* G and kùš-ki-tag-tag-ga = *pašālu* Gtn (Izi E 329–30); possibly derived from this passage are kùš^{kéš}-ki-tag-ga = *pašālu* G and kùš-⟨ki⟩-tag-tag-ga = *pašālu* Gtn (Antagal III 221, 223). In order to fit the format of Antagal (see 1.2(h)), an entry KU-KU-ru = *pešēlu* was inserted between the two entries just cited to form a triplet. The final episode of its history is a literary passage: gašan-mu...kùš ki a-ra-ab-tag-tag, translated as *aptašilki* (*OECT* VI, Pl. 19, K. 4623 r. i 1–2). The translation and even the Sumerian morphology are correct, but the text belongs to a genre that probably was composed with the help of lexical lists.

The form (b) had a more complicated life, interwoven with that of (a). The starting point is: $^{ku-uš}$U.PIRIG = *šá-a-qu*, U.PIRIG-tag = *lâpu*, U.PIRIG-tag-tag =*nâqu* (Erimhuš II 9–11). The form U.PIRIG is clear in the source CBS 328; the other available source, a Middle Assyrian one, offers a sign form that looks like PÉŠ. In the Boghazköy recension (*KBo* I 44 + XIII 1 and 1431/u + [Otten and Von Soden, *Das akkadisch-hethitische Vokabular*, Pl. I], collated by Güterbock) the sign form is ⟨⤫⤬ and the Akkadian translations are mixed up with those of the preceding section, so that this branch ends in complete confusion. In support of Erimhuš as given above, one can adduce: $^{ku-šum}$U.[PIRIG] = [x]-*a-qu*

(*Nabnitu* B 146), at the end of a very loosely organized section that violates several principles of the arrangement of lexical items in *Nabnitu*. Landsberger restored [*na*]-*a-qu*, because there is a *tanûqātu* two lines above, but since there is no consistency in the roots of the section, [*šá*]-*a-qu* seems equally acceptable, if not more. An additional item is ki-tag-ga = *lâpu* (5*R*, Pl. 16, col. i, l. 37, and dupl.). But (b) seems to have a secondary branch: ku-šu-um : BI.LUL = *šá-a-qu*, *nâqu*, *nâṣu* (A V/1 176–78) and ku-šu-um : LUL = *šá-a-qu* (A VII/4 136; Ea VII 299 has *šu-ú-q*[*um*], but the beginning of the line is broken). Do we have a sign confusion with U.PIRIG becoming LUL, or just an example of the case discussed in 1.7.1(b), with *nâqu* included by attraction next to a bona fide kušum = *šâqu* (or *šâqû*[?], see below)? Semantically, the situation is extremely confused. The verb *nâqu* B is explained by *alâku* (*AHw*, p. 744*b*), but what is the semantic difference between the two? Observe that U.PIRIG—tag is said of quadrupeds in literary contexts. One could infer from the Erimhuš style and from the similarity of the Sumerian forms that *lâpu* is roughly a synonym of *nâqu*. The problem of *šâqu* is still more complex. It may not even belong to the same semantic range as *nâqu* and *lâpu*, since its membership in the Erimhuš triplet could be justified by the common logogram U.PIRIG. On the one hand, [lú]BI.LUL is a logogram for *šâqû* in MB and later texts; on the other hand, there is a *šâqu* with unknown meaning attested in ri = *šâqu* (together with *râdu*, *râbu*, and *redû* [Erimhuš V 204–7]), and in hum, huz = *šâqu* (A V/1 15, 29). I will not attempt to solve the problem here; my point is to illustrate what happens, unfortunately too often, in the study of the lexical lists. Finally, it must still be pointed out that in S[b] I 210 kušu is translated by *bûlu*, "animal herd."

1.8. Modern Editions

The first significant block of lexical sources was published by Rawlinson in typographical facsimiles (2*R* [1866] and 5*R* [1880–84]); the handcopies of Thompson (*CT* XI [1900], XII [1901], XVIII and XIX [both 1904]) replace almost completely the older editions, adding at the same time considerable new materials. These four volumes still constitute the main core of sources published in copy. Most Assyriologists (Meissner, Thureau-Dangin, Zimmern, Scheil, Meek, Langdon, Gadd, etc.) have contributed something new in this field. Worthy of special mention are the efforts of Chiera in *Sumerian Lexical Texts* (*OIP* XI [1929]) and of Meissner in his *Studien zur assyrischen Lexikographie* ("Mitteilungen der Altorientalischen Gesellschaft" I [1925], III [1929], XI [1937], XIII [1940]). Full reconstructions were attempted only for the short basic syllabaries (see, for example, the reconstructions of S[a], S[b], and S[c] by Delitzsch in *Assyrische Lesestücke* [2d ed.; Leipzig, 1878; more complete in the 4th ed., 1901]). The systematic reconstruction of all lexical series is the result of the insight of Benno Landsberger, who, realizing their crucial importance for any serious lexicographic work, devoted a great deal of his time and effort to the enterprise from the late twenties to the time of his death in 1968. The actual realization of the project received a decisive impulse when Chiera, then head of the Assyrian Dictionary Project of the Oriental Institute of the University of Chicago, asked Landsberger to prepare the lexical series for the *CAD* files. With the collaboration of L. Matouš and H. S. Schuster, he reconstructed HAR-ra, S^b, and Ea, and collected materials for the other series. After Landsberger's publication of the fourteenth tablet of HAR-ra (*Die Fauna des alten Mesopotamien* ["Abhandlungen der Sächsischen Akademie der Wissenschaften zu Leipzig," Philol.-hist. Kl., XLII, No. VI (1934)]), the first volume of *Materialien zum sumerischen Lexikon* (*MSL*) appeared in 1937. The onset of World War II interrupted the printing of a second volume with the series Ea and á-A, of which only a few page proofs remain. The work did not start again until the late forties, and Landsberger, who had joined the Oriental Institute staff in 1948, prepared the manuscripts of all the lexical series,[29] including a completely new revision of Ea and á-A, but excluding most of the unilingual OB forerunners whose extent and importance had not yet been realized. A second volume of *MSL* (different from the one planned more than a decade before) was published in 1951. At Landsberger's death, seven more volumes had been printed. In 1968, E. Reiner and M. Civil took over the editorial task of *MSL* and four more volumes are now available. *MSL* XIV (vocabularies of the Ea group, including a re-edition of Proto-Ea) should appear in 1975. Volume XVI (*Nabnitu*) is being prepared for publication in 1976. It will be followed by Volume XV (Diri), prepared by M. Civil. With the publication of Volumes XVII (Erimhuš and Antagal) and XVIII (miscellaneous vocabularies) the main task will be finished. It is worth noting that the lexical sections of the individual entries of *CAD* have already made available to everyone perhaps as much as 70 per cent of the unpublished series.

2. AVAILABLE RESOURCES

The publication of all native lexical sources, even after the most complete indexing, is only a preliminary step in the study of the Sumerian lexicon. The contextless words of the lexical lists are as dead as the plants in a botanist's herbarium. Only by considering the words in their syntactic, literary, and cultural context can we revitalize them so that their meaning can be established as a means to capture the messages from a past that is separated from us perhaps more by linguistic and cross-cultural barriers than by millennia. As things now stand, the Sumerologist must improvise a "dictionary entry" for each word he encounters in his texts. If he is lucky, some of his colleagues will have done part of the work for him; nevertheless, it is always a painstaking task that often detracts his attention from the literary and anthropological aspects of the texts he is working on. In any case, and for several years to come, he will have to write his own private lexicon. Where he gets his materials and how he goes about it are the subject of this section.

29. Many Assyriologists helped Landsberger in this task; see the list in *MSL* IX 124, n. 3.

2.1. Classification of Lexicographic Works

The resources at the Sumerologist's disposal can be classified under the following headings: (1) Logogram Collections, (2) Dictionaries, (3) Partial or Specialized Glossaries, (4) Lexicographic Notes, and (5) Word Indexes. Admittedly, the borderline between types 3 and 4 will be somewhat fuzzy in particular cases. Naturally, I do not include in the list either etymological dictionaries based on the signs' *Urbild* and *Grundbedeutung* or comparative dictionaries that attempt to relate Sumerian to any number of other languages. An example of the first type is J. D. Prince's *Materials for a Sumerian Lexicon* (*AB* XIX [1905–8]). The discovery of many Early Dynastic texts in the 1920's marks a revival of his approach. Deimel has an opening paragraph about graphic etymology for each sign of his *ŠL*, and he left at his death an unpublished "Šumerisches etymologisches Lexikon." A series of notes "Zur Erklärung sumerischer Wörter und Zeichen" (*Or*, n.s., Vol. 13 [1944] pp. 321 ff., etc.) gives an idea of its content and style. A recent demonstration *ad absurdum* of the inanity of this approach is K. Jaritz, *Schriftarchäologie der altmesopotamischen Kultur* (Graz, 1967; see the review by R. D. Biggs, in *BiOr* XXVI [1969] 207 ff.). The graphic analysis of pictographs is an archeological problem and totally irrelevant to linguistics. The comparative glossaries range from relatively sober, if misguided, studies such as P. Rivet's *Sumérien et Océanien* (Paris, 1929), to monstrosities such as Hilaire de Barenton's *L'origine des langues, des religions, et des peuples* (Paris, 1932–37), of the purest seventeenth-century erudite style. All of these studies can be safely disregarded by the Sumerologist.[30] The same applies to recent attempts to apply glottochronological methods to Sumerian (for a recent example, see *Current Anthropology*, Vol. 12 [1971] pp. 215 ff., with discussion).

2.1.1. LOGOGRAM COLLECTIONS. After a pioneer tradition represented by J. Ménant, *Eléments d'épigraphie assyrienne* (Paris, 1864), E. de Chossat, *Classification des caractères cunéiformes babyloniens, ninivites, archaïques et modernes* (Lyon, 1878), and J. N. Strassmaier, *Alphabetisches Verzeichniss der assyrischen und akkadischen* [i.e., Sumerian] *Wörter* (*AB* IV [1886]), R. E. Brünnow published his careful and precise work, *A Classified List of All Simple and Compound Cuneiform Ideographs* (Leiden, 1887–89), which presented the final form for all subsequent logogram compilations. Everything published afterwards, although not always of the same quality, can be considered a supplement to Brünnow's list of 14,453 entries. Brünnow limited his compilation to Sumerian entries, included bound morphemes, and, except for the latter, proposed no translations other than the Akkadian ones. The indexes are complete and include a list of all verbal forms in the book. Supplements soon started to appear, the more substantial ones being C. Virolleaud, *Premier Supplément à la liste des signes cunéiformes* (Paris, 1903), C. Fossey, *Contribution au dictionnaire sumérien-assyrien*

---

30. For a partial bibliography of such studies see Sollberger, *Le système verbal dans les inscriptions "royales" présargoniques de Lagaš* (Geneva, 1952) pp. 10–11, and K. Oberhuber, "Zur Struktur des Sumerischen," *OLZ* XLIX (1954) 7.

(Paris, 1905–7), and especially B. Meissner, *Seltene assyrische Ideogramme* (*AB* XX [1910]), which included 11,521 additional entries, but again, semantic pre-occupations were lacking. In 1904, G. Howardy modestly started his publication *Clavis Cuneorum, sive Lexicon signorum assyriorum* (London, 1904–33), with a new orientation and format: facing each page of hand-copied logograms and their Akkadian translation is a page with the Akkadian words translated into Latin, English, and German, with references. The work progressed very slowly and its last fascicles were printed after the author's death in 1931 by G. R. Driver. Several scholars helped Howardy in his last days, among them Thorkild Jacobsen. This compact and quite useful book unfortunately was not imitated. The last compilation of logograms was A. Deimel, *Šumerisches Lexikon* (Rome, 1928–33), completed later with additional specialized supplements. The first part, re-edited three times with important modifications, is a list of all phonetic values;[31] the second and largest (1144 pages) is the *Vollständige Ideogramm-Sammlung*, basically an updating of Brünnow and his successors,[32] but with the addition of some unilingual material: some entries from the Fara texts which Deimel himself had published in *Die Inschriften von Fara* II ("Wissenschaftliche Veröffentlichungen der Deutschen Orient-Gesellschaft," Vol. 43 [1923]); the Pre-Sargonic words that he was studying at the time for some article in the old series of *Orientalia*; and some Ur III materials that N. Schneider was collecting in close association with Deimel. The literary material is almost completely neglected, except for the royal inscriptions.[33] For the last fascicles, A. Goetze contributed references from the Boghazköy texts. The third part gives Sumero-Akkadian and Akkado-Sumerian indexes (the latter based mostly on Bezold). No one will deny that *ŠL* has been, and still can be, a useful work for the discriminating reader, despite its many defects: it is uneven, uncritical, hastily put together in a mechanical fashion, with many incorrect quotations. There have been some proposals to revise *ŠL* and to publish a "Super-Deimel," but the wisdom of such a project appears doubtful. The time for a dictionary centered on a logogram collection is past. A full index of the native lexical lists, based on the *MSL* editions, is an absolute necessity, but it must be kept separate from the dictionary proper, since it is only one of its sources.

2.1.2. DICTIONARIES. The only serious work that can be classified as a conventional dictionary is F. Delitzsch, *Sumerisches Glossar* (Leipzig, 1914). The entries are given in transliteration (with the key signs added afterwards in typographic cuneiform) and are arranged alphabetically (if that term can be used to describe the succession   a   i   e   u   b   p   g   k   d   t   l   r   m

31. The third edition unfortunately does not include the list of sources for the sign values given in the previous editions.

32. As a matter of fact, in the first fascicles of *ŠL*, the references are given simply by the numbers used in Brünnow and Meissner.

33. The skepticism about the literary texts was of course widespread during that period; "our only safe foundation [for writing a grammar] is either the pre-Sargonic or Gudea texts" (S. A. Pallis, *The Antiquity of Iraq* [Copenhagen, 1956] p. 237).

n ǧ z s š, based on phonological considerations). The quotation of
sources by museum numbers rather than by publication makes the handling of
this glossary somewhat awkward. Nevertheless, the importance given to meaning
and a good critical sense make this work of less than 300 pages worthy of imitation. Why it has not found continuants is a mystery. This may be due in part to
its idiosyncratic format and in part to the fact that it has not been easy to integrate
the data coming from lexical lists and bilinguals (the basis for the *Sumerisches
Glossar*) with the new material from the archaic and Ur III periods that has
been pouring in since the publication of Delitzsch's work. In 1954–55, R. Jestin
and M. Lambert published two mimeographed fascicles of a *Sumericae Linguae
Thesaurus* (later entitled *Contribution au Thesaurus de la langue sumérienne*
[Paris]). Their objective was to provide a concordance with contexts, with only
secondary attention given to semantics. The project was not continued. Without
being, properly speaking, a dictionary, it would have been a mine of useful
references far superior to Deimel's work.

2.1.3. SPECIALIZED GLOSSARIES. There are several varieties of specialized
glossaries, as, for example, those accompanying a restricted corpus of texts (1),
such as A. Falkenstein, *Die neusumerische Gerichtsurkunden* III (*ABAW*, NF,
Vol. 44 [1957]), and E. Sollberger, *The Business and Administrative Correspondence under the Kings of Ur* (*TCS* I [1966]). One can also include under
this heading more modest glossaries such as the one in I. M. Price's
edition of the Gudea texts, *The Great Cylinder Inscriptions A and B of Gudea*
(*AB* XXVI [1927]), which will continue to be useful until Falkenstein's posthumous edition appears. There are also monographic studies of a particular
lexical domain with the emphasis on vocabulary (2), such as the long series of
volumes loosely inspired by the "Wörter und Sachen" school, produced by A.
Salonen. They range from the *Wasserfahrzeuge in Babylonien* (*StOr* VIII/4
[1939]) to *Die Ziegeleien im alten Mesopotamien* (*AASF* Series B, Vol. 171
[1972]). Extremely useful for a preliminary survey of a lexical field, they are
basically secondary compilations, whose quality does not always measure up to
their bulk. And finally there are monographic studies that include all the items
of a lexical field and are oriented mainly toward anthropological and material
culture aspects (3). Although such studies do not contain a formal vocabulary,
one can be extracted with the help of the indexes. Works to be included under
this subdivision range from studies such as H. Waetzoldt, *Untersuchungen zur
neusumerischen Textilindustrie* (Rome, 1972) to B. Landsberger, *The Date-Palm
and Its By-products according to the Cuneiform Sources* (*AfO* Beiheft 17 [Graz,
1967]). These studies do not need to be in book form; B. Landsberger, "Über
Farben im Sumerisch-Akkadischen" (*JCS* XXI [1967] 139–73), covers the full
field of color terms. It must be noted at this point that because of the bilingual
character of Mesopotamian civilization, it would not only be inadvisable but
downright impossible to study the *denotata* by a separate handling of the Sumerian and Akkadian sources. As a result, as soon as the studies classified under

2.1.3 and 2.1.4 leave the lexicon proper to investigate the anthropological aspects of the meanings of words, they have to deal with both languages at the same time.

2.1.4. LEXICOGRAPHIC NOTES. The main difference between lexicographic notes and the studies described in 2.1.3 is that the former investigate individual words without attempting to assign them a place in the semantic sphere to which they belong. Most published commentaries to text editions are a series of lexical notes rather than explanatory remarks on the form and content of the literary work. A typical example is Å. Sjöberg's commentary to the temple hymns (*TCS* III) with its wealth of lexical data. The lexicographic note can be considered as a partial dictionary entry, the advantage being that its author can concentrate on isolated sections of the entry (for my idea of a complete entry, see 3.3) and can expand into "encyclopedic" considerations that would be out of place in a dictionary (see 4). A close examination of the lexicographic note according to a typological classification of its range, perspective, and presentation would be in itself a fascinating study worthy of a special monograph. There is no room for it in the present context, however, so I will limit myself to some general remarks. Range would include, among other things, the degree of completeness of references. The lexicographer must of course inspect all available references to the word under study, but in the exposition of his conclusions completeness is a condition neither necessary nor sufficient. Not all occurrences are equally informative, and the indiscriminate piling up of references, even when not used as a smokescreen to avoid taking an unambiguous position, tends to obscure the semantic results. Many Sumerologists still show a certain reticence in their use of Pre-Sargonic and Ur III administrative materials, which could be extremely revealing when discussing literary texts.[34] Because of the concrete nature of these administrative texts, words occurring there have a precision of meaning that can

---

34. An article about sesame oil (F. R. Kraus, "Sesame im Alten Mesopotamien," *JAOS*, Vol. 88 [1968] pp. 112–19), for instance, forgets the existence in Ur III of the engar-geš-i-ka-(ke₄-ne); Szlechter, *Tablettes juridiques et administratives de la III᷎e dynastie d'Ur* (Paris, 1963) Pl. 55, No. 26:3, Pl. 57, No. 29:3; H. F. Lutz, *Selected Cuneiform Texts* (University of California "Publications in Semitic Philology" IX [Berkeley, 1931]) p. 200, No. 78:25; *TCL* V, No. 6038 viii 16, No. 6049 i 3; etc. The contrast with the engar-gu-ke₄-ne would have reinforced the author's thesis on the one hand and spared him the incorrect statement that "ein...*giš-i kommt nicht vor," on the other hand. The Sumerian Ur III terminology is geš-i-(ak), "the oil producing plant" (well-attested without engar); e.g., M. I. Hussey, *Sumerian Tablets in the Harvard Semitic Museum*, Part II (*HSS* IV [1915]) No. 63:7; *NRVN* I, No. 31:2; N. Schneider, *Die Drehem- und Djoḫa-Urkunden* (*AnOr*, Vol. 1 [1931]) No. 303:2; H. Holma and A. Salonen, *Some Cuneiform Tablets from the Third Ur Dynasty* (*StOr* IX/1 [1941]) No. 36:15; geš-i sur-sur, G. Reisner, *Tempelurkunden aus Telloh* (Berlin, 1901) No. 101 iv 15; še-geš-i, "the grain of this plant," and i-geš, "the vegetable oil," the last two also genitives. Note, incidentally, the Soviet claims of having found sesame grains at Urartian sites: B. B. Piotrovskij, *Vanskoje Carstvo (Urartu)* (Moscow, 1959; Italian trans. by M. Salvini, 1966) pp. 200 ff. The neglect of the Pre-Sargonic administrative texts among scholars working on Sumerian literature is almost complete.

amply compensate for the difficulties of a diachronic approach. Presentation is of course of secondary importance, and some of the most important lexical contributions, for instance those of the deservedly admired master of the genre Benno Landsberger, are often written in a somewhat obscure and rambling style which, by way of compensation, gave Landsberger the occasion to make public brilliant insights on words completely unrelated to the ones he was discussing which otherwise would have remained unsaid. Mechanical repetitions of references to lexical sources and studies can have curious results: there are instances when an author says "for the Akkadian translation *X* of Sumerian *Y* see *ŠL*," and the only reference in *ŠL* is precisely to the passage upon which he is commenting! These defects in the presentation do not affect in general the lexicographic value of the note, but a faulty perspective can. The two main distorting factors are the ethnocentric approach and the Akkadocentric approach. By the ethnocentric approach I mean the unwarranted projection on Sumerian vocabulary of semantic categories, presuppositions, and cultural classifications applicable only to the standard Western worldview, or perhaps to only part of it. To show how difficult it is to get rid of ethnocentric prejudices, it is enough to consider the problems involved in the translation of kinship terms, despite the fact that the *denotata* involved can be rigorously defined in objective terms. The implications of the lack of a term for "cousin" in Sumerian have not yet been realized by Sumerologists. The anthropologist will conclude that še š and nin₉ apply not only to siblings but to cousins as well (i.e., that the Sumerian kinship system belongs to the so-called "Hawaiian" type). The importance of this conclusion for the correct interpretation of some mythical tales cannot be overrated. By the Akkadocentric approach I mean the procedure that stops the semantic investigation of a Sumerian word as soon as its Akkadian equivalent is determined. The syntactic and/or stylistic constraints on the constructions with ú—sud (see 3.3.2–6) could hardly be inferred from the occurrences of *patānu* in Akkadian. The use of zi—túm (with terminative), "to take refuge from a mortal danger," is the equivalent of *napišta abālu*. The sense is clear from many Sumerian contexts, but it could not possibly be deduced from the rare instances of the Akkadian idiom (cf. *CAD*, Vol. A/1, p. 18*b*, with the translation "to present oneself"). In most cases the help from Akkadian is crucial, but there are also many instances in which Sumerian solves a problem for the Akkadian lexicographer. Whenever possible, however, the meaning of a Sumerian word should be sought first in Sumerian contexts.

2.1.5. WORD INDEXES. Little can be said about indexes except that the contribution they make to facilitating the lexicographer's task far outweighs the trouble and expense involved in adding a complete list of words to all text editions, and especially to journals: *Zeitschrift für Assyriologie* and *Orientalia* are to be commended in this respect. Let us hope that other journals, such as *Revue d'assyriologie* and *Journal of Cuneiform Studies*, will someday follow the same path.

3. THE SUMERIAN DICTIONARY

After seeing what the Sumerologist can expect from the past and how he is coping with the present, it is time to look at the future of his lexicographic activities. The need for a dictionary is evident, and most of the materials are at hand; the discussion therefore can happily center more on how to make the dictionary than on its feasibility. The question "how does one make a dictionary?" is not an easy one to answer. As Weinreich put it: "The indifference which lexicography displays towards its own methodology is astonishing." If dictionary-makers are notorious for their disregard of the theoretical bases of their work, the opposite approach of wasting time in interminable procedural discussions without getting down to writing more than a few sample entries is a real, if less frequent, trap to be carefully avoided. Several years ago, the writer, in collaboration with Å. Sjöberg, who was at the time a member of the Oriental Institute staff, read a paper at an American Oriental Society meeting about a dictionary project, but nothing concrete came out of it.[35] Recently, an announcement has been circulated about a project directed by K. Oberhuber, but no technical details are available. Other proposals must be around, but none has reached the execution stage. I assume, therefore, that it is still appropriate to spend a moderate amount of time and energy to ensure that the end result of a dictionary project will fulfill some of the requirements that the recent progress in the field of semantics and grammar imposes on the ones who will have the courage to engage in the tedious and long task of giving us a Sumerian dictionary.

3.1. METHODOLOGY

The appearance of the *CAD* and *AHw* has been one of the greatest, if not the greatest, accomplishments of Assyriology in the last two decades. There is no need to stress that, because of the bilingual nature of the most important native lexical lists, the writing of a Sumerian dictionary without a reliable Akkadian one at hand would be a most difficult task indeed. But what concerns us here is not this obvious fact, but the potential use of the *CAD* and *AHw* as models for a Sumerian dictionary. The *CAD* and *AHw* are, each in its own way, fine examples of a descriptive dictionary in the nineteenth-century tradition inaugurated, it is customary to assume, by the *Deutsches Wörterbuch* (Leipzig, 1852–1961) of Jacob and Wilhelm Grimm. The question before us is whether the Sumerian dictionary should follow the same path, that is, imitate *CAD* or, if a more concise format is desired, *AHw*. In my opinion the answer must be negative, for

---

35. This is somewhat inexact. At present the Oriental Institute has (1) a word index that covers most of the Sumerian literary corpus and a good deal of the administrative texts, (2) a file of 106,800 Sumerian lexical cards of various kinds, (3) a computer concordance prepared by G. Gragg of 7,000 lines, and 6,500 additional lines on punched cards, partly processed, and (4) several hundred sample dictionary articles (mostly verbs).

two main reasons: first, two great revolutions, the structuralist and the generativist, have permanently changed linguistic science as the creators and practitioners of nineteenth-century lexicography knew it; second, anthropological linguistics has refined its methods of handling cross-cultural vocabulary analysis, and these methods have been successfully tested in the study of many exotic languages. For the Sumerologist to ignore these developments is tantamount to depriving himself of powerful means to arrive at a deeper comprehension of the Sumerian vocabulary, to minimize his ethnocentric bias, and, ultimately, to get a better understanding of his texts. It is completely impossible in the present context to give an adequate idea of the new concepts and tendencies in lexicographic and semantic studies to a Sumerological audience unfamiliar, with honorable exceptions, not only with the transformational-generative approach, but even with the older structuralist methods. I will limit myself to some of the consequences of the new approach:

(1) The lexicon is an integral part of the grammar, since, for example, the choice of the types of syntactic constructions is in large measure predictable from a number of basic semantic factors. Without a grammar there cannot be a dictionary, and without a dictionary a grammar is incomplete.

(2) The usual definitional descriptions of lexical items are advantageously replaced or at least supplemented by a more strict treatment, be it in the form of sets (matrices) of contrastive or specificative features, or preferably in the form of categorical trees.

(3) The componential (*lato sensu*) analysis is incompatible with the practice of writing a dictionary in alphabetic order and "making it up as you go along." Each one of the different classes of verbs, each set of related nouns, for example, terms for parts of the human body or kinship terms, must be studied together.

(4) Only the data that account for the shape and behavior of the word in the grammar, and the data that identify the *denotata*, need to be included in the dictionary. The "encyclopedic treatment" is no part of it. See section 4.

I do not believe, however, that dictionary-making, despite all theoretical progress, is close to being a precise science; no mechanical application of clear-cut methods will be capable of solving cases such as the one described in 1.7.8. A good dictionary is still above all a work of art and cannot be created by a committee, but it can, conceivably, be made in collaboration with other people, and probably should. A good lexicographer classifies the occurrences of a word according to the variations in its meaning, and classifies them as crucial, significant, or ballast good only for a concordance, using his natural instinct and flair, a gift that does not necessarily come with academic degrees and that cannot be acquired by reading the theoreticians; both may be necessary but not sufficient.

3.2. THE COLLECTION OF DATA

Next to the lack of a grammar, the single major obstacle in the preparation of a Sumerian dictionary is the relative unavailability of a main literary corpus.

Fortunately this obstacle is in the process of disappearing. Strategically placed Sumerologists have or are in a position to have a relatively complete corpus. I am sure all texts would be made available for a serious dictionary project. There are reasons to believe that the texts at our disposal form a sample of sufficient size to give a reasonably complete picture of the vocabulary of Sumerian.[36] A practical problem is that as long as the editions have not been officially published one cannot refer to the texts by standard line numbers, even if one has a completely reconstructed text at his disposal. Variations in the line arrangement of the manuscripts, the practice of counting as lines such rubrics as ki-ru-gú, sa-gíd-da, and the like (not counted by the ancient scribes but usually counted by modern editors), different textual recensions, variable estimates of lacuna length, all make line numbering highly subjective. When a text is updated or re-edited, the new editor does not hesitate to introduce changes in the sigla of the manuscripts and in the line numbering; Sumerologists would be well-advised to imitate the editorial practices in more experienced fields such as Greek and Latin textual studies. The minor aesthetic inconveniences involved in adding line 326a after line 326, or of leaving certain line numbers vacant (as is done in *MSL*) makes an edition immediately available for

36. This affirmation is obvious, I think, in the case of administrative texts. It can be demonstrated that a substantial portion of the literary corpus has been recovered. Van Dijk, "Une variante du thème de 'l'Esclave de la Lune,'" *Or*, n.s., Vol. 41 [1972] p. 339, n. 3, may be correct in considering some of the preserved catalogues (e.g., *UET* V, No. 86) as occasional inventories of tablets. However, when one can find duplicates of a catalogue, even though it has all the appearances of an inventory (e.g., *TMH* NF III, Nr. 55, now duplicated by Ni. 1905), some other interpretation seems to be in order. I believe that this is the case for the so-called Nippur and Louvre catalogues: (1) Despite their divergencies, they show an extensive common structure, a significant fact if they come from different sites, as my examination of them leads me to believe. (2) The first three compositions (or perhaps five) of the Nippur catalogue are the only ones (with the exception of proverbs and certain short tales) which are found in type II/2 exercise tablets (for this designation see *MSL* XII 27–28). Note that the first three are all brief compositions of barely more than 100 lines and of a relatively simple structure. That seems to point to a didactic arrangement of the catalogue, at least at its beginning. (3) There are cases where a composition has as a catch-line the one which follows in the catalogue: e.g., UM 59-15-1 has the Enlil hymn (No. 5), with the Keš hymn (No. 6) as a catch-line; in UM 29-16-198, Šulgi A (No. 1) is followed by Lipit-Ištar A (No. 2); and so forth. (4) The overwhelming majority of important compositions so far recovered are represented in the catalogues. Quantitatively, of the 62 incipits listed in the Nippur catalogue, 54 are identified (with four more tentative ones), and 46 of the compositions are virtually complete. The original extent of this corpus must have been around 14,000 lines (to be compared with the 15,793 lines of the Iliad alone). Of them, *ca.* 75 per cent are preserved, although not all of them are understandable and therefore lexically useful. Although some important texts are not listed in the Nippur catalogue (among them lugal-e and an-gin$_x$, which are nevertheless mentioned in the Louvre catalogue), most of the missing ones are royal and divine hymns with a restricted vocabulary. An analysis of the catalogue of canonical liturgical series 4*R*, Pl. 53 likewise shows a similar situation, though not as favorable as the one in Nippur, but again this literary genre calls for a limited range of vocabulary. Needless to say, new discoveries may change the picture, and unusual or archaic texts of exceptional lexical interest may appear, but in any case we have more than enough to begin a Sumerian dictionary on a solid, broad basis.

quoting without reference to the individual sources, a system that clutters many lexical studies and is impossible to use in collecting data for a dictionary.

As far as the collection of data itself is concerned, the size of the corpus is not so large as to preclude simple solutions. With excellent and flexible concordance programs for computers readily available,[37] it would appear that the best way to collect and organize the material would be through a computer concordance. Experiments in this direction conducted on two different occasions in the Oriental Institute (see Figs. 1 and 2 for samples of the output) make me skeptical as to the wisdom of this solution. In the first place, a concordance is not a dictionary. All concordance programs, unless one is willing to handle outputs of enormous size, give only a limited amount of context. A reinspection of the original edition when the reference is processed for a dictionary is therefore required. There were additional reasons for suspending, at least temporarily, our computer concordance project: (a) we considered that we had found satisfactory programs and acquired enough experience in the various stages of concordance-making (encoding, key-punching, etc.) to be able to compile one any time we wished to do so; (b) a concordance makes sense only when a textually stable corpus is available; and (c) we had not found a satisfactory system for including textual variants. A program for such a purpose is technically feasible, but those proposed so far have been too cumbersome or too indiscriminating. The best returns from our computer concordances have been in the field of grammatical studies. In summary, the usefulness of mechanical concordances for Sumerian texts appears to be somewhat limited. At present it seems that the best solution to making sources easily available to the dictionary compiler would be the preparation of a list of references (this can be done by computer, of course), and the microfilming of the corpus in such a way that, given the reference, the passage and the whole of its context could be located within seconds.[38]

3.3. The Ideal Lexical Entry

3.3.1. What follows is a very tentative sketch of what a lexical entry should look like. It is given here more as a stimulus than as a paradigm. No suggestion about style or format is implied; the time to write a standard operating procedure for a Sumerian dictionary has not yet come. It is not the form that interests me here but the contents, with one exception, and that is my contention that quotations must be given in a separate section within the entry and numbered consecutively. The reason for this is, I think, obvious. If the lexicographer wants to quote the pertinent references in the different sections dealing with orthography, morphophonemics, syntax, and the like, he will find that a linear system of divisions and subdivisions of the references is not adequate. The occurrences of

---

37. The current activities in this field are reported in the journal *Computers and the Humanities*, published by Queens College of the City University of New York.

38. Note that a standard 16 mm. Recordak cartridge could easily contain some 40,000 lines!

```
LH262 U4-BI-A ZI-DU CA3 KUC2-U3 D. EN-LIL2 -LA2 -KA    LH263 U2 NAM-TI -LA =I-IM DU*    LH264 ID2-HAL-HAL-HAL -LA AMA HUR-SAG -GA2 -KE4 A
-HAL -LA AMA HUR-SAG -GA2 -KE4 A NAM-TI -LA =IM DU*    LH265 U2 NAM-TI -LA -KA KA =NAM-MI-IN GUB / KA-GUB    LH266 A NAM-TI -LA -KA
B / KA-GUB    LH266 A NAM-TI -LA -KA DUB* =NAM RIG7    LH267 U2 NAM-TI -LA -KA =HE2-IM GUB +BU +A +KA    LH268 A NAM-TI -LA *DUB =HE2
U =NAM-GA-MU-NI-IB DUG4 / CU-DUG4    LH327 U2. I-LI-IN-NU X U2 SIKIL KUR -RA -KA KI-NA2 -CE3 =MU-UN GAR    LH328 TUG2. SIG2-SU3 -E =
```

Fig. 1.—Part of the entry ú in the Oriental Institute Computer Concordance. The head word appears in the center preceded and followed by as much context as can be fitted in one line of the output. Note C represents š and * marks capitals; the verbal prefix chains are preceded by = so that they may be listed together in a special section of the concordance.

```
TUK-TUK

A761S U4-KUR2  -CE3 DAM CA3 -GA -NI =HE2-NI-IB2 TUK-TUK INIM-MA =NU-MU-UN-CI- GA2-GA2
    A A-NA MA-TI-MA MU-UT CA3*-BI-XU I-HU-US-SU U2-UL I-RA-AG-GU-UM-XI
    L ANA MATII MUTU LIBBU AHAAZU UL RAGAAMU

A763S CA3 KI-AG2 -A-NI -TA NAM-NU-GIG Ø-A-NI =IN-NE-IN TUK-TUK
    A INA RA-ME-XU QA2-AX-DU-US-SU I-HU-US-SU
    L INA RAMUU-S QADIXDUUTU QAXDUUTU AHAAZU
```

Fig. 2.—Sample of a bilingual section of the concordance. S gives the Sumerian as in Fig. 1; A gives the transliteration of the Akkadian and L the lexical transcription. Only S and L are concorded. Note that in Akkadian X represents š (and C represents ṣ), and length is represented by doubled vowel.

147

a given word in context can only be classified in several sets with multiple intersections. The limitations of the linear system can be illustrated by a relatively simple example: the very first entry in *CAD*, "*a/ā*, 'that, those, the afore-mentioned' (a demonstrative of Aramaic origin)." Using, for practical purposes, a tagmemic frame (with ± indicating an optional item), the constructions with *a/ā* can be formulated as:

Noun + *ā* ± pronomial suffix ± number ± measure. That gives eight possibilities:

	1	2	3	4	5	6	7	8
Suffix	+	+	+	+	−	−	−	−
Number	+	+	−	−	+	+	−	−
Measure	+	−	+	−	+	−	+	−

All possibilities occur, except 3 and 7, for the obvious reason that measure implies number. The references are classified by the *CAD* into four groups: (a) followed by a number; (b) followed by a number and measure; (c) without specification of quantity; and (d) determined by a pronominal suffix. Note that (d) does not exclude (a), (b), and (c), and sure enough there are examples of these three types in *CAD* under (d). This inadequacy in the entry's subdivision is the rule rather than the exception in both *CAD* and *AHw*; both dictionaries mix the morphological classification by verbal stems with a classification by subject, or object, or both. The complete entry in a sufficiently explicit dictionary should give syntactic information about the feature ± ANIMATE of agent and patient, about the presence or absence of the dative complement, about possible infixes, prefixes, spellings, and the like. This information must then be followed by the numbers identifying the pertinent references; for instance, taking as example the arrangement of the entry s u m u (Sollberger, *TCS* I 169, No. 640), one could have: conjugation prefixes: b- (1, 2, 4), m- (5–7), vocalic (3, 8, 9, etc.).

3.3.2. The information that one should expect to find in a dictionary entry includes:

(1) Orthography: all graphic shapes of the word.

(2) Morphophonemics: various forms that the word takes in different grammatical situations.

(3) Meaning: translation plus semantic structure.

(4) Syntax: syntactic environments in which the lexical item can occur, rules of the grammar which apply to the item, etc.

(5) Semantic environment: conceptual or morphological relations with other items in the lexicon: synonyms, antonyms, compounds.

(6) Stylistics: stereotypes in which the item intervenes, etc.

(7) References, numbered and translated.

(8) Native lexical sources.

(9) Homographs.

(10) Bibliography, and remarks.

Note that etymology is not even mentioned. Somewhere in the entry, the item may be marked as a compound or as +FOREIGN, if it is a loanword, and the Akkadian, or other etymon should be given. Internal etymologies are implied in the compounds, but they have no value whatsoever for *predicting* the meaning of the item.[39] The verb šu—ti may very well be "*die Hand nähern*," and šu—tag, "*die Hand berühren lassen*," but this fact is a trivial consequence of the compounding process and contributes only *retrospectively* to the understanding of the meaning. "Etymologically" šu—ti could very well have come to mean "to caress" or "to punch in the nose," instead of "to take," "to receive." Some comments on the points above are necessary:

(1) The section must include all the logograms, syllabic spellings, textual variants, and so on. In this, as in the other sections, if diachronic changes are attested, they should be indicated. One of the spellings must be chosen as the head word. Traditional, but less well founded transliterations, such as kú instead of gu_7, will be better replaced. A typical problem will be the choice of the phonological shape of the head word: To give a simple example: do we need two entries mezem and pisan? The word is written with two different logograms: [1] GÁ and [2] ŠID×A (frequently abbreviated as ŠID). The phonological information is (with the logogram indicated in brackets): bi-sa-an (Erimhuš D 11 [1]), bi-zé-èǧ (An = *anum* III 82 [2]), me-zé-èǧ (Proto-Ea, 1. 238, Vocab. Proto-Ea A f 7 ([...]-zé-èǧ) [2]), mi-ze-èǧ (Ni. 1142:7 [2]), pi-sa-an (Ea IV 234, Sᵃ 66, Hh IX 49, Hh X 332 [1], Hh VI 224 [2]). It would be absurd to list all the forms as entries in the main lexicon; pisan is the traditional form because it happened to be the first one discovered (5R, Pl. 26, 1. 61a). Note that the value for GÁ is not preserved in Proto-Ea. The initial consonant shows the alternation b∼m∼p that may be phonemicized as /ᵐb/, as I have shown elsewhere. The second consonant is an example of OB [z] ∼ late [s] (cf. *MSL* II 28). It may be conventionally represented by [ś] (or the like). The third consonant is obviously /ǧ/: from the OB spelling -èm, from spellings such as šà GÁ-gá-ka gál-la (*TCL* V, No. 6055 iv 11), or GÁ-gá ù-mu-ni-gá-ar (E. Sollberger, *TCS* I, No. 290:4),[40] and from the sign name *pisannu*, which has a genitive *pisangaku* (Ea IV 229, 235, 248). An occasional late -na after GÁ would not be sufficient to invalidate this conclusion. What form must one choose as the head word? The narrower phonological transcription is /ᵐbiśeǧ/ or /ᵐbiśaǧ/ (I cannot discuss here the vocalic reconstruction), but it is advisable to use a broader transcription since not all occurrences of /ᵐb/ can be identified because of the lack of information in the native sources. I would choose bisaǧ, adding afterwards (/ᵐbiśaǧ/).

(2) This section must tell, for example, whether a word ending in [-m] is subject to the rule [-m] → [-n] before pause, as in ezem/n, or not, as in kalam; whether a vowel can be reduced in compounds, as in sikil > skil; types of reduplication of verbal roots; and so forth.

---

39. Note that the traditional definition of the compound word is precisely "a combination of roots whose total meaning *is not explicable* in terms of the constituent parts."

40. Translated by Sollberger as "in my (tablet-)basket," but in view of the rest of the evidence I prefer to take -gá as a locative.

(3) See 3.1 (3), with regard to supplementing the definitional description with a more rigorous componential and structural one, whenever possible. Some lexical domains are more amenable to this treatment than others.[41] Generative semantics uses other means and obtains deeper results. If its assumptions about the deep semantic structure (Universal Base) of the sentence are correct, the benefits for translating would be enormous. The old dichotomy between literal translations and translations *ad sensum* simply disappears. Whenever possible, meaning has to be treated in such a way that the connection with syntactic properties rooted in semantics appears clear and natural.

(4) What kind of agents and objects, what kind of complements a verb can take are examples of the information that must be included in this section; the dictionary must give such data explicitly, without its user's having to infer it from an *ad hoc* examination of the passages quoted. For instance, for the verb geštu$_2$— gub, "to set one's mind on," it must be indicated that it takes only +ANIMATE agents; that the goal is −ANIMATE, and it takes -šè if it is a nominal phrase, and -dè if it is a verbal phrase. Furthermore, if it is a nominal phrase, it is a place name; if it is a verbal phrase, it can designate any activity, but the verb's agent must be the same as that of the main clause. The verb takes the infix -ši- only if the goal is "pronominalized," having been mentioned in a previous clause.[42] The conjugation prefix is the vocalic one, with one case of ba-ši- in Gudea, which is at the same time an exception to the previous statement about the directional infix. The verb class must also be indicated, as well as related facts, such as that ù—ku (negated) shares many peculiarities with geštu$_2$—gub, and so on. It is, of course, out of the question to formulate this information in the informal descriptive way it is given here. Appropriate symbols, used systematically, will provide the information in a clear and compact form. The format will depend on what kind of grammar the authors of the dictionary are using. Note that all the data above refer to surface structure. If a case grammar or a generative semantics approach is followed, the syntactic frames and rules that may apply will have to be formulated in a much stricter way.[43] It will not be easy to define the border between syntactic and stylistic facts: is it significant, or purely accidental, that all occurrences of geštu$_2$—gub are in the third person, or that no negative forms are attested?

(5) Some near-synonyms should probably be dealt with in the preceding section: what is the difference between šag$_5$/sig$_5$ and zíl, both = *damāqu*, or between ku$_4$-(r) and sun$_x$(= BÚR), both = *erēbu*?[44] But true synonyms, as

41. For a relatively simple illustration, see H. Landar "Seven Navaho Verbs of Eating," *IJAL*, Vol. 30 (1964) pp. 94 ff.; B. Berlin "Categories of Eating in Tzeltal and Navaho," *IJAL*, Vol. 33 (1967) pp. 1 ff.; and J. A. Frisch, "Maricopa Foods: A Native Taxonomic System," *IJAL*, Vol. 34 (1968) pp. 16 ff. These studies are anthropologically oriented and apply a distributional approach based on folk taxonomies, which would be interesting to test on, let us say, all Sumerian verbs meaning "to cut."

42. This statement is somewhat hypothetical, being based on a single passage.

43. For an example based on case grammar see R. P. Stockwell, P. Schachter, and B. H. Partee, *The Major Syntactic Structures of English* (New York, 1973) pp. 717 ff.

44. The stem sun$_x$(= BÚR) will probably turn out to be a plural.

polysemy, do exist, even if to a lesser extent than is usually assumed. The synonyms and antonyms must be listed, for example, pà-(d) opposed to ú-gu—dé, zi—gi₄ opposed to du₁₄—mú, not only because they help to clarify the meaning but also because of frequency of parallel constructions in the literature. In general some explanation must be offered for words translated by the same Akkadian equivalent: thus, in the case of bisaĝ, one should also list the other words translated by Akk. *pisannu*, namely ⁱᵐše₁₄/te₆ (= ŠID) and ᵍⁱˢdùn-lá-ig. They are not true synonyms, but an explanation must be given for the translations of them into Akkadian. The convenience derived from listing all the compounds of a given word does not need comment.

(6) As indicated above, given the abundance of stereotypes in the literature and the absence of a sufficient number of occurrences of the same lexical item in different genres, it is not easy to separate syntactic properties from stylistic uses. The verb sag-kéš—ak occurs many times in the frame N_1-e inim N_2-ak-šè (late variants -ke₄ and -∅) sag-kéš ba-ši-in-ak, "N_1 paid attention to the words of N_2," where both N_1 and N_2 are animate, and N_2 is usually superior or somehow higher in rank than N_1. Isolated occurrences show the possibility of other constructions: nig du[mu]-ne-ne sag-kéš mu-ak-e, "the bitch attracted the attention of her puppies (and said)" (direct discourse follows) and nimgir-a-ni en ᵈhendur-sag-gá-ke₄ sag-kéš mu-na-ab-ak. Note that the Akkadian translation *itʾudu* applies only to the form with ba-. Note the fact that ú—sud, "to eat," which as far as we can tell, is said only of divine agents, takes a locative, and the thing eaten is never mentioned, or that šu/šú-luh—ak, "to clean," is said exclusively of canal beds; is this due to syntactic constraints or to stylistic tradition? Clearly stylistic is the use of geštu₂—gub with the modal prefix na- in the introductions to narrative passages.

(7) The reasons for having quotations serially numbered are discussed in 3.3.1.

(8) The passages from the native lexical sources may require some critical comments, if the entry is not a straightforward one (see 2 for details).

(9) The list of words written the same way as the head word, regardless of their pronunciation, can be a time-saver and can enable the user to avoid mistakes. Thus, along with the variant spelling kùš—tag for kušu—tag (see 1.7.9), the homographs ú-tag, "part of the plow," and ú—tag, "to weave reeds for a fence," should be given; similarly, hé-ši, a variant of he-ši/še, "to be dark" could be confused with the prefix group hé-ši-.

(10) Only essential remarks relative to dubious passages, semantic confusions, and the like should be given. Encyclopedic explanations and anthropological digressions on the *denotata* are to be avoided (see 4.0).[45]

45. The experience of the *CAD* shows the danger of adding, among extremely useful information, uninformative comments of an anecdotal nature; see as an example the amusing semantic *quid pro quo* "note that Ez. 16:4 speaks of the cutting of the navel, not of the umbilical cord," (*CAD*, s.v. *abunnatu*).

3.4. Preparatory Work

All lexical studies described in 2.1.3 and 2.1.4 are, in one way or another, positive and useful contributions to a future Sumerian dictionary, but I would like to single out a type of research that has up to this point been completely neglected by Sumerologists,[46] although it is indispensable if we want a good dictionary: the systematic investigation of semantic classes of verbs, and their syntax, following the methods of different grammatical schools. Besides the direct benefits for the lexicon and grammar, the use of different types of grammar would answer the question of which theoretical grammatical framework is the most suitable to the paleolinguistic task of describing Sumerian. Not only does the absence of informants preclude the use of the most common tests of a generative grammar, but the paucity of contextual data seriously hampers the use of inductive generalizations: what can one say about a verb such as h e š i, "to be(come) dark," of which, as far as I can tell, only three occurrences are known? Will we need to content ourselves with a tagmemic approach, which does not require the use of non-sentences for its descriptions? I do not think so, but the answer can come only from the actual tests provided by the kind of studies I am suggesting. Examples of such studies are physical perception verbs; how does Sumerian express the cognitive/active contrast (see/look, hear/listen, etc.) of such verbs? By different lexical items or by different syntactic constructions? Do these verbs include in Sumerian a third descriptive subclass, as, for example, in English "it looks crooked"? Or cognitive verbs; how can the polysemy of Sum. z u, "to know," "to learn," "to teach," be resolved? Apparently the only solution is by different syntactic frames. If the vexing problem of the conjugation prefixes ever receives a satisfactory solution, it will occur in this kind of study. Some important verbs appear to be "missing" in the Sumerian lexicon. Which ones, and why? Does the lack of a verb "to begin" force us to look for inchoative forms in the verb? The frequently heard complaint that, with most of the main literary texts either edited or in the course of being reconstructed, students are running out of subjects for their dissertations thus has an obvious answer. Lexicographic dissertations are urgently needed.

4. BEYOND THE DICTIONARY

Despite the contention that the dictionary proper should not include encyclopedic information, the fact that a Sumerian dictionary describes a vocabulary across cultural barriers implies that if one cannot write a dictionary without a grammar, one cannot write one without an "encyclopedia" either. There is such a work being published in the Assyriological field, the *Reallexikon der Assyrio-*

---

46. Note, however, that several chapters about verb constructions in Falkenstein, *Grammatik der Sprache Gudeas von Lagaš* II (*AnOr*, Vol. 29 [1950]), and classified there as syntax, do in fact represent an attempt in this direction.

logie.[47] Its publication was initiated by Meissner and Ebeling in 1928, and at the onset of the Second World War two volumes, covering topics through the end of letter "E," had been published. The work was taken up again by Weidner almost two decades later. Von Soden later replaced Weidner as editor; Edzard is the present editor. The last published fascicle (1972) covers the beginning of letter "H," so that, in forty-four years, only about one-fifth of the work has been completed. Changes in editorship as well as the personal orientation of the numerous collaborators make for rather uneven coverage of the subjects ("*Granatapfel*" has 25 columns and three full plates, while "*Gerste*" is dispatched in less than two columns), to say nothing of the variations in quality. What has been said above about the need to study the items of a given semantic field at the same time and in relation to each other applies *a fortiori* to the *Reallexikon* and its alphabetized articles. The usefulness of the work is undeniable, and the overall quality of the last fascicles is outstanding but its approach belongs to another era, to the nineteenth-century *Reallexikon* genre, exemplified by Pauly-Wissowa. The lexicographer is not always able to consult it with satisfactory results, because of the fact that it is partly outdated, too little of it has been published, and it lacks systematic organization.[48] The lexicographer is thus on his own most of the time and must improvise and assemble the data related to the *denotata* from all kinds of sources.

What is needed is a global survey of Mesopotamian civilization in an anthropological frame.[49] It is certainly a difficult task, but B. Meissner, *Babylonien und Assyrien*, Vols. I and II (Heidelberg, 1920–25), shows the way.

In the study of a semantic field, the investigator may look for "etic" or "emic" (to use Pike's terminology) elements and classifications. In the first case he works in terms of his own background and the principles of his own scientific field. In the second case, he strives to discover the native's arrangement and classification of the world around him and of the words which designate it.[50] Only

47. In 1968 the title was expanded by adding "und vorderasiatischen Archäologie" (Vol. 3, Fasc. 5).

48. The problems of coordinating material culture and textual evidence can be illustrated by the article of P. Calmeyer and C. Wilcke, "Hacke," *RLA*, Vol. 4, pp. 31 ff., divided into two sections: A. In der Archäologie, B. Philologisch. Both sections are informative and prepared by competent specialists, but no expert in the history of agriculture has been consulted, except for the second-hand source A. Salonen, *Agricultura Mesopotamica* (*AASF* Series B, Vol. 149 [1968]) with the result that the typical structure of the Sumerian wooden hoe (ᵍⁱˢal), correctly determined by Thureau-Dangin, "Notes assyriologiques," *RA* XXIII (1926) 31, and the only graphic representation of it on an Akkadian cylinder seal escaped the authors' attention; see my forthcoming edition of the Debate between the Hoe and the Plow.

49. As a first step, the Sumerian dictionary entries could be coded by giving at their end a numerical classification such as Murdock's in the "Human Relations Area Files," or a similar one devised *ad hoc*.

50. The field of ethnographic semantics has progressed enormously in the last years; see, e.g., the survey by B. N. Colby, "Ethnographic Semantics: A Preliminary Survey," *Current Anthropology*, Vol. 7 (1966) pp. 3 ff., especially P. Kay's comments there, pp. 20 ff.; and H. C. Conklin, "Lexicographical Treatment of Folk Taxonomies," *IJAL*, Vol. 28 (1962) pp. 119 ff.

154 M. CIVIL

by trying to look at the world the way the ancient Mesopotamian did will the lexicographer properly understand his vocabulary.

SELECTED BIBLIOGRAPHY

There is no general, up-to-date introduction to the native lexicographic compilations. The series published in *MSL* I, II, and XII–XIV are provided with brief introductions. See also Landsberger's remarks in *MSL* IX 124–26, and *JAOS*, Vol. 88 (1968) pp. 133–47. Still useful, but partly outdated and/or incomplete, are:

Schuster, H. S. "Die nach Zeichen geordneten sumerisch-akkadischen Vokabulare." *ZA*, Vol. 44 (1938) pp. 217–70.
Soden, W. von. *Leistung und Grenze sumerischer und babylonischer Wissenschaft.* Darmstadt, 1965. Reprinted with additions from *Die Welt als Geschichte* II (1936) 411–64, 509–57.

Major Collections of Copies of Native Lexical Sources

Chiera, E. *Sumerian Lexical Texts from the Temple School of Nippur.* OIP XI. Chicago, 1929.
Matouš, L. *Die lexikalischen Tafelserien der Babyloner und Assyrer in den Berliner Museen* I. Berlin, 1933.
Meer, P. E. van der. *Syllabaries A, B¹ and B with Miscellaneous Lexicographical Texts from the H. Weld Collection. OECT* IV. Oxford, 1938.
———. "Tablets of the ḪAR-ra = ḫubullu Series in the Ashmolean Museum." *Iraq* VI (1939) 144–79.
Meissner, B. *Supplement zu den assyrischen Wörterbüchern.* Leiden, 1898.
Poebel, A. *Historical and Grammatical Texts. PBS* V. Philadelphia, 1914.
Rawlinson, H. C., and E. Norris. *The Cuneiform Inscriptions of Western Asia* II: *A Selection from the Miscellaneous Inscriptions of Assyria.* London, 1866.
Rawlinson, H. C., and T. G. Pinches. *The Cuneiform Inscriptions of Western Asia* V: *A Selection from the Miscellaneous Inscriptions of Assyria and Babylonia.* London, 1880–84. Reprinted 1909.
Thompson, R. C. *Cuneiform Texts from Babylonian Tablets in the British Museum* XI, XII, XIV, XVIII, XIX. London, 1900–1904. Reprinted 1962–65.

Editions of Native Lexical Sources

Older, partial editions are superseded by:

Materialien zum sumerischen Lexikon (later: *Materials for the Sumerian Lexicon*). B. Landsberger, ed. (1937–68). M. Civil and E. Reiner, eds. (1968——). Rome, 1937——.

Important texts not yet published in the series can be found in:

Goetze, A. "The 38th Tablet of the Series á-A-nâqu." *JCS* XIII (1959) 120–27.

Hallock, R. T. *The Chicago Syllabary and the Louvre Syllabary AO 7761. AS*, No. 7. Chicago, 1940.

Landsberger, B. "The Seventh Tablet of the Series e a-nâqu." *JCS* XIII (1959) 128–31.

————. "The Third Tablet of the Series Ea A nâqu." *JAOS*, Vol. 88 (1968) pp. 133–47. Published simultaneously as *AOS*, Vol. 53. New Haven, 1968.

Landsberger, B., and O. R. Gurney. "Igi-duḫ-a = *tāmartu*, Short Version." *AfO* XVIII (1957–58) 81–86.

————. "Practical Vocabulary of Assur." *AfO* XVIII (1957–58) 328–41.

LOGOGRAM COLLECTIONS

See above, Classification of Lexicographic Works, for older compilations.

Deimel, A. *Šumerisches Lexikon* I: *Lautwerte der Keilschriftzeichen im šumerischen, akkadischen und hethitischen Texten*. 2d ed., with indication of sources; Rome, 1930. 3d ed., with some paleographic information added but no sources; 1947. II: *Vollständige Ideogramm-Sammlung*. 1928–33. III/1: *Šumerisch-akkadisches Glossar*. 1934. III/2: *Akkadisch-šumerisches Glossar*. 1937. IV/1: *Pantheon Babylonicum*. 1950. IV/2: F. Gössmann. *Planetarium Babylonicum*. 1950.

DICTIONARIES

Delitzsch, F. *Sumerisches Glossar*. Leipzig, 1914. Reprinted 1969.

Jestin, R., and M. Lambert. *Contribution au thesaurus de la langue sumérienne*. Paris, 1954–55. Two fascicles, GAR (1954) and AK (1955), published; discontinued.

LEXICOGRAPHIC NOTES AND MONOGRAPHS

For reasons outlined above, it is not possible to give a complete listing; the following are selected for their historical or methodological value (among the older ones), or to give a sampling of current tendencies:

[T. Abusch, J. Durham, and S. Lieberman]. "Lexical Index to Jacobsen's Writings." In *Toward the Image of Tammuz and Other Essays on Mesopotamian History and Culture*. W. L. Moran, ed. *HSS* XXI. Cambridge, Mass., 1970.

Jacobsen, T. "Parerga Sumerologica." *JNES* II (1943) 117–21.

[A. L. Oppenheim, *et al.*] "B. Landsberger's Lexical Contributions." *JCS* IV (1950) 57–62. (Index of Sumerian words studied by Landsberger up to that date. A similar list for the rest of Landsberger's production by A. D. Kilmer is in preparation.)

Poebel, A. *Miscellaneous Studies. AS*, No. 14. Chicago, 1947.

————. "The Root Forms sì(m) and su$_{11}$(m), 'To Give,' in Sumerian." *JAOS*, Vol. 57 (1937) pp. 35–72.

————. *Sumerische Studien. MVAG*, Vol. 26/1. Leipzig, 1921.

————. "Sumerische Untersuchungen." *ZA*, Vol. 36 (1925) pp. 1–10, Vol. 37 (1927) pp. 161–76, 245–72, Vol. 38 (1929) pp. 81–94, Vol. 39 (1930) pp. 129–64.

————. "Eine sumerische Inschrift Samsuilunas über die Erbauung der Festung Dur-Samsuilunas." *AfO* IX (1933–34) 241–92.

Among more recent works:

Alster, B. "Sum. NAM-EN, NAM-LAGAR." *JCS* XXIII (1970) 116–17.

Civil, M. "Notes on Sumerian Lexicography I, II." *JCS* XX (1966) 119–24, and XXV (1973) 171–77.

————. "Note lexicographique sur SUḪUR/KA." *RA* LXI (1967) 63–68.

Falkenstein, A. "Su-ùd-ága." *ZA*, Vol. 52 (1957) pp. 304–7.

————. "Sumerische Bauausdrücke." *Or*, n.s., Vol. 35 (1966) pp. 229–46.

————. "Zum sumerischen Lexikon." *ZA*, Vol. 58 (1967) pp. 5–15.

Klein, J. "Sum. GA.RAŠ = Akk. *purussû*." *JCS* XXIII (1971) 118–22.

Krecher, J. "Die pluralischen Verba für 'gehen' und 'stehen' im Sumerischen." *WO* IV (1967) 1–11.

Landsberger, B. "Über Farben im Sumerisch-akkadischen." *JCS* XXI (1969) 139–73.

Limet, H. *Le travail du métal au pays de Sumer au temps de la IIIe dynastie d'Ur.* Paris, 1960.

Sjöberg, Å. "Giri$_x$(= KA)-zal." *ZA*, Vol. 55 (1963) pp. 1–10.

————. "Beiträge zum sumerischen Wörterbuch." In *Studies in Honor of Benno Landsberger. AS*, No. 16, pp. 63–70. Chicago, 1965.

————. "Beiträge zum sumerischen Wörterbuch." *Or*, n.s., Vol. 39 (1970) pp. 75–98.

————. "Zu einigen Verwandtschaftsbezeichnungen im Sumerischen." In *HSAO*, pp. 201–31. Wiesbaden, 1967.

————. "Contributions to the Sumerian Lexicon." *JCS* XXI (1967) 275–78.

Wilcke, C. "Ku-li." *ZA*, Vol. 59 (1969) pp. 65–99.

GENERAL LEXICOGRAPHY AND SEMANTICS

A general but insufficient survey of the theoretical problems is given by L. Zgusta, *Manual of Lexicography* (Prague, 1971), more interesting for its general overview of the field of dictionary-making and for its discussion of practical, concrete problems. As a general orientation for the reader who is more inclined to go to the root of the problem, the anthology edited by D. D. Steinberg and L. A. Jakobovits, *Semantics: An Interdisciplinary Reader in Philosophy, Linguistics, and Psychology* (Cambridge, 1971), contains some useful chapters. I would recommend that the reader begin with H. Maclay's "Overview" (pp. 157 ff.), continue with the section on the lexicon (pp. 370 ff.), and then tackle the more theoretical parts (pp. 183 ff.). *Studies in Linguistic Semantics*, edited by C. J. Fillmore and D. T. Langendoen (New York, 1971), may also be of interest. Older views, with more empirical information, can be found in F. W. Householder and S. Saporta, eds., *Problems in Lexicography*, Part IV of *IJAL*, Vol. 28/2 (Bloomington, 1962), and E. A. Hammel, ed., *Formal Semantic Analysis*, special publication of *American Anthropologist*, Vol. 67/2 (1965).

THE OLD BABYLONIAN EDUBA

Å. W. Sjöberg

Philadelphia

I. INTRODUCTION

é an-gin$_x$ uru$_4$ gar-ra	"A house with a foundation like heaven,
é dub-pisan-gin$_x$ gada mu-un-dul	A house which like a...vessel has been covered with linen,
é uz-gin$_x$ ki-gal-la gub-ba	A house which like a goose stands on a (firm) base,
igi nu-bad ba-an-ku$_4$	One with eyes not opened has entered it,
igi-bad ba-an-ta-è	One with open eyes has come out of it.
ki-búr-bi é-dub-ba-a	Its solution: the school."
	(Sumerian riddle)

Sumerian é-dub-ba-a[1] is translated into Akkadian as *bīt tuppi*, literally, "the tablet house." Bruno Meissner was the first one who translated *bīt tuppi* as "Schule" (school).[2]

In this article dedicated to Professor Thorkild Jacobsen, I concentrate on the curriculum in the Old Babylonian eduba. The institution of learning, the eduba,

---

1. Also written é-dub-ba. References for é-dub-ba-a have been collected by A. Falkenstein, "Der 'Sohn des Tafelhauses,'" *WO* I (1948) 174–75. The writing is puzzling; Falkenstein called it "merkwürdige Pleneschreibung." B. Landsberger (private communication) suggested that the word for "school" was written é-dub-ba-a to keep it apart from the word for "storehouse," é-DUB-ba (= é-kišìb-ba). Landsberger thought, however, that this explanation might "als künstlich gelten." Cf. also D. O. Edzard, in *AfO* XXIII (1970) 92, n. 5. In this connection, I refer the reader to Proto-Lu, ll. 40 and 42, šà-tam-é-dub-ba-a, where obviously one line should be read é-kišìb-ba-a (cf. *MSL* XII 68). See further *MSL* XII 98, 138b, [šà-ta]m-é-dub-ba-a, where it probably should be read -é-kišìb-ba-a (cf. the two preceding lines). Note also writing gi-dub-ba-a, and see, for instance, *SKIZ*, p. 24, l. 22, gi-dub-ba with var. gi-dub-ba-a; *UET* VI/2, No. 150:11, gi-dub-ba-a with var. gi-⟨dub⟩-ba-a-bi in CBS 13984, col. i.

2. *Babylonien und Assyrien* II (Heidelberg, 1925) 324.

159

is also specifically Old Babylonian, and as an institution of education, the eduba
seems to die out at the end of the Old Babylonian period.[3]

There are, however, two references to *bīt ṭuppi* in the post-Old-Babylonian
period: *mār ᵈbēl ištu* É *ṭup-pi ana ha-am-mu-[ti* x x], "the son of Bēl (Nabû) (goes)
from the *bīt ṭuppi* to (the place) where he lives as master" (*KAR*, No.
122:10),
and, in a ritual text from Boghazköy, *šīnāt imērim ina ṭīdi ša bīt ṭuppi tuballal*,
"you shall mix urine from a donkey with clay from *bīt ṭuppi*" (*ZA*, Vol. 45
[1939] p. 200, l. 4). We assume that the *bīt ṭuppi* in the first passage does not refer
to the eduba as a still living institution of learning. As a patron of the scribes,
Nabû is here connected with the old school, which in this text has a "mythological" character. The second passage is no proof of the existence of a *bīt ṭuppi*
in Boghazköy since the text is probably a copy of an Old Babylonian text.[4]

The following reconstruction of the curriculum in the Old Babylonian eduba
is based on the so-called Eduba Dialogues (to be published by M. Civil), where
we frequently meet with negative statements made by a student about one of his
classmates. But, as the reader will see, I often quote the so-called Examination
Text A, although this text, dealing with an exam in the *bīt ṭuppi*, is not from the
Old Babylonian period.[5] The oldest copies of Examination Text A are from Assur
(written about 900 B.C.), and the latest texts are Seleucid. Mention of the eduba
(l. 2, kisal-é-dub-b[a-a-ka] = *kisal* [*bīt ṭuppi*], and l. 4, é-dub-ba-a
i-ti-le-[en] = *ina bīt ṭuppi aš*[*bāt*]) shows, however, that this text reflects the
Old Babylonian curriculum. I have used this text only when I have been able to
find parallels in Old Babylonian texts dealing with the eduba.

Outside of the eduba texts, the school is mentioned in some royal
hymns, where the kings refer to their education in the eduba (see below). It is also
mentioned in three Old Babylonian letters: *ana bīt ṭuppim* (= É.DUB.BA.A)
alākam šūhissu qassu hītma usātam ina muhhišu šukun, "instruct him (my son)

---

3. We assume that the education in post-Old-Babylonian times was "private" in the sense
that fathers taught their sons. Families of scribes come into existence, claiming descent from
ancestors, some of whom are known as authors or editors of literary texts; cf. W. G. Lambert,
"A Catalogue of Texts and Authors," *JCS* XVI (1962) 59–77.

4. There is, however, one reference to an É.DUB.BA.A in a Hittite text: *Ankara Arkeoloji
Müzesinde bulunan Boğazköy Tabletleri* ("Boğazköy-Tafeln im Archäologischen Museum zu
Ankara," [Istanbul, 1948]) No. 65 rev. 8; cf. J. Friedrich, *Hethitisches Wörterbuch* (Heidelberg, 1952) p. 270; Liane Rost, "Die ausserhalb Boğazköy gefundenen hethitische Briefe,"
MIO IV (1956) 345 ff. In this connection, I should like to refer the reader to *BE* XVII, No.
31:10 (Kassite period letter), *lišânimma ana ihzi lišîbâ*, "let them (the two girls)
come out and sit for instruction"; *CAD*, Vol. I/J, p. 47a, "for instruction (in singing)";
A. L. Oppenheim, *Letters from Mesopotamia* (Chicago, 1967) p. 118, No. 62, "they can both
leave and attend school." Oppenheim's translation could lead the reader to assume the
existence of *bīt ṭuppi* during the Kassite period, but this assumption is not supported by the
passage. Even the scribal activity in the Old Scribal Quarter at Nippur in Assyrian, Neo-
Babylonian, and Achaemenian levels (D. E. McCown and R. C. Haines, *Nippur* I [*OIP*
LXXVIII (1967)] p. 149) does not prove the existence of a *bīt ṭuppi* in post-Old-Babylonian
times in that city.

5. See Sjöberg, "Examenstext A," *ZA*, Vol. 64 (1975) pp. 137–76.

to go to school; watch over his hand(writing) and help him" (*CT* II, Pl. 11, ll. 29–31);[6] *ana bīt ṭuppim* (= É.DUB.BA.A) *irumma* gá-nu *aštanassi u kammi ša* gá-nu *ša tēzibam uṭâb*, "I(!) entered the school and read (the composition beginning with) gá-nu, correcting the tablet of gá-nu, which you left" (*TLB* IV 84, ll. 21–23); and PN DUB.SAR.ZAG.GA *ša ana* PN₂ [*išš*]*aknu ana ṭupšarrūtim utīrma ana* É.DUB.BA *i*[*ru*]*b* (*PBS* VII, No. 89 rev. 36–37; courtesy of Dr. Ria de J. Ellis; translated in *CAD*, Vol. Z, p. 75, s.v. *zazakku*).

II. INSTRUCTION IN THE EDUBA

THE LANGUAGE OF INSTRUCTION

Since we concentrate on the Old Babylonian school, the question "What language was the medium of instruction in the Old Babylonian eduba?" is legitimate. C. J. Gadd assumed that instruction in the schools was given entirely in Sumerian.[7] He found it hard to understand how the Sumerian language came to be distinguished as a "subject" at all, "for the whole instruction appears to have been carried out in Sumerian, and proficiency in that language to have been both the aim and the criterion of teaching."

In this connection, I should like to refer the reader to the proverb, dub-sar eme-gi₇ nu-mu-un-zu-a inim-bal-e me-da hé-en-tùm, "a scribe who does not know Sumerian, how shall he properly convey a translation?"[8] In his commentary to this proverb, Gordon quotes a passage from an eduba text "if there is a translation to be made from the Sumerian, the Sumerian is hidden from you" (*SEM*, No. 67 i 7–8; see now the dupl. *UET* VI/2, No. 167:41–42). According to Gordon, the implication of both these passages seems to be that Sumerian was not the native tongue of these scribes and perhaps it was no longer a living language at the time these passages were composed.[9] Another proverb points in this direction, as well: dub-sar eme-gi₇ nu-mu-un-zu-a a-na-àm dub-sar e-ne, "a scribe who does not know Sumerian, what (kind of) a scribe is he?"[10] The following passages from eduba texts support the assumption that Sumerian was not a living language but had to be learned in school: ú-húb-nam-dub-sar-ra ú-ug-eme-gi₇-ra, "he is a deaf fool when it comes to the scribal art, a silent idiot when it comes to Sumerian" (Enkimansum and Girini-isag, l. 10, *UET* VI/2, No. 150:10, CBS 13984 i 6′); eme-gi₇-šè eme-zu si nu-ub-sá, "your tongue is not adapted to the Sumerian language"

---

6. See R. Frankena, *Briefe aus dem British Museum* ("Altbabylonische Briefe in Umschrift und Übersetzung," Vol. 2 [Leiden, 1966]) p. 48, No. 81 (text collated by Frankena).

7. *Teachers and Students in the Oldest Schools* (London, 1956) p. 18.

8. *SP*, p. 208, Coll. 2.49.

9. See now also J. S. Cooper, "Sumerian and Akkadian in Sumer and Akkad," *Or*, n.s., Vol. 42 (1973) pp. 239–46.

10. *SP*, p. 206, Coll. 2.47.

(Dialogue 1 [Two Scribes], l. 56); eme-gi₇-šè al-dugud eme-ni si nu-ub-sá, "he is 'heavy' for the Sumerian language, he cannot move his tongue correctly" (Enkitalu and Enkihegal, l. 97, *TMH* NF III, No. 42 ii 13 and dupl.).

We cannot deny the possibility, however, that the instruction initially was carried out in Babylonian but in more advanced classes in Sumerian. The teaching of Sumerian, now dead, also aimed at proficiency in speaking the language. In this connection I refer the reader again to an eduba text, gá-e-gin₇-nam eme-gi₇-ra-me-en, "do you, as I do, speak Sumerian?" or, literally, "are you of Sumerian language?" (Enkimansum and Girini-isag, *UET* VI/2, No. 150:66), a passage which shows, in my opinion, that bilingualism was pursued in the eduba.[11] Note also that Enkitalu, after having charged Enkihegal with not keeping the rules in the eduba, says: ᵐᵈen-ki-he-gál eme-2-àm igi-zu-uš ga-ab-du₁₁, "(and) that I will tell you in both languages, Enkihegal!" (Enkitalu and Enkihegal, l. 6).

THE CURRICULUM OF INSTRUCTION

Language

The vocabularies copied, studied, and used in the eduba seem to have been Proto-Ea = *naqû*, the tu-ta-ti series, and the series a-a, a-a-a (so-called Silbenalphabet B, not to be confused with the Vocabulary Sᵇ in *MSL* III 90–153). More advanced students copied and studied the "forerunners" of the lexical series ur₅-ra = *hubullu* and lú = *ša* and further the "forerunners" of the series diri = *atru*, izi = *išātu*, and ká-gal = *abullu*.[12]

There are two references to syllabaries in Sumerian texts from the Old Babylonian period: d[ub]-ki-e ⌜n⌝-g[i]-k ⌜i⌝-uri-ke₄ a-a me-me-ta...i-sar, "the tablets of Sumer and Akkad, from a-a (and) me-me...I have written"

---

11. See also *UET* VI/2, No. 150:61 (Enkimansum and Girini-isag, l. 61): a-ru-a-mu eme-gi₇-ra-àm dumu-dub-sar-ra-me-en, "my father speaks Sumerian, I am a son of a scribe." This passage has been translated variously, by C. J. Gadd (*Teachers and Students*, p. 33) as "Gifted with a Sumerian name, one who has written from (his) childhood am I" (Gadd read tur-ta sar-ra instead of dumu-dub-sar-ra-, see copy); by E. I. Gordon (*SP*, p. 528) as "My (special) gift is (the) Sumerian (language), (for) I am the son of a scribe!"; by S. N. Kramer (*The Sumerians* [Chicago, 1963] p. 242) as "I was raised on Sumerian." In *MNS* I 30, I translated as follows: "Mein Erzeuger (Vater) ist ein Sumerer." But a-ru-a could also be connected with im-ru-a, im-ri-a (=*kimtu*, "family"; see Å. W. Sjöberg, "Zu einigen Verwandtschaftsbezeichnungen im Sumerischen," *HSAO*, pp. 202–9). The passage is ambiguous: (1) the father was a "Sumerian" and consequently the Sumerian language was his native tongue; he had received his education in the eduba and his son followed his profession (see Å. W. Sjöberg, "Der Vater und sein missratener Sohn," *JCS* XXV [1973] 112, ll. 115–16); (2) the father has received his education in the eduba, where he learned Sumerian; Babylonian was his native tongue; (3) if a-ru-a here means "family," this passage states that his family was Sumerian, that Sumerian was their native tongue.

12. See B. Landsberger, "Zum 'Silbenalphabet B,'" *Zwei altbabylonische Schulbücher aus Nippur* (Ankara, 1959) p. 98 and n. 3.

(*UET* VI/2, No. 167:14–15, and unpub. dupls.),[13] and lú a-a nu-mu-un-da-aka-da-àm eme-kaš$_4$-kaš$_4$ me-da hé-en-tùm, "a fellow who cannot produce (the vocabulary beginning with) a-a, how will he attain fluent speech?" (*SP*, p. 207, Coll. 2.48).[14] After having mentioned a-a and me-me, the first of these two texts reads as follows: mu-didli-^{d}inanna-téš-ta en-na nì-zi-gál-eden-na zà-lú-šu-du$_{11}$ (var. lú-gašam)-šè ì-sar, which I translate, "I have written (a tablet) from the different names of Inanna up to (the names of) the animals living in the steppe (and the names of the different) artisans" (*UET* VI/2, No. 167:16–17; *Or*, n.s., Vol. 22, Pl. XLII, Ni. 9718: 2–3).[15] The first line of this eduba text indicates that the student copied and studied god lists. "(The names of) the animals living in the steppe" is at least a part of ur$_5$-ra = *hubullu*, Tablet XIV (*MSL* VIII); "(the names of) artisans" may refer to the lexical series lú = *ša*. Several other references to vocabularies occur in Dialogue 1; for example in lines 2–5 (UM 55-21-315 obv. i 2–5 and dupls. with further variants), we read:

tukum-bi nam-dub-sar-ra ì-zu a-na-àm ì-šid
mu-didli-zi-ga-nam-dub-sar-ra[16]
nì-zi-gál-eden-na zà-lú-šu-du$_{11}$-šè (var. -gašam- for -šu-du$_{11}$-)
ì-sar eger-bi gú mu-e-dù
"If you have learned the scribal art, you had recited all of it,
the different lines, chosen from the scribal art,
(the names of) the animals living in the steppe to (the names of) artisans
you have written (but) after that you hate (writing)."

Lines 54–55 (*SLTNi*, No. 116 obv. 3–4 and dupls.) have:

nam-dub-sar-ra hé-bí-šid ki-bi li-bí-ib-gi$_4$-gi$_4$[17]
nì-zi-gál-eden-na zà-lú-šu-du$_{11}$-šè ì-sar
"You may recite from the scribal art but you cannot place it in its (right) place;
you have written (the names of) the animals living in the steppe up to (the names of) artisans."

13. See Edzard, in *AfO* XXIII 93*b*, commenting on this line. And see G. R. Castellino, *Two Šulgi Hymns* (*BC*) (*StSem*, No. 42 [1972]) p. 30, Hymn B, l. 14, dub-ki-en-gi-ki-uri-ka nam-dub-sar-ra mi-ni-zu, "on tablets of Sumer and Akkad I learnt the scribal art." Accordingly, I restore *UET* VI/2, No. 165:10, [dub-ki]-en-gi-ki-uri-ka nam-[du]b-[sa]r mi-ni-dab$_5$ (dab$_5$ = *aḫāzu*, "to learn," "to understand"); see further 3 NT 386 i 7 (see below), [dub]-ki-en-gi-ki-uri-k⸢a⸣ sar-re-b⸢i⸣ mu-zu-a.

14. Cf. H. Hunger, *Babylonische und assyrische Kolophone* (*AOAT*, Vol. 2 [1968]) p. 31, 47 (VAT 10172, col. vi); *iškar* A.A.MEŠ LIBIR.RA.MEŠ (see n. 11) probably refers to the "Silbenalphabet B."

15. Cf. Bruno Meissner, "Textkritische Bemerkungen zu einem medizinischen Kompendium," *Archiv für Keilschriftforschung* I (1923) 12, l. 2; for the sixty names of Ištar.

16. Line 3 refers, in my opinion, to a tablet containing an excerpt from a literary text; zi-ga = *nishu*.

17. For this line see below, under Identification.

In line 59, we read:

inim-inim-ma-nam-dumu-é-dub-ba-a-ke₄-ne šu-za íb-ši-in-tùm

"All the vocabulary of the scribes in the eduba is in your hands."

Furthermore, lines 7–8 have:

> inim-inim-ma-nam-dumu-é-dub-ba-a-ke₄-ne
> ga-ab-šid-dè-en diri-zu-šè ì-zu
> "The whole vocabulary of the scribes in the eduba
> I will recite for you, I know it much better than you." [18]

The bilingual vocabularies are very often divided into sections consisting of a group of three Sumerian words and their Babylonian translations, as, for instance, in Erimhuš I 198–200:

> dul-lá = *redūtu* ("succession")
> é-dul-lá = *edullû* ("a building")
> lah₄-lah₄ = *šalālu* ("to lead into captivity," "to plunder")

These three lines are quoted in an *izbu* commentary as follows: dúl-lá, a-dúl-lá, lah₄-lah₄ = [*redūtu*], *etellû*, *šalālu*, *ina erim-huš qabi*, "...as said in E." [19] This commentary shows that when quoting a section containing (as here) three Sumerian words with their Babylonian translations, the Sumerian words were quoted first and then the three Babylonian equivalents. Note that the three words are not etymologically related. Whether this method of learning lexical and grammatical texts by heart was practiced in the Old Babylonian eduba remains uncertain. [20]

Legal phraseology was also a part of a schoolboy's studies. One of the compositions studied in the eduba was *ana ittišu*, an anthology of law and legal and administrative phraseology, written in Sumerian with a translation into Babylonian. We assume that this anthology was drawn up in the edubas in Nippur. [21] The famous murder trial in Isin was used as an exercise in the Old Babylonian

---

18. Inim-inim-ma = *a-ma-a-tum*, Nabnitu IV 31. Cf. *SGL* II 116, U 17900 J 2 (also *UET* VI/2, No. 150:2), inim-inim-ma-didli-me, "unsere Vokabeln"; Gadd, *Teachers and Students*, p. 30, translates this "the individual dialects." See also *UET* VI/2, No. 150:40; *VS* XVII, No. 44 iii 9, and dupl. *BE* XXXI, No. 29:12 (the same text is in *ISET* I 126, Ni. 972), inim-inim-ma-20-àm inim-inim-ma-30-àm nu-mu-un-da-si-ʳiˀg.

19. See E. Leichty, *The Omen Series Šumma Izbu* (*TCS* IV [1970]) p. 232, Commentary 0, ll. 3–4; *CAD*, Vol. E. p. 38*b*, s.v. *edulû*, and Vol. L, p. 173*b*, s.v. *libbu*.

20. Also Old Babylonian lexical and grammatical texts are sometimes divided into sections; see, for instance, *MSL* II 142–46, AO 5400, and *MSL* IV 47–55. Some sections in *MSL* IV 47–55 contain four or five lines, and others (see, for instance, *MSL* IV 51–52, ll. 401–9, 410–18, and 419–53) are very long and I doubt that they were learned by heart according to the method in the *izbu* commentary quoted above.

21. No Old Babylonian texts have been found as yet. The composition goes back probably to the dynasty of Isin; see B. Landsberger, *MSL* I, pp. II–III.

eduba.[22] The tablet YBC 2177 is a student exercise in legal phraseology.[23] Here should also be mentioned the collections of "model contracts," which are essential for the redaction of legal documents. A number of newly discovered texts belonging to the Lipitištar Code (at least three different copies of that code have now been identified) strongly support the assumption that the code was studied in the eduba; it is only natural to assume, as well, that the Code of Hammurabi was studied in school. The two copies of the Laws of Ešnunna may have been products of an eduba, recopied for instruction and education in the school in Šaduppûm, the modern Tell Abu Ḥarmal, on the outskirts of Baghdad.[24]

In connection with the study of legal phraseology, I should like to refer the reader to Dialogue 1, lines 52–53: di i-du$_{11}$ eger-bi-šè nu-mu-un-til-e-en, "you can institute legal proceedings, but afterwards you are not able to finish them" (SLTNi, No. 116:1–2, and dupls.). This passage hardly refers to the scribe's training to be an attorney but, in spite of the wording, refers to the student's study of legal phraseology for his future profession as DUMU.É.DUB.BA ša dajjāni, "the scribe of the judge" (TCL I, No. 157:75).

Letter-writing was also taught in school. In the dialogue between Enki-mansum and Girini-isag, lines 19–20, we find a reference to that subject: dub i-sar dím-ma(-aš) nu-mu-da-an-ku$_4$ ù-na-a-du$_{11}$ i-sar ki-GÌR.BAR a-ra-ab-tuku, "you have written a tablet, but you cannot penetrate (its) meaning; you have written a letter, (but) that is all you can do" (UET VI/2, No. 150:19–20 and dupl.; cf. M. Civil, in JCS XX [1966] 123). The many texts and fragments containing letters to the kings of Ur and Isin in Old Babylonian copies found at Nippur and Ur reveal the great interest in this epistolary literature.

In the Old Babylonian eduba the student also received training in writing letters in Babylonian, the native tongue of the scribe.[25] Tablets with exercises in Old Babylonian epistolary form have been found at Nippur, Sippar, Adab, Kish, and Ur.

In an eduba text we read as follows: dub AŠ še-gur-ta zà DIŠ NE GA DU/dub DIŠ udu ta zà 60+10 še-gur ŠÈ | [...] AN zà-e 10 ma-na ŠÈ (UET VI/2, No. 167:44–45 and dupl. SEM, No. 67 i 9–11 [collated]). Although these two lines are still somewhat unclear to me, they seem to refer to the training in writing "economic" texts.

22. See T. Jacobsen "An Ancient Mesopotamian Trial for Homicide," Studia Biblica et Orientalia III ("Analecta Biblica," Vol. 12 [Rome, 1959]) 130–50 (TIOT, pp. 193–214); and also A. L. Oppenheim, Ancient Mesopotamia (Chicago, 1964) p. 284.

23. Cf. J. J. Finkelstein, "Sex Offenses in Sumerian Laws," JAOS, Vol. 86 (1966) pp. 357–59; ANET Supplement, p. 89.

24. A. Goetze, The Laws of Eshnunna (New Haven, 1956) p. 14.

25. I refer the reader to F. R. Kraus's article "Briefschreibübungen im altbabylonischen Schulunterricht," JEOL, Vol. 16 (1964) pp. 16–39.

In a letter from Abaindasa to King Šulgi we read:

ìr-zu na-ab-bé-a
kala-ga-me-en lugal-mu ga-ab-ús
inim-ma-zu ra-gaba-zu hé-me-en
giš-má gub-ba giš-gisal mu-un-sì-ge
a gub-ba a mu-un-da-ak-e
im gub-ba im mu-da-ak-e
dub-sar-me-en na-rú-a ab-sar-re-en
"Your servant thus says:
'You are mighty: I will follow my king;
of your word, I will be your messenger;
standing on a boat, I will pull the oar;
standing on land(?), I will...;
I am a scribe (and) I can write a stele.'"[26]

Abaindasa states in his letter that he is able to write a stele because he is a scribe, having received his education in the eduba. The students of the "tablet house" studied formulas on steles and copied them. Several of these have been treated elsewhere.[27] One of them is written in syllabic Sumerian along with its Babylonian translation. I assume that, after transferring the Sumerian inscription into syllabic Sumerian,[28] the student translated it into Babylonian, his native tongue.[29] Also, "In Praise of the Scribal Art" contains a reference (l. 15) to the writing of a stele.[30] Some of the Old Babylonian copies of Old Akkadian inscriptions and texts relating to kings of the Third Dynasty of Ur may be products of the eduba.[31]

According to Examination Text A, lines 21 and 25–26, the student was supposed to know the "tongue" (eme = lišānu) of several classes of priests, silversmiths, jewelers, shepherds, and master shippers. These "tongues" are

26. OB copy. See F. Ali, "Sumerian Letters" (Ph. D. diss., University of Pennsylvania, 1964) pp. 53–54, B:1, ll. 8–14. Variants have not been noted.

27. There are several copies of steles; for example, SRT, No. 13, rev., is a copy of a stele of Išmedagan of Isin; another copy of a stele is published in UET VI/2, No. 192; a text from Tell Abu Ḥarmal has been published by J. J. van Dijk, "Textes divers du Musée de Baghdad," Sumer XI (1955) 110, Pl. XVI; a Hammurabi text is treated in Å. W. Sjöberg, "Ein Selbstpreis des Königs Ḥammurabi von Babylon," ZA, Vol. 54 (1961) pp. 51–70. CBS 2253 and N 1494 (both texts unpublished) contain curses at the end and are therefore copies of steles.

28. The Sumerian syllabic texts seem to have originated mostly in northern Babylonia; see M. Civil, "Remarks on 'Sumerian and Bilingual Texts,'" JNES, Vol. 26 (1967) p. 209.

29. UET VI/2 No. 150:41 (Enkimansum and Girini-isag, l. 41), na-rú-a.

30. In JCS XXIV (1972) 126–31. F. R. Kraus, Vom mesopotamischen Menschen der altbabylonischen Zeit und seiner Welt (Leiden, 1973) pp. 20–21, thinks that the passage in the letter from Abaindasa, dub-sar-me-en na-rú-a ab-sar-re-en, refers to "das Verfertigen von Modellen oder Vorzeichnungen für Inschriften."

31. H. Hirsch, "Die Inschriften der Könige von Agade," AfO XX (1963) 1–82. See, for example, PBS V, No. 40, Urnammu, and No. 68, Šusîn; cf. D. O. Edzard, "Neue Inschriften zur Geschichte von Ur III unter Šūsuen," AfO XIX (1959–60) 2, n. 26.

doubtless the technical jargon, the words and expressions peculiar to these priests and professionals. "In Praise of the Scribal Art," line 14 (*JCS* XXIV 126–27) reads as follows:

ni-zu diri-ga eme-gi₇ zu-zu-dè eme-[x] zu eme-sal [zu-zu-dè?]

ihzu šūturu šumeru ahāzu KAB-*lit lam*[*ādu x x x x*]

"to have superior knowledge in Sumerian, to learn the...tongue, to learn emesal"

So far as I know, there are no references in Old Babylonian eduba texts to the teaching of professional terminology or of Emesal; but since we have texts written in Emesal from the Old Babylonian period, it is only natural to assume that this "dialect" was taught in school.[32]

Mathematics and Surveying

Examination Text A, line 27, reads as follows:

a-rá igi igi-ba igi-gub-ba ni-ka₉ ku[ru]₇ šid-dù ga-lá á-dù-à dù-a-bi dù-a ha-la ha-la-bi a-šà si-ge-dè ì-zu-ù

arâ igî igibâ igigubbâ nikkassī piqittam paqāda adê kala epêšu zittam zâzu eqla palāku tīdē

"Do you know multiplication, reciprocals, coefficients, balancing of accounts, administrative accounting, how to make all kinds of pay allotments, divide property, and delimit shares of fields?"

Mathematical terminology is, as one would expect, found in Old Babylonian eduba texts, for example, in Dialogue 1, lines 57–58, a-rá hé-bí-šid zà-bi-šè nu-e-zu igi-diri hé-du₈ ki-ús nu-mu-ra-ab-dab₅, "you may recite the multiplication table, but you do not know it perfectly; you may solve inverted numbers, (but) you cannot...for you (*STLNi*, No. 116 obv. 6–7, *UET* VI/2, No. 155 obv. 2–3 and dupls.) and in line 6 a-rá igi-diri ni-ka₉ sahar-gar-ra zà-bi-šè ì-zu, "you have learned perfectly multiplication, inverted numbers, accounting and calculation of volume"; and in Schooldays, line 48,

---

32. Šulgi (see Castellino, *Two Šulgi Hymns*, p. 256, ll. 122 and 124) proclaims that he knows the Elamite language. In an unpublished fragment (CBS 13688, identified by M. Civil), belonging to Šulgi C 115 + ff., the language of the Amorites, which Šulgi claims to speak, is also mentioned; read in Castellino, p. 256, l. 121 (b) [eme]-mar-tu-a. Šulgi Hymn B, ll. 216–18 (pp. 52–53), di-ki-en-giᵏⁱ-ke₄ si-s[á-d]a-mu-dè 5-bi eme-bi ba-ni-ib-gⁱ¹₄-gi₄ é-gal-gá KAš₄ inim-bal-e KA (var. eme in P)-e li-bí-dù-e (text Q -e! li-bí-, hardly -zalag, as Castellino reads it). If Castellino's translation of l. 218, "(While) in my Palace no (one) else could speak (understand) foreign tongues" is correct, then "the five tongues" in the preceding line are foreign languages (cf. p. 187, where Sumerian is mentioned; I assume it is the king's first language). So far as I can see, there are no references in Old Babylonian texts to the teaching of foreign languages in the eduba. The mention of Subarian in *TMH* NF III, No. 42 viii 6–7, [e]me-ni eme-gi₇-ra nu-ub-[du₇] [e]me-ni subirᵏⁱ àm-da-[...] x, "his tongue is not fitting the Sumerian language, his tongue *chatters* the Subarian language" does not suggest the teaching of that language in school.

šid nì-šid-dè.[33] The Old Babylonian eduba also taught how to divide property and delimit shares of fields, as we read, for example, in Enkimansum and Girini-isag, lines 21–23 (*UET* VI/2, No. 150:21–23, and dupl. CBS 13984 i 17′–20′):

> gána ba-e-dè gen-na gána nu-mu-da-ba-e-en
> a-šà si-ge-dè gen-na éš-gána gi-DIŠ-ninda nu-mu-da-ha-za
> giš-gag-a-šà nu-mu-e-da-rú-e dím-ma nu-mu-e-da-ku₄
> "Go to divide a field but you won't be able to divide it,
> go to delimit a field but you won't be able to hold the tape
>   and the measuring rod,
> the pegs *of* the field you won't drive in, you are not able to
> figure out the sense."[34]

A further example ha-la dab₅ (*UET* VI/2, No. 165:27 and *TLB* II, No. 7 iii 23′, dab₅(!)), corresponds to ha-la ha-la ‖ *zittam zâzu* in Examination Text A, line 27; in these same eduba texts (Nos. 165:30 and 7 iii 24′) we find the expression a-šà si(-g) (No. 165 ⟨si⟩-) corresponding to *eqla palāku* in Examination Text A, line 27, in both texts together with a-šà-ga gíd(-gíd) (No. 165:28, a-šà mú éš-gána gi-ninda-DIŠ x a-šà-gʳaᵀ gíd; No. 7 iii 24′, a-šà éš-⟨gána⟩ si gi-DIŠ(!)-ninda a-šà-ga ì(!)-gíd-gíd), corresponding to Akkadian *eqla šadādu*, which is found in "In Praise of the Scribal Art," line 15, where it also refers to teaching: na₄-rú-a ab-sar-re-[dè a-šà]-ga gíd-e-[dè] nì-ka₉ sá-du₁₁-[ge-dè x x x] = *narâ šaṭāri eqla šadādu nikkassa kašādu* [x x x], "to write a stele, to draw a field, to settle accounts,..." (*JCS* XXIV 127).

Music

"Die Schule ist aber dafür hinaus noch die Bildungsstätte für die musischen Zweige, soweit diese an Wort und Ton gebunden sind."[35] Professor Adam Falkenstein was the first scholar to draw attention to music as a subject in post-Old-Babylonian instruction. He discovered it in an unpublished text from Babylon (VAT 17071/BE 35882, Seleucid period).[36] This text (with dupls.) is now incorporated in Examination Text A; line 28 reads as follows:

> [x] x-ga hub-dar [x x x LA]M(?) giš-zà-mí giš-balag-di giš-har-har
> giš-gù-dé-gù-dé-bi [nì-a-na-mu-sa₄]-a-bi sur-sur-re-e-dè ì-zu-ù

---

33. S. N. Kramer, "Schooldays: A Sumerian Composition Relating to the Education of a Scribe," *JAOS*, Vol. 69 (1949) p. 203. See further *UET* VI/2, No. 150:34–38 (and dupls., Enkimansum and Girini-isag; cf. Gadd, *Teachers and Students*, p. 32, translation of No. 150:34–38; Kramer, *The Sumerians*, p. 243) and No. 165:24 ff.

34. Some lines later in the text we read: gána ba-e-dè ga-gen gána mu-da-ba-e-en a-šà si-ge-dè ga-gen ki si-ge-d[è....], "let me go to divide a field and I will be able to divide the field, let me go to delimit a field and [I will be able] to delimit the place" (ll. 29–30 and dupl.).

35. A. Falkenstein, "Die babylonische Schule," *Saeculum* IV (1953) 125–37.

36. Falkenstein, in *Saeculum* IV 132, n. 28; also in *WO* I 185.

[x x x x]-*a-ti rik-bu* [*k*]*i-ṣir sa-am-mi-e tim-bu-ut-ti har-har-ri* [*u i-ni m*]*a-la ba-šu-ú ni-ba-šú-nu nu-us-su-ka ti-di-e*

"Do you know..., the *sammû*-instrument, the *timbuttu*, the *harharu* and the *inu*-instrument, as many as they are, (do you know how?) to...their designation(?)?"

According to Examination Text A, line 24 (see *ZA*, Vol. 64, pp. 137–76), a pupil was supposed to know the different names of "songs" (šìr); he should be able to divide up the different parts of a song (*pirsišunu parāsu*); and he was expected to know what antiphon, recital and finale were. An Old Babylonian eduba dialogue clearly states that music and song were taught in school (Enkitalu and Enkihegal, ll. 94–99, *TMH* NF III, No. 42 obv. ii 10–15 and dupl.):

> giš-zà-mí an-da-gál nam-nar nu-un-zu
> a-ga-aš-gi₄-gi₄-me-a-aš-e-ne
> ad-ša₄ za-pa-ág nu-sa₆
> eme-gi₇-šè al-dugud eme-ni si nu-ub-sá
> èn-du nu-mu-un-da-di ka gál nu-tag₄-tag₄
> ù za-e lú-til-me-en
> "(Even if) he had a zami-instrument he could not learn the art of
>   singing,
> he, the most backward among (his) classmates,
> has not been able to make a beautiful tremolo[37] and sound,
> he is 'heavy' for the Sumerian language, he is not able to move his
>   tongue correctly,
> he cannot sing a song, cannot open his mouth.
> and you are an accomplished man?!"

The same dialogue reads, in lines 110–13 (No. 42 obv. ii 26–29 and dupls.; variants not noted):

> nam-nar-e nu-ub-du₇ kin-gi₄-a-aš la-ba-ab-du₇
> é-lú-šè ù-un-gin lú nu-mu-e-da-sá
> á-ni gál ù-bí-in-tag₄ šìr-gíd-da nu-ub-bé
> igi-um-mi-a-ke₄-ne-šè ù-ba-tuš tigi a-da-ab nu-ub-bé
> "He is not fit for the art of singing, not fit for that task,
> when entering a house of (another) man he does not...,
> when 'opening his arm'[38] he cannot recite a širgida,
> when sitting in front of the masters he cannot recite either a tigi-song
>   or an adab-song."

37. For ad-ša₄, probably "tremolo," see *SP*, pp. 201–2; J. Renger, "Untersuchungen zum Priestertum der altbabylonischen Zeit," *ZA*, Vol. 59 (1969) p. 181, n. 820.

38. Cf. Gilgamesh and the Netherworld, l. 264 (A. Shaffer, "Sumerian Sources of Tablet XII of the Epic of Gilgameš," [Ph.D. diss., University of Pennsylvania, 1963], pp. 90, 117, and commentary, p. 150), dub-sar-sa₆-ga-ginₓ á-ni gál bí-in-tag₄ é-gal si-sá-bi ba-an-ku₄-ku₄, and Gilgamesh Epic XII 108, [*kīma ṭupšarri damqi*] *idsu petât išariš ana ēkalli irrub*, "like a good scribe his hand is at work, he enters the palace easily" (Shaffer). The activity implied by the idiom in this case must, according to Shaffer, be the writing on tablets, but the implication in our line remains uncertain.

Adam Falkenstein expressed his views on the teaching of music as follows:
"Wie das zu deuten ist, wird sofort klar, wenn wir daran denken, dass besonders
für die sumerische Literatur, grossenteils aber auch für die akkadische, eine enge
Verbindung zwischen Text und musikalischer Begleitung bestand. Weite Teile
der Literatur, vor allem alle hymnischen Gattungen, waren an die Rezitation im
Lied gebunden. Aus gewissen Andeutungen einiger Texte scheint sogar hervor-
zugehen, dass die Ausbildung zum Sängerberuf notwendig über die Schule der
Schreiber führte."[39]

Literature

The curriculum for the study of Sumerian was not confined entirely to lexical
and grammatical texts. Sumerian syntax could hardly be learned except from
connected prose and poetry. The thousands of tablets inscribed with Sumerian
literary compositions and excerpts from literary texts reveal the intensive study
of this literature during the Old Babylonian period. In the following I intend to
concentrate only on certain features in the study of Sumerian literature in the
eduba.

Dictation

The following passages show that dictation was used as a method of instruction. The teacher would dictate a text; the student would repeat it orally and at
the same time write it down: dub-sar šu ka-ta sá-a e-ne-àm dub-sar-ra-
àm, "a scribe (whose) hand rivals (his) mouth, he is indeed a scribe" (my
translation differs somewhat from that of Gordon, SP, p. 202, Coll. 2.40);
šu(-zu) ka-zu (variant has si) nu-ub-da-sá, "your hand does not rival
your mouth," Dialogue 1 (Two Scribes) line 53;[40] šu-zu hu-du₇ šu gi-dub-
ba-a nu-du₇ (var. šu gi-⟨dub⟩-ba-bi nu-dù) im-ma nu-túm-ma šu
ka-ta nu-sá (sá preserved only in CBS 13984), "your hand may be fair, but
it is not fit for the reed stylus, is not apt for the clay (tablet), (and your) hand
does not rival (your) mouth" (Enkimansum and Girini-isag, ll. 11–12, UET VI/2,

---

39. Falkenstein, in *Saeculum* IV 132. A nar, "singer," could probably not read and write
(see Renger, in *ZA*, Vol. 59, p. 184 and n. 839), but the gala-mah, the chief singer of
lamentations and dirges in a temple, had received his education in the eduba, according to
Renger (see, however, Kraus, *Vom mesopotamischen Menschen*, p. 20, n. 23). See also *CAD*,
Vol. G, pp. 19–20, galmāhu as a scribe, and Vol. K, p. 93b, kalû as a scribe in later texts.
    Šulgi of Ur claims to have studied music and the art of singing with great zeal. See
Castellino, *Two Šulgi Hymns*, p. 46, ll. 155–58; there follows an enumeration of ten musical
instruments, some of them also occurring in the Examination Text A, l. 28. It should be
noted, however, that these lines in the Šulgi hymn about his interest in music are not connected with his accomplishments in the eduba, which are mentioned in lines 13–20.
    40. These two references have been quoted by the writer, "Beiträge zum sumerischen
Wörterbuch," *Or*, n.s., Vol. 39 (1970) p. 84, UM 29-15-73 i-ii 7 (see now *MSL* XIII 114,
níg-ga, Bilingual V 7) šu ka-ta sá-a = qa-at-sú pi-šu [k]a-aš-da-tum (mistake for kašdat).

No. 150:11–12, CBS 13984 i 7′–8′; Kramer, *The Sumerians*, p. 241, translates "cannot take dictation").[41]

Composition

It has often been suggested that some literary compositions were composed in the eduba; S. N. Kramer, for instance, is positive that "Schooldays" was the creation of one of the ummia's in the eduba.[42]

The following passages from three "royal hymns" may indicate that the hymns were composed in school:

> zà-mí-zu é-dub-ba-a-ka im-e mu-e-ni-du₁₁-du₁₁
> dub-sar-e a-la hé-em-ši-ak-e gal-le-eš hé-i-i
> ár-zu é-dub-ba-a-ka mùš nam-ba-an-túm-mu
> "The clay (tablet) says your praise in the eduba,
> the scribe may...you (Lipitištar), praise you greatly,
> your glory will never cease in the eduba."[43]

> dub-sar-umún(!)-ak é-dub-⟨ba⟩-a é na-de₆-kalam-ma-ka
> zà-mí-zu gá-la nam-ba-an-dag-ge
> "The learned scribe is never going to let your
> glory cease in the eduba, the house, the counselor of the land!"[44]

> ár-nam-lugal-la-zu é-dub-ba-a ka-ka ì-gál
> "The glory of your kingship will be in (everyone's) mouth in the eduba."[45]

Another passage suggesting that hymns were composed in the eduba reads as follows:

> geštú-diri dub-ᵈnisaba-ke₄ sum-ma-zu
> é-dub-ba-a im-ma mùš nam-ba-an-túm-mu
> é-dub-ba-a-ba èš-nì-ù-tu-ginₓ ki nam-ba-silig-ge
> dub-sar-tur šu-ni íb-ši-in-tum₄ im bí-íb-sar-a
> ᵈnisaba nin-mul-a ⌈x⌉ geštú hu-mu-u[n(?)-na-sum]
> šu hu-mu-un-bad

41. Dictation is mentioned in two colophons, *PBS* I/2, No. 106 rev. 30 (see Hunger, *Kolophone*, p. 134, No. 486; hymns to various deities, first millennium), *a-na [p]i ummâni šá-ṭir gaba-ru-u la-bi-ru ul a-mur*, "written according to the dictation (lit., mouth) of the master; I have not seen the old original," and *CT* XVI, Pl. 18 rev. 5–9 (see Hunger, *Kolophone*, p. 122, No. 416), *kima labīrišu šá-ṭir-ma up-pu-[uš] a-na qa-bé-e li-gin-n[i] za-mar šu-bal-ku-ut*, "written according to the old original and read aloud; hurriedly transferred for dictation." For *uppuš* see M. Cohen, "*Balag*-Compositions to the God Enlil" (Ph.D. diss., University of Pennsylvania, 1972) p. 29, where he refers to the expression *ṭuppa epēšu*, "to read a tablet aloud"; cf. *CAD*, Vol. E, p. 224a.

42. *The Sumerians*, p. 237.

43. *SKIZ*, p. 29, ll. 59–61 and variants.

44. Enlilbani, see A. Kapp, "Ein Lied auf Enlilbāni von Isin," *ZA*, Vol. 51 (1955) p. 80, ll. 178–84; cf. *SGL* II 117.

45. Hammurabi, *ISET* I 112, Ni. 4577 rev. ii 4.

ki-nam-dub-sar-ra-ka u₄-gin$_x$ hé-en-na-è
"Your surpassing wisdom, which the tablet of Nisaba has given you,
shall never end on the clay in the eduba,
in the eduba, which is like a shrine that creates everything, a place that
    never ceases,
to the young scribe, who has 'brought his hand to it' and who has
    written a clay (tablet),
Nisaba, the lustrous lady, may give wisdom,
may she 'open (his) hand'
and may she come forth for him like the sun!"[46]

A. Falkenstein quotes the aforementioned passages from the Lipitištar and Enlil-
bani texts, which in his opinion show that the school was "im königlichen
Dienste."[47] I assume, however, that the royal court ordered hymns to the king
from the eduba and that the ummia composed the hymns for the palace
but also used them in his teaching.[48]

Identification

In Dialogue 1, line 54 we read as follows: nam-dub-sar(-ra) hé-bí-šid
ki-bi-šè nu-mu-ra-ab-gi₄ (var. ki-bi li-bí-ib-gi₄-gi₄), "you may recite
from the scribal art (the literature), but you cannot put it in the (right) place"
(*SLTNi*, No. 116 obv. 3 and dupls.). What does "you cannot put it in the (right)
place" mean? The Sumerian phrase ki-bi(-šè) gi₄ is translated into Akkadian
ana ašrišu turru, "to restore." A translation "you cannot restore it" would then
mean that the student was expected to restore a broken line or passage in an older
copy of a literary text. I believe, however, that the implication in this line is that
the pupil was supposed to identify a quoted line or passage and place it in the
right literary composition.

III. THE SCHOOL IN SOME ROYAL HYMNS

The education in the eduba is also referred to in some royal hymns:

tur-ra-mu-dè é-dub-ba-a-àm
dub-ki-en-gi-ki-uri-ka nam-dub-sar-ra mi-ni-zu
nam-tur-ra gá-e-gin₇-nam im nu-mu-sar
nam-dub-sar-ra ki-nam-kù-zu-ba lú im-mi-DU-DU
zi-zi-i gá-gá šid nì-šid-dè zà im-mi-til-til

46. *SKIZ*, p. 211, ll. 64–70.
47. *WO* I 185.
48. Cf. Kraus, *Vom mesopotamischen Menschen*, p. 24.

^{d}nanibgal-sa$_{7}$-ga ^{d}nisaba-ke$_{4}$
geštú-gizzal-la šu-dagal-la ma-ni-in-du$_{11}$
dub-sar-gál-tag$_{4}$-a nì-e nu-dab$_{5}$-bé-me-en
"Since I was a child (I was in) the eduba;
on the tablets of Sumer and Akkad I learned the scribal art;
of the young, no one could write a tablet like me;
in the place of wisdom (where) the scribal art (is learned) people...;
I am perfectly able to subtract and add,[49] (clever in) counting and
    accounting;
the fair Nanibgal, Nisaba
has lavishly provided me with wisdom and intelligence;
I am an 'open' scribe, ...am I."[50]

More informative about the curriculum in the Neo-Sumerian period is the
following passage from a Šulgi hymn:

é-geštú igi-gál-kalam-ma-ka
šul-gi lugal-ki-en-gi-ra-me-èn umún-zi-ak-me-èn
šu-mu-ù gi-kù-ga si mi-ni-íb-sá
kúr-kúr-ra ad-ša(var. -ša$_{4}$)[51] gá-gá-gá
x[...]x x IL(?) si NI x/[(...)] x šu(?) dal-la-bi
UN g^{r}á^{1}n^{r}a^{1}(?) kù-ga [éš-gána]-za-gìn a-šà-ge ra-ra-da
eburu hé-gál-la šu-íl-íli-da
gu-sag še-sag-gá KÚ DI-bi
al giš-ù-šub á-K^{r}U^{1}(?) giš-gá-gá giš-hur uš-ki-tag
maš-anše gam ki-gal hum-ma sag-tag-ga šu-gal du$_{7}$-e-me-èn
dub-za-gìn-na pa mu-ni-è
šid nì-šid (or: nì-ka$_{9}$) giš-hur-kalam-ma-ka
igi-gál-sum-mu-bi á-bi-šè in-ga-zu[52]

As seen in this text, the following subjects were taught in school: writing (ll.

49. For zi-zi-i, "to subtract," and gá-gá, "to add," see O. Neugebauer and A. Sachs,
Mathematical Cuneiform Texts (*AOS* XXIX [1945]) p. 175, *sub* zi, "to withdraw," and p.
163, *sub* gar, "to add."
50. Castellino, *Two Šulgi Hymns*, pp. 30–31, Hymn B, ll. 13–20 (translation modified).
51. This variant, in CBS 7079, was not noted by Castellino. The only Babylonian equivalent of ad-ša$_{4}$ is *nissatu* (as verb, = *nasāsu*). For ad-ša$_{4}$, "tremolo," see, above n. 37.
Van Dijk, *SGL* II 116, suggests that it may refer to "eine Fähigkeit, die mit Lesen und
Deklamieren in Verbindung steht." He reads ad ša-gá-gá-gá, but the new duplicate shows
that it is in fact ad-ša$_{4}$. I cannot concur with Castellino's translation "Foreign words to
put into songs." Note the parallel kur-kur-ra ad-ša$_{4}$ gá-gá-gá (var. omits -ša$_{4}$) in
Å. W. Sjöberg and E. Bergmann, *The Collection of the Sumerian Temple Hymns* (*TCS* III
[1969]) p. 49, l. 539, which I translated as "She (Nisaba) gives advice to all lands" (see my
commentary, *TCS* III 148), which is hardly a correct translation.
   The next line (39) is also obscure. Castellino's reading giš-dúb and translation "harp"
are dubious.
52. *SRT*, No. 14:35–47, dupl. CBS 7079 ii 16 ff., Castellino, *Two Šulgi Hymns*, p. 250,
ll. 35–47, and p. 245; see also *SGL* II 115–16.

37 and 45) field-measuring (l. 40), agriculture (ll. 41–42), construction (l. 43), and counting and accounting (l. 46). It remains uncertain what kúr-kúr-ra ad-ša might mean. Moreover, line 44 is unclear, and the meaning of igi-gál-sum-mu in line 47 remains problematic.[53]

> šud$_x$ (= KA×ŠU) é-kur-ra ki hé-ús-sa-mu-uš
> dub-sar hé-gub šu-ni hé-éb-dib-bé
> nar hé-gub gù hu-mu-un-ni-re-dé(!)
> é-dub-ba-a da-rí hur nu-kúr-ru-dam
> ki-umún da-rí hur nu-silig-ge-dam
> "May the scribe stand ready for my prayer in the Ekur...,
>   may he take it in his hand,
> may the singer stand ready for it and perform it,
> in the eduba it will never be changed,
> in the place of learning it will never cease."[54]

As I assumed above, at least some of the royal hymns were composed (and studied) in school. The lines from the Šulgi hymn just quoted are to be interpreted as stating that the scribe wrote down the prayers of the king and that they were studied in the eduba.

> ^{d}nisaba munus ul-la gùn-a
> munus-zi dub-sar nin nì-nam zu
> si-zu im-ma si ba-ni-in-sá
> šà-dub-ba-ka gu-sum mi-ni-in-sa$_6$-sa$_6$
> gi-dub-ba-a-guškin-ga šu mu-ni-in-gùn-nu
> giš-DIŠ-ninda éš-gána-za-gìn
> giš-as$_4$-lum le-um igi-gál-sum-mu ^{d}nisaba-ke$_4$
>   šu-dagal ma-ra-an-du$_{11}$
> "Nisaba, the beautiful woman,
> the true woman, the scribe, the lady who knows everything,
> has let you put your...correctly on the tablet,
> she has let you...the stylus of gold,
> the measuring rod (lustrous like) lapis lazuli,

53. Castellino: "To tame the beasts (of the steppe), to let them multiply in the Ki-gal, applying myself with perfect ability" (l. 44).
SKIZ, p. 24, l. 24 (modified reading and translation), giš-as$_4$-lum le-um igi-gál-sum-mu ^{d}nisaba-ke$_4$ šu-dagal ma-ra-an-du$_{11}$, "the aslum-cubit, the tablet,..., Nisaba has lavishly given to you (Lipitištar)." Falkenstein, in *WO* I 179, n. 27, suggested a reading igi-ku$_x$-sì as a possibility; Van Dijk, *SGL* II 116, reads *SRT*, No. 14:47 as igi-gál-sì-mu-bi and translates "die Zahlen 'einander gegenüberstellen'" (i.e., division and multiplication). Römer (p. 25) translates le-um igi-gál-sum-mu as "die Tafel, die die Weisheit schenkt." His translation is supported by *UET* VI/1, No. 99 rev. v 27, igi-gál ù-mu-un-na-sum, "(Nisaba) gave him wisdom."
54. Castellino, *Two Šulgi Hymns*, p. 62, Hymn B, ll. 311–15; see Falkenstein, in *WO* I 185.

the aslum-cubit, the tablet which bestows wisdom
Nisaba has lavishly given to you."[55]

> im-bi dub-bi
> sar-re-bi
> šu mi-ni- ⌜í⌝b-du₇-du₇-a
> ᵈnisaba nin-geštú-g⌜a⌝l⌜a⌝m-ma
> igi-gál ù-mu-un-na-sum
> šu-sa₆-[s]a₆
> hi-li-nam-dub-s⌜a⌝r-ra
> sag-e-e⌜š⌝ ⌜x⌝-[...-r]ig₇

"He is perfect in writing on clay and tablets;
Nisaba, the lady with cunning wisdom,
has given him wisdom,
a fine hand(writing), the luxury of the scribal art,
she has given to him."[56]

[nam-du]b-sar ki-nam-galam-ma-k⌜a⌝(?) [....]
[x(x)] usu bí-DU
[é]-dub-ba šid nì-šid bùru dagal x x x mu-búr
x [D]U(?) gíd gána gi-né giš-as₄-lum gi è
x-[x]-ba ki igi-íl-la x x te x x RI gá
⌜x⌝-x-ga šu-dadag g⌜á⌝-gá
[dub]-ki-en-gi-ki-uri-k⌜a⌝ sar-re-b⌜i⌝ mu-zu-a
[é-du]b-ba-a [...]⌜x⌝-ni-ta(?) ⌜x x x⌝
[x x] x dub-nam-d[ub-sar]-ra z⌜à⌝ im-mi-til-la[57]

The name of the king is not mentioned on the tablet. The subjects in this text
are writing (ll. 1, 7, 9; see n. 13 above), mathematics (l. 3), and surveying
(l. 4).[58] The next lines in this text deal with nam-nar, the art of singing and
music. The text enumerates several musical instruments, which the king obviously could play.[59] I assume that these lines refer to music taught in the eduba; this
assumption is strengthened by the mention of um-mi-a, "the master" in line

55. Lipitištar; *SKIZ*, p. 24, ll. 18–24; the readings given here have been partially modified;
for variants see *SKIZ*.
56. Sîniddinam, *UET* VI/1, No. 99 rev. v 22–30.
57. A 30230, 3 NT 386 obv. 1–9.
58. Line 3: bùru, "depth"; dagal, "width." Line 4: giš-as₄-lum also occurs above,
see n. 53. For gi = *qanû*, a measure, see *AHw.*, p. 898*b*; *CAD*, Vol. A/2, p. 70, s.v. *ammatu*
A 2.
59. The enumerated musical instruments are: sa-šu-si, giš-gù-di (= *inu*, a stringed
instrument), l. 13; giš-al-⟨gar⟩-sur_x (Akk. *algarsurrû*), giš-sa-eš, gi[š-sa-b]í-tum,
l. 14 (for giš-sa-eš, see A. Draffkorn Kilmer, "The Strings of Musical Instruments; Their
Names, Numbers, and Significance," *Studies in Honor of Benno Landsberger* [*AS*, No. 16
(1965)] p. 263*a*); giš-har-har (= *harharru*, a string instrument), see my commentary to
Examination Text A, l. 28; for za-na-ru, see Å. W. Sjöberg, "Beiträge zum sumerischen
Wörterbuch," *AS*, No. 16, pp. 64–65, l. 15.

18. I believe that this text describes Šulgi's education; as seen in Šulgi Hymn B, lines 155–74, the king showed a special interest in music.[60] Some of the musical instruments enumerated in this text recur in Šulgi Hymn B.

IV. SCHOOLS AND SCRIBAL ACTIVITY
DURING THE OLD BABYLONIAN PERIOD

Nippur.—D. E. McCown writes as follows: "There is, however, no textual evidence for private schools. The written information concerns the *edubba*, the formal institution of education. From a survey of the known find-spots of school tablets it is apparent that no such find-spots can with certainty be identified as an *edubba* and that, as at Nippur, tablet concentrations were usually in private houses. However, this evidence does not indicate whether or not individual scribes conducted small schools in their homes. The most obvious argument against this possibility is provided by the find-spots of the concentrations of tablets at Nippur. In Old Babylonian levels concentrations were found in at least four houses, three of which adjoined one another. One would not expect three schools to be located so close together."[61] The explanation for the tablet concentrations in these adjoining houses is found by McCown in "Schooldays," lines 1–11, where it is said that the schoolboy took his tablets home, and he concludes that the tablets in the concentrations were the work of individual boys who lived in the various houses where the tablets were found. We find it surprising that the excavators at Nippur did not interpret the three adjoining houses with tablet concentrations as schoolhouses; we see no reason why three schools could not be so close together. One cannot exclude the possibility that the ummia's lived in the same quarter, a scribal quarter.

In an eduba letter, which, unfortunately, is partially broken, and its unpublished duplicate, the eduba in Nippur is mentioned, nibru^ki-a é-dub-ba-a diš-àm al-me-a (var. aš-à[m] or dili-à[m], aš written over a partially erased diš), "in Nippur the eduba is unique" (*VS* XVII, No. 44 iii 12, and dupl. UM 29-13-520).

Uruk.—In the area of the palace of Sînkašid were found syllabaries, lexical texts, tables of multiplication, as well as a text with three lines from a hymn to Iddindagan of Isin and a text containing a dialogue between a dog and a fox(?).[62] "School texts" were also found in the Old Babylonian strata in the Eanna precinct. They consist of lentil-shaped tablets with writing exercises; some are inscribed with the so-called "Silbenalphabet B," other lists of personal names, and excerpts from literary compositions.[63]

60. Castellino, *Two Šulgi Hymns*, pp. 46–49. M. Civil has kindly informed me that he has identified some duplicates to this passage and that it refers to the education of King Išmedagan.

61. *Nippur* I 148–49.

62. A. Falkenstein, "Zu den Inschriftenfunden der Grabung in Uruk-Warka 1960–1961," *Baghdader Mitteilungen*, Vol. 2 (1963) pp. 41–42.

63. *Ibid.*, p. 41, n. 185.

Ur.—The excavators at Ur uncovered a house ("No. 1 Broad Street") belonging to a certain Igmil-Sîn. Nearly two thousand tablets were found in the house. Some hundreds of the tablets were the regular lentil-shaped "school texts," but there were also many religious texts, mathematical tablets, multiplication tables, all belonging to the eduba of Igmil-Sîn.[64]

Kish.—Finds of literary texts, multiplication tables, Babylonian exercises in letter-writing and lexical texts clearly point to the existence of an eduba. The texts were found in domestic quarters.[65]

Sippar.—The existence of female scribes during the Old Babylonian period is attested only at Sippar.[66]

Šaduppûm (Tell Abu Ḥarmal).—The finding of lexical and literary texts and geographical lists shows scribal activity in this city. It should be noted that the texts were found in the temple dedicated to Nisaba and her spouse Haja, patrons of scribes and the scribal art.

Larsa.—"School texts" with excerpts from literary texts were found in the palace of King Nūradad.[67]

Mari.—Two rooms, which are believed to be schoolrooms, were uncovered in the palace.[68] In one of these adjoining schoolrooms there were four, in the other three, ranges of low benches in crude brick occupying the middle of the rooms and others along the walls; the benches were of different lengths, to accommodate one, two, or four occupants. A. Falkenstein speaks about the "Schule" in Mari;[69] F. R. Kraus is more cautious: "Die Schulen in den Palästen

---

64. See L. Woolley, "Excavations at Ur, 1930–1," *Antiquaries Journal* XI (1931) 365, and *Excavations at Ur, A Record of Twelve Years' Work* (London, 1954) p. 185.

65. Cf. Gadd, *Teachers and Students,* p. 25.

66. R. Harris, "The Organization and Administration of the Cloister in Ancient Babylonia," *Journal of the Economic and Social History of the Orient* VI (1963) 138–39. *VS* X, No. 207, which has the subscript *šu*-MUNUS.DUB.SAR, may come from Sippar (cf. B. Landsberger, *MSL* IX 148). See also *CT* VI, Pl. 35*a*, last line, (witness) MUNUS.DUB.SAR (from Sippar?).

Female scribes are extremely rare during the Ur III period; see A. L. Oppenheim, *Catalogue of the Cuneiform Tablets of the Wilberforce Eames Babylonian Collection (AOS* XXXII [1948]) pp. 21–22. In this connection, for dub-sar as an epithet of the goddess Nisaba, see *SKIZ*, p. 24, l. 19; Enki and the World Order, l. 414, dub-sar-kalam-ma, "the scribe of the land" (S. N. Kramer, in *WZJ*, Vol. 9 (1960) pp. 231–56); cf. Šulgi A, l. 19, dub-sar-gal-zu-ᵈnisaba-kam-me-en, "I am the wise scribe of Nisaba"; *SKIZ*, p. 32, l. 39. Innana is ga-ša-an-dub-sar (*CT* XV, Pl. 28, l. 24) and gašan dub-sar-mah (*BL*, No. VIII obv. 6); Ninimma is dub-sar-an-na (*ISET* I 74, Ni. 4233 obv. 4).

V. Scheil, *Une Saison de fouilles à Sippar* ("Mémoires de l'Institut français d'archéologie orientale," I [Cairo, 1902]) pp. 30–54.

67. Cf. G. Dossin *apud* Falkenstein, in *Baghdader Mitteilungen*, Vol. 2, p. 41, nn. 184 and 190 end.

68. See A. Parrot, *Mission archéologique de Mari* II: *Le Palais, Architecture* (Institut français d'archéologie de Beyrouth, "Bibliothèque archéologique et historique" LXVIII [Paris, 1958]) pp. 186–91, Pls. XLI–XLII; see also Parrot, "Les fouilles de Mari, deuxième campagne (Hiver, 1934–35)," *Syria* XVII (1936) 21, Pl. III 3, 4, and "Les fouilles de Mari, troisième campagne (Hiver, 1935–36)," *Syria* XVIII (1937) Pl. VIII.

69. *Saeculum* IV 127.

von Mari und Uruk kann ich nur als Ausbildungsstätten für künftige Beamte, also in innerem Zusammenhange mit der königlichen Kanzlei sehen."[70] So far as I know, no literary, lexical or grammatical texts are reported to have been found in the two rooms that were thought to have been schoolrooms nor in other parts of the Palace.

"School texts" have also been found at Adab (Old Babylonian epistolary exercises),[71] Kisurra, and Tell ed-Dēr.[72] Likewise, the literary texts published by F. Thureau-Dangin in *Nouvelles fouilles de Telloh* (Paris, 1910–14) may be the products of an eduba at Telloh.

As to schools and scribal activity I should like to add that the schools in Babylonia may not have had the same curriculum, that the activity and manner of teaching were different in some edubas and that some may not even have been "schools" if by "school" we mean an institution of education with a full curriculum.[73]

BIBLIOGRAPHY

Dijk, J. J. A. van. "L'edubba et son esprit." *La Sagesse suméro-accadienne*, pp. 21–27. Leiden, 1953.

Falkenstein, A. "Der 'Sohn des Tafelhauses.'" *WO* I (1948) 172–86.

———. "Die babylonische Schule." *Saeculum* IV (1953) 125–37.

Gadd, C. J. *Teachers and Students in the Oldest Schools.* London, 1956.

Hallo, W. W. "Archives, Monuments and the Schools." In W. W. Hallo and W. K. Simpson, *The Ancient Near East, A History*, pp. 154–58. New York, 1971.

Kramer, S. N. *Schooldays: A Sumerian Composition Relating to the Education of a Scribe.* Philadelphia, 1949. Reprinted from *JAOS*, Vol. 69 (1949) pp. 199–215.

———. "Education: The First Schools," and "Schooldays: The First Case of 'Apple-Polishing.'" In S. N. Kramer, *From the Tablets of Sumer*, pp. 3–13. Indian Hills, Colo., 1956.

———. "Education: The Sumerian School." In S. N. Kramer, *The Sumerians*, pp. 229–48. Chicago, 1963.

———. "Die sumerische Schule." *WZJ*, Vol. 5 (1955–56) pp. 695–700.

Kraus, F. R. "Briefschreibübungen im altbabylonischen Schulunterricht." *JEOL*, No. 16 (1964) pp. 16–39.

———. "Der Schreiber, Vermittler zwischen dem altbabylonischen Menschen

---

70. In *JEOL*, Vol. 16, p. 33. See also Kraus, *Vom mesopotamischen Menschen*, p. 24.

71. There are "archaic" literary texts from Adab; see D. D. Luckenbill, *Inscriptions from Adab* (*OIP* XIV [1930]) Nos. 53–56; cf. M. Civil and R. D. Biggs, "Notes sur des texts sumériens archaïques," *RA* LX (1966) 1–5. See above, with n. 25.

72. *Texts in the Iraq Museum* VII, Nos. 236–53.

73. See Kraus, *Vom mesopotamischen Menschen*, p. 220.

und uns." In F. R. Kraus, *Vom mesopotamischen Menschen der altbabylonischen Zeit und seiner Welt*, pp. 18–32. Leiden, 1973.

Landsberger, B. "Babylonian Scribal Craft and Its Terminology." Excerpted in Denis Sinor, ed., *Proceedings of the Twenty-Third International Congress of Orientalists*, pp. 123–26. London, 1956.

———. "Zum 'Silbenalphabet B.'" In M. Çığ and H. Kızılyay, *Zwei altbabylonische Schulbücher aus Nippur*, pp. 97–116. Ankara, 1959.

———. "Scribal Concepts of Education." In C. H. Kraeling and R. M. Adams, eds., *City Invincible*, pp. 94–102. Chicago, 1960.

Sjöberg, Å. "Examenstext A." *ZA*, Vol. 64 (1975) pp. 137–76.

TOWARD A HISTORY OF
SUMERIAN LITERATURE

William W. Hallo

New Haven

To Thorkild Jacobsen, with warmth and respect

Literary history is a stepchild of literary criticism. More often than not, "leading histories of literature are either histories of civilization or collections of critical essays. One type is not a history of *art*; the other, not a *history* of art."[1] And even while proposing remedies for this situation, Wellek and Warren relegate their suggestions to the end of their *Theory of Literature*. Twenty years later, that is still the position Geoffrey Hartman assigns to the proposals he addresses "Toward Literary History."[2]

In such circumstances, extensive apologies are hardly necessary for the rudimentary state of Sumerian literary history.[3] The recovery of Sumerian literature, though it began a century ago (1873),[4] is an ongoing process that is today far from complete; every year brings first editions of newly recovered or newly reconstructed works. The only systematic attempt to subject this growing corpus to some kind of chronological order[5] is today in need of major revisions on linguistic and other grounds.[6] Indeed, the prospect of writing a literary history of Mesopotamia seems only slightly less dim[7] than that of describing its religion in the opinion of the field's more skeptical spokesmen.

1. René Wellek and Austin Warren, *Theory of Literature* (New York, 1948; 3d ed., 1963) p. 253.

2. Geoffrey H. Hartman, *Beyond Formalism* (New Haven, 1970) pp. 356–86.

3. See the Bibliography below.

4. This date is chosen, somewhat arbitrarily, as marking the first appearance of François Lenormant's *Études accadiennes* ("Lettres assyriologiques," seconde série [Paris, 1873–79]). In three volumes Lenormant offered full editions of substantial numbers of bilingual Sumero-Akkadian texts, most of them previously unedited.

5. A. Falkenstein, "Zur Chronologie der sumerischen Literatur," *CRRA* II 12–30; *MDOG*, No. 85 (1953) pp. 1–13.

6. See e.g. M. Civil, "Remarks on 'Sumerian and Bilingual Texts,'" *JNES*, Vol. 26 (1967) p. 201: "the presence alone of late grammatically incorrect forms in a text is an unreliable criterion for placing its [original] composition at a late date."

7. A. L. Oppenheim, *Ancient Mesopotamia* (Chicago, 1964) p. 255: "The literary history of Mesopotamia cannot be more than outlined, and it is open to serious doubt—and I am inclined here to side with the skeptics—whether enough material is available to embark on the venture of writing such a history."

For all that, it is not too early to assay a history of Sumerian literature on strictly literary grounds, not only for the sake of a better appreciation of Sumerian literature, but also in the service of the history of literature. For Sumerian literature meets the criterion of basic linguistic unity which has now been reinstated as a principle of literary history.[8] But beyond that it can claim distinction on the basis of three remarkable superlatives: it leads all the world's written literature in terms of antiquity, longevity, and continuity.[9] Its beginnings can now be traced firmly to the middle of the third millennium B.C.,[10] and native traditions would have it that it originated even earlier, with the antediluvian sages at the end of the fourth millennium.[11] Its latest floruit occurred at the end of the pre-Christian era, and at least one canonical text is dated as late as 227 of the Seleucid Era and 163 of the Arsacid (Parthian) Era (or 85 B.C.).[12] And in the long interval between these extreme terminals, much of it was copied and preserved with a remarkable degree of textual fidelity.

A single linguistic and literary tradition spanning two and a half or even three millennia surely deserves to be studied in terms of its own history. Moreover, it should be fairly easy to avoid some of the major pitfalls of conventional literary history[13] in connection with Sumerian literature. We are not tempted to use it for the reconstruction of national or social history given the fact that the last two millennia of Sumerian literature were produced in the admitted absence of a Sumerian nation or society and that, even before that time, the very existence of a recognizable Sumerian ethnic group has been challenged.[14] Nor are we prone to offer, in the guise of literary history, a series of disconnected essays on individual authors, given the fact that the vast majority of Sumerian literary works are anonymous or at best pseudonymous in authorship.

We are thus virtually forced to devote our attention to the proper concerns of literary history, beginning with "the establishment of the exact position of each

---

8. Hartman, *Beyond Formalism*, pp. 356–86.

9. For the nearest competition, see Hellmut Brunner, *Grundzüge einer Geschichte der altägyptischen Literatur* (Darmstadt, 1966). See also the reviews by V. Wessetzky, *BiOr* XXIV (1967) 156–57 and by G. Björkman, *BiOr* XXIX (1972) 178.

10. R. D. Biggs, "The Abū Ṣalābīkh Tablets: A Preliminary Survey," *JCS* XX (1966) 73–88; M. Civil and R. D. Biggs, "Notes sur des textes sumériens archaïques," *RA* LX (1966) 1–16; and below, n. 36. For the chronological question, see Hallo, "The Date of the Fara Period," *Or*, n.s., Vol. 42 (1972) pp. 228–38. The definitive edition of the literary and lexical texts from Abū Ṣalābīkh (and parallels from Fara) has now appeared; see R. D. Biggs, *Inscriptions from Tell Abū Ṣalābīkh* (*OIP* XCIX [1974]).

11. Hallo, "On the Antiquity of Sumerian Literature," *JAOS*, Vol. 83 (1963) pp. 167–76, esp. 175–76.

12. G. A. Reisner, *Sumerisch-babylonische Hymnen nach Thontafeln griechischer Zeit* (Berlin, 1896) No. 55. No. 49 may even be dated four years later. See also below, n. 46.

13. Wellek and Warren, *Theory of Literature*, p. 253.

14. F. R. Kraus, *Sumerer und Akkader, ein Problem der altmesopotamischen Geschichte* (Amsterdam, 1970), esp. ch. vii. J. S. Cooper, "Sumerian and Akkadian in Sumer and Akkad," *Or*, n.s., Vol. 42 (1973) pp. 239–46.

work in a tradition."[15] From there it is a logical step to the "morphological approach," that is, "the history of genres" or the "problem of the development of a type."[16] Finally the extensive perspective afforded by our corpus leads naturally to a meaningful periodization which, while "embedded in the historical process,"[17] is based in the first instance on the cumulative evidence of major periods of creativity, adaptation, and consolidation of the literary material.

So ambitious a programme can at this stage be tackled only by means of illustrative examples. But by selecting the examples widely from a representative genre, it is intended to validate the general approach and to encourage more systematic efforts along similar lines.

In the long history of transmission, each genre tended to undergo different treatment. If these different treatments are to be compared, it must be done according to some common scale. Admittedly there will inevitably be a subjective bias in the choice of such a scale. The one chosen here is that of fidelity to the received text. On this basis, it is possible to grade the genre histories from an extreme of slavish fidelity on one hand, via various degrees of organic expansion and creative adaptation, all the way to total suppression or displacement. As we shall see, however, the extremes join in the case of the occasional late recovery of an early text that had not survived in the tradition. I will begin my survey with a rather extreme example of textual fidelity in the context of a continuing tradition.

The Exploits of Ninurta is the name currently given to the composition known anciently by its incipit as lugal-(e) u₄ me-lám-bi nir-gál. Modern classifications assign it to the genre of myth, since its protagonists are drawn from the divine realm, and its story, however interpreted, clearly presents a legendary occurrence as a paradigm for a continuing experience, whether in the human sphere or in nature. But in the native system, it figures rather as a hymn of praise to the deity, concluding with the requisite doxology: "Oh Ninurta, it is good (or, in the late version: exalting) to praise (zà-mí) you," and this is true of all the texts to be considered in this section.

The text of the composition, virtually complete in over 700 lines, has been reconstructed by J. van Dijk from some 130 exemplars.[18] Nearly two-thirds of these date from the Old Babylonian scribal schools at Nippur and (to a lesser extent) Ur, which flourished in the eighteenth and nineteenth centuries, respectively. At least three bilingual texts from Assur may belong to the library of Tiglath-Pileser I (1115–1077 B.C.), according to Weidner.[19] The rest date

---

15. Wellek and Warren, *Theory of Literature*, p. 259.

16. *Ibid.*, p. 261.

17. *Ibid.*, p. 265. See in this connection Fawzi Rasheed, "Sumerian Literature: Its Character and Development," *Sumer* XXVIII (1972) 9–15.

18. I am indebted to him for his transliteration in manuscript form. The first 180 lines are preserved on the large Yale tablet YBC 9867 (Old Babylonian).

19. E. F. Weidner, "Die Bibliothek Tiglatpilesers I.," *AfO* XVI (1952–53) 197–215.

from the first millennium, particularly the royal Assyrian libraries in the seventh century. A comparison of the three versions is instructive. In the overwhelming majority of cases, the late text reproduces the early text with no more orthographic variants than can be found among various exemplars of the early text itself. In other cases, the original sense of the text has been lost, and the later version substitutes a wholly new one in both Sumerian and Akkadian. In those relatively few instances where all three periods are represented, the Middle Assyrian versions vary with the later and against the earlier.

Within limits, a similar situation characterizes the shorter epic of Ninurta called Angim. The edition by J. Cooper shows, however, that the late version is occasionally closer to the early version than is the intermediate version.[20]

In attempting to account for the striking tenacity of this particular textual tradition, it is necessary to pursue the literary history of the two compositions further back than their earliest written manifestations in Old Babylonian times. Both deal with Ninurta; both allude in mythological terms to campaigns against the "mountains." In Lugale, the victory of Ninurta is reconstructed in detail; in Angim, this victory is presupposed and, in its aftermath, the spoils of war are donated in Nippur. It is difficult to escape the conclusion that real historical events provide the background.[21] Already Hrozný had argued that Lugale contained an explicit allusion to Gudea (XI 13-16 = lines 475-78 of the combined text) in the context of (the so-called ki-a-nag) offerings to the statues of deceased rulers and grandees.[22] Several almost verbatim correspondences between Lugale and the inscriptions of Gudea of Lagash have been noted and the same can be said for Angim.[23] Given the historical datum of Gudea's campaigns against Anshan and Elam, we may well have before us the mythological version of these events. The compositions probably owe their incorporation into the Nippur curriculum to the substitution of Ninurta of Nippur for his Lagashite equivalent Ningirsu[24] and their preservation beyond

20. Chiefly *KAR*, Nos. 12 and 18. I am indebted to Professor Cooper for an advanced copy of his revised working text (May, 1973) of the edition. As he points out in his introduction (May, 1975), however, the only fully preserved subscript of the composition labels it a šìr-gíd-da of Ninurta.

21. Cf. Hallo and Van Dijk, *The Exaltation of Inanna* (*YNER*, Vol. 3 [1968]) p. 66.

22. Friedrich Hrozný, "Sumerisch-babylonische Mythen von dem Gotte Ninrag (Ninib)," *MVAG*, Vol. 8/5 (1903) p. 64. Cf. A. Falkenstein, in *CRRA* II 14; *Die Inschriften Gudeas von Lagaš* I (*AnOr*, Vol. 30 [1966]) pp. 45, 139; *RLA*, Vol. 3 (1971) p. 677.

23. Note especially the reference, by name, to the divine weapons šar-gaz, šar-ùr, etc., in both Angim (e.g. ll. 129 f. = III 24 f.) and Gudea's date formulas and inscriptions; see simply Falkenstein, *AnOr*, Vol. 30, p. 111, n. 4. For other correspondences, see B. Landsberger, "Einige . . . Nomina des Akkadischen," *Wiener Zeitschrift für die Kunde des Morgenlandes*, Vol. 57 (1961) p. 12. Note that the same weapons still occur in the inscriptions of Esarhaddon.

24. Such substitutions therefore have greater significance than is assigned to them by B. Alster, *Dumuzi's Dream: Aspects of Oral Poetry in Sumerian Myth* (Copenhagen, 1972) p. 44, and "'Ninurta and the Turtle,' *UET* 6/1 2," *JCS* XXIV (1972) p. 120 and n. 2. For Ninurta in connection with both Nippur and Lagash, cf. already *SLTNi*, No. 61 (ed. M. E. Cohen, in *WO* VIII [1975] 22-36) ll. 58-87, esp. l. 64.

Old Babylonian times precisely to the sublimation of specific historical allusions into mythological forms.

What is here suggested then is that these (and possibly other)[25] myths to Ninurta were commissioned in their original form at the court of Gudea, or at least inspired by his exploits shortly after his reign, and that they helped to perpetuate his memory thereafter.[26] The suggestion cannot be proved as yet, but it can be buttressed by various considerations. Gudea appears as patron of Sumerian literary (and artistic) creations of the highest order (the Cylinders of Gudea; the statue inscriptions, etc.).[27] He enjoyed posthumous worship in the Ur III period in the form of ki-a-nag offerings;[28] and he figured in the Old Babylonian canonical literature of Nippur[29] and Larsa.[30]

Royal patronage of Sumerian literature did not, however, begin with Gudea. As early as the Sargonic period, not only can we point to Sargon or Naram-Sin as probable patrons but we can identify the author whom they commissioned. Enheduanna, daughter of the former and older contemporary of the latter, claimed the authorship of two significant cycles of hymns, and there is little reason to deny the claim. For although pseudepigraphical attribution is not a priori to be excluded, it is noteworthy that Enheduanna's principal contemporary monument was still standing in Old Babylonian Ur as is evident from the copy identified by Sollberger,[31] thus making her an unlikely candidate for legen-

25. Cf. also *TMH* NF IV, No. 49 and Alster, in *JCS* XXIV 120–25. This text reads more like a parody than a serious hymn to Ninurta, though A. J. Ferrara, *Nanna-Suen's Journey to Nippur* (Rome, 1973) p. 4, n. 7 calls it "Ninurta's Journey to Eridu." See also M. E. Cohen, in *JCS* XXV (1973) p. 208 f., n. 29, for multiple allusions to Ninurta myths in late Ninurta balag-laments.

26. Cf. Falkenstein, *AnOr*, Vol. 30, p. 45: "although the passage [above, n. 22] does not mention Gudea by name, it was clear to anyone familiar with Babylonian history to whom it alluded" (translation mine).

27. Falkenstein, *AnOr*, Vol. 30.

28. N. Schneider, "Die Urkundenbehälter von Ur III und ihre archivalische Systematik," *Or*, n.s., Vol. 9 (1940) p. 23, and above, n. 22.

29. Hymn to Nanshe (*SLTNi*, No. 67 and duplicates); tigi-hymn to Baᵓu (*STVC*, No. 36): cf. Falkenstein, *AnOr*, Vol. 30, pp. 44–45, and Hallo, "Royal Hymns and Mesopotamian Unity," *JCS* XVII (1963) 115; Temple Hymn No. 20: cf. C. Wilcke, "Der aktuelle Bezug der Sammlung der sumerischen Tempel-hymnen und ein Fragment eines Klageliedes," *ZA*, Vol. 62 (1972) pp. 48–49. Cf. now also G. Gragg, "The Fable of the Heron and the Turtle," *AfO* XXIV (1973) 51–72, l. 19.

30. E. Sollberger, "The Rulers of Lagash," *JCS* XXI (1967) 282, ll. 198–99. This text, which Sollberger dates to the middle Old Babylonian (i.e., Larsa) period, is clearly a kind of polemic against the canonical Sumerian King List as tradited at Nippur, which ignored both Lagash and Larsa. It thus accomplished for Lagash what the W-B 62 recension (Langdon, *OECT* II, Pl. VI) did in its way for Larsa, and both documents presumably originated from the latter city. That Gudea himself ruled over Larsa was still unknown to Falkenstein, *AnOr*, Vol. 30, pp. 42–46, but is now highly probable in light of the new French excavations, which have turned up a brick to Nanshe and a clay nail to Ningirsu inscribed by Gudea on the site; see D. Arnaud, "Nouveaux jalons pour une histoire de Larsa," *Sumer* XXVII (1971) 43–44.

31. *RA* LXIII (1969) 180 (ad *UET* I, No. 289).

dary status at that time. Moreover, there is increasing evidence for women, and especially royal princesses, as authors of major Sumerian literary works. Thus, the widow of Ur-Nammu has been proposed as the author of the hymn memorializing his death and burial,[32] and the daughter of Sin-kashid of Uruk is the author of an important letter-prayer to Rim-Sin of Larsa.[33] In addition, there are various love songs and lullabies purportedly sung to the kings of Ur III (notably Shu-Sin) by their wives or mothers.[34]

The two Enheduanna cycles are related to each other, although different in character. The first, consisting of Inanna and Ebih, in-nin šà-gur$_x$-ra, and The Exaltation of Inanna, constitutes hymns of praise to Inanna, patron deity of the Sargonic kings, in which their triumphs over foreign enemies and internal rebellions are thinly disguised as the *res gestae* of the goddess. In the second, the temples of Sumer and Akkad are apostrophized in a manner calculated to put royal solicitude for them in the best possible light: having triumphed in war and crushed Sumerian political aspirations, the Sargonic kings are nevertheless depicted as defenders of the traditional Sumerian faith.[35] This conception of Enheduanna's work as glorifying her king in war and peace can be compared, in the visual arts, with the famous Standard of Ur from the Royal Cemetery at Ur some three centuries earlier. It also provides a model for the anonymous Ninurta hymns dated (above) nearly two centuries later, since Lugale focuses on military exploits and Angim on their cultic consequences. Yet the actual history of the Enheduanna corpus was quite different from that of the latter.

This history begins as early as *ca.* 2500 B.C. at Abū Ṣalābīkh, among whose literary tablets, R. D. Biggs has identified not only "an archaic Sumerian version of the Kesh Temple Hymn"[36] but also fragments of briefer temple hymns more closely related to the later cycle of Enheduanna.[37] She is expressly described as the compiler of the cycle in its colophon, and it thus seems reasonable to suppose that she adapted and incorporated, at least in part, pre-existing hymns to individual temples such as those from archaic Abū Ṣalābīkh. But the colophon also credits her with creating what "no one has created (before)," using the terminology of child-bearing, as does The Exaltation of Inanna,[38] to describe the

32. C. Wilcke, "Eine Schicksalsentscheidung für den toten Urnammu," *CRRA* XVII 86. For her identity, see either Sollberger, "Ladies of the Ur-III Empire," *RA* LXI (1967) 69 (Watartum?) or Civil, "Un nouveau synchronisme Mari–IIIe dynastie d'Ur," *RA* LXI (1962) 213 (Tarām-Uram; cf. Hallo, in *RLA*, Vol. 4 [1972] pp. 13 f.).

33. Hallo, "The Royal Correspondence of Larsa" (forthcoming).

34. S. N. Kramer, in *ANET* (3d ed., 1969) pp. 644–45, 651–52.

35. Hallo and Van Dijk, *Exaltation*, ch. i; C. Wilcke, in *ZA*, Vol. 62, pp. 35–61. Wilcke's study, like mine of 1970 (below, note 49), investigated the "Sitz im Leben" of Sumerian poetry and concluded (by a process of elimination) that the Temple Hymns survived in the courtly ceremonial as implicit praise for any given king who was solicitous of the temples.

36. R. D. Biggs, "An Archaic Version of the Kesh Temple Hymn from Tell Abū Ṣalābīkh," *ZA*, Vol. 61 (1971) pp. 193–207.

37. *Ibid.*, p. 195 f.; cf. Å. Sjöberg and E. Bergmann, *The Collection of the Sumerian Temple Hymns* (*TCS* III [1969]) p. 6.

38. Hallo and Van Dijk, *Exaltation*, pp. 61–62.

process of poetic creativity. Presumably, it was the composition of the cycle as a whole that represented her creative contribution.[39]

The oldest actual exemplar used in reconstructing the temple hymn cycle is dated by Sjöberg to the Ur III period.[40] At this period, the text was still apparently to some degree in flux: a Sargonic date for its original composition can be reconciled with its form in the Old Babylonian version only on the assumption that, in the interim, it was expanded to admit the inclusion of hymns to temples built in neo-Sumerian times. This is particularly evident in the case of Temple Hymn No. 9 in honor of the palace of Shulgi. The internal development of the cycle of Enheduanna's hymns to Inanna is somewhat different. All known exemplars date from Old Babylonian times, and variants among them are relatively minor.[41] In the case of Innin-šagurra, some of the later Old Babylonian exemplars are written in syllabic Sumerian and include an interlinear translation into Akkadian.[42]

What both cycles have in common, however, is their complete disappearance from the canon after Old Babylonian times. Unlike the Ninurta hymns, it may be argued, they failed to sublimate their historical particulars sufficiently to qualify for enduring and universal interest in the cuneiform curriculum. Though their allusions may be obscure enough to lead to very different modern interpretations,[43] they did not end as proper myth. At best it can be said that one of their themes, the exaltation of Inanna to equal rank with An at the head of the pantheon, was taken up in very different form in the bilingual poem Ninmah-ušuni-girra. Traditionally, this poem is ascribed to Taqīsha-Gula, a lamentation-priest and scholar of Nippur,[44] who is said to date back to the time of Abi-eshuh in the late Old Babylonian period.[45] But its extant exemplars date from the seventh to the fourth centuries B.C.[46] and show little evidence of pre-Kassite origins.

At best; but the suggestion just offered is much better illustrated in another instance. If we have so far dealt with the two extremes of textual preservation—

39. Sumerian KA-kèš-da, "compiler," is used of Enheduanna in the colophon of the Temple Hymns just as *kāṣiru*, its Akkadian equivalent, is used of the author of the Erra Epic; cf. Sjöberg, *TCS* III 150.

40. Sjöberg and Bergmann, *TCS* III 6; see copies, Pls. XXXVII f.

41. For some of the more significant ones, see Hallo and Van Dijk, *Exaltation*, pp. 41 and 97 f.

42. J. J. A. van Dijk, "Textes divers du Musée de Baghdad," *Sumer* XI (1955) 110, Pl. VI, and *Sumer* XIII (1957) 69–79.

43. Compare, e.g., the interpretation of The Exaltation of Inanna offered in Hallo and Van Dijk, *Exaltation*, with that of Kramer, in *ANET* (3d ed., 1969) pp. 579–82.

44. W. G. Lambert, "A Catalogue of Texts and Authors," *JCS* XVI (1962) 75–76.

45. Van Dijk, *UVB* XVIII (1962) 51 *ad* line 15.

46. B. Hruška, "Das spätbabylonische Lehrgedicht 'Inannas Erhöhung,'" *ArOr*, Vol. 37 (1969) pp. 473–522. I fail to see the basis for Hruška's statement (p. 477) that one of the exemplars, which he dates to 316 B.C., is the latest bilingual literary text known (see above, n. 12). Cf. also W. G. Lambert, "L'exaltation d'Ishtar," *Or*, n.s., Vol. 40 (1971) pp. 91–95.

slavish fidelity and total obliteration—we must consider now the large intermediate area within which preservation was achieved by means of a greater or lesser degree of adaptation. We may begin with The Curse of Agade, since this composition, like the cycles already considered, arose out of a specific historical context. It too dealt with the Sargonic dynasty; it too formally constituted a hymn of praise to Inanna; it too dates back to Ur III times on the evidence of several of its exemplars[47] and then enjoyed considerable popularity in the Old Babylonian curriculum. Beyond that, its history ran a middle course between the extremes illustrated above. It was neither totally eliminated from the canon nor simply perpetuated. Instead it was creatively transformed to meet the ideological requirements of a new age, the vehicle for (or at least concomitant of) the transformation being, in this case, translation into Akkadian. Specifically, the historical viewpoint and major outlines of the plot of the original composition (which seem most at home in a neo-Sumerian milieu) are reproduced in the fragmentary Weidner Chronicle, with certain significant alterations. Notably they substitute Babylon and Marduk for Nippur and Enlil as the aggrieved city and its avenging deity respectively.[48] But both agree that Naram-Sin was the victim of the divine retribution (though in point of historical fact he probably was not), and the Gutian hordes its instrument.

The Weidner Chronicle pursues the theme of divine intervention in the fate of empires by applying it in turn to the Gutians themselves. Although this topic is beyond the scope of The Curse of Agade, it has a corresponding model in the inscription of Utu-hegal of Uruk, which is equally a literary document, albeit less well attested. Here too, the Sumerian Enlil is replaced in the Akkadian text by Marduk, but the human agent remains the same Utu-hegal. These examples illustrate the same ideological modernizing within a documented textual tradition which was posited above for the transition from an assumed and perhaps oral original from Lagash dealing with Ningirsu to an attested written version, chiefly of Nippur, centered on Ninurta. They show that specific historical allusions were not, as such, an insuperable obstacle to the preservation of literary materials provided their mythical settings were updated.

Having thus constructed in some detail a paradigm for the category of "history into myth," we may deal more briefly with that of "history into legend," or what in modern terms is generally regarded as epic. Again, however, it should be remembered that the modern distinction is not observed in the ancient texts themselves. Rather these end, as do "myths" with the typical hymnic

47. A. Falkenstein, "Fluch über Akkade," *ZA*, Vol. 57 (1965) p. 44.

48. Hallo, "Gutium," *RLA*, Vol. 3 (1971) p. 709. Similarly the stele's version of the prologue to the Laws of Hammurapi has substituted Babylon and Marduk for Nippur and Enlil in the version published by D. J. Wiseman, "The Laws of Hammurabi Again," *Journal of Semitic Studies* VII (1962) 161–72. The latter version preserves the oldest formulation according to R. Borger, *Babylonisch-Assyrische Lesestücke* II (Rome, 1963) 7; cf. also A. Finet, *Le Code de Hammurapi* (Paris, 1973) pp. 31–32.

doxology except that now the praise is addressed, not to the deity, but to the deceased heroic mortal.[49]

As is well known, the principal subject of the Sumerian epic tales is the First Dynasty of Uruk, to be dated in the Early Dynastic II period (*ca.* 2700–2500 B.C.), probably in its second quarter (*ca.* 2650–2600).[50] The lords of distant Aratta and the last kings of the First Dynasty of Kish also figure in the epics, while other literary sources, notably the History of the Tummal, reveal the links of both Uruk and Kish with the First Dynasty of Ur.[51]

The common distinctive feature of the Sumerian epic corpus is that it deals with heroic rulers of a distant past, in a form reduced to writing long after the events described, most likely in the Ur III period, and very conceivably on the basis of a pre-existing oral tradition. It is this feature that best accounts for the considerable range of variation in different Old Babylonian recensions of given epics[52] and for their preservation, beyond Old Babylonian times, in much the same variety of ways as already detailed for the mythology. Specifically, these ways include: (1) more or less literal transmission into neo-Assyrian times together with a verbatim interlinear translation into Akkadian (Lugalbanda epic);[53] (2) scattered allusions in later Akkadian and classical sources (Enmerkar cycle);[54] (3) organic transformation of the original Sumerian episodes into components of new Akkadian compositions on the same themes. This last characterization applies in the first instance to the bulk of the material dealing with Gilgamesh.[55] A special case is represented by the twelfth chapter (tablet) of the canonical Akkadian Gilgamesh epic, which is a literal translation of one of the pre-existing Sumerian episodes, and as such the principal exception to the

49. Hallo, "The Cultic Setting of Sumerian Poetry," *CRRA* XVII 117. Cf. the listing by W. Heimpel in *JAOS*, Vol. 92 (1972) p. 290, n. 8. Note that some exemplars of the Lugalbanda epic write his name with the divine determinative: C. Wilcke, *Das Lugalbandaepos* (Wiesbaden, 1969) pp. 51–52.

50. Hallo and Simpson, *The Ancient Near East: A History* (New York, 1971) p. 47. Note that Sollberger dates (En)mebaragesi of Kish about 2630–2600 B.C. (*Inscriptions royales sumériennes et akkadiennes* [Paris, 1971] p. 39). In my scheme, the latter is contemporary with Gilgamesh (Hallo and Simpson, *The Ancient Near East*, p. 46).

51. Hallo and Simpson, *The Ancient Near East*, p. 46; cf. Sollberger, "The Tummal Inscription," *JCS* XVI (1962) 40 ff.

52. Notably, e.g., in the case of Gilgamesh and the Land of the Living. See in detail H. Limet, "Les chants épiques sumériens," *Revue belge de philologie et d'histoire* L (1972) 3–24, esp. 8–9.

53. *CT* XV, Pls. 41–43, edited by Wilcke, *Das Lugalbandaepos*, pp. 90–98. See pp. 23–28 for the textual history of this epic.

54. See the references collected by T. Jacobsen, *The Sumerian King List* (*AS*, No. 11 [1939]) pp. 86–87, n. 115. For the *apkallu* text cited there, see more recently E. Reiner, "The Etiological Myth of the 'Seven Sages,'" *Or*, n.s., Vol. 30 (1961) pp. 1–11.

55. The classic study on this subject is Kramer's "The Epic of Gilgameš and Its Sumerian Sources," *JAOS*, Vol. 64 (1944) pp. 7–23. Since then the material has been reviewed by Aaron Shaffer, "Sumerian Sources of Tablet XII of the Epic of Gilgameš" (Ph.D. diss., University of Pennsylvania, 1963), and by J. H. Tigay, "Literary-Critical Studies in the Gilgameš Epic" (Ph.D. diss., Yale University, 1971).

general rule that straightforward Akkadian translations of Sumerian originals (outside the area of wisdom literature)[56] appear only in the form of bilinguals, that is, in combination with their Sumerian originals.[57]

It is debatable whether any of the Dumuzi material fits into this category. In the first place, it is not certain whether Dumuzi reflects the Urukian ruler of the King List tradition or the antediluvian king of Bad Tibira. Second, the bulk of the Dumuzi texts are generically cultic songs according to their subscripts. Only The Descent of Inanna ends, like the epics, with the zà-mí notation, and this is addressed, not to Dumuzi, but to Eresh-kigal.[58] At best we can regard the Akkadian myth of The Descent of Ishtar (and possibly that of Nergal and Eresh-kigal) as preserving elements of a Sumerian tradition which may have dealt in epic fashion with the exploits of a historic ruler of Uruk.

We have so far dealt with hymns of praise (zà-mí), which can be argued to have recast recent history into cosmological terms (myth) or more remote events into heroic ones (epic), in both cases inextricably interweaving the human and divine realms of experience. But this is not intended to deny that the hymnic genre was equally capable of concentrating on either one of these realms in its own right. As long ago as 1944, Kramer collected and classified Sumerian mythology into myths of origins, myths of Kur (the netherworld), and miscellaneous myths.[59] As he interpreted them, these myths took place almost entirely in the divine sphere, though of course often with an etiological motive, that is, to account for a continuing situation observed in the human condition, preferably in terms of its origins. From the point of view at issue here, what is most striking about these and similar myths is that almost without exception they have no literary history at all. They appear in fixed form in copies (sometimes numerous copies) datable to a relatively short span of time, normally within the Old Babylonian period,[60] occasionally earlier.[61] Only rarely are the

56. Cf. e.g., E. I. Gordon, "A New Look at the Wisdom of Sumer and Akkad," *BiOr* XVII (1960) 127, n. 46, and 129 f., n. 57.

57. This rule has been generally overlooked, except by W. von Soden (*Zweisprachigkeit in der geistigen Kultur Babyloniens* [Graz, 1960] p. 9), who noted that the Akkadian translator "die Übersetzungen in der Regel nicht für sich allein, sondern zusammen mit dem sumerischen Original abschrieb." See now also W. G. Lambert, "DINGIR.ŠÀ.DIB.BA Incantations," *JNES*, Vol. 33 (1974) p. 270: "though it is common to find Sumerian texts with interlinear Akkadian translations, the translations did not usually circulate alone." Lambert offers another exception to the rule.

58. *UET* VI/1, No. 10 rev. 14 f.; cf. Kramer, in *PAPS*, Vol. 107 (1963) p. 515.

59. *Sumerian Mythology* (Philadelphia, 1944; rev. eds., 1961, 1972).

60. Notably the myths of Enlil and Ninlil, Enki and Ninhursag, Enki and Inanna, and The Marriage of Martu. Note, however, that the last text is, generically speaking, an antiphonal poem (lum-a-lam-a) and may reflect a princely wedding or other historic event; cf. Hallo and Van Dijk, *Exaltation*, p. 84, and G. Buccellati, *The Amorites of the Ur III Period* (Naples, 1966) p. 339.

61. For the Old Sumerian myths of Enlil and Ninhursag (*MBI*, No. 1) and Enlil and Ishkur (S. N. Kramer, *From the Tablets of Sumer* [Indian Hills, 1956] p. 106, Fig. 6A), see

themes of these myths taken up in recognizably similar forms in Akkadian; in the most striking case, that of the Flood Narrative, it has even been implied that the Sumerian version may be later than and dependent on the earliest Akkadian one.[62] Even rarer is the transmission of the Sumerian text, intact and with an Akkadian translation, into the first millennium, as exemplified best by the myth of Enlil and Sud.[63] Two of the principal themes of the older mythology, the loves and travels of the Sumerian deities, apparently ceased to interest the later periods by and large, while the third, etiology, was worked into the cosmological preamble (the prologue in heaven, as it were) of genres such as incantations more often than it was left in independent hymnic form. Only the traditions surrounding Dumuzi continued to exercise their full fascination on later audiences.

The history of royal hymnography is equally instructive. For fully five centuries (*ca.* 2140–1640 B.C.), some seven successive dynasties were apparently rewarded for their cultic deference to the national Sumerian shrines at Nippur through hymns composed in their honor by the Nippur priesthood and tradited wherever Sumerian scribal schools adopted the Nippur curriculum.[64] These hymns included many essentially divine hymns with only incidental mention of the king (chiefly in the context of short prayer-refrains invoking the divine blessings on the ruler then controlling Nippur), which were most likely at home in the temple liturgy:[65] of these more presently. Here we are concerned with the royal hymns properly speaking, that is, those concluding with the typical zà-mí doxology, spoken by, to or of the living king in first, second or third person. In the last case, the formal analogy with epics about the deceased rulers of Uruk is particularly clear, and it is conceivable that these epics served as models for what, in sum, added up to virtual hymnic biographies of the contemporary rulers.[66] Like the epics, these compositions lack all liturgical notations and were most likely at home not in the temple, but in the courtly ceremonial, where they may well have functioned in the context of the official (biennial?) proclamation of the royal date formulas.[67] Given all these links to

---

Sjöberg and Bergmann, *TCS* III 7 with notes 7 and 8. For the mythical fragment Urukagina 15, see most recently Hallo, "Antediluvian Cities," *JCS* XXIII (1970) 65 f.; Wilcke, *Das Lugalbandaepos*, p. 132; B. Alster, "En-ki nun-ki: Some Unobserved Duplicates, Ni 4057, etc.," *RA* LXIV (1970) 189–90.

62. M. Civil *apud* W. G. Lambert and A. R. Millard, *Atra-ḫasīs: The Babylonian Story of the Flood* (Oxford, 1969) pp. 138–45.

63. O. R. Gurney and P. Hulin, *The Sultantepe Tablets* II (London, 1964) Nos. 151–54; see the partial edition by M. Civil, in *JNES*, Vol. 26, pp. 200–205. Note also the myth of Enki and Ninmah, for which see most recently Carlos A. Benito, "'Enki and Ninmah' and 'Enki and the World Order'" (Ph.D. diss., University of Pennsylvania, 1969).

64. Hallo, in *JCS* XVII 112–18.

65. Hallo, "New Hymns to the Kings of Isin" *BiOr* XXIII (1966) 239–47.

66. Hallo, "The Coronation of Ur-Nammu," *JCS* XX (1966) 135.

67. Hallo, in *CRRA* XVII 118–19. A different conclusion was reached by Daniel Reisman ("Two Neo-Sumerian Royal Hymns" [Ph.D. diss., University of Pennsylvania, 1969] pp. 39–40), who regarded hymns of type B (including some addressed to deities without explicit reference to any king) as also belonging to the temple cult, though perhaps used at royal coronations and the like.

specific historic and political situations, it is a tribute to the literary taste and cosmopolitanism of the Old Babylonian schools that they tradited the royal hymns at all, regardless of their current dynastic affiliation.[68] It should cause little surprise that later ages, with their wholly new ideologies of kingship, ceased to preserve these compositions.[69] Even the genre as such can at most claim a remote successor in the Akkadian poems celebrating the achievements of the Middle Assyrian kings.

It was somewhat otherwise with the royal hymns in the wider sense (Römer's Type A),[70] that is, the liturgical hymns of various genres. Two of these, the adab- and tigi-genres, were particularly favored vehicles for incorporating prayers on behalf of the reigning king in the context of hymns to deities. These genres survived at least to the extent of occupying a prominent place in two literary catalogues of Middle Babylonian and Middle Assyrian date (ca. 1500 and 1100 B.C.), respectively.[71] The earlier catalogue listed by title (incipit) and deity up to eleven tigi-hymns (the individual entries are, however, largely lost) and fifteen adab-hymns; among the latter, three titles[72] can be identified with reasonable assurance as the opening words of adab-hymns for Nanna in honor of the city of Ur,[73] for Nergal in honor of Shu-ilishu of Isin, and for Ninurta in honor of Lipit-Ishtar of Isin.[74] The later catalogue[75] listed at least four collections (*iš-ka-ra-a-tu*) comprising numerous tigi-songs (*za-ma-ru*[meš] *te-ge-e*) (though the eighteen incipits actually preserved remain so far unidentified) and "five Sumerian adab-songs (forming) one collection" (5 *za-ma-ru il-ti-a-at* GIŠ.GÀR *a-da-pa šu-me-ra*). Of the latter, one title belongs to a hymn for An in honor of Ur-Ninurta of Isin.[76]

Thus, cultic hymns associated with the early kings of Isin were preserved into the second half of the second millennium, even though there is no evidence whatever for any interest in such relatively obscure kings as Shu-ilishu, Lipit-

---

68. Hallo, in *JCS* XVII 117 with notes 95–99.

69. Daniel Reisman, Kramer Anniversary Volume (*AOAT*, in press) has identified *OECT* I, Pls. 36–39 (and duplicates) as a royal hymn of the zà-mí type (though in some respects intermediate between types A and B) dedicated to Ishbi-Irra of Isin, and M. Civil has identified 4R, Pl. 35, l. 7 as a duplicate (see Reisman). But in spite of its Kuyunjik number (K. 4755), it may be questioned whether the fragment is neo-Assyrian.

70. *SKIZ*, pp. 5 f. Cf. my review in *BiOr* XXIII 240 f.

71. Hallo, in *JAOS*, Vol. 83, p. 169, Nos. 9 and 10.

72. *TMH* NF III (1961) No. 58, 11. 62, 70 and 67; see the edition by I. Bernhardt and S. N. Kramer, "Götter-Hymnen und Kult-Gesänge der Sumerer auf zwei Keilschrift-'Katalogen' in der Hilprecht-Sammlung," *WZJ*, Vol. 6 (1956–57) p. 392.

73. *SLTNi*, No. 58, edited by Sjöberg, *MNS* I 35–43. Add now *ISET* I 157, Ni. 4467 (see also p. 58).

74. Nos. *4 and *26 in *SKIZ*, ch. 3 and pp. 6–9, respectively.

75. *KAR*, No. 158; see the partial edition by A. Falkenstein, "Sumerische religiöse Texte," *ZA*, Vol. 49 (1949) pp. 91 and 103.

76. *SKIZ*, No. *31, edited on pp. 10–17, and see p. 58, n. 16; Falkenstein, *ZA*, Vol. 49, p. 88, No. 2 and n. 2; Hallo, in *BiOr* XXIII 242 and n. 44.

Ishtar or Ur-Ninurta at this late date.[77] But the explanation for this seeming paradox is not far to seek. So far from preserving specific biographical data like the true royal hymns, these cultic hymns allude to the king, when at all, only in the most general terms. The royal name is, in fact, of such secondary importance in these contexts that it is very often abbreviated almost beyond the point of recognition.[78] It may well be that such abbreviations, or the generic term for king (lugal), once substituted for the proper name, freed the composition of any vestige of historical or political particularism and smoothed its entry into the general curriculum. And another genre used in this connection, the antiphonal song (balbal-e), provides yet another model for the same process: the antiphonal song for Inanna which, in a Louvre version, invokes blessings on Ishme-Dagan of Isin,[79] in a Yale version substitutes a reference to Dumuzi, suggesting that it was suitable for *any* king performing the role of Dumuzi in the sacred marriage rite.[80]

For such reasons, then, the royal hymns of "Type A" survived longer than those of "Type B," but not by much. The libraries of the first millennium have not preserved cultic compositions with the traditional generic labels (tigi, adab, balbal-e, šìr) with one apparent exception: a tigi-song for Ninurta mentioned on a small fragment from the library of Assurbanipal at Nineveh.[81] But this exception only proves the rule, for the fragment involved has been successfully joined to five others published in the same volume[82] on the basis of a comparison with an Old Babylonian duplicate from Nippur published in 1967.[83] And the two versions, whose breaks can be largely restored with each other's help, prove that the late text is a reliable copy from the older one (or from a duplicate of it), and that we may in essence accept the statement of its colophon which can be restored on the basis of parallels to read "[copy] of Nippur written out according to its old prototype and [checked against the original]." We need only correct the subscript: it should have read tigi-song for Nintu, not Ninurta. The hymn thus recovered, nearly in its entirety, is interesting in its own right: it apostrophizes Nintu, patroness of childbirth, for putting her talents at the disposal of Enlil by giving birth to the high priest and the king,[84] so that the "chief executive" of the

---

77. There is, for example, no trace of the Laws of Lipit-Ishtar in copies of post-Old-Babylonian date. The only Isin kings recalled in the late historical tradition are Irra-imitti and Enlil-bani.

78. Hallo, "The Road to Emar," *JCS* XVIII (1964) 67, n. 11. Add possibly the spelling Sa (for Samsu-iluna) in a literary catalogue (*UET* V, No. 86, entry No. 6) according to Bernhardt and Kramer, in *WZJ*, Vol. 6, p. 394, n. 4.

79. *SKIZ*, No. *18, edited on pp. 21–29.

80. Hallo, in *BiOr* XXIII 244–45.

81. *Ibid.*, p. 242 with notes 35 f., referring to S. Langdon, *BL*, No. 97.

82. *BL*, Nos. 95, 102, 107, 111, 127; my letter of February 17, 1969, to Dr. Sollberger, who confirmed the joins by letter of February 26, 1969.

83. *TMH* NF IV (1967) No. 86; cf. Sjöberg, in *Or*, n.s., Vol. 38 (1969) p. 355, who independently identified this text with four of the Langdon fragments.

84. Assuming that lagal/lagar is a mistake for lugal in the Old Babylonian version; so Gertrud Farber-Flügge, *Der Mythos "Inanna und Enki"* (*StP*, Vol. 10 [1973]). The neo-Assyrian copyist mistook the sign for si; see my forthcoming edition of the text.

gods can assign these offices to his favorite mortals.[85] This is the traditional ideology of kingship, already on the wane when the Old Babylonian copy was written.[86] Yet the neo-Assyrian copyist resurrected the tigi-genre which was its vehicle and, more than a millennium later, copied the text with all the accuracy and objectivity that a modern Assyriologist would bring to the task. This example allows us to derive a more general principle: that the rediscovery of lost texts may be added to the preservation or adaptation of surviving texts as means whereby the literary heritage of the third and second millennia passed into the first within Mesopotamia.[87]

The literary histories we have traced to this point, selected from the hymnic genres, already point to at least one useful generalization: although the original creative impulse most often arose out of and in response to a specific historical situation, the long process of canonization (that is, the incorporation of the text in fixed form in the generally accepted curriculum of the scribal schools) tended to suppress allusions to these situations. If a composition resisted such sublimation or ideological updating, it tended to disappear from the canon. Thus, the history of Sumerian hymnography repeatedly illustrates the conversion of history into myth or, more generally, the triumph of religious over historical interests. The same process can be seen at work in the various kinds of prayer in Sumerian. This is not the place to repeat the long history of individual prayer in Sumerian, which has been traced elsewhere,[88] nor that of collective prayer as illustrated by the "congregational laments."[89] Suffice it to say that both histories involve the transformation of specific petitions or celebrations of particular one-time occasions into recurrent cultic services or commemorations. Consistent with the increasingly cultic orientation of Sumerian literature in the first millennium, the corpus of laments and prayers, both individual (ér-šà-hun-gá) and collective (balag, ér-šem-ma, šu-íl-la), tended not only to preserve material dating as far back as the very beginning of the second millen-

---

85. An edition of the combined text is in preparation.

86. For the unique addition of a prayer for the ruling king at the end of a late bilingual šu-íl-la composition, see J. S. Cooper, "A Sumerian šu-íl-la from Nimrud with a Prayer for Sin-šar-iškun," *Iraq* XXXII (1970) 51–67. For other late bilingual and Akkadian hymns, prayers and rituals of various kinds with blessings for reigning (neo-Assyrian) kings, see, e.g., W. von Soden in Falkenstein and Von Soden, *Sumerische und akkadische Hymnen und Gebete* (Zurich, 1953) passim; more recently R. Borger, "Baurituale," in M. A. Beek, *et al.*, eds., *Symbolae . . . de Liagre Böhl* (Leiden, 1973) pp. 50–55.

87. On the implications of this principle, also for comparative biblical studies, see my "Problems in Sumerian Hermeneutics" in Byron L. Sherwin, ed., *Perspectives in Jewish Learning* V (Chicago, 1973) 1–12. See also below, note 96, for an example of an Old Babylonian literary text rediscovered and copied (according to its colophon) in neo-Babylonian times.

88. Hallo, "Individual Prayer in Sumerian: The Continuity of a Tradition," *JAOS*, Vol. 88 (1968) pp. 71–89.

89. *SKly*; R. Kutscher, "A-ab-ba hu-luh-ha: The History of a Sumerian Congregational Lament" (Ph.D. diss., Yale University, 1966; to appear as *YNER*, Vol. 6).

nium[90] but also to grow by imitation and new additions to the very end of the first.[91]

Nor is this the place to review the arguments recently advanced in favor of the oral prehistory of much of Sumerian literature, based inevitably, as they largely are, on a combination of hypotheses and analogies from later, in part much later, world literature.[92] Rather, the object here, while remaining within the limits of the written evidence, is to extend the scope of the inquiry beyond the confines of canonical literature in order to gain a fuller picture of both the creative impulse and the process of canonization. Elsewhere, I have already assembled some of the evidence to show the large variety of *monumental* genres which found their way into the canon, among them cadastres, law codes and royal inscriptions.[93] (The copying of such monuments from the original steles is now in fact known to have been a prescribed part of the scribal curriculum.[94]) And I used this evidence to argue that the typical royal, divine and temple hymn may often go back to a monumental origin as well. Indeed, this origin is implicit or explicit in a growing number of cases.[95] Even incantations on occasion originated on "stone steles."[96]

What deserves special attention at this time, however, is the creation of canonical literature out of *archival* prototypes. On the most basic level, this involved the orderly abstraction of lexical entries, grammatical forms and legal formulations from documentary sources to form the core of the perennial cuneiform lexical tradition. This was then assimilated to the hymnic genre by the simple device of appending a concluding doxology addressed to Nisaba (and sometimes her consort Haia) as divine patron(s) of the scribal art. While the meaning of zà-mí in this connection is closer to "glory" or "praise" (Akk. *tanittu*) than to "hymn" (Akk. *sammû*),[97] the generic connotation may not have been totally excluded, for example, at the end of various collections of model contracts.[98] These contracts with their specific tallies, prices and personal names strongly suggest that they were copied from actual archives. They differ

90. J. Krecher, "Zum Emesal-Dialekt des Sumerischen," *HSAO*, p. 88, and "Die sumerischen Texte in 'syllabischer' Orthographie," *ZA*, Vol. 58 (1967) pp. 19–22 ad *NFT*, Nos. 202–12.

91. M. E. Cohen is preparing new editions of the balag and ér-šem-ma compositions.

92. See especially Alster, *Dumuzi's Dream*.

93. In *CRRA* XVII 121.

94. Sjöberg, "In Praise of the Scribal Art," *JCS* XXIV (1972) 129 *ad* "Examination Text D," l. 15.

95. E.g., *UET* VIII, Nos. 62, 65 and 79, with Sollberger's comments in the Descriptive Catalogue.

96. B. Alster, "A Sumerian Incantation against Gall," *Or*, n.s., Vol. 41 (1972) pp. 349–58.

97. Both equivalents are attested; see H. Hartmann, *Die Musik der sumerischen Kultur* (Frankfurt, 1960) pp. 71–73.

98. Ist.Ni. 10194, 10570. Differently NBC 7800: til[sic]-la ᵈNisaba ù ᵈHa-ià (cf. *YOS* I, No. 28 end: ti-la ᵈNisaba ù ᵈHa-ià). An edition of the whole genre is in preparation.

from functional documents only in two respects: they are arranged on "Sammeltafeln" in a conscious order, probably for didactic purposes, that foreshadows
later compendia of legal formulations such as *ana ittišu*; and they substitute for
the original list of witnesses and date the notations "its witnesses, its date
(literally: year)."

These clues help to illuminate the evolution of somewhat more genuinely
literary genres, such as the collections of letters and related documents. Whether
dealing with the royal houses of Ur, Isin or Larsa, they concentrate on a single
thread of interest running through them. In the Ur correspondence, this is the
relation of the king to one of his high officials,[99] in that of Isin, the dispute with
Larsa over water rights,[100] in that of Larsa a variety of political and personal
problems involving chiefly Sin-iddinam and Rim-Sin.[101] While these particular
collections went out of fashion with the end of the Old Babylonian schools,
another survived: the corpus of "scribal letters" revolving around high officials
at Nippur in neo-Sumerian times was still taught at Ugarit and Hattusha in the
middle of the second millennium.[102] The many prosopographic interconnections
among these scribal letters, as also among certain compositions usually classed
with the wisdom literature (e.g. the Message of Lu-dingira to His Mother and the
Pushkin Elegies), suggest that we have here the makings of, as it were, several
novellas of family life in aristocratic circles at Nippur; though perhaps never
actually put into this form, such novellas can almost be reconstructed with their
help.[103]

In much the same way, the Old Babylonian copies of neo-Sumerian royal
inscriptions seem to concentrate by preference on the "triumphal inscriptions"[104]
of Shu-Sin of Ur as if in preparation for a connected history of his campaigns
in the East. In the event, this too proved to be beyond the interest or capacity of
Babylonian writers, and it remained for Assyrian historiography to exploit the
potential of the genre.

To sum up: even a cursory glance at the Sumerian texts defined in the native
sources as hymns shows the possibilities inherent in a historical approach to

99. The royal correspondence of Ur is the subject of a forthcoming Ph.D. thesis by P.
Michalowski (Yale).

100. See for now Letter Collection B in F. A. Ali, "Sumerian Letters," (Ph.D. diss.,
University of Pennsylvania, 1964). Cf. also M. B. Rowton, "Water Courses and Water
Rights in the Official Correspondence from Larsa and Isin," *JCS* XXI (1967) 267–74.

101. Above, note 33.

102. J. Nougayrol *et al.*, *Ugaritica* V (1968) 23, *ad* No. 15; cf. Krecher, "Schreiberschulung in Ugarit: die Tradition von Listen und sumerischen Texten," *UF*, Vol. 1 (1969) pp.
131–58, esp. 152–54.

103. For a modern reconstruction, see e.g. Hallo, "The House of Ur-Meme," *JNES*,
Vol. 31 (1972) pp. 87–95.

104. For this useful addition to the typology of royal inscriptions, see J.-R. Kupper,
"Les inscriptions triomphales akkadiennes," *Oriens Antiquus* X (1971) 91–106; cf. E.
Sollberger and J.-R. Kupper, *Inscriptions royales sumeriennes et akkadiennes* (Paris, 1971)
pp. 32–33. The suggestion is criticized by G. van Driel, "On 'Standard' and 'Triumphal'
Inscriptions," *Symbolae . . . de Liagre Böhl* (Leiden, 1973) pp. 99–106.

Sumerian literature. The approach could and should be extended to other broad categories slighted or ignored above. It promises new insights and implications for all cuneiform literature and for the history of literature in general. Here there is room only for a general hypothesis about the periodization of the literary process.

Employing a variety of cultural criteria which cannot be defended in detail here, the nearly two and a half millennia of Mesopotamian literary history referred to at the outset may be conveniently divided into eight equal installments of three centuries each and labelled according to their dominant cultural factor as follows (all dates are approximate):

> 2500–2200 B.C.: Old Sumerian (OS)
> 2200–1900 B.C.: Neo-Sumerian (NS)
> 1900–1600 B.C.: Old Babylonian (OB)
> 1600–1300 B.C.: Middle Babylonian (MB)
> 1300–1000 B.C.: Middle Assyrian (MA)
> 1000–700 B.C.: Neo-Assyrian (NA)
> 700–400 B.C.: Neo-Babylonian (NB)
> 400–100 B.C.: Late Babylonian (LB)

In order to fit the Sumerian component into this framework, one must also take into account the bilingual and dialectal (Emesal) traditions, which directly reflect Sumerian models, and the unilingual Akkadian tradition, which often reflected them indirectly. Nor should one lose sight of the possible existence, at all times, of an oral tradition. All these traditions deserve fuller study in their own right.[105] I have previously suggested four distinct canons of cuneiform literature, of which three involved Sumerian;[106] the examples given above may now be used as a starting-point to elaborate on the suggestion.

The Old Sumerian canon drew on the literature created from the Fara period to the end of the high Sargonic age (*ca.* 2500–2200 B.C.). This period included the pre-Sargonic dynasties of Lagash (Lagash I), where the literary dialect achieved an early flowering as a vehicle not only for monumental inscriptions but also for mythology and wisdom.[107] This first canon was adapted in neo-Sumerian times which, for literary and linguistic purposes, includes the late Sargonic or Gudea

---

105. Dialectal Sumerian has been studied in some detail by Krecher: *SKly*; in *HSAO*, pp. 87–110; in *ZA*, Vol. 58, pp. 16–65; "Die pluralischen Verba für 'gehen' und 'stehen' im Sumerischen," *WO* IV (1968) 252–77; "Verschlusslaute und Betonung im Sumerischen," *Lišān mithurti* (*AOAT*, Vol. 1 [1969]) pp. 157–97. On Sumero-Akkadian bilingualism, see in general W. von Soden, *Zweisprachigkeit in der geistigen Kultur Babyloniens* (Vienna, 1960). For the earliest Akkadian literary originals, see Hallo and Simpson, *The Ancient Near East*, p. 62, n. 68; and add now the alleged prototype of "A Naram-Sin Text Relating to Nergal" edited by W. G. Lambert, *BiOr* XXX (1973) 357–63. For what may be the earliest monumental text in Akkadian, see Sollberger's remarks on *UET* VIII, No. 2 (p. 1). The text AO 5477, described by F. Thureau-Dangin (*RA* VIII [1911] 139) as the oldest bilingual, is a copy of a Sargonic monumental text, probably of Old Babylonian date; see H. Hirsch, "Die Inschriften der Könige von Agade," *AfO* XX (1963) 13, *sub* Rimuš b 12 (2).

106. Hallo, in *JAOS*, Vol. 88, p. 72, and *JAOS*, Vol. 83, p. 167.

107. Above, n. 61; see now Biggs, "Pre-Sargonic Riddles from Lagash," *JNES*, Vol. 32 (1973) pp. 26–33.

period (Lagash II), the Ur III period, and the early Isin period (*ca.* 2200–1900 B.C.). The process of adaptation may be illustrated by the expansion of the Cycle of Temple Hymns to include references to structures built under the Ur III kings (above). In Old Babylonian times (*ca.* 1900–1600 B.C.), the portions of the Old Sumerian corpus deemed fit to survive were given their final fixed form in the schools, that is, the corpus became a canon in the limited sense in which the latter term is employed here. In the process, some texts were already provided with translations into Akkadian. These early examples of (non-interlinear) bilinguals, notably from the realm of wisdom literature, include both proverbs and instructions (na-ri-ga) going back to Fara and Abū Ṣalābīkh. They are also (apart from lexical texts) the only Old Sumerian materials that survived in any form after their canonization in Old Babylonian times. The Kesh Temple Hymn, though of equal antiquity, and the cycles of hymns attributed to Enhe-duanna in the high Sargonic period are more typical of this corpus in that they did not survive.

The neo-Sumerian canon preserved the creations of the neo-Sumerian period (as defined above). Again some of the finest literary Sumerian of the period originated at the court of Lagash, but Shulgi of Ur, who claimed the founding of the great scribal schools at both Ur and Nippur, was also a devoted patron of literature and the arts. In this he was emulated by his successors both at Ur and among the early kings of Isin. The rich materials of this neo-Sumerian corpus provided the bulk of the curriculum for the Old Babylonian schools, which freely adapted them in one of two ways. Either a received tradition, conceivably still in oral form, was "modernized" to make it more congenial to the current Nippur theology, as has been argued above for the myths about Ninurta. Or, if the text was already received in fixed, written form, and yet needed updating, as in the case of The Curse of Agade/Utu-hegal sequence, it might be recast completely by a free rendering or loose imitation in Akkadian. The same technique, whether the source or the result of the concomitant beginnings of the Akkadian canon (see presently), is illustrated by the earliest Akkadian epi-sodic tales about Gilgamesh, which go back to Old Babylonian times when the Sumerian versions were still being copied in the schools. The canonization of the neo-Sumerian corpus presumably took place in Middle Babylonian times, specifically during the period of the "First Kassite Empire" (*ca.* 1600–1300 B.C.).[108] This is the likeliest setting for the illustrious ancestors who were claimed as eponymous founders by the later scribal guilds or families. It was also a time when Akkadian came fully into its own, even assuming an international impor-tance. Scribal schools as far way as Hattusha, Alalakh, Ugarit, Megiddo and Amarna taught the standard Mesopotamian curriculum.[109] It was in these circumstances that the neo-Sumerian corpus took its final form. We may

108. K. Jaritz, "Die Geschichte der Kassitendynastie," *MIO* VI (1958) 202–25.

109. See Jerrold S. Cooper, "Bilinguals from Boghazköy," *ZA*, Vol. 61 (1971) pp. 1–22; Vol. 62 (1972) pp. 62–81, for examples of Old Babylonian unilingual Sumerian texts provided with Akkadian (and sometimes Hittite) translations at Hattusha, as well as examples of new bilingual compositions going back at most to Kassite times. In his Introduction (*ZA*, Vol. 61, pp. 1–8), Cooper surveys the history of Sumerian literature from this vantage point.

picture the Kassite scribes as weeding out whatever had failed to undergo suitable adaptation at the preceding stage and providing the rest with a literal, interlinear translation into Akkadian. At the same time they must have begun to introduce such external structural features as chapters, sections, incipits, explicits and the like. The myths of Ninurta may again serve as examples here, as well as the epics of Lugalbanda.

The Old Babylonian period, so active in both canonization of the Old Sumerian heritage and adaptation of the neo-Sumerian tradition, was not demonstrably a creative period in its own right, as far as Sumerian is concerned. True, new compositions clearly originated in this period, for example, royal hymns and other genres involving the kings of Larsa and, to a lesser extent, of Babylon. In the case of Larsa, one may suspect a substantial contribution from Lagash, whose traditions were somehow kept alive in Old Babylonian Larsa,[110] and which thus for the third time contributed significantly to the Sumerian literary scene. But the new texts are so completely cast in the familiar neo-Sumerian molds that they represent the epigone of that canon rather than the herald of a new one. The Old Babylonian period deserves instead to be regarded as the source of the principal Akkadian literary canon. Previously Akkadian had been considered fit only for administrative texts, for royal monuments (chiefly translations or imitations of Sumerian prototypes), and for the merest handful of literary fragments (see n. 105). Now, however, a whole new literary dialect was created for Akkadian, and its products freed from excessive dependence on Sumerian models.[111] The resulting corpus probably followed a pattern not unlike its Sumerian precursors, being adapted and greatly enlarged in Middle Babylonian and especially Middle Assyrian times and organized by fixed text and sequence in the great libraries of the neo-Assyrian kings.[112]

There was, however, a final flowering of Sumerian literature, or rather of bilingual texts. This is the corpus which Falkenstein has described as post-Old-Babylonian (see n. 5) and which I prefer to label simply post-Sumerian (see n. 106). It is readily distinguished from the earlier canons by both form and content. Its language violates many known standards of classical Sumerian and often reflects the native Akkadian speech of its author when it is not in fact actually a secondary translation from the Akkadian. It displays an increasing tendency to employ dialectal (Emesal) Sumerian, even substituting it for the

110. I hope to demonstrate this more fully in another connection. See for now Hallo and Simpson, *The Ancient Near East*, pp. 92–93, and above, n. 30. See also Hallo, "Choice in Sumerian," *Journal of the Ancient Near Eastern Society of Columbia University*, Vol. 5 (The Gaster Festschrift, 1973) p. 110.

111. See most recently Römer, "Studien zu altbabylonischen hymnisch-epischen Texten," *HSAO*, pp. 185–99, *JAOS*, Vol. 86 (1966) pp. 138–47, *WO* IV (1967) 12–28.

112. Merely to illustrate the constant additions to this dossier: the Middle Assyrian laws have hitherto been known only in copies from Assur of Middle Assyrian date (*ca.* 1100 B.C.), but a fragmentary duplicate, presumably from Nineveh and presumably of neo-Assyrian date, has now been discovered and demonstrates, for the first time, a historical dimension for this particular tradition; see J. N. Postgate, "Assyrian Texts and Fragments," *Iraq* XXXV (1973) 19–21.

Approximate Date (B.C.)	Cultural Period	Old Sumerian Literature	Neo-Sumerian Literature	Akkadian Literature	Bilingual (Post-Sumerian) Literature
2500–2200	Old Sumerian	created			
2200–1900	Neo-Sumerian	adapted	created		
1900–1600	Old Babylonian	canonized	adapted	created	
1600–1300	Middle Babylonian		canonized	adapted	created
1300–1000	Middle Assyrian		canonized	adapted	created
1000–700	Neo-Assyrian			canonized	adapted
700–400	Neo-Babylonian			canonized	adapted
400–100	Late Babylonian				canonized

Fig. 1. Tentative Periodization of the Canons of Sumer and Akkad.

main dialect of the ancestral text-type, as when the earlier letter-prayers were replaced by the ér-šà-hun-gá laments. Religious texts in general and cultic texts in particular assumed a dominant place in this canon, with congregational laments especially prominent. This corpus presumably originated after the fall of the Old Babylonian dynasty of Babylon, when Sumerian scholars and scholarship apparently fled to the Sealand, and the great scribal schools of Nippur and Babylon were closed. But the Kassites, determined to assimilate the ancient culture that they conquered, encouraged the new scribal guilds to take up the task, and the result, though inferior, kept some knowledge of Sumerian alive for another millenium and a half. Although the intervening stages are not clearly attested, it is this late bilingual corpus which served as the canon of the very latest surviving cuneiform scriptoria in Uruk, Babylon and perhaps other Babylonian centers of the Selecuid and Arsacid periods.

With all due allowance for the shortcomings of such a schematic representation, the above may be charted as a point of departure for future refinements (Fig. 1).

SELECTION OF LITERARY WORKS AND GENRES CITED

a-ab-ba hu-luh-ha
adab-hymns
ana ittišu
An-gim dím-ma
bal-bal-e hymns
Curse of Agade
Descent of Inanna
Descent of Ishtar
Dumuzi texts
Enki and Inanna
Enki and Ninhursag
Enki and Ninmah
Enlil and Ishkur
Enlil and Ninhursag
Enlil and Ninlil
Enlil and Sud
Enmerkar cycle
Exaltation of Inanna
Exaltation of Ishtar
Exploits of Ninurta (lugal-e)
Flood narrative
Gilgamesh
Gudea cylinders
Gudea statue inscriptions
Inanna and Ebih
in-nin šà-gur$_x$-ra
Kesh temple hymn

Laments
lexical texts
Lipit-Ishtar laws
Love songs
Lugalbanda epic
lullabies
Marriage of Martu
Message of Lu-dingira
Model contracts
Nanshe hymn
Nergal and Eresh-kigal
nin-mah ušu-ni gìr-ra (see Exaltation of Ishtar)
Ninurta and the Turtle
Pushkin Elegies
Rim-Sin letter-prayer
royal correspondence
Rulers of Lagash
scribal letters
Temples of Sumer and Akkad
tigi-hymns
triumphal inscriptions
Tummal history
Ur-Nammu's death and burial
Utu-hegal inscription
Weidner Chronicle

BIBLIOGRAPHY

A useful survey of Sumerian literature, with some attention to historical considerations, is provided by D. O. Edzard and Claus Wilcke in the sixteen articles on as many different genres listed below; an earlier survey, by M. Lambert, recognized fifteen major, but only partially comparable, genres. In English, the material has been assembled at regular intervals by S. N. Kramer, notably in the articles listed below. The standard chronology of Sumerian literature is that of Falkenstein, and I have dealt with various aspects of the subject.

Edzard, D. O. "Der Leidende Gerechte." *Kindlers Literatur Lexikon* IV, col. 1176–77. Zurich, 1965–71.

———. "Sumerische Beschwörungen." *Kindlers Literatur Lexikon* VI, col. 2109–10. Zurich, 1965–71.

———. "Sumerische Briefe an Götter und vergöttlichte Herrscher." *Kindlers Literatur Lexikon* VI, col. 2110–11. Zurich, 1965–71.

———. "Sumerische Fabeln." *Kindlers Literatur Lexikon* VI, col. 2116. Zurich, 1965–71.

———. "Sumerische Gebete." *Kindlers Literatur Lexikon* VI, col. 2116–17. Zurich, 1965–71.

———. "Sumerische Gesetzessammlungen." *Kindlers Literatur Lexikon* VI, col. 2117–18. Zurich, 1965–71.

———. "Sumerische historische Kompositionen." *Kindlers Literatur Lexikon* VI, col. 2118–23. Zurich, 1965–71.

———. "Sumerische Sprichwörtersammlungen." *Kindlers Literatur Lexikon* VI, col. 2150–51. Zurich, 1965–71.

———. "Sumerische Unterweisungen." *Kindlers Literatur Lexikon* VI, col. 2154–55. Zurich, 1965–71.

Edzard, D. O., and Claus Wilcke. "Sumerische Mythen." *Kindlers Literatur Lexikon* VI, col. 2142–47. Zurich, 1965–71.

Falkenstein, A. "Der sumerische Gilgameš-Zyklus." *Kindlers Literatur Lexikon* III, col. 804–7. Zurich, 1965–71.

———. "Inannas Gang zur Unterwelt." *Kindlers Literatur Lexikon* III, col. 2475–79. Zurich, 1965–71.

———. "Zur Chronologie der sumerischen Literatur." *CRRA* II 12–30. Leiden, 1951.

———. "Zur Chronologie der sumerischen Literatur. Die nachaltbabylonische Stufe." *MDOG*, No. 85 (1953) pp. 1–13.

Hallo, William W. "New Viewpoints on Cuneiform Literature." *Israel Exploration Journal*, Vol. 12 (1962) pp. 13–26.

———. "The Royal Inscriptions of Ur: A Typology." *HUCA* XXXIII (1962) 1–43.

———. "Royal Hymns and Mesopotamian Unity." *JCS* XVII (1963) 112–18.

————. "On the Antiquity of Sumerian Literature." *JAOS*, Vol. 83 (1963) pp. 167–76.

————. "New Hymns to the Kings of Isin." *BiOr* XXIII (1966) 239–47.

————. "The Coronation of Ur-Nammu." *JCS* XX (1966) 133–41.

————. "Individual Prayer in Sumerian: The Continuity of a Tradition." *JAOS*, Vol. 88, pp. 71–89. Published simultaneously as *AOS*, Vol. 53. New Haven, 1968.

————. "The Cultic Setting of Sumerian Poetry." *CRRA* XVII 116–34. Han-sur-Seure, 1970.

————. "Problems in Sumerian Hermeneutics." In Byron L. Sherwin, ed., *Perspectives in Jewish Learning* V 1–12. Chicago, 1973.

Kramer, S. N. "Sumerian Literature: A General Survey." *The Bible and the Ancient Near East: Essays in Honor of William Foxwell Albright*. Ed. by G. E. Wright. Garden City, New York, 1961.

————. "Literature: The Sumerian Belles-Lettres." *The Sumerians: Their History, Culture and Character*. Chicago, 1963.

Lambert, M. "La littérature sumérienne, à propos d'ouvrages récents." *RA* LV (1961) 177–96, LVI (1962) 81–90, 214.

Wilcke, Claus. "Sumerische Epen." *Kindlers Literatur Lexikon* VI, col. 2111–16. Zurich, 1965–71.

————. "Sumerische Königshymnen." *Kindlers Literatur Lexikon* VI, col. 2123–26. Zurich, 1965–71.

————. "Sumerische Kultlieder." *Kindlers Literatur Lexikon* VI, col. 2126–35. Zurich, 1965–71.

————. "Sumerische Lehrgedichte." *Kindlers Literatur Lexikon* VI, col. 2135–42. Zurich, 1965–71.

————. "Sumerische Schulsatiren (Schulgedichte)." *Kindlers Literatur Lexikon* VI, 2147–50. Zurich, 1965–71.

————. "Sumerische Streitgedichte." *Kindlers Literatur Lexikon* VI, col. 2151–54. Zurich, 1965–71.

FORMALE GESICHTSPUNKTE IN DER SUMERISCHEN LITERATUR

CLAUS WILCKE

München

Seit Texte in sumerischer Sprache lesbar und verständlich wurden, haben Forscher den dichterischen Gestaltungswillen in den einzelnen Literaturwerken festgestellt und ihre strophische Gliederung und—inspiriert durch Untersuchungen zur hebräischen Metrik—metrische Struktur herauszufinden gesucht. Dazu kam noch der Vergleich mit der alttestamentlichen Literatur. Die Ergebnisse dieser Untersuchungen fasste B. Meissner, *Die babylonisch-assyrische Literatur* (Wildpark und Potsdam, 1930) S. 25 zusammen.

In den folgenden Jahren trat der Vergleich mit der hebräischen Literatur in den Hintergrund—ohne Zweifel eine Folge von B. Landsbergers Forderung, der "Eigenbegrifflichkeit" der babylonischen Kultur Rechnung zu tragen. Erst in neuerer Zeit findet diese Methode in den Werken von S. N. Kramer und W. W. Hallo wieder Verwendung.

Die metrische Struktur wurde ebenfalls nicht wieder Gegenstand der Forschung, da man erkannte, wie wenig man erst über die Aussprache des Sumerischen wusste. Auch hier zeigt sich in allerneuester Zeit ein Wandel (s.u., 2.4). Vielmehr wandten sich die Sumerologen in verstärkter Weise der Untersuchung von Grammatik und Lexikon und vor allem der mühevollen Wiedergewinnung grösserer Literaturwerke aus kleinen und kleinsten Fragmenten zu.

Einen neuen Zugang zur literarischen Analyse hatte A. Falkenstein in seiner Dissertation *Die Haupttypen der sumerischen Beschwörung literarisch untersucht* (*LSS* NF I [1931]) gefunden: die thematische Gliederung gekoppelt mit der Untersuchung der Redeformen (Beschreibung, Bericht, Forderung) und Zeitstufen ı präsentisch, präterital). Dieser Weg wurde aber später nicht wieder beschritten, obwohl er die formal nicht zu rechtfertigende, in der Literatur gängige[1] Unterscheidung von Mythen und Epen (je nach dem, ob der Text von Göttern oder Menschen handelt) hätte verhindern können.

Ebenfalls stilistische Kriterien benützte Th. Jacobsen in seiner Ausgabe der sumerischen Königsliste (*The Sumerian King List* [*AS*, Nr. 11 (1939)]), um die

---

1. Siehe zuletzt C. Wilcke, *Das Lugalbandaepos* (Wiesbaden, 1969) S. 2–3, Anm. 12; *Kindlers Literatur Lexikon*, Bd. 6 (Zürich, 1971) Sp. 2111; B. Alster, *Dumuzi's Dream: Aspects of Oral Poetry in a Sumerian Myth* (Copenhagen, 1972) S. 13.

Quellen zu unterscheiden, auf denen dieses Werk über die babylonische Geschichte fusst.

Im Abschnitt *"form and affinities"* in seiner Bearbeitung von "Inanna und
Bilulu" (Jacobsen und Kramer, in *JNES* XII [1953] 160–63 [*TIOT*, S. 52–54])
hat Th. Jacobsen m.w. als erster Sumerologe einen ganzen Text auf Stil und
strophische Struktur untersucht. A. Falkensteins Analyse der Zylinderinschrif-
ten Gudeas von Lagaš (*AnOr*, Bd. 30 [1966] S. 178–87) zeigte dann, wie enge
Grenzen einer solchen Untersuchung gesetzt sein können.

Zu wesentlich gesicherteren Ergebnissen kam A. Falkenstein aber in dersel-
ben Monographie durch die Gliederung des Textes in einzelne konstituierende
Abschnitte, die Aufbau und Struktur der Gudea-Zylinder zeigte. Leicht modi-
fiziert verwendete auch C. Wilcke dieselbe Methode in seiner Dissertation *Das
Lugalbandaepos* (Wiesbaden, 1969), gefolgt von B. Alster, *Dumuzi's Dream*
(Copenhagen, 1972). Ähnlich gingen auch W. W. Hallo und J. van Dijk, *The
Exaltation of Inanna* (*YNER*, Bd. 3 [1968]) vor; s. auch C. Wilcke und D. O.
Edzard in *Kindlers Literatur Lexikon*, Bd. 6 (1971) Sp. 2109–55.

Den Versuch, strophische Einheiten durch die Beobachtung verschiedener
Satztypen abzugrenzen, machte C. Wilcke, *Das Lugalbandaepos*, S. 17–22, und
in *AfO* XXIV (1973) 8.[2]

Monographische Untersuchungen einzelner formaler Fragen in der sumeri-
schen Literatur sind selten: A. Falkenstein untersuchte Unterschriften und
Rubriken in hymnischen Texten (*ZA*, Bd. 49 [1950] S. 80–105) und gab in
SAHG, S. 7–37, einen Überblick über Form und Geschichte der sumerischen
Hymnen und Gebete. Ebenfalls 1953 zeigte J. J. A. van Dijk, *La Sagesse
suméro-accadienne* (Leiden) S. 31–85, die formalen Regeln der Streitgedichte auf.
W. Heimpel untersuchte 1968 in *Tierbilder in der sumerischen Literatur* (*StP*, Bd.
2 [1968]) die sumerische Bildersprache, ein Thema, das im folgenden Jahr auch
von S. N. Kramer behandelt wurde (*JAOS*, Bd. 89 [1969] S. 1–10). Schliesslich
hat 1972 B. Alster in *Dumuzi's Dream*, S. 15–27, der Frage der mündlichen
Überlieferung von Literaturwerken ein Kapitel gewidmet.

Eine Darstellung und Analyse der formalen Prinzipien, die in der sumerischen
Literatur Verwendung finden, steht noch aus. Sie sollte von einem Literaturwissenschaftler gegeben werden—ein Eindruck, der sich aufdrängt, wenn man
K. Heckers Besprechung von W. Heimpels *Tierbildern* liest (*Zeitschrift der
Deutschen Morgenländischen Gesellschaft*, Bd. 122 [1972] S. 274–77). Da aber
nicht zu hoffen ist, dass die Literaturwissenschaft sich von sich aus der sumerischen Literatur zuwenden wird, will ich im folgenden versuchen, das zusammen-
zustellen, was bekannt ist oder nachgewiesen werden kann.

---

2. H. Saurens Artikel, "Zur poetischen Struktur der sumerischen Literatur," *UF*, Bd. 3
(1971) S. 327–34, enthält zahlreiche nützliche Beobachtungen. Er zeigt aber auch eine
erstaunliche Missachtung der Grammatik, wenn z.B. S. 333, Anm. 28, vorgeschlagen wird,
das Zeichen KA in der Bedeutung "Wort" nicht inim sondern du₁₁ zu lesen, wenn das
"Metrum" ein einsilbiges Wort verlange. Das wäre dasselbe, als wenn man im Deutschen
aus metrischen Gründen "Wort" durch "gesprochen" (nicht "Gesprochenes," das wäre
du₁₁-ga) ersetzen wollte.

1. MERKMALE LITERARISCHER TEXTE

Es ist eine erstaunliche Tatsache, dass Sumerologen in der Lage sind, kleinste Fragmente, die oft keinen vollständigen Satz, ja keine einzige vollständige Verbalform enthalten, als literarisch zu klassifizieren.

Hierfür ist zunächst ein negativer Grund zu nennen: Da Form und Formular nichtliterarischer Texte, d.h. der Rechts- und Wirtschaftsurkunden, weitgehend bekannt sind, kann man Fragmente, die sich in ein derartiges Formular nicht einfügen lassen, als nicht nichtliterarisch, also als literarisch einordnen. Dazu kommt die Sprache (das Sumerische) in Verbindung mit dem paläographisch annähernd bestimmbaren Datum als Kriterium: Die meisten sumerischen literarischen Texte sind in Abschriften aus altbabylonischer Zeit überliefert, einer Zeit, in der man Briefe in akkadischer Sprache abfasste.

Auch die Beobachtung der äusseren Form der Keilschrifttafeln kann die Bestimmung erleichtern: Nichtliterarische Texte wurden ganz überwiegend auf einkolumnigen Tafeln niedergeschrieben, sodass jedes Fragment einer Mehrkolumnentafel aus altbabylonischer Zeit in sumerischer Sprache mit grosser Wahrscheinlichkeit von einem literarischen Text stammt. Dazu kommen noch andere Kriterien wie die Verwendung des Emesal-Dialekts, der auf literarische Texte beschränkt ist, die Wortwahl, Phraseologie und Grammatik; dazu s.u.

1.1. DIALEKTE

Sumerische literarische Texte können in zwei verschiedenen Dialekten abgefasst sein, dem Hauptdialekt (auch in Rechts- und Verwaltungsurkunden verwandt) und dem Emesal-Dialekt. Letzterer erscheint nur in literarischen Texten.[3] Ein Text kann ganz in einem der beiden Dialekte abgefasst sein oder beide Dialekte verwenden.

Die Verteilung der Dialekte ist noch nicht restlos geklärt. Der Emesal-Dialekt wird von Frauen, nicht dagegen von Männern benutzt (mit Ausnahme der Reden männlicher Sprecher in balag- und ér-šèm-ma-Kompositionen, die durchweg im Emesal stilisiert sind, vielleicht weil sie von gala-Priestern vorgetragen wurden).[4] Frauen können aber in literarischen Texten auch den Hauptdialekt benutzen (in nichtliterarischen Texten tun sie es immer)—so in den

---

3. Siehe A. Falkenstein, *Das Sumerische* (*Handbuch der Orientalistik* II [Leiden, 1959]) S. 18; *SKly*, S. 12–14, 35–36; J. Krecher, "Zum Emesal-Dialekt des Sumerischen," *HSAO*, S. 87–110. Siehe aber *TMH* NF I–II, Nr. 27:10, da-ab-su(?) bí-du₁₁, "Sie hat gesagt: 'Ich will es ersetzen!'": Kohortativ-Präformativ des Emesal in einer Rechtsurkunde der Ur III-Zeit; m.W. singulär.

4. Zum gala als Sänger der Emesal-Texte s. zuletzt *SKly*, S. 27. Siehe aber auch das šìr-nam-gala an Meslamtaea und Lugalgirra für den letzten König der III. Dynastie von Ur, Ibbi-Sîn, das ganz im Hauptdialekt abgefasst ist (Å. Sjöberg, "Hymns to Meslamtaea, Lugalgirra and Nanna-Suen in Honour of King Ibbisuen (Ibbisîn) of Ur," *OrS* XIX/XX [1970–71] S. 142–44); in dem šìr-nam-gala auf Nininsina für Lipit-Eštar von Isin (*UET* VI/1, Nr. 96, 97) findet sich das Emesal nur in der Rede der Göttin.

Gudea-Zylindern, den Werken der Enhedu'anna, der Tochter Sargons von
Akkade, etwa in der Sammlung der Tempelhymnen (*TCS* III), den Dichtungen
nin-me-šár-ra (*YNER*, Bd. 3) und in-nin-šà-gur₄-ra oder dem Epos
"Inanna und Ebeh."

Wenn ich zurecht das zweite bal-bal-e-Lied auf der Sammeltafel *TMH* NF
IV, Nr. 7 der Enhedu'anna zugeordnet habe (Wilcke, in *JNES*, Bd. 31 [1972]
S. 38, Anm. 2; *Kollationen ... Jena* ["Abhandlungen der Sächsischen Akademie
der Wissenschaften zu Leipzig," Philol.-hist. Kl., Bd. 65 (Berlin, im Druck)])
liegt bereits ein Emesal-Text aus so früher Zeit vor. Wenig später (Gudea-Zeit)
ist wahrscheinlich lugal ud melam-bi nir-gál zu datieren; dort findet
sich der Emesal-Dialekt bei weiblichem Sprecher in Tafel VIII 43–IX 12. Ebenso
in dem wohl aus derselben Zeit stammenden an-gim dím-ma, Z. 110–12
(MS J. Cooper). Wenig später auch in Urnammu's Tod, Z. 207–15.

Ist die Verwendung des Emesal-Dialekts bis zum Beginn der Ur III–Zeit bei
Frauen nicht vorhersagbar, so scheint von der Regierungszeit Šulgi's an sich die
Tendenz durchzusetzen, dass weibliche Personen das Emesal zu benutzen haben.

1.2. WORTSCHATZ

Fast jedes Wort, das sich in einem nichtliterarischen Text findet, kann auch in
literarischen Texten erscheinen. Diese Regel ist aber nicht umkehrbar. Da ein
sumerisches Lexikon noch fehlt, kann dies im einzelnen allerdings nicht nachgewiesen werden. Der Grund für die Unterschiede im Wortschatz ist gewiss
zum grossen Teil der, dass Privatbriefe in sumerischer Sprache gänzlich fehlen
(die einzigen Beispiele gehören zu den sogenannten "Letter Collections," sind
also literarisch tradiert). Wir dürfen aber annehmen, dass gewisse semantische
Bereiche wie der des Numinosen (s. *SAHG*, S. 29–35) der literarischen Sprache
vorbehalten waren. Dazu gehören auch die Namen von Göttern und "Heroen,"
soweit sie Träger von Handlung sind. Eine systematische Untersuchung dieser
Frage ist ein dringendes Desideratum. Zu beachten ist aber, dass Eigennamen
den literarischen Wortschatz benutzen.

1.3. PHRASEOLOGIE

Der Unterschied von literarischen und nichtliterarischen Texten wird besonders in der Phraseologie deutlich. Auch diese Frage ist noch nicht untersucht.
Auf Grund der Phraseologie kann man z.B. ein so schlecht erhaltenes Fragment
wie den Ur III-Text *HLC* III 140, Nr. 371, als literarisch (Streitgedicht?)
bestimmen.

1.4. GRAMMATIK

Die sumerischen literarischen Texte sind den Regeln der sumerischen Grammatik unterworfen. Dabei ist aber stets zu beachten, dass diese Regeln weitestgehend aus literarischen Texten (einschliesslich der Königsinschriften) abgeleitet
sind. Der Gebrauch einiger grammatischer Regeln (z.B. der vorausgestellte

Genitiv und der Genitiv ohne Regens) ist in nichtliterarischen Texten sehr selten, andere scheinen auf literarische Texte beschränkt zu sein.

Letzteres betrifft vor allem die freie Wortstellung im Satz: sämtliche Beispiele, die A. Falkenstein, *Das Sumerische*, S. 52e, für den Agentiv oder ein dimensionales Objekt als letztes Satzglied (also nach dem finiten Verbum) zitiert, sind literarischen Texten entnommen. Ein sehr ähnliches Phänomen ist die Stellung der Apposition eines Satzgliedes nach dem finiten Verbum, wobei Beziehungswort und Apposition das Kasuszeichen tragen, z.B. *TMH* NF IV, Nr. 11:4–5 (= 18–19 = 28–29, Refrain in Šulgi F)[5]

ur-sag ama-ni-e ur$_5$-re ba-an-tu ^{d}nin-suna$_x$(= SÚN)-ke$_4$
šul-gi ama-ni-e ur$_5$-re ba-an-tu ^{d}nin-suna$_x$(= SÚN)-ke$_4$
"Den Helden hat seine Mutter darum geboren, Ninsuna,
Šulgi hat seine Mutter darum geboren, Ninsuna."

In normaler Satzstellung müssten die beiden parallelen Sätze lauten: *ama-ni ^{d}nin-suna$_x$(= SÚN)-ke$_4$ ur-sag (/šul-gi) ur$_5$-re ba-an-tu. Ausser der Nachstellung der Apposition zum Subjekt (Agentiv) beobachten wir auch, dass das Akkusativobjekt an den Satzanfang gerückt ist. Daraus resultiert die Einrahmung des Satzes durch die beiden Namen Šulgi (in der ersten Zeile vertreten durch ein Epitheton) und Ninsuna, d.h., die Namen von Sohn und (göttlicher) Mutter.

Wiederum etwas anders geartet ist die Nachstellung des Subjekts in "2. Urklage," Z. 172–73 (*UET* VI/2, Nr. 128:23–24, *PBS* X/4, Nr. 6:10–11)

kù ^{na_4}za-gìn(-bi ^{giš})má-gal-gal-la(/e) bal-šè ì-ak-e
nin nì-ga-šè(/ra-ni) hul(-lu) ti-la-a(/àm) kù-^{d}nin-MAR.KI-ke$_4$
"Sein (des Heiligtums) Silber und Lapislazuli lässt sie auf grosse Schiffe laden, die Herrin, die wegen ihrer Habe traurig dasitzt, die reine Nin-MAR.KI."

Hier ist die zweite Zeile das nachgestellte Subjekt zu dem Satz in Z. 172. Diese zweite Zeile ist in den beiden Textzeugen verschieden konstruiert: in *PBS* X/4, Nr. 6:11 ein Nomen mit appositioneller Partizipialkonstruktion, das Ganze im Agentiv (ti-la-a ⟨ *ti-la-e), dazu parallel der Name im Agentiv mit vorgestelltem Attribut; in *UET* VI/2, Nr. 128:24 steht ein Nominalsatz mit Kopula und danach der Name im Agentiv mit vorgestelltem Attribut. In normaler Satzstellung müsste dies aber lauten: *kù-^{d}nin-MAR.KI nì-ga-ra-ni hul {-lu}[6] ti-la-àm. Um den Namen nachstellen und aus dem Nominalsatz herausnehmen zu können, musste der Dichter hier ein Epitheton einfügen, das

---

5. Nach Kollation sind die Lesungen von J. Klein, "Sum. ga-raš = Akk. *purussû*," *JCS* XXIII (1970) 118 (ár-re) und von Th. Jacobsen (ub-ri, von J. Klein in hektographierten Nachträgen zu seinem Artikel mitgeteilt) ausgeschlossen; der Text schreibt klar HAR-re, i.e., ur$_5$-re, "dafür," bezogen auf die finalen /ed-e/ Formen in den Zeilen 1–29.

6. Das /*e/ in hul-lu (nur *UET* VI/2, Nr. 128) kann ich nicht erklären, da "traurig dasitzen" parallel zu ul-ti, "froh dasitzen," in Urnammu's Tod, Z. 15 (S. N. Kramer, "The Death of Ur-Nammu and His Descent to the Netherworld," *JCS* XXI [1967–69] 113) hul-ti heisst.

in der normalen Satzstellung überschüssig wäre; ähnlich auch in *PBS* X/4, Nr. 6, doch ist dort die Lösung mit den beiden parallelen Agentiven glatter. Welche der beiden Versionen die ursprüngliche ist, wissen wir freilich nicht.

Wir wissen auch nicht, ob die grössere Freiheit der literarischen Texte in der Wortstellung dem gesprochenen Sumerisch näher steht als die relativ feste Wortstellung der nichtliterarischen Texte. Das Fehlen von Privatbriefen macht sich hier besonders negativ bemerkbar. Vielleicht lässt sich das Problem eines Tages durch die Analyse von Erklärungen unter Eid in juridischen Texten lösen. Dasselbe gilt auch für verschiedene modale Präformative wie ša-, na- (affirmativ), nu-uš-, né-eš- (s. *CT* XV, Taf. 14, Z. 36–37), die (ebenso wie die Äquativpostposition) in nichtliterarischen Texten fehlen.

1.5. BILDERSPRACHE

Ein weiteres Merkmal der literarischen Texte ist der Gebrauch der Bilder-sprache, d.h., von Vergleich und Metapher, die W. Kayser, *Das Sprachliche Kunstwerk* (15. Aufl.; Bern, München, 1971) S. 112, "die dichterischste Figur des uneigentlichen Sprechens" nennt.[7]

Der Vergleich wird grammatisch bezeichnet durch die Postposition -gim, die an eine nominale Kette oder einen nominalisierten Satz angefügt wird. Sehr häufig wird aber der Vergleich über die grammatisch bezeichnete Grenze hinaus fortgeführt und schliesst oft das Prädikat des Satzes mit ein; z.B. Šulgi D: *MBI*, Nr. 3 ii 16–17 = UM 29–16–235 ii 1 (J. Klein, "Šulgi D: A Neo-Sumerian Royal Hymn" [Ph.D. diss., University of Pennsylvania, 1968] Taf. 1) = N 3654 ii 2 (Klein): ^{giš}eren-duru$_5$ ha(-šu)-úr-re mú-a-gim gissu-du$_{10}$-ga-me-èn, "Wie eine grüne Zeder, die bei(?) Zypressen gewachsen ist, hast du ange-nehmen Schatten (verbreitet)." Hier gehört der Schatten semantisch noch zum Bereich der Bäume, grammatisch aber bereits zu dem des angesprochenen Königs Šulgi. Beispiele derartiger Vergleiche bietet Heimpel, *Tierbilder*, S. 36–42. Der Schritt von ihnen zur Metapher ist nur gering.

Metaphern können syntaktisch sehr verschieden ausgedrückt werden: als Apposition, als nominales (mit und ohne Kopula) oder verbales Prädikat, als dimensionales oder Akkusativobjekt, als Genitivverbindung und schliesslich ohne Nennung eines Beziehungswortes.

(a) Apposition: Šulgi D, *MBI*, Nr. 3 i 1–2

lugal-mu   gu$_4$-gal   á-gú-nu
muš-huš [igi]-pirig-gá
"Mein König, grosser Stier, der die Hörner funkeln lässt,
schreckliche Schlange, mit den [Augen] eines Löwen, . . ."

Zeilen 11–12

pirig-tur-bàn-da ga-zi kú-a
gu$_4$ á-gur$_8$ pirig-gal-šè tu-da

---

7. Siehe W. Heimpel, *Tierbilder in der sumerischen Literatur* (*StP*, Bd. 2 [1968]); S. N. Kramer, "Sumerian Similes," *JAOS*, Bd. 89 (1969) S. 1–10.

"wilder junger Löwe, mit der richtigen Milch genährt,
Stier mit mächtigen Hörnern, geboren, um ein grosser Löwe zu sein, . . ."

(b) Nominales Prädikat ohne Kopula: Šulgi G, *CT* XXXVI, Taf. 26, Z. 9

gal bí-du$_{11}$ šà-ga-ni i$_7$-mah a-na-àm D[U]-a-bi
"Er sprach Grosses—sein Sinn ist ein mächtiger Fluss—was hat er gebracht?"

(c) Nominales Prädikat mit Kopula: Šulgi D, *MBI*, Nr. 3 ii 9–12 (zusammen
mit einem Vergleich)

^{giš}ildág ki-en-du zà-bi dù-a-gim
á-guruš-a-me-èn
mes-zi kurùn-na gùn-a-me-èn
u$_6$-di-du$_{10}$-ga-me-èn
"Wie eine ildág-Pappel, die am Rande eines Gartens gepflanzt ist,
bist du die Kraft der jungen Männer;
du bist ein wohlgewachsener mes-Baum, mit Früchten bunt (geschmückt),
bist ein erfreulicher Anblick, . . ."

(d) Verbales Prädikat: Šulgi B, Z. 53 = 79 = 116 = 152 (G. R. Castellino,
Two Šulgi Hymns (BC) [*StSem*, Nr. 42 (1972)]; die Metapher schliesst das
Akkusativobjekt mit ein)

kala-ga-gá(/mu) mu-bi á bí-sù-ud (Var. mu-bi ga-bí-[sù-ud])
"Der Ruhm meiner Stärke ist weit geeilt (wörtl.: Der Name meiner Stärke
    hat die Arme lang gemacht; Var.: Kohortativ)."

SLTNi, Nr. 61:17–19 (vgl. 20–26)

ur-sag kur-gul-gul
uru^{ki} DU.DU
ki-bal-šè bí-du$_7$-du$_7$
"Held, der die Bergländer zerstört,
der die Städte plündert,
du hast auf das Bergland eingestossen."[8]

(e) Akkusativobjekt: Šulgi F, *TMH* NF IV, Nr. 11:49 (s. auch oben d)

an-né ki-e ubur(?)-bi bí-íb-sù-ud
"Der Himmel liess seine Zitzen zur Erde herabhängen."

(f) Dimensionales Objekt: Šulgi F, *TMH* NF IV, Nr. 11:21

nì-erím na$_4$-mah-nu-me-a engur-ra tab-e-dè
"Das Böse, wenngleich es kein riesiger Stein ist, im "Süsswasserozean"
    festzuhalten, . . ."

(g) Genitivverbindung: Šulgi B, Z. 82 (Castellino, *Two Šulgi Hymns*)[9]

8. Zum Verbum du$_7$-du$_7$ s. Heimpel, *Tierbilder*, S. 300–307.
9. Siehe auch die ähnlichen Beispiele in *CRRA* XIX 189, Anm. 36–43 (unser Zitat dort
Anm. 42).

(d)šul-gi dingir-nam-guruš-a sag-rib-erén-na-me-èn
"Šulgi, der Gott der jungen Männer, der erste der Truppe bin ich!"

(h) Freies Vorkommen: Šulgi D, *ISET* I 79, Ni. 4571 iv 13–17 (Der Gott, von dem die Rede ist, ist Ningublaga, der aber nicht mit Namen genannt wird):

am-gal-šè tu-da pirig ne-ba gub-ba
ibila-kala-ga-šul-ᵈsuᵓen-[na x x]
dumu-ur-sag-ᵈaš-ím-bab[bar-ra x x]
sún-zi zà-gᵗáˡb-bu-ni-a ba-ᵗx-xˡ [x x]
šul-gi sipa-zi-[ki-en-g]i-ᵗraˡ-da [gìri-a ba-da-gen]
"Der dazu geboren ist, ein grosser Ur zu sein, der Löwe, der in seiner Stärke
    dasteht,
der starke Erbsohn [des] jugendlichen Suᵓen,
der heldenhafte Sohn Ašimbab[bar's . . .],
das rechte Leittier . . . zu seiner Linken,
[ging] zusammen mit Šulgi, dem rechten Hirten von [Sum]er, [auf dem
    Wege (zur Schlacht)]."

Bis auf eines sind alle Beispiele Texten um Šulgi entnommen, um die Vielfalt der Formen in einem homogenen Material nachzuweisen. Bei dem unter (g) zitierten Beispiel, Šulgi B, Z. 82, könnte man dingir, "Gott," auf die Vergött-lichung des Königs beziehen und nicht als Metapher ansehen. Ein Text schreibt tatsächlich ᵈšul-gi. Da aber die übrigen Texte das Gottesdeterminativ nicht zeigen, ist Šulgi B wohl vor der Vergöttlichung des Königs entstanden. Im zweiten Beispiel unter (d), *SLTNi*, Nr. 61:17–19, beschreibt das Verbum du₇-du₇ den Angriff eines gehörnten Tieres, hier übertragen auf einen Gott, da Götter nach altmesopotamischer Anschauung Hörnerkronen tragen; s. Heimpel, *Tierbilder*, S. 300–307, besonders S. 307.

2. FIGUREN

Die meisten der von den sumerischen Dichtern verwendeten Figuren zeigen sich bei der Analyse auf der Wort- und Satzebene, wie ich es im Exkurs dar-zustellen versuche. Aber auch die Gliederung eines Textes in formal und inhalt-lich zusammengehörige Abschnitte und die Beobachtung der Wechselbezie-hungen zwischen ihnen kann die ornamentale Form eines ganzen Textes verdeutlichen; s. Wilcke, *Lugalbandaepos*, Kap. III; *Kindlers Literatur Lexikon*, Bd. 6 (1971) Sp. 2112. Für fast alle Werke der sumerischen Literatur fehlen derartige Untersuchungen.

2.1. EPISCHE WIEDERHOLUNG

Die weitaus am häufigsten—und auch am einfachsten—zu beobachtende Figur ist die der Wiederholung (Repetition). Dabei ist zu unterscheiden zwischen der epischen Wiederholung, einem Stilmittel der Verzögerung, das die Spannung des Lesers oder Hörers erhöht und ihm gleichzeitig bereits Gesagtes ins Gedächtnis ruft, und der überwiegend in Liedern auftretenden rein ornamentalen Wiederholung einzelner Zeilen oder Zeilengruppen, meist in Verbindung mit leichter Abwandlung.

Die epische Wiederholung betrifft meist wörtliche Reden, die etwa im Botenbericht mehrfach erscheinen, Vorsatz und Ausführung des Vorhabens oder die Wiederholung einer Rede vor verschiedenen Zuhörern. Sie kann das einem Text zugrundeliegende Strukturprinzip sein oder als ein Stilmittel unter vielen verwandt werden.

So lässt "Inanna und Ebeḫ" die Göttin zunächst ihr Vorhaben im Selbstgespräch erzählen, es dann nach einem kurzen erzählenden Passus vor dem höchsten Gotte An wiederholen und berichtet dann—aber mit anderen Worten —die Ausführung. In "Gilgameš, Enkidu und die Unterwelt"[10] wird im ersten Teil dieselbe Geschichte dreimal erzählt: das erste Mal vom Erzähler in der 3. Person und im Hauptdialekt, das zweite Mal (Emesal) von der Göttin Inanna in der 1. Person vor ihrem Bruder Utu, das dritte Mal (Emesal) von der Göttin vor Gilgameš. Der zweite Teil gebraucht dann dieses Stilmittel sparsamer, auf kurze Abschnitte beschränkt. Sehr kunstvoll verwendet das Enmerkarepos[11] die epische Wiederholung: Abschnitte, die dreimal, zweimal und nur einmal vorkommen, sind ineinander verschachtelt und in den Wiederholungen mit anderen verbunden. Der Hauptteil des Epos handelt von den Botschaften, die sich Enmerkar und der e n von Aratta durch einen Boten gegenseitig übermitteln. Dabei lässt der Dichter aber den Boten nicht immer die ganze Botschaft wiederholen und oft heisst es nur, dass er sie übermittelt habe. So entsteht ein Wechsel von Bewegung und Ruhe, Spannung und Entspannung, wobei Bewegung und Spannung immer mehr zunehmen, je mehr das Werk seinem Höhepunkt zusteuert.

Ganz anders gebraucht das Lugalbandaepos (Lugalbanda II)[12] die epische Wiederholung. Sie findet sich in den beiden Teilen des Epos jeweils nur einmal, gegen Ende der beiden Abschnitte. Hier benutzt der Dichter noch ein anderes, der Wiederholung verwandtes Stilmittel—ebenfalls in jedem der Teile einmal: die dichte Folge ähnlicher Passagen, die jeweils mit einer Art Refrain schliessen. Im ersten Teil sind dies die Angebote des Anzu an Lugalbanda, im zweiten ist es die Beschreibung von Enmerkar's Suche nach einem Boten, den er nach Uruk schicken kann. Beide Male gehen diese Sequenzen der oben beschriebenen epischen Wiederholung voraus.

10. A. Shaffer, "Sumerian Sources of Tablet XII of the Epic of Gilgameš" (Ph.D. diss., University of Pennsylvania, 1963); C. Wilcke, *Kollationen . . . Jena* ("Abhandlungen der Sächsischen Akademie der Wissenschaften zu Leipzig," Philol.-hist. Kl., Bd. 65, Heft 4 [Berlin, im Druck]) zu III 13–14.

11. S. N. Kramer, *Enmerkar and the Lord of Aratta* (Philadelphia, 1952). Neuausgabe durch S. Cohen in Vorbereitung.

12. Wilcke, *Das Lugalbandaepos.* Zur Terminologie Lugalbanda II s. Wilcke, "Der Titel u₅ giš-gi-kù-ta in zwei sumerischen Literaturkatalogen," *AfO* XXIV (1973) 50.

2.2. Ornamentale Wiederholung

Bei der Wiederholung einzelner Zeilen oder Zeilengruppen meist in Liedern, seltener in epischen Texten, lassen sich die folgenden Schemata feststellen (R = Repetition):

R-1: Folge von Zeilen *a*, *a'*, *a''*, etc., *b*, etc., in der ein Teil von *a*, meist ein Epitheton, in *a'*, *a''*, etc., durch ein anderes Wort oder eine Gruppe von Wörtern, meist einen Namen, ersetzt wird. Wird dieses Schema über eine längere Passage ausgedehnt, kann man von einer Litanei mit gleichbleibendem Refrain sprechen, die für den modernen Leser recht ermüdend sein kann, von den sumerischen Hörern (oder Lesern) aber anscheinend nicht so empfunden wurde.

R-1': Folge von Zeilen *a*, *b*, *a'*, wobei *a'* die Zeile *a* leicht variiert wiederholt. Dieses mit R-1 verwandte Schema kann auch als unvollständiges Schema R-2/3 aufgefasst werden.

R-2: Folge von Zeilen *a*, *b*, *c*, etc., *a'*, *b*, *c*, etc., wobei *a'* ein Wort, meist einen Namen, am Anfang der Zeile zum Text von *a* hinzufügt. Varianten sind in der Wiederholung *a'*, *b'*, *c'*, etc., oder *a*, *b'*, *c*, etc.

R-3: Dieselbe Abfolge von Zeilen wie in R-2 aber mit Ersatz eines Wortes, meist am Zeilenanfang, durch ein anderes, meist einen Namen.

R-4: Wiederkehr eines Wortes, wieder meist eines Namens, in mehr oder weniger regelmässigen Abständen.

R-5: Wiederholung eines (kurzen) Satzes oder eines Satzteiles in éiner Zeile, überwiegend an deren Anfang.

Diese Figuren, die meist am Beginn der Zeilen zu beobachten sind (seltener am Zeilenende), können als Anapher oder Epipher (R-1–4) beschrieben werden; bei R-5 handelt es sich um eine Epanalepsis.

Da wir sie als Hinweise auf die äussere Gliederung des Textes in Zeilengruppen, d.h. Strophen, verstehen, werden Beispiele für R-1–4 bei der Erörterung der Strophe angeführt. Der Typ R-5 findet sich ebenfalls an der Strophengrenze, meist am Anfang. Beispiele für diese Figur sind: Keš-Hymne, Z. 1 (*TCS* III 167 = *ZA*, Bd. 61 [1971] S. 200), nám-nun-e nám-nun-e é-ta nam-ta-ab-è (ohne Varianten); Keš-Hymne, Z. 58 (*TCS* III 170), uru in-ga-àm uru in-ga-àm šà-bi a-ba mu-zu (ohne Varianten); Gudea Zyl. A i 24–25 = iii 22–24, ga-na ga-na-ab-du₁₁ ga-na ga-na-ab-du₁₁ inim-ba ha-mu-da-gub; *TMH* NF III, Nr. 25:13, gá-e ga-ri-ib-zu-zu$^{lu-uq-bi-ki}$ gá-e ga-ri-ib-zu-zu; *TCL* XV, Nr. 20:66, ba-lam ba-lam-lam hi-is-sar-àm a ba-an-du₁₁; *SRT*, Nr. 31:1-2, lu-bi-mu lu-bi-mu lu-bi-mu / la-bi-mu la-bi-mu làl-ama-ugu-na-mu; *TMH* NF IV, Nr. 7 iv 19 = *ISET* I 62, Ni. 9788, 1 lu-lu-a-bi lu-lu-a-bi ú-šim^{ki-ma} ki-dar-re-dam. Für ein Beispiel von R-5 am Zeilenende s.u. zur Strophe (bal-bal-e für Ninazu). Das Vorkommen dieses Typs in der Keš-Hymne, einem der ältesten bislang datierbaren Literaturwerke (Fara-Zeit), zeigt sein grosses Alter.

2.3. Refrain

Eine Sonderform der ornamentalen Wiederholung ist der Refrain. Hier beobachten wir zwei verschiedene Typen:

(*a*) Folgen von Zeilen, die jeweils gleich enden. Dieser Typ ist eng verwandt mit R-1. Er findet sich z.B. in der litaneiartigen Einleitung zur "1. Urklage"[13] im 1. und 2. ki-ru-gú-Abschnitt, dann auch im 6. ki-ru-gú. Sehr ähnlich ist der Fall, in dem jede zweite Zeile eines Textes den Refrain bietet, so z.B. weite Passagen in "Nanna's Fahrt nach Nippur,"[14] dort gekoppelt mit dem System des alternierenden Refrains: Auf ein Zeilenpaar mit einem Refrain, der mit ᵈnanna-ᵈsuˀen beginnt, folgt eins mit dem Namen ᵈaš-ím-babbar;[15] dieser Text verwendet aber auch noch andere Refrains. Ein weiteres Beispiel für den alternierenden Refrain behandle ich im Exkurs. Eine andere Form dieses Refrain-Typs ist die Verbindung eines festen Gliedes mit einem variablen, wie z.B. in "Reiher und Schildkröte," Z. 12–21 (s.u. 3.2).

(*b*) Wiederkehr einer Zeile oder Zeilengruppe in meist unregelmässigen Abständen. Diese Art des Refrains findet sich in der bereits für die Fara-Zeit nachweisbaren Keš-Hymne[16] und erscheint in verschiedenen Šulgi-Texten: Šulgi B,[17] Z. 52–55 = 78–81 = 115–18 = 151–54; Šulgi C,[18] Z. 18–20 = 32–34 = 48–50 = 80–82 = 110–12 = [125–27?] = 141–43 = Text I 17'–19' (= Text G 13–15) = Text I Rs. 16'–18' = Text F 19'–21'; Šulgi D (nur im einleitenden Hymnus),[19] MBI, Nr. 3 i 22–31 (+ Dupl.) = ii 18–23 (+ Dupl.) = iii 21–[26]; Šulgi F,[20] Refrain 1 in TMH NF IV, Nr. 11:4–5 = 18–19 = 28–29; Refrain 2 in TMH NF IV, Nr. 11:59–60 = SLTNi, Nr. 78 Rs. ii 18–19 = Rs. iii 18(?)–19(?) (= BE XXXI, Nr. 24 iv 3 = ISET I 80–81, Ni. 4564, Z. 29–30) = Ni. 4564, Z. 55–56; ähnlich auch in dem Išbi-Erra-Text bur-šu-ma-gal[21] Z. 36 = 44 = 64 = 79; vgl. auch den Refrain in dem šìr-nam-ur-sag-gá der Ninsianna,[22] der zunächst dem Typ *a* folgt, sich dann aber mit dem Wachsen

13. S. N. Kramer, *Lamentation over the Destruction of Ur* (*AS*, Nr. 12 [1940]). Siehe die Zusammenstellung weiterer Textzeugen bei Wilcke, *Kollationen . . . Jena*, zu IV 18+.

14. A. J. Ferrara, *Nanna-Suen's Journey to Nippur* (*StP* M, Bd. 2 [1973]). S. auch C. Wilcke, "Sumerische literarische Texte in Manchester und Liverpool," *AfO* XXIV (1973) 2 ff.

15. Alle drei Namen bezeichnen den Mondgott.

16. Gene Gragg, "The Keš Temple Hymn," in Å. W. Sjöberg und E. Bergmann, *The Collection of the Sumerian Temple Hymns* (*TCS* III [1969]) S. 157–88. R. D. Biggs, "An Archaic Sumerian Version of the Keš Temple Hymn from Tell Abū Ṣalābīkh," *ZA*, Bd. 61 (1972) S. 193–207. S. auch C. Wilcke, in *JNES*, Bd. 31 (1972) S. 41–42; D. O. Edzard, "Zur sumerischen Hymne auf das Heiligtum Keš," *Or*, NS, Bd. 43 (1974) S. 103–13.

17. G. R. Castellino, *Two Šulgi Hymns* (*BC*) (*StSem*, Nr. 42 [1972]). Bearbeitung dort: S. 9–242. Dort nicht verwertete Texte: *ISET* I 163, Ni. 4538 = Šulgi B, Z. 231–37, 345–50; Ni. 4335 (mir durch eine Kopie von F. W. Geers bekannt, aber z. Zt. nicht zugänglich) = Šulgi B, Z. 212–23, 260–73, 302–16, ca. 360 ff.

18. Castellino, *Two Šulgi Hymns*, S. 243–94.

19. J. Klein, "Šulgi D: A Neo-Sumerian Royal Hymn" (Ph.D. diss., University of Pennsylvania, 1968). Zur Rekonstruktion C. Wilcke, "Der aktuelle Bezug der Sammlung der sumerischen Tempelhymnen und ein Fragment eines Klageliedes," *ZA*, Bd. 62 (1972) S. 42, Anm. 13*a*; *CRRA* XIX 198, Anm. 87.

20. Siehe vorläufig Wilcke, *Kollationen . . . Jena*, zu IV 11.

21. D. Reisman, "Two Neo-Sumerian Royal Hymns" (Ph.D. diss., University of Pennsylvania, 1969) S. 103 ff.

22. *SKIZ*, Kap. IV; Reisman, "Two Neo-Sumerian Royal Hymns," S. 147 ff.

der Abstände zwischen den Refrain-Zeilen zum Typ *b* entwickelt. Wenn man die Sammlung der Tempelhymnen[23] als einheitliches Literaturwerk auffasst, kann der stereotype Schluss der einzelnen Hymnen als Refrain verstanden werden. Ähnlich auch die formelhafte Wendung, mit der die sumerische Königsliste[24] den Übergang der Königsherrschaft von einer Dynastie auf eine andere beschreibt, doch wird damit der Begriff des Refrains überstrapaziert.

Die durch einen Refrain vom Typ *b* abgeschlossenen Abschnitte sind meist auch inhaltlich von den vorausgehenden und folgenden unterschieden. Dass sie auch von den antiken Schreibern als Einheiten aufgefasst wurden, zeigt z.B. die Überlieferung von Šulgi C. Dort beginnen die einkolumnigen Auszugstafeln B, D und I (in I ist allerdings der Anfang zerstört)[25] mit der ersten Zeile eines solchen Abschnitts und enden mit dem Refrain, dem sie eine weitere Zeile als Stichzeile anfügen; dabei umfasst jeder von ihnen mehrere durch den Refrain abgeschlossene Einheiten.

Während man in Šulgi D und F in den einleitenden Hymnen die durch den Refrain bezeichneten Einheiten ohne Bedenken als Strophen auffassen wird, verbietet sich das aber in Šulgi B, C und im Hauptteil von Šulgi F angesichts der Länge dieser Abschnitte.

Die Verwendung des Refrains ist nicht auf bestimmte Texttypen beschränkt. Er findet sich in Litaneien wie in der "1. Urklage" (s.o.), in Klageliedern, wie dem ér-šèm-ma Mullil's im-kur-ra igi-gá,[26] in Hymnen, die in der ersten (Šulgi B, C, im Hauptteil von Šulgi F), der zweiten (Šulgi D, Einleitung) oder der dritten Person (Šulgi F, Einleitung) stilisiert sind, in Liebesliedern (kun-gar Inanna's, s. Exkurs), in Streitgedichten (Reiher und Schildkröte, s.u.) und Texten mit epischer Grundhaltung (Nanna's Fahrt nach Nippur; s.o.; Gilgameš, Enkidu und die Unterwelt).[27]

Ein Text kann durch die stete Wiederkehr eines Refrains bestimmt sein (Keš-Hymne; s.o.) oder durch die Verwendung verschiedener Refrains (Nanna's Fahrt nach Nippur; Reiher und Schildkröte; im-kur-ra igi-gá). Die Refrains

23. Sjöberg und Bergmann, *TCS* III 5–154.

24. Th. Jacobsen, *The Sumerian King List* (*AS*, Nr. 11 [1939]). F. R. Kraus, "Zur Liste der älteren Könige von Babylonien," *ZA*, Bd. 50 (1952) S. 29–60; J. J. Finkelstein, "The Antediluvian Kings," *JCS* XVII (1963) 39–51; W. W. Hallo, "Beginning and End of the Sumerian Kinglist," *JCS* XVII (1963) 52–57; M. Civil, "Texts and Fragments," *JCS* XV (1961) 79–80, N 3368.

25. Sigla nach der Edition G. Castellinos. Bei Text I hat G. Castellino Vorder- und Rückseite vertauscht (nur Umschrift; *Two Šulgi Hymns*, S. 243, 258, 260). Ein weiteres gemeinsames Merkmal ist die Wahl des Zeichens -èn, nicht -en. Zu einem anderen Typ scheint Text A zu gehören (auch Schreibung mit -èn), eine Mehrkolumnentafel, die aber ohne Refrain (und Stichzeile) schliesst, obwohl auf der letzten Kolumne dafür noch reichlich Platz vorhanden ist. Die Texte C und G nehmen keine Rücksicht auf den Refrain; E, F und B' (unveröff.) sind nur fragmentarisch erhalten.

26. *CT* XV, Taf. 7–9 = Wilcke, in *AfO* XXIV 15–16. Das ér-šèm-ma verwendet verschiedene Refrains des Typs *a*.

27. Shaffer, "Sumerian Sources." Hier in den Fragen Gilgameš's an Enkidu am Ende des Epos. Siehe auch oben "Epische Wiederholung" zum Lugalbanda-Epos.

können aber auch auf Teile eines Textes beschränkt sein (Šulgi B, D, F, Gilgameš, Enkidu und die Unterwelt, kun-gar Inanna's).

Schliesslich sei noch darauf hingewiesen, dass in "Enkihegal und Enkita" (Dialogue 2) und im "Streitgedicht zweier Frauen" (Dialogue 5) die Reden der Kontrahenten Refrain-artig enden; "und du bist ein Mensch," "du streitest mit mir," "du (willst) wie ich geschaffen sein," etc.

An Refrains gemahnen schliesslich auch Fälle, in denen innerhalb eines Textes eine Zeile (mit Variation) noch einmal erscheint, wie nin-me-šár-ra Z. 42, nin kur(/an/šár[?])-ra diri-ga a-ba ki-za(/zu) ba-an-tùm (/tum₄/túm), "Herrin, grösser als das Bergland, wer kann es so weit bringen wie du?" und Z. 59, nin an-ra diri-ga a-ba(-a) ki-za ba-an-tùm, "Herrin, die den Himmel(sgott An) überragt, wer kann es so weit bringen wie du?"[28]

2.4. REIM, ALLITERATION UND ASSONANZ

Der Reim wird in sumerischen Literaturwerken häufig verwendet, hat aber anders als in den neueren europäischen Literaturen keine Funktion innerhalb der Strophenbildung. Daher wird man ihn am besten nur als die Zeilengrenze überschreitende Form von Alliteration und Assonanz auffassen. Daneben findet sich aber auch der Binnenreim und eine dem Reim verwandte Form von Anklängen an den Zeilenanfängen; s. R. R. Jestin, "La rime sumérienne," *BiOr* XXIV (1967) 9–12, "La rime interne en sumérien," *RA* LXIII (1969) 115–20; Wilcke, *Lugalbandaepos*, S. 18–20; Castellino, *Two Šulgi Hymns*, S. 20–21. Der Gebrauch des (End)reims ist vielleicht oft nur ein Nebenprodukt der Reihung parallel gebauter Zeilen wie z.B. in Šulgi A, Z. 1–19, wo alle Zeilen auf -me-en, meist sogar -a-me-en enden; ähnlich Šulgi C, Z. 1–7, wo wir neben dem Endreim in Z. 1–4 auch beobachten, dass jeweils die Enden der ersten Zeilenhälften paarweise miteinander reimen. Diese Reimstellen stimmen mit den Zeilenenden in Text A[29] überein, der Kurzzeilen in Kästchen (Normalzeile; s. dazu unten) schreibt. Ausserdem haben die Zeilen 3–4 vor dem Endreim noch eine Assonanz:

lugal-me-èn am á-pà-da-me-èn / pirig ka-du₈-ha-me-èn
šul-gi-me-èn am á-pà-da-me-èn / pirig ka-du₈-ha-me-èn
u₄-gal an-ta šu-ba-ra-gim / me-lám sù-sù-me-èn
a-zi ᵍᵘ₄nindá a-ru-a-gim / sag-bar gùn-gùn-me-èn
"Ich, der König, bin ein Ur, der (dem Angreifer) die Hörner gezeigt hat,[30]
    bin ein Löwe, der das Maul aufgerissen hat,

---

28. Vgl. G. Castellino, "Incantation to Utu," *Oriens Antiquus* VIII (1969) 20, Z. 147, ᵈutu di-ku₅-mah an-ki-bi-da ki-zu nam-ba-(da-a[n])-túm, und S. 26, Z. 57, ᵈutu di-ku₅-mah-an-ki-bi-da-m[e-e]n ki-za nam-ba-e-tùm, "Utu, (du bist) der höchste Richter von Himmel und Erde, zu dir wird er gebracht werden."

29. S.o. Anm. 25.

30. Gemeint ist, dass der Ur dem Feind die gesenkten Hörner entgegenstreckt. Zu á, "Horn," s. Heimpel, *Tierbilder*, S. 93–94.

Ich, Šulgi, bin ein Ur, der (dem Angreifer) die Hörner gezeigt hat, bin ein
Löwe, der das Maul aufgerissen hat.
Wie ein grosses Licht, das herableuchtet, verbreite ich weitreichenden
Schreckensglanz,
Wie der rechte Same, den ein Zuchtstier gezeugt hat, habe ich einen bunten . . .
Kopf."

Alliteration und Assonanz finden sich häufig. Um sie aber in jedem Einzelfalle
nachweisen zu können, müssten wir besser über das Phoneminventar des
Sumerischen informiert sein. Alliterationen sind meist auf kürzere Abschnitte
einer Zeile beschränkt; längere Folgen wie Šulgi C, Z. 76, níg-ge-ge-na-aš
gu_4-gal-gal-gim... sind selten. Für ein Beispiel von Assonanz s. Šulgi
B, Z. 4, á-na zà-mí-bi(-im) kala-ga-na šìr-bi(-im), wo sich das Vokal-
schema wiederholt. Ein Textzeuge (b 3') schreibt hier zà-mí-ba und stört
das Klangbild.

2.5. Chiasmus, Antithese und Klimax

Der Chiasmus findet sich häufig, oft wird er mit anderen Figuren verbunden.
So etwa in Šulgi D, *MBI*, Nr. 3 i 11–12, zusammen mit der Antithese:

pirig-tur-bàn-da ga-zi kú-a
gu_4 á-gur$_8$ pirig-gal-šè tu-da
"Wilder junger Löwe, mit der richtigen Milch genährt,
Stier mit mächtigen Hörnern, geboren, um ein grosser Löwe zu sein."

In Verbindung mit einer Klimax findet sich wenige Zeilen später wieder ein
Chiasmus, *MBI*, Nr. 3 i 17–21, UM 29–16–235, Z. 3–5 (Klein, "Šulgi D." Taf. 1)

lú an-né mu-du$_{10}$-ga sa$_4$-a
sipa-zi á-sum-ma-(/)^{d}en-líl-lá
šul-gi ^{d}nin-líl-lá (/) ki-ág-šà-ga-na
"Mann, den An mit einem guten Namen benannt hat,
rechter Hirte, von Enlil mit Kraft begabt,
Šulgi, den Ninlil's Herz liebt."

Hier bilden die Namen der Götter und deren Verhalten Šulgi gegenüber einen
doppelten Chiasmus, den der Dichter durch die Verwendung verschiedener
grammatischer Konstruktionen erreicht: in der ersten Zeile durch eine soge-
nannte "Mesannepada Konstruktion," in der zweiten durch den *genitivus
subjectivus* und in der dritten durch den vorausgestellten Genitiv.
Mit dieser Bewegung kontrastiert das gleichmässige Fortschreiten der Klimax
am Zeilenanfang: Farbloses Epitheton "Mann," festgelegtes, "richtiges"
Epitheton (s. *SAHG*, S. 29), Name. Auf diese Zeilen folgt dann der Refrain.
Schematisch lässt sich der Schluss dieses ersten Abschnitts des einleitenden
Hymnus von Šulgi D folgendermassen darstellen:

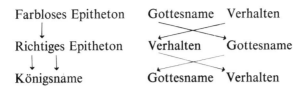

Refrain

Für ein weiteres Beispiel der Klimax s.u. "Reiher und Schildkröte," Z. 19–21.

2.6. PARALLELE REIHUNG

Sehr beliebt ist in sumerischen literarischen Texten die parallele Reihung gleich oder ähnlich konstruierter Sätze oder Satzteile. Sie findet Verwendung in Litaneien, aber auch in Hymnen; z.B. Šulgi A im einleitenden Passus: vgl. etwa Z. 4–6

lugal-an-ub-da-limmu-ba-me-en
na-gada sipa-sag-gi₆-ga-me-en
nir-gál dingir-kur-kur-ra-me-en
"Ich bin der König der vier Weltgegenden,
ich bin der Hüter, der Hirte der Schwarzköpfigen,
Ich bin der angesehene, der Gott aller Länder, ..."

Darauf folgt dann eine lange Reihe von Aussagen des Tenors "ich bin der ... des Gottes. ..."

Auch epische Texte verwenden diese Figur, meist in den Einleitungen. Ein Beispiel aus dem Hauptteil eines Epos ist das erste Angebot des Anzu im Lugalbandaepos (Lugalbanda II), Z. 135–40.[31]

2.7. AUFZÄHLUNG

Aufzählungen sind der parallelen Reihung ähnlich. Sie finden sich häufig in Dialogen; s. z.B. unten 3.3 (Schreiber und missratener Sohn). Die Grenze zur parallelen Reihung ist z.B. in an-gim dím-ma, Z. 129–46 (MS J. Cooper) in der Aufzählung der Waffen Ninurta's fliessend. Dort heisst es: "Zu meiner Rechten habe ich meine šár-ùr-Waffe, / zu meiner Linken habe ich meine šár-gaz-Waffe," worauf bis Z. 146 eine Aufzählung der Waffen folgt, jeweils formuliert als "ich habe (mu-da-an-gál-la-àm; jung: mu-e-da-gál-la-àm) meine...-Waffe, die. ..."

3. VERS UND METRUM

In *SAHG*, S. 27, stellte A. Falkenstein fest "Die kleinste Einheit des sumerischen Liedes ist der Vers" und postulierte die Übereinstimmung von Vers und

---

31. Neues Duplikat, *CT* LI, Nr. 181 Rs. ii 3 (zu Z. 135).

Zeile. Er begründete dies mit dem Schreibgebrauch, nur wenige Schriftzeichen auf einer Zeile mit grossen Zwischenräumen unterzubringen und andererseits dort, wo der verfügbare Raum einer Zeile der Tafel nicht ausreiche, sich mit eingerückten Zeilen zu behelfen. Ausserdem verwies er auf die Zeile als syntaktische Einheit, sei es, dass die Zeilengrenze mit der Satzgrenze übereinstimmt, sei es, dass sie zugleich Ende eines Satzgliedes (Kette) ist, falls sich der Satz über mehrere Zeilen erstreckt. Sein Urteil hinsichtlich des Metrums (*SAHG*, S. 28) fiel negativ aus. Ein quantitierendes Metrum schloss er aus.

3.1. VERS

A. Falkensteins Beobachtungen zum Vers sind nicht in Zweifel zu ziehen; sie lassen sich auch stützen durch die Tatsache, dass in der ganz überwiegenden Zahl von Fällen, in denen ein oder mehr Duplikate vorliegen, diese dieselben Zeilengrenzen zeigen. Die nicht sehr häufigen Ausnahmen von dieser Regel zwingen jedoch zu einer Einschränkung seiner Forderung, Vers und Zeile miteinander gleichzusetzen:

1. Textzeugen, die dieselben Zeilengrenzen aufweisen, können gelegentlich dergestalt voneinander abweichen, dass der eine von ihnen zwei Zeilen des anderen auf einer Zeile zusammenfasst. Sehr viel seltener ist der Fall, dass sich die Divergenz über mehr als zwei Zeilen erstreckt oder dass der Text von zwei Zeilen in zwei verschiedenen Quellen unterschiedlich abgeteilt wird. Als Beispiele hierfür mögen zwei Zitate aus Šulgi F dienen:
A = *TMH* NF IV, Nr. 11; B = *TCL* XVI, Nr. 86

A (Z. 71!–72!) ^{d}nanna-ar mu-na-ku$_4$ me ki-bi-e gi$_4$-gi$_4$-dè // húl-la-da na-du-du en dumu-KA-an-kù-ga

B (Z. 3–5) ^{d}nanna-ar mu-na-an-ku$_4$ // me-e ki-bé gi$_4$-gi$_4$ ⌜húl⌝-la-da na-du$_{11}$-du$_{11}$ // [en] dumu-KA(?)-an-kù-ga

"Zu Nanna trat er ein, sagte ihm(?) freudig (zu), die göttlichen Kräfte wiederherzustellen, (der) Herr, (der) Enkel des reinen An. . . ."

Hier ist unklar, wer das Versprechen abgibt, der König oder der Gott. In letzterem Falle wäre en dumu-KA-an-kù-ga nachgestelltes Subjekt, wogegen aber der fehlende Agentiv spricht. Ist der König Subjekt zu na-du-du (oder na-du$_{11}$-du$_{11}$), fehlt hinter en-dumu-KA-an-kù-ga entweder das Dativzeichen (so bei dieser Interpretation Text A) oder aber das Agentivzeichen, wenn es Subjekt zum folgenden ist (in Text A wohl ausgeschlossen).
A = *TMH* NF IV, Nr. 11, B = *TCL* XVI, Nr. 86

A (Z. 77!–78!) [dumu]-sag-^{d}en-líl-lá me-gal-gal-la-kam // [hi-l]i-é-kur-ra-kam u$_6$-di-da-ni nì-du$_{10}$-ga-à[m]

B (Z. 10–11) dumu-sag-^{d}en-líl-lá me-gal-gal-la-ka hi-li-é-kur-ra-ke$_4$ // u$_6$(!)-di-da-ni nì-du$_{10}$-ga(!)-àm

"Der erstgeborene Sohn Enlils besitzt die grossen göttlichen Kräfte, ist die Wonne des Ekur, ihn anzuschauen, ist angenehm."

Die Unterschiede in der Zeilentrennung lassen sich am ehesten erklären, wenn man annimmt, dass beide Textzeugen (oder ihre Vorläufer) auf einer Kurzzeilen-Version beruhen, die sie unterschiedlich interpretierten.

2. Gelegentlich finden sich Duplikattexte, die regelmässig zwei Zeilen einer Tafel mit "normaler" Zeilenlänge auf einer Zeile zusammenfassen wie etwa das von Å. Sjöberg erkannte (*OrS* X [1961] 3–12) Duplikat zu dem Urnammu-Text *SRT*, Nr. 11. Da bei solchen Texten die Kolumnenbreite der Tafel nur selten ausreicht, um die "Langzeile" aufzunehmen, verwenden sie häufig eingerückte oder durch Trennstriche abgeteilte Doppelzeilen. Welche der beiden Versionen dann die Einheit "Vers" mit der Einheit Zeile ausdrückt, wird man nicht entscheiden können, solange eine metrische Bestimmung der Einheit "Vers" noch unmöglich ist. Statt "Vers" und "Halbvers" oder "Vers" und "Doppelvers" ziehe ich daher vorläufig die Bezeichnungen "Normalzeile" und "Langzeile" vor.

Ausser der "Langzeile" gibt es noch eine andere von der "Normalzeile" abweichende Schreibweise: die Verteilung des Textes einer "Normalzeile" über zwei oder mehr "Kurzzeilen" auf Mehrkolumnentafeln mit geringer Kolumnenbreite.

Ein Beispiel für das Vorkommen der drei verschiedenen Zeilentypen bei demselben Text ist der Anfang von "Nanna's Fahrt nach Nippur."[32] (Siehe S. 222–23.)

Die Texte A und C (letzterer aber ab C, Z. 4 mit einer abweichenden Version) verwenden Normalzeilen, B hat Langzeilen und D Kurzzeilen. Dabei fällt noch auf, dass die Zeilengrenzen von Text A (und, soweit übereinstimmend, Text C) und die jeweils zweite Zeilengrenze von D mit dem Beginn der eingerückten Zeilen in Text B übereinstimmt. Entweder in B oder in A und C sind Zeile und Vers identisch. Die Zeilen von Text D können unmöglich den Vers vertreten, da D, Z. 1, z.B. nur einen Namen enthält. Die Kurzzeilen müssen also eine Einheit unterhalb der des Verses, vielleicht sogar des Halbverses sein. Was aber ist deren Funktion und wie ist dieser Schreibgebrauch entstanden?

Dem Schreiben auf Zeilen geht historisch der Brauch voraus, den Text, der dann später einer Zeile entspricht, in Kästchen anzuordnen, die in schmale Kolumnen gesetzt sind. Dieser Brauch hält sich bei literarischen Texten länger als bei Urkunden, die etwa mit Beginn der Akkadzeit die Zeile dem Kästchen vorzuziehen beginnen. Demgegenüber verwenden die Zylinder Gudea's und die nur in Abschriften überkommenen Steleninschriften von Šū-Sîn und eine Abschrift von Šulgi C (Text A der Edition) noch das Kästchen.

Während anfangs und noch bei Gudea nur die letzte "Zeile" innerhalb eines Kästchens eingerückt sein konnte, beobachteten wir in den Stelenabschriften Šū-Sîn's das Auftreten von eingerückten "Zeilen" innerhalb eines Kästchens; so z.B. in UM 29-15-566+ i 8′ (M. Civil, "Šū-Sîn's Historical Inscriptions:

---

32. Sigla nach der Edition von A. J. Ferrara, *StP* M, Bd. 2. Hier und im folgenden bedeutet / : Beginn einer eingerückten Zeile; // : Beginn einer neuen Zeile (bei Texten, die Kurzzeilen verwenden).

Nanna's Fahrt nach Nippur, Anfang:

Text A

1 ur-sag-e uru-ama-n[a-šè]
2 ^{d}nanna ^{d}su᷃en-e gešt[ú-ga-ni na-an-gub]
3 ^{d}su᷃en-e uru-ama-n[a(!)-šè]
4 ^{d}aš-ím-babbar-re geštú-ga-n[i na-an-gub]
5 uru-ama-na-šè a-a-[na-šè]
6 ^{d}nanna ^{d}su᷃en-e geštú-ga-[ni na-an-gub]
7 ^{d}en-líl-lá-šè ^{d}nin-l[íl-lá-šè]
8 [^{d}aš-ím-babb]ar-re [geštú-ga-ni na-an-gub]

Text B

1 u[r-sag-e uru-ama-na-šè] / [^{d}nanna ^{d}su᷃en-e geštú-ga-ni na-an-gub]
2 ^{d}su᷃en-e⌉ [uru-ama-na-šè] / ^{d}⌈aš⌉-ím-[babbar-e geštú-ga-ni na-an-gub]
3 uru^{ki}-ama-n[a-šè a-a-na-šè] / ^{d}nanna ^{d}[su᷃en-e geštú-ga-ni na-an-gub]
4 ^{d}en-líl-lá-šè ^{d}[nin-líl-lá-šè] / ^{d}aš-ím-babbar-e [geštú-ga-ni na-an-gub]
5 ur-sag-m⌈e-e⌉n gá-⌈e⌉ [uru-mu-šè ga-gen] /
6 a-[a]-mu-šè g⌈a⌉-[an-ši-gen] / ^{d}su᷃e[n-me-en] gá-e ur⌈u⌉-[mu-šè ga-gen] /
7 ⌈a-a⌉-mu-[šè ga-an-ši-gen]

Text C

[Anfang abgebrochen]

1 [^{d}nanna ^{d}su᷃en-e geštú-ga-ni n⌈a⌉-[an-gub]
2 [^{d}en-l]íl-šè ^{d}nin-líl-[šè]
3 ^{d}⌈aš⌉-ím-babbar-e geštú-ga-a-[ni] / na-an-gub
4 ur-sag-me-en gá-e uru^{ki}-mu--uš-šè / ga-an-DU.DU
5 gá-e uru^{ki}-mu-uš-šè ga-an-gen / a-a-mu-uš-šè ga-an-ši-DU-en
6 ^{d}su᷃en-me-en gá-e uru^{ki}-mu-uš-šè / ga-an-gen
7 gá-e uru^{ki}-mu-uš-šè ga-an-gen / a-a-mu-uš-šè ga-an-ši-DU-en

Text D

1–2 [^{d}aš-ím]-babbar-e // geštú-ga-ni na-an-gub
3 ur-sag-me-en gá-e //
4 uru-mu-šè ga-gen //
5 a-a-mu-šè ga-an-ši-gen //
6 ^{d}su᷃en-me-en gá-e //
7 uru-mu-šè ga-gen //
8 a-a-mu-šè ga-an-ši-gen //

9 a-a-mu ᵈen-líl-lá-šè ga-an-ši-gen

10 gá-e uru-mu-šè ga-gen

11 a-a-mu-šè ga-an-ši-gen

[Text B bricht ab]

8 a-a-mu ᵈen-líl-lá-šè ga-an-gen

9 gá-e ⌜uruᵏⁱ-mu-uš-šè⌝
   g[a-an-ši-DU-en] /
   [Text C bricht ab]

"Der Held—[auf] die Stadt sei[ner] Mutter
[richtete] Nanna-Su'en [wirklich seinen Sinn].
Su'en—[auf] die Stadt sei[ner] Mutter
[richtete] Ašimbabbar [wirklich] sei[nen] Sinn.
Auf die Stadt seiner Mutter, [auf die seines] Vaters
[richtete] Nanna-Su'en wirklich sei[nen] Sinn.
Auf die Enlils, [auf die] Ninlil[s]
richtete Ašimbabbar wirklich seinen Sinn:
'Ich bin ein Held, ich will zu meiner Stadt gehen, zu meinem Vater will ich gehen!
Ich bin Su'en, ich will zu meiner Stadt gehen, zu meinem Vater will ich gehen!
Zu der meines Vaters Enlil will ich gehen!
Ich will zu meiner Stadt gehen, will zu meinem Vater gehen!...'"

Collection B," *JCS* XXI [1967] 25). Hier konnte der Schreiber auf der ersten Zeile des Kästchens offenbar nicht die Kette u l ù - m a h - z i - g a - g i m unterbringen und rückte darum -z i - g a - g i m ein.[33]

Dass der Grund für das Einrücken an dieser Stelle die Einheit der Kette ist, überrascht nicht. Denn das entspricht der Übung in Texten, die Zeilen, nicht Kästchen verwenden und von geringen Ausnahmen abgesehen eine Kette nie über zwei Zeilen verteilen. In den Stelenabschriften Šū-Sîn's entspricht auch innerhalb der Kästchen eine Zeilengrenze stets dem Ende einer Kette. Eine Ausnahme von dieser Regel sind nur längere Genitivverbindungen (z.B. Civil, in *JCS* XXI 31, Kol. iv, Z. 37 f., k i - s u r - r a - //n i b r u^{ki}- k a), die über zwei Zeilen geschrieben sein können. In den etwas älteren Gudea-Zylindern dagegen fallen die Ketten- und die Zeilengrenze innerhalb eines Kästchens höchstens zufällig zusammen.

Die Verwendung von Kurzzeilen in altbabylonischen literarischen Texten erscheint als Fortsetzung der Schreibweise in Šū-Sîn-Stelenabschriften—nur dass die Einteilung in Kästchen aufgegeben wurde. Dies stellt den modernen Leser derartiger Texte vor das vorläufig oft unlösbare Problem, die alten "Vers-" oder "Halbversgrenzen" wiederzufinden. Den antiken Schreibern der Texte bereitete dies aber offenbar keine Schwierigkeit, da die Einheit Vers sonst ganz verlorengegangen wäre. Die Duplikate mit Normal- und Langzeilen zeigen aber, dass dies nicht der Fall war.

Der Grund für die Verteilung eines Verses über mehrere Kurzzeilen kann der Vortrag gewesen sein: man unterteilte den Vers in Abschnitte, die in einem Atemzug gesprochen werden konnten, bezeichnete mit den Zeilenenden also die Sprechpausen.

3.2. METRUM

Da die Beobachtung der Pausen von Bedeutung für die Erschliessung der metrischen Regeln oder doch des Rhythmus (Kola) sein kann, will ich im folgenden einige hervorstechende Beispiele zusammenstellen, in denen die Schreiber

---

33. Dieser Schreibgebrauch findet sich häufiger in den Jenaer Stelenabschriften Šū-Sîn's, die D. O. Edzard, "Neue Inschriften zur Geschichte von Ur III unter Šusuen," *AfO* XIX (1959–60) 1–32 mit Taf. I–IV veröffentlicht hat. Die Kästchengrenzen sind dort in der Umschrift nicht eigens bezeichnet, die Zeilen (soweit nicht eingerückt) sind gezählt. Als Beispiel aus diesem Text seien das 8., 7. und 6. Kästchen in Kol. ii, gezählt vom Kolumnenende, angeführt: ii "25–32." (Zu ii "32" s. M. Civil, "Šū-Sîn's Historical Inscriptions: Collection B," *JCS* XXI [1967] 38).

 8 v.u. [^{d}š]u-^{d}su^{ɔ}en // lugal mu-pà-/da-an-na(!)-ke$_4$ // á-mah-sum-ma- // ^{d}en-líl-lá-ke$_4$

 7 v.u. u$_4$-da- eger-/bi-šè // a-ar-bi

 6 v.u. ka-ta nu-šub-/bu-dè // šu-a bal(?)-e-/dè(!)

 "[Š]ū-Sîn, der König, den ʾAn mit Namen gerufen hat, den Enlil mit höchster Kraft begabt hat—

 damit in künftigen Tagen das Preislied darauf (Sieg und Gaben an die Götter aus der Beute)

 nicht aufhöre gesungen zu werden, dass es tradiert werde. . . ."

die Pausen unterschiedlich setzen oder der Schnitt mitten durch eine Kette geht:

(a) Derselbe Schreiber unterteilt denselben "Vers" verschieden: Šulgi D, Refrain (A = *MBI*, Nr. 3; D = UM 29–16–235 und E = N 3654 [J. Klein, "Šulgi D," Taf. 1]). A verwendet Kurzzeilen, D und E Normalzeilen. (Siehe S. 226).

Der Schreiber von Text A unterteilt die Zeilen des Refrains bei der Wiederholung jeweils einmal weniger als beim ersten Mal. Vielleicht hielt er es für ausreichend, die erste Pause beim ersten Vorkommen des Refrains jeweils bezeichnet zu haben. Dass in den ersten beiden Zeilen dann die zweite Unterteilung beibehalten wurde ist wohl eine Folge von Platzmangel. Diese zweite Pause stimmt mit dem Beginn der eingerückten Zeile in Text E überein. (Text D verwendet hier keine eingerückten Zeilen.) Eingerückte Zeilen können also auch Sprechpausen bezeichnen (s.o. zu "Nanna's Fahrt nach Nippur").

(b) Verschiedene Schreiber, die denselben "Vers" verschieden unterteilen: "Isin-Hymne" *7 (*SKIZ*, S. 209–35); A = *TCL* XVI, Nr. 88; B = *SRT*, Nr. 52. Beide Texte gebrauchen Kurzzeilen

A (ii 25–iii 2) [har-ra-an-kas]kal-e // [si] bí-sá // [su-ka]lam-ma mu-
e-du$_{10}$

B (ii 7–9)   har-ra-an-kaskal-la si bí-sá // su-kalam-ma mu-e-du$_{10}$
"Du hast die Strassen und Wege in Ordnung gebracht, hast das Land sich wohlfühlen lassen."

A (iv 9–12) sig$_4$-$^{\lceil}$é$^{\rceil}$-[kur-ra]-ke$_4$ // ša$_6$-ga-zu // ^{d}e[n-líl] ^{d}nin-líl-ra // hu-mu-ni{-in}-íb-bé

B (iv 2–6)   [sig$_4$]-é-kur-ra-[ke$_4$] // ša$_6$-ga-[zu] // ^{d}en-líl // ^{d}nin-líl-ra // hu-mu-{un}-ne-[x-b]é
"Die Ziegel des Ekur mögen zu Enlil und Ninlil von deinen guten (Taten) sprechen!"

A (iv 13–14) KA-ša$_6$- ga-//an-^{d}en-líl-lá-ta

B (iv 7–9)   KA-ša$_6$-ga-//an-//^{d}en-líl-lá-ta
"Entsprechend den freundlichen Worten von An und Enlil. . . ."

Im ersten der Beispiele unterteilt Text A einen Satz, während Text B ihn als Einheit behandelt. Die Trennung in A erfolgt nach der ersten nominalen Kette; die zweite wird zum finiten Verbum gezogen (ähnlich A, Kol. iv, Z. 17–18 = B, Kol. iv, Z. 12). Im zweiten und dritten Beispiel (ähnlich auch A, Kol. iv, Z. 6–8 = B, Kol. vi, Z. 4–7) unterscheiden sich die Textzeugen in der Behandlung appositioneller Ketten: Text A behandelt sie als Einheit; Text B verteilt sie auf zwei Zeilen und scheint jeder von ihnen das gleiche Gewicht zuzumessen.

Das dritte Beispiel zeigt ausserdem eine Genitivverbindung, die sich über zwei (A) oder drei Zeilen (B) erstreckt.

(c) Genitivverbindungen: s.o. unter (b). Ein weiteres Beispiel für eine sich über drei Zeilen erstreckende Genitivverbindung ist Šulgi R (A = *STVC*, Nr. 60+54; B = *STVC*, Nr. 99(+); s. Wilcke, in *AfO* XXIV 18)

Šulgi D, Refrain

A (i 22–24)   lugal-mu za-gim // a-ba an-ga-kalag // a-ba an-ga-a-da-sá
A (ii 18–19 = iii 21–22)   lugal-mu za-gim a-ba an-ga-kalag // a-ba an-ga-a-da-sá
D (6 = Rs. 2) = E (ii 3)   lugal-mu za-gim a-ba an-ga-k[alag] / a-ba an-ga-a-da-sá

A (i 25–27)   a-ba za-gim // šà-ta geštú-ga // šu-dagal mu-ni-in-du$_{11}$
A (ii 20–21 = iii 23–[24])   a-ba za-gim šà-ta geštú-ga // šu-dagal mu-ni-in-du$_{11}$
D (7 = Rs. 3) = E (ii 4)   a-ba za-gim šà-ta geštú-[ga] / šu-dagal mu-ni-in-du$_{11}$

A (i 28–29)   [n]am-ur-sag-zu-ù // pa hé-è-è
A (ii 22)   nam-ur-sag-zu-ù pa hé-è-è
D (8 = Rs. 4) = E (ii 5)   nam-ur-sag-zu-ù pa hé-[è-è]

A (i 30–31)   nam-kala-ga-zu-ù // mí-du$_{10}$ hé-e
A (ii 23)   nam-kala-ga-zu-ù mí-du$_{10}$ hé-e
D (9 = Rs. 5)   nam-kala-ga-zu-[ù mí-du$_{10}$ hé-e]

"Mein König, wer ist so stark wie du? Wer kann sich mit dir messen?
Wer ist wie du vom Mutterleibe an mit Verstand so reichlich begabt?
Alle deine Heldentaten sollen bekanntgemacht werden!
Von deiner Stärke soll man freundlich sprechen!"

A (Rs. 10) giš-gi-tum-ma-al^{ki}-^{d}en-líl-lá-ka á mu-$^⌈$x$^⌉$[   ]

B (ii 1–4) g$^⌈$i$^⌉$š-gi-//tum-ma-al^{ki}-//^{d}en-líl-lá-ke$_4$ // á mu-sù-sù-e

"Im Röhricht von(?) Enlils Tummal eilt (das Schiff) dahin."

Weitere Beispiele für über zwei Zeilen verteilte Genitivverbindungen sind Šulgi D (A = *MBI*, Nr. 3 i 18–19, D = UM 29–16–235, Z. 4); nin mul-an-gim (W. W. Hallo, in *CRRA* XVII 123–28), Z. 6, 12, 13, 18, 29; A. Kapp, in *ZA*, Bd. 51 (1955) S. 80, Z. 180–81.

(d) Substantiv und Attribut: Beispiele aus nin mul-an-gim (A = W. W. Hallo, in *CRRA* XVII 123–28)

A (Z. 4–5) gi-DI-//imin-e ka ba-a

me-gal-//ninnu-e šu-du$_7$-a

"Die den sieben Rohrflöten den Mund geöffnet hat,

Die die fünfzig grossen göttlichen Kräfte vollkommen gemacht hat."

Ähnlich auch Z. 19, 28 und 34. Ausser in Z. 28 ist jeweils das zweite Attribut abgetrennt. In Z. 4(?), 5, 19 und 28 ist die erste "Zeile" zweisilbig; die Lesung in Z. 34 ist unklar.

(e) Finites Verbum: Ich kenne nur ein Beispiel, in dem eine finite Verbalform sich möglicherweise über zwei Zeilen erstreckt. Angesichts des fragmentarischen Erhaltungszustands kann eine eingerückte Zeile nicht ausgeschlossen werden, sie ist aber in Anbetracht der Raumverhältnisse unwahrscheinlich: Šulgi R, Z. 46 (A = *STVC*, Nr. 60+54; B = *ISET* I 84, Ni. 13203(+); s. Wilcke, in *AfO* XXIV 18)

A (Z. 46) [x bá]ra-kù-ga dúr im-mi-in-gá(!)-re-éš(!) níg(!) mi-ni-

íb-[   ]

B (i 1–4) [x bára-k]ù-ga(!) // [dúr im-mi]-gá-re-éš // [níg mi-n]i-íb-

// [gu-ul-g]u-ul-ne

"[. . .] setzten sich auf den hellen [Hoch]sitz und tischten dabei

grossartig auf."

Die Beobachtung der Sprechpausen beim Vortrag, wie sie die Texte mit Kurzzeilen (Kola) bezeichnen, ist ein möglicher Weg zur Wiedergewinnung der metrischen Regeln. Sie müsste Hand in Hand gehen mit der Analyse der Verteilung der Worte und Ketten auf einer Tafel innerhalb der Kolumne. Dafür ist aber in der Mehrzahl der Fälle eine Autopsie der Keilschrifttexte von Nöten. Ausserdem bedarf diese Methode der Ergänzung durch andere.

Eine mögliche solche Ergänzung ist der von W. Heimpel, in *Or*, NS, Bd. 39 (1970) S. 492–95, eingeschlagene Weg, das Zählen der Silben. Heimpel stellte fest, dass Gruppen von fünf Silben häufig in literarischen Texten vorkommen– verbunden mit Gruppen mit freier Silbenzahl.

Dieser Methode steht freilich ein grosses Hindernis entgegen. Denn obwohl die meisten Lesungen jetzt annähernd festgelegt sind, handelt es sich doch bei ihnen um die isolierten Formen, wie sie die Syllabare und lexikalischen Listen bieten. Über Kontextformen wissen wir nur wenig. Und dort, wo man sie unorthographisch geschriebenen Texten entnehmen kann (s. A. Falkenstein, in *AfO* XVI [1952/53] 60–64; in *ZA*, Bd. 55 [1963] S. 11–67; *MNS* I, Nr. 8–10; Å. Sjöberg, in *OrS* X 3–12; E. Bergmann, in *ZA*, Bd. 56 [1964] S. 1–43, in *ZA*, Bd. 57 [1965] S. 31–42; J. Krecher, in *ZA*, Bd. 58 [1967] S. 16–65, in *WO* IV [1968] 252–72; *Lišan mithurti* [*AOAT*, Bd. 1 (1969)] S. 157–97; M. Civil, in *JNES*, Bd. 26 [1967] S. 209–11), ist stets damit zu rechnen, dass es sich um Besonderheiten des Emesal-Dialekts handelt und obendrein die belegten Formen durch den Kontext und eventuell auch durch die metrische Struktur des Textes, dem sie entnommen wurden, beeinflusst sind.

Die Untersuchung W. Heimpels hat trotz dieser Hindernisse zeigen können, dass die Silbenzahl eine wichtige Rolle spielt; s. auch unten im Exkurs. Dieses Ergebnis können auch weitere Beobachtungen zu den Gudea Zylindern, auf denen Heimpel wesentlich fusst, stützen. So scheint in Gudea Zyl. A xxviii 3–12 das Vorkommen der Postposition -ta von der Silbenzahl abzuhängen. Ein weiteres Beispiel ist Gudea Zyl. A xxv 24–xxvi 14. (Siehe S. 229.)

Wir haben den Text in drei Kolumnen angeordnet, von denen die erste die Orte der Handlung (Gebäude im Tempelkomplex), die zweite die Objekte und die letzte die Handlung enthält. In xxv 28 und xxvi 2 stimmt diese Einteilung allerdings nicht mit den Kästchengrenzen überein. In der ersten Kolumne schwankt die vermutliche Silbenzahl zwischen 7, 8 und 9. In der letzten beträgt sie mit Ausnahme von xxvi 5 (ist dort im Kontext ein Vokal elidiert, etwa *immadasge?) regelmässig 4. Die Silbenzahl in der mittleren Kolumne ist in den ersten drei Zeilen schwankend, von der vierten bis zur siebten Zeile regelmässig 8. Diese Zahl 8 ist gewollt und nicht zufällig, da sie in xxvi 4 verglichen mit xxvi 7 nur durch das Weglassen der enklitischen Kopula und, worauf mich D. O. Edzard aufmerksam machte, in xxvi 10 (vgl. xxvi 13) nur durch die Unterdrückung des -da von -bi-da, "zusammen mit," erreicht wird.

Als letztes Beispiel für die Relevanz der Silbenzahl möchte ich den Refrain der Zeilen 12–21 von "Reiher und Schildkröte" heranziehen, der sich jeweils aus einem variablen und einem festen Glied zusammensetzt. Die Lage ist hier durch teilweise divergierende Duplikate (Sigla nach der Edition von G. Gragg, in *AfO* XXIV [1973] 51 ff.) etwas kompliziert.

12 ([na]m-)di$_4$-di$_4$-lá	du$_{10}$-ga-àm
13 nam-ki-sikil	du$_{10}$-ga-àm
14 nam-guruš[34]	du$_{10}$-ga-àm
15 é-gi$_4$-a	du$_{10}$-ga-àm
16 TUR-bàn-da	du$_{10}$-ga-àm
17 nam-ab-ba[35]	du$_{10}$-ga-àm

---

34. Text B schreibt n⌈a⌉m-x-guruš. Dabei ist das Zeichen vor guruš ein unvollständig geschriebenes GURUŠ, das der Schreiber zu tilgen vergass, als er das Zeichen guruš an das Ende der Zeile rückte (Rest eingerückte Zeile).

35. Die Variante nam-ab-ba-ke$_4$ (so G. Gragg, "The Fable of the Heron and the Turtle," *AfO* XXIV [1973] 61, Anm. 17.2) kann ich auf dem Photo von Text B nicht verifizieren.

Gudea Zyl. A xxv 24–xxvi 14

xxv 24 a-ga-tukul-lá ká-mè-ba	25 ur-sag-šeg$_9$-bar sag-imin SAG.AR-bi	26 im-ma-ab-dab$_5$-bé	8/10(?)/4
27 igi-uru^{ki}-šè ki-ní-íL-ba	28 ur-sag-imin-àm	im-ma-ab-tuš-e	8(?)/5+4
xxvi 1 šu-ga-lam ká-me-lám-ba	2 búr-ša$_6$-bi	im-ma-ab-dab$_5$-bé	7/3+4
3 igi-u$_4$-è ki-nam-tar-re-ba	4 šu-nir-^{d}utu sag-alim-ma	5 im-ma-da-si-ge	9/8/5
6 ká-sur-ra igi-u$_6$-di-ba	7 ur-mah ní-dingir-re-ne-kam	8 im-ma-ab-tuš-e	8/8/4
9 tar-sír-sír ki-á-ág-ba	10 ku-li-an-na urudu-bi	11 im-ma-ab-tuš-e	7/8/4
12 a-ga-^{d}ba-ba$_6$ ki-šà-kúš-ba	13 má-gi$_4$-lum gu$_4$-alim-bi-da 14 im-ma-ab-tuš-e		8/8/4

"In seiner Halle, in der die Waffen hängen, dem Tor der Schlacht, lässt er den Helden 'Wildschwein mit sieben Köpfen' und ... (Platz) nehmen.

Gegenüber der Stadt, an seinem Ort, der sich erhebt(?), setzt er die sieben Helden hin.

Am Šugalam, seinem 'Tor Schreckensglanz,' lässt er die schönen bur-Gefässe (Platz) nehmen.

Gegenüber dem Sonnenaufgang, an seinem Platz, an dem die Schicksale entschieden werden, errichtet er das Emblem Utu's mit dem Wisentkopf.

Am Kasurra, seiner staunenswerten Fassade, setzt er den Löwen, die Furcht der Götter, hin.

In seinem Tarsirsir, dem Ort, an dem Weisungen erteilt werden, setzt er den 'Freund des An' zusammen mit dem (gewaltigen) Kupfer hin.

In der Halle Baba's, seinem Ort, an dem vertraulich beraten wird, setzt er das Magilum und den Ur-Stier hin."

18 nam-um-ma	du$_{10}$-ga-àm
19 gù-dé-a	du$_{10}$-ga-àm
20 nam-lugal(-la)	du$_{10}$-ga-àm
21 dumu-lugal(-la)	du$_{10}$-ga-àm

Der Refrain hat in Z. 14, 15, 17, 18 und 19 jeweils 5 Silben. Dazu kommt noch Z. 12, wenn wir die Variante [na]m-di$_4$-di$_4$-lá von Text A als (von den anderen Bildungen auf nam- abhängigen) Fehler betrachten. In Z. 13 scheinen 6 Silben vorzuliegen, doch ist für KI.SIKIL auch eine Lesung kiskil bezeugt (s. A. Falkenstein, in *ZA*, Bd. 53, S. 100 mit Anm. 24; J. Krecher, in *AOAT*, Bd. 1, S. 193), mit der wir ebenfalls zu 5 Silben kommen. TUR-bàn-da (Z. 16) wird gewöhnlich dumu-bàn-da gelesen (A. Falkenstein, in *ZA*, Bd. 57, S. 78), aber soweit ich weiss, ist die Lesung des ersten Zeichens nicht gesichert, sodass wir mit der Möglichkeit rechnen können, dass hier ebenfalls 5 Silben vorliegen. Diese Beobachtung der gleichen Silbenzahl im Refrain der Z. 12–19 bietet uns die Erklärung, warum in Z. 12 (Text B), 15 und 16 das Abstrakta-Präfix nam- fehlt: Es hätte zu einer überzähligen Silbe geführt. Der Refrain in Z. 12–19 hat dann dieselbe Silbenzahl wie der in Z. 1–9 (mú-a-bi du$_{10}$-ga-àm, "der es wachsen liess, ist gut") und Z. 26–30 // 73–77 (zà im-ma-ni-in-tag, "er stiess ihn zurück"). Die übrigen Refrains des Textes haben dagegen sechs Silben: Z. 39–47 // 80–86: nunuz ki ba-ni-in-tag, "er legte Eier"; Z. 49–59: du$_{14}$ ga-nam mu-da-mú, "sie hat mit ihm wirklich Streit angefangen," und Z. 89–98 lú-har-ra-an-gig-ga-ke$_4$ "die, der die Wege bitter sind."

Ab Z. 19 steuert unser Refrain einer Klimax zu: in Z. 19 ist die Silbenzahl noch fünf, aber im variablen Glied des Refrains ist ein semantischer Wechsel eingetreten. Handelte es sich in Z. 12–18 um Gruppen verschiedenen Personenstandes (Kinder, Status der jungen Frau, Status des jungen Mannes, ⟨Status der⟩ Schwiegertochter, ⟨Status des⟩ jungen Mädchens, Status des alten Mannes, Status der alten Frau), so ist es in Z. 19–21 eine einzelne Person, von der die Rede ist: "der Berufene," "der des Königtums" = der, dem das Königtum zukommt), "der Königssohn."[36] Die Klimax in diesen Ausdrücken wird durch das Ansteigen der Silbenzahl unterstützt: Z. 19 noch 5 Silben, Z. 20: 6 Silben, Z. 21: 7 Silben.

36. Text D schreibt nam-lugal und dumu-lugal; A und B haben nam-lugal-la und dumu-lugal-la. Da in Z. 21 dumu-lugal-la(-k) grammatisch korrekt ist, ist auch in Z. 20 A und B der Vorzug zu geben. Nam-lugal-la(-k) ist dann regensloser Genitiv.

G. Gragg fasste gù-dé-a in Z. 19 als Namen auf. Dies würde—da hierfür nur Gudea von Lagaš in Frage käme—historische Konsequenzen haben (s. *AfO* XXIV 51, Anm. 1). Denn nur hier würden wir erfahren, dass Gudea ein Königssohn war—wir kennen ihn aber als Schwiegersohn Urbabas, seines Vorgängers im Amte eines ensí von Lagaš. Ausserdem müssten die am Anfang des Textes aufgezählten Sumpfgebiete Teil seines Reiches gewesen sein, was möglich ist. Hinsichtlich der Literaturgeschichte würde es ausserdem bedeuten, dass "Reiher und Schildkröte" das älteste bekannte Streitgedicht ist.

Gegen diese Annahme spricht aber, dass der Name nicht am Anfang, sondern am Ende einer Klimax stehen sollte, da sie sonst im Leeren verpuffen würde. Eine Folge "der Berufene," "der, dem das Königtum zukommt," "der Königssohn" ist dagegen eine echte Klimax, die durch die steigende Silbenzahl noch unterstrichen wird.

Wir können also festhalten, dass die Silbenzahl von Bedeutung für die metrischen Regeln der sumerischen Dichtung war. Sicher können wir andererseits ausschliessen, dass sie das metrische Grundprinzip war, wie etwa in der japanischen Poesie. Denn dafür sind die angeführten Beispiele zu vereinzelt. A. Falkenstein, in *SAHG*, S. 28, hatte eine quantitierende Metrik ausgeschlossen— sein Argument, das Sumerische kenne keine langen Vokale, ist aber nicht unwidersprochen geblieben (D. O. Edzard, in *HSAO*, S. 33, Anm. 9; Krecher, in *AOAT*, Bd. 1, S. 169). Sein Hinweis auf den "ausgesprochenen Druckakzent" des Sumerischen behält aber weiterhin seine Gültigkeit und spricht für akzentuierende Metren. Da unsere Kenntnis des Akzents im Sumerischen aber noch ganz mangelhaft ist (s. Krecher, in *AOAT*, Bd. 1, S. 157–97), ist vorläufig nicht damit zu rechnen, dass es gelingen wird, die genauen metrischen Regeln wiederzugewinnen—dies besonders, da auch in gut bekannten modernen Sprachen die Diskussion von Metrik und Rhythmus wieder in Bewegung geraten ist (s. R. Wellek und A. Warren, *Theorie der Literatur* [2. Aufl.; Frankfurt, 1972] Kap. 12).[37]

3.3. PROSA UND POESIE

Bis jetzt haben wir die sumerischen literarischen Texte so betrachtet, als gebe es nur Poesie und nicht auch Prosa. Der Nachweis, dass ein Text in Prosa verfasst ist, lässt sich nicht leicht führen. Denn wir kennen die metrischen Regeln der Poesie nicht. Da die Schreiber beim Kopieren von Vorlagen meist auch deren Zeileneinteilung übernahmen, können wir auch bei Werken, die von vornherein als Prosatexte verdächtig sind, wie der sumerischen Königsliste als "wissenschaftlichem Werk" oder den literarisch tradierten Briefen, die Entscheidung Prosa oder Poesie nicht treffen. In einem Sonderfall scheint es aber möglich zu sein: Im Dialog "Schreiber und missratener Sohn," Z. 148–52 (Å. W. Sjöberg, "Der Vater und sein missratener Sohn," *JCS* XXV [1973] 105–69) weichen die einzelnen Textzeugen in der Aufzählung der Schimpfwörter, die der Vater seinem Sohn an den Kopf wirft, hinsichtlich der Zeilengrenzen so sehr voneinander ab, dass es naheliegt, hier Prosa zu vermuten.[38]

---

37. Ich gehe darum auf die metrische Gliederung einzelner sumerischer literarischer Texte von H. Sauren, "Beispiele sumerischer Poesie," *JEOL*, Bd. 22 (1971/72) S. 255–306, und seine Bemerkung in "Les épopées sumeriennes," *Orientalia Lovaniensia Periodica*, Bd. 3 (1972) S. 36, "les vers présentent un mètre classique: dactyle, spondée, trochée et d'autre pieds connus" nicht ein.

38. Siehe den Kommentar Å. W. Sjöbergs, in *JCS* XXV (1973) 133–37. Zu is-háb s. *CAD*, Bd. I/J, S. 189, s.v. *ishappu*. Zu sag-ùr-ùr ist vielleicht das in *MSL* XII 168, OB Lú Recension A, Z. 336, neben anderen, z.T. auch in unserem Textabschnitt erscheinenden Schimpfwörtern stehende lú š[u]-ùr-ùr = *uš-šu-šum* zu vergleichen, das in *MSL* XII 194 OB Lú Recension C₃, Z. 17 (wieder neben auch in unserem Passus auftauchenden Schimpfwörtern) als [lú š]u-ùr-ùr = *lu-uš-šu-*[*x*] wiederkehrt. Die akkadischen Ausdrücke sind mir unklar; ist in Rec. A vielleicht ein *lu-* ausgefallen oder dieses *lu-* in Recension C zu tilgen? Ist das in beiden Fällen teilweise beschädigte Zeichen šu vielleicht ein Fehler für das sag unseres Textes?

Siglen nach Å. W. Sjöberg, in *JCS* XXV 107-9.

Ur$_5$	(9)	lú-ıM lú-la-ga è-bùr-bùr // (10) lú-sikil-dù-a is-[...] //
E iv	(8)	[l]ú-ıM lú-la-ga é-bùr(!)-bùr(!) // (9) lú-sikil-dù-a is-háb-ba-àm //
G iv'	(7)	lú-lú(!)-ıM lú-la-ga é-bùr-bùr // (8) lú-sikil-dù-a lú-is(?)-háb(?)-àm //
K v	(29)	[lú-ıM lú-la]-ga é-bùr-bùr // (30) [...]
LL v	(27)	l[ú-x-x lú-l]a-ga é-bùr-bùr-x // (28) [...]-˹a˺ is-h˹a˺b-ba(!)-àm //
TT	(5)	lú-lú-ıM lú-l˹a˺-g˹a˺ é-bùr-[...] // (6) lú-[sikil]-dù-a is-háb-ba-àm
UU	(2)	lú-ùlu-ıM lú-l˹a˺-g˹a˺ é-bùr-bur-bùr(?) lú-s˹i˺k˹i˺l-dù-a is-h˹á˺b-[...] //

Ur$_5$	(11)	na-gá-ah lú-m[ú-da] // (12) eme(!) zà-ga bar-bar šu-gig bí-ib-du$_{11}$-ga //
E iv	(10)	na-gá-ah lú-mu-da // (11) eme zà-ga bar-bar // (12) sag šu-zi bí-du$_{11}$-ga //
G iv'	(9)	na-gá-ah lú-mu-da // (10) eme(?) zà-ga bar-bar // (11) sag šu-zi bí-in-du$_{11}$-ga //
K v		na]-gá-ah // (31) [...-g]a bar-bar // (32) [...]
LL v	(29)	[...l]ú-mu-da // (30) [...-g]a bar-bar // [Rest abgebrochen]
TT		...] // (7) lú-lú-mu-d˹a˺ // (8) [...] bar-bar // (9) [...]˹x˺ du$_{11}$-g˹a˺ //
UU	(3)	na-gá-ah lú-[...z]à-ga bar-bar // (4) sag šu-zi-d[a(?)...
OO Rs.		[..] // (1) [x x x x] x [...] //

Ur$_5$	(13)	sag ùr-ùr lú-hu(!)-h[u-nu] //
E iv	(13)	sag ùr-ùr lú-hu-hu-nu //
G iv'	(12)	sag ùr-ùr lú-hu-hu-nu //
K v		...-ù]r // [Rest abgebrochen]
UU		..]-ur$_4$ lú-hu-hu-nu //
OO Rs.	(2)	[...] lú-hu-hu-[nu] //

Falscher Kerl, Räuber, Einbrecher—der Gehässige ist ein Tölpel—Dummkopf, Beleidiger, Verleumder, ewig Gestriger(?)... Schwächling, (...).

4. STROPHE

Nur selten geben die Keilschrifttexte direkte Hinweise auf die strophische Gliederung. Soweit sie es tun, gebrauchen sie zwei verschiedene Mittel:

(a) Die Abtrennung der Strophen voneinander durch kräftiger eingedrückte oder doppelt gezogene Striche wie z.b. in *SRT*, Nr. 52 Vs. In ähnlicher Weise werden auch die Reden der Kontrahenten in Streitgesprächen oder die (beschreibende) Einleitung einer Beschwörung von der (epischen) Marduk-Ea-Formel und der folgenden Ritualanweisung getrennt (Wilcke, in *AfO* XXIV, Taf. II). Derartige Trennstriche können auch Rubriken ersetzen wie in den Ur-Texten zur Sammlung der Tempelhymnen (s. Wilcke, in *JNES*, Bd. 31, S. 38), in dem šìr-nam-gala Nanna's CBS 8084 = UM 29-15-58 (Å. Sjöberg, "Miscellaneous Sumerian Hymns," *ZA*, Bd. 63 [1974] S. 31 ff.) oder dem šìr-nam-gala Nininsina's *UET* VI/1, Nr. 96 = 97.

(b) Die abgekürzte Schreibung wiederholter Zeilen (Verse) in Texten, die die Wiederholungsschemata R–2 oder R–3 verwenden (s.o. 2.2), wie z.B. in *STVC*, Nr. 36, einem tigi-Lied auf Baba für Gudea. Manchmal fassen die Schreiber dann diese abgekürzt geschriebenen Zeilen auf einer Zeile zusammen wie z.B. in *CT* XXXVI, Taf. 33–34, einem tigi-Lied auf Inanna, wobei der optische Eindruck von der Strophengliederung wieder verlorengeht.

Meist aber verzichten die antiken Schreiber darauf, derartige Hilfsmittel zu geben—sehr zum Leidwesen des modernen Lesers. So ist es oft unmöglich zu sagen, ob ein Text in Strophen gegliedert war oder nicht.

Moderne Bearbeiter sumerischer literarischer Texte bieten diese oft in Strophen unterteilt. Aber nur Jacobsen und Kramer, in *JNES* XII 162, Anm. 5, Falkenstein, in *SGL* I 9–10, und Hallo und van Dijk, in *YNER*, Bd. 3, S. 44–45, begründen die vorgenommene Gliederung.[39] Falkenstein und Hallo und van Dijk beobachteten ausser der auch von Jacobsen verwendeteten Methode der

---

39. In der assyriologischen Literatur herrscht einige Verwirrung in der Terminologie hinsichtlich der Einheit Strophe: Th. Jacobsen und S. N. Kramer, "The Myth of Inanna and Bilulu," *JNES* XII (1953) 162, Anm. 5 (*TIOT*, S. 334–35) bezeichnet mit "strophe" den Vers oder Halbvers. Zwei oder drei "strophes" bildeten als "distich" oder "tristich" eine "stanza," mehrere "stanzas" dann eine "megastrophe." W. W. Hallo und J. van Dijk, *The Exaltation of Inanna* (*YNER*, Bd. 3 [1968]) S. 44, setzen die Zeile einem Stichos oder Kolon gleich, während sie die Strophen als bicola oder tricola bezeichnen. Als "stanza" verstehen sie dann Gruppen von *ca.* vier "Strophen." A. Falkenstein, in *SGL* I 9, spricht dagegen nur von Strophen, worunter er Gruppen von 2 oder mehr Zeilen versteht.

Der Terminus Kolon, der eine rhythmische Einheit innerhalb des Verses bezeichnet, sollte ganz aus der Diskussion der Strophe verschwinden. Da die Stanze auf vorhersagbare Reimschemata festgelegt ist, halte ich die Einführung dieses Ausdrucks in die Beschreibung der sumerischen Literatur nicht für glücklich. Ob man Stichos oder Zeile sagt, mag auf den ersten Blick gleich sein, doch muss man sich die oben beschriebenen verschiedenen Zeilentypen vor Augen halten und entscheiden, auf welchen man den Terminus anwenden will. Hier sind die Ausdrücke "Kurzzeile," "Normalzeile" und "Langzeile" präziser. Für die dem Vers übergeordnete Einheit bietet sich die nicht durch formale Definitionen festgelegte Strophe an. Zu der Strophe übergeordneten Einheiten s.u. 5.

Zusammenfassung paralleler Zeilen Beginn und Ende von Auszugstafeln, da zu erwarten ist, dass diese mit der Strophengrenze übereinstimmen. Diese rein objektive Methode enthält aber hinsichtlich der Tafelenden einen Unsicherheitsfaktor, da viele Texte nicht eigens gekennzeichnete Stichzeilen schrieben, die Strophe dann also eine Zeile früher enden muss. Ausserdem ist sie nur auf längere Kompositionen anwendbar und hängt von der Zahl der vorhandenen Auszugstafeln ab.[40]

Ein weiteres objektives Kriterium ist die Beobachtung der Wiederholungsschemata (s.o. 2.2), von denen R–2 und R–3 immer Strophen bilden. R–1 und R–5 erscheinen meist am Anfang einer Strophe, aber auch am Ende. Die Stellung von R–4 innerhalb der Strophe scheint nicht so festgelegt zu sein, es ist aber zu erwarten, dass sie innerhalb eines Textes gleichbleibt.

Ein Beispiel eines Textes, der ausser R–2 und R–3 alle übrigen Wiederholungstypen verwendet, ist das b a l - b a l - e -Lied auf Ninazu, das J. van Dijk in *SGL* II 57–80 bearbeitet hat:[41]

(a) Das grundlegende Schema ist die Wiederholung der Phrase e n ^{d}n i n - a - z u - m u (R–4) am Anfang der Zeilen 3, 7, 12, 17, 22, 28 und am Ende der letzten Zeile, Z. 31, also jeweils am Ende einer Strophe.

Zusätzlich finden sich die folgenden Wiederholungen:

(b) Z. 1–2, 16–17 und 20–21 zeigen die Folge a, a′ (R–1), die in Z. 16–17 mit der durch R–4 bezeichneten Strophengrenze übereinstimmt (in den übrigen Fällen ist das Schema erweitert, s.u., (d)).

(c) In Z. 3 (lies e n ^{d}n i n - a - z u - m u u n [ù - b i z a - e - m e - e n u] n [ù - b i z a] - e - m e - e n), 12, 22 und 28 wird eine Phrase am Ende der Zeile wiederholt (R–5), was mit der durch R–4 gekennzeichneten Strophengrenze übereinstimmt.

(d) In Z. 1–3, 11–12, 16–17, 20–22 und 27–28 finden sich (refrainartige) Epiphern, wobei die zweite (und in Z. 1–3 und Z. 20–22 auch die dritte) einer Gruppe von Zeilen den Schluss der ersten wiederholt.

(e) An einen Refrain erinnert, dass in Z. 7 und Z. 16–17 die Phrase ^{d}n a n n a h é - e - d a - h ú l am Zeilenende erscheint.

Die verschiedenen Arten der Wiederholung zeigen alle dieselben Strophengrenzen:

A = Z. 1–3	(3 Zeilen)	E = Z. 18–22	(5 Zeilen)
B = Z. 4–7	(4 Zeilen)	F = Z. 23–28	(6 Zeilen)
C = Z. 8–12	(5 Zeilen)	G = Z. 29–31	(3 Zeilen)
D = Z. 13–17	(5 Zeilen)		

40. Hallo und van Dijk, *YNER*, Bd. 3, S. 44, versuchen—wenn auch mit Vorbehalten—diese Methode auch auf die Kolumneneinteilung von Mehrkolumnentafeln zu übertragen, was jedoch wenig überzeugt. So beginnt z.B. auf der 4-Kolumnentafel *ISET* I 64, Ni. 9660 + *ISET* I 164, Ni. 4590 + *BE* XXXI, Nr. 41 + *SLTNi*, Nr. 64 (Texte d, C und H der Edition in *YNER*, Nr. 3, wo Ni. 4590 noch nicht verwertet werden konnte; Joins von J. Klein freundlicherweise während eines Aufenthaltes in Istanbul bestätigt) Kol. ii mit der letzten Zeile einer Strophe, und Kol. iii endet mitten in einer anderen.

41. Die im folgenden begründete Stropheneinteilung weicht von der von J. van Dijk in seiner Bearbeitung vorgenommenen ab.

Die so gewonnenen Strophen zeigen beträchtliche Unterschiede im Umfang; s. bereits *SAHG*, S. 27, Jacobsen und Kramer, in *JNES* XII 162, Anm. 5.[42]

Eine andere Möglichkeit, Strophen zu isolieren, bietet die syntaktische Analyse, da Strophen häufig einem bestimmten syntaktischen Muster folgen. Die folgenden Typen lassen sich unterscheiden:

(a) Nominal stilisierte Zeilen, sei es als appositionelle Fügungen, sei es als Nominalsätze (einschliesslich infiniter Verbalformen).

(b) Wie a, aber mit der enklitischen Kopula.

(c) Verbal stilisierte Zeilen (finite Verben). Hier kann noch nach grammatischen Kategorien wie Person und Modus unterschieden werden, der Gebrauch der dimensionalen Präfixe kann von Bedeutung sein; auch die Konstruktion des nominalen Satzteiles kann Hinweise auf die Einheit Strophe geben.

(d) Verbindung von Typen a–c.

Dass die Beobachtung dieser Kriterien zur Abgrenzung von Strophen führen kann, möchte ich an einem kurzen Text, der durch den Wiederholungstyp R–2 klar in Strophen gliedert ist, einem tigi-Lied auf Nintu, demonstrieren. Texte: A = *TMH* NF IV, Nr. 86 (kollationiert); B = *BL*, Nr. 102; C = *BL*, Nr. 127; D = *BL*, Nr. 95; E = *BL*, Nr. 97. Text A ist altbabylonisch; B–E stammen aus der Bibliothek Assurbanipals. Die Strophen bezeichne ich mit kursiven Versalien.

A   1 nin ᵈa-ru-ru-é-kèšᵏⁱ-a
      2 hur-sag ki-sikil-la ù-tu-da
      3 ᵈnin-tu ama-mah-kur-kur-ra-[ka]ᵃ
A'   4 ama ᵈnin-tu nin ᵈa-ru-ru-é-kèšᵏⁱ-aᵇ
      5 hur-sag ki-sikil-la ù-tu-da
      6 ᵈnin-tu ama-mah-kur-kur-ra-kᵀaᵀᶜ
B   7 su-zi-pirig-gá-ka ši-mi-ni-in-è
      8 en mu-un-ù-tu lagar mu-ᵀuᵀn-ù-tu
      9 lugal bára-kù-ga ᵈnin-tu-rᵀeᵀ bí-in-ù-tu
B'   10 ᵈnin-tu su-zᵀi-pirig-gá-kaᵀ ši-mi-ni-in-è
     11 [en] mᵀu-un-ùᵀ-tu lagar mu-un-ù-tu
     12 [luga]l bára-kù-ga ᵈnin-tu-re bí-in-ù-tu
C   13 [(x)]ᵀxᵀ-ZU nì sag-bi-šè è-a
     14 [ᵈni]n-tᵀuᵀ-re sag-gá ša-mu-ni-in-gál
     15 [(x) hi-l]i-a tu ki-ús-sa
C'   16 [ama ᵈn]in-t[u] ᵀxᵀ-ZU nì sag-bi-šè è-a
     17 [ᵈni]n-tu-⟨re⟩ sag-gá ša-mu-ni-in-[gál]
     18 [ᵈnin-tu] ᵀxᵀ hi-li-a tu ki-ús-sa
     19 sa-gíd-da-àm

42. Darum kann H. Saurens Feststellung, "Als Strophe ist die literarische Einheit anzusehen, deren äussere Form, die Zeilenzahl, im Werk stets wiederkehrt" (in *UF*, Bd. 3, S. 328), nicht richtig sein.

D 20 [nin gaba]-gál nam-nun-an-ki-a
   21 [x] ᵈnin-tu ù-tu-da
   22 [x] abzu-ta nun-e gar-ra
   23 kur-gal ᵈen-líl-da šu-sá-a
D′ 24 ᵈnin-tu nin gaba-gál nam-nu[n-an-ki-a]ᵈ
   25 [x] ᵈnin-tu ù-[tu-da]ᵈ
   26 [x ab]zu-ta nun-e [gar-ra]ᵉ
   27 [kur-gal ᵈen-líl-da šu-sá-a]ᵉ
E 28 [áb am]ar-bi-ta gù-nun mu-na-ab-béᶠ
   29 [am]a ᵈnin-tu-re i-lu-bi-ta mu-un-na-an-kin(!)-e(!)
   30 ama ᵈnin-tu nin-mah-kèškⁱ-a
   31 kur-gal ᵈen-líl-da šu-sá-a
E′ 32 ᵈnin-tu áb amar-bi-ta gù-nun mu-na-ab-bé
   33 [ama ᵈnin-tu-re i-lu-bi-ta mu-u]n-na-kin(?)-eᵉ
   34 ama ᵈnin-tu nin-mah-keškⁱ-a
   35 kur-gal ᵈen-líl-da šu-sá-a
F 36 dúr-kù-giriₓ(= KA)-zal-la ki-tuš nì-lu-lu-aᵍ
   37 ama(!) ᵈnin-tu bára tuš-a-ni
   38 me-mah guškin-ga-àm me-te-un-lu-a
   39 nam-en nam-lugal ᵈen-líl-šè gál-la
F′ 40 ᵈnin-tu [k]i-tʳuˡš-[gir]iₓ(= KA)-zal-la ki-tuš nì-lu-lu-aʰ
   41 ama ᵈnin-tu bára tuš-a-ni
   42 me-mah guškinⁱ me-te-un-lu-a
   43 [na]m-en nam-lugal ᵈen-líl-šè gál-la
   44 sa-gar-ra-àmʲ
   45 ti[gi-ᵈn]in-tu-ra-kamᵏ
Kolophone: B [. . .]-šú-ma // [. . .l]i-hal-li-qu
           E nibrukⁱ-a sar-ma [. . .]

(a) So A nach Z. 6; B: ke₄.   (b) So B; A: -é-kèš-a.   (c) So A; B ke₄.
(d) Zeile in A und C; D om.   (e) Zeile in A; D om.   (f) So D; in A unsichere
Spuren.   (g) So D; A:]-lu-a; vgl. Z. 40.   (h) So A; D(+?)E ᵈnin-tu
giriₓ(= KA)-zal-la ki-tuš nì-lu-lu-a.   (i) So A; D guš]kin-àm.   (j) In
A selbständige Zeile; in E eine Zeile mit Z. 43.   (k) So A; E: ˹x˺-BALAG AN.
KÈŠ(?) ᵈnin-urta [(. . .)] (bedarf der Kollation).

A Die Herrin Aruru vom Hause Keš,
     im Gebirge, dem reinen Ort geboren,
     Nintu, die die grösste Mutter aller Länder ist,
A′ die Mutter Nintu, die Herrin Aruru vom Hause Keš,
     im Gebirge, dem reinen Ort geboren,
     Nintu, die die grösste Mutter aller Länder ist,
B hat sich wirklich mit dem haarsträubenden Schrecken eines Löwen bekleidet,
     hat den en-Priester geboren, hat den lagar-Priester geboren,
     den König hat Nintu auf dem reinen Hochsitz geboren.

B′ Nintu hat sich wirklich mit dem haarsträubenden Schrecken eines Löwen
    bekleidet,
    hat den [en-Priester] geboren, hat den lagar-Priester geboren,
    den [Köni]g hat Nintu auf dem reinen Hochsitz geboren.

C   Das [...], das alles überragt,
    hat [Ni]ntu ihm(?) wirklich aufs Haupt gesetzt,
    [...], die das Gebären in [Wonn]e gegründet hat(?)

C′ [die Mutter N]in[tu] (hat) das ..., das alles überragt,
    [Ni]ntu hat es ihm(?) wirklich aufs Haupt [gesetzt],
    [Nintu], die ..., die das Gebären in Wonne gegründet hat(?)
    sa-gíd-da ist es.

D [Die Herrin, die sich (dem Feind) entgegen]stellt, die die Fürstlichkeit von
    Himmel und Erde (besitzt),
    [...] Nintu geboren,
    [...], das der Fürst vom Abzu her gesetzt hat,
    die mit dem grossen Berg Enlil gewetteifert hat(?),

D′ Nintu, die Herrin, die sich (dem Feind) entgegenstellt, die die Für[st]lichkeit
    [von Himmel und Erde (besitzt)],
    [...] Nintu [ge]bo[ren],
    [...], das der Fürst vom [Ab]zu her [gesetzt hat],
    [die mit dem grossen Berg Enlil gewetteifert hat(?)]—

E [Die Kuh] ruft laut zu ihr wegen ihres [Kal]bes,[43]
    [Die Mut]ter Nintu sucht nach ihm wegen ihrer Klage,[44]
    die Mutter Nintu, die grösste Herrin von Keš,
    die mit dem grossen Berg Enlil gewetteifert hat,

E′ Nintu—die Kuh ruft laut zu ihr wegen ihres Kalbes,[45]
    [Die Mutter Nintu] sucht nach ihm [wegen ihrer Klage],[46]
    die Mutter Nintu, die grösste Herrin von Keš,
    die mit dem grossen Berg Enlil gewetteifert hat.

F (Auf) dem reinen Wohnsitz der Wonne, dem Wohnsitz, an dem sie alles
    zahlreich gemacht hat,
    als die Mutter Nintu auf dem Hochsitz Platz nahm,
    war sie es, die die höchsten göttlichen Kräfte, die golden sind, die Zierde des
    zahlreichen Volkes,
    das en-Priestertum und das Königtum für Enlil dasein liess,

F′ Nintu—(auf) dem Wohnsitz der Wonne, dem Wohnsitz, an dem sie alles
    zahlreich gemacht hat,

---

43. Zeile grammatisch unklar: Nach áb kein Agentiv, darum vielleicht amar-bi-ta,
"zusammen mit ihrem Kalb." Für das Dativpräfix der Personenklasse kommt anscheinend
nur Nintu als Bezugsperson in Frage; s. aber Anm. 44.

44. Zeile grammatisch unklar. Da ᵈnin-tu-re Agentiv ist, muss sich das Dativpräfix auf
eine andere Person beziehen, vielleicht aber trotz der Personenklasse auf das Kalb.

45. Siehe Anm. 43.

46. Siehe Anm. 44.

als die Mutter Nintu auf dem Hochsitz Platz nahm,
war sie es, die die höchsten göttlichen Kräfte, die golden sind, die Zierde des
    zahlreichen Volkes,
das e n-Priestertum und das Königtum für Enlil dasein liess.
s a - g a r - r a ist es.
Ein t i [g i]-Lied der [N]intu ist es.
Kolophone: B: [. . ., den mög]en [Assur und Ninlil] stürzen und [seinen Namen
            und seine Nachkommenschaft im Lande] vernichten! [s. H.
            Hunger, *Babylonische und assyrische Kolophone* (*AOAT*, Bd. 2.
            [1968]) Nr. 319–20.]
          E: In Nippur geschrieben und [kollationiert].
Die Stropheneinteilung ist durch die variierende Wiederholung (R–2) festgelegt. Die syntaktischen Schemata der Strophen sind:
A und A': Nominal: Z. 1/4: Genitivverbindung; Z. 2/5: infinite Verbalform
(*hamṭu*); Z. 3/6: Genitivverbindung mit (zu /a/ verkürzter) Kopula.
B und B': Verbal: jede Zeile endet in eine finite Verbalform (Z. 7/10 *hamṭu*,
die beiden folgenden auf *hamṭu* oder *marû* nicht festlegbar). Die Präfixketten sind
unterschieden: Z. 7/10: Präformativ š i - + (i m) m i n i n ; Z. 8/11: kein Präformativ, Konjugationspräfix m u - (Gegensatz zu Z. 7/10, wo wahrscheinlich ì -,
und Z. 9/12, wo kein Konjugationspräfix); Z. 9/12: kein Präformativ, kein
Konjugationspräfix, dimensionales Präfix b í - des Lokativ-Terminativs wie in
Z. 7/10.
C und C': Nominal und verbal: Z. 13/16 und 15/18 enden auf infinite Verbalformen (*hamṭu*); Z. 14/17 auf eine finite (ebenfalls *hamṭu*) mit Präformativ š a -
und Konjugationspräfix m u - (vgl. B und B', wo das Präformativ in der ersten
Zeile steht, das Konjugationspräfix aber ebenfalls in der mittleren).
D und D': Nominal: Z. 20/24: infinite Verbalform (*marû*)+Genitivverbin-
dung; Z. 21–23/25–27: infinite Verbalformen (*hamṭu*).
E und E': Verbal und nominal: Z. 28–29/32–33: finite Verbalformen (*marû*)
mit Konjugationspräfix m u - und Dativpräfix. Z. 30–31/34–35: nominal, aber
unterschiedlich: Z. 30/34: Genitivverbindung; Z. 31/35: infinite Verbalform;
an den Zeilenanfängen jeweils Epitheton und Name.
F und F': Nominal, aber jede Zeile anders stilisiert: Z. 36/40: Genitivverbindung und infinite Verbalform (*hamṭu*); Z. 37/41: pronominale Konjugation
(*hamṭu*); Z. 38/42 Nominalsatz mit Kopula; Genitivverbindung; Z. 39/43:
infinite Verbalform (*hamṭu*).
Die Rubriken s a - g a r - r a - à m und s a - g í d - d a - à m teilen das Lied in zwei
Teile, die hinsichtlich der Zahl der Strophen symmetrisch sind, nicht jedoch in
der Zahl der Zeilen, da jede der drei Doppelstrophen des s a - g a r - r a -Teils um
zweimal eine Zeile länger ist als die des s a - g í d - d a -Teils:
s a - g í d - d a : 3 mal 3 + 3 Zeilen
s a - g a r - r a : 3 mal 4 + 4 Zeilen.
Auch die Abfolge der syntaktischen Schemata ist nicht symmetrisch in den
beiden Teilen:

sa-gíd-da: nominal:verbal:gemischt
sa-gar-ra: nominal:gemischt:nominal

Hilfreich bei der Suche nach Strophengrenzen kann noch die Beobachtung von Sprecherwechseln sein. Diese Methode führt aber nur in wenigen Fällen zu sicheren Ergebnissen, da Sprecherwechsel auch innerhalb von Strophen zu finden sind.

Trotz der hier dargestellten Kriterien zur Abgrenzung von Strophen verbleibt eine beträchtliche Anzahl von Texten, die sich vorläufig einer den ganzen Text erfassenden Strophengliederung sperren, so besonders die epischen Texte, aber auch z.B. das tigi auf Ninlil für Šulgi (*STVC*, Nr. 60+54 und Dupl.). Hier bleibt nur der Rückgriff auf die thematische Struktur als wenig verlässliche Methode.

5. EINHEITEN OBERHALB DER STROPHE

Oben zum Refrain sind wir bereits grösseren durch einen Refrain vom Typ *b* zusammengehaltenen Einheiten begegnet, die angesichts ihres Umfanges nicht als Strophen angesehen werden können. Ähnliches gilt für die durch Rubriken bezeichneten Abschnitte in tigi- (s.o.), a-da-ab-, šir-nam-gala-, šir-nam-ur-sag-gá-, balag-Liedern und anderen ki-ru-gú-Kompositionen. Auch wo solche äusseren Anzeichen fehlen, kann man—allerdings weitestgehend nach inhaltlichen Gesichtspunkten—solche grösseren Einheiten feststellen, die strophisch gegliedert sind (s.u. im Exkurs), oder doch einzelne deutlich strophische Teile enthalten (*SGL* I, Nr. 1; Wilcke, *Lugalbandaepos*, S. 9–22). Einen einheitlichen Terminus für diese Abschnitte kann ich nicht vorschlagen. Es bedarf auch noch der Untersuchung, ob es sich in allen diesen Fällen um dasselbe Phänomen handelt.

6. PROLOG

Eine oft selbständige Einheit innerhalb eines Literaturwerkes ist die Einleitung, der Prolog, der sich besonders bei umfangreicheren Texten findet, aber kein konstituierendes Element einer bestimmten Gattung darstellt. Prologe können sehr kurz sein und nur eine Strophe (*CT* XXXVI, Taf. 31–32, Z. 1–5 = *VS* X, Nr. 145:1–5) oder nur ein Zeilenpaar (*KAR* I, Nr. 15:1–2 = 16:1–2) umfassen, sie können aber sehr ausführlich abgefasst sein und wie in nin-me-šár-ra fast den Umfang des Hauptteiles erreichen. Je nach der Stilisierung können wir zwei Grundtypen des Prologs unterscheiden: den erzählenden und den liedhaften. Wird letzterer ausführlich gestaltet, so kann er auch erzählende Abschnitte enthalten wie z.B. nin-me-šár-ra, Z. 43–57.

(a) Der erzählende Prolog ist, soweit ich sehe, mit nur einer Ausnahme (s.u.) an erzählende Texte gebunden. Das älteste mir bekannte Beispiel ist der altsumerische Text *MBI*, Nr. 1 (s. J. van Dijk, in *Acta Orientalia* XXVIII [1964] 34–39). Meist führt der Erzähler in diesem Abschnitt seinen Hörer in eine graue Vorzeit, die er in einer zunächst losen Aneinanderreihung[47] von Einzelheiten beschreibt, die sich langsam zu einem Zusammenhang verdichten, der für sich genommen eine kurze Erzählung sein kann wie die Einleitung zu "Gilgameš, Enkidu und die Unterwelt"[48] und die Ausgangssituation der Erzählung entweder vorbereitet oder schon beschreibt. Diese Abschnitte bestehen oft aus (oder beginnen mit) einer Reihe von Zeilen, die auf -a-ba, "als," enden (ähnlich *SEM*, Nr. 58 i 1–6, ì-me-a . . .nu-me-a, "als es gab, als es nicht gab"). Der Übergang zum Hauptteil, der eigentlichen Erzählung, kann bruchlos erfolgen wie in "Enki's Fahrt nach Nippur,"[49] wo auf die vorausstehenden "als"-Sätze unmittelbar der die Erzählung beginnende Hauptsatz folgt. Es kann aber auch eine Zäsur vorliegen, z.B., wenn die Erzählung mit u₄-ba/bi-a, "damals," beginnt. Sehr beliebt in dieser Art des Prologs ist die Verwendung des bekräftigenden Präformativs na-.

Der Rückgriff auf die ferne Vergangenheit ist nicht das einzige Mittel, mit dem der Erzähler die Geschichte, die er erzählen will, vorbereitet. So bedient er sich in "Enlil und Ninlil"[50] der Beschreibung des Schauplatzes, an dem die ersten Ereignisse stattfinden werden, der Stadt Nippur und eines Kanals dort, wobei er gleich in den ersten drei Zeilen sein Publikum mit den Worten "wir wohnen dort" in seine Erzählung mit einbezieht. Die Beschreibung der Stadt endet mit der Vorstellung der Hauptgestalten, der Götter von Nippur, und leitet mit u₄-ba, "damals," die eigentliche Erzählung ein.

Um die unmittelbare, von den Hörern des Textes zum grossen Teil wohl noch miterlebte Vergangenheit geht es in der "2. Urklage."[51] Hier umfasst der Prolog den ganzen ersten ki-ru-gú-Abschnitt, Z. 1–115, und schildert den Entschluss der Götter, das Land und das Königtum von Ur zu vernichten, und in allgemeinen Wendungen die Auswirkungen dieses Entschlusses. Dabei gebraucht der Dichter, der Ur "meine Stadt" nennt (Z. 53), dreimal die u₄-ba-Formel, ohne aber dann mit der Erzählung zu beginnen (Z. 75, 83, 103). Im ersten Falle werden die Zerstörer, deren sich die Götter bedienen, eingeführt, im zweiten beginnt so die Beschreibung der kosmischen Ausmasse der Katastrophe, im letzten die der Auswirkungen auf das Königtum. Der Hauptteil des Textes wird dann nicht durch u₄-ba eingeleitet, sondern beginnt unmittelbar mit dem Namen einer Stadt.

47. Siehe D. O. Edzard, in *Kindlers Literatur Lexikon,* Bd. 6 (1971) Sp. 2142.
48. Shaffer, "Sumerian Sources."
49. A. A. al-Fouadi, "Enki's Journey to Nippur" (Ph.D. diss., University of Pennsylvania, 1964).
50. Prolog und 4 Zeilen des Hauptteils bearbeitet von A. Falkenstein, "Untersuchungen zur sumerischen Grammatik," *ZA,* Bd. 47 (1942) S. 194–97; s. auch S. N. Kramer, *Sumerian Mythology* (Philadelphia, 1944) S. 43–47. Siehe dazu bereits Th. Jacobsen, in *JNES* V (1946) 133 f., Anm. 8 (*TIOT,* S. 354, Anm. 8).
51. Übersetzung von S. N. Kramer, in *ANET* (3. Aufl.) S. 611–19; Literatur bei Wilcke, *Kollationen . . . Jena,* zu IV 26.

Ganz anders wiederum ist die Einleitung zu Gudea Zyl. A, die mit einem "als"-Satz beginnt und mythisches Geschehen berichtet. Der Übergang zur Erzählung wird dadurch vorbereitet, dass der Gott zu seinem Tempel von dem spricht, was Gudea, die handelnde Person der folgenden Erzählung, tun wird. Ähnlich der u_4-ba-Formel beginnt diese mit den Worten (Zyl. A i 17–18):[52] "Seinen König, den Herrn Ningirsu, schaute Gudea an diesem Tage im Traum."

Von dem oben beschriebenen Schema weicht die Einleitung zu Šulgi B, einer in der 1. Person stilisierten Hymne, völlig ab:[53]

1 lugal-e mu-ni nì-du₇-e
2 u₄-sù-rá-ka pa-è AK-dè
3 šul-gi lugal-uríᵏⁱ-ma-ke₄
4 á-na zà-mí-bi-imᵃ kala-ga-na šìr-bi-imᵇ
5 gal-an-zu nì-sag-bi-šè è-a-naᶜ mu-da-rí-bi-imᵈ
6 šà-bal-bal-aᵉ eger-u₄-da-ka šu-a bal-e-dè
7 kala-ga dumu-ᵈnin-sunaₓ(= SÚN)-kaᶠ-raᵍ
8 geštú-eger-ra-biʰ igi-šè mu-unⁱ-na-DU
9 á-niʲ šìr-ra silim-šè mu-un-e
10 dím-ma nì-sa₆-ga šà-ta DU-a-niᵏ nì-bi ì-balag-eˡ

(a) So B, C, c; A: zà-mí-bi; a:]-bi; b: zà-mí-ba.
(b) So A, B, C; b: šìr(!)-bi.
(c) So A [nì], C [bi], c; B nì-sag-bi-šè è-⌜x⌝; a:]-bi-šè è-a-me-en; ii:]-en.
(d) So B, C; A, c: mu-da-rí-bi; ii:]-bi; a: mu-[.
(e) So B, C, d; b, c: -b]al-bal-a; A: -ba]l-bal; a om. Zeile.
(f) -ka in B, C, a; A: NE.   (g) So A, B, C; ii: ke₄(?).
(h) -bi in A, B, C, a, d; b: [ge]štú-eger-ra.
(i) -un- in A, B, a; C: mu-na-.
(j) Castellino liest lú; die Kopien haben durchweg -ni; B (Photo) unklar.
(k) A: DU-a; B, C: DU-a-ni; ii:]⌜x⌝.
(l) Castellino liest ì-il-e (s. dazu Two Šulgi Hymns, S. 112–13).[54]

1 Damit der König seinen Namen gebührlich
2 für die (Zeit) ferner Tage berühmt mache,
3 damit Šulgi, der König von Ur, es
4 —es ist das Preislied seiner Kraft, ist das Lied auf seine Stärke,
5 ist die ewige Kunde seiner alles überragenden Klugheit—
6 den Nachkommen für die Zukunft überliefere,

52. *SAHG*, S. 138.
53. Castellino, *Two Šulgi Hymns*, Text ii, Kol. i 1′ ff. entspricht Z. 5 ff.
54. Das fragliche, von Castellino "il" gelesene Zeichen sieht überall dort, wo Photo oder Kopie ein deutliches Zeichen bieten, wie BALAG aus: A i 10, 52, ii 23; B i 10, iii 4; C 10; F iii 8; K iii 14; M 28; h Rs. 6; k ii 18; t 9; hh ii 3. Zu nì-balag (oder bulugₓ) s. Wilcke, *Lugalbandaepos*, S. 156 mit Anm. 426; *Kollationen . . . Jena*, zu III 15–17 bei Z. 23–24 mit Anm. Meine Lesung "dúb" (*Lugalbandaepos*, S. 180 zu Z. 170) lässt sich angesichts der neuen Texte nicht aufrecht erhalten, da die Mehrzahl von ihnen ein von DÚB unterschiedenes BALAG schreibt. Dagegen sprach schon immer die Schreibung des folgenden /e/ als -e, nicht -bé.

7 habe ich dem Starken, dem Sohn der Ninsuna,
8 diese Kunde(?) für die Zukunft vor Augen geführt.—
9 Seine Kraft preist er im Liede,
10 den Verstand, die gute Sache, die ihm eigen ist, rühmt(?) er: . . . .

Hier wendet sich der Dichter unmittelbar an sein Publikum und legt dar, aus welchen Gründen er den Text verfasst hat. Er lässt keinen Zweifel daran, dass er der Verfasser ist. Die Fiktion, der König habe den Selbstpreis selbst gedichtet, ist von vornherein ausgeschlossen. Um so bedauerlicher ist es, dass der Dichter seinen Namen nicht nennt.

Ein solcher Prolog unterscheidet sich von den übrigen erzählenden Einleitungen, in denen sich ein (beliebiger) Erzähler an seine Zuhörer wendet, auch dadurch, dass er die schriftliche Form voraussetzt. Denn wenn ein vom Dichter verschiedener Sänger den Prolog mitvortrüge, so machte er sich eines wohl auch zu dieser Zeit nicht erlaubten Plagiats schuldig.[55]

55. B. Alster in seiner Untersuchung zur mündlichen Tradition der sumerischen Literatur (*Dumuzi's Dream*, Kap. I) scheint anzunehmen, dass das Gros der Werke der sumerischen Literatur im mündlichen Vortrag wurzelt und erst wesentlich später aufgezeichnet wurde. Die Beziehungen der sumerischen literarischen Texte zu mündlicher Tradition sind unverkennbar, besonders in der Phraseologie. Hieraus lassen sich m.E. jedoch nicht so weitreichende Schlüsse ziehen. Denn die sumerischen Dichtungen, die wir kennen, sind keine Volkspoesie, sondern, soweit wir sehen, auf die Bereiche Palast, Tempel und Schule beschränkt. M.E. war zu der Zeit, als man begann, sumerische Literaturwerke aufzuschreiben, vermutlich in der Fara-Zeit, der Schatz der geprägten Formulierungen und der Gebrauch von Stilmitteln wie der epischen Wiederholung längst Gemeingut der Dichter und wurde auch in schriftlich verfassten Literaturwerken benutzt. Man vergleiche nur die lange Tradition der sumerischen und akkadischen Briefeinleitungsformeln, die in der mündlichen Übermittlung von Botschaften wurzeln, aber durch Jahrhunderte in schriftlich verfassten Briefen Verwendung fanden.

Wir wissen zudem durch Schultexte, dass das Studium der Literaturwerke zur Ausbildung der Schreiber gehörte. Ein schreibender Dichter kannte also die Literatur. Ausserdem sind moderne Vorstellungen vom geistigen Eigentum nicht auf die Antike übertragbar und was uns heute als Plagiat erscheinen mag, kann damals als poetischer Kunstgriff verstanden worden sein, der die Bildung des Dichters demonstrierte. Siehe W. Kayser, *Das sprachliche Kunstwerk* (15. Aufl.; Bern, 1948) S. 15 (Hervorhebung durch mich): "Gerade die leichte Erkennbarkeit lässt das Plagiat in solchem Falle (= Verwendung eines Motivs von Händel durch Beethoven) eher *als gewollten Hinweis und als Huldigung* verstehen. . . ., dass der Begriff des geistigen Eigentums und seines Schutzes recht jung ist und dass frühere Zeiten darin anders urteilten als wir."

Damit schliesse ich nicht aus, dass der schriftlichen Überlieferung von Literaturwerken eine mündliche parallel lief. Ich glaube aber der systematischen Durchformung der uns überkommenen Texte entnehmen zu können, dass die schriftliche Fassung eines Stoffes das Werk éines Dichters ist, der lange Zeit hindurch tradierte Sagen oder Mythen (wohl auch Märchen) in eine bestimmte Form brachte. Dies schliesst nicht aus, dass derselbe Stoff von verschiedenen Dichtern unterschiedlich gestaltet wurde.

Zum Problem "schriftlicher" und "mündlicher" Literatur siehe jetzt R. Finnegan, "How Oral Is Oral Literature?" in *Bulletin of the Schools of Oriental and African Studies* XXXVII (1974) S. 52–64, die die wechselseitige Beeinflussung dieser beiden Produktions- und Traditionsarten von Literatur betont, und deren Schlussfolgerungen zu äusserster Vorsicht beim Gebrauch des Begriffs "Oral Literature" zwingen.

Inhaltlich lässt sich zur Einleitung von Šulgi B am ehesten der Epilog der Sammlung der Tempelhymnen vergleichen.[56]

(b) Anders als der erzählende ist der Prolog in Form eines Liedes an keine besondere Textart gebunden. Er findet sich z.B. in dem a-da-ab-Lied auf Nininsina, *ISET* I 113, Ni. 9496, Z. 1–12; im tigi-Lied auf Enki, *CT* XXXVI, Taf. 31–32, Z. 1–5 = *VS* X, Nr. 145:1–5; im šìr-nam-šub auf Nininsina, *KAR* I, Nr. 15:1–2 = Nr. 16:1–2 (erzählender Text!); im šìr-nam-šub auf Nanna, *CT* XLIV, Nr. 16:1–22 = *ISET* I 224, L 1499, Z. 1′–17′; *TCL* XV, Nr. 12:1–16 (es folgt ein Hymnus Urnammu's in der 1. Person); in Epen wie "Inanna und Ebeḫ," Šulgi A, D und F. In all diesen Fällen ist der Prolog hymnisch gehalten. Daneben gibt es auch den klagenden Prolog, wenn der Gegenstand der Dichtung Anlass zur Klage gab wie die "1. Urklage" (Kramer, *AS*, Nr. 12), "Dumuzi's Tod" (Alster, *Dumuzi's Dream*), das damit eng verwandte ér-šèm-ma für Inanna und Dumuzi (Scheil, in *RA* VIII [1911] 162–63 = *VS* II, Nr. 2 i 1–iii 22 = *TCL* XVI, Nr. 78), die bis auf die klagenden Prologe gleichlautenden ér-šèm-ma für Gula (*CT* XLII, Nr. 7 i 1–iii 41) und Inanna (*CT* XLII, Nr. 16 + Dupl.; s. Krecher, in *ZA*, Bd. 58, S. 32–65, *WO* IV 255–59).[57]

Die inhaltliche Verbindung zwischen einleitendem Lied und Hauptteil kann sehr eng sein wie im tigi-Lied auf Enki, dem a-da-ab auf Nininsina oder den erzählenden Texten wie "Inanna und Ebeḫ," Šulgi A, D und F, wo der Hymnus die Hauptperson der Erzählung besingt. Sehr lose ist dagegen der Zusammenhang im šìr-nam-šub auf Nanna (s.o.) oder in *TCL* XV, Nr. 12, wo den in der 3. oder 1. Person stilisierten Hymnen auf Urnammu ein Preis auf die Stadt Ur, die Residenzstadt des Königs, vorausgestellt ist (in der 2. bezw. 3 Person stilisiert); ähnlich Šulgi O,[58] wo aber in Z. 25 die Erzählung mit [lugal(?)]-bi, "sein (= Ur's) [König,]" beginnt und so der Zusammenhang hergestellt ist.

Der Übergang vom Prolog zum Hauptteil kann bruchlos und so glatt erfolgen, dass—wie in Šulgi A—eine Grenze nur schwer festzulegen ist. Meist ist aber ein deutlicher Einschnitt zu beobachten, sei es durch den Wechsel der Person, in der von der Hauptperson gesprochen wird, durch einen auf das einleitende Lied beschränkten Refrain oder durch eine abschliessende Preisformel. Oft treten zwei dieser Kriterien zusammen auf, wie im tigi auf Enki (Personenwechsel und Preisformel), in "Inanna und Ebeḫ" (ebenso) oder in Šulgi D (Personenwechsel und Refrain). Die oben zum erzählenden Prolog beobachtete Einleitung des

---

56. Sjöberg und Bergmann, *TCS* III 49, Z. 543–44; dazu Wilcke, in *ZA*, Bd. 62, S. 46–47.

57. Neues Duplikat *ISET* I 209, Ni. 13237. Der von J. Krecher in seiner Bearbeitung in zwei Teile zerlegte Text dieses Berichts der Inanna(/Gula) von ihrer Intervention bei Enlil zugunsten ihres Mannes(/Sohnes) ist eine Einheit. Der 2. Teil ("Die sumerischen Texte in 'syllabischer' Orthographie," *WO* IV [1968] 255–59) beginnt mit der Antwort Enlils an Inanna/Gula: dumu(!)-mu, etc., "Mein Kind, etc."

58. *SLTNi*, Nr. 79; *ISET* I 85, Ni. 4101, 130, Ni. 4112 (s. M. Civil, "Supplement to the Introduction to *ISET* I," *Or*, n.s., Bd. 41 [1972] S. 83); s. Th. Jacobsen, "New Sumerian Literary Texts," *BASOR*, Nr. 102 (1946) S. 15–16; *MNS* I 108–18; D. O. Edzard, "Enmebaragesi von Kiš," *ZA*, Bd. 53 (1959) S. 20–21; Klein, "Šulgi D," S. 32–33, Anm. 39.

Hauptteils durch u₄-ba, "damals," findet sich auch bei liedhaftem Beginn. In Šulgi F (*TMH* NF IV, Nr. 11:30) lässt sich das vielleicht daher erklären, dass der Refrain von der Geburt Šulgi's handelt—der folgende erzählende Text hat dann allerdings seine Investitur als König zum Gegenstand. Anders verhält es sich mit dem Prolog zu lugal ud me-lám-bi nir-gál, der hymnisch beginnt (Z. 1–16), dann aber ähnlich den erzählenden Prologen in Z. 17–21 eine Reihe von "als"-Sätzen anfügt ("pronominale Konjugation" und temporale Lokative), die die Hauptperson, den Gott Ninurta, als Subjekt haben, von dem dann die folgende Zeile 22, eingeleitet durch u₄-bi-a, auch spricht. Da der hymnische Passus in der 2. Person stilisiert ist, die Z. 17–21 aber in der dritten, ist der liedhafte Prolog mit Z. 16 abgeschlossen. Die folgenden Zeilen kann man als zusätzlichen erzählenden Prolog ansehen, man kann aber auch daran denken, dass die Erzählung bereits mit Z. 17 anfängt und das sonst die Zäsur markierende u₄-bi-a in den Hauptteil hinein verlagert ist.[59]

(c) Die Mehrzahl der Lieder und eine weniger grosse Zahl von epischen Texten verzichtet auf einen Prolog und geht sofort *medias in res*. In einigen Fällen kann man bei den Epen daran denken, dass es sich um die Fortsetzung einer mit Prolog eingeleiteten Erzählung handelt,[60] in anderen gemahnt ein in parallelen Reihungen gestalteter Anfang an die erzählenden Prologe wie z.B. in "Inanna's Gang zur Unterwelt"[61] oder der ganz ähnlich gestalteten Einleitung zu "Inanna und Šukaletuda."[62] Diese Frage lässt sich für "Inanna's Gang zur Unterwelt" entscheiden, denn dieser Text gebraucht in seinen ersten drei Zeilen eine Formel, mit der ein Epos beginnt, das auf den Prolog sicher verzichtet, während bei einem weiteren ebenfalls prologähnliche Reihungen zu beobachten sind:

---

59. Siehe die Zusammenstellung der Literatur bei R. Borger, *HKL*, S. 147 zu S. Geller, *Die sumerisch-assyrische Serie* Lugal-e ud me-lam-bi nir-gál ("Altorientalische Texte und Untersuchungen," Bd. 1/4 [1917]); Wilcke, *Kollationen . . . Jena*, zu IV 78. Altbabylonische Textzeugen für den Anfang sind: *SLTNi*, Nr. 6, 7, *ISET* I 168, Ni. 9495. Junge zweisprachige Version: J 5326 (Umschrift bei S. Geller); *TCL* XVI, Nr. 82; *ASKT*, Nr. 10, K 133; O. R. Gurney und P. Hulin, *The Sultantepe Tablets* II (London, 1964) Nr. 150; J. V. Kinnier Wilson, "Lugal ud melambi nirgal: New Texts and Fragments," *ZA*, Bd. 54 (1961) S. 73a, 74, BM 83–1–18,488. Einsprachig akkadisch: Th. Meek, "Some Explanatory Lists and Grammatical Texts," *RA* XVII (1917) 151, K 7604.

60. Siehe Wilcke, *Lugalbandaepos*, Kap. 2; J. Klein, in *JAOS*, Bd. 91 (1971) S. 296–97; S. N. Kramer, in *Acta Orientalia* XXXIII (1971) 367 ff. Meine Folgerungen aus dem Erscheinen eines Titels u₅ giš-gi-kù-ta in Literaturkatalogen haben sich nicht bestätigt (Wilcke, in *AfO* XXIV 50), da mit diesen Worten nicht nur der zweite Teil von Lugalbanda II anfängt, sondern auch "Nanše und die Vögel"; s. jetzt D. I. Owen, "Texts and Fragments," *JCS* XXIV (1972) 177.

61. S. N. Kramer, "'Inanna's Descent to the Netherworld' Continued and Revised," *JCS* V (1951) 1–17; "Cuneiform Studies and the History of Literature: The Sumerian Sacred Marriage Texts," *PAPS*, Bd. 107 (1963) S. 510–16; A. Falkenstein, "Der sumerische und der akkadische Mythos von Inannas Gang zur Unterwelt," *Festschrift W. Caskel* (Leiden, 1968) S. 96–110. Siehe auch Alster, *Dumuzi's Dream*, passim; Wilcke, *Kollationen . . . Jena*, zu III 2.

62. Siehe C. Wilcke, "Der Anfang von 'Inanna und Šukalletuda,'" *AfO* XXIV (1973) 86.

"Gilgameš und Huwawa,"[63] Z. 1

en-e kur-lú-ti-la-šè geštú-ga-ni na-an-gub

"Nanna's Fahrt nach Nippur," Z. 1–2

ur-sag-e uru-ama-n[a-šè] // ᵈnanna-ᵈsuʾen-e [geštú-ga-ni na-an-gub]

"Inanna's Gang zur Unterwelt," Z. 1

[an-gal-t]a [ki-g]al-šᵉˈèˈ geštú-ga-ni na-an-gub

Diese Formel scheint typisch zu sein für Texte, deren Gegenstand eine Reise ist,[64] und unmittelbar die Erzählung einzuleiten. Trotzdem gewinnt man in "Inanna's Gang zur Unterwelt" und "Nanna's Fahrt nach Nippur" den Eindruck, dass der Dichter bestrebt war, den Einleitungspassus in Anlehnung an die Prologe ausführlicher zu gestalten.

Eine vergleichende Untersuchung der Anfänge literarischer Texte, besonders der erzählenden, ist ein dringendes Desideratum.

7. EPILOG

Eine deutlich abgegrenzte Einheit Epilog lässt sich weitaus seltener beobachten. Sie scheint mit Ausnahme der Tempelhymnensammlung der Enheduʾanna, in der sich die Verfasserin in den letzten Zeilen an ihren König wendet (*TCS* III 49, Z. 543-44; s. Wilcke, in *ZA*, Bd. 62, S. 46–47), auf erzählende Texte beschränkt zu sein. So z.B. nin-me-šár-ra, Z. 143–53 (Wechsel der Person bezüglich Inanna und Enheduʾanna), "Nanna's Fahrt nach Nippur," Z. 349–52,[65] wo sich der Dichter dem König zuwendet und die Quintessenz aus der erzählten Geschichte zieht.

63. S. N. Kramer, "Gilgamesh and the Land of the Living," *JCS* I (1947) 1–46; J. van Dijk, "Le dénouement de 'Gilgameš au bois de cèdres' selon LB 2110," *CRRA* VII 69–81; A. Falkenstein, "Zur Überlieferung des Epos von Gilgameš und Ḫuwawa," *JNES* XIX (1960) 65–71; Wilcke, *Kollationen . . . Jena*, zu III 12.

64. Siehe Ferrara, *StP* M, Bd. 2, S. 107.

65. A. J. Ferraras Auffassung dieser Zeilen als "Benison" und seine Übersetzung, *StP* M, Bd. 2, S. 106, kann ebensowenig überzeugen wie die meine in *CRRA* XIX 187, Anm. 12, wo ich die Variante u₄-imin-e in *UET* VI/1, Nr. 25 Rs. ii′ 6/8 (= Z. 350/352) übersehen habe. In derselben Zeile ist Ferraras Lesung "hé-a-ši-ib-tu" nicht korrekt; die Texte schreiben:

	Z. 350:		Z. 352:	
C	hé-a-ù-tu	C	hé-a-ù-tu	
U	[-t]u	U	hé-b[í-]	
V	[ ]	V	hé-[ ]	
W	ši-bí-a-ù-tu	W	[ ]-t[u]	

Mir erscheinen nur zwei Deutungen der Zeilen als möglich:

Mein König (Urnammu?), die (Gaben) Enlil's hat Nanna-Suʾen für deinen Hochsitz in(?) sieben Tagen geschaffen, für deinen reinen Hochsitz hat der Herr Ašimbabbar die (Gaben) der grossen Mutter Ninlil in(?) sieben Tagen geschaffen!

oder:

Mein König (Urnammu?), für deinen Hochsitz hat der (Sohn) Enlil's, Nanna-Suʾen, (diese Gaben) in(?) sieben Tagen geschaffen, für deinen reinen Hochsitz hat der (Sohn) der grossen Mutter Ninlil, der Herr Ašimbabbar (diese Gaben) in(?) sieben Tagen geschaffen.

Einen liedhaften Epilog zeigt "Inanna und Bilulu," Z. 176–84,[66] wo die Thematik des Prologs wieder aufgenommen wird—beides sind Klagen, in denen dieselben Ortsnamen verwandt werden. Liedhaft scheint auch der Schluss von lugal ud me-lám-bi gestaltet zu sein, soweit sich das den fragmentarischen Textzeugen[67] entnehmen lässt. Auch Lugalbanda II 413–16 ist ein hymnisch stilisierter Epilog.

In einigen Fällen ist der Epilog mit der abschliessenden Doxologie so eng verknüpft, dass man ihn als eine erweiterte Doxologie ansehen kann.

8. DOXOLOGIE

Der Abschluss eines Textes, sei er liedhaft oder erzählend, durch eine Doxologie ist sehr beliebt. Die Doxologien enthalten zwei konstituierende Elemente: einen Namen und das Wort zà-mí, "Preis." Je nachdem ob sie in der 1., 2. oder 3. Person stilisiert sind, beobachten wir drei Grundtypen:

(a) Name (+Epitheta) zà-mí, "dem X sei Preis," passim.

(b) Name (+Epitheta) zà-mí-zu du₁₀-ga-àm, "X, dein Preis ist angenehm," z.B. *TCL* XV, Nr. 7 Rs. 22′; *SGL* II 110, Z. 24.

(c) Name (+Epitheta)+Kopula der 1. Pers. zà-mí-mu du₁₀-ga-àm, "mein, des X, Preis ist angenehm", z.B. *TCL* XV, Nr. 12:115. Hier kann der Name auch fortfallen, da der Bezug durch das Possessivsuffix der 1. Pers. bereits eindeutig festgelegt ist, z.B. in Šulgi B, Z. 348.

Diese Grundtypen können in vielfältiger Weise variiert werden, sei es, dass das Adjektiv du₁₀, "angenehm," durch ein anderes ersetzt wird (mah, "höchster," in ᵈen-líl sù-DU-šè), sei es, dass der Doxologie eine längere Reihe von Epitheta vorausgestellt ist, die man als Hymnus auffassen kann, wie in an-gim dím-ma, oder dass der Preisformel eine Begründung vorausgeht, wie oft in Streitgedichten, in Gudea Zyl. A xxx 6–14, verbunden mit einem hymnischen Epilog (Hymnus auf das Eninnu) und Zyl. B xxiv 9–15 (ebenfalls mit hymnischem Epilog), ähnlich auch ᵈen-líl sù-DU-šè, Z. 165–71:[68]

Dafür, dass von Ninlil—die Herrin von Himmel und Erde, die Herrin aller
    Länder ist sie—
im Preis des grossen Berges freundlich gesprochen worden ist—
Gewaltiger, dessen Wort feststeht,
dessen erster und zweiter Ausspruch unabänderlich sind—

---

66. Jacobsen und Kramer, in *JNES* XII 160–88.

67. *SRT*, Nr. 21 iv 14–24 = *BE* XXIX, Nr. 13 Vs. 6–14, Rs. 1–6 = *BE* XXIX, Nr. 10 Rs. 1–6.

68. *SGL* I 5–79; D. Reisman, "Two Neo-Sumerian Royal Hymns," S. 41–102. Mah-àm auch in an-gim dím-ma, F. Hrozný, "Sumerische-babylonische Mythen von den Gotte Ninrag (Ninib)," *MVAG*, Bd. 8/5 (1903) Taf. VIII, K 4829 (nach dem MS J. Coopers haben die aB-Texte du₁₀-[g]a-àm).

was seinen Mund verlässt, geht (allem) voran,
was er aufzeichnet, legt die Worte fest—
grosser Berg, Vater Enlil, ist dein Preis der höchste!

In diesen Fällen gilt die Doxologie stets der zentralen Figur eines Textes (in den Streitgesprächen dem Gott, der das Urteil fällt). Anders verhält es sich in Šulgi A, Z. 96–103,[69] wo der Preis für den mit Bezug auf den König in der 1. Person stilisierten erzählenden Text der Göttin Nisaba gilt; in dem mit der Doxologie verbundenen hymnischen Epilog wird vom König in der 3. Person gesprochen:

"Dafür, dass sie von der höchstens Kraft des Königs freundlich gesprochen hat,
dass von dem, dem Suʾen im Ekišnugal
Kriegertum, Stärke und angenehmes Leben geschenkt hat,
dem von Nunamnir höchste Kraft verliehen worden ist,
von Šulgi, der die Feindländer vernichtet, der das Volk sicher wohnen lässt,
die, die die göttlichen Kräfte von Himmel und Erde (besitzt), die keinen
   Widerpart hat,
die angesehene Tochter An's von Šulgi freundlich gesprochen hat,
sei Nisaba Preis!"

Hiermit ist der Schluss von *STVC*, Nr. 37 (*SGL* II 144–59) zu vergleichen:
Der, die den Leiter der Ratsversammlung Nusku gepriesen hat,
der rechten [Frau], die den gestirnten Himmel zu Rate zieht,
Nisaba sei Preis![70]

Wiederum anders verhält es sich mit der Doxologie zur Nisaba-Hymne nin mul-an-gim,[71] die dem Gott Enki gilt, dem der abschliessende hymnische Passus in den Mund gelegt wird. Unklar ist mir dagegen, warum in *TCL* XV, Nr. 25 (*SGL* II 81–107), einem in der 2. Person stilisierten bal-bal-e-Lied auf Ningizzida, die Doxologie den vorher nicht erwähnten Enki preist; s. auch die

---

69. A. Falkenstein, "Sumerische religiöse Texte, 2. Ein Šulgi-Lied," *ZA*, Bd. 50 (1952) S. 70–73; Klein, " Šulgi D," S. 174, 182–83.

70. Analog wohl auch *TMH* NF IV, Nr. 49+88 Rs. i 5′ und *MNS* I, Nr. 6 Rs. 17 zu ergänzen. Auch der zweite Teil der Tempelhymne 42 (*TCS* III 48–49, Z. 535–42) preist die Göttin Nisaba als Verfasserin des Preisliedes. Trotz der Bedenken Å. Sjöbergs, in *TCS* III 147 ("hardly comes into consideration"), lese ich jetzt Z. 535, zà-mí munus-e gar-ra (-àm); darauf folgen in Z. 536–41 Epitheta der Nisaba und in Z. 542 die Formel ᵈnisaba zà-mí. Ich übersetze dann: "Dafür, dass die Frau das Preislied 'gesetzt' hat, sei der (Reihe von Epitheta), Nisaba Preis!" Hierauf folgt in Text B unmittelbar die Rubrik "13 Zeilen, Haus der Nisaba in Ereš," die (mit verschiedenen Zeilenzahlen) die Texte A, O und Q erst nach den beiden folgenden Zeilen, in denen sich Enheduʾanna der Kompilation (oder Dichtung) der Tempelhymnen rühmt (s.o. zum Epilog), bieten. Ob munus in Z. 535 auf die Göttin oder bereits auf Enheduʾanna bezogen werden muss, kann ich nicht entscheiden, halte aber ersteres für wahrscheinlicher.

71. W. W. Hallo, "The Cultic Setting of Sumerian Poetry," *Actes de XVIIᵉ Rencontre Assyriologique Internationale* (Brüssel, 1970) S. 123–33.

Doxologie der "Hendursanga-Hymne"; dazu D. O. Edzard und C. Wilcke, in Festschrift S. N. Kramer (*AOAT* Sonderreihe [im Druck]).

Mit den hier besprochenen Doxologien—und besonders denen von Šulgi A und *STVC*, Nr. 37—die zum Text der Dichtungen gehören, darf die Schreiber-doxologie "Nisaba sei Preis," die Nisaba als Göttin der Schreibkunst gilt, nicht verwechselt werden.

9. HALTUNG

Die drei dichterischen Grundhaltungen, das Lyrische, das Epische und das Dramatische, sind in der sumerischen Literatur nicht gleichmässig vertreten. Sind Epos und Lyrik gut bezeugt, so fehlt gänzlich die Dramatik, will man nicht die Streitgedichte als dramatische Dichtungen verstehen.

Die Gruppe der Streitgedichte als ganze zur Dramatik zu rechnen, ist aber angesichts der in vielen von ihnen erscheinenden erzählenden Elemente wie der Einleitungs- und Schlussformeln der Reden nicht möglich. Nur die relativ kleine Gruppe der Schulstreitgespräche (Dialoge in der Terminologie M. Civils), die auf alles Erzählende verzichtet—soweit ich sehe—liesse sich als dramatisch verstehen. Daraus den Schluss zu ziehen, es habe (sonst) kein sumerisches Schauspiel gegeben, wäre sicher falsch. Offenbar hat man aber die "Text-bücher" der Bühnenkunst nie aufgeschrieben.[72]

Die erzählende Grundhaltung definiert die Epik. Je nachdem ob der Gegen-stand der Erzählung ein Mythos, eine historische Begebenheit oder eine Ge-schichte ist, die um den gerade regierenden König kreist, können wir von mythologischen, historischen oder Königsepen sprechen. Je nach der Gestaltung des Prologes können wir aber auch historisierend, hymnisch, klagend oder gar nicht eingeleitete Epen unterscheiden. Dabei fällt auf, dass die Königsepen Šulgi's (Šulgi A, D, F, O) durchweg den liedhaften Prolog aufweisen, während sich in "Urnammu's Tod" und im Utuhegalepos[73] kein und in den ihrer

72. H. Sauren rechnet auch epische Texte wie Lugalbanda oder Enmerkar zur Dramatik (*Orientalia Lovaniensia Periodica*, Bd. 3, S. 35 ff.). Die Einführung eines "Spielleiters," dem er die erzählenden Passagen zuweist, scheint mir durch nichts gerechtfertigt.

Dabei hat aber Sauren die durch die Wechselreden bedingte Verwandtschaft von Epos und Drama richtig erkannt—ein Problem, mit dem sich bereits Aristoteles in der "Poetik" ausführlich auseinandergesetzt hat (ohne dass Aristoteles den homerischen Epen einen 'Spielleiter' zugeordnet hätte); s. die zusammenfassende Darstellung bei M. Fuhrmann, *Einführung in die antike Dichtungstheorie* (Darmstadt, 1973), S. 38–54. Von literar-historischem Interesse mag in diesem Zusammenhang aber sein, dass gerade das Merkmal der wörtlichen Reden, die in der altorientalischen Epik so stark hervortreten, Aristoteles veranlasst hat, den homerischen Epen eine Zwischenstellung zwischen Epik und Dramatik zuzuweisen (Poetik, Kap. 3). Steht Homer vielleicht in altorientalischer Tradition? Wurzelt gar, setzt man die aristotelische Entwicklungstheorie voraus, das griechische Drama im altorientalischen und damit letztlich im sumerischen Epos?

73. F. Thureau-Dangin, "La fin de la domination gutienne," *RA* IX (1912) 111–20; "Notes assyriologiques," *RA* X (1913) 98–100.

Haltung nach ebenfalls epischen Gudea-Zylindern ein erzählender und ein hymnischer Prolog finden.[74] Ein Sonderfall epischer Dichtung ist Šulgi A. Hier folgt auf einen in der ersten Person stilisierten hymnischen Prolog die ebenfalls in der ersten Person gehaltene Erzählung, die in der Beschreibung des Gewitters gipfelt. Erst der mit der Doxologie verknüpfte Epilog zerstört die Fiktion, dass der König wirklich selbst spricht. Innerhalb der Gruppe der Epen nehmen die epischen Streitgedichte historischen, mythologischen oder naturkundlichen Inhalts eine Sonderstellung dadurch ein, dass sie durch besondere Formmerkmale bestimmt sind.[75]

Die sumerische Epik verwendet mit besonderer Vorliebe die direkte Rede, oft verbunden mit dem Stilmittel der epischen Wiederholung. Ihr gegenüber kann die Erzählung stark zurücktreten und weitgehend auf die Redeeinleitungen beschränkt werden. Auch beschreibende Abschnitte und Lieder oder Gebete können sich in einem Epos finden.

Die stilistischen Unterschiede innerhalb der sumerischen Epik sind beträchtlich. So haben wir einerseits das fast nur auf Rede und Gegenrede basierende Epos "Gilgameš und Agga"[76] und andererseits das—im Umfange etwa entsprechende—Utuhegalepos, das die wörtliche Rede nur sparsam verwendet. Beide aber zeichnen sich durch eine äusserst straffe Führung der Handlung aus. Ganz anders das Lugalbandaepos, das in Beschreibungen verweilt und auch in Passagen wie den vergeblichen Angeboten Anzu's oder Enmerkar's wiederholter Suche nach einem Boten retardierende Elemente einbaut. Gudea Zyl. A beginnt mit einem regelmässigen Wechsel von Erzählung und Rede. Darauf folgt dann ein nur erzählender Abschnitt, in den mehr und mehr beschreibende Unterbrechungen eingestreut werden, bis schliesslich eine ausführliche Beschreibung folgt, an die die kurze berichtende Überleitung zum Epilog mit Doxologie anschliesst. Zyl. B zeigt anfangs noch eine wörtliche Rede (Gebet), ist dann aber ganz überwiegend beschreibend (Aufgaben des Hofstaates) mit refrainartig wiederkehrenden erzählenden Einschüben. Darauf folgt ein Abschnitt, in dem die Erzählung im Vordergrund steht, und zum Schluss dominieren wieder die Reden. Die Unterschiede zwischen dem Lugalbandaepos und den Gudea Zylindern einerseits und "Gilgameš und Agga" und dem Utuhegalepos andererseits lassen sich mit denen zwischen Roman und Novelle vergleichen.

W. Kayser, *Das sprachliche Kunstwerk* (15. Aufl.) S. 191, definiert die Lyrik als "monologische Aussprache eines Ich." Ausserhalb von Hymnen und Gebeten verwendeten die Dichter gern das Rollengedicht, z.B. in bal-bal-e-Liedern der Inanna, dem tigi der Inanna *TMH* NF III, Nr. 25 (s. Wilcke, in *AfO* XXIII [1970] 84–87) oder den šìr-nam-šub der Inanna *CT* XLII, Nr. 13 und 22 (s.

---

74. Siehe oben 6*a*. Vielfach hat man von der Haltung des Prologs auf das ganze Werk geschlossen und es dementsprechend klassifiziert.

75. *SSA*, S. 31–42; Wilcke, in *Kindlers Literatur Lexikon*, Bd. 6, Sp. 2151–54.

76. S. N. Kramer und Th. Jacobsen, "Gilgamesh and Agga," *AJA* LIII (1949) 1–18; A. Falkenstein, "Zu 'Gilgameš und Agga,'" *AfO* XXI (1966) 47–50.

S. N. Kramer, in *PAPS*, Bd. 107 [1963] S. 503–5), doch fällt auf, dass die Dichter diese Form anscheinend nur bei der Göttin Inanna gebrauchen.

Die drei lyrischen Grundhaltungen, Nennen, Ansprechen und liedhaftes Sprechen (W. Kayser, *Das sprachliche Kunstwerk*, S. 338 ff.) finden sich auch in den sumerischen Gedichten. Ihre Anwendung auf sie scheint mir jedoch nicht immer zu glücklichen Ergebnissen zu führen. So ist die Hymne *per definitionem* auf die Ansprache beschränkt. Da sich aber bei Texten, die in der zweiten (eigentliche Hymnen), der dritten (Nennen) oder der ersten Person (liedhaftes Sprechen) stilisiert sind, keinerlei stilistische Unterschiede feststellen lassen, ziehe ich es vor, von in den verschiedenen Personen stilisierten Hymnen zu sprechen.

Die sumerische Lyrik verwendet überwiegend die Beschreibung und kann in Dialogform gehalten sein. Daneben finden sich aber auch (liedhafte) Ich-Erzählungen, die auch einen Dialog umfassen können. Hymnen enthalten oft kurze Du- oder Er-Erzählungen.

Lyrische und epische Erzählung unterscheiden sich dadurch, dass die Lyrik den Reden keine Einleitungsformel vorausstellt, dass also kein Erzähler erscheint. Wo sie dennoch auftreten, muss mit der Möglichkeit gerechnet werden, dass hier ein Redaktor durch die Einfügung einer epischen Formel den Text verdeutlicht hat, wie ich es im Exkurs an einem Beispiel zeige. In allen Fällen wird sich dies aber kaum nachweisen lassen, und darum ist damit zu rechnen, dass auch in einem lyrischen Gedicht bisweilen ein Erzähler spricht. Zumindest haben die Redaktoren, die die epischen Formeln einfügten, dies nicht als Stilbruch angesehen.

Zur weiteren Unterscheidung dient, dass die lyrische Erzählung sich auf eine Episode beschränkt und keine Geschichte von Anfang bis Ende erzählt.

Trotz dieser Kriterien ist es oft schwierig oder gar unmöglich, einen bestimmten Text auf die lyrische oder epische Haltung festzulegen.

10. GATTUNG

Will man nicht die Terminologie und die damit verbundenen Definitionen moderner oder anderer antiker Literaturen der sumerischen aufpfropfen, so muss die Gliederung der Werke in Gattungen aus ihnen selbst gewonnen werden. Auf diesem Gebiet sind erst wenige erste Schritte unternommen worden—nur einige wenige Gattungen haben sich feststellen lassen.

Besonders gut sind wir dank den Untersuchungen von J. van Dijk[77] über die Streitgedichte informiert. Heute lassen sich zwei Hauptgruppen unterscheiden: die epischen Streitgedichte und die Schulstreitgespräche, die der Dramatik nahestehen.

Die epischen Streitgespräche beginnen mit einem erzählenden Prolog historischen oder mythologischen Inhalts, der einen beträchtlichen Umfang

77. Siehe oben, Anm. 75.

erreichen kann.[78] Darauf folgt die Vorstellung der Kontrahenten und des Gegenstandes ihres Streites. Der Streit selbst nimmt dann den Hauptteil der Dichtung ein. Meist ist er in mehrere Wechselreden gegliedert; er kann jedoch auch Handlungen einschliessen. Sonderfälle sind "Dumuzi und Enkimdu," wo sich die (einzige) Streitrede Dumuzi's nicht an den Gegner, sondern an das Streitobjekt, die Göttin Inanna, richtet, (darauf folgt eine Handlung Dumuzi's gegen seinen Kontrahenten und dessen [einzige] Rede, in der er Verzicht leistet) und "Enmerkar und Suhkešdaanna," wo auf je eine Streitrede der Gegner ein epischer Bericht folgt.[79] Den Abschluss bilden die Streitentscheidung durch einen Gott oder den König[80] und die Versöhnung, gefolgt von der Doxologie: "Dass A und B miteinander gestritten haben, dass A den B übertroffen hat, dafür sei dem Gotte X Preis!"[81]

Im Prinzip analog sind die Schulstreitgespräche gebaut, nur dass dort stets der Prolog, jegliche Handlung und die Versöhnung fehlen. Ort des Streites ist stets die Schule (Ausnahme vielleicht der "Streit zweier Frauen"). Während in den epischen Streitgedichten der König eine Rolle (aktiv oder passiv) spielen kann (Urnammu in "Silber und Kupfer"; Šulgi in "Baum und Rohr" und "Vogel und Fisch"; Ibbi-Sîn in "Sommer und Winter"), wird er in die Schulstreitgespräche nicht miteinbezogen.

Verwandt mit den Schulstreitgesprächen ist eine Gruppe von Texten, die mit der Anrede des Schülers beginnen, der dann über den Alltag in der Schule und seine Ausbildung berichtet.[82] Da diese Texte—soweit mir verständlich oder rekonstruierbar—durchweg satirisch sind, möchte ich sie als Schulsatiren bezeichnen.

Eine formale Bestimmung der Gattung Hymne ist mir nicht möglich; dasselbe gilt von der Klage.

Anders verhält es sich mit den Gebeten,[83] bei denen wir drei Typen unterscheiden können. Zunächst beobachten wir in verschiedenen epischen Texten Gebete, mit denen sich ein Mensch die Hilfe der Götter sichern will (Gudea-Zylinder, Lugalbanda I, "Gilgameš und Huwawa," "Gilgameš, Enkidu und die Unterwelt," "Dumuzi's Tod," "Inanna's Gang zur Unterwelt," ér-šèm-ma

---

78. "Dumuzi und Enkimdu" (s. *SSA*, S. 67, Z. 55 ff.) beginnt anscheinend ohne Prolog. Ist *SRT*, Nr. 3 eine weitere Tafel vorausgegangen oder das Gespräch Utu's mit seiner Schwester Inanna einem Prolog gleichzusetzen?

79. Siehe S. N. Kramer und Th. Jacobsen, "Enmerkar and Ensukišširanna," *Or*, NS, Bd. 23 (1954) S. 232–34.

80. Fehlt in "Dumuzi und Enkimdu" wegen des bereits geleisteten Verzichts und in "Enki und Ninmah" (C. Benito, "Enki and Ninmah" [Ph.D. diss., University of Pennsylvania, 1969]).

81. Ähnlich in "Enki und Ninmah":
Ninmah konnte es dem grossen Herrn Enki nicht gleichtun.
Vater Enki, dein Preis ist angenehm!
In "Baum und Rohr" entscheidet der König Šulgi den Streit, die Doxologie gilt aber Enlil.

82. Siehe Wilcke, in *Kindlers Literatur Lexikon*, Bd. 6, Sp. 2147–50.

83. A. Falkenstein, in *RLA*, Bd. 3, S. 156–60.

von Dumuzi und Inanna, Utuhegalepos, etc.). Hier wird das Anliegen frei formuliert.

Die zweite Form ist das offizielle Gebet für den König, meist in Texten mit den Unterschriften tigi oder a-da-ab. Die Bitte oder der in Form einer Feststellung geäusserte Dank sind stets in eine Hymne eingeschlossen oder schliessen sie ab. Bitte oder Dank beziehen sich auf Leben und Regierungszeit des Herrschers. Individuelle Anliegen fehlen. Der Herrscher bittet nicht selbst, vielmehr leistet eine ungenannte Person (ein Priester) Fürbitte für ihn.

Der dritte Typ ist das individuelle Anliegen, das dem Gott vorgetragen wird. Hierfür verwendete man zwei verschiedene Formen, den Brief an die Gottheit[84] oder die an oder auf einer Weihgabe formulierte Bitte. Der Brief an die Gottheit ist durch das Briefformular festgelegt. Die Anrede wird oft zu einem kleinen Hymnus ausgestaltet, wobei der eigentliche Anlass in den Hintergrund treten kann. Derselben Form bediente man sich auch bei Anliegen, die man dem König zu Gehör bringen wollte. Die Briefform des Gebets wurzelt in dem Brauch, einer Weihgabe eine Botschaft an die Gottheit mitzugeben, wie dies F. Thureau-Dangin, *Die sumerischen und akkadischen Königsinschriften* (*VAB* I) S. 64–65, Kol. ii, Z. 2–6, Gudea Stat. B vii 21–25 und besonders J. van Dijk, in *JCS* XIX (1965) 5–10, Z. 41–163 und 164–240 bezeugen.

Die Briefform fehlt aber bei der Weihung eines Hundes an Nintinugga durch Lugal-nisag-e (Letter Coll. B 18) und der einer Axt an Nergal durch den Kaufmann Nibru^{ki}-ta-lú (Wilcke, *Lugalbandaepos*, S. 58, Anm. 210). Beide beginnen mit dem Namen des Spenders, nennen oder beschreiben den geweihten Gegenstand. Lugal-nisag-e bietet als nächstes die Bitte, die der Hund vortragen soll, Nibru^{ki}-ta-lú sagt den Ersatz zu, falls die Axt verloren geht oder beschädigt wird. Beide Texte schliessen mit der Formel "Solange ich lebe, möge sie/er ihn/es anschauen, wenn ich sterbe, möge ich(?) in der Unterwelt . . . -Wasser trinken!" (s. M. Civil, in *RA* LXIII [1969] 180).

Andere formal bestimmbare Gattungen sind die Beschwörungen (s. Falkenstein, *LSS* NF I) und z.B. die Gebete für den König, die enden "NN (= Königsname), mein König!" (*UET* VI/1, Nr. 102–6, mit Unterschrift šud$_x$ (= BUM)-dè an in *UET* VI/1, Nr. 102; in *UET* VI/1, Nr. 103 [...]-ma-ká-gal-mah-ku$_4$-ra-kam, "[...] beim Eintreten durch das 'grösste Stadttor'"; *TCL* XVI, Nr. 61).

11. UNTERSCHRIFTEN UND RUBRIKEN

11.1. RUBRIKEN UND LITERARISCHE EINHEIT

Eine grosse Zahl von Texten weist Unterschriften und Rubriken auf, die zuletzt von A. Falkenstein, in *ZA*, Bd. 49 (1950) S. 83–105, *SAHG*, S. 20–26, H. Hartmann, "Die Musik der sumerischen Kultur" (Diss.; Frankfurt, 1960) S.

---

84. W. W. Hallo, "Individual Prayer in Sumerian: The Continuity of a Tradition," *JAOS*, Bd. 88 (1968) S. 71–89; R. Borger, in *RLA*, Bd. 3, S. 575–76.

192–252, und J. Krecher, in *SKly*, S. 18–36, untersucht worden sind. Diese Klassifizierungen durch die antiken Schreiber beziehen sich—soweit wir sehen—weitestgehend auf den musikalischen Vortrag und dürfen darum *a priori* ebensowenig als literarische Kategorien angesehen werden wie etwa die Bezeichnungen Arie und Rezitativ. Andererseits beobachten wir, dass Rubriken häufig an Zäsuren im Text stehen, dass also die ihnen vorangehenden Abschnitte literarische Einheiten sind.

Als Beispiele lassen sich hierfür anführen: (a) Die "2. Urklage," in der die ki-ru-gú-Notierung jeweils die folgenden Abschnitte voneinander trennt: 1. Prolog, 2. Aufgabe der Städte durch ihre Götter, 3. Ur als letzte Stadt, die dem Feind widersteht, und Fürbitte Nanna's bei Enlil für Ur, 4. Ablehnung der Bitte und Fall von Ur, erneute Fürbitte Nanna's und Einlenken Enlil's, Rückkehr der Götter nach Ur, 5. Epilog. (b) A-da-ab-Lied Nanna's (*SLTNi* 58 + *ISET* I 157, Ni. 4467 + 138, Ni. 4274): Der sa-gíd-da-Teil ist ein Hymnus auf Nanna (in der 2. Pers. stilisiert). Der sa-gar-ra-Teil nennt Städte und ihre Götter (Refrain uru an-né ki-gar-ra, "Stadt, die An gegründet hat"), an erster Stelle Ur. Die Antiphone dazu handelt von Ur und den Enki- und Ninki-Gottheiten. Das uru$_x$(= ULÙ)-EN-bi-im nimmt die erste Zeile des sa-gar-ra wieder auf und variiert sie nach dem Schema R–2. Nach dem Ende des sa-gíd-da-Teiles wird Nanna nicht wieder erwähnt. Der sa-gar-ra-Teil (und das uru$_x$(= ULÙ)-EN-bi-im) sind durch den Refrain deutlich vom sa-gíd-da-Teil abgesetzt. (c) Tigi Enlil's für Urnammu: Der sa-gíd-da-Teil enthält eine Erzählung mit beschreibenden Einschüben (Typ lyrische Erzählung). Der sa-gar-ra-Teil ist hymnisch gehalten und deutlich strophisch gegliedert (R–3). Dabei spricht zunächst der Gott Enlil, dessen Rede im sa-gíd-da-Teil bereits in den letzten drei Zeilen summarisch erwähnt ist. Darauf folgt ein beschreibender Abschnitt.

Diese wenigen Beispiele mögen genügen, um zu zeigen, dass die Rubriken inhaltlich und formal verschiedene Teile einer Dichtung trennen können. Dies ist aber keine feste Regel, denn es finden sich auch Texte, in denen die Rubriken Zusammengehöriges trennen—oft in unmittelbarer Nähe einer Zäsur. So finden wir in der Eriduklage (s. C. Wilcke, in *ZA*, Bd. 62, S. 50–52) eine Rede der Damgalnunna, die den erhaltenen Teil des 6. ki-ru-gú-Abschnitts, die Antiphone dazu und die ersten drei Zeilen des 7. ki-ru-gú umfasst, ohne dass sich an dieser Stelle ein Einschnitt fände. Das Gegenteil ist der Fall: Die letzte Zeile des 6. ki-ru-gú und die erste des 7. bilden eine Einheit (R–1), unterbrochen durch die Antiphone. Der Einschnitt findet sich erst nach der dritten Zeile des 7. ki-ru-gú. In dem a-da-ab auf An für Urninurta enthält der sa-gíd-da-Teil eine (lyrische) Erzählung, die aber anders als im oben erwähnten tigi auf Enlil für Urnammu bis zur zweiten Zeile des sa-gar-ra-Teils fortgesetzt wird. Darauf folgt dann eine wörtliche Rede An's (wie im tigi auf Enlil), die aber über die Begrenzung des sa-gar-ra-Abschnittes hinaus auch den (sonst selbständigen) uru$_x$(= ULÙ)-EN-bi-im-Abschnitt mit umfasst. Die Frage, ob die Übereinstimmung von literarischer Einheit und durch die Rubriken festgelegter musikalischer oder liturgischer Unterteilung oder die Abweichung davon die grössere Kunst des Dichters verrät, können wir angesichts unserer Unkenntnis der musikalischen Darbietung und der metrischen Struktur nicht entscheiden.

11.2. Hierarchie der Rubriken

In einigen Texten beobachten wir das Fehlen von Rubriken, dort wo wir sie erwarten, oder in einem Duplikattext, der hierin von dem anderen abweicht; auch Unterschriften können fehlen. Dabei ist danach zu unterscheiden, ob die Rubriken nach der Struktur der Texte sicher ergänzt werden können oder nicht. Im a-da-ab auf Baba, *CT* XXXVI, Taf. 39–40, fehlen die Rubriken sa-gar-ra-àm und uru$_x$(= ULÙ)-EN-bi-im. Da aber die letzten drei Zeilen dem für das uru$_x$(= ULÙ)-EN-bi-im typischen Schema R–1 folgen, sind diese Rubriken sicher zu ergänzen. Ähnlich verhält es sich mit dem a-da-ab auf Inanna für Rīm-Sîn, *UET* VI/1, Nr. 100, wo das giš-gi$_4$-gál zum sa-gar-ra fehlt, dem auf Su'en für Šū-Sîn, *TMH* NF IV, Nr. 12 (ebenso) und dem auf Su'en für Ibbi-Sîn (Å. Sjöberg, in *OrS* XIX/XX [1970–71] 147–49), wo die Rubrik sa-gar-ra nicht geschrieben ist. In diesen Fällen erlaubt die festgelegte Form des uru$_x$ (= ULÙ)-EN-bi-im die sichere Ergänzung der Rubriken.

Anders das a-da-ab auf Nergal für Šū-ilišu (Å. Sjöberg, in *ZA*, Bd. 63, S. 2 ff.). Hier notiert *SRT*, Nr. 12 (= A) die Rubriken bar-sù-àm, šà-ba-TUK-àm, bar-sù-MIN-kam-ma-àm, šà-ba-TUK-MIN-kam-ma-àm, bar-sù-EŠ$_5$-kam-ma-àm vor der Notiz [sa]-bar-sù-da-àm. CBS 14074 (= B) hat aber nur die der letzten von A entsprechende Rubrik sa-gíd-da-àm und lässt die übrigen fort, ohne dass sich deren Notwendigkeit aus dem Text selbst ergibt. Dies berechtigt zu dem Schluss, dass die Notierung von bar-sù und šà-ba-TUK fakultativ, die von sa-gíd-da (/sa-bar-sù-da) aber obligat ist. Ausserdem können wir diesem Text entnehmen, dass sich die Rubrik sa-gíd-da auf den gesamten ihr vorhergehenden Text bezieht, nicht nur auf die Zeilen zwischen der letzten šà-ba-TUK- oder bar-sù-Rubrik und der Notiz sa-gíd-da. So ist es denn auch nicht verwunderlich, wenn zwischen den Rubriken šà-ba-du-ga und sa-gíd-da-àm im tigi auf Nanāja für Išbi-Erra nur eine Zeile steht (W. W. Hallo, in *BiOr* XXIII [1966] 243, Z. 19–20). Diesen Befund bestätigt das šìr-nam-ur-sag-gá der Ninsianna (in ki-ru-gú unterteilt), wo die Rubrik šà-ba-TUK-àm (Z. 132) sich in Text A, nicht aber in B und F findet.[85]

11.3. Rubriken und strophische Gliederung

Die Rubriken sa-gíd-da, sa-gar-ra und uru$_x$(= ULÙ)-EN-bi-im stehen— soweit ich sehe—stets an einer Strophengrenze. Auch ki-ru-gú-Vermerke fallen in der Regel mit Strophengrenzen überein; doch siehe das oben erwähnte Beispiel aus der Eriduklage, wo der erhaltene Teil des 6. ki-ru-gú-Abschnitts durch einen Refrain deutlich in Strophen gegliedert ist, die letzte Zeile aber inhaltlich und nach dem Wiederholungsschema R–1 zur ersten Strophe des 7.

---

85. *SKIZ*, Kap. IV; Reisman, "Two Neo-Sumerian Royal Hymns," S. 147 ff.

ki-ru-gú gehört—ob die Zeile der Antiphone hier Teil der Strophe ist oder nicht, lässt sich nicht entscheiden.

Die Rubriken bar-sù und šà-ba-TUK können ebenfalls mit der Strophengrenze übereinstimmen wie im a-da-ab auf Ningublaga für Iddin-Dagān (*SLTNi*, Nr. 85) oder dem auf Nergal für Šū-ilišu (Å. Sjöberg, in *ZA*, Bd. 63, S. 2 ff.) Im a-da-ab auf An für Lipit-Eštar (*SKIZ*, S. 10–14) aber trennt die Rubrik bar-sù-2-kam zwei parallel gebaute Zeilenpaare eines Vierzeilers. Ähnlich wird im a-da-ab auf An für Ur-Ninurta (*SKIZ*, S. 10–16) durch die Rubrik šà-ba-TUK-àm die letzte Zeile eines Vierzeilers (Z. 20) abgetrennt.

Die "Antiphone," giš-gi$_4$-gál-bi, gehört in der Regel (zu einer möglichen Ausnahme s.o.) nicht zu der vorhergehenden oder folgenden Strophe und bildet eine selbständige Einheit.

Dort, wo Rubriken durch Trennstriche ersetzt sind, dürfen wir wohl annehmen, dass die so bezeichneten Einheiten auch Strophen sind.

11.4. Belegte Unterschriften und Rubriken

Die altbabylonische Serie Proto-Lu bietet in den Zeilen 587–621a eine Aufzählung von Ausdrücken, die wir zum grossen Teil aus Textunterschriften und Rubriken kennen. Darunter finden sich auch Termini, die aber aller Wahrscheinlichkeit nach keine solche Funktion haben wie Z. 602–5. Andere wie Z. 615 ma-al-ga-tum und 619 za-am-za-am kennen wir nur als Bezeichnung von Musikinstrumenten.

Die uns bekannten und eine sonst noch nicht belegte Unterschrift (šìr-nam-sipa-da) sind das Anordnungsprinzip des mittelbabylonischen(?) Katalogs (Bibliotheksinventar, kaum Bibliographie) HS 1447 aus Jena (I. Bernhardt und S. N. Kramer, in *WZJ*, Bd. 6 [1956/57] S. 391–92; *TMH* NF III, Nr. 53). Auch der grosse Hymnenkatalog aus Assur *KAR*, Nr. 158 bietet bekannte neben unbekannten Bezeichnungen.

Eine Aufzählung von bezeugten Unterschriften findet sich auch in Šulgi E, Z. 28–30 (*PBS* X/2, Nr. 7:28–30)

šu-SU$_4$(?)-a ki-gìri-gen-na-ke$_4$
šìr-gíd-da ár-nam-lugal-la
sumun-DU kun-gar bal-bal-e ga-mu-ši-gar-gar-ra
Das, was ich mit...Händen auf den Wegen(?)[86]
alles setzen will, das šìr-gíd-da, den Preis des Königtums,
das sumun-DU, das kun-gar (und das) bal-bal-e,....

Šìr-gíd-da, kun-gar und bal-bal-e kennen wir als Unterschriften. Sumun-DU wird wahrscheinlich in Proto-Lu, Z. 614 (vor ma-al-ga-tum) genannt und ist entweder eine Textunterschrift oder ein Musikinstrument (oder beides); s. Šulgi E, Z. 21–22 (*TCL* XV, Nr. 14 i 21–22 = *PBS* X/2, Nr. 7:21–22 = *ISET* I 147, Ni. 4378, Z. 5–6)

---

86. Castellino, *Two Šulgi Hymns*, S. 141–42, fasst gìri-gen-na als "run of a series."

inim-nin-mu-ᵈgeštin-an-na-ka-ta
a-da(-ab) ᵏᵘˢ⁽ʔ⁾balag (sumun-DU) ma-al-(ga-)tum(-bi-[da])
 mu-ši-gar-gar-re-eš
"Adab, Harfe, sumun-DU und ma-al-ga-tum haben sie
auf das Wort meiner Herrin(?) Gestinanna hin vor mich gestellt"
oder:

"(für) das Adab die Harfe, (für) das sumun-DU das ma-al-ga-tum (etc.)."

Siehe auch Šulgi B, Z. 174 (Castellino, *Two Šulgi Hymns*) sumun-DU ur₅-
ša₄(-e) i-si-iš gá-gá im Zusammenhang mit verschiedenen Musikinstrumenten genannt; s. ferner Dialog 2, Z. 112–13 (*TMH* NF III, Nr. 42 ii 28–29 =
ISET I 148, Kol. ii, Z. 5–6)

á-ni gál ù-⟨bí-⟩in-*tag₄ šìr-gíd-da nu-*ub-*bé
igi-dumu-um-mi-a-ka-šè ù-*ba-*tuš tigi a-da-ab nu-ub-bé
"Breitet er seine Arme aus, so spricht er doch kein šìr-gíd-da,
sitzt er vor dem Lehrer, so spricht er weder tigi noch a-da-ab."

Eine umfangreichere Aufzählung findet sich dann in Šulgi E, Z. 52–60
(A = *TCL* XV, Nr. 14 ii 10–18; B = *PBS* X/2, Nr. 7:52–56; C = *ISET* I
162, Ni. 4519 i 2–10; D = *STVC*, Nr. 71:2–9; teilweise behandelt von A.
Falkenstein, in *ZA*, Bd. 49, S. 84)

èn-du-gáᵃ a-da-ab hé-emᵇ
ᵏᵘˢ⁽ǃ⁾balag ma-al-ga-tum hé-emᶜ
šìr-gíd-da-aᵈ a-arᵉ-nam-lugal-laᶠ
sumun-DUᵍ kun-gar bal-bal-e hé-em
gi-gíd za-am-za-amʰ hé-em
geštú nu-díbⁱ ka-ta nu-šub-dèʲ
KI.GIŠ-gá lú-ùᵏ nam-bí-ibˡ-tag₄-tag₄-a
é-kur-za-gìn-na muš naᵐ-ba-an-túm-mu
ᵈen-líl-ra èš-u₄-SAR-ra-ka-na hé-na-TUK

(a) B: gá; A: mu.
(b) In B und D eine Zeile mit der folgenden (53).
(c) A, C: hé-em; B: hé-dù.   (d) So A; D:]-a; B: šìr-gíd-da.
(e) A, D: a-ar; C: -a]r; B ár.   (f) So B; A, C: nam-lugal.
(g) So B; A: ša-mu-DU.
(h) So B; A: za-za-am; C:]-àm; D: -z]a-àm.
(i) So A; D:]ᵣxˋ-b[é(?)].   (j) So A, C; D: nu-šub-[bu]-dè.
(k) So A; D: l]ú.   (l) So C, D; A: íb.   (m) So A; D nam.

Unter meinen Liedern sei das Adab—
Harfe und ma-al-ga-tum seien (dabei),
sei das šìr-gid-da (und[?]) der Preis des Königtums,
das sumun-DU, das kun-gar und das bal-bal-e—

Flöte und za-am-za-am-Trommel seien (dabei)!
Damit sie am Ohr nicht vorbeigehen, nicht in Vergessenheit geraten,
(damit) sie niemand in meinem . . . zurücklasse,
sollen sie im strahlenden Ekur kein Ende finden,
sollen sie für Enlil in seinem Neumondhaus gespielt werden!

An diesem Textabschnitt ist die Zuordnung von Musikinstrumenten zu den Unterschriften bemerkenswert:

Adab: Melodieinstrument Harfe und Rhythmusinstrument Malgatum;
šìr-gíd-da, Preis des Königtums, sumun-DU, kun-gar, bal-bal-e:
   Melodieinstrument Flöte und Rhythmusinstrument zamzam.

Ausserdem zeigt dieser Abschnitt, dass èn-du, "Lied," den anderen Begriffen übergeordnet ist und dass Texte mit den genannten Unterschriften zum Kult gehören, wobei a-ar-nam-lugal-la vielleicht epische Texte wie Šulgi A, D, F und O meint.
Ferner fällt in den Aufzählungen Šulgi's und den lexikalischen und Katalog-texten das Fehlen der Klagelieder aber auch einer so häufigen auf den König bezogenen Gruppe wie der tigi-Texte auf. Letztere erscheinen allerdings in den Katalogen und in Dialog 2.
Versucht man nun die tatsächlich als Textunterschriften belegten Bezeich-nungen und die in diesen Texten zu beobachtenden Rubriken einander zuzuord-nen, so ergibt sich das folgende Bild (o = obligat, f = fakultativ). In die Tabelle habe ich nicht aufgenommen èn-du, vielleicht belegt als Unterschrift zur 1. Urklage, aber sehr zweifelhaft; s. J. Krecher, in *OLZ*, Bd. 67 (1972) Sp. 252; šud$_x$(= BUM)-dè-AN aus *UET* VI/1, Nr. 102, igi-du$_8$-a-lugal aus *UET* VI/1 Nr. 104 und die Beschwörungen. Da sich mitunter in der Literatur die Ansicht findet, die zà-mí-Formel sei ein den übrigen Unterschriften vergleichbarer Schluss, gebe ich auch an, wo sich eine solche Doxologie in Texten mit Unterschrift findet. Siehe die Tabelle auf Seite 258.

Die Bedeutungen der Unterschriften sind in der Mehrzahl und die der Rubriken zum Teil vordergründig klar, ihre exakte Bedeutung und klassifi-zierende Funktion ist aber weitestgehend unklar. Nur beim a-da-ab—verglichen mit dem tigi—lässt sich ein formales Merkmal im Text feststellen: der durch die Rubrik uru$_x$(= ULÙ)-EN-bi-im abgeschlossene Schluss, der fast immer 3 Zeilen umfasst, die nach dem Schema R–1 gebaut sind (s. die Tabelle).
Die Unterschriften lassen sich ihrer Bedeutung nach in drei Gruppen einteilen:
(a) Nach Musikinstrumenten sind benannt a-da-ab (s. *CAD*, Bd. A/1, S. 102; Šulgi E, Z. 21–22), balag, wahrscheinlich kun-gar, tigi, wozu noch ér-šèm-ma als mit dem Namen eines Instruments zusammengesetzt kommt. Die Bezeichnungen beziehen sich auf Rhythmus- (a-da-ab, šèm, tigi und vielleicht kun-gar) und Melodieinstrumente (balag).
(b) Als Lieder sind bezeichnet: šìr-gíd-da, "lang gemachtes Lied," šìr-

Unterschriften	Rubriken									Literatur/Quellen
	sa-gíd-da	sa-gar-ra	uru$_x$(= ULÙ)-EN-bi	bar-sù	šà-ba-TUK	giš-gi$_4$-gál	ki-ru-gú	ki-šú	zà-mí-Schluss	
a-da-ab	o	o	o	f	f	f	-	-	-	s. u. Tabelle
bal-bal-e	-	-	-	-	-	f	-	-	f[a]	s. u. Tabelle
balag	-	-	-	-	f[b]	f	o[c]	o[d]	-	s. u. Tabelle
ér-šèm-ma	-	-	-	-	-	-	-	-	-	s. u. Tabelle
kun-gar	-	-	-	-	-	-	-	-	-	unten Exkurs
šìr-gíd-da	-	-	-	-	-	-	-	-	f[e]	s. u. Tabelle
šìr-kal-ka[1]	-	-	-	-	-	-	-	-	-	Alster, *Dumuzi's Dream*
šìr-nam-gala	-	-	-	-	f[f]	o[g]	o	o	f[h]	s. u. Tabelle
šìr-nam-šub	-	-	-	-	-	f[i]	f[j]	f[i]	-	s. u. Tabelle
šìr-nam-ur-sag-gá	-	-	-	-	f[k]	o	o	-	o[k]	s. o. Anm. 85
tigi	o	o	-	f[l]	f[l]	f	-	-	f[m]	s. u. Tabelle
ù-lu-lu-ma-ma	-	-	-	-	-	-	-	-	f[n]	s. u. Tabelle
ù-líl-lá	-	-	-	-	-	-	-	-	?[o]	*JNES* XII 160-88
Ohne Unterschrift, aber mit Rubriken:										
UM 29-16-51	x	x	-	-	-	x	?[p]	-	-	*RSO* XXXII 95-102
UET VI, Nr. 101	-	-	x[q]	-	-	x[q]	-	-	x[q]	
1. Urklage	-	-	-	-	-	x	x	(x[r])	-	Kramer, *AS*, Nr. 12
2. Urklage	-	-	-	-	-	x	x	-	-	*ANET* (1969) S. 611-19
Eriduklage	-	-	-	-	-	x	x	[-	-]	*ZA*, Bd. 62, S. 49-61
Nippurklage	-	-	-	-	-	x	x	-	-	*Eretz Israel* IX 89 ff.
Nanna's Fahrt nach Nippur	-	-	-	-	-	-	-	x	-	Ferrara, *StP* M, Bd. 2
Texte in akkadischer Sprache										
Aguŝaja[s] (Hammurapi)	-	-	-	-	-	x	x	-	-	*VS* X, Nr. 214; *RA* XV 169-82
Nanaja-Samsuiluna	-	-	-	-	-	x	-	-	-	*ZA*, Bd. 44, S. 30-44
Ištar-Ammiditana	-	-	-	-	-	x	-	-	-	*SAHG*, S. 235-37

(*a*) In den bal-bal-e auf Ningizzida *UET* VI/1, Nr. 70, *ISET* I 187, Ni. 9808 und *TCL* XV, Nr. 25.

(*b*) So, falls *CT* XXXVI, Taf. 43–44 eine balag-Komposition ist; geschrieben šà-ba-a-TUK (ii' 17, 21').

(*c*) Teilweise durch Trennstriche ersetzt, z.B. *CT* XLII, Nr. 15.

(*d*) In *CT* XLII, Nr. 3 fehlen sowohl die Rubrik ki-šú-bi-im als auch die Unterschrift balag. Kol. vi, Z. 60 scheint jedoch die šud$_x$(= BUM)- ... gi$_4$-gi$_4$-Zeile (s. dazu *SKly*, S. 22 und 30) zu sein, die für das ki-šú-bi von balag-Kompositionen typisch ist.

(*e*) Šìr-gíd-da-Lieder enden mit Ausnahme von *STVC*, Nr. 34 (zuletzt D. Reisman, in *JCS* XXIV [1971] 3–10) stets auf eine zà-mí-Doxologie.

(*f*) Nur im šìr-nam-gala auf Nininsina für Lipit-Eštar (*UET* VI/1, Nr. 96, 97).

(*g*) Alle mir bekannten šìr-nam-gala haben giš-gi$_4$-gál Rubriken; dies kann aber durch den Zufall der Überlieferung bedingt sein.

(*h*) Nur im šìr-nam-gala auf Meslamtaea und Lugalgirra für Ibbi-Sîn (Å. Sjöberg, in *OrS* XIX/XX 142–44).

kal-kal, ". . .-Lied," šìr-nam-gala, "*kalû*-Priester-Lied," šìr-nam-šub,
". . .-Lied," und šìr-nam-ur-sag-gá, "Helden/Krieger-Lied"; dazu kommt
das im Katalog *TMH* NF III, Nr. 53:48 belegte šìr-nam-sipa-da, "Hirten-
lied" (der Inanna). Anzuschliessen ist auch ér-šèm-ma "Weinen zur šèm-
Pauke." In dieser Gruppe fällt die Verbindung mit Personenbezeichnungen auf:
kalû-Priester, eine Gruppe von Sängern der Kultlieder im Emesaldialekt, ur-sag,
"Helden oder Krieger," sipa, "Hirten." Dabei ist aber unklar, ob es sich um
die Sänger handelt (z.B. Soldatenchor) oder die Takt, Rhythmus, Begleitung
und Melodie festlegende Art des Liedes (z.B. Marschmusik; von D. O. Edzard
gesprächsweise vorgeschlagen für šìr-nam-ur-sag-gá).

   (c) Völlig unklar: bal-bal-e,[87] ù-lu-lu-ma-ma und ù-líl-lá.

   In der Gruppe der Rubriken finden wir zunächst das durch das Wort sa =
pitnu, "Saite," zusammengehaltene Paar sa-gíd-da (mit Var. sa-bar-gíd/
sù-da in *VS* X, Nr. 199 i 29, *SRT*, Nr. 12:36 [sa] und *TMH* NF IV, Nr. 12:37
[sa]; s. Falkenstein, in *ZA*, Bd. 49 S. 87–88, Anm. 1) und sa-gar-ra. Die
vermutliche Opposition von gíd und gar in diesen Ausdrücken lässt sich bei

---

   87. Bal-bal-e wird mit *atmû*, "mit jemandem/einander sprechen," geglichen; s. *CAD*,
Bd. A/2, S. 86. B. Landsberger hatte die Unterschrift als "Gespräch," "Duett" verstanden
("Jahreszeiten in Sumerisch-Akkadischen," *JNES* VIII [1949] 295, Anm. 151). Dem hat
S. N. Kramer, in *BiOr* XI [1954] 171, Anm. 6, mit Hinweis auf Texte mit nur einem Sprecher
widersprochen. Falls die bal-bal-e-Lieder in einen grösseren Zusammenhang gehören,
in dem verschiedene Lieder vorgetragen wurden, liesse sich B. Landsbergers Deutung
aufrecht erhalten. Ob die Unterschrift bal-bal-e-dam in *SRT*, Nr. 3 (Dumuzi und Enkimdu) zur Rubrik bal-bal-e zu stellen ist, kann ich nicht entscheiden.

   (*i*) Das šìr-nam-šub auf Ninurta (*SLTNi*, Nr. 61) hat in Z. 111 die Notiz giš-gi₄-
gál-bi-im, was auf eine ausgelassene Rubrik (ki-ru-gú) schliessen lässt. In Z. 184 steht
ki-šú-bi-im.

   (*j*) S.o. Anm. *i*; *MNS* I, Nr. 7; dazu vielleicht die Trennstriche in *CT* XLII, Nr. 13 und 22.

   (*k*) S.o. bei Anm. 85; die zà-mí-Formel steht nicht am Ende des Textes, sondern 2 oder
3 Zeilen vor der ausgefallenen (in allen Texten!) Rubrik ki-ru-gú-10-kam-ma-àm.

   (*l*) Tigi auf Ninurta für Šū-Sîn (*BE* XXIX, Nr. 1 i 1 ff.) und auf Nanaja für Išbi-Erra
(Hallo, in *BiOr* XXIII [1966] 243).

   (*m*) Tigi auf Ninurta für Šulgi (*BE* XXIX, Nr. 1 iii 6′–36′) und auf Enki für Ur-Ninurta
(Falkenstein, in *ZA*, Bd. 49 [1949] 112–16).

   (*n*) *MNS* I, Nr. 6; Sjöberg, in *OrS* XIX/XX 145–47; vielleicht auch *STVC*, Nr. 124.

   (*o*) Falls in Jacobsen und Kramer, in *JNES* XII 178, Z. 185–86 gelesen werden kann:
ᵈbi-lu-lu ug₅-[ga] // ᵈinanna zà(!)-m[í] (nach der Kopie nicht ausgeschlossen).

   (*p*) Der Text scheint in Z. 42 eine Rubrik ki-UD-ru-gú-dam zu haben (= ki-ru-gú?).
Z. 70 hat noch einmal ein giš-gi₄-gál-bi-im, vor dem eine Rubrik ausgefallen zu sein
scheint.

   (*q*) Die Rubrik uruₓ(= ULÙ)-en-bi-im bezieht sich anscheinend auf die davorstehenden
letzten vier Zeilen: Z. 54–55 Typ R-1; Z. 56–57 Doxologie (2. Pers.) für Enki, der das Lied
ganz gross gemacht habe (mah). Nach dem uruₓ(= ULÙ)-en-bi folgt noch eine Zeile und
dann die Notiz giš-gi₄-gál-bi-im.

   (*r*) Der Text *ISET* I 205, Ni. 9586 hat eine Unterschrift, die aussieht wie [. . . ᴇ]N-bi-im
zà-[. . .]; vielleicht [k]i(!)-šú(!)-bi-im zà-[til-la-bi].

   (*s*) Unterschrift (der 2. Tafel) DUB(?).BI(?).IM(?) *a-gu-ša-ja*. Hier nehme ich nur akkadische Texte auf, die dieselben Rubriken zeigen wie die sumerischen.

einem Ansatz gíd, "lang," nicht erklären. Darum frage ich mich, ob gíd hier nicht "anziehen" im Sinne von "spannen" bedeutet und gar, "hinsetzen," mit konkreter Bedeutung "loslassen." Diese Bezeichnungen könnten sich dann auf die Spannung des Fells des Schlaginstruments oder die Stimmung des Melodieinstruments beziehen, sofern dies ein Saiteninstrument war. Die Variante sa-bar-gíd/sù-da-àm bezeichnet die Saite als "äussere," was gut zu einem Saiteninstrument passen könnte, doch kann damit auch eine am Resonanzkörper eines Schlaginstruments aussen befestigte Saite, die das Trommelfell spannt, gemeint sein.

Die Rubrik uru$_x$(= ULÙ)-EN-bi-im hat zuletzt A. Falkenstein, in *ZA*, Bd. 52 (1957) S. 69–72 ausführlich behandelt. Er deutete sie als "seine bezwingenden Worte." Dieser Ansatz passt gut dazu, dass in den so bezeichneten Zeilen oft eine Bitte ausgesprochen wird. Da dies dann aber die einzige inhaltlich bestimmte Rubrik wäre, möchte ich die Deutung lieber offen lassen.

Die Rubriken šà-ba-TUK und bar-sù sind durch die Opposition šà, "Inneres," und bar, "Äusseres," verbunden. Für sù in bar-sù bieten sich die Bedeutungen "weit, fern" und "nackt" an: auf dem ferner liegenden äusseren Teil oder dem "unbekleideten," d.h., nicht mit dem Fell bespannten Teil des Schlaginstruments zu begleiten. Der als šà-ba-TUK-àm/šà-ba-du-ga/šà-ba-a-TUK bezeichnete Abschnitt wäre dann der mitten auf dem Instrument zu begleitende Teil: "ist in seiner Mitte gespielt."

Hier ist auch der Zusatz zu der Rubrik sa-gar-ra-àm in *BE* XXIX, Nr. 1 iii 5 zu nennen: šu-ta e-ne-di-[dam], "[ist] mit der Hand [zu] spielen," was sich wohl auf ein Schlaginstrument bezieht (oder bezeugt es den Gebrauch eines Plektrums bei Saiteninstrumenten?).[88]

Die Rubrik giš-gi$_4$-gál (mit Variante giš-ki-gál) ist mit *me-her za-ma-ri* und *mi-ih-rum šá za-ma-ri*, "Gegenstück zum Gesang," geglichen (*CAD*, Bd. Z, S. 35); daher die Deutung als "Antiphone," zu der passt, dass sich die so bezeichneten Zeilen oder kurzen Zeilengruppen nicht sicher in die strophische Struktur der Texte einordnen lassen. Der sumerische Ausdruck ist aber für sich genommen unklar: "Holz zurückkehren(?) (oder: zur[?] Erde[?]) lassen" —vielleicht "ohne Begleitung"?

Die Rubrik ki-ru-gú ist in *KAR*, Nr. 100 ii 5 mit *še-e-ru*, "Lied," geglichen, was zu der oben notierten inhaltlichen Einheit ki-ru-gú (s. aber die Ausnahme!) passt. Diese bereits von H. Zimmern, *Ištar und Ṣaltu* (Leipzig, 1916) S. 5, Anm. 2, notierte Gleichung erklärt den sumerischen Ausdruck aber nicht. Im Anschluss an Falkenstein, in *ZA*, Bd. 49, S. 105, versteht man ihn meist als "der Erde entgegenneigen," "Verbeugung," "niederknien," also als liturgischen Ausdruck; es wäre aber die einzige auf die Liturgie bezogene Angabe in den Texten, was an dieser Deutung zweifeln lässt. Eine einleuchtende auf die musikalische Begleitung bezogene Erklärung kann ich aber nicht vorschlagen.

---

88. E-ne-di, "spielen," mit Bezug auf ein Musikinstrument ist belegt in *TMH* NF III, Nr. 25:16 (s. dazu C. Wilcke, "Die akkadischen Glossen," *AfO* XXIII [1970] 84–85).

Da ki-šú-bi-im stets als letzte Rubrik erscheint, ist es sicher mit šú = *katāmu* (*ŠL* 545:12) "bedecken" zu verbinden, sei es, dass es sich auf den Text bezieht und meint "ist das Deckelstück (= der Schluss) davon," sei es, dass es sich um die musikalische Darbietung handelt und bedeutet "ist die Stelle davon, an der man das Instrument wieder zudeckt," oder ähnlich. J. Krecher, in *SKly*, S. 30, Anm. 60*a*, führt noch 3 weitere Belege für ki-šú an: *VS* II, Nr. 30 iv; *VS* X, Nr. 118 ii 4′ und *TLB* II, Nr. 7 iv. Dazu kommt noch *VS* II, Nr. 1 ii 8. An diesen Stellen scheint ki-šú (in *TLB* II, Nr. 7 iv 16′, ki-šú-bi) "zu Ende" zu bedeuten. Darauf folgt dann eine Summe der Zeilen des Textes ohne einleitendes šunigin oder mu-šid-bi o.ä.

11.5. Unterschriften und Haltung

Untersucht man die Texte mit Unterschriften auf die ihnen zugrundeliegende Haltung, so zeigt sich das folgende Bild:

LYRISCH	EPISCH	GRENZFÄLLE
a-da-ab	—	—
bal-bal-e	—	—
balag	—	balag^a
ér-šèm-ma	ér-šèm-ma^b	ér-šèm-ma^c
kun-gar^d	—	—
šìr-gíd-da^e	šìr-gíd-da^f	—
—	šìr-kal-ka[l]^d	—
šìr-nam-gala^g	šìr-nam-gala^h	—
šìr-nam-šub	šìr-nam-šub^i	—
—	—	šìr-nam-ur-sag-gá^{d,j}
tigi	—	—
ù-lu-lu-ma-ma^k	(ù-lu-lu-ma-ma^l)	ù-lu-lu-ma-ma^m
—	ù-líl-lá^d	—

(*a*) Das balag Dumuzi's *CT* XLII, Nr. 15 (e-ne-eĝ$_x$(= ÁG)-gá-ni i-lu-i-lu) ist zwar, soweit erhalten und verständlich, lyrisch gehalten; trotzdem wird eine Geschichte erzählt: Dumuzi's Befreiung durch Inanna.

(*b*) Ér-šèm-ma für Inanna und Dumuzi (Scheil, in *RA* VIII 162 ff. = *VS* II, Nr. 2 i 1–iii 22 = *TCL* XVI, Nr. 78) und für Iškur (*CT* XV, Taf. 15–16 mit Teilduplikat *CT* XLII, Nr. 10).

(*c*) Die bis auf den Prolog weitgehend übereinstimmenden ér-šèm-ma für Inanna und Gula (s.o., 6. mit Anm. 57) sind zwar lyrisch gehalten, erzählen aber eine Geschichte: Inanna's/ Gula's Intervention bei Enlil für Dumuzi (vgl. Anm. *a*).

(*d*) Nur ein Vertreter der Unterschrift.

(*e*) Z.B. die šìr-gíd-da auf Martu (*SGL* I 120–40) und Nusku (*SGL* II 108–43, 144–59).

(*f*) Šìr-gíd-da auf Nininsina (*SRT*, Nr. 6, 7), Ninurta (Reisman, in *JCS* XXIV 3–10), an-gim dím-ma (nach dem MS von J. Cooper ebenfalls ein šìr-gíd-da Ninurta's).

Die oben angeführten ki-ru-gú-Kompositionen ohne Unterschrift, die Ur-, Eridu- und Nippurklagen, sind trotz der—auf ihre Rezitation im Kult weisenden —Antiphonen in ihrer Haltung episch; ebenso die akkadische Dichtung *Agušaja*, der—wie auch in Sumerischen Epen—ein hymnischer Prolog vorausgeht (1. und 2. ki-ru-gú).

Dieser Überblick zeigt deutlich, dass den Unterschriften nichts über die Haltung des Textes entnommen werden kann—mit der Ausnahme von a-da-ab, bal-bal-e und tigi, die anscheinend—angesichts der grossen Zahl von Texten (s. die Tabellen)—auf die lyrische Haltung beschränkt sind.

11.6. Unterschriften und Gattung

Bei Unterschriften, die Texte verschiedener Haltung klassifizieren, ist es von vornherein ausgeschlossen, dass sie eine Gattung bezeichnen. Aber auch bei a-da-ab, bal-bal-e und tigi lässt sich keine für die jeweilige Unterschrift typische Gattung feststellen:

Als a-da-ab werden Hymnen auf Götter und in solche Hymnen gekleidete Gebete für den König bezeichnet. Allerdings sind Hymnen ohne Bitt- oder Dankgebet für den König in der Minderzahl (s. Tabelle). Wir kennen aber auch zwei a-da-ab, in denen sich die Hymne auf den Gott auf den sa-gíd-da-Teil beschränkt, während der sa-gar-ra-Teil den Gott überhaupt nicht erwähnt.

Die Unterschrift bal-bal-e steht überwiegend bei recht profan anmutenden Liebesliedern—aber auch bei Hymnen auf Götter und bei Gebeten (*TMH* NF IV, Nr. 7 ii [6]–iii 6, iii 7–iv 19; *ISET* I 95, Ni. 4105, dazu S. 210, Ni. 4403 und der unveröff. Text 3 NT 500). Nur eines der Gebete ist auf den König bezogen. Die beiden anderen spricht eine en-Priesterin in eigener Sache.

Auch tigi-Texte können Götterhymnen oder mit solchen verbundene Gebete für den König sein. In zwei Fällen (M. Civil, in *JAOS*, Bd. 88 [1968] S. 3–14; *STVC*, Nr. 60+54 und Dupl.) ist aber im sa-gíd-da-Teil nicht die Gottheit, sondern ein Weihgegenstand angeredet. Ausserdem werden als tigi Liebeslieder bezeichnet wie (als Ich-Erzählung gestaltet) *TMH* NF III, Nr. 25.

11.7. Serienbildung

Die Zusammenfassung verschiedener Texte mit Unterschrift zu grösseren Einheiten (Serien) beobachten wir an Hand von Sammeltafeln und Stichzeilen.

(*g*) Šìr-nam-gala für Meslamtaea/Lugalgirra (Å. Sjöberg, in *OrS* XIX/XX 142–44) und Nanna (ders., *ZA*, Bd. 63, *S*. 31–36).

(*h*) Šìr-nam-gala für Nininsina (*UET* VI/1, Nr. 96, 97).

(*i*) Šìr-nam-šub der Nininsina (*KAR*, Nr. 15, 16).

(*j*) Reisman, "Two Neo-Sumerian Royal Hymns," S. 147 ff. Die Haltung ist überwiegend lyrisch. Es wird jedoch minutiös ein Fest beschrieben.

(*k*) *MNS* I, Nr. 6.

(*l*) Das Fragment *STVC*, Nr. 132 könnte einen epischen Text enthalten haben.

(*m*) Das ù-lu-lu-ma-ma auf Suʾen für Ibbi-Sîn ist zwar überwiegend lyrisch, es erzählt aber von einer Fürbitte des Gottes für den König bei Enlil.

Sammeltafeln können Lieder an einen Gott bei verschiedener Unterschrift zusammenfassen (wie *BE* XXIX, Nr. 1), Lieder an einen Gott bei gleicher Unterschrift (wie *TMH* NF IV, Nr. 7; *ISET* I 118–19, Ni. 4569), Lieder an verschiedene Götter bei gleicher Unterschrift (so sehr wahrscheinlich Kramer, in *PAPS*, Bd. 107 [1963] S. 524, Ni. 4452) oder Lieder mit verschiedener Unterschrift an verschiedene Götter (*VS* X, Nr. 199). Ein System der Serienbildung lassen die Sammeltafeln nicht erkennen.

Stichzeilen finden sich bei Texten mit den Unterschriften a-da-ab, bal-bal-e und tigi. Nur in einem Fall können wir mit Sicherheit den Anschlusstext identifizieren (s. Tabelle a-da-ab, Anm. *g*). Dieser Text hat aber in seinem erhaltenen Teil (41 Zeilen!) keine Rubriken, und sein Ende—und damit die mögliche Unterschrift—fehlt.

Trotz dieser negativen Feststellungen ist eindeutig, dass in der altbabylonischen Zeit, aus der die uns vorliegenden Abschriften der Lieder stammen, damit begonnen wurde, die Einzeltexte in Gruppen oder Serien zusammenzufassen. Ob dabei liturgische, musikalische oder literarische Prinzipien zugrundegelegt wurden oder weitgehend der Zufall regierte, können wir vorläufig nicht feststellen.

11.8. Übersicht über Texte mit Unterschrift

Im folgenden gebe ich eine Übersicht über die Texte mit Unterschriften, beschränke mich dabei aber weitestgehend auf altbabylonische Abschriften, da ich zu den jüngeren Exemplaren keine ausreichenden Sammlungen besitze. Bei a-da-ab, bal-bal-e und tigi versuche ich ausser der Analyse nach den Redeformen und Sprechern auch eine Gliederung in Strophen anzuschliessen.

Spalte König: BS = Būr-Sîn; Gg = Gungunum; Gudea = Gudea von Lagaš; ID = Išme-Dagān; IdD = Iddin-Dagān; IS = Ibbi-Sîn; LE = Lipit-Eštar; RS = Rīm-Sîn; Š = Šulgi; ŠI = Šū-ilišu; ŠS = Šū-Sîn; UNa = Urnammu; UNi = Ur-Ninurta.

Spalte Redeform: D = deskriptiv; H = heischend (Wunschsätze und Kohortative); N = narrativ (episch und lyrisch nicht unterschieden).

Spalte Person: Zahlen beziehen sich auf 1., 2., 3. Person mit Bezug auf den in der Unterschrift genannten Gott.

Spalte Sprecher: (nicht bei a-da-ab und tigi). Bei bal-bal-e: 1f = ein weiblicher Sprecher (eme-sal-Dialekt); 1m = ein männlicher Sprecher (Hauptdialekt); 1(f) = ein dem Kontext nach weiblicher Sprecher, aber Hauptdialekt. In den übrigen Tabellen: Sänger = Sänger (nicht unterschieden nach Sänger oder Erzähler) oder Dichter; Gott/Göttin (a) = in der Unterschrift genannte Gottheit; Gott/Göttin (b, c) = nicht in der Unterschrift genannte Gottheiten.

Spalte Katalog: As = *KAR*, Nr. 158 (mittelassyrisch); JA = *TMH* NF III, Nr. 54 (Bernhardt und Kramer, in *WZJ*, Bd. 6, S. 389–91: altbabylonisch); JB = *TMH* NF III, Nr. 53 (*WZJ*, Bd. 6, S. 391–93: mittelbabylonisch?); 4*R*, Taf. 53: neuassyrisch; *VS* X, Nr. 216: altbabylonisch; *Y* = W. W. Hallo, in

JAOS, Bd. 83 (1963) S. 167 ff. (Ur III-Zeit). Die Kataloge As und JB bezeugen die Tradition von a-d a-a b, b a l-b a l-e, š ì r-n a m-š u b und t i g i bis in mittel-babylonische/mittelassyrische Zeit. Auch ein š ì r-n a m-š u b in mittelassyrischer Abschrift liegt vor. Mit a n-g i m d í m-m a ist ein š ì r-g í d-d a sogar in neu-babylonisch/neuassyrischer Überlieferung erhalten.

Spalte Strophische Gliederung: R-1 − 5 = ornamentale Wiederholungsschemata; S = syntaktische Struktur; Sprecher = Sprecherwechsel; T = thematische Struktur.

Übersicht über die Tabellen

Tabelle a-da-ab   S. 266–73
Tabelle bal-bal-e   S. 274–80
Tabelle ér-šèm-ma   S. 282–84
Tabelle balag   S. 285–86
Tabelle šìr-gíd-da   S. 287
Tabelle šìr-nam-gala   S. 288
Tabelle šìr-nam-šub   S. 288
Tabelle ù-lu-lu-ma-ma   S. 289
Tabelle tigi   S. 290–92

Tabelle a-da-ab

Gott	Kö-nig	Quellen	Über-setzung Bear-beitung	Kata-log	Anfang	Rubriken bar-sù	šà-ba-TUK	bar-sù-2	šà-ba-TUK-2	bar-sù-3	sa-gíd-da	giš-gi₄-gál
An[a,b]	ŠS	*STVC*, Nr. 65 iii 1'-iv 11'	--	--	[. . .]	[ ]	x	x	[			]
An[a]	ŠI	*STVC*, Nr. 65 iv 12'-v [28']	--	--	an me-gal-ḫuš-a	[				x]		x
An[a,c,d]	LE	*STVC*, Nr. 65 ii; *VS* X, Nr. 199 i 1-ii 8	*SKIZ*, S. 10-14	--	[an]-maḫ zà-dib me-galam u$_x$-r[u]	x	x	x	x	-	x	x
An[a,c,e]	Uni	*STVC*, Nr. 65 i; *VS* X, Nr. 199 ii 9-iii 7	*SKIZ*, S. 10-17	JA 11 As III 36	an u$_x$-ru-gal-dingir-re-e-ne	x	x	-	-	-	x	-
Baba[f]	--	*CT* XXXVI, Taf. 39-40	*SAHG*, Nr. 9	--	dumu-an-na an-gal ki-gal-ta	-	-	-	-	-	x	x
Baba[g]	ID	*PBS* X/2, Nr. 14; *STVC*, Nr. 72 obv. + *ISET* I 210, Ni. 9774 obv.	*SKIZ*, S. 236-65	--	nin ní-íl-[ ]	-	-	-	-	-	x	x
Dagān[h]	ID	N 3367	*ZA*, Bd. 63, S. 1-55	--	[. . .]	[						]
Enki	ID	UM 29-15-6	*ZA*, Bd. 63, S. 1-55	--	[. . .]	[					] x	x
Enlil[i]	Š	*CT* XXXVI, Taf. 26-27	--	--	^{d}en-líl gal-di	-	-	-	-	-	x	x
Enlil	ID	*TCL* XV, Nr. 22	--	--	[. .] IM u$_5$ nun-dingir-re-e-ne	-	-	-	-	-	x	x
Enlil[j]	ID	*TCL* XV, Nr. 18 i-ii [?]	--	--	[. . .]	[					] x	x
Enlil[j]	ID	*TCL* XV, Nr. 18 ii [?]-iii 2	--	--	[. . .]	[					] x	-
Enlil[k]	BS	NBC 9034; *ISET* I 110, Ni. 4050	*BiOr* XXIII 246-47	--	[. .] an-ki-šè dili-ni dib	-	-	-	-	-	[x]	[?]
Inanna[l]	UNi	VAT 9205	*ZA*, Bd. 52, S. 56-75	--	in-nin zà-díb-a-nun-ke$_4$-ne	x	-	-	-	-	x	x

Rubriken				Redeform					Person, bezogen auf Gott					Versuch einer Gliederung in Strophen von n Zeilen			Strophengliederung nach
sa-gar-ra	giš-gíd-gál	uru$_x$(=ULÙ)-EN-bi	a-da-ab-DN	sa-gíd-da	giš-gíd-gál	sa-gar-ra	giš-gíd-gál	uru$_x$(=ULÙ)-EN-bi	sa-gíd-da	giš-gíd-gál	sa-gar-ra	giš-gíd-gál	uru$_x$(=ULÙ)-EN-bi	sa-gíd-da	sa-gar-ra	uru$_x$(=ULÙ)-EN-bi	
x̣	x!	x	x	D	[ ]	?	?	D?	3	[	]?	?	3	?	?	3	R_1 (uru$_x$(=ULÙ)-EN-bi)
x	x	[	]	D	?	DH	?	?	?	?	2	?	[ ]	?	6,3,4,6	[3]	R_4
x	x	x	x	DN	H	NH	H	?	3	3	3	3?	3	2,3,3, 4,4,4, 4	5,5,5,6	3	S, T; R_3 in sa-gíd-da; R_1: uru$_x$(=ULÙ)-EN-bi
x	-	x	x	DN	-	NH	-	d	3	-	3	-	(1)	4,4, 6!,3, 4,4	2,4,4,4, 4	3	R_3, R_4, S, T; R_1: uru$_x$(=ULÙ)-EN-bi
⟨x⟩	-	⟨x⟩	x	D	D	D	-	D	2	2	2	-	3	4!,6, 6,4,2, 7	4,4,4,4, 4	3	$R_{2/3}$, Refrain; R_1: uru$_x$(=ULU)-EN-bi
x	-	x	x	D	H	NH	-	H	2	3	2	-	2	4,4,4, 3,4,3, 4,4	5,4,2,5, 5,5	3	T, R_1: uru$_x$(=ULÙ)-EN-bi
x	x	x	x	[		]H?	?	H?	[	]	2	?	2	?	?	3	R_1: uru$_x$(=ULÙ)-EN-bi
x̣	[		]	D?	H	D	?	[ ]	2	?	2	?	[ ]	?	4,3,3,5	[ ]	T, R_4
x	x	x	x	DN	N	D	D	D	3	3	3	3	3	4,4,6, 6,4,6	7,7,7,7	3	T, S; R_1 in uru$_x$(=ULÙ)-EN-bi
x	-	x	x̣	DH	H	DH	-	H	2	2	2	-	2	6,6,6	?	3	T, S
x̣	[		]	D?	H	DH?	[	]	2	2	2	[	]	?	4,4,5,4, 4,5	[ ]	T; R_1 in uru$_x$(=ULÙ)-EN-bi?
x	x	[x]	x̣	DH	-	DH	D	?	2	-	2	2?	2?	?	?	3	R_1: uru$_x$(=ULÙ)-EN-bi
x	x	x	x	DN?	[ ]	[?]H	D	H	3	[ ]	2	2?	?	4,5,4 [+?]	[?+]4,4	3	T, S
x	x	x	x	DH	D	DH	H	D	2	2	2	2	2	4,4,3, 3,3,3	5,5	3	S, T; R_4: sa-gar-ra; R_1: uru$_x$(=ULÙ)-EN-bi

267

Tabelle a-da-ab

Gott	König	Quellen	Übersetzung Bearbeitung	Katalog	Anfang	bar-sù	šà-ba-TUK	bar-sù-2	šà-ba-TUK-2	bar-sù-3	sa-gíd-da	giš-gi$_4$-gál
Inanna^m	RS	UET VI, Nr. 100	--	--	[. . .k]i-ág-an-na	x[						]
Iškur^n	?	STVC, Nr. 57	--	--	am u$_4$-da u$_5$-a	[						
Iškur	UNi	VS XVII, Nr. 40	--	--	ur-sag nam-ḫé-a	x [						]
Nanna^o	--	SLTNi, Nr. 58 + ISET I 157, Ni. 4467 + 138, Ni. 4274	MNS I 35-43	JB 62	en-zi nam-tar-ra	-	-	-	-	-	x	-
Nanna^p	Gg	CBS 2135 + 19829; N 3324	ZA, Bd. 63, S. 1-55	--	[. . .]	x	x	[				]
Nanna^q	ID	ISET I 96-97, Ni. 2781	--	--	[. . .] im-mi-ẋ-ẋ	-	-	-	-	-	x	x
Nergal^r	Š	BL 195 B	SGL II 13-15	--	[. . .]	[x	x]	x	x	-	x!	ẋ
Nergal^s	ŠI	SRT, Nr. 12; CBS 14074	ZA, Bd. 63, S. 1-55	JB 70 (?)	en u$_4$-ḫuš-du$_7$-ru	x	x	x	x	x	x	x
Nergal	ID	STVC, Nr. 73	--	--	[en am-du$_7$-du$_7$ (?)]	-	-	-	-	-	x	x
Ningublaga^t	IdD	SLTNi, Nr. 85	--	--	[e]n? u$_4$-šúr-ḫuš	x	x	x	[			]
Nininsina^u	[?]	ISET I 113, Ni. 9496	--	JB 75	nin an-gal-e zi-dè-eš tu-da	-	-	-	-	-	[x	?
Ninlil^v	--	AfO XXIV, Taf. II	AfO XXIV 6-9	JB 80	dnin-líl me-šár-ra	-	-	-	-	-	x	x
Ninlil	Š	BE XXXI, Nr. 4	--	--	munus-zi gá-al-ga-sù-dingir-re-ne	-	-	-	-	-	[x	?]
Ninlil^j	ID	TCL XV, Nr. 18 iii 3-iv; Rd?	--	--	[. . .]-nir-ra sag-íl	-	-	-	-	-	x	-
Ninšubura?	Š	SLTNi, Nr. 76	--	--	[. . .]	[						]

268

Rubriken				Redeform					Person, bezogen auf Gott					Versuch einer Gliederung in Strophen von n Zeilen			Strophengliederung nach
sa-gar-ra	giš-gi$_4$-gál	uru$_x$(=ULÙ)-EN-bi	a-da-ab-DN	sa-gíd-da	giš-gi$_4$-gál	sa-gar-ra	giš-gi$_4$-gál	uru$_x$(=ULÙ)-EN-bi	sa-gíd-da	giš-gi$_4$-gál	sa-gar-ra	giš-gi$_4$-gál	uru$_x$(=ULÙ)-EN-bi	sa-gíd-da	sa-gar-ra	uru$_x$(=ULÙ)-EN-bi	
x	⟨x⟩	x	x	D	[	]H	H	H	2	[ ]	2?	2	2	?	?	3	R_1: uru$_x$(=ULÙ)-EN-bi
	]	x	x	D[				]	3	[			]	?	?	?	?
x	x	x	x	D[		]N	?	D	3	[ ]	3?	?	3?	?	?	3	R_1: uru$_x$(=ULÙ)-EN-bi
x	x	x	x	DH	-	D	D	D	2	-	0	0	0	4,4,4 [ ],?	9 (1 Strophe!)	3	T, S, Refrain; R_1: uru$_x$(=ULÙ)-EN-bi
x	-	x̣	x	D	[ ]	H	-	H	2	[ ]	2	-	2	?	?	3	
x	x	x	x	D	D	DH	H	D	2	3?	2	?	2	?	?	3	R_1: uru$_x$(=ULÙ)-EN-bi
[			]x̣	D	?	[		]	2	?	[		]	[?], 4?,4, 3,3,4, 3,3	[	]	R_1, R_1,, T
x	-	x	x	DH	H	DH	-	D	2	2	2 3	-	2	4,6,4, 6,4,6	?	3	S, T, R_4; R_1: uru$_x$(=ULÙ)-EN-bi
x	-	[x	x]	D	H	DH	-	D?	2	2	2	-	2	?	6?,5?, 5?,3,3, 3,3	3	T, R_1 (die drei Teile)
x	x	x	x	D	[ ]	DH	H	H	2	[ ]	2	2	2	4,4,4, 4,4,4, 4,[ ]	[ ],4,4, 4,4,4,4	3	R_2; R_1: uru$_x$(=ULÙ)-EN-bi
x]	x̣	x	x	DH	[?	?]	?	D	3	[?	?]	?	3	12,16, [...]	?	3	R_3; R_1: uru$_x$(=ULÙ)-EN-bi
x	x	x	x	D	D	[]DH	D	D	2	2	2	3?	2	4,4,2	[ ],3	3	S, T; R_1: uru$_x$(=ULÙ)-EN-bi
x	x	x	-	DN	[?]	N	D	H	2	[?]	0	0	0	4,3,4, 3, [...]	?	3	$R_{2/3}$; R_1: uru$_x$(=ULÙ)-EN-bi
[			]	DH	-	N[		]	3?	-	3	[	]	?	?	?	?
x	-	x	-	?	[ ]	?	-	H	?	[ ]	?	-	3	?	?	3	R_1: uru$_x$(=ULÙ)-EN-bi

Tabelle a-da-ab

Gott	Kö-nig	Quellen	Über-setzung Bear-beitung	Kata-log	Anfang	Rubriken						
						bar-sù	šà-ba-TUK	bar-sù-2	šà-ba-TUK-2	bar-sù-3	sa-gíd-da	*(?)*
Ninurta[w]	ID	*STVC*, Nr. 72 rev. + *ISET* I 210, Ni. 9774 rev.	--	--	[. . .]	[				]	x	x
Ninurta[x,y]	LE	*ISET* I 100, Ni. 9695	*SKIZ*, S. 6-9	JB 67	ur-sag á-gál-a-nun-ke₄-ne	x	x	x	-	-	x	x
Ninurta[x]	UNi	*TCL* XV, Nr. 19	*ZA*, Bd. 49, S. 116-22	--	ur-sag ušum ní-ri	x	x	x	-	-	x	x
Ninurta[z]	BS	*BE* XXIX, Nr. 1 iii 37-iv	--	--	[. . .] kur-gal-e tu-da	-	-	-	-	-	x	x
Ninurta[hh]	--	*BE* XXIX, Nr. 5	--	--	[. . .]	-	-	-	-	-	x	-
Nuska[aa]	ID	UM 29-16-21; *ISET* I, 98-99, Ni. 4464	*ZA*, Bd. 63, S. 1-55	--	[. . .]	-	-	-	-	-	x	[
Su'en[x,bb]	ŠS	*TMH* NF IV, Nr. 12	--	(Y 6)	x̱ še-er-ri idim-ta	x	x	x	x	-	x	x
Su'en[cc]	IS	CBS 8526	*OrS* XIX/XX 147-49	--	[xx]-an-ki sù-DU-ág	-	-	-	-	-	x	-
Utu[dd]	--	*ISET* I 114, Ni. 4450	--	--	[. . .]	[				]	x	-
Utu	Š	*SRT*, Nr. 15	--	--	[. . .]	[-	-	-	-	-]	x	x
?[ee]	ID	*ISET* I 136, Ni. 4157	--	--	[. . .]	[						
?	?	*ISET* I 134, Ni. 4141	--	--	[. . .]	[						
?[ff]	?	*ISET* I 127, Ni. 4058	--	--	[. . .]	[				]	x	x
?[ff]	?	*ISET* I 129, Ni. 4088	--	--	[. . .]	[				]	x?	[
?[ff,gg]	ID	*SRT*, Nr. 36:45-61	--	--	èš nibru[ki] abzu-a ab-diri	-	-	-	-	-	x	

Rubriken				Redeform					Person, bezogen auf Gott					Versuch einer Gliederung in Strophen von n Zeilen			Strophen-gliederung nach
sa-gar-ra	giš-gi$_4$-gál	uru$_x$(=ULÙ)-EN-bi	a-da-ab-DN	sa-gíd-da	giš-gi$_4$-gál	sa-gar-ra	giš-gi$_4$-gál	uru$_x$(=ULÙ)-EN-bi	sa-gíd-da	giš-gi$_4$-gál	sa-gar-ra	giš-gi$_4$-gál	uru$_x$(=ULÙ)-EN-bi	sa-gíd-da	sa-gar-ra	uru$_x$(=ULÙ)-EN-bi	
[			]	?	?	?	[	]	?	?	?	[	]	?	?	[?]	?
x	x	x	x	ND	H	DH	H?	H	2	2	2	2	2	3,7,3,7	?	3	T; R$_1$: uru$_x$(=ULÙ)-EN-bi
x	x	x	x	DH	H	D	H	H	2	2	2	2	2	4,3,3,3,3,4	4,3,3,4,3,3	3	T, S; R$_1$: uru$_x$(=ULÙ)-EN-bi
x	x	x	x	DH	H	D	?	?	3	3	2	?	2	?	6,?	3	R$_1$
x	[-		]	D	-	D	[	]	2	-	0	[	]	?	12	[ ]	Refrain
	]			D	H?	DH	[	]	2	?	?	[	]	?	?	[ ]	?
x	⟨x⟩	x	[?]	D	H	DN?	H?	H?	3	2	2?	?	2?	6,5,5,??	6?,4?,4?,4?,4	3	T, S; R$_1$: uru$_x$(=ULÙ)-EN-bi
⟨x⟩	x	x	x	D	-	N?	D?	D	3	-	3	3	3	10,10,10,10	4,4,4,4,4	3	R$_3$; R$_1$: uru$_x$(=ULÙ)-EN-bi
x	-	x	x	D	-	D	-	D?	2?	-	1	-	2?	[ ],?,2,3	1+3,11,3	2	Refrain, totale Rep.
x	x	[	]	DH	H	DH	D	D?	3	2	3?	3	?	[ ],6?,5?,6?	?	3?	S, T, R$_4$; R$_1$: uru$_x$(=ULÙ)-EN-bi
	]	x̣	[ ]														
]	x	-	[ ]	[	]	DH	-	[ ]	[	]	2	-	[?]	[...]	?	2 + [1]	
[			]														
			]														

(*a*) *STVC*, Nr. 65 ist eine Sammeltafel mit a-da-ab-Kompositionen auf An; Kol. v, Z. 29 – Kol. vi, Z. 5 und Kol. vi, Z. 6–31 sind noch nicht identifiziert.

(*b*) In Kol. iv, Z. 6 ist giš-gi₄-gál-sa-gíd-da-[kam] Schreibfehler für giš-gi₄-gál-sa-gar-ra-kam; in Kol. iv, Z. 4 ist nur sa-[. . .] erhalten.

(*c*) *VS* X, Nr. 199 ist eine Sammeltafel mit 2 a-da-ab und 2 bal-bal-e.

(*d*) Zweites bar-sù nach zweitem šà-ba-TUK. *VS* X, Nr. 199 schreibt sa-bar-suₓ(= GÍD)-da-àm statt sa-gíd-da-àm in *STVC*, Nr. 65. Die 2. Person im giš-gi₄-gál zum sa-gar-ra kann sich auf den König beziehen.

(*e*) Im sa-gar-ra beginnende Rede An's im uruₓ(= ULÙ)-EN-bi-im fortgesetzt. Heischend nur die beiden letzten Strophen des sa-gar-ra und das uruₓ(= ULÙ)-EN-bi-im. Rubrik šà-ba-TUK innerhalb einer Strophe. Der Königsname (nur *VS* X, Nr. 199) wird abgekürzt geschrieben: ᵈur.

(*f*) Rubriken sa-gar-ra-àm und uruₓ(= ULÙ)-EN-bi-im nicht im Text; nach dem Schema der drei letzten Zeilen (R-1) ergänzt. Namentlich nicht genannter König (lum-ma, lugal-lum-ma, "üppiger (König)"); anders Kramer, in *BiOr* XI 172, Anm. 19). Formen wie mu-u₈-da-mah-di (Z. 33) sprechen für ein spätes Datum des Textes.

(*g*) Stichzeile en eš-bar-galam-dingir-rᵀe-e-neᵀ sig-nim-ma uₓ(= ULÙ)-ru-bi ist Anfang von UM 29–16–3 (Å. Sjöberg, in *ZA*, Bd. 63, S. 40 ff.), wo im erhaltenen Teil (die ersten 41 Zeilen) keine Rubrik.

(*h*) Der Herausgeber dieses Fragments, Sjöberg, in *ZA*, Bd. 63, S. 19 ff., zieht es zum a-da-ab auf Nusku (s.u.). Stichzeile: [. . . dingir]-re-ne igi-šè [. . .].

(*i*) Letzte Teilbearbeitung: Å. Sjöberg, "Die göttliche Abstammung der sumerisch-babylonischen Herrscher," *OrS* XXI (1973) 103–5. Im giš-gi₄-gál zum sa-gar-ra ist der König in der 2. Person angeredet (sonst 3. Person).

(*j*) *SKIZ*, S. 2, fasst *TCL* XV, Nr. 18 als nur eine "Königshymne" auf. Dies ist unmöglich, da in Kol. iii, Z. 1 die Unterschrift [uruₓ(= ULÙ)-EN-bi-im a-da-ab-ᵈen-1]íl-lá-kam steht. Wiederholungen von sa-gíd-da und sa-gar-ra innerhalb eines Textes kommen beim a-da-ab (sonst) nicht vor. Darum ist *TCL* XV, Nr. 18 eine Sammeltafel mit a-da-ab-Liedern auf Enlil und Ninlil für Išme-Dagān. Trennstriche finden sich im ersten a-da-ab auf Enlil vor den Rubriken sa-gíd-da-àm und giš-gi₄-gál-sa-gíd-da-bi-im; im zweiten a-da-ab auf Enlil vor und nach Kol. ii, Z. 3 und vor und nach den Rubriken sa-gíd-da-àm, sa-gar-ra-àm und [uruₓ(= ULÙ)-EN-bi-im a-da-ab-ᵈen-1]íl-lá-kam; im a-da-ab auf Ninlil vor und nach der Rubrik sa-gíd-da-àm und Kol. iii, Z. 28. Der Schluss des Textes (l. Rd.) ist unklar.

(*k*) Die 2. Person im sa-gar-ra bezieht sich in Rs. 1′–4′ auf den Gott, in Rs. 5′–9′ aber auf den König.

(*l*) Text schreibt a-tab für a-da-ab. Die letzten Zeilen von sa-gíd-da und sa-gar-ra sind identisch.

(*m*) Lesungen [uruₓ(= ULÙ)-E]N-bi-im und [a-da-a]b-ᵈinanna-kam durch freundliche Kollation von A. Shaffer bestätigt. Rubrik giš-gi₄-gál-sa-gar-ra-kam fehlt, kann aber nach dem Schema der letzten drei Zeilen restituiert werden (R-1); s. Anm. *f, bb, dd.*

(*n*) Nur ganz kleines Fragment.

(*o*) Sa-gar-ra nur eine Strophe mit gleichem Refrain, der im uruₓ(= ULÙ)-EN-bi-im wieder aufgenommen wird. Hier wird der Gott nicht erwähnt; vgl. unten Ninurta: *BE* XXIX, Nr. 5.

(*p*) N 3324 kann auch zu einer anderen Dichtung gehören.

(*q*) Stichzeile: [x x (x)]-ÍL-mah-zu an-ki nam-nir-ra šu-du₇.

(*r*) Da der Schluss fehlt, kann der Text auch ein tigi sein.

(*s*) Bar-sù, šà-ba-TUK und uruₓ(= ULÙ)-EN-bi-im-Rubriken in CBS 14074 ausgelassen. *SRT*, Nr. 12 schreibt [sa]-bar-sù-da-àm (s.o., Anm. *d*). Der Name des Gottes erscheint alle zwei Zeilen. Dieses Prinzip wird nur aufgegeben, wenn an dieser Stelle der Königsname steht. Erste und zweite Strophe beginnen mit fast denselben Worten. Rubriken im sa-gíd-da-Teil stimmen mit Strophengrenzen überein.

(*t*) Rubriken sa-gar-ra-àm und uru$_x$(= ULÙ)-EN-bi-im fehlen; s. aber giš-gi$_4$-gál-sa-gar-ra-bi-im in Rs. 26.

(*u*) Heischend nur im Prolog (2 Strophen).

(*v*) Sänger nennt die Göttin nin-mu, "meine Herrin."

(*w*) Fragmentarisch, vielleicht auch tigi; hier aufgenommen, da die Vs. der Sammeltafel ein a-da-ab enthält. Ist die Stichzeile im Duplikat zur Vs. (s.o., Anm. *g*) der Anfang dieses Liedes?

(*x*) Strophengrenzen und Rubriken stimmen überein.

(*y*) Trennstriche vor der Rubrik bar-sù, vor und nach der letzten Zeile des sa-gar-ra und vor der Notiz uru$_x$(= ULÙ)-EN-bi-im.

(*z*) Trennstrich vor Rubrik sa-gíd-da-àm. *BE* XXIX, Nr. 1 ist eine Sammeltafel, die auch tigi-Texte enthält.

(*aa*) Siehe oben, Anm. *h*.

(*bb*) Text schreibt [sa]-bar-sù-da-àm für sa-gíd-da-àm; s.o. Anm. *d*. Der Sprecher gebraucht die 1. Person: "mein Šū-Sîn," "mein König." Die Rubrik giš-gi$_4$-gál-bi-im nach dem sa-gar-ra fehlt, kann aber nach dem Schema der letzten drei Zeilen ergänzt werden (R–1); s. auch Anm. *f* und *m*.

(*cc*) Rubrik sa-gar-ra-àm ausgelassen, kann aber wegen giš-gi$_4$-gál-bi-im in Z. 62 restituiert werden. Sprecher gebraucht die 1. Person: "mein Ibbi-Sîn."

(*dd*) Die 2. bis 4. Zeile des sa-gar-ra identisch mit dessen letzten 3 Zeilen (Einrahmung der mittleren Strophe). Die 1. Zeile nach der Rubrik sa-gíd-da-àm könnte darum das giš-gi$_4$-gál zum sa-gíd-da sein. Da sie jedoch denselben Refrain zeigt wie die mittlere Strophe, gehört sie wahrscheinlicher bereits zum sa-gar-ra. Die 11 Zeilen der mittleren Strophe enden alle in NAGA-e ú-a (mir unverständlich); sie können auch als abgekürzte Schreibungen für Strophen verstanden werden, die analog der ersten (und letzten) gebaut wären. Dieser Text enthält das einzige uru$_x$(= ULÙ)-EN-bi mit nur 2 Zeilen Umfang.

(*ee*) Stichzeile: AN [. . .].

(*ff*) Oder tigi? Texte fragmentarisch; *SRT*, Nr. 36:45–61 unvollständig gelassen.

(*gg*) Ein dem a-da-ab verwandter Text (hinsichtlich der Rubriken) ist UM 29–16–51 (S. N. Kramer, "Hymn to the Ekur," *RSO* XXXII [1957] 95–102). Er notiert: sa-gíd-da-àm (Z. 28), giš-gi$_4$-gál-bi-im (Z. 30), ki-UD-ru-gú-dam (Z. 42), [sa-gar-r]a-àm (Z. 53), giš-gi$_4$-gál-bi-im (Z. 55), wahrscheinlich eine ausgelassene Rubrik nach Z. 68, giš-gi$_4$-gál-bi-im (Z. 70, letzte Zeile). Die Abschnitte vor den einzelnen Rubriken (mit Ausnahme der jeweiligen giš-gi$_4$-gál) sind durch verschiedene Refrains gekennzeichnet. Die Rubrik ki-UD-ru-gú-dam und den langen Passus nach dem sa-gar-ra-Abschnitt kenne ich anderweitig nicht.

(*hh*) Vorder- und Rückseite der Tafel zu vertauschen oder Sammeltafel?—Ersteres wahrscheinlicher. Sa-gar-ra-Teil nur eine Strophe mit festem Refrain: nun-e dúr-gar-ra. Der Gott wird in diesem Teil nicht erwähnt. Vom uru$_x$(= ULÙ)-EN-bi-Abschnitt (oder giš-gi$_4$-gál zum sa-gar-ra) ist nur das 1. Zeichen erhalten, Rest abgebrochen. Zum Typ dieses Textes vgl. das a-da-ab auf Nanna *SLTNi*, Nr. 58+ (s.o. bei Anm. *o*).

Gott	König	Quellen	Übersetzung/ Bearbeitung	Katalog
Baba[a]	ŠS	*SRT*, Nr. 23	*WO* I 43-50; *JCS* VII 46-47	JA 21
Enki[b]	ID	*ISET* I 95, Ni. 4105, 210, Ni. 4403, 3 NT 500	--	--
Inanna[c]	ŠS	*ISET* I 90, Ni. 2461	*Belleten* XVI 345-65; Jacobsen und Wilson, *Most Ancient Verse*, S. 11	--
Inanna[d]	ŠS	*PAPS*, Bd. 107, S. 521, N 3560, N 4305	*PAPS*, Bd. 107, S. 508	--
Inanna?[e]	ŠS?	*ISET* I 118, Ni. 4569 i 15 ff.	--	As II 50?
Inanna[f]	Ur III König	*TAD* VIII/2, Taf. 29, Ni. 4563	--	--
Inanna[g]	ID	*TCL* XVI, Nr. 97; YBC 6409	*BiOr* XXIII 244-45	--
Inanna	--	*SRT*, Nr. 9:1-21	--	JA 18
Inanna[h]	--	*SRT*, Nr. 5; *PAPS*, Bd. 107, S. 521, N 4305 Rs. i 1'-ii 3'; CBS 8037	--	--
[Inanna][h']	--	*UET* VI, Nr. 121 Vs., 122; *STVC*, Nr. 107; *PAPS*, Bd. 107, S. 521, N 4305 ii 1-9; *ISET* I 118, Ni. 4569 i 1-14	*PAPS*, Bd. 107, S. 510	As II 49?
[Inanna][i]	--	*TMH* NF IV, Nr. 55	--	--
Inanna[j]	--	*TCL* XV, Nr. 20:66-76; *UET* VI, Nr. 121 Rs.	*PAPS*, Bd. 107, S. 508-9	As II 52
Inanna[k]	--	*PAPS*, Bd. 107, S. 522-23, UM 29-16-8, 524, Ni. 4552	*PAPS*, Bd. 107, S. 509-10	--
Inanna	--	*PBS* XII, Nr. 39	--	--
Inanna	--	*BE* XXX, Nr. 4; *PAPS*, Bd. 107, S. 521, N. 4305 i	*SSA*, S. 65-85	--
Inanna[l]	--	*SRT*, Nr. 31	Kramer, *Sacred Marriage*, S. 104-06	--
Inanna[m]	--	*ISET* I 118, Ni. 4569 ii [?]-[39']; *SLTNi*, Nr. 90	--	--
(Inanna)	--	*ISET* I 118, Ni. 4569 ii [34']-iii 23	--	--

274

Anfang	Rubriken		Stichzeile	Sammeltafel*	Redeform	'Geschlecht' und Zahl der Sprecher	Person, bezogen auf Gott	Versuch einer Gliederung in Strophen	Strophengliederung nach
	bal-bal-e-DN	giš-gi₄-gál							
kù-ga-àm in-tu-ud	x	–	–	–	DH	1m, 1f	0	6,6,6,4,5	Sprecher, T, Refrain
[. . .]	x	x	x	–	DH	?	2?,1?	?	?
mu-tin šà-gá	x	–	–	–	H	1f	0	4,4,6,4,3,2 4,2	R₂, R₄
siki-mu ḫi-is-sar-àm	x	–	–	B	D	nf, 1m	1	?	?
[. . .]x x in-tu-ud	[-]	[-]	–	A	D	?	0?	?	? (Refrain)
[. . .]	x	x?	–	–	D?	?	3?	?	?
áb KA-du₁₀-ga	x	–	–	–	H	1m?	2	3,6,6,8,7,6	R₂, R₄, Refrain
u₄-ḫuš-gal-m[è-a]	x	–	–	D	D	1m	2	2,4,4,4,4,2	R₁, T, S
nin₉-mu é-a a-na-àm mu-e-[ak]	x	(x)	–	B	D	2f, 1m	2,1	2,3,3,4,3,3, 4,4,6,6,2, 5,2	Sprecher, R₄, Refrain
x lam-lam-ma [. . .]	x	–	–	A,B, C	DH	nf, 1f	1	2,6,4?,4	Refrain
[. . .]	[ ]	[ ]	–	–	D	?	?		
ba-lam ba-lam-lam ḫi-is-sar-àm a ba-an-du₁₁	x	–	–	C,E	D	1f	1	4,4,2	Refrain
[. . .]	x	⟨?⟩	–	F	N	1f, (1m)	1,(2)		
ga-ša-an-ĝen gi-rin-e u₆ ga-e-da-du₁₁	x	–	–	–	DH	1f	1	4,4,[...]..	R₄
šeš-e nin₉-ra mí na-mu-e	x	–	–	B	DH	1m, 1f	2,1	2,2,3,3,3,2, 3,2,3,2,3,2, 3,2,3,2,2,6,6	Sprecher, Refrain
lu-bi-mu lu-bi-mu	x	–	–	–	DH	1m, 1f	2,1	3,3,3,3,4,4, 6,6	Refrains, Sprecher, S
[. . .]	x	–	–	A	DH	1f	1	[...],5,5,4, ...	Refrain
[. . .]	–	–	–	A	D	1f	1		

Tabelle bal-bal-e

Gott	König	Quellen	Übersetzung/ Bearbeitung	Katalog
Inanna[n]	--	*ISET* I 118, Ni. 4569 iii 24-iv [45]; *TCL* XV, Nr. 20:1-65; *VS* X, Nr. 156	Civil in *Studies . . . Oppenheim*, S. 67-80	--
(Inanna)	--	*TMH* NF III, Nr. 24 ii 1'-4'	--	--
(Inanna)	--	*TMH* NF III, Nr. 24 ii 5'-13'	--	--
(Inanna)[o]	--	*TMH* NF III, Nr. 24 iii; *PAPS*, Bd. 107, S. 524, Ni. 4552 Rs. 1'-10'	--	--
(Inanna)[p]	--	*TMH* NF III, Nr. 24 iv 1'	--	--
(Inanna)	--	*TMH* NF III, Nr. 24 iv 2'-14'	--	--
Inanna[q]	--	*VS* X, Nr. 199 iii 8-41; *PAPS*, Bd. 107, S. 521, N. 4305 Rs. ii 4'-[36']	Römer, *Or* n.s. 38, S. 97-104	--
Nanna-Suen[r]	(König)	*SRT*, Nr. 9:22-82; *TCL* XV, Nr. 21; *TMH* NF IV, Nr. 7 i 1'-ii [5]	*MNS* I 13-34	JA 2
Nanna[s]	--	*TMH* NF IV, Nr. 7 ii [6]-iii 6	--	(JA3)
Nanna[t]	(Enḫeduanna)	*TMH* NF IV, Nr. 7 iii 7-iv 18	--	--
Nanna[u]	UN?	*TMH* NF IV, Nr. 7 iv 20-[58?]; *ISET* I 62, Ni. 9788	--	--
Nanše	--	*VS* X, Nr. 199 iii 42-iv 23	--	--
Ninazu[v]	--	*PBS* XIII, Nr. 41	*SGL* II 57-80	JA 17
Ningizzida[w]	--	*UET* VI, Nr. 70; *ISET* I 187, Ni. 9808	--	--
Ningizzida[x]	--	*TCL* XV, Nr. 25	*SGL* II 81-107	--
Ninkasi[y]				
Ninurta[z]	--	*SLTNi*, Nr. 62	*SAHG*, Nr. 1; *ANET* (1969) S. 576-77	--

276

Anfang	Rubriken		Stichzeile	Sammeltafel*	Redeform	'Geschlecht' und Zahl der Sprecher	Person, bezogen auf Gott	Versuch einer Gliederung in Strophen	Strophen-gliederung nach
	giš-gíd-gál	bal-bal-e-DN							
a-zal-le ù-tu-da	x	-	-	A,E	D,H	1m? nf, 1f	(1)	4,4,4,4,4,4, 4,4,4,4,4,4, 10,5,5,11	R$_2$, S
[. . .]	-	-	-	G	?	?	1		
[ama?-u]gu-mu za-a-ra gá-a im-mi-in-tu-ud-en	-	-	-	G	?	1f	1	2,2,2,[...]	R$_1$
[. . .]	-	-	-	G,F		1f	1	[...],4?,2,2, 3,3,4	
[. . .]	-	-	-	G					
[. . .] na mu-un-ri	-	-	-	G			1	4?,4?,5?,[..]	Refrain
a-mu an ma-an-zé-eĝ$_x$ (= ÁG)	x̣	-	-	H,B	D	1f	1	9,4,4,4?,12	Refrain, S, T
me-a lu áb me-a lu-lu	x	-	x	D,I	N,D H	2?m, 1f	3,2,1	2,4,4,4,2,4, 4,2,6,4,4,4, 2,4,4,4,2	S, T, Sprecher
(me-a-am-ra me-e mu-u[n- . . .])	x	-	-	I	H	1m, 2?f	2,3	[...]...,4,5	T, S, Sprecher
é u$_4$-gim è-a ki-en-gi-ra	x	x	-	I	D,H	1(f)	3,2	?	?
lu-lu-a-bi lu-lu-a-bi ú-šim ki-dar-re-dam	x	-	-	I	D	2?m	3	5,4,5?,5?,4, 5, . . .	T, S
[. . .]x̣ šu-du$_7$-a	x	-	-	H	D	1?, 1f	3,1	...[...],6?, 6,8,2	T, S, Sprecher
lugal uru áb-gim lu-a [. . .]	x	-	-	-	D	1m	2	3,4,5,5,6,3	R$_1$, R$_4$, R$_5$
en me-te-kù-ga ní-ḫuš gal gùr-ru	x	-	-	-	D	1m	2	6,2,2,3,...	R$_4$, (R$_1$)
[ur]-sag en šà-túm a-gàr ur-maḫ kur-sù-da	x	-	-	-	D	1m	2	8,5,...,4,3	R$_4$
a-zi-da numun-zi-da	x	-	-	-	D,H	1m	2	4,3,3,3, [...],2?,8	R$_2$, R$_4$, Refrain

* Sammeltafeln: A = *ISET* I 118–19, Ni. 4569; B = Kramer, in *PAPS*, Bd. 107, S. 521, N 3405; C = *UET* VI/1, Nr. 121; D = *SRT*, Nr. 9; E = *TCL* XV, Nr. 20; F = Kramer, in *PAPS*, Bd. 107, S. 524, Ni. 4452; G = *TMH* NF III, Nr. 24; H = *VS* X, Nr. 199; I = *TMH* NF IV, Nr. 7.

(*a*) Zum quasi-Duplikat *ISET* I 118, Ni. 4569 i 15–33 s.u. zu Inanna (bei Anm. *e*). Die Göttin Baba ist im (erhaltenen) Text nicht genannt. Sprecher reden Königin und König an.

(*b*) Stichzeile [. . .]⸢x⸣ SIG₇ lugal an-kù [. . .]. Text fragmentarisch. Ni. 4105 Vs. redet den Gott an (2. Pers.); Rs. 4′–6′ zeigt Dative der 2. Pers. und einen der 1.: anscheinend redet der Gott zum König. Die letzten 4 Zeilen nennen den König in der 3. Pers.

(*c*) Göttin im Text nicht erwähnt. Sie könnte die Sprecherin sein, obwohl wir erwarten, dass dies eine junge Frau, vielleicht eine lukur-kaskal-la, ist. Auffällig die Kohortative mit ga- in Z. 6, 8 und 12; ferner dingir (nicht dìm-me-er) in Z. 24; s. auch unten, Anm. *h*.

(*d*) Sprecher von Vs. 1–12 und Rs. 4′–5′ gebraucht den Hauptdialekt (9, 10: lú; Rs. 4′: igi). Dem Inhalt zufolge scheint aber Inanna die Zeilen zu sprechen. In Rs. 1′–3′ (eme-sal) sprechen die Schwestern.

(*e*) Quasi-Duplikat zu *SRT*, Nr. 23 (s.o., Anm. *a*). Da alle identifizierbaren Texte auf der Sammeltafel A bal-bal-e der Inanna sind, ordne ich dieses Lied der Inanna zu. Der Name des Königs ist im erhaltenen Teil nicht genannt; vielleicht Šū-Sîn wie in *SRT*, Nr. 23. Anfang vielleicht zu ergänzen nach Katalog As ii 50, lál-li lál-li lál-li im-du-ud.

(*f*) Der fragmentarische Text bezieht sich auf einen König von Ur, da l. Rd. 3–4 die göttlichen Eltern der Ur III-Könige nennt: [. . .ᵈ]⸢ù-mu⸣-un-bàn-da // [. . .ᵈga-š]a-an-sún-na. Rubrik giš-gi₄-gál erscheint vielleicht verschrieben vor der Unterschrift und dem doppelten Schlusstrich: ⸢x⸣ GÁL.GIŠ.KI(?) [. . .].

(*g*) Unterschrift bal-bal-e fehlt in *TCL* XVI, Nr. 87, wo aber eine Zeile hinzugefügt. Die vorletzte Zeile weicht von der letzten des Duplikats ab. Da die letzte Zeile den Satz der vorletzten fortzusetzen scheint (s. *SKIZ*, S. 22), handelt es sich wohl nicht um eine Stichzeile.

(*h*) Rubrik giš-gi₄-gál-bi-im und die damit gekennzeichneten letzten 2 Zeilen nur in *SRT*, Nr. 5, dort aber nach der Unterschrift. N 4305 gibt eine Summe von 52 Zeilen an, d.h. 7 Zeilen mehr, als *SRT*, Nr. 5 vor der Unterschrift hat. Das unveröff. Dupl. CBS 8037 (von M. Civil identifiziert) erwähnt Å. Sjöberg, in *JCS* XXV (1973) 131. Sprecher sind Utu (Bruder Inanna's: Z. 1–2, 21, 23–28, 47–48?), Inanna (Z. 3–18, 39–45) und Baba (hier Schwester Inanna's: Z. 19–20, 22, 29). Auffällig sind die Kohortative des Hauptdialekts (ga-, nicht da-) in Z. 41 und 43, wo wegen des Inhalts der Aussage nur eine weibliche Person als Sprecherin möglich ist.

(*h′*) Vgl. Katalog As ii 49, ni-ig-li AN-al-la-am-ma a-ma-gu-un-na-ki.

(*i*) Hier angeführt wegen des Refrains auf (. . .-me) hé-me-en.

(*j*) Katalog As ii 52, ba-lam ba-lál-li hi-is-sa-me(-)e pa-t[u(?!)]. Reihenfolge der beiden letzten Zeilen in den Dupl. verschieden. Z. 1–4 eme-sal (ág in Z. 4, s. aber gar in Z. 2); Z. 5–10 Hauptdialekt (lú, in, giri). Unterschrift in *TCL* XV, Nr. 20 (2 bal-bal-e-ᵈinanna) bezieht sich auch auf a-zal-le ù-tu-da; s.u. bei Anm. *n*.

(*k*) Soweit erhalten, spricht nur die Göttin Inanna, die die Worte ihres Liebhabers zitiert. Die beiden letzten fragmentarischen Zeilen nach der Unterschrift können zu einem giš-gi₄-gál gehören, auch wenn diese Rubrik nicht erscheint. Siehe jetzt die Neubearbeitung durch Th. Jacobsen, "The Sister's Message," *Journal of the Ancient Near Eastern Society*, Bd. 5 (1973) S. 199–212, der den Text als Dialog zwischen Geštinanna und Dumuzi versteht.

(*l*) In Z. 13–16 und 25 heisst na-áĝ-erím ma-ku₅-dè-en wahrscheinlich "Du wirst mir schwören, dass du . . ." (assertorischer Eid) und nicht "und dennoch verfluchst du mich" (A. Falkenstein, "Tammuz," *CRRA* III 62) oder "you have been decreed an evil fate" (S. N. Kramer, *The Sacred Marriage Rite* [Bloomington, London, 1969] S. 105).

Die Strophengliederung des von Inanna gesprochenen zweiten Teils (Z. 13–32) kann sich an den Refrains orientieren: Z. 13–16 nam-eŕim ma-ku₅-dè-en; Z. 17–20 šeš-i-bí-sa₆-sa₆-mu (teilweise ergänzt; auch Z. 18 so?); Z. 27–32 hi-li-zu zé-ba-àm. (Die Zeilen 21–24 enden in finite Verbalformen, die darauf folgenden beiden Zeilen 25–26 bringen die Refrains von Z. 13–16 und 17–20.)

Anders der von Dumuzi gesprochene erste Teil (Z. 1–12). Hier wechseln von Zeile zu Zeile (ab Z. 3) die Refrains ka-làl-ama-na-mu und gen nin₉-ki-ág-mu. Die syntaktische Struktur zwingt aber m.E. zu einer mit der Refrain-Folge nicht übereinstimmenden Strophenabtrennung: Z. 1–3 je Zeile 3 Vokative mit Suffix -mu; Z. 4–6 "Von deinem . . . (= Körperteil) das . . . (= Tätigkeit) ma-du₁₀" vor Refrain; Z. 7–9 "Von deinem . . . (= Sache) hast du das . . . (= Produkt?) in-du₁₀" vor Refrain; Z. 10–12 fragmentarisch. Graphisch lässt sich das Verhältnis von Refrains und Strophengrenzen in diesem ersten Abschnitt so darstellen:

Zeile	1	2	3	4	5	6	7	8	9	10	11	12
Refrain a		x			x		x	x			x	
Refrain b				x		x		x		x		x

(*m*) *SLTNi*, Nr. 90 lässt Z. 26–28 von Ni. 4569 ii aus.

(*n*) *VS* X, Nr. 156 hat nach Z. 48 einen Trennstrich, der in beiden Duplikaten fehlt. Vor diesem Einschnitt ist der Text im Hauptdialekt abgefasst und in Strophen vom Typ R–2 gegliedert. Nach Z. 48 finden sich eme-sal-Formen, und die strophische Gliederung nach R-2 ist aufgegeben. Ausserdem wechselt der Text von der hymnischen Beschreibung (angeredet Ninkasi) zu heischenden Formen und dem Erscheinen einer 1. Pers. Pl. und zum Schluss auch einer 1. Pers. Sing. Zur Unterschrift in *TCL* XV, Nr. 20 s.o., Anm. *j*. *VS* X, Nr. 156, l. Rd. kann nach H. Zimmerns Kopie [. . . ᵈnin-k]a-si-kam gelesen werden. Nach freundlicher Kollation von H. Freydank sind die Spuren nicht so deutlich und eine Lesung [. . .-ᵈ]⌈i⌉nann⌈a⌉-kam kann nicht ganz ausgeschlossen werden.

(*o*) In Ni. 4552 folgt ein weiterer Text, vielleicht ebenfalls ein bal-bal-e mit Anfang šul ᵈnanna-mu lú-⌈x⌉[. . .].

(*p*) Letzte und einzige erhaltene Zeile: [. . .]-r⌈a-ab-bé⌉-en; danach Trennstrich.

(*q*) Unterschrift (nur *VS* X, Nr. 199): [. . .]-ᵈinanna-kam. Bereits H. Zimmern (Einleitung zu *VS* X), gefolgt von A. Falkenstein, in *SAHG*, Nr. 7, und S. N. Kramer, in *ANET* (3. Aufl.) S. 579, ergänzte [bal-bal-e]. Dagegen W. H. Ph. Römer, in *SKIZ*, der den Text als šir-nam-šub ansieht. Für die Ergänzung bal-bal-e spricht das in *VS* X, Nr. 199 folgende bal-bal-e der Nanše und dass Ni. 4305—soweit identifizierbar—nur bal-bal-e-Kompositionen enthält.

(*r*) Vgl. Katalog As ii 51 ma-a-al-lu ki nam al-la-ma-an-gu, Titel eines anderen, wohl mit me-a lu beginnenden Liedes. Unser Text hat zwei Sprecher: einen Erzähler (wohl auch Fragesteller in Z. 1.2) und einen Sänger (wohl auch Antwortgebender in Z. 3–6). Der Erzähler gebraucht den epischen Stil und berichtet wörtliche Reden von Ninlil und ihrem Sohn Nanna (mit Redeeinleitungsformeln). Von Nanna spricht er als "mein Herr" (lugal-mu). Die dem Sänger zuzuordnenden Abschnitte (Z. 3–6, 21–24, 33–36, 45[?]–60) heben sich deutlich durch ihren hymnischen Stil ab. Z. 60 spricht von einem von Nanna unterschiedenen lugal; dies kann nur ein irdischer König sein. Unterschrift in *SRT*, Nr. 9 bal-bal-e-ᵈsu'en-na-kam; in *TCL* XV, Nr. 21, bal-bal-e-ᵈna[nna-kam]; dort auch die Stichzeile me-a-am-ra me-e mu-u[n-...], vielleicht der Anfang des nächsten Liedes in unserer Liste.

(*s*) Anfang ergänzt nach der Stichzeile in *TCL* XV, Nr. 21 und Katalog JA 3, da JA 2 me-a lu der Anfang von *TCL* XV, Nr. 21 und dem in der Sammeltafel *TMH* NF IV, Nr. 7 unserem Text vorangehenden bal-bal-e ist; s. auch das eme-sal-Wort me-a-am (s.u., Exkurs), das zweimal in unserem Text erscheint. Zunächst ist Ningal angeredet und von Nanna in der 3. Pers. gesprochen; die letzten 5(?) Zeilen reden Nanna in der 2. Pers. an. Sprecher ist eine en-Priesterin Nanna's in Ur, vielleicht Enheduʾanna, die Tochter Sargons von Akkade.

(*t*) Text fragmentarisch, nur Hauptdialekt. Angesprochen ist die Stadt Ur mit ihrem Tempel Ekišnugal. Nur in den letzten 3 Zeilen wird der Gott angeredet. Sprecher ist Enhedu-ʾanna (s.o., Anm. *s*). Sie nennt den Gott lugal-mu, "mein Herr." Rubrik giš-gi₄-gál-bi-im vor der Unterschrift.

(*u*) Wegen der engen Parallele zu "The Coronation of Urnammu" (W. W. Hallo, in *JCS* XX [1966] 139–41) ist der in Z. 19 erwähnte König vielleicht Urnammu. Der Text nennt auch eine "Frau" (munus), ist eine Priesterin gemeint?

(*v*) Katalog JA schreibt lugal-mu uru áb-gim lu-⌜x⌝. Zur strophischen Gliederung s.o. 4. Der Sprecher/Sänger redet den Gott als "mein Herr" und "mein Herr (en) Ninazu" an.

(*w*) Sprecher nennt Gott "mein Herr." Texte bedürfen der Kollation. Doxologie am Schluss.

(*x*) Beachte die Doxologie an Enki, nicht Ningizzida, am Schluss.

(*y*) Siehe oben bei Anm. *n* zu a-zal-le ù-tu-da.

(*z*) Sprecher nennt Gott "mein Herr." Heischende Redeform: Kohortativ: "Ich will deinen Namen nennen!"

Tabelle ér-šèm-ma

Gott	Quellen	Literatur
Baba[a]	*CT* XV, Taf. 22; *VS* II, Nr. 2 iv 10-44	*HKL*, S. 226
Dingirmaḫ[b]	*VS* X, Nr. 198	--
Dingirmaḫ	*RIAA*, S. 19, 0.17	*ZA*, Bd. 32, S. 56-57
Dumuzi[c]	*CT* XV, Taf. 18; CBS 145	*HKL*, S. 226
Dumuzi	*CT* XV, Taf. 19	*HKL*, S. 226
Dumuzi[d]	*CT* XV, Taf. 20-21	*HKL*, S. 226
Dumuzi	*TMH* NF III, Nr. 26; *PRAK* C 118 Rs. iii	--
(Enlil)[e]	*CT* XV, Taf. 10; *ISET* I 185, Ni. 9798	*HKL*, S. 226
Enlil[f]	*CT* XV, Taf. 7-9; *AfO* XXIV, Taf. III	*HKL*, S. 226; *AfO* XXIV 15-16
Enlil[g] (Ninurta)	*CT* XV, Taf. 11-12; *VS* II, Nr. 2 iii 23-iv 9; *BA*, Bd. 5, S. 632, K 11174	*HKL*, S. 226
Enlil	*CT* XV, Taf. 12-13; *BL* 144; 4R, Taf. 28* Nr. 4 Rs. 5-70; *SBH*, Nr. 46:27-29, Nr. 70 + 85 + VAT 1803; *CT* XLII, Nr. 26 Rs. 11-12	*HKL*, S. 226; J. Krecher, *SKly*, S. 29-30, Anm. 58-59
Enlil[m] (Utu)	*Bab* III 75-76; *VS* II, Nr. 69-71; *ISET* I 219, L 1486	Schollmeyer, *Šamaš*, Nr. 34
Gula	*CT* XXXVI, Taf. 41-42	--
Gula[h]	*CT* XLII, Nr. 7 i-iii 41	*WO* IV 253-59; *ZA*, Bd. 58, S. 32-65
[Gula]	*CT* XLII, Nr. 19	--
Inanna[i]	*VS* II, Nr. 94, 95, 182, *CT* XLII, Nr. 16, XLIV, Nr. 15; *ISET* I 209, Ni. 13237	*WO* IV 253-59; *ZA*, Bd. 58, S. 32-65
Inanna	*ISET* I 221, L 1492	--
Inanna und Dumuzi	*RA* VIII, Taf. vor S. 161; *VS* II, Nr. 2 i-iii 22; *TCL* XVI Nr. 78	*HKL*, S. 646
Iškur[j]	*CT* XV, Taf. 15-16	*HKL*, S. 226
Iškur[k]	*CT* XLII, Nr. 10	--
Martu	*CT* XLII, Nr. 7 iv	--
Nergal	*CT* XV, Taf. 14	*HKL*, S. 226
Ningirgilu[l]	*CT* XV, Taf. 23	*HKL*, S. 226
Nisaba	*ISET* I 220, L 1489	--
Su'en	*CT* XV, Taf. 16-17; *SBH*, Nr. 38; *VS* X, Nr. 109	*MNS* I 44-54

Anfang	Katalog	Redeform	Person	Sprecher*
uru a gi$_{16}$-sa	--	D	1/3	Göttin (a), Sänger
[ù-u$_8$]-a ama-gan ù-u$_8$-a dumu-ni	--	D	3/1	Sänger, Göttin (a)
[x x a]-ši-ir-zu SAR AB ba ši [x x]	(4R, Taf. 53 iii 40?)	D	2/1/3?	Sänger, Göttin (a)
[am-mu-ra nu-un-ti] am-mu-ra nu-un-ti	4R, Taf. 53 iii 31	D H	3/1?/2	Sänger, Göttin (b), Gott (a)
šeš-e KU-a-na uru-a ér-ra na-nam	--	D N	3	Sänger, Göttinnen (b, c), Fliege
[. . . dab$_5$-ba] e-en gig-ga [. . .]	--	D N	3/1	Sänger, Göttinnen (b, c), Dämonen
[. . .]	--	D (N)	3/1	Sänger, Göttin (b), Gott (a)
ù-mu-un na-áĝ-zu-ka-na-áĝ-[ĝá] še-er-ma-al-ní-te-na	--	D	2	Sänger
im-kur-ra igi-gá	4R, Taf. 53 ii 36	D	3	Göttin (b), balag-di-Sänger
en-zu sa-mar-mar lú (/mu-lu) ta-zu mu-un-zu	VS X, Nr. 216, Vs. 10, Rs. 17	D	3	Sänger, Gott (b)
tilmun$^{(ki)}$ nigin-ù	4R, Taf. 53 ii 23-24, 38, iii 22	H D	3	Sänger
^{d}utu è-ma-ra ^{d}utu-mu ḫé-me-en	4R, Taf. 53 ii 26	H, D	2/1?	Sänger, Gott (a)?
[. . .]	--	D H	1	Göttin (a)
[xx]x a-ra-li-me-en áĝ-mu áĝ-gal-la-àm	--	DN (H)	1/2	Göttin (a), Gott (b)
ama-bi aš-tar-ra-na dumu-ni me-ta ba-an-GAM ù-x[. . .]	--	D	3/1/2	Sänger, Göttin (a) Gott (b)?
ù-u$_8$ ga-àm-du$_{11}$	--	DN (H)	1/2	Göttin (a), Gott (b)
[a é-an-na a gi$_6$-pàr-kù]	4R, Taf. 53 ii 43	D	1/2	Göttin (a), Sänger (?)
(e)-en gig-ga-bi na-áĝ-dam-a/ma-na	--	D N	3/2/1	Sänger, Göttin (a), Göttin (b), Gott (a), Dämonen
[gu$_4$-maḫ pa]-è-a mu-zu an-zà-šè	4R, Taf. 53 ii 27	D N	2/3	Sänger, Gott (b)
SIG-an-na gù-d[é-dé-aš]	4R, Taf. 53 i 27?	D N	3/2/1	Sänger, Gott (b) Gott (a)
[. . .]	--	D N	3/1?	Sänger(?), Gott (a)
[ù lú-lirum-m]a lirum-ta me-a	--	D	2/1?	Sänger, Göttin (b), Gott (a)?
ul-e pa-pa-al-ta	--	DN (H)	2/1	Sänger, Gott (b) Göttin (a)
[. . .]	--	N D	3/1	Sänger, Göttin (a)
má-gur$_8$-kù-an-na	?	D (N)	2/3	Sänger

* "Gott/Göttin (a)" bezieht sich auf die in der Unterschrift genannte Gottheit; "Gott/
Göttin (b, c)" auf andere Götter als Sprecher.

(a) Derselbe Schreiber wie *CT* XV, Taf. 20–21; junge Texte mit Zusätzen. Abweichungen
hinsichtlich der Sprecher.

(b) Unterschrift: [ér-šèm-m]a(?)-dingir-mah-a-kam.

(c) Siehe M. Civil, "A Hymn to the Beer Goddess and a Drinking Song," *Studies Presented to A. Leo Oppenheim* (Chicago, 1964) S. 80.

(d) S.o. Anm. *a*.

(e) Unterschrift nur ér-šèm-ma.

(f) Katalog: im-kur-ra šèg-gá. Die Göttin ist Šerida.

(g) Nach der Unterschrift ér-šèm-ma Enlil's. Nach *VS* X, Nr. 216 Rs. 17–18 aber
Ninurta-Lied. Dieser Gott ist angeredet.

(h) Bis auf den Prolog weitestgehend gleichlautend mit dem Inanna-Text unten bei Anm.
i.

(i) S.o. Anm. *h*.

(j) Vgl. *CT* XLII, Nr. 10.

(k) Vgl. *CT* XV, Taf. 15–16. Wenn zu Recht auf den Katalogeintrag bezogen, war das
Lied in junger Zeit ein balag.

(l) Wozu gehören die Zeilen nach der Notiz ér-šèm-ma-ᵈnin-gir-gi-lu?

(m) Laut Katalog ér-šèm-ma Enlil's; angeredet ist Utu.

Tabelle balag

Gott	Quellen	Literatur	Anfang	Katalog	Rubriken					
					šà-ba-a-TUK	ki-ru-gú	giš-gi4-gál	ki-šú	šudx(= BUM)-Schluss	balag
Dingirmaḫ	RA XVII 50	HKL, S. 452; SKly, S. 30, A. 63	(eden líl-lá šà-mu líl-lá)	--	-	x	-	x	x	x
Dumuzi[a]	CT XLII, Nr. 15; BE XXX, Nr. 8	PAPS, Bd. 107, S. 476, A. 7	[. . . im-m]a(?)-an-nú	--	-	(x)	x	x	-	x
Enlil[b]	VS II, Nr. 11; Bab III 241 ff.	HKL, S. 646; SKly, S. 17, 31, A. 65, 67	e-lum gu4-SÚN mu-zu kur-kur-šè	4R, Taf. 53 i 13	-	x	-	x	x	-
Enlil	PBS I/1, Nr. 8	SKly, S. 30-31, A. 64-65	ᵈutu-gim è-t[a . . .]	4R, Taf. 53 i 5, 35	-	[	]	x	x	-
[Gula?]	CT XXXVI, Taf. 43-44	--	[. . .]	--	x	x	-	[		]
[Inanna?]	CT XXXVI, Taf. 45-46	--	[. . .]	--	-	x	-	[		]
Inanna	CT XXXVI, Taf. 35-38	SKly, S. 30, A. 64	[. . .]	--	-	x	-	x	-	x
(Inanna)[c]	VS II, Nr. 26, 27, 45?; PRAK C 8, D 41	PAPS, Bd. 107, S. 478, A. 16	[eden-na ú-sag-gá]	4R, Taf. 53 i 52?	-	x	-	-	-	-
?[d]	CT XLII, Nr. 3	--	[. . .]	--	-	x	-	-	-	x̣?
?	MAH 16066	SKly, S. 30, A. 60, 61	?		?	x	?	x	x	x
?[e]	TCL XV, Nr. 8; CT XV, Taf. 26-27, 30	HKL, S. 154, 226	g̃-mu-un-e [dum]u-nun-gal an-ki-šè maḫ-àm	--	-	x	x	-	-	-
Inanna[f]	BL viii; ASKT, Nr. 17; K 3328; SRT, Nr. 46; CT XLII, Nr. 48; VS II, Nr. 29	SAHG, Nr. 46; RA LXVIII 95-96	urú àm-ma-ir-ra-bi	4R, Taf. 53 i 45; Rit. Mari ii 19	-	-	-	-	-	-

Vorbemerkung: Grundsätzlich zu den balag-Texten s. *SKLy*, S. 19–23, 30–31. Nur wenige altbabylonische Texte tragen die Unterschrift balag; es ist aber zu vermuten, dass eine grosse Zahl von in ki-ru-gú-Abschnitte gegliederten Texten ohne Unterschrift zu dieser Gruppe gehört; dazu kommen solche mit Trennstrichen anstelle von Rubriken. In einigen Fällen lässt sich dies nachweisen—sei es durch Katalogeinträge, sei es durch den für eine Gruppe innerhalb der balag-Lieder typischen Schluss šu d$_x$ (= BUM)-bi . . . na-(an-)gi$_4$-gi$_4$-ra; s. dazu *SKLy*, S. 22, 30. Ich führe hier nur altbab. Texte auf.

(*a*) Texte weichen erheblich voneinander ab. Anfang und Rubriken nur in *CT* XLII, Nr. 15; *BE* XXX, Nr. 8 hat Trennstriche. Titel in junger Überlieferung: e-ne-eḡ$_x$(= ÁG)-gá-ni i-lu i-lu.

(*b*) Rubriken nur in S. Langdon, "A Fragment of a Nippurian Liturgy," *Bab* III (1910) 241 ff. (Unterschrift al-til e-lum-gu$_4$-SÚN); in *VS* II, Nr. 11 nur Trennstriche.

(*c*) Verschiedene Versionen. Rubriken nur in *PRAK* C 8 und D 41; in *VS* II 26 und 27 nur Trennstriche.

(*d*) Unterschrift: [. . .] ᶠx–xˀ-kam (vielleicht: [balag]-ᶠ$^{d(?)}$inannaˀ(!)-kam. Text handelt von Lulal (12. und 13[?]. ki-ru-gú).

(*e*) Der Text handelt von der Mutter Dumuzi's (oder eines mit ihm verwandten Gottes). Unterschrift: [. . .]-BU zà-ba mah-àm; vielleicht [^{d}ù-bu]-bu zà⟨-mí⟩-zu(!) mah-àm. Unsicher, ob balag, da sonst einziger Text mit Doxologie.

(*f*) Zur Textrekonstruktion s. M. Civil, in *RA* LXVIII [1974] 95–96.

Tabelle šìr-gíd-da

Gott	Quellen	Literatur	Anfang	Redeform	Person	Sprecher
Lulal	*HAV*, S. 431, Nr. 5	--	ur-sag nam-šul-la zà-díb-ba kala-ga sag-gi$_4$-a	D[?]	2[?]	Sänger, [?]
Martu	*SRT*, Nr. 8	*SGL* I 120-40	ur-sag šul-maḫ kur-idim-ma zà-bi-šè til-la	D	3	Sänger
Nininsina	*SRT*, Nr. 6; 7	*AOAT*, Bd. 1, S. 284-91	[nin-me-ḫuš-a bará-m]aḫ-a dúr-gar-ra	D, N	3/2/1	Sänger, Göttin (a), Kranker
Ninurta	*STVC*, Nr. 34	*JCS* XXIV 3-9	[. . . é-kur-t]a è-a	N, (D)	3/2	Sänger, Gott (b)
Ninurta[a]	*TCL* XV, Nr. 7; *ISET* I, 145, Ni. 4346	--	ur-sag dumu-nir-gál- ^{d}en-líl-lá	D	2	Sänger
Ninurta	*TMH* NF IV, Nr. 49 + 88 [?]-Rs. i' 6	--	[. . .]	?	3(?)	?
Ninurta	*TMH* NF IV, Nr. 49 + 88 Rs. i' 7-ii [?]	--	uru ^{giš}ig-gal-ki-en- gi-r[a]	D,N(?)	3(?)	Sänger, [?]
Ninurta	s. C. Wilcke, *Koll.* . . . *Jena*, zu iv 68; Edition durch J. Cooper in Vorbereitung		an-gim dím-ma	D,N,H	3/2/1	Sänger, Gott (a), Gott (b) Göttin (c)
Nusku	*STVC*, Nr. 37	*SGL* II 144-59	[lugal] t[u-d]a-z[u] é-kur-ta ^{d}e[n-líl-le bí]-in-du$_{11}$-g[a]	DH	2	Sänger (= Göttin (b))
Nusku	*JCS* IV 138-39	*SGL* II 108-43	[. . .]	D	2	Sänger

(*a*) Siehe J. Bauer, in *RA* LXVIII [1974] 91.

Tabelle šìr-nam-gala und šìr-nam-šub

Gott	Kö-nig	Quellen	Literatur	Anfang	Rede-form	Per-son	Sprecher	Rubriken šà-ba-TUK	ki-ru-gú	giš-gi₄-gál	ki-šú
a) šìr-nam-gala											
Meslamtaea /Lugalgirra	IS	UM 29-13-609; CBS 14053	OrS XIX/XX 142-44	[. . .]	D H	2/3	Sänger	-	x	x	x
Nanna	--	CBS 8084 UM 29-15-58	ZA, Bd. 63, S. 1-55	dumu-nun nir-an-na kur-BÀD-na dagal bú[ru]	D	2	Sänger	-	x	x	ẋ
Nininsina	LE	UET VI, Nr. 96 = 97	--	[ᵈnin-ì]-si-na du[mu]-an-na é-gi₄-a-gal nir-ẋ[. . .]	N H D	2/3/1	Gott (b), Sänger, Göttin (a)	x	x	x	⟨x⟩
[Inanna?]	UNi	CT XXXVI, Taf. 28-30	ZA, Bd. 49, S. 106-13	[. . .]	N H	3/1	Sänger, Göttin (a) Götter (b,c,d)	-	x	x	ẋ?
b) šìr-nam-šub											
Inanna[a]	--	CT XLII, **Nr. 13**	PAPS, Bd. 107, S. 503	[di-d]a-mu-dè	D	1/2	Göttin (a) ?	-	(x)		-
Inanna[a]	--	CT XLII, **Nr. 22**	--	ma-a(-)a(-)u₅(-)ĝen-na	D H	1	Göttin (a) ? (pl.)	-	(x)	(x)	-
Nanna[a]	UN	CT XLIV, **Nr. 16;** ISET I **224-25**	--	uru bàd-kù-bi-ta ḫi-li gùr-ru	D (H) N	3	Sänger	-	(x)	-	-
Nininsina[b]	--	JCS XVI 79	--	ì-li-a ì-li-a ì-li ḫé-en-na-DU na-áĝ-ì-li-a	D	3	Sänger	-	-	-	-
Nininsina	--	KAR, Nr. 15 = 16	HKL, S. 97	[dumu]-maḫ-a[n-uraš]	H N	3/2?	Sänger, Gott (b)	-	-	-	-
Ninurta[c]	--	SLTNi, Nr. 61	--	[ur-sag gú-za] mùš-bi ši-du₈	D	2/3	Sänger	-	⟨x⟩	x	x
Nisaba	--	VS II, Nr. 65; PRAK C 39	ZA, Bd. 56, S. 4	[. . .]	D N	1/3/2	Sänger, Göttin (a) Gott (b)	-	-	-	-
Su'en	--	VS II, Nr. 68	MNS I 80-88	an-gim sù-DU-e k[i-]	D N	3/2	Sänger, Göttin (b)	-	-	-	-

(a) Trennstriche = ki-ru-gú?
(b) Katalog JB 2 (-3).
(c) Katalog JB 18; lies dort [ur-sag g]ú-za mùš-ʳbiꜞ ⟨ši⟩-du₈.

Tabelle ù-lu-lu-ma-ma

Gott	König	Quellen	Bearbeitung	Anfang	Redeform	Person	Sprecher
Nanna	--	*TCL* XV, Nr. 30	*MNS* I 70-79	en giri$_x$(= KA)-zal-an-na	D	2/3	Sänger
Ningublaga	--	*STVC*, Nr. 124	--	[. . .]	?	?	?
Ningublaga	--	*STVC*, Nr. 132	--	si$^?$-ga-dè ir[i$^?$-in-ga-àm-me] gù-nun iri-in-ga-àm-me	N?	3	Sänger
Su'en	IS	CBS 11168	*OrS* XIX/XX 145-47	en-gal giš-ḫé-ta sag-íl še-er-zi x̱-a	D N H	3	Sänger, Gott (a) Gott (b)?

Gott	Kö-nig	Quellen	Übersetzung/ Bearbeitung	Kata-log	Anfang	bar-sù	šà-ba-TUK	bar-sù-2
Baba[a]	Gud.	STVC, Nr. 36	SAHG, Nr. 16	--	nin-mu ša$_6$-ga	-	-	-
Enki[b]	UNi	CT XXXVI, Taf. 31-32; VS X, Nr. 145	ZA, Bd. 49, S. 112-16	JA 7 As III 3	en me-galam-ma	-	-	-
Enlil[c]	UNa	SRT, Nr. 11; TCL XV, Nr. 38	ZA, Bd. 53, S. 106-18; OrS X 3-12	--	^{d}en-líl maḫ-[ ]	-	-	-
Enlil[d]	ID	CBS 6136	JAOS 88, S. 3-14	--	^{giš}gigir-maḫ	-	-	-
Inanna[e]	--	CT XXXVI, Taf. 33-34	ZA, Bd. 48, S. 105-13	--	nin ^{d}nin-gal-e	-	-	-
Inanna[f]	--	TMH NF III, Nr. 25	AfO XXIII 84-87	--	ga-ša-an-ĝen	-	-	-
Inanna[g]	--	TMH NF IV, Nr. 89	--	--	[. . .]	[-	-	-
Inanna[h]	--	TCL XVI, Nr. 70	PAPS, Bd. 107, S. 495-96	JA 19	ú-MÙŠxA.DI.MÙŠxA.DI-e MÙŠ.DI			
Nanaja[i]	IE	YBC 9859	BiOr XXIII 243	--	nin me-nun-na	x	x	x
Nergal[j]	--	TCL XV, Nr. 23	SGL II 7-34	As III 6?	en ní-ÍL-an-ki	-	-	-
Ninlil[k]	Š	STVC, Nr. 60 + 54; STVC, Nr. 99 + PBS XIII, Nr. 40 + ISET I 84, Ni. 13203 + 159, Ni. 4492	--	--	[m]á? [^{d}]en-ki-ke$_4$	-	-	-
Nintu		TMH NF IV, Nr. 86; BL 95, 97, 102, 127,	s. oben 4. Strophe	--	nin ^{d}a-ru-ru-é-kèški-a	-	-	-
Ninurta	?	TCL XVI, Nr. 84	--	--	[. . .]	[		
Ninurta[l]	Š	BE XXIX, Nr. 1 iii 6'-36'	--	--	en nam-ur-sag-gá šu-du$_7$-a	-	-	-
Ninurta[m]	ŠS	BE XXIX, Nr. 1 i 1-ii 17; CBS 15208	(s. AfO XXIV 36)	(JA 33)	ur-sag utaḫ-gal-le-eš	x	x	-
Ninurta[n]	ŠS	BE XXIX, Nr. 1 ii 18-iii 5	--	JA 30	GIŠ.GA.RU.RU	-	-	-
Su'en[o]	--	PBS X/4, Nr. 7; CBS 7140	ZA, Bd. 63, S. 1-55	--	lugal-mu sug-ga(/a)-na	-	-	-
Su'en[p]	IS	UM 29-16-43	OrS XIX/XX 144-45	JA 20 As III 4	en me-⟨PA⟩.GAN nu-di	-	-	-
?[q]	Š	TCL XV, Nr. 32	--	--	[. . .]	[		

Rubriken								Redeform				Person, bezogen auf Gott				Versuch einer Gliederung in Strophen von n Zeilen		Strophengliederung nach
šà-ba-TUK-2	bar-sù-3	sa-gíd-da	giš-giá-gál	sa-gar-ra	giš-giá-gál	tigi-DN	Stichzeile	sa-gíd-da	giš-giá-gál	sa-gar-ra	giš-giá-gál	sa-gíd-da	giš-giá-gál	sa-gar-ra	giš-giá-gál	sa-gíd-da	sa-gar-ra	
··	-	[x]	-?	x	-	x	-	D	-	D	-	2	-	2	-	8,8,8	8,6,6	R_3, S, T
-	-	x	x	x	-	x	-	DH	H	DH	-	2	2	2	- /3	5,7,4,4	5,4,6,4,3	S, T
-	-	x	-	x	-	x	-	N	-	HN	-	3	-	3	-	3,3,3,4,5, 5,5,5	6,6,2,4,4, 4,4,3	T, S; R_3, R_4 nur in sa-gar-ra
-	-	x	-	x	-	x	-	ND	-	D	-	3	-	3	-			
-	-	x	-	x	-	x	-	D	-	D	-	2	-	2	-	4,4,4,4,4, 4,4	8,8,10	R_2, R_3
-	-	x	-	x	-	x	-	N	-	N	-	1	-	1	-	4,4,6,4	?[...]?,4, 6,4	T, Sprecher, R_2, R_3 in sa-gar-ra
-	-]	x	-	[x	]			?	-	?	-	?	-	?		?	?	? ($R_{2/3}$?)
-	-	x	-	x	-	x?	-	N	-	NH	-	3	-	3	-	2,2,2,2,2, 14	2,2,2,2,3, 3,3,2,2	R_2, Refrain
x	-	x	x	x	-	x	-	DH	H	D	-	2	2	2	-	2,2,2,4,2, 2,2,3,1	3,2,3,3,2	R_4, S
-	-	x	-	x	-	x	-	D	-	DH	-	2	-	2	-	10,10,10	5,5,5,5,5, 5	R_2: sa-gíd-da; S, T: sa-gar-ra
-	-	x	-	x	-	-	x	ND	-	NH	-	3	-	3	-	?	?	?
-	-	x	-	x	-	x	-	D	-	D	-	3	-	3	-	6,6,6	8,8,8	R_2, S
	x]	x	-	x	-			D	-	D	-	2	-	3?	-	[...],2,2, 2,2,[...]	[...],2	R_2(?)
-	-	x	-	x	x	x		D	-	DH	d	2	-	2?	2	6,5,5 (?)	?	R_4
-	-	x	x	x	-	[?]	-	DH	H	DH	-	2	2	2	-	2,2,2,5,2, [..].,2	6,?,6,6,6	R_4: sa-gíd-da R_2: sa-gar-ra
-	-	x	-	x	-	-	-	?	-	DH?	-	?	-	2	-	?	2,2,[...]	R_2(?)
-	-	x	-	x	-	x	-	D	-	D	-	3	-	2	-	5,4,4,2	8,8,8	R_4: sa-gíd-da R_2: sa-gar-ra
-	-	x	-	x	-	x	-	D	-	DH	-	3	-	3	-	?	?	R_2 Anfang sa-gar-ra
	]	x	-	x	-	-	x	N	-	?	-	?	-	2	-	?	?	?

(*a*) Sprecher nennt Göttin "meine Herrin."

(*b*) Rubrik sa-gar-ra in *CT* XXXVI verstellt; richtig: *VS* X. Sprecher gebraucht die 1. Pers. im Prolog.

(*c*) Sprecher nennt König "mein König/Herr."

(*d*) Im sa-gíd-da-Teil ist der Wagen des Gottes angeredet; s.u., Anm. *k*.

(*e*) Die Stelle des Königs nimmt hier der Gott Amaušumgalanna ein.

(*f*) Alle Reden sind Teil der Erzählung.

(*g*) Wahrscheinlich ein tigi. Wechsel von eme-sal und Hauptdialekt.

(*h*) Unterschrift unleserlich, wahrscheinlich t⌈igi⌉-ᵈ⌈i⌉[nanna-k]a.

(*i*) Text schreibt ša-ba-du-ga statt des zu erwartenden ša-ba-ᴛᴜᴋ-2-kam-ma. Rubriken und Strophengrenzen stimmen überein.

(*j*) Text erwähnt "Regierungszeit langer Tage" und den "Thron, den du gründest"; gehört also zur königlichen Sphäre.

(*k*) Stichzeile: lugal me-lám-huš gú bí-è = Katalog Y 21 (vgl. auch Katalog JB 59). Im sa-gíd-da-Teil ist das Schiff der Göttin angeredet; s.o., Anm. *d*.

(*l*) Sprecher nennt den König "mein König/Herr"; Unterschrift [ti-g]i-ᵈnin-urta-kam; vgl. Gudea Zyl. B xviii 12; unten Anm. *o*. *BE* XXIX, Nr. 1 ist eine Sammeltafel.

(*m*) Sprecher nennt den König "mein König/Herr"; *BE* XXIX, Nr. 1 ist eine Sammeltafel.

(*n*) Nach der Rubrik sa-gar-ra-àm fügt der Text (Sammeltafel) hinzu: šu-ta e-ne-di-[dam], "mit der Hand zu spielen"; s.o. bei Anm. 88. "Mein König/Herr" in den 3 letzten Zeilen: Bezug unklar.

(*o*) Unterschrift in CBS 7140: [ti-g]i-ᵈsuˀen-[na-kam]; s.o. Anm. *l*. Dieser Text kürzt den sa-gar-ra-Teil und bietet eine andere Reihenfolge der Zeilen. Sprecher nennt den Gott "mein Herr." Dies ist das einzige tigi, in dem mit Sicherheit ein Wechsel in der Person, in der vom Gott gesprochen wird, zu beobachten ist.

(*p*) Sprecher nennt den König "mein Ibbi-Sîn."

(*q*) Stichzeile: [ur-sag šà]-kù-ta pirig-gim gú-peš-ša = Katalog Y 19.

EXKURS: EIN kun-gar-LIED INANNA'S

Sumerische literarische Texte sind—soweit ich weiss—bis heute nicht in das Corpus von Texten aller Zeiten und Räume miteinbezogen, die von der Literaturwissenschaft erforscht werden; und doch ist die sumerische Literatur—zusammen mit der ägyptischen—die älteste Literatur der Welt und ist—mittelbar über die akkadische—gewiss nicht ohne Einfluss auf die Literaturen der klassischen Antike und damit auf die Literatur bis zum heutigen Tage geblieben.

Der Grund dafür, dass die moderne Literaturwissenschaft sich dieses Gegenstandes noch nicht bemächtigt hat, ist die Sprachbarriere—und diese gleich in dreifacher Weise:

Wohl kein moderner Literaturwissenschaftler beherrscht das Sumerische, soweit es z. Zt. erforscht ist, und er kann die Texte nicht unmittelbar nach dem Keilschrifttext lesen. Nur ein Bruchteil der Werke der sumerischen Literatur liegt aber in einigermassen adäquater moderner philologischer Bearbeitung vor. Auch diese Bearbeitungen sind aber für den, der des Sumerischen nicht mächtig ist, nicht benutzbar, da sie auf Schritt und Tritt die Kenntnis von Grammatik und Wortschatz des Sumerischen voraussetzen. Übersetzungen sind nur sehr beschränkt verwertbar, da sie über die Stellung eines Satzgliedes—um nur ein Beispiel zu nennen—innerhalb eines Satzes nichts aussagen. Die literarische Analyse der Texte von Seiten der Sumerologen schliesslich ist nur in rudimentären Ansätzen vorhanden.

Letzteres ist den Sumerologen nicht anzulasten, denn wie den Literaturwissenschaftlern die Kenntnis von Schrift, Grammatik und Wortschatz des Sumerischen abgeht, so fehlt ihnen das literaturwissenschaftliche Rüstzeug: keiner—oder kaum einer—hat die Methoden dieser Wissenschaft von Grund auf studiert. Auch der Verfasser dieser Zeilen ist keine Ausnahme von dieser Regel.

Da aber nicht zu hoffen oder erwarten ist, dass sich die Literaturwissenschaft von sich aus der sumerischen Literatur zuwenden wird, muss es die Aufgabe der Sumerologen sein, ihr diese Materie nahezubringen. Dies kann in zweierlei Weise geschehen:

Einmal sollten sumerische Texte in einer Form ediert werden, die es dem Literaturwissenschaftler erlaubt, mit ihnen umzugehen, d.h., sie müssen grammatisch und lexikalisch erschlossen werden. Ein möglicher Weg hierzu ist die formalisierte Umschrift als grammatische Analyse zusammen mit einem Lexikon des Textes, wie ich versuche, sie unten zu bieten.

Zum anderen sollte der Sumerologe auch den Versuch der literarischen Analyse unternehmen, um den reichen Formenschatz der sumerischen Literatur und ihre Gegenstände zu verdeutlichen.

In der folgenden Bearbeitung eines recht willkürlich herausgegriffenen kurzen Textes versuche ich, einen Schritt in diese Richtung zu gehen, wobei ich bewusst Fragen, die den Sumerologen als Philologen in erster Linie interessieren, nur knapp behandele.

Texte: A = UM 29-16-37 (Photo, Kramer, in *PAPS*, Bd. 107, S. 517–18)
B = *PRAK* C 94 obv.(?) (identifiziert durch J. Krecher)
Bearbeitung: Kramer, in *PAPS*, Bd. 107, S. 493–95; nur A
Übersetzung: Kramer, in *ANET* (3. Aufl.) S. 637–38; nur A

1 A ama-me-da-nu-me-a sila-a MI-eden-na i-iĝ$_x$(= ÁG)-ĝi$_6$-in-SAR-re

2 A šul-e ama-me-da-nu-me-a sila-a MI-eden-na i-iĝ$_x$(= ÁG)-ĝi$_6$-in-SAR-re

3 A ama-mu ^{d}ga-ša-an-gal-da-nu-me sila-a MI-eden-na i-iĝ$_x$(= ÁG)-ĝi$_6$-in-SAR-re

4 A ^{d}ga-ša-an-gi-kù-ga-da-nu-me-a sila-a MI-eden-na i-iĝ$_x$(= ÁG)-ĝi$_6$-in-SAR-re

5 A a-a ^{d}su$^{\textgamma}$en-da-nu-me-a sila-a MI-eden-na i-iĝ$_x$(= ÁG)-ĝi$_6$-in-SAR-re

6 A šeš-mu ^{d}utu-da-nu-me-a sila-a MI-eden-na i-iĝ$_x$(= ÁG)-ĝi$_6$-in-SAR-re

7 A lú ki-sikil du$_{14}$-gim na-an-mú-mú-un

8 A ^{d}inanna inim-gim ga-àm-me-en-dè-en

9 A ^{d}inanna du$_{14}$-gim na-an-mú-mú-un

10 A ^{d}nin-é-gal-la ad-gim ga-àm-gi$_4$-dè-en

11 A a-a-mu a-a-zu-gim in-ga-dím

12 A ^{d}⌜ina⌝nna inim-gim ga-àm-me-en-dè-en

13 A ⌜ama-mu⌝ ama-zu-gim ⌜i⌝n-ga-dím

14 A ^{d}nin-é-gal-la a[d-gim ga-à]m-gi$_4$-dè-en

15 A ^{d}g⌜eštin-a⌝n-na ^{d}n[i]n-⌜é⌝(?)-nu-n[a(?)]-gim in-ga-dím

16 A ^{d}inanna inim-gim ga-àm-me-en-dè-en

17 A gá-e ^{d}utu-gim in-ga-dím-me-en

18 A ^{d}nin-é-gal-la ad-g⌜im ga⌝-àm-gi$_4$-dè-en

19 A ^{d}en-ki ^{d}su$^{\textgamma}$en-gim in-ga-dím

20 A ^{d}inanna inim-gim ga-àm-me-en-dè-en

21 A ^{d}du$_x$(= BU)-tur ^{d}nin-gal-gim in-ga-dím

22 A ^{d}nin-é-gal-la ad-gim ga-àm-gi$_4$-dè-en

23 A inim bí-in-eš-a inim-hi-li eš-àm

24 A du$_{14}$-mú-mú-d⌜a⌝-a h⌜i⌝-li-šà-ga-na-ke$_4$

25 A ^{na_4}šuba-k⌜e⌝$_4$ ^{na_4}šuba-ke$_4$ ^{na_4}šuba na-ur$_x$(= URU$_4$)-ru

26 A ^{d}ama-ušumgal-⌜an-na⌝ ^{na_4}š⌜uba⌝-ke$_4$ ^{na_4}šuba na-ur$_x$(= URU$_4$)-ru

27 A $^{[n]a_4}$šuba-n⌜a⌝(?) ^{na_4}šub⌜a⌝-[tu]r-tu[r-b]i [x x x (x)]

28 A $^{[na_4]}$šu[ba-n]a(?) ^{na_4}šuba-[gal-gal]-bi s[a$_6$-x x (x)]

29 A   [x x x a ùr]-ra lá-lá a ùr-ra mu-na-ab-lá-[lá]

30 A   [x x x a bà]d-da lá-lá a bàd-da mu-na-ab-lá-lá

31 A   M[UNUS.x x x (x) ^{d}]ama-ušumgal-an-na-ra gù mu-na-dé-[e(?)]

32 A ^{na_4}š⌜uba⌝-[ur$_x$(= URU$_4$)]-r⌜u⌝ ^{na_4}š⌜u⌝ba-ur$_x$(= URU$_4$)-ru   / a-ba-a mu-[na]-ur$_x$(= URU$_4$)-ru

  B(1) šub$_x$(= ŠUBA)-bi-ù-ru-[ur   šub$_x$(= ŠUBA)-bi-ù-ru-ur]   / a-b[a mu-na-ù-ru]

33 A ^{d}ama-ušumga[l-an-na ^{na_4}šuba]-ur$_x$(= URU$_4$)-ru   / a-ba-a mu-na-ur$_x$(= URU$_4$)-ru

  B(2) ušumgal-an-na šub$_x$(= ŠUBA)-bi-ù-ru-ur / a-ba mu-na-ù-ru

34 A ^{na_4}šuba-[na] $^{[n]a_4}$š[uba]-tur-tur-bi ši-pa-áǧ-me NE-a

  B(5) [šub$_x$(= ŠUBA)-b]i-z⌜a⌝ šub$_x$(= ŠUBA)-bi-tur-tur-bi ši-pa-áǧ-me N⌜I⌝-[a]

35 A ^{na_4}šuba-na ^{na_4}š[uba]-gal-gal-bi gaba-kù-me NE-a

  B(6) [šub$_x$(= ŠUBA)-bi-za šu]b$_x$(= [ŠUB]A)-⌜bi⌝-gal-gal-b[i] / [gab]a-kù(!)-me NI-a

36 A ^{d}ama-ušumgal-an-na⟨-ke$_4$⟩ n⌜u-u$_8$-gig⌝-ra inim mu-ni-ib-gi$_4$-gi$_4$

  B   . . . .

37 A   n⌜u-u⌝$_8$-gig-ga-àm dam-mu nu-u$_8$-gig-ga-àm e-ne-er mu-na-ur$_x$(= URU$_4$)-ru

  B(3) nu-u$_8$-gig-ga-àm dam-mu nu-u$_8$-gig-ga-àm / e-IM mu-na-ù-ru

38 A   kù-^{d}inanna-ke$_4$ nu-bar-ra e-ne-er mu-na-ur$_x$(= URU$_4$)-ru

  B(4) kù-^{d}inanna-mu nu-u$_8$-b[ar](?)-ra ⌜e-I⌝M(?) mu-na-ù-ru

39 A ^{na_4}šuba-na-ke$_4$ ^{na_4}šuba-na-ke$_4$ ^{na_4}šuba na-ur$_x$(= URU$_4$)-ru

40 A ^{d}ama-ušumgal-an-na-ke$_4$ ^{na_4}šuba-na-ke$_4$ ^{na_4}šuba na-ur$_x$(= URU$_4$)-ru

41 A ^{na_4}šuba-ur$_x$(= URU$_4$)-ru ^{na_4}šuba-ur$_x$(= URU$_4$)-ru a-ba-a mu-na-ur$_x$(= URU$_4$)-ru

42 A ^{d}ama-ušumgal-an-na ^{na_4}šuba-ur$_x$(= URU$_4$)-ru a-ba-a mu-na-ur$_x$(= URU$_4$)-ru

43 A   ma-ab-dù-da-a-gá$^{ba-a-ni-i}$ ma-ab-dù-da-a-gá su$_6$-a-ni ^{na_4}za-gìn-na

44 A   me-a-am an-né ma-ab-dù-da-a-gá su$_6$-a-ni ^{na_4}za-gìn-na

45 A   ezen(?)-e su$_6$-a-ni ^{na_4}za-gìn-na su$_6$-a-ni ^{na_4}za-gìn-na

46 A   kun-gar-^{d}inanna-kam

47 A   gi-dub-ba-gi-ta sar-ra

1 Wäre nicht unsere Mutter—er würde...-Pflanzen der Steppe sich auf der Strasse hin und her biegen lassen!

2 Wäre nicht unsere Mutter—der junge Mann würde...-Pflanzen der Steppe sich auf der Strasse hin und her biegen lassen!

3 Wäre nicht meine Mutter Gašangal—er würde die. . .-Pflanzen der Steppe
    sich auf der Strasse hin und her biegen lassen!

4 Wäre nicht Gašangikuga—er würde die. . .-Pflanzen der Steppe sich auf der
    Strasse hin und her biegen lassen!

5 Wäre nicht Vater Suʾen—er würde die. . .-Pflanzen der Steppe sich auf der
    Strasse hin und her biegen lassen!

6 Wäre nicht mein Bruder Utu—er würde die. . .-Pflanzen der Steppe sich auf
    der Strasse hin und her biegen lassen!

7 Mensch, Mädchen! Du sollst nicht etwas wie Streit anfangen!

8 Inanna, lass uns etwas wie (vernünftige) Worte reden!

9 Inanna, Du sollst nicht etwas wie Streit anfangen!

10 Ninegala, lass uns so etwas wie ein Gespräch führen!

11 Mein Vater ist ebenso geformt wie dein Vater—

12 Inanna, lass uns etwas wie (vernünftige) Worte reden!

13 Meine Mutter ist ebenso geformt wie deine Mutter—

14 Ninegala, lass uns etwas wie ein Gespräch führen!

15 Geštinanna ist ebenso geformt wie N[i]nhenun[a](?)—

16 Inanna, lass uns etwas wie (vernünftige) Worte reden!

17 Ich bin geformt wie Utu—

18 Ninegala, lass uns etwas wie ein Gespräch führen!

19 Enki ist geformt wie Suʾen—

20 Inanna, lass uns etwas wie (vernünftige) Worte reden!

21 Duttur ist geformt wie Ningal—

22 Ninegala, lass uns etwas wie ein Gespräch führen!

23 Die Wörter, die sie gesprochen haben—die Wörter der Wonne sind dreissig—

24 (Sie), die dabei war, Streit anzufangen, (er), die Wonne ihres Sinns.

25 Der mit den šuba-Steinen, der mit den šuba-Steinen, pflügt wirklich die
    šuba-Steine!

26 Amaušumgalanna, der mit den šuba-Steinen, pflügt wirklich die šuba-
    Steine!

27 Die kleinen unter seinen šuba-Steinen [sind. . .],

28 die grossen unter seinen šuba-Steinen [sind] sch[ön].

29 [. . .], der(?) [Wasser] auf das(?) [Dach] trägt(?), trägt(?) für ihn Wasser auf
    das Dach,

30 [. . .], der(?) [Wasser] auf die(?) [Maue]r trägt(?), trägt(?) für ihn Wasser
    auf die Mauer.

31 Die [. . .] sprich[t] zu Amaušumgalanna:

32 Der šuba-Stein-Pflüger, der šuba-Stein-Pflüger—für wen pflügt er,

33 Amaušumgalanna, der šuba-Stein-Pflüger—für wen pflügt er

34 Die kleinen unter seinen šuba-Steinen, die unsere Kehle geschmückt haben,

35 Die grossen unter seinen šuba-Steinen, die unsere helle Brust geschmückt
    haben?

36 Amaušumgalanna antwortet der Hierodule:

37 Sie ist eine Hierodule, meine Ehefrau ist eine Hierodule—für sie pflügt er!

38 Für meine helle Inanna, die n u - b a r—für sie pflügt er!

39 Der mit den š u b a -Steinen für sie, der mit den š u b a -Steinen für sie pflügt wirklich die š u b a -Steine,

40 Amaušumgalanna, der mit den š u b a -Steinen für sie pflügt wirklich die š u b a -Steine!

41 Der š u b a -Stein-Pflüger, der š u b a -Stein-Pflüger—für wen pflügt er,

42 Amaušumgalanna, der š u b a -Stein-Pflüger—für wen pflügt er?

43 Der Bart dessen, der es für mich erbauen wird, dessen der es für mich erbauen wird, ist aus Lapislazuli,

44 der Bart meines Hirten, der es für mich bis zum Himmel erbauen wird, ist aus Lapislazuli!

45 Auf, zum Fest! Sein Bart ist aus Lapislazuli! Sein Bart ist aus Lapislazuli!

46 Ein k u n - g a r Inanna's ist es.

47 Mit einem Schreibrohr aus Rohr geschrieben.

GRAMMATISCHE ANALYSE (FORMALISIERTE UMSCHRIFT)

Sigla

.a	Lokativ-Element in Verbalpräfix (auch für Dativ)	-ed	Verbalsuffix: unvollendeter Aspekt (?); modale Nuance des Sollens
-a₁	Postposition: Lokativ	-en	Subjektszeichen der 1./2. Pers. Sg. bei transitivem (Agentiv, Präs. Fut.) und intransitiv/passivem Verbum
-a₂	Suffix an infiniten Verbalformen (vollendeter Aspekt?)		
-a₃	Nominalisator: macht Sätze syntaktisch einem Nomen gleichwertig	-enden	dito der 1. Pers. Pl.
A	Adjektiv	-eš	Siehe -n-...-eš
-ak	Postposition: Genitiv	ga-	Präformativ: Kohortativ
-b-	Agentiv/Akkusativ-Zeichen der 3. Pers. Sg. der Sachklasse (Agentiv nur Präteritum)	-gim	Postposition: Äquativ
		î	"Konjugationspräfix"
		inga-	Präformativ: ?
-b.	Personenzeichen der 3. Pers. Sg. der Sachklasse in dimensionalen Präfixen	Kop.	Kopula
		mu-	"Konjugationspräfix"
		n.	Personenzeichen der 3. Pers. Sg. der Personenklasse in dimensionalen Präfixen
-da	Postposition: Komitativ		
.e	Lokativ-Terminativ-Element in dimensionalem Verbalpräfix	N	Name
		na₁	Präformativ: Affirmativ
		na₂	Präformativ: Vetitiv
-e₁	Postposition: Agentiv; Verbalsuffix: Agentivzeichen der 3. Pers. Sg.	-n-...-eš	Agentivzeichen der 3. Pers. Pl. der Personenklasse bei transitiven Präterita
-e₂	Postposition: Lokativ-Terminativ		

nu-	Präformativ: negativer Indikativ (vor finiten und infiniten Verbalformen)
p	Personenklasse (bei Pronomina)
pl	Plural (1pl = 1. Person Plural)
PR	Personalpronomen
PRi	Interrogativpronomen
PRp	Possessivpronomen (enklitisch)
-ra	Postposition: Dativ (mit Morphemvariante /r/ nach Vokal)
.s	Sachklasse (bei Pronomina)
S	Substantiv
sg	Singular (1sg = 1. Pers. Singular)
V	Verbum (Basis)

Z	Zahl
( ), [ ]	Ketten innerhalb von Ketten
(-)	Verbindung von appositionellen Ketten
/	Grenze zwischen selbständigen Ketten
-	Verbindung von Gliedern einer Kette
.	Verbindung eng zusammengehöriger Glieder einer Kette (reduplizierte verbale Basis oder Personenzeichen + dimensionales Element im Präfix)
?	unbekanntes (vokalisches) Personenzeichen der 1. Pers. Sg. in dimensionalen Präfixen

1 S_1-PRp_{1p1}-da-([nu-V_1]-a_2)   / S_2-a_1 / S_3-S_4-ak / î-b.e-b?-V_2-$e_1{}^a$
2 S_5-e_1 / S_1-PRp_{1p1}-da-([nu-V_1]-$\langle a_2 \rangle$) / S_2-a_1 / S_3-S_4-ak / î-b.e-b?-V_2-e_1
3 S_1-PRp_{1p1}(-)N_1-da-([nu-V_1]-a_2)   / S_2-a_1 / S_3-S_4-ak / î-b.e-b?-V_2-e_1
4 N_2-da-([nu-V_1]-a_2)   / S_2-a_1 / S_3-S_4-ak / î-b.e-b?-V_2-e_1
5 S_6(-)N_3-da-([nu-V_1]-a_2)   / S_2-a_1 / S_3-S_4-ak / î-b.e-b?-V_2-e_1
6 S_7-PRp_{1sg}(-)N_4-da-([nu-V_1]-a_2)   / S_2-a_1 / S_3-S_4-ak / î-b.e-b?-V_2-e_1
7 S_8(-)S_9 / S_{10}-gim   / na_2-b?-V_3.V_3-en
8 N_5 / S_{11}-gim   / ga-î-b-V_4-enden
9 N_5 / S_{10}-gim   / na_2-b?-V_3.V_3-en
10 N_6 / S_{12}-gim   / ga-î-b-V_5-enden
11 S_6-PRp_{1sg} / S_6-PRp_{2sg}-gim / inga-V_6
12 N_5 / S_{11}-gim   / ga-î-b-V_4-enden
13 S_1-PRp_{1sg} / S_1-PRp_{2sg}-gim / inga-V_6
14 N_6 / S_{12}-gim   / ga-î-b-V_5-enden
15 N_7 / N_8-gim   / inga-V_6
16 N_5 / S_{11}-gim   / ga-î-b-V_4-enden
17 PR_{1sg} / N_4-gim   / inga-V_6-en
18 N_6 / S_{12}-gim   / ga-î-b-V_5-enden
19 N_9 / N_3-gim   / inga-V_6
20 N_5 / S_{11}-gim   / ga-î-b-V_4-enden
21 N_{10} / $N_{1'}$-gim   / inga-V_6
22 N_6 / S_{12}-gim   / ga-î-b-V_5-enden
23 S_{11} / (b.e-n-V_4-eš)-a_3 / S_{11}-S_{13}-ak / Z_1-Kop_{3sg}
24 S_{10}-V_3.V_3-ed-a_2-e_1 / S_{13}-([S_{14}-$PRp_{3sg.p}$]-ak)-e_1

25 S_{15}-ak-e_1 / S_{15}-ak-e_1 / S_{15} / na_1-V_7-e_1^b

26 N_{11} / S_{15}-ak-e_1 / S_{15} / na_1-V_7-e_1^b

27 $(S_{15}$-$PRp_{3sg.p})$-ak / $(S_{15}$-A_1.$A_1)$-$PRp_{3sg.s}$ / A_x···

28 $(S_{15}$-$PRp_{3sg.p})$-ak / $(S_{15}$-A_2.$A_2)$-$PRp_{3sg.s}$ / A_3-···

29 ···$[S_{16}$-$(S_{17}$-$a_1)$-V_8.$V_8]$-e_1 / S_{16} / S_{17}-a_1 / mu-n.a-V_8.V_8-e_1

30 ···$[S_{16}$-$(S_{18}$-$a_1)$-V_8.$V_8]$-e_1 / S_{16} / S_{18}-a_1 / mu-n.a-V_8.V_8-e_1

31 S_{19}-(...)-e_1 / N_{10}-ra / S_{20} / mu-n.a-V_9-e_1

32 S_{15}-V_7-e_1^c / S_{15}-V_7-e_1^c / $PRi_{3sg.p}$^d / mu-n.a-V_7-e_1

33 N_{11} / S_{15}-V_7-e_1^c / $PRi_{3sg.p}$^d / mu-n.a-V_7-e_1

34 $(S_{15}$-$PRp_{3sg.p})$-ak^e / $(S_{15}$-A_1.$A_1)$-$PRp_{3sg.s}$ / S_{21}-PRp_{1p1} / V_{10}-a_2

35 $(S_{15}$-$PRp_{3sg.p})$-ak^e / $(S_{15}$-A_2.$A_2)$-$PRp_{3sg.s}$ / S_{22}-PRp_{1p1} / V_{10}-a_2

36 N_{11}-e_1 / S_{23}-ra / S_{11} / mu-n.e-b-V_5.V_5-e_1

37 S_{23}-Kop_{3sg} / S_{24}-PRp_{1sg} / S_{23}-Kop_{3sg} / $PR_{3sg.p}$-ra / mu-n.a-V_7-e_1^f

38 $(A_4$-$N_5)$-PRp_{1sg}^g(-)S_{25}-ra^h   / $PR_{3sg.p}$-ra / mu-n.a-V_7-e_1^f

39 $(S_{15}$-$PRp_{3sg.p})$-ak-e_1 / $(S_{15}$-$PRp_{3sg.p})$-ak-e_1 / S_{15} / na_1-V_7-e_1

40 N_{11} / $(S_{15}$-$PRp_{3sg.p})$-ak-e_1 / S_{15} / na_1-V_7-e_1

41 S_{15}-V_7-e_1^c / S_{15}-V_7-e_1^c / $PRi_{3sg.p}$ / mu-n.a-V_7-e_1

42 N_{11} / S_{15}-V_7-e_1^c / $PRi_{3sg.p}$ / mu-n.a-V_7-e_1

43 $([mu$-?.a-b-V_{11}-ed-$e_1]$-a_3-$PRp_{1sg})$-ak / $([mu$-?.a-b-V_{11}-ed-$e_1]$-a_3-$PRp_{1sg})$-ak
     / S_{26}-$PRp_{3sg.p}$ / S_{27}-ak

44 S_{28}(-)S_{29}-e_2(-)$([mu$-?.a-b-V_{11}-ed-$e_1]$-a_3-$PRp_{1sg})$-ak / S_{26}-PRp_{3sg} / S_{27}-ak

45 S_{30}-e_2 / S_{26}-PRp_{3sg} / S_{27}-ak / S_{26}-PRp_{3sg} / S_{27}-ak

46–47 Unterschrift

(*a*) Die hier vermutete Morphemvariante /n/ zum Akkusativzeichen der Sachklasse /b/ (graphisch nicht geschieden vom /n/ der Personenklasse) ist umstritten. Als spontaner Übergang ist sie nur denkbar in einer Umgebung, die die Nasalierung des /b/ ermöglicht und gleichzeitig eine Dissimilierung zum dentalen Nasal gestattet. Dies ist der Fall in einer rekonstruierten Präfixkette î-b.e-b-, in der das Konjugationspräfix immer die Nasalierung des ersten /b/ bewirkt. Die Nasalierung des zweiten /b/ scheint fakultativ zu sein (ist zumindest heute noch nicht für bestimmte Fälle voraussagbar), ist aber immer gekoppelt mit der Dissimilation zu /n/: Eine Kette *im-mi-im- ist nicht zu belegen. N.B., dass die Artikulation des Konjugationspräfixes /î/ noch nicht feststeht: im Hauptdialekt verändert es /b/ zu /m/; im Emesal aber zu /ğ/.

(*b*) Oder na_2-V_7-e_1 (Prohibitiv)?

(*c*) Die Variante ù-ru-ur in Text B kann nur als unorthographische Schreibung für ur_x(= URU₄)-ur_x verstanden werden: Vokativ mit reduplizierter Basis. B hat auch in Z. 34–35 (B, Z. 5–6) eine 2. Pers. gegenüber der 3. Pers. von A. Da die Verbalform eine 3. Pers. Sg. zeigt (s. Anm. *f*) und sich das Dativpräfix ebenfalls auf eine 3. Pers. bezieht, halte ich eine 2. Pers. hier für ausgeschlossen.

(*d*) Das Fragepronomen a-ba(-a) wird in Z. 37–38 mit dem Dativ e-ne-er, "für sie/ihn," beantwortet. Darum und weil auch kein anderer Bezug für das Dativpräfix -n.a- zu erkennen ist, fasse ich es als Dativ auf. S. auch den Dativ a-ba-a in *CT* XXI, Taf. 40, Kol. i, Z. 9–10, 14–15, 19–20, 23–24, [za-e] a-ba-a / [mu-na]-

gub-bé-en = *at-ta ma-an-na-am* / *tu-qá-a*, "auf wen wartest du." Einen Dativ *a-ba-ra kann ich nicht belegen. Ob das -a in a-ba-a (Text A) einen dimensionalen Kasus ausdrückt (s. A. Poebel, in *GSG* § 235), kann ich nicht entscheiden.

(*e*) Variante in Text B: (S_{15}-PRp$_{2sg}$)-ak; s.o. Anm. *c*.

(*f*) Man erwartet eine 1. Person beim Verbum. Da der Text (A) aber sonst stets das /n/ in der 1. und 2. Pers. Sg. und der 1. Pers. Pl. im Auslaut schreibt, kann mu-na-ur$_x$(= URU$_4$)-ru nicht für *mu-n.a-V$_7$-en stehen (so auch in Z. 32–33, 41–42; s.o. Anm. *c*).

(*g*) So Text B; A: (A$_4$–N$_5$)-e$_1$ (Agentiv). Text A kann nicht korrekt sein, da nach Z. 32–33 und 41–42 Amaušumgalanna der "šuba-Stein-Pflüger" ist.

(*h*) So beide Texte. Man erwartet die Kopula parallel zu Z. 37. Da diese nicht geschrieben ist, muss der Dativ hier und in e-ne-er doppelt bezeichnet sein.

WORT-EBENE

Es erscheint angebracht, die ersten Schritte der formalen Analyse des Textes auf der Wortebene zu unternehmen. Zu diesem Zweck sei zuerst der Wortschatz untersucht:

Tabelle Wortschatz

Substantive

S_1 ama, "Mutter," 1, 2, 3, 13 (2×), (N$_{11}$[a])

S_2 sila, "Strasse," 1, 2, 3, 4, 5, 6

S_3 MI, "...(?),"[b] 1, 2, 3, 4, 5, 6

S_4 eden, "Steppe," 1, 2, 3, 4, 5, 6

S_5 šul, "junger Mann," 2

S_6 a-a, "Vater," 5, 11 (2×)

S_7 šeš, "Bruder," 6

S_8 lú, "Mensch," 7

S_9 ki-sikil, "junge Frau," 7

S_{10} du$_{14}$, "Streit," 7, 9, 24

S_{11} inim, "Wort(e)," 8, 12, 16, 20, 23 (2×), 36

S_{12} ad, "Rat," (in ad-gi$_4$, "sich beraten"), 10, 14, 18, 22

S_{13} hi-li, "Anziehungskraft," "Wonne," 23, 24

S_{14} šà, "Sinn," 24

S_{15} na$_4$šuba, "ein Edelstein,"[c] 25 (3×), 26 (2×), 27 (2×), 28 (2×), 32 (2×), 33, 34 (2×), 35 (2×), 39 (3×), 40 (2×), 41 (2×), 42

S_{16} a, "Wasser," 29 ([1]+1×), 30 ([1]+1×)

S_{17} ùr, "Dach," 29 ([1]+1×)

S_{18} bàd, "Mauer," 30 ([1]+1×)

S_{19} M[UNUS-...], "...(?)," 31

S_{20} gù, "Stimme," (in gù-dé, "(an)sprechen") 31

S_{21} ši-pa-ág, "Kehle," (Emesal) 34

S_{22} gaba, "Brust," 35

S_{23} nu-u$_8$-gig, "Hierodule," 36, 37 (2×)

S_{24} dam, "Ehefrau," 38

S_{25} nu-bar, "eine Priesterin," 39

S_{26} su$_6$, "Bart," 43, 44, 45 (2×)

S_{27} na$_4$za-gìn, "Lapislazuli," 43, 44, 45 (2×)

S_{28} me-a-am, "Hirte,"[d] 44

S_{29} an, "Himmel," 44 (N$_7$, N$_{11}$, N$_5$)

S_{30} ezen, "Fest," 45

Nur in Namen:

S_{31} gašan, "Herrin," (Emesal) N$_1$, N$_2$

S_{32} nin, "Herrin," N$_1$, N$_5$

S_{33} gi, "Rohr," N$_2$

S_{34} geštin, "Wein(rebe)" N$_7$

S_{35} en, "Herr," N$_9$

S_{36} hé-nu(n), "Überfluss," N$_8$

S_{37} ki, "Erde," N$_9$

S_{38} ušumgal, "einzig Grosser," N_{11}

Namen

N_1 ᵈga-ša-an-gal : Mutter Inanna's (Emesal), 3

$N_{1'}$ ᵈnin-gal : Mutter Inanna's, 21

N_2 ᵈga-ša-an-gi-kù-ga : Schwester Inanna's oder Beiname Inanna's,ᵉ 4

N_3 ᵈsuᵓen : Vater Inanna's (Mondgott), 5, 19

N_4 ᵈutu : Bruder Inanna's (Sonnengott), 6, 17

N_5 ᵈinanna (Göttin des Venus-sterns), 8, 9, 12, 16, 20, 38

N_6 ᵈnin-é-gal-la : Beiname Inanna's, 10, 14, 18, 22

N_7 ᵈgeštin-an-na : Schwester Amaušumgalanna's, 15

N_8 ᵈn[i]n-hᵣé˥-nu-n[a(?)] : Schwester Inanna's,ᵉ 15

N_9 ᵈen-ki : Vater Amaušum-galanna's (Gott des Süsswassers), 19

N_{10} ᵈdu$_x$(= BU)-tur : Mutter Amaušumgalanna's, 21

N_{11} ᵈama-ušumgal-an-na (Gott der Herden),ᵃ 26, 31, 33, 36, 40, 42

(N_3, N_4, N_{10} sind nicht, oder nicht sicher in einzelne Wörter zu zerlegen)

Adjektive

A_1 tur, "klein," 27, 34, (N_{10}?)

A_2 gal, "gross," 28, 35, (N_1, $N_{1'}$)

A_3 sa$_6$, "gut," 28

A_4 kù, "hell," "leuchtend," "rein," 35, 38, (N_2)

A_x nicht erhalten, parallel zu sa$_6$, 27

Verben

V_1 me, "sein," 1, 2, 3, 4, 5, 6

V_2 SAR, "hin und herbiegen(?),"ᵇ 1, 2, 3, 4, 5, 6

V_3 mú, "wachsen, (lassen)," in du$_{14}$-mú, "streiten," 7, 9, 24

V_4 e, "sprechen," (Basis des Präs. Fut. und des Pl. im Prät.) 8, 12, 16, 22, 23

V_5 gi$_4$, "wenden," in ad-gi$_4$, "beraten," und inim-gi$_4$, "antworten," 10, 14, 18, 22, 36

V_6 dím, "formen," "geformt werden," 11, 13, 15, 17, 19, 21

V_7 ur$_x$(= URU$_4$), "pflügen," 25, 26, 32, 33, 37, 38, 39, 40, 41, 42

V_8 lá, "tragen (?)," 29, 30

V_9 dé, "ausgiessen," in gù-dé, "(an)sprechen," 31

V_{10} ne, "leuchten(?),"ᶠ 34, 35

V_{11} dù, "bauen," 43, 44

Zahlwort

Z_1 eš, "dreissig," 23

Pronomina

gá-e, "ich," 17

-mu, "mein," (g̃u$_{10}$) 3, 6, 11, 13, 37 (B), 38 (B), 43 (2× : gá), 44 (gá)

-me, "unser," 1, 2, 34, 35

-zu, "dein," 11, 13, 34 (B: za), 35 (B: za)

e-ne, "er/sie,"ᵍ 37, 38

-a-ni, "sein/ihr," 24, 27, 28, 34, 35, 39, 40, 43, 44, 45 (2×)

a-ba, "wer," 32, 33, 41, 42

-bi, "sein/ihr (pl.)," (Sachklasse) 27, 28, 34, 35

(a) In ᵈama-ušumgal-an-na ist ama ursprünglich nicht "Mutter"; s. zuletzt Wilcke, *Lugalbandaepos*, S. 41–42, Anm. 96; Heimpel, *Tierbilder*, S. 19–21. Text B lässt ᵈama fort parallel zu der möglichen Auslassung von en in den Namen der En-Priester; s. D. O. Edzard, in *ZA*, Bd. 53, S. 19. Ob ama in dieser Verbindung zur Zeit der Abfassung unseres Textes als "Mutter" verstanden wurde, sei dahingestellt.

(b) Kramer, in *PAPS*, Bd. 107, fasst MI-eden-na als Lokativ parallel zu sila-a auf. Da das Verbum jedoch transitiv ist (Agentiv: šul-e in Z. 2), benötigen wir einen Akkusativ. Dieser kann nur MI-eden-na sein, das demnach genitivisch zusammengesetzt sein muss. MI-eden(-na) kommt ausser in unserem Text noch vor in:

Gudea Zyl. A xxviii 23–24

kiri$_6$ MI-eden é-šè si-ga-bi kur geštin bi-bi-zé ki IM.NE-e SAR-àm

"Sein (des Eninnu) Garten mit den...der(!) Steppe, die bei dem Hause eingepflanzt sind, ist ein Berg, der Wein träufelt, ein Ort, (an dem) der...-Wind(?)...." (Oder: "sind an einem Ort, an dem viel Regen fällt, gewachsen": i m-šeg₆ für i m-šèg; s. *MSL* XIII 242, Z. 157-62).

TCL XV, Nr. 20:67-68 (Kramer, in *PAPS*, Bd. 107, S. 508-9)

kiri₆ MI-eden-na gú-gar-gar-ra-na sa₆-ga-ama-na-mu
še ab-sín-ba hi-li-a si-a-mu hi-is-sar-àm a ba-an-du₁₁

"In seinem Garten, (in dem er) die...der Steppe hat den Nacken beugen lassen, hat mein Liebling seiner Mutter
Meine Gerste, die in ihren Saatfurchen attraktiv aussieht, wie Salat bewässert."

PBS V, 76 vi 12-15

ᵈutu-ra an-na-ab-bˈéˈ / lú ᵍⁱˢmá-mu ab-bal / kiri₆ MI-eden-na / i-in-SAR(?)-s[AR]

"Er sagt zu Utu: "Jemand hat mein Schiff an das andere Ufer gebracht, einen Garten mit(?)...der Steppe hat er...(unklar).""

Gilgameš und Huwawa, Z. 56-57 (*SEM*, Nr. 27:4-5 = UM 29-13-473, Z. 7-8, *JCS* I [1947] 26 = UM 29-15-364, Z. 9-10, *JCS* I 27)

kiri₆ MI-eden(!)-na giri-ni bí-[in-gub]
ᵍⁱˢˈereˈn(?) ⁽ᵍⁱˢ⁾ha-lu-ùb ᵍⁱˢhašhur ᵍⁱˢtaskarin x[...] / im-ma-ni-[...]

"In(!) den Garten mit den...der Steppe [trat] er ein und [fällte(?)] Zedern(?), Eichen(?), Granatapfelbäume, Buchsbäume...."

Die Verbindung von MI-eden-na mit kiri₆, "Garten," geštin, "Wein(rebe)," Bäumen, hi-is-sar, "Salat," und auch še, "Gerste," (oder steht še hier für PA.ŠE = išin, "Spross"?) legt die Deutung auf eine Gartenpflanze nahe (Baum, Strauch; kaum Gemüse). Bei Gudea und in *PBS* V, Nr. 76 ist es mit dem Verbum SAR verbunden—wie in unserem Text. Während man dort geneigt ist, mú "wachsen (lassen)" zu lesen, scheidet dies in unserem Text wegen des Auslautes auf -r aus. Das Wort sar = *kuššudum*, "vertreiben," kann nicht vorliegen, wenn es sich um eine Pflanze handelt. Darum vermute ich in sar das Verbum, das auch in ÉŠ.HÚLᵉ⁻ˢᵉ⁻ᵐⁱⁿ-sar-ra = MIN (= *mēlulu*) *šá kep-pe*-[e], "mit dem Springseil spielen," ešemenₓ(= KI.E.NE.DI.ᵈINANNA)-gim sar-sar = *kīma keppê šutakpû*, "sich wie ein Springseil hin und her bewegen lassen," "GIŠ.MEŠ" sar-sar = *keppâ mēlulu*, "mit dem Springseil spielen," vorliegt; s. die Belege in *CAD*, Bd. K, S. 312; ferner "Inanna und Ebeh" Z. 38 = 97 (*PBS* X/4, Nr. 9 Rs. 12 = *SEM*, Nr. 103 Rs. 8 = *STVC*, Nr. 90 iii 1 = *UET* VI/1, Nr.13:5 = Nr. 15:3)

húb(!) ga-mu-un-šú(/šub) KI.E.NE.⟨DI⟩.ᵈINANNA-kù ga-mu-ni-in-sar

"Ich will rennen und dabei das Springseil auf und ab tanzen lassen."

Zu diesem Ansatz passt auch das in *TCL* XV, Nr. 20:67 erscheinende gú-gar; s. gú ki-šè gar = *ke-pu-u ša amēli* (*CAD*, s.v. *kepû*).

MI-eden-na sar wird in unserem Text eine Metapher für das Verhalten Amaušumgalanna's bei seiner Begegnung mit Inanna und ihren Schwestern sein; sei es, dass er sich vor ihnen verrenkt, um ihre Aufmerksamkeit zu erhaschen, sei es, dass er aufschneidet, "dass sich die Balken biegen"—in jedem Falle nicht das eines Mannes würdige Verhalten. Besteht ein Zusammenhang mit NE.MI-eden-na = *anqullu*, 4R, Taf. 24, Nr. 2:21-22 (s. *CAD*, s.v.); Kramer, *AS*, Nr. 12, S. 36, Z. 188?

Siehe aber *MSL* XIII 181: Izi D iii 3'-5' (akk. Entsprechungen nicht erhalten): sila-dagal-[la], sila-MI-eden-[na], sila-limmu-ba. Siehe ferner den von Falkenstein, in *ZA*, Bd. 55, S. 57 erwähnten Beleg

VS II, Nr. 11 vi 8 ᵈlama-sa₆-ga-sila-MI-eden-na
CT XLII, Nr. 3 v 3 ᵈlama-sa₆-ga-sila-MI-dè-na.

Von dieser MI-eden-na-Strasse ist unser Beleg wegen des in sila-a offenbar vorliegenden Lokativs zu trennen. Jacobsen, in *Journal of Ancient Near Eastern Studies*, Bd. 5, S. 203, liest sila A-mi-edin-na.

(c) Text B schreibt ŠUBA-bi für ⁿᵃ⁴šuba, wohl šubₓ-bi zu lesen; s. Å. Sjöberg und E.

Bergmann, in *TCS* III 96, zu unorthographischen Schreibungen für šUBA (darunter: su-bi).

(*d*) Me-a-am kann hier nicht aufgrund der unorthographisch geschriebenen Gleichung [me]-a-am = *a-ji-[ki-am]*, "wo" (*MSL* IV 13, Emesal II 11; s. *CAD*, Bd. A/1, S. 232) verstanden werden. Falsch ist auch die Wiedergabe C. Wilckes durch "Wie! Wildstier" in *AfO* XXIII 87 (ähnlich S. N. Kramer, in *ANET* [3. Aufl.] S. 640 mit Anm. 2).

Ausser in unserem Text kommt das Wort vor in:

TMH NF III, Nr. 25:9 (Inanna redet Dumuzi an)

me-a-am šu-bar-mu-u₈ é-me-šè da-gen

"..., lass mich frei! Ich will nach Hause gehen!"

TCL XV, Nr. 21 Stichzeile = *TMH* NF III, Nr. 54 i 3 (Katalogeintrag; vielleicht der verlorengegangene Anfang von *TMH* NF IV, Nr. 7 ii [6]–iii 6)

me-a-am-ra me-e mu-u[n-...]

"Zum ... ich."

TMH NF IV, Nr. 7 ii 30′ // 32′

me-a-[am] ⌜x⌝-me-da nu-me-a (...)

ᵈnan[na x x (x)-za]lag-ga-da nu-me-a

"ohne unseren...(...)

ohne den [...leuch]tenden Nan[na]."

TMH NF IV, Nr. 7 iii 4–5

ù-mu-un-mu ⌜x⌝-[tù]r-nun-na me-e du₅-mu-r[a-...]

me-a-am u₆-di-d⌜è⌝ du₅-mu-ra-da-[...]

"Mein Herr, das...der fürstlichen Hürde will ich dir...,

..., zum Bestaunen will ich damit zu dir...!"

TMH NF IV, Nr. 89:11 Rs. 2

[...]AN.SÙ.BA(?)ˣˡ⁻ᵇᵘ⁻ᵘʳ me-a-am UD ⌜x⌝[....]

Das Wort gehört zur Personenklasse, wird als Anrede oder Bezeichnung für Amaušumgalanna und Nanna (mit Bezug auf seine Stallungen) gebraucht und erscheint nur in Emesal-Kontext. Darum ist es sehr wahrscheinlich mit der Gleichung des Emesal-Vokabulars *MSL* IV 13, Emesal II 11, [x]-a-am = SIP⌜A⌝ = *ri*-JA-[*x x*] zu verbinden und dort [me]-a-am = SIP⌜A⌝ = *re-ju-[ú-um]* zu ergänzen und "Hirte" zu übersetzen. Die in *MSL* IV vorgeschlagene Ergänzung [ri]-a-am ist ganz unwahrscheinlich, da m.W. akkadische Wörter nicht ins Emesal entlehnt sind und zudem eine Entlehnung im Akkusativ mit Mimation nicht belegbar ist.

(*e*) ᵈGa-ša-an-gi-kù-ga kann entweder eine Schwester Inanna's sein—dann ist aber unklar, warum ihr Name nicht neben dem von Amaušumgalanna's Schwester Geštinanna wieder in Z. 15 genannt wird—oder es ist ein Beiname Inanna's. Den Namen kann ich sonst nicht nachweisen.

(*f*) Das Verbum ne (Text B: né) gehört vielleicht zusammen mit Lugal ud melambi XIII 16, zitiert in *MSL* IX 118 mit unveröff. jungem Dupl. (aB Texte: *UET* VI/1, Nr. 7:4; *SRT*, Nr. 21 i 11; *BE* XXXI, Nr. 8:6)

ⁿᵃ₄maš-da ⁿᵃ₄dub-ba-an ga-an-zi-ir(/⌜i⌝s(?) [...]) NE-a

jung: [...]NE-[xx]

ⁿᵃ₄MIN ⁿᵃ₄MIN *nab-lu nap-hu-ú-tum*

"M.-Stein, D.-Stein, leuchtende Flammen" (wörtlich: "entzündete Flammen").

Eine Lesung ne für NE = *napāhum* ist allerdings nicht bezeugt (s. *MSL* IX 117–19), eine Hiatusschreibung barₓ-a in lugal ud melambi in dem aB Text (nur in *UET* VI/1, Nr. 7:4 erhalten) wäre aber befremdlich.

(*g*) J. Krecher, in *HSAO*, S. 106, schlägt für die Variante e-IM in Text B die Lesung e-ĝerₓ (= MÍR) als Emesal-Form für e-ne-er vor. Da Amaušumgalanna Sprecher der Zeilen ist und der Text bei den Sprechern regelmässig den Dialekt wechselt (B ist allerdings nur ein kleines Fragment), ist dies zweifelhaft. Ich habe aber keine andere Erklärung dieser Variante.

Die kurze Dichtung von 45 Zeilen verwendet 30 Substantive (oder 38, wenn Wörter, die nur als Bestandteile von Namen vorkommen, mitgezählt werden), 11 Namen, davon einer in dialektisch verschiedenen Formen, 4 [+1] Adjektive, 11 Verben, 1 Zahlwort, 3 selbständige und 5 enklitische Pronomina; alles in allem 66 verschiedene Wörter. Dass das Verhältnis der einzelnen Wortarten zueinander in literarischen Texten beträchtlichen Schwankungen unterworfen ist und darum etwas über den Stil aussagen kann, sei im Vergleich mit zwei weiteren Texten desselben Umfangs demonstriert, dem bal-bal-e Inanna's. *SRT*, Nr. 5 = Kramer, in *PAPS*, Bd. 107, S. 521, N 4305 Rs. i' 1–ii' 3 und dem oben in Umschrift wiedergegebenen tigi-Lied auf Nintu; Zahlen = %:

Text	Subst.	Adj.	Name	Zahlw.	Pron.	Interj.	Adverb	Verb
kun-gar	46,5	7,6	16,8	1,6	12,2	——	——	16,8
bal-bal-e	48,0	14,3	1,8	1,8	10,9	0,9	0,9	21,8
tigi	61,5	7,2	9,0	——	3,6	——	——	19,5

Dieser Vergleich zeigt, dass das Schwergewicht in unserem Text auf den Namen zu liegen scheint, dass Verben eine relativ geringe Rolle spielen, Substantive und Adjektive nahe der unteren Grenze der "Norm" angesiedelt sind, während die Pronomina über dem Durchschnitt liegen. (Dieses Bild freilich—gewonnen aus drei Texten etwa desselben Umfanges—könnte durch eine Untersuchung auf breiterer Basis erheblich verändert werden.) Vielleicht sollte man statt vom Schwergewicht besser von der Vielfältigkeit und Variation des Ausdrucks sprechen.

Beim Übergang vom Vergleich ganzer Kompositionen zur Einzelanalyse zeigt sich freilich, dass die oben gebotenen Prozentzahlen noch wenig aussagen: In unserem Text (kun-gar) sind die Adjektive beschränkt auf zwei Zeilenpaare und eine weitere Zeile: Z. 27/28, 34/35, 38, allgemeiner gefasst: auf die zweite Hälfte des Textes. Andererseits ist die Gruppe der Namen ganz überwiegend in der ersten Hälfte vertreten, während nur ein Name in beiden Teilen erscheint und einer nur im zweiten Teil. D.h., nur 5 von 45 Zeilen enthalten Adjektive, und diese 5 Zeilen gehören zum zweiten Teil des Textes; der grossen Zahl von 10 Namen im ersten Teil stehen nur zwei im zweiten Teil gegenüber.

Betrachten wir die Wörter nach semantischen Gesichtspunkten, so zeigt sich wieder die Zweiteilung des Textes:

(1) In Z. 1–22 dominieren die Ausdrücke für Verwandtschaft aus der Sicht des Kindes: Mutter, Vater, Bruder gekoppelt mit den Namen der Verwandten. Demgegenüber erscheint nur in Z. 37 noch einmal ein Terminus der Verwandtschaft: dam-mu, "meine Ehefrau." War es im ersten Teil die Blutsverwandtschaft, so handelt es sich hier um eine neu zu gründende Familie.

(2) In Z. 2 und 7 werden die Kontrahenten šul, "junger Mann," und ki-sikil, "junge Frau," genannt. Diese Sphäre der Altersgruppe wird nicht wieder angesprochen. Vielmehr ist im zweiten Teil die Rede von nu-u₈-gig, "Hierodule," nu-bar, "nu-bar-Priesterin," und me-a-am, "Hirte," d.h., von Berufen.

(3) Der Gegensatz von "Strasse" (sila), als Teil der Stadt und damit der

Herkunft Inanna's, zu "Steppe" (eden) als Herkunft Amaušumgalanna's (Z. 1–6) kehrt im zweiten Teil nicht wieder.

(4) Die Opposition du_{14}, "Streit,"—inim, "(vernünftiges) Wort" / ad-gi$_4$, "sich beraten," "ein Gespräch führen," fehlt im zweiten Teil.

(5) Die mögliche semantische Differenzierung im Wechsel der Namen ^{d}inanna / ^{d}nin-é-gal-la (letzteres = "Herrin des Palasts") wird im zweiten Teil nicht wieder aufgenommen.

(6) Die Bezeichnungen von Körperteilen (ši-pa-ág, "Kehle," gaba, "Brust," und su$_6$, "Bart") hat kein Gegenstück im ersten Teil; ebenso die Bauausdrücke ùr, "Dach," und bàd, "Mauer."

(7) Die Edelsteine ^{na_4}šuba und ^{na_4}za-gìn, "Lapislazuli," zusammen mit dem dazugehörigen Verbum ur$_x$(= URU$_4$)-ru finden sich nur im zweiten Teil.

(8) Ein möglicher Gegensatz zwischen den beiden Teilen besteht in den Ausdrücken MI-eden-na sar und su$_6$-a-ni ^{na_4}za-gìn-na, wenn ersteres eine eines Mannes unwürdige Haltung beschreibt (s. Tabelle Wortschatz Anm. *b*) und letzteres einen "richtigen" Mann.

Betrachten wir nun die Wörter daraufhin, wie der Dichter mit ihnen seinen Text gestaltet, so ist im ersten Teil das Arrangement der Namen und Verwandtschaftsbezeichnungen von Interesse, wobei wir zwei mögliche Schemata unterscheiden müssen, je nachdem, ob ^{d}ga-ša-an-gi-kù-ga als Beiname der Inanna verstanden wird oder als Name einer Schwester der Göttin; um das Bild des ersten Teils vollständig darzustellen, seien sie zusammen mit dem des Refrains dargestellt:

	1	2	3	4	5	6	7	8	9	10	11
Mutter	x	x	x								
EGO				x							
Vater					x						x
Bruder/Schwester						x					
Refr. sila-a...	x	x	x	x	x	x					
Refr. du$_{14}$-mù								x	x		
Refr. inim-e							x				
Refr. ad-gi$_4$										x	
Mutter	x	x	x								
Schwester				x							
Vater					x						x
Bruder/EGO						x					
	12	13	14	15	16	17	18	19	20	21	22
Mutter		x								x	
EGO						x					
Vater							x				
Bruder/Schwester				x							
Refr. sila-a...											
Refr. du$_{14}$-mú											
Refr. inim-e	x				x			x			
Refr. ad-gi$_4$			x				x				x
Mutter		x								x	
Schwester				x							
Vater							x				
Bruder/EGO				x							

Ob nun das untere oder das obere der mit dem Refrain hier zusammengestellten Schemata der Familien richtig ist, wir beobachten den Gegensatz zwischen
der gleichmässig fortschreitenden Reihe in Z. 1–6 und der wellenförmigen
Bewegung in Z. 11–21—unten (ᵈga-ša-an-gi-kù-ga, Schwester Inanna's) 2
Gipfel und 2 Täler, oben (ᵈga-ša-an-gi-kù-ga, Inanna) 3 Gipfel und 3 Täler.

Mit diesen verschiedenen Bewegungen harmonieren die Refrains: in Z. 1–6
erscheint stets derselbe Refrain und unterstreicht so die Gleichförmigkeit des
Fortschreitens. Ab Z. 7 aber wird die Refrain-Ebene bewegt und erreicht rasch
(mit Z. 10) eine gleichmässige Wellenform, die mit der oberen (ᵈga-ša-an-gi-
kù-ga, Inanna) Wellenform harmonisiert.

Den Kontrast von gleichförmigem Fortschritt und Wellenbewegung im
Wiederkehren der Verwandtschaftstermini und damit verbundenen Namen
erzielt der Dichter unseres Textes durch die Kombination zweier verschiedener
Familiensysteme: in Z. 1–6 die Gliederung nach Geschlechtern (Mutter-Tochter,
Vater-Sohn), in Z. 11–21 aber nach Generationen (Vater-Mutter, Tochter-Sohn)
und durch die Wiederholung des Paares Vater-Mutter (Z. 19 und 21), die gleichzeitig bewirkt, dass die 1. Person "ich" nicht die Reihe als Höhepunkt abschliesst
sondern (bescheiden) darin eingeschlossen wird.

Im zweiten Teil (Z. 25–45) lassen sich keine ornamentalen Strukturen beobachten, die denselben Prinzipien folgen wie die des ersten Teiles. Vielmehr
zeigen sich drei andere formale Besonderheiten, von denen die dritte allerdings
bereits zur Satzebene gehört, hier aber angeschlossen wird, um das Bild des
zweiten Teiles zu vervollständigen; siehe die Tabelle auf Seite 307.

(a) Wir beobachten, dass dasselbe Substantiv (oder ein nominalisierter Satz)
innerhalb einer Zeile (= 1 Satz) mehrfach vorkommen kann, meist gefolgt von
einer Zeile, die einen Namen und das Substantiv (n−1) mal nennt.

(b) Innerhalb einer Zeile (= eines Satzes) mit finitem Verbum kann dieses
Verbum ein- oder zweimal auch im nominalen Satzteil erscheinen.

(c) Paare von Sätzen kehren (z.T. leicht verändert) wieder.

Abschnitt (a) der Tabelle zeigt, dass die Folge Substantiv n mal—Name+
Substantiv (n−1) mal in unserem Textabschnitt dominiert und als Mittel der
Steigerung zum Ende und damit Höhepunkt benutzt wird: Die Folge Substantiv
3×—Name+Substantiv 2× findet sich nur zweimal, in Z. 25–26, d.h., dem
ersten Zeilenpaar des zweiten Teiles, den wir hier untersuchen, und in Z. 39–40.
Auf diese beiden Zeilenpaare folgen jeweils zwei Paare des Schemas Substantiv
2×—Name+Substantiv 1×. Während aber in Z. 39–44 diese Gruppierungen
ohne Unterbrechung aneinander anschliessen, liegen in Z. 25–38 jeweils einige
Zeilen dazwischen: Z. 27–31 = 4 Zeilen à 2 Substantive (+1 Zeile, die dem
Wiederholungsschema nicht folgt, die Redeeinleitung), Z. 34–36 = 2 Zeilen (+1
Zeile, die dem Wiederholungsschema nicht folgt, wieder Redeeinleitung); der
Abstand nimmt also um zwei Zeilen ab und schmilzt dann bei gleicher Abnahme
zwischen Z. 38 und 39 auf Null zusammen.

Abschnitt (b) zeigt ein mit dem oben beschriebenen Schema der Substantive
kontrastierendes System der Prädikate, den Gegensatz zwischen Zeilen (=
Sätzen) mit und ohne finites Verbum: Die Zahl der Zeilen mit finitem Verbum,

	25	26	27	28	29	30	31	32	33	34
(a)										
Substantiv 3×	x									
Name + Substantiv 2×		x								
Substantiv 2×			x	x	(x)	(x)		x		x
Name/Epitheton + Substantiv 1×									x	
Keine Wiederholung							x			
(b)										
Verbum infinit 2×								x		
Verbum infinit 1×					x	x			x	
Verbum infinit O×	x	x					x			
Kein finites Verbum			[x]	[x]						x
(c)										
^{na_4}šuba-ke$_4$ na-ur$_x$(= URU$_4$)-ru	x	x								
^{na_4}šuba-na ^{na_4}šuba-tur-tur/gal-gal-bi			x	x						x
a lá					x	x				
^{na_4}šuba-ur$_x$(= URU$_4$)-ru. . .a-ba-a								x	x	
e-ne-er mu-na-ur$_x$(=URU$_4$)-ru										
su$_6$-a-ni ^{na_4}za-gìn-na										
(Redeeinleitung)							x			

	35	36	37	38	39	40	41	42	43	44	45
(a)											
Substantiv 3×				x							
Name + Substantiv 2×					x						
Substantiv 2×	x		x				x		x		x
Name/Epitheton + Substantiv 1×				x				x		x	
Keine Wiederholung		x									
(b)											
Verbum infinit 2×							x				
Verbum infinit 1×								x			
Verbum infinit O×			x	x	x	x	x				
Kein finites Verbum	x								x	x	x
(c)											
^{na_4}šuba-ke$_4$ na-ur$_x$(= URU$_4$)-ru						x	x				
^{na_4}šuba-na ^{na_4}šuba-tur-tur/ gal-gal-bi		x									
a lá											
^{na_4}šuba-ur$_x$(=URU$_4$)-ru. . .a-ba-a								x	x		
e-ne-er mu-na-ur$_x$(=URU$_4$)-ru				x	x						
su$_6$-a-ni ^{na_4}za-gìn-na									x	x	x
(Redeeinleitung)			x								

die jeweils einer Gruppe von Zeilen mit nominalem Prädikat vorausgehen, steigt von 2 über 4 (+1 = Z. 31: Redeeinleitung) zu 6 (+1 = 36: Redeeinleitung) um jeweils zwei Zeilen (dieselbe Einheit wie in Abschnitt a) an. Die Häufigkeit der Nennung des Verbums im nominalen Satzteil scheint keine Rolle zu spielen.

Abschnitt (c) schliesslich, das System der Wiederholung von (teilweise modifizierten) Zeilenpaaren, ähnelt in seinem Verlauf dem oben dargestellten Schema der Verwandtschaftsbezeichnungen: Z. 25–33 gleichmässiges Fortschreiten (unterbrochen durch die Redeeinleitung in Z. 31), gefolgt von einer Wellenbewegung (2 Gipfel, 3 Täler; in Z. 36 noch einmal durch die Redeeinleitung unterbrochen), die in den drei letzten Zeilen auszulaufen scheint. Dabei könnte die sich über drei Zeilen erstreckende Nennung des Bartes aus Lapislazuli das Pendant zu den ersten drei Zeilen unseres Textes sein, in denen die Mutter erscheint.

War der erste Teil auf die beiden gegensätzlichen Familienstrukturen gegründet und die Verwendung von Refrains, so scheinen im zweiten Teil grammatische Kategorien (Substantiv, Prädikat) das Formprinzip zu sein, gekoppelt mit der an Refrains anklingenden Verwendung von Wiederholungen von Zeilenpaaren.

Satz-Ebene

Mit der Einbeziehung ganzer Sätze in die Untersuchung, aber auch schon durch die Verwendung von Begriffen wie Prädikat und finites Verb, haben wir in dieser Untersuchung bereits die Satz-Ebene betreten. Das erste aber, das bei der Betrachtung der Sätze auffällt, ist, dass jede Zeile einen Satz enthält—mit Ausnahme von Z. 23–24, wo zwei ineinander verschachtelte Sätze zwei Zeilen beanspruchen. Dieses Prinzip scheint auch in Z. 34–35 nicht zur Anwendung zu kommen, da diese beiden Zeilen nachgestellte Akkusativobjekte zu den Verben von Z. 32/33 zu sein scheinen. Isoliert betrachtet sind diese beiden Zeilen aber auch selbständige Sätze. Die meisten Sätze besitzen ein finites Verbum als Prädikat (s. Tabelle, Abschnitt b), nominale Prädikate erscheinen nur in insgesamt sieben Zeilen (15,5%). Die Kopula "sein" erscheint nur dreimal (Z. 23 und 37 [2×]).

Der Gebrauch der Modi in den beiden Teilen unseres Textes ist recht unterschiedlich:

Indikativ, Präs.-Fut. 1–6, 29–31, 32–33 (Frage), 36–38, 41–42 (Frage)
Indikativ, Präteritum 23/24
Prohibitiv 7, 9
Kohortativ 8, 10, 12, 14, 16, 18, 20, 22
Affirmativ 25, 26, 39, 40
in-ga- 11, 13, 15, 17, 19, 21
Nominales Prädikat, Modus-neutral 27, 28, 34, 35, 43, 44, 45

Mit Ausnahme der beiden Zeilenpaare Z. 25/26 und 39/40, in denen der Affirmativ auf na- vorliegt, ist der zweite Teil ganz im Indikativ verfasst (Aussagesätze und Fragen). Demgegenüber findet sich der Indikativ nur in Z. 1–6 im ersten Teil—alle anderen Zeilen weisen ein "Präformativ" auf, sind also modal differenziert (die modale Nuance von in-ga- ist noch unbekannt). Aber auch Z. 1–6 sind nur der äusseren Form nach indikativisch stilisiert: Mutter, Schwester (oder EGO), Vater und Bruder sind ja vorhanden, die Bedingungssätze sind also irreal.

Die Anzahl der funktional relevanten Satzglieder, der Ketten, schwankt zwischen drei und sechs je Satz. Dabei fällt besonders die grosse Gruppe der Zeilen 7–22 auf, die aus je drei Ketten zusammengesetzt sind.

	1	2	3	4	5	6	7	8	9	10	11	12	13	14	15
3:							x	x	x	x	x	x	x	x	x
4:	x		x	x	x	x									
5:		x													
6:															

	16	17	18	19	20	21	22	23	24	25	26	27	28	29	30
3:	x	x	x	x	x	x	x					x?	x?		
4:										x	x				
5:														x?	x?
6:								(x)							

	31	32	33	34	35	36	37	38	39	40	41	42	43	44	45
3:															
4:	x	x	x	x	x	x		x	x	x	x	x	x		
5:							x							x	x
6:															

Der erste Teil ist abgesehen von der Schwankung bei Z. 2 und dem Schritt von 4 Ketten zu nur 3 Ketten von Z. 6 zu Z. 7 sehr einheitlich gestaltet. Im zweiten Teil dagegen beobachten wir eine gewisse Unruhe, obwohl auch dort ein Typ (4 Ketten) überwiegt. Ganz aus dem Rahmen fallen Z. 23–24.

Dieses Bild der Einheitlichkeit des ersten Teils im Gegensatz zur Bewegtheit des zweiten wird auch noch anderweitig gestützt: In Z. 1–6 wird jeweils nur ein Teil der ersten Kette variiert (oder in Z. 2 eine Kette hinzugefügt), in Z. 7–22 bleibt die dritte Kette jeder zweiten Zeile unverändert, und jede zweite Kette steht im Äquativ.

Demgegenüber erstrecken sich parallel konstruierte Zeilen im zweiten Teil jeweils über nur zwei Zeilen.

Auch im Gebrauch des Genitivs bestehen Unterschiede: im ersten Teil findet sich der Genitiv nur in Z. 1–6 in MI-eden-na. Der zweite Teil macht weit häufiger Gebrauch vom Genitiv und benutzt obendrein Genitive ohne Regens und vorausgestellte Genitive.

DIALEKT-EBENE

Unser Text gebraucht die beiden Dialekte eme-sal und den Hauptdialekt, eme-gi₇, von denen der erstere weitestgehend auf weibliche Sprecher (und eine Gruppe von Priestern) beschränkt ist. Den Hauptdialekt verwenden demgegenüber überwiegend männliche Sprecher.

A. eme-sal: Verwendung des Phonems /ĝ/ in Präfixketten in Z. 1–6; s. J.

Krecher, in *HSAO*, S. 104–5; ga-ša-an, "Herrin," statt Hauptdialektform nin in Z. 3 und 4; ši-pa-ág, "Kehle," statt zi-pa-ág in Z. 34; me-a-am, "Hirte," statt sipa in Z. 44.

B. Hauptdialekt: lú, "Mensch," statt eme-sal mu-lu in Z. 7; ᵈinanna statt ᵈga-ša-an-an-na in Z. 8, 9, 12, 16, 20, 38; Präformativ ga- statt dafür den Kohortativ in Z. 10, 12, 14, 16, 18, 20, 22; nin, "Herrin," statt ga-ša-an in Z. 14, 15, 18, 22; ᵈgeštin-an-na statt ᵈmu-tin-an-na in Z. 15; gá-e statt me-e in Z. 17; ᵈen-ki statt ᵈam-an-ki in Z. 19; ᵈduₓ(= BU)-tur statt ᵈzé-er-tur in Z. 21; šà-g statt šà-b in Z. 24; nu-u₈-gig statt mu-gi₄-ib in Z. 36, 37; nu-bar statt (?) (s. *MSL* IV 18, Emesal II 82) in Z. 38.

Die Verteilung der Dialekte über unseren Text zeigt, dass wir es mit männlichen und weiblichen Sprechern zu tun haben. Zwar hat J. Krecher, in *HSAO*, S. 87–110, nachgewiesen, dass in eme-sal-Texten auch Wörter des Hauptdialekts Verwendung finden können—der Beweis, dass dann kein Sprecherwechsel vorliegt, muss aber in jedem Einzelfall geführt werden.

SPRECHER UND HALTUNGEN

Die einzelnen Sprecher lassen sich durch die Verwendung der Dialekte, den Gebrauch der Pronomina, der Person beim Verbum und der Vokative bestimmen; Sicherheit ist hierbei freilich nicht immer zu gewinnen. Ausserdem können wir die in ihren Worten ausgedrückte Haltung beschreiben.

Z. 1–2: Sprecher eine oder mehrere Schwestern der Inanna: eme-sal-Dialekt; ama-me, "unsere Mutter." Die Haltung ist ironisch beschreibend, vielleicht gar sarkastisch. Sie sprechen von einem jungen Mann, d.i. Amaušumgalanna.

Z. 3–6: Sprecher Inanna: eme-sal-Dialekt; Bezug auf die 1. Pers. Sing. in ama-mu, "meine Mutter," und šeš-mu, "mein Bruder." Die Haltung ist dieselbe wie in Z. 1–2. Auch sie spricht von dem jungen Mann.

Z. 7–22: Sprecher ist (der noch nicht mit Namen genannte) Amaušumgalanna: Hauptdialekt; Bezug auf Mitglieder seiner Familie; Gebrauch der 1. Person in diesem Zusammenhang. Angeredet ist Inanna (Vokative, Gebrauch der 2. Pers. Sing.). Die Haltungen sind fordernd, heischend und beschreibend.

Z. 23–24: Sprecher ist eine ungenannte Person. Die Haltung ist kommentierend. Inanna, ihre Schwester(n) und Amaušumgalanna sind nicht angeredet.

Z. 25–30: Eine oder mehrere Personen, die von Amaušumgalanna in der 3. Person sprechen; wahrscheinlich Inanna, da in Z. 32–35 die Schwester(n) sprechen. Möglich auch, dass in diesem Abschnitt noch einmal ein Sprecherwechsel stattfindet (nach Z. 26 oder nach Z. 28). Auf wen sich das Dativpräfix in Z. 29–30 bezieht, ist nicht festzustellen. Wenn Inanna spricht, kann es nur Amaušumgalanna sein; sprechen die Schwester(n), können es Amaušumgalanna oder Inanna sein. Der Bezug auf eine andere Person (etwa Mutter, Vater, Bruder oder Schwester) ist weniger wahrscheinlich, da diese im zweiten Teil sonst nicht mehr erscheinen. Die Haltung ist beschreibend.

Z. 31: Ungenannter Sprecher wie in Z. 23–24. Die Haltung ist erzählend.

Z. 32–35: Sprecher eine oder mehrere Schwestern Inanna's, die von Amaušum-galanna in der 3. Pers. Sing. reden: eme-sal-Dialekt; Possessivsuffix -me, "unser." Die Haltung ist fragend beschreibend.

Z. 36: Wie Z. 31.

Z. 37–38: Sprecher Amaušumgalanna: Hauptdialekt; Gebrauch der 1. Pers. Sing. Da von Inanna in der 3. Pers. Sing. geredet wird, sind die Schwestern angeredet. Er spricht aber auch von sich selbst in der 3. Pers. Sing. im verbalen Satzteil. Die Haltung ist beschreibend, feststellend.

Z. 39–42: Sprecher eine oder mehrere Personen; da Inanna in Z. 43–45 spricht, wahrscheinlich die Schwester(n). Ein Sprecherwechsel nach Z. 40 ist aber nicht auszuschliessen; dann spricht Inanna die Z. 39–40, und die Schwester(n) sprechen Z. 41–42. Die Haltung ist beschreibend und fragend.

Z. 43–45: Sprecher Inanna: eme-sal-Dialekt; Possessivpronomen der 1. Pers. Sing.; von Amaušumgalanna ist in der 3. Pers. Sing. gesprochen. Angeredet müssen darum die Schwester(n) sein. Die Haltung ist beschreibend und heischend (Z. 45: ezen-e, "zum Fest!").

Wir haben es also mit vier Sprechern zu tun: Inanna, ihren Schwester(n) (auch bei nur einer Schwester wäre die erste Pers. Pl. berechtigt, wenn sie Inanna miteinbezieht), Amaušumgalanna und dem Kommentator/Erzähler.

Während die ersten drei miteinander sprechen und die Worte, die eine der drei Parteien an eine andere richtet, stets auch von der dritten mit gehört werden und anscheinend auch für ihre Ohren bestimmt sind, nimmt der Kommentator/

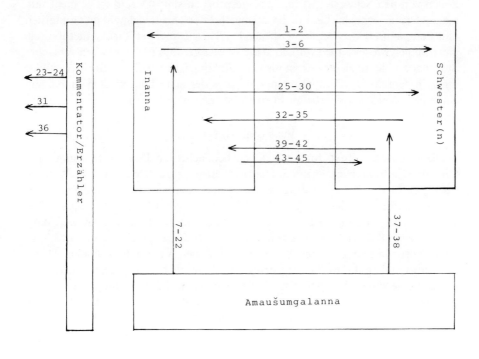

Erzähler an dem Gespräch nicht teil. Seine Worte sind vielmehr an den Hörer
oder Leser des Textes gerichtet.

Aber warum notiert er nur zweimal den Sprecherwechsel? Gehört das, was
er sagt, ursprünglich zum Text, oder ist es sekundär, was die Untersuchung auf
der Wort- und Satz-Ebene nahezulegen scheint?

Die Lösung dieser Fragen finden wir in den Z. 23–24. Hier sagt der Kommentator, die Wörter der Wonne seien dreissig. Hat er wirklich die Wörter gezählt?
Er hat es tatsächlich getan: Die Zahl der Wörter, die in Z. 1–22 gebraucht sind,
ist tatsächlich dreissig (wenn man ^{d}ga-ša-an-gal und ^{d}nin-gal als verschiedene
Wörter zählt und die enklitischen Possessivpronomina unberücksichtigt lässt):

> ama, me, sila, MI, eden, SAR, šul, ^{d}ga-ša-an-gal,
> ^{d}ga-ša-an-gi-kù-ga, a-a, ^{d}su^{ʾ}en, šeš, ^{d}utu, lú, ki-sikil,
> du$_{14}$, mú, ^{d}inanna, inim, e, ^{d}nin-é-gal-la, ad, gi$_4$, dím,
> ^{d}geštin-an-na, ^{d}n[i]n-h^{ʾ}é^{ʾ}-nu-n[a(?)], gá-e, ^{d}en-ki,
> ^{d}du$_x$(= BU)-tur, ^{d}nin-gal.

Ausserdem bezeichnet er in diesen Zeilen die gesprochenen Wörter als solche
von hi-li—ein Ausdruck, dessen Bedeutung nicht exakt festzulegen ist (Perücke,
Reiz, sex appeal), den wir aber hier gern als "Spannung zwischen Liebenden"
verstehen würden. Inanna und Amaušumgalanna sind nach seinen Worten "die,
die dabei war, Streit anzufangen" und "hi-li ihres Sinnes," wo wir hi-li gern
mit "Wonne" wiedergeben würden. Er übersieht völlig, dass die ersten beiden
Zeilen von den Schwester(n) Inanna's gesprochen sind. Darum ist er nicht mit
auf der Szene, wenn das Gespräch stattfindet. Er erscheint vielmehr erst hinterher
und kommentiert den bereits vorliegenden Text. Dabei verfährt er methodisch
ganz ähnlich wie wir: auch wir haben die Wörter gezählt, und wir haben versucht,
Sprecher zu identifizieren. Er ist also ein Philologe, der auch um die literarische
Analyse bemüht ist. Dies ist meines Wissens der erste Fall, in dem es gelingt,
einen philologischen Bearbeiter in so früher Zeit nachzuweisen.

VERS UND METRUM

Die in unserem Text durchgehend zu beobachtende Übereinstimmung von
Satz- und Zeilengrenze (s.o. zur Satzebene) berechtigt zu dem Schluss, dass dieses
kun-gar-Lied in Versen geschrieben ist—mit Ausnahme der Zeilen, die wir dem
Kommentator zugewiesen haben. Ist aber jede Zeile ein Vers? Wir können den
Beweis weder hierfür noch für das Gegenteil führen. Es fällt aber auf, dass
in den Zeilen 1–6 der Refrain jeweils die zweite Hälfte einer Zeile einnimmt, was
dazu führt, dass in Z. 3 und 4 eingerückte Zeilen Verwendung finden. Demgegenüber stehen die Refrains in den Z. 7–22 jeweils auf einer eigenen Zeile.

Als Folge dieser Schreibweise ist der Unterschied im Umfang der Zeilengruppen 1–6 und 7–22 recht gross; gemessen an der (vermutlichen) Silbenzahl
entsprechen zwei Zeilen des zweiten Abschnittes jeweils ungefähr einer des
ersten:

Z. 1: 7+11? Silben	Z. 7: 9? Silben
	Z. 8: 9 Silben
Z. 2: 9+11? Silben	Z. 9: 8 Silben
	Z. 10: 9 Silben
Z. 3: 9+11? Silben	Z. 11: 10 Silben
	Z. 12: 9 Silben
Z. 4: 9+11? Silben	Z. 13: 10 Silben
	Z. 14: 9 Silben
Z. 5: 8+11? Silben	Z. 15: 12? Silben
	Z. 16: 9 Silben
Z. 6: 8+11? Silben	Z. 17: 9 Silben
	Z. 18: 9 Silben
	Z. 19: 8 Silben
	Z. 20: 9 Silben
	Z. 21: 8 Silben
	Z. 22: 9 Silben

Diese Silbenzahlen sind teilweise nur Annäherungswerte, da die Lesung von MI in MI-eden-na unbekannt ist (Z. 1–6), ki-sikil in Z. 7 auch /kiskil/ gelesen werden kann und die Lesung des Gottesnamens in Z. 15 nicht ganz sicher ist. Die ungefähre Übereinstimmung des Zeilenumfangs in Z. 1–6 mit dem von 2 Zeilen in Z. 7–22 ist auffällig, besonders, wenn man berücksichtigt, dass jede zweite Zeile in Z. 7–22 einen Refrain enthält.

Nach Z. 24, d.h. im zweiten Teil, geht die Einheitlichkeit des Umfangs verloren; dort wo die Silbenzahl sicher festzustellen ist, schwankt sie zwischen 11 (Z. 25) und 18 (oder 17, wenn a-ba-a nur zweisilbig ist, in Z. 33 und 42; 17 Silben auch in Z. 40).

Wir können nicht entscheiden, ob der Schreiber nach Z. 6 feststellte, dass er genügend Platz auf der Tafel zur Verfügung hatte, um den Refrain, der Teil der grösseren Einheit "Vers" ist, auf eine eigene Zeile zu schreiben, oder ob die Verse nach Z. 6 erheblich kürzer sind.

Diese Frage könnte vielleicht gelöst werden, wenn sich feststellen liesse, ob die Zeilen jeweils eine metrische Einheit sind—davon sind wir aber noch weit entfernt.

Dafür, dass unserem Text eine metrische Gliederung zugrundeliegt und dass diese etwas mit der Zahl der Silben zu tun hat, sprechen die Zeilen 2–6: In Z. 2–4 zählen wir in der ersten Zeilenhälfte jeweils 9 Silben. Diese Zahl 9 wird in Z. 3 aber nur durch die Weglassung des—grammatisch an sich notwendigen—Nominalisators -a erreicht. Ähnlich verhält es sich mit Z. 5. Dort fällt das Fehlen des Possessivsuffixes -mu hinter a-a auf: "Vater," nicht "mein Vater," was zu Silbenzahl 8 (statt 9, was zu den vorangehenden Zeilen passen würde) führt, die mit der der folgenden Zeile übereinstimmt.

In Z. 5 kann aber die Silbenzahl nur ein Nebenprodukt und die beabsichtigte Wirkung die Stellung der ersten den Akzent tragenden Silbe im Vers gewesen sein, da nach J. Krecher, in *AOAT*, Bd. 1, S. 194, § 41, 2, zweisilbige Wörter vor Affixen stets auf der zweiten Stammsilbe betont werden—freilich wissen wir nicht, wo der Ton in a-a, "Vater," in der freien Form sass, doch kann dies die erste Silbe gewesen sein; s. zur möglichen Anfangsbetonung zweisilbiger Wörter J. Krecher, in *AOAT*, Bd. 1, S. 177–79, § 33*b*.

Strophische Gliederung

Wir haben bereits oben die Gliederung unseres Textes in zwei grössere Abschnitte beobachtet, die formal verschieden gestaltet sind. Innerhalb des ersten Teiles lassen sich dank der Refrains kleinere Einheiten isolieren, die man als Strophen ansprechen kann:
Z. 1–6 (eventuell noch unterteilbar wegen des Sprecherwechsels in Z. 1–2, 3–6); 7–10, 11–14, 15–18, 19–22. Z. 23–24, die vom Kommentator stammen, entfallen: 6 (2+4), 4, 4, 4, 4 Zeilen.
Im zweiten Teil, in dem es keinen Refrain gibt, ist nicht mit gleicher Sicherheit abzuteilen. Nimmt man an, die Folge Substantiv n mal – Name + Substantiv $(n-1)$ mal erscheine jeweils am Beginn einer Strophe—die erste des zweiten Teiles beginnt so— ergibt sich das folgende Bild: Z. 25–30 (Z. 31 entfällt), 32–35 (Z. 36 entfällt), 37–38, 39–40, 41–42, 43–45. Das ist aber wegen der nur zweizeiligen Strophen gegen Ende zu wenig wahrscheinlich. Vielleicht beginnen die Strophen jeweils mit dem Paar [na4]šuba-..., [d]ama-ušumgal-an-na...Dann sind die Strophen Z. 25–30, 32–38 (ohne Z. 36), 39–45, d.h., 6, 6 und 7 Zeilen. Dies würde bedeuten, dass innerhalb der zweiten und der dritten Strophe des zweiten Teils jeweils ein Wechsel der Sprecher stattfände.

Inhalt

Unser Text enthält ein Gespräch zwischen drei Parteien, der oder den Schwester(n) Inanna's, Inanna und Amaušumgalanna. Er beginnt unmittelbar mit einer Rede und überlässt die Rekonstruktion der Situation, in der das Gespräch stattfindet, ganz dem Hörer oder Leser—es sei denn, diese Situation ist durch die Einbettung des Textes in ein Ritual vorgegeben.
Die Ausgangssituation ist die Begegnung der Mädchen mit dem ihrem Milieu fremden Amaušumgalanna, der—vielleicht werbend—versucht, ihre Aufmerksamkeit zu erhaschen. Sein Verhalten scheint dabei nicht das eines Mannes würdige zu sein, denn die Mädchen spotten über ihn. In seiner Erwiderung behauptet Amaušumgalanna seine Ebenbürtigkeit mit ihnen.
Das Gespräch schlägt nun um in die Erörterung, für wen Amaušumgalanna die (kostbaren) šuba-Steine "pflüge"—er sagt, dass er es für seine Frau, die nu-u8-gig, d.h., für Inanna tue—und es endet mit einem Preis Inanna's auf "den Hirten, der es für mich bis zum Himmel erbauen wird," der einen Lapislazulibart trage, also ein richtiger Mann sei.

Beschrieben wird also der Sinneswandel Inanna's, die Amaušumgalanna zunächst (gemeinsam mit ihrer/n Schwester[n]) ablehnt und sich schliesslich zu ihm bekennt. Zwei Einzelheiten, die anscheinend für das exakte Verständnis des Textes von Bedeutung sind, bleiben weithin unklar: Der Gebrauch des Verbums "pflügen" im Zusammenhang mit den šuba-Steinen und das fehlende Objekt zu dem "bauen" in Z. 43–44.

Während ich für die zweite der Fragen keine Lösung weiss, lässt sich die erste wenigstens annäherungsweise beantworten. Das Verbum "pflügen" wird noch an einer anderen Stelle mit den šuba-Steinen verbunden: *SRT*, Nr.6:66–71 = Nr. 7:3–8, bearbeitet von W. H. Ph. Römer, in *AOAT*, Bd. 1 (1969) S. 293–94 (mit Bezug auf unsere Stelle)

u_4-ba unu$_6$-šuba nu-gál-la-àm
unu$_6$-šuba gú-a nu-gál-la-àm
^{d}nin-in-si-na-ke$_4$ KA-e bí-in/ib-sè-ge
šuba na-ur$_x$(= URU$_4$)-ru numun-e-eš na-gá-gá
in-nin$_9$ nu-(u$_8$-)gig-gal-an-na-ke$_4$
unu$_6$-šuba KA-e bí-ib-sè-ge
Damals gab es noch keinen šuba-Schmuck,
gab es noch keinen šuba-Schmuck am Halse;
Nininsina erfindet(?) ihn.
Sie pflügt wirklich die šuba(-Steine) und legt sie als Samen hin.
Die Herrin, die grosse Himmelshierodule,
erfindet(?) den šuba-Schmuck.

Hier ist das "Pflügen" eindeutig auf die Gewinnung der Steine bezogen—freilich in einem Bild, das der Feldbestellung entlehnt ist, so dass "Pflügen" kaum eine besondere Technik des Abbaus der Edelsteine beschreiben kann. [K.Z.: Es handelt sich sehr wahrscheinlich um das Auffädeln der Edelsteine zu einer Halskette, für das das Fallen der Saatkörner nacheinander in die Furche beim Säh-Pflügen als Metapher gebraucht wird.] Keinesfalls aber lässt sich diesem Zitat, wie W. H. Ph. Römer schon gesehen hat, eine sexuelle Nuance des "Pflügen"s entnehmen, die S. N. Kramer, in *PAPS*, Bd. 107, S. 495, in unserem Text zu finden glaubte—vielleicht wegen des Ausdrucks "die Vulva pflügen" in dem von ihm in *PAPS*, Bd. 107, S. 505–8 (Kopie S. 519–20) veröffentlichten Text (ii 25–31).

UNTERSCHRIFT

Zur Unterschrift kun-gar s.o., 11.5. Dass der Schreiber hervorhebt, er habe den Text mit einem "Schreibrohr aus Rohr" geschrieben, lässt darauf schliessen, dass zur Zeit der Niederschrift des uns vorliegenden Exemplars auch Griffel aus anderem Material gebraucht wurden.

BIBLIOGRAPHIE

Auf die Literaturzusammenstellung zum Aufsatz W. W. Hallos sei generell verwiesen; sie wird hier nicht wiederholt; ferner:

ALLGEMEINES

(jeweils mit ausführlicher Bibliographie)

Kayser, Wolfgang. *Das sprachliche Kunstwerk*. 15. Aufl. Bern, München, 1971.

Richter, Wolfgang. *Exegese als Literaturwissenschaft*. Göttingen, 1971.

Wellek, René, und A. Warren. *Theorie der Literatur*. 2. Aufl. Frankfurt, 1972.

Wilpert, Gero von. *Sachwörterbuch der Literatur*. 5. Aufl. Stuttgart, 1969.

SUMERISCHE LITERATUR

Alster, Bendt. *Dumuzi's Dream: Aspects of Oral Poetry in a Sumerian Myth*. Kopenhagen, 1972.

Cooper, Jerrold. "New Cuneiform Parallels to the Song of Songs." *Journal of Biblical Literature* XC (1971) 157–62.

Dijk, Johannes J. A. van. *La Sagesse suméro-accadienne*. Leiden, 1953.

Falkenstein, Adam. *Die Haupttypen der sumerischen Beschwörung literarisch untersucht*. LSS NF I. Leipzig, 1931.

———. "Drei Hymnen auf Urninurta von Isin." *ZA*, Bd. 49 (1950) S. 80–150.

———. *Die Inschriften Gudeas von Lagaš* I: *Einleitung*. AnOr, Bd. 30. Rom, 1966.

Falkenstein, Adam, und Wolfram von Soden. *Sumerische und akkadische Hymnen und Gebete*. Zürich, Stuttgart, 1953.

Gordon, Edmund I. "Sumerian Proverbs, Collection Four." *JAOS*, Bd. 77 (1957) S. 67–79.

———. "Sumerian Proverbs and Fables." *JCS* XII (1958) 1–21, 43–75.

———. *Sumerian Proverbs: Glimpses of Everyday Life in Ancient Mesopotamia*. "Museum Monograph." Philadelphia, 1959.

———. "A New Look at the Wisdom of Sumer and Akkad." *BiOr* XVII (1960) 122–52.

Hartmann, Henrike. "Die Musik der sumerischen Kultur." Frankfurt am Main, 1960. (Diss.).

Heimpel, Wolfgang. *Tierbilder in der sumerischen Literatur*. StP, Bd. 2. Rom, 1968.

———. "Observations on Rhythmical Structure in Sumerian Literary Texts." *Or*, NS., Bd. 30 (1970) S. 492–95.

Jacobsen, Thorkild. *The Sumerian King List*. AS, Nr. 11. Chicago, 1939.

———. "The Myth of Inanna and Bilulu." *JNES* XII (1953) 160–87. Nachdruck in *TIOT*, S. 52–71.

Krecher, Joachim. *Sumerische Kultlyrik*. Wiesbaden, 1966.

Limet, Henri. "Les Chants épiques sumériens." *Revue Belge de philologie et d'histoire* L (1972) 3–24.

Römer, Willem H. Ph. *Sumerische "Königshymnen" der Isin-Zeit*. Leiden, 1965.

Wilcke, C. *Das Lugalbandaepos*. Wiesbaden, 1969.